MILWAUKEE: THE HISTORY

OF A CITY

CITY HALL

MILWAUKEE

THE HISTORY OF A CITY

By Bayrd Still

PROFESSOR OF HISTORY IN
NEW YORK UNIVERSITY

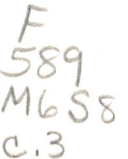

MADISON
THE STATE HISTORICAL SOCIETY OF WISCONSIN
1948

COPYRIGHT 1948

STATE HISTORICAL SOCIETY OF WISCONSIN

MANUFACTURED BY
THE NORTH AMERICAN PRESS
MILWAUKEE

TO MY

MOTHER AND FATHER

Foreword

IT IS significant that as this book goes to press the centennial of the statehood of Wisconsin is being celebrated in a Wisconsin city of some 600,000 people, the thirteenth largest of the nation. It is appropriate that this full-scale history of that city should appear during the State's centennial year.

The massive record of material achievement of the past century in the United States nowhere in Wisconsin finds fuller exemplification than in her largest city. Here the problems of urbanization, which Jefferson so greatly feared, find their clearest expression within the borders of our State. Here the growth of huge enterprises, the phenomenal march of productivity, the lengthening payrolls of prosperity, and the increasing concentration of real and personal wealth are matched by the growing threat of blighted areas, the constant pressure to keep abreast of the needs of a metropolis constantly expanding both in population and in dimensions, the needs not only for bigger schools, better fire protection, and wider streets and sewers, but for adequate recreational facilities, public health services, municipally sponsored cultural activities, city planning, and solutions for the urgent problems of depression. The story of Milwaukee is in some degree the story of any large American Midwestern city. It parallels the story of the smaller Wisconsin cities. Yet it has its own distinctive flavor, based chiefly on the cultural and political heritage of its citizens of European origin, and on the nature of its hinterland. And Milwaukee, like Wisconsin, was a pioneer in the Midwest in certain types of public service.

This study, the first to treat of some of the larger aspects of the municipal problems of Milwaukee, is trebly welcome as a study of the urbanization of one important area of our nation, an analysis of the growing rivalries between neighboring urban centers in an era of cheap and rapid transportation of goods and people, and as a contribution to the history of Wisconsin. No one can follow Dr. Still's story of the city from the days of Solomon Juneau to recent times without a better understanding of some of the major and often hidden factors in the growth of American cities and a growing comprehension of the vital problems of the modern metropolitan center.

State Historical Society of Wisconsin   CLIFFORD L. LORD
October 15, 1948

Preface

THE story of the growth of Milwaukee to metropolitan stature transcends local interest not alone because of the city's nationwide reputation for honest and effective municipal administration nor because of the Germanic and socialistic ingredients of its culture which in the popular mind have differentiated it from the other major cities of the nation. The townsite promotion in its early history demonstrates an important, if frequently neglected, aspect of the westward movement of population in the United States. Its evolution from *Deutsch-Athen* to American metropolis reveals the role of the city both in the transmission of ideas from the Old World and in their transformation in the New. And inasmuch as its rise to metropolitan proportions coincided almost exactly with the occurrence of this phenomenon in the wider nation, the city's adjustments to the problems of urban living reflect the details of a significant and pervasive contemporaneous activity in the United States at large. In short, its experience recapitulates in many ways the as yet unwritten history of the city in American life.

The attempt to delineate the broad span of city building within the limits of a single volume has been deliberate. By so doing it is possible to disclose the outlines of the evolving urban entity with a clarity that rarely results when the concern is with all-inclusive institutional and biographical detail. Such compression has imposed the necessity of selection and generalization, practices which present especial hazards in the writing of urban history. This follows from the scarcity of monographic studies in the local field and from the want of available personal papers, a situation which exists in part because of the intimate and informal relations prevailing in the urban community and in part because persons of local consequence usually have not been regarded as of sufficient historical importance to justify having their correspondence preserved. Lacking such evidence of the nature and motivation of urban action, it has been necessary to rely, more than otherwise would be warranted, on such potentially biased and frequently inaccurate records as newspaper reports, census returns, campaign arguments, trade association figures, and recollections and memoirs.

Because of the relatively undigested character of so voluminous a body of source material, I have been particularly dependent upon the guidance of local specialists for aid in research. The personnel of the Reference Department of the Milwaukee Public Library, including Miss Mamie E. Rehnquist, Miss Gretchen DeWitt, Mr. John Dulka, Mr. Peter J. McCormick, and Mr. Albert Strobl, have given unstinting and resourceful assistance, as have Mr. William Slayton and Mrs. Lucile Perry of the Municipal Reference Library in the city hall. No less cooperative in making available the highly useful materials at their disposal were Mrs. Alice M. Schramm and Miss Betty Wallace of the Milwaukee *Journal* Library, Mr. Theodore Mueller of the Milwaukee County Historical Society, and Miss Alice Smith, chief of research of the State Historical Society of Wisconsin. For the benefit of their understanding of special phases of the Milwaukee social scene, I am indebted to Dr. Joseph L. Baron, Mrs. Helen Dressel, the Rev. John F. Fedders, Mr. Paul Gauer, the Rev. Roscoe Graham, Mr. Frederic Heath, Rabbi Samuel Hirshberg, the late Dr. Louise Phelps Kellogg, Mrs. Felicia Kwasie-Borski, Dr. Albert Lepawsky, Mrs. Paula Lynagh, Mr. Frederick I. Olson, Mr. Edmund G. Olszyk, Professor Selig Perlman, Professor Philip H. Person, Mr. Hugo W. Rohde, Dr. Marian Silveus, and Mr. Szymon St. Deptula. Grateful mention should be made of the subsidy provided by the Duke University Research Council and of the encouragement of Professor Frederic L. Paxson and Professor W. T. Laprade through the years. I should like to express an especial debt of gratitude to two of my former students: to Mr. William H. Herrmann, who shared in the tedious task of newspaper research and in the selection of illustrations, and to Mr. Philip K. Lundeberg, who verified the sources for much of the manuscript and compiled the data for most of the charts. Professor Bessie L. Pierce and Miss Livia Appel contributed helpful counsel and criticism. And throughout the period of writing I have profited from the enthusiasm, the broad knowledge, and the comprehending insight of Mr. Norman N. Gill, director of the Citizens' Governmental Research Bureau of Milwaukee, an expert observer of the local political and administrative scene. To all these, as well as to Miss Lillian Krueger and Mr. John C. Sammis of the State Historical Society of Wisconsin and the many others who have given unselfish service in preparing the manuscript for the press, my hearty thanks.

New York, 1948 BAYRD STILL

Contents

I. THE VILLAGE

1. Fur Trade and Townsite Promotion	3
2. Village Politics and Internal Improvements	33
3. Commercial Foundations	52
4. The Social Fabric of the Village	70
5. The Beginnings of Urban Services	96

II. THE EXPANDING CITY: 1846–1870

6. The Nationality Background	111
7. Local Politics and National Issues	133
8. When Commerce Was King	168
9. The Pattern of Culture	200
10. The Extension of Urban Services	230

III. THE EMERGING METROPOLIS: 1870–1910

11. Nationality Ingredients	257
12. The Play of Politics	279

13. Industrial Foundations 321

14. Signs of a Municipal Conscience 356

15. The Metropolitan Mold 396

IV. THE MATURE METROPOLIS: 1910–1940

16. The Structure of Society 433

17. The Economic Base 476

18. Politics and Urban Maturity 515

Appendix: Tables and Charts 569

Bibliographical Note 601

Index 611

Illustrations

City Hall, photograph from the Milwaukee *Journal*
                                                                           Frontispiece

Land Purchases (1835) on Which Original Townsites Were Based, map prepared with the assistance of Robert A. Campbell and John L. Wernette, Office of the City Engineer, Milwaukee   16

Pioneer Promoters of the Townsite Era: photographs of Juneau, Kilbourn, and Walker from Conard's *History of Milwaukee,* Martin from the State Historical Society of Wisconsin, Rogers from the Milwaukee County Historical Society   36

Map of Milwaukee in 1836 as Recalled by Early Settlers, from Buck's *Pioneer History of Milwaukee*   60

Milwaukee in 1853, from a lithograph in the possession of the Milwaukee County Historical Society   128

Leading Figures of the Developing City: photographs of Mitchell, Plankinton, and King from Buck's *Pioneer History of Milwaukee,* Holton from the State Historical Society of Wisconsin, Huebschmann from Conard's *History of Milwaukee*   144

It "Made Milwaukee Famous," photographs from the Milwaukee *Sentinel*   188

Milwaukee in the Eighties, photograph from the Milwaukee *Journal*   266

Personalities of the Early Metropolitan Period: photograph of Allis from the Allis-Chalmers Industrial Press, Milwaukee, Pabst from Pabst Brewing Company, Grottkau and Rose from the Milwaukee County Historical Society, Beggs from the State Historical Society of Wisconsin 292

Urban Services of the Later Nineteenth Century, photographs from the Milwaukee *Journal* 360

Milwaukee in 1938, aerial photograph by Ray P. Knaup, Midwest Airways, Incorporated, Milwaukee 436

Representative Citizens of the Twentieth-Century Metropolis: photographs of Weber, Bruce, and Berger from the Milwaukee County Historical Society, Falk from the Allis-Chalmers Manufacturing Company, Kruszka from J. A. Kapmarski, the *Kuryer Polski* 464

Architectural Contrasts: photograph of the Cottage Inn from Buck's *Pioneer History of Milwaukee,* Schroeder Hotel from the Milwaukee *Journal* 472

Changes in the Heavy Metal Trades: nineteenth-century photograph from the Allis-Chalmers Industrial Press, twentieth-century photograph from the Milwaukee *Journal* 488

Milwaukee's First Socialist Mayors: photographs of Hoan (1916) and Seidel from Milwaukee County Historical Society, Hoan (1940) from the Milwaukee *Journal* 522

Twentieth-Century Urban Services, photomontage from Milwaukee Municipal Reference Library 552

PART I

The Village

"A correspondent at the mouth of the Milwauky, speaks of their having a town already laid out; of selling quarter acre lots for five, and six hundred dollars, and says that by fall there will be one hundred buildings up;... that some 50 to 100 people are living there! A gentleman supports a school at his own expense. A clergyman is about taking up his abode among them; ... Land speculators are circumambulating it, and 'the Milwauky' is all the rage."—Green-Bay Intelligencer, and Wisconsin Democrat, June 27, 1835.

"The way we speculate in this country is this: Buy lands at ten shillings per acre and sell the same at two and one-half or three dollars per acre, with the purchase money down and the rest in three or six months, and then come again, and keep it going, making one hundred per cent. in four or six months, sometimes longer.... This government land speculation is the surest, but there is not so much to be made as there is in town property."—E. W. Edgerton to Elisha Edgerton, August 31, 1836.

CHAPTER 1

Fur Trade and Townsite Promotion

A CITY was in the making when Jacques Vieau beached his canoe at the mouth of the Milwaukee River one summer day toward the close of the eighteenth century.[1] The wild rice swamp, steep bluffs, and looming forest gave little hint of the metropolis by which this wilderness solitude would be replaced before a hundred years had passed. His accompanying Mackinaw boat weighed down with goods for the Indian trade, this young agent of the North West Fur Company was not the first white trader to live among and traffic with the motley band of natives then dwelling near the point at which the meandering Milwaukee joins the waters of Lake Michigan. But the somewhat more continuous contacts of the French-Canadian newcomer and those of his better-known successor, Solomon Juneau, broadened and secured the trading-post foundations from which the American city was presently to rise.

Today remnants of mounds, once shaped like birds and animals, are the meager reminder of the aboriginal civilization which preceded white settlement at the mouth of the Milwaukee.[2] For the Indian, as later for the white man, the confluence of lake and river dictated human occupation; and here French missionaries, touching the area in the last quarter of the seventeenth century, found Foxes, Mascouten, and Potawatomi inhabiting lands which, to judge from the nature of the mounds,

[1] The recollections of his sons place his arrival in August 1795. "Narrative of Andrew J. Vieau, Sr.," Wisconsin Historical Society, *Collections*, 11:218-33 (1888); "Narrative of Peter J. Vieau," Wisconsin Historical Society, *Collections*, 15:458-69 (1900).

[2] On this subject, see Will C. McKern, "The First Settlers of Wisconsin," *Wisconsin Magazine of History*, 26:153-69 (December 1942). According to McKern, Wisconsin's Indian inhabitants occupied the area for "many hundreds, probably thousands, of years" before the coming of European man.

Winnebagoes had occupied in prehistoric times.[3] The assertion of French control in the region, a reality between 1671 and 1760, gave the natives an opportunity for commerce with the outside world. Even before 1700, occasional traders may have visited the native settlement to offer rum and trinkets in exchange for peltries; but by the middle of the eighteenth century such activities were a certainty. The first known resident trader was one St. Pierre, who was living among the Indians as early as 1764 and as late as 1779 when Samuel Robertson, piloting the sloop "Felicity," touched "Millwakey Bay."[4] Between then and the early years of the nineteenth century others known to have engaged in the trade included Alexander and François La Framboise, John B. Beaubien, Antoine Le Claire, Joseph St. Pierre, Laurent Fily, Joseph La Framboise, Joseph La Croix, and Captain Thomas G. Anderson, as well as the earlier mentioned Vieau.[5] Anderson, who arrived in 1803, reported that, counting Le Claire and La Framboise, each of whom had "two or three relatives or other hangers on," there was "quite a society of its kind" at the river's mouth.[6] The blacksmith Mirandeau, with his Ottawa wife and three or four children, was part of this company.[7]

There was only the promise of a permanent community, however, in the activities of Le Claire, La Framboise, Vieau,

[3] Joseph Schafer, *Four Wisconsin Counties: Prairie and Forest* (Madison, 1927), 20-21. The locality, spelled Melleoiki, is first mentioned specifically by Father Zenobius Membré, a Recollect missionary traveling with La Salle in 1679. Father Marquette and two companions encamped under the bluffs of the Milwaukee in the fall of 1674. Jean François Buisson de St. Cosme, one of the three Seminary priests sent in the summer of 1698 by François Laval, bishop of Canada, to set up missions among the Indians, entered the Milouakik River, October 9, 1698, and feasted two days in the Indian village. W. A. Titus, "Early Milwaukee: A Polyglot Village That Became a Metropolis," *Wisconsin Magazine of History*, 10:425 (June 1927); Louise P. Kellogg, *The French Régime in Wisconsin and the Northwest* (Madison, 1925), 205, 261-62.

[4] "Papers from the Canadian Archives—1778-1783: A Voyage on Lake Michigan—1779," Wisconsin Historical Society, *Collections*, 11:210 (1888). Quaife asserts that St. Pierre, who possibly was related to the well-known Canadian family of Le Gardeur St. Pierre, was "the city's first known white inhabitant." Milo M. Quaife, *Lake Michigan* (Indianapolis, 1944), 199-200.

[5] Charles E. Snyder, "Antoine LeClaire, the First Proprietor of Davenport," *Annals of Iowa*, 3d series, 23:80-81 (October 1941).

[6] "Narrative of Capt. Thomas G. Anderson," Wisconsin Historical Society, *Collections*, 9:153 (1909).

[7] "Antoine Le Clair's Statement," Wisconsin Historical Society, *Collections*, 11:240-41 (1888).

and their kind. Assisted by French-Canadian *engagés* who cut wood, gardened, or wintered at outlying points with the Indians, their chief interest was in the peltries and maple sugar which they bartered with the natives for scarlet and blue cloth, striped gartering, vermilion paint, sleigh bells, tobacco, needles, scissors, and scalping knives. La Framboise and Vieau took their furs to Mackinac; Le Claire carried his to Detroit. There the latter selected his supplies in the spring, shipping them in May on a sailing vessel which delivered goods to traders at the mouth of the St. Joseph and at Chicago, as well.[8] Vieau, who made almost annual contacts with the Milwaukee post in spite of the fact that he retained his homestead in Green Bay, would set out for Mackinac each spring with the winter's peltries, not to return with another supply of "store goods" until the following August.[9] By 1818 the American Fur Company had replaced the North West Fur Company in the Wisconsin country; and the Milwaukee traders were serving American rather than British fur-trading interests. In that year there entered the Milwaukee trade a young French-Canadian, Solomon Juneau, whose activities were ultimately to effect the transition from Indian trading post to American urban community at the mouth of the Milwaukee. When Vieau relinquished his agency in 1819, young "Solomo," as the natives called the strapping newcomer, became the "trader-king" of this wilderness domain.[10]

[8] *Ibid.*, 238-41.
[9] "Narrative of Andrew J. Vieau, Sr.," Wis. Hist. Soc., *Colls.*, 11:223. A fuller picture of the fur-trading activities of the period awaits a careful study of the Grignon, Lawe, and Porlier papers in the Wisconsin Historical Society Library.
[10] Because of inaccuracies in the recollections of Vieau's sons, it is difficult to reconstruct the relationship between Juneau and Vieau. Juneau was born on August 9, 1793, in the village of Repentigny, adjoining the island of L'Assomption which was formerly credited as his birthplace. He was descended from a family from La Rochelle, which had been in Canada since the seventeenth century. After several years of employment with the Hudson's Bay Company, to whom he incurred a debt of $300, he came to Prairie du Chien in 1817. There his uncle loaned him money to pay his debt and furnished him an outfit with which he began trading with the Menominee Indians in the vicinity of Milwaukee. In the spring of 1818, the United States factor, John W. Johnson, staked him to cash and goods. According to Juneau's assertion, he first met Vieau in this year. Juneau may have become Vieau's clerk at this time; for it was in this period that he married Vieau's daughter, Josette. He began to learn English in 1831. To his wife's insistence is attributed his removal in 1852 to Dodge County where he founded the village of Theresa. He died while attend-

Juneau's Indian compatriots, whom he scolded when they were tipsy and regaled with abundance when they had goods to trade, made a heterogeneous group. Compiling the Indian census of 1817, John Bowyer called them "renigadoes from all the tribes about them, viz., the Saques, Foxes, Chippewas, Menomonies, Ottawas, Winnebagoes, and Potawatomies estimated at three hundred warriors."[11] Although the evidence of the effigy mounds points to the presence of Winnebago Indians in the Milwaukee area in prehistoric times, by the second half of the seventeenth century the region probably belonged to the Miami. By the eighteenth, the Potawatomi, reported in the Wisconsin country as early as 1652,[12] appear to have been the most numerous type in an aboriginal population which included Chippewa and Ottawa as well.[13] An early friendliness for the French and Spanish on the part of these Indians of the "Mahn-a-wau-kie" paved the way for their adherence to the Patriot cause in the conflict between the American colonies and England. Visiting George Rogers Clark soon after his capture of the Illinois posts, the principal chief of the Potawatomi, called Letourneau by the French, entered into an alliance with the Americans—a move which prompted the commander of the British post at Michilimackinac to refer in 1779 to "those runagates of Milwakie—a horrid set of refractory Indians." Clark's victory over Hamilton in that year cemented the loyalty of the Indians for the "Bostonnais"; and despite British efforts to destroy American influence, "the Milwaukee villagers never wavered in their attachment to the Spanish-American cause."[14] In the early nineteenth cen-

ing a "payment" on the Menominee reservation, November 14, 1856. Louise P. Kellogg, "The Society and the State," *Wisconsin Magazine of History*, 21:246 (December 1937); John H. Fonda, "Early Wisconsin," Wisconsin Historical Society, *Collections*, 5:218 (1868); Joseph Tassé, *Les Canadiens de l'Ouest* (2 vols., Montreal, 1878), 1:216-17; P. L. Scanlan, "The Founder of Milwaukee at Prairie du Chien," *Wisconsin Magazine of History*, 22:3-5 (September 1938). See also Isabella Fox, *Solomon Juneau* (Milwaukee, 1916); *Dictionary of American Biography*, 10:247-48; "Narrative of Peter J. Vieau," Wis. Hist. Soc., *Colls.*, 15:458-69; "Narrative of Andrew J. Vieau, Sr.," Wis. Hist. Soc., *Colls.*, 11:218-37.

[11] Schafer, *Four Wisconsin Counties*, 35.
[12] Kellogg, *French Régime*, 96.
[13] Schafer, *Four Wisconsin Counties*, 20.
[14] A. S. De Peyster's "Speech to the Western Indians," in "The British Régime in Wisconsin," Wisconsin Historical Society, *Collections*, 18:384, 384n

tury, the Menominee showed their friendship for the United States when Onaugesa, or "Old Flour," attempted to restrain his people from aiding the British in the War of 1812. This was the more unusual considering the rather general sympathy for the British in the Wisconsin country at the time and the fact that Vieau appeared to be supporting the European government.[15] During the Black Hawk War in 1832, the Milwaukee region was designated as a refuge for Indians friendly to the United States, and many erected wigwams on the river banks.

It was with this polyglot people, becoming increasingly lazy and debauched through their contact with white civilization, that Juneau carried on his trade.[16] With Juneau and his brother they constituted the Indian village and two families near the "Milwalky River" which John Farmer pictured on his map of the territories of Michigan and Wisconsin, published in 1830.[17] But neither Indian village nor transient trader could provide the basis of a really permanent community. In fact, it was the absence rather than the presence of the Indians that made possible urban beginnings in the Milwaukee area. This was foreshadowed when the defeat of Black Hawk removed an Indian obstacle against which the expanding American farmer frontier had been pressing for some years with relentless force. With the close of the Black Hawk War, the Sauk and Foxes ceded all their lands south of the Fox-Wisconsin waterway. Already the Menominee treaty of February 8, 1831, had brought into American hands the Indian lands north and east of the Milwaukee River. On September 26, 1833, the Chippewa, Ottawa, and Potawatomi relinquished their claim to the territory east of the Winnebago cession and south of that ceded by the Menominee.[18] Thus was southeastern Wisconsin cleared of the red man's claim. The treaty negotiations were not followed,

(1908); Louise P. Kellogg, *The British Régime in Wisconsin and the Northwest* (Madison, 1935), 155-56, 178. Chippewa, Potawatomi, and Ottawa were all here at this time.

[15] *Ibid.*, 311-12.

[16] "Narrative of Andrew J. Vieau, Sr.," Wis. Hist. Soc., *Colls.*, 11:227.

[17] Edwin S. Mack, "The Founding of Milwaukee," Wisconsin Historical Society, *Proceedings*, 1906, p. 196.

[18] Louise P. Kellogg, "The Story of Wisconsin," *Wisconsin Magazine of History*, 3:190 (December 1919); Milo M. Quaife, "The Chicago Treaty of 1833," *ibid.*, 1:287 (March 1918); William F. Raney, *Wisconsin: A Story of Progress* (New York, 1940), 73.

however, by the immediate disappearance of the Indians. In 1838, a caravan of teams conveyed many of them westward according to treaty stipulations. But until that time, groups of Indian wigwams were a customary sight in the midst of the developing American community; and as late as the 1850's blanketed Indians on the streets of the lakeside village were a vivid reminder of the long years of Indian occupation and fur-trading contacts, dimly descried through a haze of history and legend, which gave way to American town-making on Milwaukee Bay.[19]

New and unexpected responsibilities came to young "Solomo" in 1833 and 1834. The chances are that the genial trader would have been content indefinitely to dispense his "store goods" and dominate the uneventful Indian village from his trading post with its "floors, stools, tables all riven out and finished with the axe and auger."[20] But with the Indian cessions of 1831 to 1833, the Milwaukee country had caught the attention of westward-moving America, of speculators and settlers touched by the "Wisconsin phase" of the migrating fever of the Middle Period; and Juneau had to become a city-maker almost despite himself. Major S. C. Stambaugh, exploring the country ceded by the Menominee Indians in 1831, publicized the fine mill privileges on the Milwaukee River and reported "attractions to the agriculturist rarely to be found in any country."[21] Nature had marked the mouth of the Milwaukee for a townsite; and now the time was ripe for man to forge the foundations of a city there. The ubiquitous speculator was quick to see a "future metropolis" at a spot where two rivers—in this instance the Milwaukee and the Menomonee, which joined the latter a mile and a quarter from its mouth—flowed from a rich hinterland into Lake Michigan. But the two who caught the most enduring vision of city building there were Morgan L.

[19] Louise Phelps Kellogg told the author that her grandmother recalled visits of Potawatomi chiefs to her kitchen in Milwaukee about 1837 or 1838. "She gave them doughnuts and sometimes bread and butter. Once a chief came in drunk and men on the street told Grandfather Kellogg to hurry home and look after his womenfolks. Grandfather said, 'Puckagee,' the word for 'get out,' and the Indians left."

[20] Reminiscence of L. Goodrich Loomis, quoted in John G. Gregory, *History of Milwaukee, Wisconsin* (4 vols., Chicago, 1931), 1:52. See also Fonda, "Early Wisconsin," Wis. Hist. Soc., *Colls.*, 5:218-20, 230-31, 234.

[21] Schafer, *Four Wisconsin Counties*, 49-50.

Martin, the Green Bay land speculator and promoter, and Byron Kilbourn, Yankee assistant to the surveyor general of Michigan Territory.

Martin's excursions about the territory in search of untouched opportunities brought him to the mouth of the Milwaukee River in July 1833.[22] He later wrote:

My visit was one of exploration, and my observations were limited to the examination of the outlet of the stream to ascertain whether a harbor could be constructed at this point. . . . Previous to my tour of observation, Michael Dousman had agreed to share with me any purchase I should make, with a view to laying out a town at the point where Milwaukee now stands.[23]

What he saw about him he sketched in his "Map of Milwaukie," dated August 1833: the wide bay at the confluence of lake and river, the forested banks of the Milwaukee, the Indian village on the Menomonee west of its junction with the larger stream, and solitary dwellings labeled "S. Juneau, P. Juneau, and J. Vieau."[24] Since Juneau was in Chicago at the time, negotiations between the speculator and the local trader had to await a meeting in October 1833. On this occasion the basis of the town-

[22] Morgan L. Martin was born in 1805 in Martinsburgh, New York. In 1826 he went to Detroit where he read law in Henry S. Cole's office and was admitted to the bar. The following year, at the age of twenty-two, he went to Green Bay as the protégé of his cousin James D. Doty. From 1831 to 1835 he served as a member of the legislative council of Michigan Territory and from 1838 to 1844 in that of the territory of Wisconsin. From 1845 to 1847 he represented the territory in Congress, in 1847-48 he was president of the State constitutional convention, in 1855 he was elected to the State assembly, and in 1858 he was chosen for the senate. His greatest promotional achievement was the development of the Fox-Wisconsin waterway which effected a continuous line of transportation from Green Bay to the Mississippi. He died in 1887. In a letter to the Old Settlers' Club, written in 1882, he claimed to have first visited Milwaukee in June 1833. Reuben G. Thwaites, "Sketch of Morgan L. Martin," Wisconsin Historical Society, *Collections,* 11:380-81 (1888); Gregory, *History,* 1:147.

[23] "Narrative of Morgan L. Martin," Wisconsin Historical Society, *Collections,* 11:404 (1888); Morgan L. Martin to James S. Buck, Sept. 1, 1876, quoted in James S. Buck, *Pioneer History of Milwaukee* (2 vols., Milwaukee, 1890, 1881), 1:40-41. The volume one of Buck's work used in this study is the revised edition (1890) of the original volume one, which was published in 1876. Buck continued his work with two volumes titled, *Milwaukee under the Charter.* The first of these, called volume 3, was published in Milwaukee in 1884; the second, called volume 4, was published in Milwaukee in 1886. This work will hereafter be cited as Buck.

[24] The original of this map is in the possession of the Wisconsin Historical Society.

promotion activities of Martin and Juneau was laid. For $500 Juneau was to relinquish a half-interest in his pre-emptive claim to the river front property that was to be the core of the promotion plan—the future northeast quarter of section 29, township 7 North, range 22 East. Martin was to share in the expense of getting pre-emption to the land; and, as it proved, Juneau was to assume much of the managerial responsibility. It was a verbal agreement, but one which continued to the last to inspire the respect of both parties. The combination of French-Canadian trader and Yankee speculator-politician was a fortunate one. Juneau undoubtedly benefited, for unaware of the prospective value of his holding, he might well have been the victim of land sharks.[25] But Martin secured a canny if somewhat open-handed agent in permitting Juneau to share in the profits, at the same time safeguarding his own interests by binding the trader not to dispose of his portion without asking the speculator's advice. Juneau's personal enthusiasm and his knowledge of and identification with the locality and Martin's sound judgment, experience with real estate operations, and political influence at the territorial and national capitols were mutually important contributions to the speculative venture.[26]

The correspondence between the Green Bay speculator and his trader-partner during these formative years reveals the methods which characterized the speculative townsite promotion of the Jacksonian period. In December 1833, shortly after the

---

[25] "Narrative of Morgan L. Martin," Wis. Hist. Soc., *Colls.*, 11:406.

[26] Little is to be gained in trying to decide who was the real "founder" of Milwaukee. There is no doubt that Martin first envisioned the townsite possibilities of the location and considerable evidence that at the time he proposed his plan to Juneau the latter was not a permanent resident of the place. Martin contends in his *Narrative* that not until 1835 or 1836 did Juneau think of residing permanently in Milwaukee; he wrote in 1882 that at his meeting with Juneau in Chicago, in October 1833, the trader offered to sell out his "possession"; and according to Andrew Vieau, Juneau's clerk, the trader's homestead remained in Green Bay "until about 1834 or 1835, when Milwaukee began to grow and Juneau platted the village and settled there permanently." Louise P. Kellogg and Edwin S. Mack recognize Martin as the directing spirit of the enterprise. H. W. Bleyer comes to the conclusion that Juneau was the founder because he was the first United States citizen to become a property-owner there. Gregory, *History*, 1:147; "Narrative of Andrew J. Vieau, Sr.," Wis. Hist. Soc., *Colls.*, 11:224; Louise P. Kellogg, "The Beginnings of Milwaukee," *Wisconsin Magazine of History*, 1:417 (June 1918); Mack, "The Founding of Milwaukee," Wis. Hist. Soc., *Proc.*, 1906, p. 198; H. W. Bleyer, "The Founder of Milwaukee," Milwaukee *Sunday Sentinel*, Nov. 11, 1906.

partnership had been formed, Juneau reported the steps he had taken to secure their claim. On the east side of the river, site of his trading post, he had enclosed "the best parts" of the land; across the river, at Martin's suggestion, a tract had been enclosed and posts planted. "This winter I shall have logs drawn upon the spot, and early next spring I will build an handsome little building, as a Dwelling house," the trader wrote. "This improvement will substantiate more for the right Claims." Speaking through the "discreet person" whom he had commissioned to write the letter, he expressed his gratitude for the "sensible and generous offer" Martin was making.[27] Meanwhile, Martin, then sitting as a member of the territorial council of Michigan, at Detroit, was exerting political pressure to clear the townsite enterprise of legal obstacles. His major concern was to secure the privilege of pre-emption for the lands which Juneau was occupying, thus forestalling the designs of other speculators upon the place, and to press the survey of the area so that real estate operations could get under way. In part as a consequence of his influence, Congress passed a law in June 1834 reviving the pre-emption law of 1830 so as to allow pre-emption on lands which settlers had cultivated in 1833. The following January, Martin wrote M. T. Williams, surveyor general of Michigan Territory, asserting the rights of Juneau and his brother Peter under this law and urging immediate survey of the region. Settlements were being "continually" established "on and near the Milwaukie river," he complained; and the owners were "liable to . . . encroachments from persons desirous of settling near their possessions." About two weeks later Williams replied that contracts for the survey had been let.[28]

The danger of encroachment on Juneau's claim was not mere fancy. In December 1833, he warned his partner of the presence in the area of a rival claimant for their land; and a year later the impulsive trader-speculator was forced to "throw down" a building constructed by a group of interlopers backed by James Kinzie of Chicago. "He tells me to inform you,"

[27] Solomon Juneau to Morgan L. Martin, Dec. 1, 1833, Morgan L. Martin Papers, Wisconsin Historical Society Library.
[28] M. L. Martin to M. T. Williams, Jan. 15, 1835, and M. T. Williams to M. L. Martin, Jan. 28, 1835, Martin Papers.

wrote Juneau's clerk to Martin, "that he will hold possession at the Peril of his life until he has advice from you."[29] By November 1833, other white men had made their way into the Milwaukee country. Four of them—Albert Fowler, R. J. Currier, Andrew J. Lansing, and Quartus G. Carley—arrived from Chicago on November 18. They spent the winter in an old log cabin, the only whites, save Juneau, at the river's mouth. The following spring, Currier and Carley started a mill, and Fowler entered the employ of Juneau whom he served until 1836.[30] While on their way to the Milwaukee, this quartet had come upon another pioneer who was later to figure significantly in the city's growth. Virginia-born George H. Walker had set out for the Milwaukee country in October 1833, but having lost his way, he remained at Skunk Grove for the winter, trading with the Indians. He reached the Milwaukee on March 20, 1834, and located south of the river in what was later called "Walker's Point." There he engaged in the Indian trade, ultimately assuming in the development of Milwaukee's South side a role similar to that of Juneau and Martin on the east and Kilbourn on the west sides of the river.[31] By December 1834, other new-

[29] Albert Fowler to M. L. Martin, Dec. 13, 1834; Feb. 5, 1835, Martin Papers.

[30] Albert Fowler's westward migration had taken him from Massachusetts, where he was born in 1802, to New York and thence, at the age of thirty, to Chicago, where he speculated in corner lots and engaged in the Indian trade. The Indians called him "Red Cap" while he was working for Juneau. Against his protests, Doty and Martin got him a commission as justice of the peace. Denying that he was qualified for the position, he nevertheless wrote Martin that "Our exposed situation and the advice of my friends have induced me to accept it should I be appointed." Albert Fowler to M. L. Martin, Feb. 5, 1835, Martin Papers; Gregory, *History*, 1:74; Buck, 1:27-35 (rev. ed.).

[31] Born October 22, 1811, in Lynchburg, Virginia, Walker pioneered westward with his father at the age of fourteen, settling at Gallatin, Illinois. Activities in connection with the Indian trade had brought him to Juneau's trading post in the fall of 1833, and it was while attempting to return to the Milwaukee country with stores a few months later that he made his winter's sojourn at Skunk Grove. Arriving at Milwaukee in 1834, he located south of the river, the first white man, according to J. S. Buck, to build in that area, and there his trading activities with the Indians rivaled those of Juneau. Attempts were made to cover his claim with "floats," but he held out resolutely against all interference with his "squatter's right" until 1849 when his title to the land was recognized. The region in which he located soon came to be identified as Walker's Point and the young trader a "power" south of the river. He was early chosen supervisor, was elected to the territorial legislature in 1842 and 1844, acted as register of the Milwaukee land office from 1845 to 1849, and served as both alderman and mayor of Milwaukee. He was also identified with many projects for public improvements, such as the Prairie du Chien railroad and the city's first

comers, including Horace Chase, William Burdick, and Samuel Brown, had driven the stakes and piled the basswood logs that established the claims they later were to occupy.[32]

A more aggressive competitor for townsite profits than any of these, however, had spied the Milwaukee country in May of 1834. This was Byron Kilbourn, young Ohio engineer, whose commission from the surveyor general directed him not only to survey the area but also to be on the alert for desirable townsites between Fort Dearborn and Green Bay.[33] An excursion by horseback along the lake shore gave the ambitious surveyor's assistant his first glimpse of the site of Milwaukee. He was immediately impressed with the urban promise of the spot, free from conflicting interest with Green Bay and Chicago, and like those settlements possessed of its "own appropriate" hinterland. As he later wrote in the first issue of the Milwaukee *Advertiser*, in his opinion the region "*naturally* united to Milwaukee by common interest" was "at least equal in extent and fertility" and would sustain "a more dense population than either of the others."[34] For several reasons Kilbourn turned his speculative attentions to the lands on the west side of the river. Not only was Juneau in possession of the opposite side, but that territory, hemmed in between river and lake, appeared to be too limited for the young Ohioan's expansive ambitions. The rectangular tract bounded on the east by the Milwaukee, on the south by the Menomonee, and opening westward into a rich agricultural hinterland was more to his liking. He determined to buy it as soon as the sales opened, counting on Williams to advance the necessary funds and on his own ingenuity to get the lands at the

street railway. He died September 20, 1866. Gregory, *History*, 1:142-43; Howard L. Conard, ed., *History of Milwaukee from Its First Settlement to the Year 1895* (3 vols., Chicago, n.d.), 1:23-24 (hereafter cited as Conard); William G. Bruce, ed., *History of Milwaukee City and County* (3 vols., Milwaukee, 1922), 1:102-3; obituary, Milwaukee *Daily Sentinel*, Sept. 21, 1866.

[32] Buck, 1:51 (rev. ed.).

[33] Born in Granby, Connecticut, on September 8, 1801, Kilbourn had been brought to Worthington, Ohio, at the age of two. He profited from a good schooling until he was thirteen; and after clerking in his father's store and studying mathematics, history, and law, he took up surveying on the Ohio canals and served as resident engineer in the construction of the Miami Canal. In 1833, he received the commission as surveyor of public lands which brought him to Wisconsin in May 1834. Mack, "The Founding of Milwaukee," Wis. Hist. Soc., *Proc.*, 1906, p. 199; Gregory, *History*, 1:138.

[34] Milwaukee *Advertiser*, July 14, 1836.

minimum price.³⁵ He apparently rejected the offer of Martin and Juneau to combine their speculative ventures.³⁶

Regardless of their decision to develop separate townsites, the two sets of promoters were equally interested in having the lands opened to public sale. With the survey a matter of concern both to Williams, surveyor general of the territory, and to Martin, a member of the legislative council, it is not surprising that by February 1835 the Menominee cession (fractional townships 7 and 8 in range 22) and even a portion of the lands reserved to the Potawatomi until 1836 had been surveyed and made ready for public sale.³⁷ Kilbourn wrote Martin in January that he had succeeded in *prevailing* upon the surveyor general to include four fractional townships of the Potawatomi cession in the survey by pointing out

the peculiar situation and wants of that section of country, and the public advantage which would flow from that tract being brought into market as early as possible. . . . The wishes of those interested will thus be met and a public benefit confered [sic] in the facilities thus offered for the more immediate settlement of not only that strip of country but of the interiour [sic], in connection with it.³⁸

"Those interested" were quite obviously the Martin and Kilbourn enterprisers, for the time being cooperating with one another. It was not, however, until late July 1835, when squatters had already taken possession of the site "in swarms" and Juneau was selling quarter-acre lots at five and six hundred dollars each in anticipation of purchase, that the register of the Green Bay land office could offer the Milwaukee lands for sale.

Prospects for profit had begun to brighten six months before the lands were put on the open market.³⁹ Assured of his right to buy the land at the minimum price and certain of acquir-

---

³⁵ Conard, 1:21-22; Gregory, *History*, 1:119.

³⁶ In the fall of 1834, Kilbourn spent a few days with Martin and James D. Doty, at Juneau's trading house; and early in 1835, Martin and Juneau proposed to Kilbourn a union of their interests. "Narrative of Morgan L. Martin," Wis. Hist. Soc., *Colls.*, 11:405-6; Kellogg, "Beginnings of Milwaukee," *Wis. Mag. of Hist.*, 1:418 (June 1918).

³⁷ Conard, 1:29.

³⁸ Byron Kilbourn to M. L. Martin, from Columbus, Ohio, Jan. 8, 1835, Martin Papers.

³⁹ Albert Fowler to M. L. Martin, Dec. 13, 1834, Martin Papers.

ing title, Juneau had thirty-six lots laid out and surveyed. Purchases made of Juneau were sure to "stick," with no risk of eviction after the lands were offered at public auction—a strong selling point for the Juneau-Martin enterprise. As the day of sale approached, the ambitions of the speculators swelled. Martin became involved with Sheldon Thompson, a Buffalo forwarder, and eleven others in a $20,000 scheme for the purchase and improvement of "lands at the mouth of the Milwauky River . . . or at any other point or points which possess some extraordinary value by reason of Mill-Site, quarry of Stone, Minerals, Timber, etc."[40] In May, Martin and Juneau turned down an offer from "a company of rich merchants," acting through James D. Doty, as a result of which the original promoters would have relinquished all but one-tenth of the profits from their claim. Even at this late date, the whole-souled French-Canadian exhibited a casual indifference to impending speculative profits when he left the decision in the matter to Martin's judgment. "I told him that what you would do for our common interest would be agreeable to me," he wrote his partner. "With the reservation of 4 lots for me and 2 lots for my brother you can do what pleases you. . . . I have referred it entirely to you to do as you please but I hope you will ask a good price."[41] However, at this stage of the speculation, Martin, like Kilbourn, was reluctant to share with others the potential profits of what appeared to be a highly promising enterprise; thus when the lands were first offered for sale, control of the projected townsite development remained with the three original promoters and the handful of investors on whom they counted to provide them with financial aid.

The plat based on the survey by William A. Burt in 1835 and the abstract of lands sold at the Green Bay land office in late July and August of that year make graphic the process by which the Kilbourn and Martin-Juneau interests gained possession of nearly every acre of their respective townsites—and hence of what became the business center of the modern city—at a cost of no more than approximately $1.25 an acre. As has been pointed out, the promoters were primarily interested in the portions

---

[40] Power of attorney, dated March 2, 1835, Martin Papers.
[41] Juneau to Martin, May 6, 1835, Martin Papers.

of four sections in township 7 North, range 22 East, contiguous to the Milwaukee River north of its junction with the Menomonee. As the Milwaukee flows southward towards its confluence with the smaller stream, it bisects the southeast quarter of section 20 and the eastern half of section 29. Between these sections and Lake Michigan lie fractional sections 28 and 21. These four sections were the object of the speculators' first attention. Implemented with his pre-emptive right to the northeast quarter of fractional section 29 (called fractional because of the presence in it of the river bed), Juneau was able to purchase for only $165.82 a tract of 132.65 acres in what was to become the heart of modern Milwaukee—the entire portion of the present-day city bounded by Juneau Avenue on the north, Broadway on the east, Wisconsin Avenue on the south, and a point between North Fifth and North Sixth streets on the west.[42] Of this one-day million-dollar domain, Juneau was most interested in the 48½ acres which lay east of the river, this being the tract on which his trading post was located. Southeast of this were situated the 156.85 acres (lots 2, 3, and 4 of fractional section 28) to which Peter Juneau had a pre-emptive right. By using this claim, Juneau and Martin obtained for $196.07 all the land now bounded roughly by the lake on the east; Wells Street, Wisconsin Avenue, and Broadway on the north and west; and Menomonee Street on the south. "Floating rights" were laid on the remaining pieces in section 28, by which means Asa Sherman secured the west half of the northwest fractional quarter (80 acres) and John T. Read, lot 1 of the northwest fractional quarter (62.88 acres). Speculators with whom Martin had dealings appear to have been connected with the latter purchase. The same two—Ebenezer Childs and A. G. Ellis—were also involved in the purchase, through the use of Simeon Gammon's "floating right," of the 71.61 acres directly to the north (the west half of the southwest fractional quarter of section 21). And Martin himself appears to have patented the adjoining 80 acres (the east half of the southwest quarter of section 21) after it had been purchased through the use of Paul and Christiana Grignon's "floating right." The remaining 21 acres of river property in the southeast quarter of

---

[42] Juneau's affidavit, claiming right of pre-emption, is in National Archives.

LAND PURCHASES (1835) ON WHICH ORIGINAL TOWNSITES WERE BASED

section 29 were part of a parcel purchased by Kilbourn. These he relinquished to Juneau and Martin in return for that portion of Juneau's original purchase (northeast quarter of section 29) which lay west of the river.

The "floating right" was in a sense pre-emption "once removed." Land law provided that in case two persons claimed a pre-emptive right to the same quarter section they might divide it equally and receive from the government a certificate permitting each to enter an additional 80 acres elsewhere in the same land district so long as he did not interfere with occupants who had settled before 1834. This purchase could be made at the minimum price. Since such certificates were transferable, speculators bought them from the original holders and used them to secure, at the minimum price, land on which in some cases squatters had already settled. Kilbourn, lacking pre-emptive rights of his own, on which to base his townsite purchases, resorted to the expedient of using the "floating rights" of others to acquire land at the minimum price. The legal record shows that he made contacts with settlers possessed of such rights and arranged that these be placed upon tracts essential to his townsite plan. In this way he acquired the southeast quarter of section 29, site of the junction of the Milwaukee and Menomonee rivers. He used the "floating right" of Peter Chalifon to purchase 61.40 acres of it (lot 5) and that of John B. Genor (lots 2 and 6, southeast quarter, section 29) to acquire the remaining 67.42 acres. Thus for a total of $161.03 Kilbourn came into possession of the immensely valuable river front property between Wisconsin Avenue and East Erie Street, including both sides of present-day North Water Street and extending west to North Sixth. He acquired lands to the northwest and northeast of this tract at the minimum price through the use of the "floating rights" of Lewis Rouse (east half, southwest quarter, section 20—80 acres) and Joseph Jourdain (north half, southeast fractional quarter, section 20—72.65 acres). All four pieces were patented to Kilbourn on January 20, 1836.[43] On December 13,

---

[43] Records of the Green Bay land office, now in the National Archives, illustrate the method by which Kilbourn used the "floating rights" of the French-Canadian settlers to acquire his lands. On July 30 and 31, 1835, respectively, Peter Chalifon and Joseph Jourdain made claim for pre-emption in the form of depositions that each had cultivated several acres of wheat, oats,

1835, Williams, the surveyor general, bought a half-interest in the lands patented by his young assistant as the nucleus of their speculative scheme.[44]

Thus, through resort to pre-emption, "floating right," and patent, the townsite promoters acquired for what must have been close to the minimum price every acre of river front land, but for one 70-acre tract, on their respective sides of the river in sections 28, 29, 20, and the pertinent portion of section 21. The 70-acre tract, being the south half of the southeast quarter of section 20, was purchased with the "floating right" of Increase Claflin and, according to the record, patented to John McCarty on January 20, 1836. The same McCarty purchased by his own "float" a valuable tract west of Kilbourn's holdings, the east half of the southwest quarter of section 29. Use of the "floating rights" of the French-Canadian pioneers of the land district enabled Kilbourn to dispossess a number of the American arrivals of 1834, including Albert Fowler, Samuel Brown, and the firm of White and Evans. He justified these acquisitions by saying that they were indispensable to his townsite project and compensated some of the losers, as in the case of Fowler, by deeding them other lands.[45] What the speculators did for the French-Canadian farmers whose "floating rights" fitted so

corn, and vegetables, built a dwelling house, and enclosed lands during 1833 in the northwest fractional quarter of section 23, township 24 North, range 21 East, and that each was living on the said tract on June 19, 1834. Both claims for pre-emption were granted. In the next step in the negotiation each made affidavit that the other also cultivated the same tract in 1833 and resided thereon on June 19, 1834. On the basis of this joint occupancy each claimed a "floating right" for eighty acres. The final step took place when Chalifon requested that his floating pre-emption right be laid upon lot 5 in section 29, township 7, range 22 (61.40 acres). Chalifon made his mark, J. Jourdain was his witness, and Kilbourn swore to the customary statement that inspection of the tract showed the absence of residents, cultivation, or pre-emptive right thereto "either under the act of 29 May 1830, or that of 19 June 1834." Significantly enough, the entire affidavit was in Kilbourn's handwriting. Records of the General Land Office. Affidavits filed with Green Bay Cash Entry 19, in National Archives, Washington, D.C.

[44] Gregory, *History*, 1:119. For information on the identification of the boundaries of the original purchases with the present streets of the city, the author is indebted to Joseph P. Schwada, city engineer, and Robert A. Campbell, chief draftsman, of the office of city engineer, Milwaukee. See map showing the boundaries of the original purchases, as prepared in the office of the city engineer (Chap. 1, p. 16). See also list of original purchasers drawn from *Abstract of Lands Sold at the Land Office at Green Bay, M.T.*, July 30 through August 9, 1835 (Chap. 1, pp. 20-21).

[45] Gregory, *History*, 1:148.

admirably their acquisitive schemes the record does not show; but the claims possessed by these long-forgotten folk were a fundamental part of the speculative foundations on which the city was ultimately to rise.

Acquisition of the land was only the first step, however, in the process of townsite development. Next came the problem of drawing and filing the plats of the towns and, more important, that of attracting purchasers for the newly described lots. The plat for Juneau's side was in use early in 1835, but it was not recorded until September 8 of that year. Presumably this plat, signed by B. H. Edgerton on August 20, 1835, was based in part on an original survey made by William S. Trowbridge in 1834. The plat was entitled "Milwaukee East Side River"; the proprietor's certificate read, "Plat of the Village of Milwaukee in the Territory of Michigan." The plat for the West side was not recorded until October 9, 1835. Made by Kilbourn, Archibald Clybourn (a Chicago speculator), McCarty, Fowler, and Juneau, it was entitled "A Plat of the Town of Milwaukee on the West Side of the River." Apparently the survey of this community was made by Garret Vliet sometime in July or August 1835.[46]

The two sets of speculators had cooperated in pressing for the survey and sale of lands; Juneau had even joined in filing the plat of the West-side community; but in the ensuing real estate operations cooperation between the Kilbourn-Williams interests and the Martin-Juneau enterprise was at an end. Now it was each side for itself, with a resultant competitive sectionalism that was not only to find violent expression in the formative years of city development but indeed to endure, in some measure, even to the present day. The river, which provided an adjunct traditionally indispensable to every great city, was for the moment the barrier that gave equal hopes of prosperity to the communities on either of its banks. It thus became the aim of each group of promoters to draw settlers to its village and bar them from that of its rival. The East-siders had the advantage of a head start; and the generous trader-speculator was openhanded in offering inducements to settlers.[47] On visits to Chi-

[46] *Ibid.*, 1:123-24; John B. Vliet, "The Story of a Wisconsin Surveyor," *Wisconsin Magazine of History*, 8:57 (September 1924).
[47] Buck, 1:112 (rev. ed.).

ABSTRACT OF LANDS SOLD AT THE LAND OFFICE

When Sold 1835		By Whom Purchased	Residence	Recpt. No.	Section		Twp.	Range
July 30		Daniel Darnall	Brown City	2	Fractional	33	7	22
"	"	Increase Claflin	"	"	3	Lot #2, SE¼ & SE fr. SE¼	20	7	22
"	"	Francis Laventure	"	"	5	N½ NE fl. ¼	32	7	22
"	"	Ebenezer Childs	"	"	6	Lot #2 NE¼	32	7	22
"	31	John Smith	"	"	8	E½ NW¼	29	7	22
"	"	Asa Sherman	"	"	9	W½ NW fl. ¼	28	7	22
August 1		John McCarty	"	"	11	E½ SW¼	29	7	22
"	"	John B. Genor	"	"	12	Lots #2&6SE¼	29	7	22
"	"	John T. Read	"	"	14	Lot #1, NW fl.¼	28	7	22
"	"	Simeon Gammon	"	"	15	W½ SW fl. ¼	21	7	22
"	"	Peter Juneau	"	"	16	Lots #2, 3, 4 fl.	28	7	22
"	"	Solomon Juneau	"	"	17	NE¼ fl.	29	7	22
"	3	Peter Chilifon [Chalifon]	"	"	19	Lot #5	29	7	22
"	"	Joseph Jourdain	"	"	20	N½ SE fl. ¼	20	7	22
"	"	Linus Thompson	"	"	22	Lot #3 SE fl. ¼	32	7	22
"	"	James Vieux	"	"	24	NW¼	31	7	22
"	4	Paul Grignon and Christiana, wife	"	"	29	E½ SW¼	21	7	22
"	"	Amable Durocher	"	"	30	W½ NW¼	29	7	22
"	5	Lewis Rouse	"	"	36	E½ SW¼	20	7	22
"	9	Laurent Fortier	"	"		W½ SW¼	29	7	22

AT GREEN BAY, M.T., JULY 30, 1835, to AUGUST 9, 1835

Acres	Price Per A.	Purchase Price	Penciled Notation	Ink Notation
77.70	$1.25	$ 97.12½		Float
70.76	"	88.45	Patented to John McCarty, 20 Jan. '36	Float
44.79	"	55.99		Float
42.60	"	53.25	Morgan L. Martin	Float
80.	"	100.00		Float
80.	"	100.00		Float
80.	"	100.00		Float
67.42	"	84.28	Patented to Byron Kilbourn, 20 Jan. '36	Float
50.30	"	62.88	Ebzr Childs and Albert G. Ellis	Float
71.61	"	89.52	Do. Do. Do. Do.	Float
156.85	"	196.07	Morgan L. Martin Pre-emption Act, 1834	
132.65	"	165.82	Pre-emption Act, 1834	
61.40	"	76.75	Patented to Byron Kilbourn, 20 Jan. '36	Float
72.65	"	90.81	Patented to Byron Kilbourn, 20 Jan. '36	Float
57.60	"	72.00		Float
160.00	"	200.00	Pre-emption Act, 1834	
80.	"	100.00	Morgan L. Martin	Float
80.	"	100.00	Morgan L. Martin	Float
80.	"	100.00	Patented to Byron Kilbourn, 20 Jan. '36	Float
80.	"	100.00	John Lawe	Float

From National Archives, *Abstract of Lands.*

cago and Green Bay, Juneau recruited carpenters and builders with offers of lots, jobs, and free transportation to his village.[48] He frequently accosted visitors, as he did George W. Lawe, with such a greeting as "George, you ought to come to Milwaukee to live. This is going to be a big town."[49] Occasionally he encouraged prospective buyers by guaranteeing that their lots would double in value in a year.[50] Meanwhile, he was active in townsite improvement: grading and improving streets, exerting pressure to have the courthouse and land office located on his side of the river, making plans for a burying ground, supervising the erection of a hotel, and organizing the Milwaukee Steamboat Company as a means of improving transportation to the village.[51] To get the land office was worth a sacrifice, he thought, for, as he wrote Martin, ". . . you know that it is of great importance that it should be on our side."[52] An additional impetus to settlement was provided by the improvements built by others interested in the promotion. Dousman was a man of wealth; and he built a warehouse, a store, and one or two dwelling houses. Martin made a similar contribution to the "going" appearance of the new community.[53]

On the other side of the river, Kilbourn's strategy was not only to improve and advertise his community, but if possible to starve out Juneautown by monopolizing the supply of settlers. This he hoped to do by making it virtually impossible for newcomers to reach the Juneau-Martin village. His bridge across the Menomonee was designed to divert to the West side the traffic on the Chicago road which terminated at Walker's Point and connected with the East side only by ferry.[54] Should the East-siders attempt to bridge the river, "I will take good care that they shall have no use of it," he wrote his Cincinnati partner; "for we can construct a couple of steamboats for harbor

[48] Nelson Olin, "Reminiscences of Milwaukee in 1835-36," *Wisconsin Magazine of History*, 13:206-7, 209 (March 1930).
[49] Milwaukee *Sentinel*, July 14, 1937.
[50] *Evening Wisconsin* (Milwaukee), Oct. 15, 1895.
[51] Juneau to Martin, Sept. 20, 1836, Martin Papers.
[52] *Ibid.*
[53] Byron Kilbourn to M. T. Williams, Feb. 27, 1837, in Gregory, *History*, 1:127.
[54] Laurence M. Larson, "The Sectional Elements in the Early History of Milwaukee," Mississippi Valley Historical Association, *Proceedings*, 1907-8, 1:125.

use, and pass them through the bridge so frequently that it can never be closed."⁵⁵ Moreover, the West-siders maintained a lighter service to pre-empt, for their community, passengers arriving by steamer in Milwaukee Bay.⁵⁶

The Milwaukee *Advertiser*,⁵⁷ founded by a group of West-siders in 1836, was aptly named, for most of its news was obviously designed to attract settlers to the growing village west of the river. The issue of July 21, 1836, discounted rumors that the Indians were warlike; that of August 11 expanded upon the easy connections between Milwaukee and the outside world. Two weeks later the paper reported that the proprietors were spending "large sums of money" improving streets, removing hills, and draining and filling lands—leaving nothing undone that would make "Milwaukee a desirable place of residence." Appeals to mechanics told of the high wages with which they could "render themselves independent."⁵⁸ Subsequent issues praised the Milwaukee harbor for its capacity to "afford protection to vessels in any storm"⁵⁹ and emphasized the fertility of the area by offering premiums for fruits and vegetables of phenomenal size.⁶⁰ In each issue a notice of Kilbourn's General Land Agency was prominently displayed. A map of Milwaukee, published in Cincinnati in 1836 at the instance of the West-siders, ignored the East side, picturing a country road traversing it diagonally and giving the impression that it was without habitation.⁶¹

Like the proprietors on the East side and, admittedly, "to counter-balance in some degree" their efforts, Kilbourn under-

---

⁵⁵ Kilbourn to Williams, Feb. 27, 1837, in Gregory, *History*, 1:128.
⁵⁶ "The 'Badger' was built by the westward of the town—and has been the cause of much quarreling between the two sides of the river, as she was formerly run exclusively for the benefit of the westward. Passengers for the eastward could find some other conveyance or land on the west side and cross over." I. A. Lapham to Darius Lapham, July 30, 1840. This is one of a series of Lapham letters published in the Milwaukee *Sentinel*, Oct. 16, 1895. These letters will hereafter be identified by reference to this issue of the *Sentinel*.
⁵⁷ The Milwaukee *Advertiser* was founded in July 1836 by Daniel H. Richards and edited for the first six months by Hans Crocker. I. A. Lapham, J. H. Tweedy, and Byron Kilbourn were frequent contributors. In March 1841, it was sold to Josiah A. Noonan and styled *Courier*.
⁵⁸ Milwaukee *Advertiser*, Aug. 25, 1836.
⁵⁹ *Ibid.*, Oct. 13, 1836.
⁶⁰ *Ibid.*, Oct. 27, Nov. 17, 1836.
⁶¹ Mack, "The Founding of Milwaukee," Wis. Hist. Soc., *Proc.*, 1906, p. 204.

took costly public improvements, as a means of enhancing the attractiveness of the townsite. By February 1837, he had spent $13,000 in the construction of buildings and probably more than a like sum on roads and streets.[62] His own dwelling had become the nucleus of settlement; he urged his partner to subsidize construction that would fill up certain vacant spaces and "give a connected appearance to the town." A good building on the corner of block 47 and a warehouse or storehouse on the corner of block 49, he wrote, would "give tone to improvements in that quarter and enhance the value of other surrounding property more than the cost of buildings—and the buildings would rent for a fair interest." The construction of improvements "would be money well expended, even if no return should ever be had from it direct."[63]

For the first few months after the original purchase of the townsite property the land business boomed, for the Milwaukee country was one of the focal points for victims of the current "land-fever." As Caroline M. Kirkland wrote of the period in her volume, *Western Clearings* (1845): "The man with one leg, or he that had none, could at least get on board a steamer, and make for Chicago or Milwaukee; the strong, the able, but above all, the 'enterprising,' set out with his pocket-map and his pocket-compass, to see with his own eyes."[64] "Government land speculation is surest," wrote B. H. Edgerton, then in Juneau's employ, "but there is not so much to be made as there is in town property."[65] As early as a month before the original land sales, all the lands within two miles of the proposed villages had been claimed; and newcomers desirous of acquiring property were forced to buy of the promoters. Lots had begun to change hands before the ink was dry on the register of sales; and by the end of August, Daniel Wells reported that already much money

[62] According to a letter from a local settler, written September 6, 1836, Juneau and Kilbourn together had 150 men "at work grading and improving the streets . . . upon which they will spend $40,000 this year." Buck, 1:145 (rev. ed.).
[63] Byron Kilbourn to M. T. Williams, Feb. 27, 1837, in Gregory, *History*, 1:126-29.
[64] Excerpt from Caroline M. Kirkland, *Western Clearings*, in *American Local-Color Stories*, ed. by Harry R. Warfel and G. Harrison Orians (New York, 1941), 46.
[65] Gregory, *History*, 1:90.

had "been made in speculating in lots."⁶⁶ By September, quarter-acre lots were selling for five and six hundred dollars, and, according to the Green Bay *Intelligencer* "Milwauky" was "all the rage."⁶⁷ In October, real estate dealers in various parts of the country were offering Milwaukee lands for sale.⁶⁸

The speculative mania mounted to its peak during the first half of 1836. In January, Juneau reported that every day brought new opportunities for sales.⁶⁹ In March, Andrew Vieau was offered $1,000 for a lot Juneau had sold him for $800; but he held out for $1,400 and thought he would get it.⁷⁰ By the close of the month, the twelve acres Juneau had sold for $2,000 an acre at the mouth of the Menomonee River could command between $3,000 and $4,000 an acre.⁷¹ By the last of April, Juneau pressed Martin to buy the twenty acres belonging to Amable Durocher. He suggested paying from $1,500 to $2,000, half down and the balance in one year, confident that the property would be worth $500 an acre in six months.⁷² Three weeks later: "You must buy up Durocher without fail if you had to pay him 5 or 6000 dollars. It will be worth 2000 dollars per acre in six weeks."⁷³ Such speculators as George Reed were acting as agents for both the Martin-Juneau lands and Kilbourn's real estate⁷⁴ and making payments, at least to the owners of the former, with mortgages on valuable land.

The promise of this speculator's paradise impressed an optimistic young Ohioan who was destined to make a marked con-

⁶⁶ Daniel Wells to Friend Kimball, Aug. 30, 1835, in Buck, 1:76 (rev. ed.). "The settlers will all get their claims for $1.25 per acre, as it is considered very mean to bid against them; some of them have already sold their claims at high figures, in one case for $8,000."

⁶⁷ A. C. Wheeler, *Chronicles of Milwaukee* (Milwaukee, 1861), 32.

⁶⁸ A Chicago auctioneer promised the "mechanic and workingman" that "a few hundred dollars" in Milwaukee lands "in the course of two years at farthest" would make him "worth thousands." The chance for "speculating" exceeded that of the Chicago sale and foreigners were "particularly invited to go and examine the premises prior to the day of sale." Bill of A. Ganett, Oct. 8, 1835, in Buck, 1:80 (rev. ed.).

⁶⁹ Juneau to Martin, Jan. 20, 1836, Martin Papers.

⁷⁰ Andrew J. Vieau to Peter Grignon, March 30, 1836, Martin Papers.

⁷¹ Juneau to Martin, March 31, 1836, Martin Papers.

⁷² Juneau to Martin, April 24, 1836, Martin Papers.

⁷³ Juneau to Martin, May 15, 1836, Martin Papers. The abstract of conveyances shows that Martin had made the purchase on May 14, 1836.

⁷⁴ Juneau to Martin, April 24, 1836, Martin Papers.

tribution in succeeding years to the intellectual as well as the material development of the new community. Journeying toward Milwaukee through a "world of speculators," Increase Lapham added the map of Milwaukee to the many plats of new towns already suspended on the barroom walls of the hotels at which he stopped.[75] Arriving on July 1, 1836, he found a village of fifty houses, mostly on the east side of the river, seething with bustle and activity. He reported that town lots were bringing from $500 to $5,000[76] and that about 1,208 people were residing where, to his amazement, "18 months ago there *were but two* families—!"[77] "Everyday, almost, new frames were erected," wrote Lucius Barber. "Men's hats were crammed with maps of paper towns."[78] Even ground room was valuable. High rents were paid for the privilege of selling goods on vacant lots.[79] And as Caroline Kirkland described it, profits could be made even by *"standing around;* i.e., watching the land-market for bargains."[80] Juneau was now reported to be worth $100,000, with the likelihood of doubling his wealth with the spring demand for land. His clerks were taking in $8,000 to $10,000 daily in return for goods and land, and the town-maker was beginning to buy back at greatly increased prices lots he had sold for a song.[81] Milwaukee was going to be a metropolis and no doubt about it. Optimistic newcomers saw an advantage over

[75] Increase to Darius Lapham, June 21, 1836, I. A. Lapham Papers, Wisconsin Historical Society Library. Increase Lapham, Wisconsin's first scholar, was born in Palmyra, New York, in 1811. The son of an engineering contractor, he gained a self-made engineering education working on canals in Ohio and Kentucky. Intellectual and scholarly interests, and keen powers of observation, were reflected in his study of botany, zoology, and scientific agriculture as a young man. An early acquaintance with Byron Kilbourn was responsible for bringing him to Milwaukee in 1836 to help in the construction of the Rock River Canal. He speedily became interested in advancing the educational facilities of the young community and his *Catalogue of Plants and Shells, Found in the Vicinity of Milwaukee, on the West Side of Lake Michigan,* published in 1836, and his gazetteer of Wisconsin, published at Milwaukee in 1844, establish him as one of the earliest writers and scholars of the Middle West. Milo M. Quaife, "Increase Allen Lapham, First Scholar of Wisconsin," *Wisconsin Magazine of History,* 1:4-9 (September 1917).
[76] I. A. to D. Lapham, July 7, 1836, Lapham Papers.
[77] I. A. Lapham to Dr. C. W. Short, Aug. 17, 1836, Lapham Papers.
[78] Quoted in Milwaukee *Sentinel,* July 14, 1937.
[79] Gregory, *History,* 1:72.   [80] *American Local-Color Stories,* 46.
[81] Alexander F. Pratt, "Reminiscences," in *Evening Wisconsin,* Oct. 15, 1895.

FUR TRADE AND TOWNSITE PROMOTION   27

Chicago in its "higher ground, . . . freedom from swamp and mud, and . . . promise of a better harbor."[82] A correspondent summed up current sentiments when he wrote: "In five years its population will outnumber Chicago's. . . . Nature has given it a marked superiority in every particular essential to the growth of a great city."[83] It looked as if all that delayed the immediate realization of a metropolis was the lack of lumber to construct the buildings. [84]

Something more than the lack of building materials was soon, however, to halt this quondam mushroom growth.[85] By the fall of 1836, the city's promoters had begun to feel the pressures that were to contribute to country-wide depression in the coming year. As early as June 15, 1836, Martin's cousin, writing from New York, had counseled him to get out of land speculation.[86] By September, Juneau was hard put for funds to pay the bills for street improvement and construction of the courthouse.[87] Money was "dam scarce," according to his report in November, and buyers with cash, non-existent.[88] December brought a demand for a $2,000 payment on the vessel for which Juneau's Milwaukee Steamboat Company had contracted.[89] The hope that spring sales would bring relief proved to be unfounded; and by May 1837 conditions were more than ever depressed. Many people were arriving, "but without any money."[90] "We feel the pressure of the times here in the

[82] Amherst W. Kellogg, "Recollections of Life in Early Wisconsin," *Wisconsin Magazine of History*, 7:480 (June 1924). Hereafter, to distinguish the writings of Amherst W. Kellogg from those of Louise P. Kellogg, he will be referred to as A. W. Kellogg.

[83] Buck, 1:145 (rev. ed.).

[84] Increase Lapham wrote his father on July 27, 1836, that the town was "improving as fast as the supply of lumber will allow. . . . Many other buildings would be put up if the necessary supply of building material could be procured. . . . If I had nothing else to do, I think I might make good wages here at engineering; there are many mill sites to be leveled and roads to be laid out." I. A. to Seneca Lapham, July 27, 1836, Lapham Papers.

[85] I. A. to Darius Lapham, Feb. 25, 1837, Lapham Papers.

[86] Ph. P. Freeman to Morgan L. Martin, June 15, 1836, Martin Papers. "The pressure in the money market is greater here than was ever known before. Consequently, real estate has come to a full stop and all business rather dull."

[87] Juneau to Martin, Sept. 20, 1836, Martin Papers.

[88] Juneau to Martin, Nov. 5, 14, 1836, Martin Papers.

[89] Juneau to Martin, Nov. 19, 1836, Martin Papers.

[90] Juneau to Martin, May 30, 1837, Martin Papers.

'woods,' " Lapham confessed to his brother in September. Available currency was of the "wild-cat" type, not good for purchases at the land offices,[91] and the lack of money necessitated forfeiture at great sacrifices. According to the reminiscences of a contemporary, many a city lot for which $500 to $1,000 had been paid was traded for a barrel of flour to ward off starvation.[92]

There were mixed opinions as to the ultimate effect of the "economic revulsion" on young Milwaukee. The editor of the *Sentinel* contended that the western city would be less hard hit than eastern communities, for it was supposed that the distresses there would "send crowds of the very bone and sinew of society to our harbor, seeking employment and bringing into speedy cultivation the . . . healthful regions in the interior."[93] But it was increasingly apparent that town building in advance of a developed hinterland was economically unsound. As early as February 1837, Increase Lapham had admitted to his brother that the country had not "kept pace with the town in its onward march."[94] "It will be no proof of our prosperity to erect buildings faster than the wants of the community and the business of the country will warrant," the *Sentinel* warned in July; and by February 1838, one of its correspondents, echoing sentiments expressed earlier in the Chicago *American,* stressed the importance of multiplying the production of the rural hinterland if the hard times were to be overcome and the city were to realize "that state of golden magnificence which the fond prophecy of its inhabitants has marked out for its destiny."[95]

Despite brave professions of returning prosperity on the turn of the forties, it was 1842 or 1843 before recovery from the aftermath of the "land-fever" was assured. "The times continue to be hard," wrote Increase Lapham on June 24, 1838, "which is not strange when we reflect how much money we have to send away for provisions."[96] A sign of potential recovery was

[91] I. A. Lapham to ——, Sept. 27, 1837, Milwaukee *Sentinel,* Oct. 16, 1895.
[92] A. W. Kellogg, "Recollections of Life in Early Wisconsin," *Wis. Mag. of Hist.,* 7:484 (June 1924).
[93] Milwaukee *Sentinel,* July 4, 1837.
[94] Increase to Darius Lapham, Feb. 25, 1837, Milwaukee *Sentinel,* Oct. 16, 1895.
[95] *Ibid.,* July 11, 25, 1837; Feb. 13, 1838.
[96] Increase Lapham to ——, June 24, 1838, *ibid.,* Oct. 16, 1895.

seen in the land sales of 1839 when actual settlers rather than speculators obtained most of the land.[97] Although the *Sentinel* remarked a revival of business in May 1839,[98] the Milwaukee *Advertiser* continued to notice the sale of many lots for taxes.[99] Money was "far from plentiful" in the fall of 1840, in spite of contentions that the prospects of the town were "never more encouraging than at the present."[100] By May 1841 the *Courier* reported substantial evidences of prosperity. Goods to the value of about $100,000 had been sold in the past twelve months, and there was a great demand for houses and real estate in the business part of the town.[101] In July, according to Lapham, it looked as if the farmers this year would "begin to come out."[102] It was not, however, until 1843 that there were such positive signs of recovery as to mark a turning point in the economic history of the young community. "Nearly every tenement of every description" was occupied, wrote the editor of the *Courier;* "the stores of our merchants are well supplied with as fine assortments of goods as can be found in the west, and our streets are thronged day after day with teams from the interior, bringing to market the produce of the country."[103] Juneau noted a new flow of immigration that was sending newcomers north and west of the settlement in search of land.[104] With its some 3,000 villagers, the Milwaukee of 1843 was not the metropolis of which the speculators had dreamed a half-dozen years earlier. But the economic revulsion had passed, and the village stood ready to receive the flood of population that the forties were to bring.

[97] Increase to Darius Lapham, March 17, 1839, *ibid.,* Oct. 16, 1895. Lapham reported that nearly $600,000 had been received and that "about all the land in the county" had been bought from the government at not more than $1.25 an acre. "Actual settlers have obtained their farms, and very little of the land was bought by speculators."
[98] *Ibid.,* May 14, 1839. "Milwaukee is rapidly recovering from the pecuniary depression under which she has suffered for the last two years."
[99] Milwaukee *Advertiser,* Sept. 14, 1839; Juneau to Martin, Nov. 30, 1839, Martin Papers.
[100] Milwaukee *Sentinel,* Oct. 6, 1840.
[101] Buck, 2:109, 111.
[102] Increase Lapham to ——, July 24, 1841, Milwaukee *Sentinel,* Oct. 16, 1895.
[103] Milwaukie *Journal,* Feb. 9, 1842.
[104] Juneau to American Fur Company, May 28, 1843, "Calendar of the American Fur Company's Papers," 2 parts, published by the American Historical Association as volumes 2 and 3 of its *Annual Report,* 1944, pt. 2, pp. 1311-12.

The periodic reckonings in which the promoters indulged shed some light on the financial aspects of the speculation which had given the city its start. By February 1837, Kilbourn had bought out Archibald Clybourn of Chicago, one of his associates in platting his village, and was in sole charge of the West-side project. A statement of receipts and expenditures, made for his partner M. T. Williams as of December 31, 1836, showed a balance due the surveyor general amounting to $9,875.70. Although Kilbourn professed to have almost this amount on hand, he proposed to use it "for the present in payment for work now progressing, . . . to be refunded out of future receipts." His own share had been "entirely consumed and a little more" in building (which had cost $13,000) and road and street expenditures.[105] In August 1837, Juneau and Martin made a similar accounting with the Mackinac speculator who had agreed to share expenses with Martin. What Michael Dousman contributed to the expense of promotion, beyond the construction of buildings, is a question; but at the time of striking the balance he was deemed to merit a quarter of the profits. The accounting showed that the partners had received $14,243 in cash on lots and that $48,466.43 was due, held in notes. Notes were transferred to Dousman in the amount of $12,295.52; and for his share of the cash, less a $1,400 obligation he owed Juneau and Martin, they gave him a note for $2,000.[106] A month later, George Reed, one of their land agents, professing to draw a "salutary lesson" from the "late hard times," inquired of Martin how much land he would take in "fraction six" in exchange for a discharge from all the liabilities to Martin and Juneau which they at that time held.[107]

To judge from Martin's accounts for 1841, he and Juneau made a division of notes in 1838 and again in 1841.[108] Throughout this period there was also continuous transfer of property by deed from Martin and Juneau to other purchasers and from Martin and Juneau to one another. Mortgages on lots, held by

[105] Kilbourn to Micajah T. Williams, Feb. 27, 1837, in Gregory, *History*, 1:126-27.
[106] Statement of accounts, Martin Papers.
[107] George Reed to M. L. Martin, Oct. 17, 1837, Martin Papers.
[108] Martin Papers, March 1841.

Martin, ranged in value from $400 to $2,500. On many occasions, Juneau assigned mortgages to Martin in parcels aggregating as much as $12,000 at one time. On April 16, 1842, Martin deeded a large parcel of lots to Juneau. A few were deeded in 1843 and 1846.[109] In the intervening years, Juneau continued to serve as Martin's agent, in addition to his fur-trading activities with the American Fur Company; and in the former capacity he collected debts, paid taxes, redeemed property that had been sold for taxes, attempted, when possible, to raise funds, protected their holdings against interlopers, and managed such joint interests as the steamboat enterprise and the Milwaukee House. Their correspondence reveals the mutual understanding and confidence of the two promoters, in spite of Juneau's occasional impatience at having the brunt of responsibility to bear. Martin honored his judgment and, whenever possible, tried to comply with his requests; and Juneau shared in a number of other promotional schemes in which the Green Bay speculator was involved.[110]

It is obviously impossible to construct a balance sheet on the operations of the pioneer promoters in developing their Milwaukee holdings. By comparison with what they paid the government for the land, their returns were, at least on paper, great. But so, too, were the obligations they incurred in developing the townsites; for example, Juneau and Martin claimed to have spent as much as $100,000 in improving the East side.[111] Moreover, it is difficult to separate the profits and losses incurred in the Milwaukee enterprise from other promotional projects of at least territorial scope with which the Milwaukee operations were inextricably interwoven. It is quite true that the speculators took land to which other settlers had an equally good, if not better, right and drew momentarily large profits from the transaction. Yet it must not be forgotten that both groups of town-makers "followed through," thus becoming victims as well

[109] Abstract of conveyances, Martin Papers.
[110] In connection with a speculative venture in the Rock and Catfish River region, Juneau wrote: "With respect to having a share in the purchases of land that you have made as you mentioned in your letter, that's what I always understood and I desire to have a share." Juneau to Martin, Sept. 30, 1835, Martin Papers.
[111] Bleyer, "The Founder of Milwaukee," Milwaukee Sentinel, Nov. 11, 1906.

as beneficiaries of a boom that collapsed before they had had time to recover the sums they had sunk in the overhead costs of the promotional enterprise.[112] And certainly their individual contribution to the growth of the city was not inconsiderable. The continuous personal identification of Juneau and Kilbourn with the welfare of their respective communities, their rivalry in striving for the advantages speculation offered, and the aggressiveness and ingenuity with which they and their financial backers pressed the improvement of the region and stimulated its settlement account in large measure for the solid, though somewhat interrupted, progress toward cityhood achieved in the young village on the Milwaukee by the middle years of the 1840's.

[112] As profits from land speculation declined, Juneau gave renewed attention to the fur trade. But this pursuit, too, was fraught with difficulties because of the increased number of competing traders in the area and the growing indolence and dissipation of the Indians. In the spring and summer of 1843 Juneau came momentarily to the conclusion that he would give up the fur trade; in the fall he determined to give it another try; but in April 1844 he reported to the American Fur Company that he was bankrupt, with $20,000 against him. Juneau to American Fur Company, May 28, July 17, Aug. 15, 18, 1843; April 25, 1844. See "Calendar of the American Fur Company's Papers," Amer. Hist. Assoc., *Ann. Rept.*, pt. 2, pp. 1311, 1322, 1329-30, 1366.

CHAPTER 2

Village Politics and Internal Improvements

POPULAR participation in government, competition and rivalry between the East and West sides, and a characteristically western concern for the development of internal improvements set the tone of politics in the young communities spawned by speculation on either side of the Milwaukee River. The political philosophy of village Milwaukee was reflected in the first issue of the *Sentinel,* when it was asserted that "rigid enforcement of and prompt obedience to the popular will" was "the most vital principle of Representative Government."[1] This political conviction was early manifested in connection with the first local election, when it was resolved that all actual settlers should have the privilege of voting for the choice of township officials at Juneau's house on September 17, 1835.[2] The most liberal suffrage qualification then prevailing in the territory limited electors to "free white male inhabitants . . . above the age of twenty-one" who had resided for three months in the territory. But in this first election in Milwaukee all possible male voters, including nineteen-year-old Talbot Dousman and Joe Oliver, Juneau's colored cook, were pressed to participate.[3] Democracy—or tradition—demanded many officers, almost more than there were eligible men to supply. Thirty-nine electors chose twenty-four township officials; and

---
[1] Milwaukee *Sentinel,* June 27, 1837.
[2] Records of first election, quoted in Buck, 4:416.
[3] "An act to enable the people of Michigan to form a constitution and state government" (Jan. 26, 1835), section 2, in *The Michigan Constitutional Conventions of 1835-36,* Harold M. Dorr, ed. (Ann Arbor, 1940), 585; Gregory, *History,* 1:237; Buck, 1:73 (rev. ed.). Milwaukee County was set off from Brown County on September 6, 1834. On March 17, 1835, an act authorizing township govern-

in several instances a trusted settler had to fill more than one position. Dr. Enoch Chase was made assessor, poundmaster, and school commissioner; Benoni Finch was to serve in similar threefold capacity as road commissioner, director of the poor, and fence viewer; and Juneau and Walker were the recipients of two offices apiece. Walker was chosen as supervisor, and Horace Chase as town clerk.[4] Frequent resort to public meetings showed a continuing concern for popular decisions in civic matters. The problem of town incorporation was proposed to the body politic by the *Advertiser* in October 1836. "It is important that our town be incorporated," wrote the editor, "and we would wish the people to decide on what manner it should be done."[5]

In spite of agitation in 1836 for village organization that would include the communities on both sides of the river, the separatism of the two rival settlements was revealed in February 1837 when the settlers met on their respective sides of the river to incorporate and choose officers for "The Town of Milwaukee" (Juneautown) and "The Town of Milwaukee on the West Side of the River" (Kilbourntown). This was done on the authority of a general law, passed by the Wisconsin territorial legislature on December 6, 1836, which provided that a community of 300 persons could be incorporated as a town upon the two-thirds vote of a meeting open to the white male inhabitants, twenty-one or above, who had resided there for six months.[6] The original town on the East side was hemmed in by the Milwaukee River and the lake, and stretched from what is now Brady Street on the north to a point east of Greenfield Avenue on the south. The more spacious West-side community, bounded by the present North Avenue on the north and the Menomonee River valley on the south, extended west from the river to a line that ran along what is now 27th Street

ment was passed, with provision for an election in September. County organization was provided by an act of August 25, 1835. Mack, "The Founding of Milwaukee," Wis. Hist. Soc., *Proc.*, 1906, p. 205.

[4] Milwaukee *Sentinel*, July 14, 1937; Buck, 4:416.
[5] Milwaukee *Advertiser*, Oct. 13, 1836.
[6] "An act to incorporate the inhabitants of such towns as wish to be incorporated," *Wisconsin Territorial Laws*, 1836 [1837, 1838] (Reprint, 1867), 65-70.

to Lisbon and thence to 20th.[7] The administration of village affairs on each side of the river was vested in a president and a board of trustees; and as in the case of township management, the "founding fathers" of the villages assumed the major municipal offices. Juneau was made president of the East-side trustees for 1837 and 1838, and Kilbourn served in like capacity for the West side. Juneau's associates were Samuel Henman, William A. Prentiss, George D. Dousman, and Daniel Wells, Jr.; while Kilbourn's included such prominent West-side personalities as James H. Rogers, John H. Tweedy, William R. Longstreet, and Daniel H. Richards.[8] The first-named of the Westsiders—James H. Rogers—early became a promoter of pre-eminent influence in the young settlement. By 1835 this thrifty New Yorker had sensed the potentialities of the Wisconsin community. In the spring of 1836 he set out with his family in a four-horse wagon and undertook the sixty-day journey to the West. Possessed of some means, he made astute real estate purchases on either side of the river, acquiring valuable properties on what are now Prospect and Wisconsin avenues. Thereafter he assumed such a role in the commercial and political development of Milwaukee as to qualify as one of its foremost promoters and one—unlike Kilbourn and Juneau—whose interests, extending to the communities on both sides of the river, transcended the sectional rivalries of the original town-makers.[9]

The costs of maintaining two separate village governments in time of depression must have prompted a movement late in 1837 to consolidate the two settlements. As a result, a law was

[7] This information was supplied by J. P. Schwada, city engineer, and R. A. Campbell, chief draftsman.

[8] Wheeler, *Chronicles of Milwaukee*, 83.

[9] Rogers was born in Troy, New York, January 11, 1794. He had a successful mercantile career in that State before deciding to migrate to the West. He was identified with almost every significant financial enterprise in the first decade of the city's growth; contributed markedly to the physical development of the community in building a hotel and many business blocks; inaugurated the improvement of what was then Grand Avenue; and supported many worthy undertakings such as the Milwaukee County Agricultural Society and Milwaukee College. James S. Buck credits Rogers with building the best buildings in the village. "If there was a promise of money in any new contemplated project, he always took a chance in [it], if he could, always going for the lion's share, and usually managed to get it." Conard, 1:337-39; Buck, 2:221.

approved, on January 16, 1838, constituting a "village of Milwaukee" to include three districts: the first, south of the Milwaukee and Menomonee rivers; the second, east and north of the Milwaukee; and the third, west and north of the two streams.[10] The existence of legislation limiting incorporations to an area of two square miles made void the 1838 enactment; but on March 11, 1839, a law was passed joining the two original villages as the East and West wards, respectively, of the town of Milwaukee.[11] On February 12, 1845, the limits of the town were extended by the addition of Walker's Point as the South Ward. The first election in the newly-organized town took place on May 1, 1839, and soon thereafter the five trustees from each ward joined in selecting a presiding officer. As might have been predicted, Juneau was the first president of the consolidated village;[12] and in the remaining years of villagehood, H. M. Hubbard (1840), J. H. Rogers (1841 and 1842), and Lindsey Ward served in the same capacity. As was characteristic of young urban communities, the most prominent merchant-speculator leaders of the settlement shouldered the responsibilities of trusteeship during these formative days; and there is no evidence that their choice constituted a perversion of the prevailing faith in popular government. Among those who served were Dr. Lucius I. Barber, Horatio N. Wells, Henry Miller, B. H. Edgerton, Daniel Wells, Jr., George D. Dousman, William A. Prentiss, Albert Fowler, D. H. Richards, Elisha Starr, Increase A. Lapham, John Hustis, Matthias Stein, D. A. J. Upham, E. D. Holton, Moses Kneeland, George H. Walker, Lemuel W. Weeks, Alexander Mitchell, Levi Hubbell, and James H. Brown. The suffrage qualification under the charter of 1839 was liberal by comparison with the tax qualifications demanded of voters in Cleveland and Chicago in the middle thirties. In the village of Milwaukee, elections were open to all free white male inhabitants, twenty-one years of age, who had resided in the town six months previous to the

[10] "An act to change the corporate powers of the village of Milwaukee," *Wisconsin Territorial Laws*, 1838 [1836, 1837] (Reprint, 1867), 258.

[11] *Wisconsin Territorial Laws*, 1838-39, p. 114, cited in Mack, "The Founding of Milwaukee," Wis. Hist. Soc., *Proc.*, 1906, p. 206.

[12] Conard, 1:49.

PIONEER PROMOTERS OF THE TOWNSITE ERA. Top row: Solomon Juneau and Morgan L. Martin, Eastside promoters. *Middle row:* Byron Kilbourn and George H. Walker, promoters, respectively, of the West and South sides. *Bottom row:* James H. Rogers, pioneer promoter and real estate speculator.

election and were inhabitants of the ward in which they voted. These qualifications were more liberal than those ultimately accorded the voters under the first city charter, when alien inhabitants desiring to vote were obliged to have declared their intention of becoming citizens and to meet certain other requirements. However, the charter of 1839 stipulated that the village trustees must be citizens of the United States; whereas under the charter of 1846, the councilmen need only be residents and voters in the ward from which they were elected.[13]

The union of the villages did not, however, put an end to the sectional rivalry induced by the speculative origins of the towns and fostered by the existence of the river barrier. Both sides insisted on a kind of local self-rule or ward autonomy which was to complicate Milwaukee politics for many years. Except for common ward expenses, money was to be spent in the ward where it was raised; and rules or ordinances affecting one ward alone were to have the consent of three of the five trustees of that ward.[14] Either ward could contract debts for which the town was not responsible, and the old village debts were carried as ward obligations.[15] As E. D. Holton reported, "the doctrine of State Rights prevailed in these little commonwealths," a situation that was to lead to bloodshed before the days of villagehood had passed.[16]

The politics of the village community were conditioned almost exclusively by the consuming desire of its leaders for improved facilities for commercial intercourse. Local rivalries

[13] *Ibid.* Complete lists of village officers are unavailable. Gregory, *History,* 1:238; *Wisconsin Territorial Laws,* 1838-39, p. 115.
[14] Larson, "Sectional Elements," Miss. Vall. Hist. Assoc., *Proc.,* 1907-8, 1:124.
[15] Laurence M. Larson, *A Financial and Administrative History of Milwaukee* (University of Wisconsin, Bulletin no. 242, *Economics and Political Science Series,* vol. 4, no. 2, Madison, 1908), 14. This bulletin will hereafter be cited as Larson, *Financial and Administrative History,* with references to specific pages of the bulletin itself.
[16] Edward D. Holton, "Commercial History of Milwaukee," Wisconsin Historical Society, *Collections,* 4:272 (1859). Holton reports the feeling on opposite sides of the river in the early forties: "every man, and especially every woman, on the east side," declared "that on the west side the ague went forth bodily at night, and that the pestilence stalked at noon-day, while they on the west side threw back the taunt, declaring their side was as good any day as the east side, and others kept courage by bold denunciation."

in this respect almost always separated the two sides in territorial politics. Thus, in the contest for territorial delegate in 1839, Kilbourn won the support of the West side with promises of a canal of benefit to the western section of the town.[17] But many East-siders, not averse to obstructing the development of this rival ward, gave their backing to the ultimately victorious James D. Doty, a Green Bay politician associated with Martin's interests, who favored a different internal improvements scheme.[18]

As early as 1840, the villagers were expressing their allegiances along national party lines. Encouraged by the national if not local success of their presidential candidate, the local Whigs on January 1, 1841, consumed roast ox and cider in honor of Harrison's victory. Not to be outdone, the Democrats followed suit on Washington's birthday, when "the real log cabin residents," as the Milwaukee *Advertiser* called them, paraded with band and banners and toasted the hero of the Democracy: "Thomas Jefferson—The Apostle of Democracy—the expounder of our political faith." Although among the thirteen toasts was one to "Woman—the only sovereign the Democrats acknowledge," there was none to the village of Milwaukee.[19] The increasing interest in national politics did not, however, submerge the political rivalries induced by the conflicting interests of the speculator factions in the opposing wards. In September 1840 the *Advertiser* contended that the East side was maneuvering to get "both members of the [territorial] Council just as they have for two years past." The people had been "dupes of management and deception long enough," wrote the West-side editor. "We shall see whether they will longer submit to the Dictation of Lawyers, East Siders, or Fag-Ends."[20] In the hotly-contested election of 1842, the issues were still largely "Kilbourn and anti-Kilbourn, Doty and anti-Doty";[21] but by 1844, as the new arrivals of the middle forties began to change the social complexion of the commun-

[17] Milwaukee *Advertiser,* July 20, 1839.
[18] *Ibid.,* July 27, 1839.
[19] *Ibid.,* Feb. 27, 1841.
[20] *Ibid.,* Sept. 22, 1840.
[21] Buck, 2:147.

ity, the original speculator alliances had things somewhat less their own way. The promoter-founders nevertheless continued to exhibit an active interest in local politics. Kilbourn and Walker were elected to the territorial assembly in 1844, and Juneau was chosen register of deeds. Both Rogers and Kilbourn had been elected to the board of trustees from the West Ward in 1842.[22]

A contest over facilities for commerce was basic to the most outspoken manifestation of the rivalry between the wards—the so-called "Bridge War" of 1845. From the outset of speculative competition, it had been Kilbourn's strategy to discourage the building of bridges across the Milwaukee River so as to isolate Juneau's community from overland migration from the south. To this cause of antagonism was added the objections of those West-siders whose dependence on river transport led them to oppose the building of bridges as an illegal obstruction of navigable streams. As Increase Lapham wrote, "the bridge question" had "always been a matter of dispute between the east and west parts of our town."[23] In spite of the legislature's authorization of bridge construction, work was delayed until the spring of 1840, when the expense was put upon the county, and a bridge was built spanning Chestnut (now West Juneau) Street on the West side and Division Street on the East.[24] Completed by the summer of 1841, it presented, according to Lapham, an almost complete bar to navigation of the river above it.[25] In 1842, Rogers, fostering closer connections between the villages, replaced the Spring Street ferry with a bridge connecting Wisconsin and Spring streets; and when it was destroyed by a freshet in the following year, a subscription of $700 was raised to build another, boasting floating bastions and a large draw which turned on a pivot. In 1844 a bridge was constructed between Oneida (now East Wells) Street on the East and Wells on the West side. Save for a bridge across the Menomonee, built by Kilbourn to attract trade which formerly had gone to the East side by ferry, the bridges had been kept in re-

[22] *Ibid.,* 2:136.
[23] I. A. Lapham to ——, June 21, 1840, Milwaukee *Sentinel,* Oct. 16, 1895.
[24] *Ibid.*
[25] I. A. Lapham to ——, July 24, 1841, *ibid.*

pair for the most part by the East Ward. To the citizens of Juneautown, the West side was shirking a civic responsibility; to the West-siders, the bridges were a nuisance and an obstruction to their legitimate commerce. In the face of these differences of opinion the bridges became a symbol of contention between the already litigious rival "sides."[26]

The issue came to a head in a meeting of the board of village trustees on May 7, 1845, the first occasion on which representatives of the South Ward met with those of the other two. Trouble began when a member from the West Ward asserted the Chestnut Street bridge to be a nuisance and proposed the removal of so much of it "and all appendages thereto as occupy or in any manner obstruct the free navigation of the Milwaukee River west of the middle of the river." In spite of the contention of some of the trustees that the whole town should decide matters concerning the rivers, the West-siders claimed sole jurisdiction to the middle of the stream and came to their decision without the others voting.[27] On the following day, the East-siders were amazed to find that the portion of the Chestnut Street bridge standing in the West Ward had been removed as a nuisance and that as a result the unsupported east portion had fallen into the water.[28] Moreover, removal of the West-side approach to the Oneida Street bridge had made that thoroughfare impassable, as well. For the moment it looked as if the residents of the East Ward would "proceed to violence," but upon the advice of sober citizens they planned a public meeting and retired.[29] A compromise was effected at a subsequent, and more conciliatory, meeting of the trustees on May 15, when it was decided with but one dissenting vote that the Chestnut Street bridge should be repaired with either a permanent or floating draw and that the Oneida Street bridge should be discontinued as a public bridge.[30]

[26] Holton, "Commercial History of Milwaukee," Wis. Hist. Soc., Colls., 4:272-73.
[27] Excerpt from Courier report of "Corporation Proceedings" for May 7, 1845, in Gregory, History, 1:214-17.
[28] Holton, "Commercial History of Milwaukee," Wis. Hist. Soc., Colls., 4:274.
[29] Milwaukie Daily Sentinel, May 9, 1845.
[30] Excerpt from Courier report of "Corporation Proceedings" for May 15, 1845, in Gregory, History, 1:222-23.

VILLAGE POLITICS AND INTERNAL IMPROVEMENTS   41

The residents of Juneautown, however, were not to be so easily avenged. Mobocracy gained the upper hand; and on May 19, despite East-side counsels decrying the sectional rivalry, the Spring Street bridge was destroyed and some damage was done to the one across the Menomonee. Cannons and guns were fired, and some of the participants were injured.[31] It was now the turn of the West Ward to be indignant. The village board was the gathering place of the hostile representatives. But order prevailed, and a committee appointed to investigate the question recommended the building "of three good and permanent bridges across the . . . river, so constructed as to present the least possible obstacle to navigation."[32] The disrepair of the bridges continued to present a problem until the fall of 1845; but with this compromise a truce in the bridge hostilities was reached. Actually, this most violent proof of its sectionalism was not without some advantage for the developing community. Despite the unfortunate publicity it gave the settlement abroad, it hastened the movement for a municipal government that would overcome "the jealousies and rivalries" of "a new and growing settlement" and foster such a "concert of action among our citizens" as to "improve the advantages we enjoy."[33]

In the relations of young Milwaukee with the federal government, as in its local politics, the concern for internal improvements was uppermost. With the exception of travel on the lake, approaches to the new village were crude and undependable. Rather than venture on any of the three overland trails from Chicago to Milwaukee in the thirties, one party built a scow, to accommodate six persons, and poled their

[31] *Ibid.*, 1:223-24.
[32] Excerpt from *Courier* report of "Corporation Proceedings" for June 2, 1845, *ibid.*, 1:225-27.
[33] Milwaukie *Daily Sentinel*, Dec. 2, 1845. The *Sentinel* reported on June 3, 1845, that immigrants were advised at Racine to land there, since bridge communication with the interior had been destroyed at Milwaukee. The editor took occasion to "remind our own citizens of the importance of taking all precautionary measures against the occurrence of any proceedings similar to those which have taken place in this town within the last few days, as they tend to destroy the good feelings of our own citizens towards each other and our good reputation abroad." Quoting a comment on the bridge war from the Baltimore *Sun*, the *Sentinel* pointed to the loss of capital and enterprise that was bound to flow from unfavorable publicity. *Ibid.*, June 3, July 8, 1845.

way along the lake shore.³⁴ To go west from the village one had to traverse an almost sunless slit in heavy timber;³⁵ and for the four-day journey northward to Green Bay there was a choice of two regularly traveled trails, with blazed timber as a guide and rough puncheon and log bridges over the unfordable streams.³⁶ It is small wonder that at their first public meeting in December 1835 the citizens passed resolutions asking Congress for a donation of land to subsidize the construction of internal improvements that would promote their contact with the outside world.

The short-lived day of the canal was on the wane, but Kilbourn's backer had stipulated that the prospective metropolis must lie where a canal could be "constructed providing communication by water with the Mississippi";³⁷ and impressed by New York's fortunate experience in this respect, the West-side promoter originally lent his support to that mode of transportation. Preliminary surveys for such a waterway, made by Kilbourn and Increase Lapham, were followed by the publication of a series of essays in the *Advertiser* during the summer of 1837 calling attention to the enterprise.³⁸ On January 5, 1838, the territorial legislature incorporated the Milwaukee and Rock River Canal Company with a capital stock of $100,000.³⁹ Kilbourn, Juneau, and Rogers were among the seven directors ultimately elected by the stockholders.⁴⁰ As president of the company, Kilbourn succeeded in getting Congress to pass an act on June 18, 1838, granting to Wisconsin Territory in trust for the enterprise the odd sections of a strip ten miles wide along the proposed course. This tract of some 140,000 acres was to be sold at $2.50 an acre in the interest of the canal.⁴¹ It was estimated that the

---

[34] Gregory, *History*, 1:264; 2:1243.
[35] *Ibid.*, 1:202.   [36] *Ibid.*, 1:270-71.
[37] *Evening Wisconsin* (Milwaukee), Oct. 15, 1895.
[38] William R. Smith, *The History of Wisconsin in Three Parts, Historical, Documentary, and Descriptive* (Part 1 of this work, *Historical*, constitutes volume 1. Part 2, *Documentary*, is volume 3. Volume 2 was never issued. Madison, 1854), 3:355.
[39] "An act to incorporate the Milwaukee and Rock river canal company, January 5, 1838," *Wisconsin Territorial Laws*, 1836 [1837, 1838] (Reprint, 1867), 181-91.
[40] Milwaukee *Advertiser*, March 16, 1839.
[41] Raney, *Wisconsin: A Story of Progress*, 107.

project would cost close to $800,000.⁴² Reporting the eagerness with which the capital stock of $100,000 had been subscribed, the *Sentinel* asserted that construction was of "great importance as well to the eastern cities as to our own Milwaukee."⁴³

Many obstacles, however, stood in the way of acquiring the necessary funds. Opposition to the undertaking appeared from various quarters. The territorial legislature, only lukewarm to the project from the outset, decreed that purchasers need make a down-payment of only 10 percent of the cost of the lands, a concession which cut to $12,000 the returns from the sale of 43,000 acres in July 1839. Promoters of railroads, friends of the Fox-Wisconsin improvement, such enemies of Kilbourn as Alanson Sweet who championed the cause of the squatters on the canal lands, and East-side interests identified with Judge Doty⁴⁴ conspired with the hard times following 1837 to make it difficult for the company to borrow money or sell lands.⁴⁵ According to Smith's *History of Wisconsin*, the legislature waged a "perpetual war" against the canal company and disbursed more than $120,000 of the funds from the sale of its lands for such public purposes as constitutional conventions.⁴⁶ Doty's elevation to the governorship of the territory in October 1841 brought the activities of the company to an end. Payments due it from the sale of canal lands were stopped in the following February.⁴⁷ Already the purchasers of canal lands and bonds were complaining that the promised benefits, in the form of interest and access to markets, had not been forthcoming.⁴⁸ The only tangible result of an otherwise abortive project was the dam which provided a source of water power in the Second Ward. Thus the current financial depres-

---

[42] Smith, *History of Wisconsin*, 3:360.
[43] Milwaukee *Sentinel*, Feb. 13, 1838.
[44] According to the editor of the Milwaukee *Advertiser*, "had the project been one to advance Racine or Green Bay, the editor of the *Sentinel* would doubtless have expressed regret at its failure, but as it is only one which benefits Milwaukee and the West, he is greatly pleased that it cannot move at present, for the reason that his master, Judge Doty, cares nothing for the interests of this part of the country." Milwaukee *Advertiser*, Oct. 12, 1839.
[45] Raney, *Wisconsin: A Story of Progress*, 108.
[46] Smith, *History of Wisconsin*, 3:423, 442.
[47] Raney, *Wisconsin: A Story of Progress*, 108.
[48] Milwaukie *Journal*, Dec. 8, 1841.

sion and the political dominance of territorial interests hostile to the Milwaukee venture brought the untimely end of a project which had been prompted by a natural desire of the town-promoters, especially on the West side, to attract the trade of the expanding West. The increasing agitation for railroads showed, however, that this ambition was not dead.

While the canal enterprise had been running its politics-ridden course, the desire for improved connections to the eastward was exciting agitation for nationally subsidized harbor improvement, a matter of primary consequence for a community largely dependent upon water connections with the outside world and one which, like the canal, soon became involved in local politics. The confluence of the river with a natural bay had been an early attraction to settlement—the harbor had excited Martin's original interest—but although the mouth of the river was capable of improvement without great expense, it was on the upper side of the bay and thus distant from the property developed by the founders of the town. In the absence of an inner harbor, immigrants were forced to rely, at extra cost, upon small harbor boats which plied regularly to and from the lake vessels. Charges of from 25 to 50 cents for this service, in addition to the fare from Buffalo, were thought to deter settlers from stopping at the Wisconsin port.[49] Moreover, because of the lack of an inner harbor, shipping in the vicinity frequently was buffeted and lost in storms and gales.

As early as 1834, steamboat owners trading out of Milwaukee began to petition the federal government for relief, asserting that a harbor could be built for $15,000.[50] In January 1836, Kilbourn attempted to exert pressure on a member of the Senate committee on commerce, to this end; but beyond undertaking some surveys in 1837 the federal government was slow to act.[51] To the gratification of the business interests of the existing town, the surveyors recommended a point 3,000

[49] Gregory, *History*, 2:1303.

[50] Ralph G. Plumb, "Early Harbor History of Wisconsin," Wisconsin Academy of Sciences, Arts, and Letters, *Transactions*, vol. 17, pt. 1, p. 189 (pub. 1914).

[51] Lake Michigan was just beginning to assume prominence as a highway of commerce in this period. Prior to 1837 the federal government had spent only $162,601 on Lake Michigan—at Chicago and St. Joseph exclusively; and as late

VILLAGE POLITICS AND INTERNAL IMPROVEMENTS 45

feet north of the outlet of the river, a spot which Kilbourn endorsed, as the site of the harbor.[52] Here a "straight cut" would permit a connection with the Milwaukee River, which at this place flowed within 300 feet of the lake. Alanson Sweet, whose opposition to Kilbourn was later manifested in his championship of the squatters on the canal lands, attempted to obtain an injunction against effecting the "straight cut," alleging that it was proposed in the interest of Juneau's and Kilbourn's speculation. The *Advertiser* countered by asserting that it was really Sweet who wanted to speculate and denied that Juneau and Kilbourn had any more interest in this development than "all the rest of the town in proportion to their property and business." It was the opinion of the editor that together these promoters probably did not own "one-eighth part of the whole," and possibly not "even a sixteenth."[53]

The acceleration of navigation following 1836 increased the popular demand for harbor improvement. At a "great harbor meeting" in December 1839 much was made of the large sums which the citizenry had paid the federal government in return for land, and harbor improvement was demanded "as a matter of right, justly our due, and too loudly called for by public necessity and the general good to be longer disregarded."[54] In 1841, the editor of the Milwaukie *Journal* cited "sacrifices of life and property to the 'economy' of Congress" and urged the citizens to "prompt and vigorous action." Several boats had recently passed by "without landing the goods or passengers with which they were freighted for this place," and Buffalo shippers were reported to be reluctant to take on goods for Milwaukee.[55] Some of the local hotheads appealed to sectional prejudice and asserted that if Congress refused to appropriate money to construct harbors the West "must take the matter into their own hands . . . go in for nullification, . . . excite the slaves in the South to insurrection. . . . secede from the Union, . . . establish an

as 1853 "only one-eighth of the river and harbor appropriations, taken as a whole, had been devoted to the Great Lakes." *Ibid.*
[52] Wheeler, *Chronicles of Milwaukee*, 98.
[53] Milwaukee *Advertiser*, Dec. 17, 1836.
[54] *Ibid.*, Dec. 7, 1839.   [55] Milwaukie *Journal*, Oct. 27, 1841.

Indian government on Doty's purchase, and make Doty our Chief."[56] Finally, in 1842, the drowning of two men who were attempting to deliver a load of wood to a steamboat lying at anchor in the bay prompted an indignation meeting at which the people determined to wait no longer for Congressional appropriation but to make plans to raise the needed sum by voluntary subscription.[57] The *Sentinel and Farmer* (Milwaukee) nevertheless continued to agitate for a federal loan, predicting that it would be returned "ten fold in a few years through the medium of the land offices."[58]

The long-awaited appropriation came on March 3, 1843, when $30,000 was allotted; but to the disappointment of the leading property holders, and amid charges of bribery, the engineers disregarded the proposed "straight cut" and spent the money at the natural outlet.[59] Exasperated at this turn of events, Kilbourn now took matters into his own hands and in June 1843 sent a hundred men to dredge a channel through the "straight cut" in a mistaken hope that the river would deepen the proposed new entrance.[60] In April of the following year the State legislature authorized the village to borrow money to be used for harbor improvements at the "cut"; but inasmuch as results began to appear at the river mouth, nothing was done.[61] In 1845, an additional appropriation of $25,000 for harbor improvement was secured by Morgan L. Martin, then delegate to Congress; but it, too, was expended at the mouth of the river.[62] In the early fifties, the federal government finally abandoned its activities at this spot, and in due time a harbor was developed in accordance with the original promoters' plans.[63]

[56] *Ibid.*, Dec. 29, 1841. "What is the use of periling our lives, our fortunes . . . here in the West," wrote the editor, "without reaping some little benefit from the Government? Give us an appropriation—or else we will kick up a muss here with the Indians, that will be worse than a Florida war." *Ibid.*, Feb. 9, 1842.

[57] I. A. Lapham to ——, April 17, 1842, Milwaukee *Sentinel*, Oct. 16, 1895. This proposal apparently did not go beyond the planning stage.

[58] *Sentinel and Farmer* (Milwaukee), June 4, 1842.

[59] Bruce, *History*, 1:275-76.

[60] A. T. Andreas, pub., *History of Milwaukee* (Chicago, 1881), 448.

[61] Larson, *Financial and Administrative History*, 19.

[62] Gregory, *History*, 1:314.

[63] Plumb, "Early Harbor History," Wis. Acad. of Sci., Arts, and *Letters, Trans.*, vol. 17, pt. 1, p. 194.

Meanwhile, individual ingenuity had found a partial substitute for the lack of a safe and conveniently located harbor. During 1842-43, Horatio G. Stevens, using outside capital, extended a pier, 1,200 feet long and 49 wide, into the lake just north of the foot of Huron Street and close to the business district of the East side. Here vessels of deep draft could land their passengers and cargoes in comparative safety. After the "Cleveland" landed there, on June 1, 1843, the pier began to do a flourishing business;[64] and soon it was the model for others in the vicinity. These piers became important incidents in the development of the forwarding business and were a source of revenue to their owners through dockage charges, levied at the rate of five to six dollars for a drayload of trunks and other baggage. Warehouses and hotels, in the dock area, accommodated the traffic in commodities and migrants; and in the forties, during the season of navigation, the piers constituted the principal passenger and commercial depot for the city.[65] The approach of a boat was the signal for the assembling of dozens of runners from the different hotels at the outer end of the piers, and once the traveler had worked his way through these noisy solicitors he found himself in a maze of carts, hackney coaches, and omnibuses.[66] Amid such confusion, Milwaukeeans greeted visitors from afar, the immigrant made his first contact with the West, and the traffic in exported and imported commodities took place.

In this age of water transport in the West, the arrivals and departures of the lake vessels were events of social as well as economic importance in the life of the village, and their captains were lionized in its society. The ninety-ton "Solomon Juneau," built in 1837 by Captain George Barber, was the first vessel to be launched at the Wisconsin village. In the same year Juneau organized a stock company for the construction of the "Milwaukee," a costly vessel which was to ply exclusively between Milwaukee and Buffalo and which came to

[64] Holton, "Commercial History of Milwaukee," *Wis. Hist. Soc., Colls.*, 4:264; Wheeler, *Chronicles of Milwaukee*, 98; Gregory, *History*, 1:315.
[65] Henry Bleyer, "The Old Milwaukee Lake Landings," quoted *ibid.*, 1:315-17.
[66] Albany *Evening Journal*, quoted in Milwaukie *Daily Sentinel*, July 14, 1845.

an untimely end in 1841 on a sand bar in the river's mouth.[67] By 1845 Milwaukee could boast a "fleet" of one steam and twenty-six sailing vessels, of an aggregate burden of 2,475 tons. This did not include the innumerable vessels owned on the lower lakes that daily touched the village wharves on their upward and downward trips. Nor did it count the line of Buffalo steamers and Buffalo and Oswego propellers, some one of which might be seen alongside the piers at almost any hour of the day. Already the expansive Milwaukeean foresaw the future "commercial power and glory of Milwaukee, when, by more direct and enlarged channels of communication" she would send "her mendant fleet upon the Atlantic, the Pacific, the Baltic, and the Mediterranean, to hold intercourse and trade with all the nations of the earth."[68]

In the absence of adequate overland transport, lake shipping and harbor improvement were vital to a community whose economy depended so largely upon the exchange of commodities with the settled East. For example, in September 1845, wheat commanded 87 cents a bushel in Buffalo, but for lack of shipping facilities to get it there it was bringing only 62 cents in Milwaukee.[69] During the winter months, when the lake was frozen and navigation closed, the economy of the community was further jeopardized. Barred from easy contact with eastern sources of supply, Milwaukeeans ran the risk that save for the chance arrival of prairie schooners from the south a shortage of foodstuffs or a corner on an essential commodity might result in exorbitant prices or actual distress. This dependence on a kind of transportation that was likely to be incapacitated by freezing for nearly a third of the year explains the early interest of Milwaukeeans in developing the railroads and other improved highways which might guarantee more reliable connections with other parts of the nation.

Milwaukee was born into a world in which the railroad was a new and exciting idea. In the middle thirties the only completed line in the State of New York was a seventeen-mile stretch from Albany to Schenectady; yet the residents of the Wisconsin village proposed this improvement with all the

[67] Milwaukee *Sentinel*, July 14, 1937.
[68] Milwaukie *Daily Sentinel*, June 27, 1845.   [69] *Ibid.*, Sept. 29, 1845.

VILLAGE POLITICS AND INTERNAL IMPROVEMENTS 49

optimistic and self-confident enthusiasm that characterized their approach to other schemes for community promotion and personal profit. Byron Kilbourn was the secretary of a meeting, held on September 22, 1836, at which resolutions for a railroad to the Mississippi and one to the "city" of Superior were proposed. The committee of fifteen to promote the enterprise contained familiar names, among them Juneau, Hans Crocker, Prentiss, Longstreet, and Rogers.[70] But the further progress of railroad schemes had to await recovery from the panic of 1837 and the realization that the Milwaukee and Rock River Canal was not destined to be completed. By 1842 railroad communication had become a matter of territorial concern, being pressed in no small degree by representatives of the lead region and the interior who sought an outlet at the lake. As with canal and harbor construction, government aid was solicited. A convention of delegates from Wisconsin and Iowa territories, assembling on January 26, 1842, memorialized the legislature to facilitate the construction of a railroad from Lake Michigan to the Mississippi and to give the canal lands as a bonus to a company to build the road forthwith. To this proposal prominent Milwaukeeans like Prentiss, Rogers, Joshua Hathaway, and Harrison Ludington agreed. The Milwaukie *Journal* lent its support, asserting that a railroad would not freeze over in winter, could be constructed more cheaply than a canal, would pay a liberal return on the investment, and, drawing patronage from the lead region, even if built only to Madison, "would greatly contribute to the business and prosperity of Milwaukie."[71]

The movement for a railroad became increasingly spirited in the early months of 1845. Editors pressed the point that to be "the Eastern terminus of this great improvement" would "make Milwaukee a large city" as with a "wand of enchantment"; and the *Sentinel* warned that "our neighbors at Racine" would "effect the desired object, unless we go to work immediately, harmoniously, and energetically to secure it to ourselves."[72] The culmination of a series of public meetings

[70] Buck, 1:131 (rev. ed.).
[71] Milwaukie *Journal*, Jan. 12, 1842.
[72] Milwaukie *Daily Sentinel*, Jan. 23, 28, Feb. 12, Dec. 3, 1845.

on the subject came on December 3, 1845, when the railroad was considered along with such other urgent community problems as fire protection and the condition of the common schools. The committee to investigate the matter included Kilbourn, Prentiss, Crocker, and Peter Yates. Within two years a railroad company had been authorized.[73]

Amid the agitation for these monumental schemes of internal improvement, both the city promoters and the farmers of the interior continued to be concerned about improving the roads between Milwaukee and its agricultural hinterland. Early in 1844 the *Courier* spoke of improved roads as only second in importance to the construction of a harbor;[74] and farmers from "south and west," complaining about the roads leading into the city,[75] were bending every effort to attract highways from Milwaukee in their direction. A correspondent to the *Sentinel* wrote in 1843 that "whenever the people of Milwaukie bestir themselves in earnest to secure the travel of Beloit and vicinity to Milwaukie . . . they will find the citizens of Beloit and others living along the way ready to contribute their share of the expense."[76] As usual, the first construction was the result of a private subscription. This small sum made possible a wagon track northwest to Fond du Lac in 1841, improved in meager fashion by bridging the streams and swamps with poles and logs.[77] Public meetings held in May 1844 resulted in the appointment of a committee, including Harrison Ludington, Rogers, Holton, Walker, and J. S. Fillmore, to raise the $2,000 considered necessary for the construction of a road from Milwaukee to Waukesha.[78] A road to Muskego, built by private subscription, was recognized to have brought "a large share of trade to Milwaukie, which formerly went to Racine and Southport." But to judge from comments in the *Sentinel* the roads continued bad in spite

[73] Gregory, *History*, 1:229.
[74] *Evening Wisconsin*, Oct. 15, 1895.
[75] *Commercial Herald* (Milwaukee), April 6, 1844, quoted in Gregory, *History*, 1:214.
[76] Milwaukie *Sentinel*, Sept. 23, 1843.
[77] Edward D. Holton, "Avenues to the Town," quoted in Gregory, *History*, 1:279-80.
[78] Buck, 2:214.

of a stagecoach advertisement which asserted that "Now comparatively good roads traverse the country in every direction, and the gay stagecoach, a miniature world within itself, freighted with stalwart manhood and feminine beauty, goes rolling along, the noisy tread of its wheels as they press the turf of the prairie forming a strange contrast with the hideous whoop of the Indian warrior."[79]

A type of improved highway which provided a practical substitute for the abortive canal and the still unrealized railroad was the plank road built at private expense. The first of these was the work of the Milwaukee and Watertown Plank Road Company, incorporated in 1846 to build a smooth-surfaced road of timber or plank, similar to an over-sized sidewalk, from the lake shore city to its western neighbor.[80] This undertaking was pushed to completion in 1847 by Elisha Eldred, Hans Crocker, Joshua Hathaway, Eliphalet Cramer, and others, cost about $119,000, and was soon providing its promoters with tolls of as much as $1,300 a week. The financial success of this kind of thoroughfare led to the building of similar roads in other directions. Their popularity waned only as the steam railroad—first operated in the area in the early fifties—provided a more modern answer to the demand of the young urban community for highways that would serve its growing commerce and give it more effective contact with the men and markets of the outside world.

[79] Gregory, *History,* 1:284.

[80] "To make a plank road they lay first 3-inch oak beams on both sides and about five feet apart, and then equally strong 8-9 feet long planks are laid thereupon and shoved together as tightly as possible so that they cannot get loose. On such a road one drives and walks, of course, as on a sidewalk but it has the effect upon horses which traverse it for a long time that they become stiff, and unshod oxen easily slip upon the plank and therefore are very unwilling to go upon them." "Christian Traugott Ficker's Advice to Emigrants (II)," *Wisconsin Magazine of History,* 25:352 (March 1942).

CHAPTER 3

Commercial Foundations

ON A WINTRY Saturday in January 1845, the editor of the *Sentinel* stood on Water Street, surveying the village scene. He counted 265 sleighs before deciding that "their number was legion." Loads of wood, hay, pork, and potatoes mingled with the gilded cutter and the sleigh and four. "On swept, with locomotive speed, the living multitude," he wrote, "swaying to and fro like the torrent of a restless river,"[1] activity which suggested that even before her village days were over Milwaukee had become "the Commercial Emporium of a rapidly settling country."[2] Indeed, the decade of villagehood witnessed a remarkable elaboration of the commercial fabric of the young Wisconsin community. For as in most young cities commerce was the foundation upon which the settlement at the junction of river and lake was based: merchandising and outfitting, to meet the needs of village settler and transient pioneer; money-lending, to facilitate the purchase of land and the shipment of goods; traffic in the produce of the hinterland, sometimes processed for export to the East; and the servicing pursuits attending the activities of a community occupied primarily with commerce and trade.

The first merchandising in the area was connected with the Indian trade; and stocks originally intended for barter with the natives were an early source of supply for the Yankee migrants. On the eve of white settlement, Juneau, as agent of the American Fur Company, received his supplies through Samuel Abbott, the company's factor at Mackinac, or William Brewster, its agent at Detroit.[3] By the spring of 1835, he pro-

[1] *Milwaukie Daily Sentinel,* Jan. 20, 1845.
[2] *Ibid.,* April 18, 1845.
[3] Ramsay Crooks to William Brewster, Nov. 4, 1834 [Calendar #60], American Fur Company Papers, in the New York Historical Society.

52

COMMERCIAL FOUNDATIONS 53

posed the sale of these goods to the white immigrants and requested that the Company provide him with such commodities as the migrating pioneers were sure to need: pork, butter, cheese, figs, lard, rice, raisins, white fish, mackerel, codfish, lump sugar, pepper, cinnamon, allspice, cloves, almonds, coffee, tea, wine, whiskey, brandy, gin, rum, lamp oil, putty, white lead, door latches, linseed oil, axes, scythes, hammers, spades, shovels, needles of all sizes and kinds, thread, and sewing silk.[4] The president of the Company, regretting the encroachment of farmer competition, reluctantly sanctioned this trade with the white newcomers;[5] but Juneau appears to have had little cooperation in this respect until the late spring of 1836.[6]

Store buildings were the first sign of business in the American community, and during the period of speculation, heavy rent was paid even for the privilege of selling goods on vacant lots and corners. In the boom days a supply of goods was frequently exhausted within a week;[7] and many a pioneer later prominent in the political and economic life of the growing city made his start through selling commodities brought in from the East in these expansive times. Wares obtained in Chicago became the basis of A. O. T. Breed's merchandising activities.[8] Uriel B. Smith, setting up in 1835 as a tailor, found such a demand for overcoats as to use up his supply of cloth before the opening of navigation.[9] In the summer of 1837 Juneau bought out the entire holdings of a store in Waukesha County and disposed of his purchase in Milwaukee.[10] Joseph and Lindsey Ward, arriving in 1838, soon extended their merchandising to the rural hinterland.[11] A stock of goods purchased by E. D. Holton in Buffalo, where he had

[4] Solomon Juneau to Ramsay Crooks, March 27, 1835 [Calendar #336], American Fur Company Papers.
[5] Ramsay Crooks to Samuel Abbott, April 17, 1835 [Calendar #390]; Crooks to Juneau, June 6, 1835 [Calendar #554]; Crooks to Abbott, June 22, 1835 [Calendar #598], all in the American Fur Company Papers.
[6] Juneau to Crooks, Dec. 16, 1835 [Calendar #1101]; Crooks to Juneau, May 11, 1836 [Calendar #1590], American Fur Company Papers.
[7] J. H. Kennedy, "Financial and Commercial Growth of Milwaukee," *Magazine of Western History*, 6:314 (May 1887).
[8] Gregory, *History*, 1:417.
[9] *Ibid.*, 2:1254.
[10] "Narrative of Andrew J. Vieau, Sr.," Wis. Hist. Soc., *Colls.*, 11:230-31.
[11] Gregory, *History*, 1:428.

served as accountant and cashier in a large forwarding and commission house, was the basis of the store which he opened in 1840. Within three years this commercial pioneer had become a leader in the social and business life of the young community.[12] By 1842 it was asserted that twenty-five stores were in operation, doing a business of $70,000 to $150,000 annually.[13] In June 1845, Rufus King reported that several of the merchants of the village had done a retail business in the last two years amounting to forty or fifty thousand dollars.[14]

The original lack of agricultural development in the vicinity, the curtailment of lake navigation during the winter months, and the pressure of migration combined frequently to produce serious shortages in necessary commodities. In 1835 milk could not be purchased at any price; a year later it sold for 20 cents a quart. Potatoes from Ohio and Indiana brought $3.50 to $6.00 a bushel at retail until local production by 1840 made it possible to procure them for 50 cents. In the early days butter was worth 50 to 65 cents a pound and flour from $18 to $27 a barrel.[15] In the face of potential shortages, farsighted businessmen occasionally attempted to corner the supply of flour, apples, or salt or to forestall chance "Easterners" coming in by ox-team with supplies from Indiana or Illinois.[16] On one occasion in 1842, Frederick Wardner sent one of his clerks out on the road to Chicago to intercept a farmer traveling from Indiana with four loads of merchandise. The employee paid cash at 10 cents a pound for his supply of bacon, ham, and poultry, almost all of which Wardner sold before nightfall at 25 cents a pound.[17]

But more than the vital necessities were available in the "urban" market even in these village years. On June 17, 1837,

[12] Kennedy, "Financial and Commercial Growth of Milwaukee," *Mag. of Western Hist.*, 6:455 (May 1887).
[13] Buck, 2:117.
[14] Rufus King, as correspondent for Albany *Evening Journal*, June 30, 1845.
[15] Milwaukee *Sentinel*, Oct. 16, 1895.
[16] In 1842, Dr. L. W. Weeks bought up all the available salt in the community, stored it, and held it for $10 a barrel. To Weeks's chagrin, Alanson Sweet broke the "corner" by sending a schooner to Chicago to obtain a supply. Buck, 2:149.
[17] Gregory, *History*, 1:440-42.

Miss S. E. Chamberlin announced the opening of her millinery and dressmaking shop where "misses fancy Grecian-colored straws," artificial flowers, ladies' silk and cotton hose, whale-bone and chip double and single foundations, and assorted belt ribbons vied for feminine favor, and hat repairs "in the most fashionable style" could be made at shortest notice. Nor did the outfitters of this period leave the public in doubt as to what they had to offer. Signs symbolical of the wares offered within were prominently displayed at the front of every store. The tobacconist's wooden Indian, the fur dealer's stuffed bear, and the signs of the "mill saw and the stove," "the large teakettle," the "horse and trunk," and the "golden hoopskirt" not only attracted prospective purchasers but also suggested the speed with which, in the face of urban development and immigrant demand, specialized merchandising was supplementing the role of the village general store.

As in most frontier communities, the money to facilitate commercial transactions was frequently as scarce as the goods desired. The paper of western banks went current as long as someone like Juneau would endorse it;[18] but the real test of its validity was its acceptance beyond the local market. In March 1838, Increase Lapham wrote his brother to inquire whether "Michigan money" could be used in Ohio without loss, "especially paper of the Safety Fund Banks, or 'Wild Cat' as it is here universally called." This and the notes of the Bank of Wisconsin (at Green Bay) were about all he could procure, for other funds were "hoarded up by merchants and others" who had payments to make "at the East."[19] In 1841, merchants were accepting bills on western banks at a 12 percent discount, whereas eastern money and specie commanded a 10 to 12 percent premium in commercial transactions.[20] Eastern money was brought into the community by immigrants, speculators, and representatives of eastern capital. Typical of the last were Eliphalet Cramer, graduate of Union College in

[18] Kennedy, "Financial and Commercial Growth of Milwaukee," *Mag. of Western Hist.*, 6:309 (May 1887).
[19] I. A. to Darius Lapham, March [n.d.] 1838, Lapham Papers.
[20] Daniel, Jr., to Charles Wells, April 7, 1841, in Buck, 1:191 (rev. ed.).

1834, who arrived in Milwaukee three years later as the agent of eastern money interests,[21] and James B. Martin, a native of Baltimore, who came in 1845, bringing money for western investment.[22] The arrival of Germans with a supply of gold currency provided a dramatic moment in the commercial life of the community in the early forties.[23] In the absence of either specie or acceptable paper, barter became a universal practice, especially from 1837 to 1840 and to a considerable extent to 1843. Tickets were issued "good for a drink," a "shave," or a "pound of tea."[24] Not only were newspaper subscriptions and doctors' bills paid in garden truck, but wages were carried home in a market basket. For a consideration from the storekeeper a contractor would agree to pay his workers with orders on a local store. This made it possible for the merchant to receive cash or credit for his goods, while at the same time he added to the cost of the commodities what he paid the contractor to make the transaction possible. James S. Buck, pioneer historian, worked for D. S. Hollister under this system in 1838. His stated wage was $12 a month. It was paid in a pair of pants which he worked five weeks to earn.[25]

Lacking cash, the western settler resorted to borrowing. This was true of urban as well as of rural development; and since the land offices no longer offered credit, the major source was the money lender or the bank. Agents of eastern capital provided squatters with funds to buy improved lands, charging heavy rates of interest and frequently exacting a mortgage for twice the amount of the loan.[26] Local merchants, real estate dealers, and private individuals were a source of limited credit; but the most natural reservoir was the local bank. The Bank of Milwaukee, first bank in the village, was incorporated by the territorial legislature on December 2, 1836, and approved by Congress, March 3, 1837. From the outset it came under

[21] Gregory, *History*, 1:394.
[22] *Ibid.*, 1:396.
[23] William F. Whyte, "The Settlement of the Town of Lebanon, Dodge County," Wisconsin Historical Society, *Proceedings*, 1915, p. 109.
[24] James D. Butler, "Alexander Mitchell, the Financier," Wisconsin Historical Society, *Collections*, 11:436 (1888).
[25] Buck, 1:218n (rev. ed.).
[26] Gregory, *History*, 2:1260.

the restraints with which Jacksonian Democracy, already suspicious of banking activities, was curtailing credit operations. Stockholders were to pay one-tenth of their subscription in specie, the balance at the director's call. The debt of the bank was not to exceed three times the amount of the capital stock paid in, plus the specie on deposit.[27] Congress added the proviso that there should be no issue of notes or bills for circulation until half the amount of stated capital should actually have been received.[28] Despite these restrictions, the Bank of Milwaukee proved ultimately to be the most speculative of the four banks chartered by the territorial government.[29]

Subscription books for the Bank of Milwaukee were opened in June 1837, under the superintendence of Rufus Parks, Horace Chase, James Sanderson, Giles S. Brisbin, Sylvester W. Dunbar, George Bowman, Jesse Rhodes, Cyrus Hawley, and Solomon Juneau.[30] Able directors were chosen, and at first they appeared to be pursuing a conservative banking policy. The stock sold slowly; it was difficult to collect more than the original down payment of one-tenth; and soon the directors were resorting to the extension of short-term loans, presumably their own notes and possibly the capital stock of the bank itself.[31] In December there entered the "fly-by-night" figure so frequently associated with the "wild-cat" banking of the period. In that month Francis K. O'Farrall purchased the 1,984 shares of stock remaining unsold and became fiscal agent and cashier. His payment for the stock was apparently a book transaction; and when on February 19, 1838, the directors ordered him to give bond and exhibit the records, he failed to appear. On July 2, 1838, the directors, torn with faction among themselves, declared forfeit all stock on which a 40 percent assessment had not been paid; in 1839 the charter was annulled by the legislature; and in October of that year

[27] *Wisconsin Territorial Laws*, 1836 [1837, 1838] (Reprint, 1867), chap. 15.

[28] Leonard B. Krueger, *History of Commercial Banking in Wisconsin* (University of Wisconsin, *Studies in the Social Sciences and History*, no. 18, Madison, 1933), 11.

[29] *Ibid.*, 19.

[30] Kennedy, "Financial and Commercial Growth of Milwaukee," *Mag. of Western Hist.*, 6:311 (May 1887).

[31] *Ibid.*

the directors voted to dispose of the bank.[32] The pressure of the times had prevented the Bank of Milwaukee from being the credit agency it might otherwise have become. Although the bona fide subscription of stock was never sufficient to warrant the issuance of notes, the bank had received deposits and discounted paper to the amount of $5,000 for the citizens of Milwaukee.[33] The O'Farrall incident aggravated the existing hostility to banking operations, and the difficulties of the bank in general contributed to the suspicion with which banks of issue were viewed in the West following the crisis of 1837.

The continuing need for credit and a circulating medium was supplied, in a sense by indirection, by the Wisconsin Marine and Fire Insurance Company, which had been incorporated on May 7, 1839. Its first board of commissioners, as appointed by the legislature, included Daniel Wells, Jr., Hans Crocker, William Brown, Jr., James H. Rogers, Allen W. Hatch, George Smith of Chicago, and Alexander Mitchell, a young Scotchman whom Smith brought to Milwaukee as secretary of the enterprise.[34] Wells had become acquainted with Smith in 1835 in connection with land speculation. In 1838, the Chicago financier, with the help of Wells, who was then a member of the legislative council, succeeded in getting the legislature to charter the proposed corporation.[35] Its capital set at $500,000, ostensibly it was to do an insurance business, but the charter contained a clause permitting the organization to "receive money on deposit" and loan the same on security. This, however, did not prevent the legislature from prohibiting banking activities, just as it had in chartering the Milwaukee and Watertown Plank Road Company and the First Congregational Church of Milwaukee.

Smith's insurance company issued a few policies, but almost immediately it began doing a general banking business; and its certificates of deposit payable to bearer circulated widely from Detroit to Cincinnati on no better security than

[32] *Ibid.*, 313; L. B. Krueger, *Commercial Banking in Wisconsin*, 21.
[33] *Ibid.*, 35.
[34] Buck, 1:232 (rev. ed.).
[35] Gregory, *History*, 1:188-90; Butler, "Alexander Mitchell, the Financier," Wis. Hist. Soc., *Colls.*, 11:436-37.

the credit of Smith and Mitchell.[36] The aggregate circulation amounted to $11,918 in 1840, to $79,721 in 1845, and to $1,470,235 by December 1, 1852.[37] One of the major activities of the bank was its purchase of farms for newcomers under an agreement by which the land would be deeded to the farmer at the end of four years or sooner at a moderate advance over the government price.[38] In 1844, most of the company's capital stock of $224,475 was owned by people residing in England and Scotland. Wisconsinites had invested only to the amount of $1,925.[39]

Objections to "George Smith's money" on grounds of opposition to absentee ownership and to banks of issue in general led to overtures in the territorial legislature to destroy the "soulless being." In 1846 this movement was successful; but the repeal of the charter did not interrupt the business of the company, for Mitchell insisted that a court of law rather than the legislature should determine whether or not the corporation was exceeding the powers granted in its charter.[40] Meanwhile, business interests in Milwaukee, sensing the value of dependable banking facilities, attempted to come to the institution's rescue. In February 1845, Juneau and sixty other citizens remonstrated against legislative interference and proposed a plan for consolidating the old (and now annulled) Bank of Milwaukee and the insurance company with its "quasi-banking powers."[41] On February 7, 1845, the *Sentinel* seconded this plan, stressing the service of stable banking to the business relations of "our enterprising merchants, forwarders, manufacturers, and vendors and purchasers of lead, copper, and agricultural products." The territorial council refused to warm the "dead bank into life lest it stings the people of the territory,"[42] but the banking activities of the

[36] The certificates of deposit were printed forms reading: "**Wisconsin Marine and Fire Insurance Co.** This is to Certify that ———— has deposited with this Institution **Ten Dollars** which will be paid on demand to bearer. Milwaukee, [Date]. [signed] *Alex Mitchell   Geo Smith*"   Buck, 1:234-35 (rev. ed.).
[37] L. B. Krueger, *Commercial Banking in Wisconsin*, 48.
[38] Butler, "Alexander Mitchell, the Financier," Wis. Hist. Soc., *Colls.*, 11:439.
[39] L. B. Krueger, *Commercial Banking in Wisconsin*, 44.
[40] *Ibid.*, 49-51.   [41] *Ibid.*, 35-36.
[42] Milwaukie *Daily Sentinel*, Feb. 18, 1845.

company continued until it was organized as a State institution under the free banking law of 1852.[43] Profiting from an adequate capital foundation, responsible leadership, knowledge of the dangers of the "wild-cat" period, and a virtual monopoly on banking activities in a decade of rapid expansion, the Wisconsin Marine and Fire Insurance Company provided a source of credit and a circulating medium which greatly facilitated the development both of the farming hinterland and of the commercial operations within the growing city during Milwaukee's formative years.[44]

Trade was the principal excuse for the rise of cities on the frontier; and in this respect the Wisconsin village was no exception. "Milwaukee is the key to the vast section of the country in the interior," wrote one of the community's promoters in 1845. "Produce must pass through the city on its way to market."[45] However, until an exportable surplus could be produced in the hinterland beyond, merchandising operations were confined largely to outfitting settlers and supplying the needs of the growing urban community. Import and export operations were at the outset transacted in the extremely personal fashion that characterized such activity in a frontier environment. In 1835, Nelson Olin collected hides in the vicinity of the village, carried them to Chicago, and with the proceeds from their sale purchased twelve barrels of flour, on which he realized a 50 percent gain upon his return.[46] Trade with the hinterland was carried on in a similarly individual way. In the fall of 1838, Lucius G. Fisher of Beloit traveled to

[43] L. B. Krueger, *Commercial Banking in Wisconsin*, 51.

[44] George Smith, coming from Scotland to Chicago, profited from real estate speculation there and in Milwaukee from 1834 to 1836. Returning to Scotland in 1837, he enlisted Scotch capital in the organization of the Scottish-Illinois Land Investment Company. He influenced the migration of other Scotsmen, among them Alexander Mitchell, who settled in various parts of the Middle West. Smith's willingness to buy out stockholders made timid by threats to the institution brought him a large share of the profit from the company's lending activities, at interest rates of from 10 to 12 percent. In 1852, Smith sold out to Mitchell and returned to Scotland with a fortune estimated at $10,000,000. Buck, 1:286-87 (rev. ed.); Gregory, *History*, 1:186, 188.

[45] Milwaukie *Daily Sentinel*, July 30, 1845.

[46] Olin, "Reminiscences of Milwaukee in 1835-36," *Wis. Mag. of Hist.*, 13:216 (March 1930).

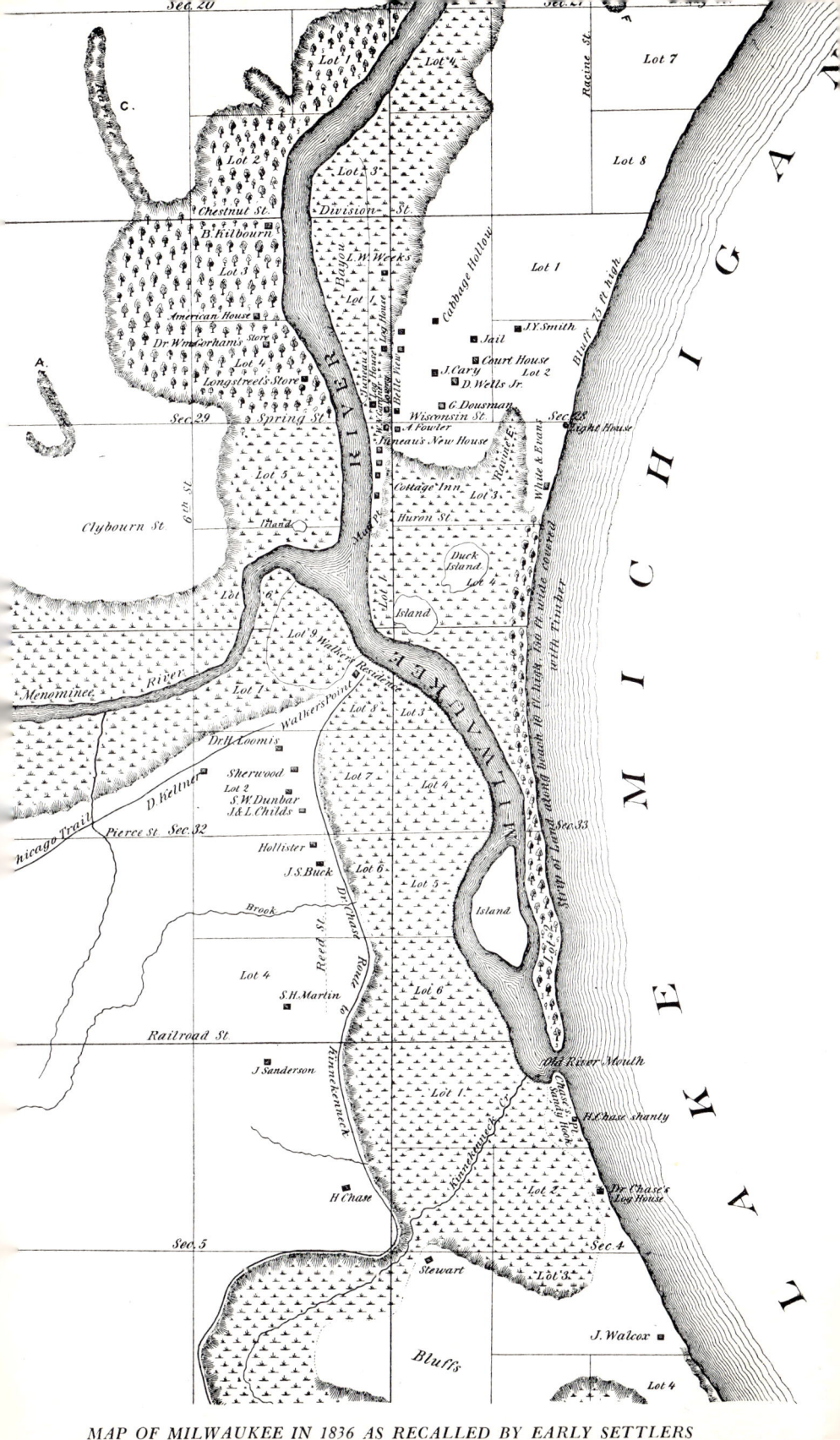

MAP OF MILWAUKEE IN 1836 AS RECALLED BY EARLY SETTLERS

COMMERCIAL FOUNDATIONS 61

Milwaukee where he "arranged with a merchant for stoves, boots, and shoes to sell on commission, and with one team . . . drove them to Beloit and sold them at a good profit to the settlers who were coming in almost every day."[47] By the late thirties and early forties, a marketable surplus began to appear, subject to available transportation facilities from the interior to the lake port. But throughout the village period the goods imported by Milwaukeeans far exceeded in value those which the young community was able to export to the outside world. The total value of imports during the period 1835 to 1841 was close to $6,000,000; whereas the value of exports hardly reached half a million.[48] As late as 1849, imports were worth close to $4,000,000 while exports were valued at little more than $2,000,000.[49] By the close of the village period Milwaukee was exporting wheat, flour, barley, corn, lead, broom corn, brooms, wool, ashes, hides, furs, rags, pails, and some merchandise;[50] but the 157 tons of merchandise exported in 1846 was small by comparison with the 8,886 tons imported in the following year, when 4,000 barrels of fruit, 2,500 barrels of whiskey, 1,400 tons of stoves and iron, and 2,700 kegs of powder were also brought into the city.[51] The *Sentinel* reported that 4,000,000 feet of lumber had been imported in 1842.[52]

[47] Lucius G. Fisher, "Pioneer Recollections of Beloit and Southern Wisconsin," *Wisconsin Magazine of History*, 1:281 (March 1918).

[48] Ray H. Whitbeck, *The Geography and Economic Development of Southeastern Wisconsin* (Wisconsin Geological and Natural History Survey, Bulletin no. 58, Madison, 1921), 59.

[49] Conard, 1:282.

[50] Exports from Milwaukee, 1846:

Wheat	213,448 bu.	Wool	10,562 lbs.
Flour	15,756 bbls.	Ashes	16,250 lbs.
Barley	5,384 bu.	Hides	5,513 lbs.
Corn	1,685 bu.	Furs	198 pkgs.
Lead	1,770,650 lbs.	Rags	140 tons
Broom corn	107,545 lbs.	Pails	295 doz.
Brooms	50,425	Merchandise	314,143 lbs.

Milwaukee City Directory, 1847-48, p. 71.

[51] *Milwaukee City Directory, 1848-49*, p. 23.

[52] Milwaukie *Sentinel*, April 26, 1843. See also *Statement of the amount of Imports and Exports of the port of Milwaukee, in the Territory of Wisconsin from 1835 to Jan. 1, 1842; made by I. A. Lapham in pursuance of a Resolution of the Trustees of said town.* This pamphlet is in the possession of the Milwaukee Public Library.

Lead, mined in northwestern Illinois and southwestern Wisconsin, was one of the first products of the hinterland that made its way to Milwaukee for export to eastern markets. The customary outlet for this commodity was by way of the Mississippi, but the promoters of the lakeside village hoped to attract a considerable portion of it to the faster and ultimately cheaper Great Lakes and Erie Canal route. As early as 1836 some lead began to arrive, and by January 1842, the Milwaukie *Journal* was applauding attempts to induce the New York legislature to abolish tolls on lead from Wisconsin passing through the Erie Canal.[53] By economy in the overland haul, the cost of shipment to New York could be reduced to about $20 a ton; whereas by the Mississippi River route shipping charges ranged from $30 to $40. While the exporting of lead never assumed the proportions its promoters hoped it might, some 2,200,000 pounds of lead and 250,000 pounds of shot were shipped from the Wisconsin port in 1843.[54] The drivers of the lead teams—or "bull-whackers" as they were called—clad in red shirts and pants of Kentucky jeans, lent a colorful touch to the village society when their great ox-drawn, canvas-covered prairie schooners were in town.[55]

By 1839, the surrounding countryside was producing enough wheat to warrant its sale in the Milwaukee market, and in 1841 Holton and Goodall exported a consignment of 4,000 bushels to Canada.[56] As the demand for the commodity increased, Milwaukee dealers circularized the farmers in the vicinity and often lined the roads as far out as Hales Corners to negotiate with the incoming producers.[57] Warehouses sprang up along the waterfront, and commission merchants undertook to channel the trade to eastern ports. The nature of these forwarding operations is suggested in the advertisement of L. J. Higby and Company, one of the most active commission firms of the period:

L. J. Higby and Company—Agents for the Insured Transportation line on the Erie Canal. Running day and night in connection

[53] Milwaukie *Journal*, Jan. 5, 1842.
[54] Whitbeck, *Geography of Southeastern Wisconsin*, 58. See also Milwaukie *Journal*, Jan. 12, 1842.
[55] Buck, 2:225.
[56] Gregory, *History*, 1:454.
[57] *Ibid.*, 1:287.

with the Albany and canal line of towboats on the Hudson river, which leave New York, foot of Broad Street, daily at 5 o'clock P.M. On the Erie Canal, one boat will leave Albany and Buffalo, immediately after the arrival of the steamboats, every day, well-fitted for freight and passengers. On Lake Erie, the above line is connected with a daily line of steam freight boats and vessels, one of which will leave Buffalo every day, wind and weather permitting, for Cleveland, Detroit, and the intermediate ports. Merchandise will be forwarded with care and despatch to the different ports on Lake Huron and Michigan by schooners and brigs of the first class. The above line is also connected on the Ohio canal with a daily line of boats, one of which will leave Cleveland every day for Massillon and Portsmouth, by steamboats to the various landings on the Ohio, southern, and western rivers. Liberal advances made upon produce of all kinds in store, upon the line of the Erie or Ohio canals, or Ports of Lake Erie, Huron, or Michigan, and all property consigned to Messrs. E. W. Barnard and company, commission merchants, 16 South-street, N. Y., . . . will receive prompt attention.[58]

By negotiations of this sort, involving the farmer-producer, the local bank and forwarder, and the New York agent, the exportable commodities of the hinterland reached a more receptive market, the farmer received an immediate, if momentarily partial, return on his crop, and the business life of the village was invigorated through commercial traffic and exchange.

It was not long before ingenious Milwaukeeans began to process some of the raw materials of the hinterland either for local use or in anticipation of export. Flour mills were early established on the "water power" made available by the completed portion of the abortive Milwaukee and Rock River Canal. Here stood a dam, 480 feet in length and 18 feet high, and from it water was conveyed through a guard lock into a canal running parallel to the river and thence to the portion of the city where the power was needed. The flour milling industry received its start with the mill established in 1844 by John Anderson and Dr. E. B. Wolcott.[59] According to the Milwaukee city directory for 1848-49, the four mills in operation were turning out 800 barrels of flour daily; with the completion of two new

[58] Milwaukee *Advertiser*, Jan. 28, 1837.
[59] Gregory, *History*, 1:532.

mills, the output was to be increased to 1,200 barrels.[60] Milwaukee exported 7,550 barrels of flour in 1845 and in the following year more than double this figure.[61] With the increase in cattle and hogs, local butchers began to pack pork and beef for export, the first such sale taking place in November 1845.[62] John Plankinton, who set up a butcher shop in 1844, and Frederick Layton, who began a similar business with his father in 1845, built their packing fortunes on this foundation.[63] In 1852, Plankinton and Layton formed a partnership for the packing of pork and beef and, supplied with $3,000 as capital, built a slaughter and packing house in the Menomonee valley.[64]

The turning of lumber into forms useful for building as well as the manufacture of bricks from the clay of the river banks were forms of processing to be expected in a community which had to be constructed from the ground up. Of the twenty-five mills and factories on the "water power" in 1848, at least half were turning mills or sash, door, and blind factories. The first cream-colored bricks, from whence came the reason for identifying Milwaukee as the "Cream City," were made by some of the employees of Solomon Juneau in 1835. Prominent among those who followed the trade of brick-making were George and Jonathan L. Burnham.[65] The most specialized manufacturing of this early period was R. W. Pierce's establishment for the production of friction matches. Pierce had learned the process in his cousin's factory in Massachusetts. By 1847 he employed a dozen men in his shop and had three agents on the road to distribute his goods to peddlers and advertise his product. His matches were widely used throughout the Middle West.[66] The ale brewery of Richard Owens, William Pawlett, and John Davis, in operation as early as 1840, and the first German lager brewery, established by the Württemberger, Reutelshöfer, in 1841, were pioneer establishments in an in-

[60] *Milwaukee City Directory, 1848-49*, p. 19.
[61] Buck, 3:213.
[62] Milwaukee *Sentinel*, Oct. 16, 1895.
[63] Gregory, *History*, 1:535; Buck, 2:211-12.
[64] Milwaukee *Sentinel*, Oct. 16, 1895.
[65] Gregory, *History*, 1:512-14.
[66] *Ibid.*, 1:517.

COMMERCIAL FOUNDATIONS 65

dustry traditionally associated with the city's history.[67]

The self-assertiveness of the skilled artisans of the village, and their increasing specialization, were early exhibited in one of the most fundamental industries of a developing community —the building trades. The plasterers and bricklayers, meeting on December 31, 1836, adopted resolutions opposing the tendency of "some of the carpenters of this place . . . to monopolize our business. . . . We expect an equal standing with other mechanics of the place," they said, "and the privilege of presenting our bills to the owners of the work for our pay."[68] December 30, 1842, saw the organization of a Mechanic's Protection Society with a shoemaker, an engineer, and a cabinet-maker on the committee for organization. Three years later, the mechanics organized an "association" or "trades union," together with a literary and scientific society. This move on the part of the artisans in the village was commended in the *Sentinel* as proof that "Labor must and will have its rights asserted and secured and reap a fair and liberal reward, if all classes of operatives so will it."[69]

But services beyond those of land speculators, merchants, forwarders, millers, carpenters, and mechanics were needed in the developing commercial community. As a way-station on the route of westward migration, it had to have accommodations for travelers, with their motley accompaniment of servants, draymen, and runners. To the log tavern of John and Luther Childs were added soon the Cottage Inn, Juneau's Belleview (later Milwaukee) House, Daniel Wells's City Hotel, Rogers' United States Hotel, and specialized hostelries like the Cross-Keys Hotel with its appeal for English settlers, The Lakes of Killarney for the Irish, the Caledonian for the Scotch, St. David's for the Welsh, and Theodore Wettstein's *Zum Deutschen Haus*. Both Kilbourn and Juneau encouraged the provision of such facilities for travelers by offers of lots and other premiums.[70] According to a correspondent of the Albany *Evening Journal*,

---

[67] Rud. A. Koss, *Milwaukee* (Milwaukee, 1871), 118. According to Gregory, this name was spelled Reuthlichberger. Gregory, *History*, 1:538.
[68] Milwaukee *Advertiser*, Jan. 28, 1837.
[69] Buck, 2:150; Milwaukie *Daily Sentinel*, Feb. 11, 1845.
[70] Gregory, *History*, 2:684-88.

in 1845, the Milwaukee House, the American House, and the City Hotel were first-rate hostelries; there were a score of the second-rate variety.[71]

Skilled builders like Victor Schulte made possible the construction of bridges and other public works. George Guild, "at his residence near Byron Kilbourn's," was ready, according to his announcement, "to attend to drawing plans . . . for buildings of every description."[72] The structures of these early years were frequently of as speculative stability as the value of the lots on which they were placed. The courthouse which, as an inducement to settlers, Juneau won for the East side, was a frame building described as of a Tuscan order surmounted by a "belvedere." But aside from this and a few brick buildings, most of the dwellings were mere shells inclosed with siding, their flimsiness not infrequently disguised by a false front. The lack of lumber forced the repeated removal of houses from one side of the river to the other; and poor construction was one cause of the extreme fire hazard of the day.

Servicing the transportation facilities upon which the young city depended were the blacksmiths, the livery stable owners, the feed dealers, and those who supplied the lake steamers with the cordwood necessary for making steam. Amherst W. Kellogg wrote that his father, using a large scow propelled by men with poles, would "go up the rivers and along the lake shore, load the scow with wood procured from the farmers or choppers on the banks, pole it out to the boat anchored in the lake . . . , discharge his cargo of wood, and take a load of freight from the boat to warehouses on the river."[73]

And finally there was the press, significant not only for servicing the community but for promoting its growth as well.[74] According to Daniel H. Richards, who founded it in July 1836, the West side's Milwaukee *Advertiser* was "part and parcel of

[71] Albany *Evening Journal*, quoted in Milwaukie *Daily Sentinel*, July 14, 1845.
[72] Milwaukee *Advertiser*, Dec. 18, 1838. See also Alexander C. Guth, "Early Day Architects in Milwaukee," *Wisconsin Magazine of History*, 10:17-28 (September 1926).
[73] A. W. Kellogg, "Recollections of Life in Early Wisconsin," *Wis. Mag. of Hist.*, 7:489 (June 1924).
[74] Cincinnati *Gazette*, quoted in Milwaukee *Sentinel*, June 10, 1859.

the project of building a city at this point and settling the then new Territory of Wisconsin."[75] Richards' original intention had been to purchase the Chicago *Democrat*, but after having been induced to visit the site of Milwaukee late in 1835, he decided to lend his support to the building of the Wisconsin village.[76] The columns of the *Advertiser* were a medium through which Kilbourn agitated for the internal improvements sought by the young community, and quite likely most of its copies were mailed out by the promoters of the West side for the purpose of attracting immigrants from settled localities in the East.

The village on the other side of the river soon countered with a rival news organ. Backed financially by Juneau and Achilles J. Rousseau of Troy, New York, the *Sentinel* appeared in June 1837, published at first by John O'Rourke, former journeyman in the office of the *Advertiser,* and later by Harrison Reed.[77] Rivals in urban promotion, the two papers championed respectively the opposing camps in territorial politics. The *Advertiser* was Democratic, supporting Henry Dodge, while the Whig-minded *Sentinel* bolstered the growing strength of James D. Doty. In fact, the political aspect of Milwaukee journalism soon superseded its specifically promotional nature. Richards' sale of the *Advertiser* to Josiah Noonan in March 1841 was prompted by the desire on the part of the Democrats "for a more efficient party newspaper." The new management renamed the paper the Milwaukee *Courier*. Meanwhile, hoping to silence Whig opposition to Dodge's candidacy for Congress, the Democrats took advantage of Reed's momentary absence from the city and succeeded in aligning the *Sentinel* with the Democratic cause. The Whigs hastened to recover their journalistic voice by establishing the short-lived Milwaukie *Journal* in August

---

[75] Letter from D. H. Richards, Wisconsin Editorial Association, *Proceedings: First, Second, and Third Sessions* [1857, 1858, 1859], 19-20.

[76] Two earlier newspapers had preceded the *Advertiser* in the territory: the Green Bay *Intelligencer*, which first appeared on December 11, 1833, and the *Wisconsin Free Press*, established in August 1835. Douglas C. McMurtrie, *Early Printing in Milwaukee* (Milwaukee, 1930), 13, 15.

[77] *Ibid.*, 18-19; *Annotated Catalogue of Newspaper Files in the Library of the State Historical Society of Wisconsin* (Madison, 1911), 395.

1841, printed on forms which its editor, Elisha Starr, had obtained through buying out the Chicago *Tribune*. Starr soon took over the *Sentinel*, restored to its Whig allegiance; and 1843 saw a virulent hostility between it and Noonan's *Courier* which was characteristic of politics in the young frontier community. This natural rivalry was aggravated when a new national administration elevated Noonan to the postmastership, a post which had long been held by Juneau. From August 1843 to September 1844, Charles Sholes published the Milwaukee *Democrat*, which he renamed the *American Freeman* upon his conversion to the antislavery cause.[78]

By 1844, less than ten years from its founding, the community had grown to such an extent as to warrant the publication of a daily newspaper. On December 9, John S. Fillmore and David M. Keeler, succeeding Starr, brought out the first issue of Wisconsin's first daily, the Milwaukee *Daily Sentinel*. Commenting on its appearance, the editor of the Richmond, Virginia, *Star* marveled at the idea of a daily paper "published way off in the wilds of Wisconsin, . . . among wild Injuns and Bears." By September 1845, less than a year after the founding of the daily, ownership of both the daily and weekly *Sentinel* fell to Rufus King, formerly of the Albany, New York, *Gazette*. King's subsequent career was to give striking evidence of the role of newspaper leadership in promoting the material, cultural, and civic development of the community. In February 1846 the *Sentinel* was merged with William D. Wilson's *Daily Gazette*, which had first appeared in October 1845. In June 1847, the *Courier*, after an unsuccessful attempt at daily publication during 1846, was sold to William E. Cramer and Joseph Curtis, who changed its name to the *Weekly Wisconsin*. Thus, as village gave way to city, Milwaukee was already being served by both Whig and Democratic newspapers, two of them dailies, and by a German journal, the *Wiskonsin-Banner*, founded as a weekly in 1844, as well.[79]

Like the practitioners of other frontier pursuits, the jour-

[78] McMurtrie, *Early Printing in Milwaukee*, 22.

[79] *Ibid.*, 27-31. In 1847, King and Wilson founded a second German newspaper, the *Volksfreund*, which they sold to Frederick Fratny in the fall of the same year. In 1855 the *Volksfreund* merged with the *Wiskonsin-Banner*.

nalist of the village period had to be a jack of all trades. Harrison Reed reported that during the panic of 1837 he was at once "editor, printer, and purveyor," and that with the approach of winter he obtained a barrel of flour in return for printing and advertising that required him to work all night as "type-setter, roller boy, and pressman."[80] The prevailing lack of capital resulted in the use of second-hand equipment and recourse to purchasing on credit; and the rapid turnover in ownership reflected the fluctuating state of western society. But despite these difficulties, Milwaukee's newspapers demonstrated, from the outset of villagehood, the integral relationship of the press to urban growth. In the frontier period they served primarily to encourage settlement or to advance a political party toward public office; but even before Milwaukee had become a city, they began to play an ever more vigorous role in fostering the development of commerce and industry, implementing the transmission of culture, and stimulating the civic improvement of a community which was destined, according to many of its journalistic promoters, to become the chief commercial and manufacturing metropolis of the West.[81]

[80] Gregory, *History*, 2:1006-7.

[81] Albany *Evening Journal,* June 30, 1845. The editor of the *Sentinel* had written as early as June 2, 1840: "It is of the first importance to this place that the trade of the southwest as well as of the west and northwest be secured. This cannot be done except by holding out greater inducements than other places." Of the role of the press in urban promotion the Cincinnati *Gazette,* quoted in the *Sentinel,* June 10, 1859, asserted that a newspaper served the founders of towns by acting as a kind of credential to the reality of the inchoate city, and as a light to direct the pioneer to a new home and to direct business and emigration into new channels.

CHAPTER 4

The Social Fabric of the Village

RUFUS KING, the most distinguished of Milwaukee's early newspapermen, visited the lakeside village for the first time in 1845. Reporting his western journey for the Albany *Evening Journal,* he was hard put to impress his readers with the growth of a community which "only ten years ago . . . was not." By the date of his visit, a town of 8,000 inhabitants was centered upon the quarter section where, ten years before, Juneau's cabin alone had stood.¹ The boom years of the middle thirties had brought more than 1,000 settlers to the river's mouth; and by 1840 the census takers enumerated 1,712. Six years later the population approached 10,000; and by 1850, with 20,061 residents listed, it had more than doubled.² Although by the time of King's arrival a third of the population was already drawn from the Teutonic migration that before another decade was to make a *Deutsch-Athen*³ of the Wisconsin city, until the middle forties Milwaukee was predominantly a Yankee-Yorker village. Only an occasional Finnegan or Daugherty, Vieau or Juneau suggested the variety that Irish migrants and French-Canadian traders lent to a society that was predominantly of the eastern seaboard; only an occasional Diedrich or Weisner foreshadowed the coming Germanic flood.⁴

It was a rare Milwaukeean of the thirties who had not known in his youth the stony soil of New England or the rolling

¹ Albany *Evening Journal,* quoted in Milwaukie *Daily Sentinel,* July 14, 1845.
² Milwaukee *Sentinel,* July 14, 1937.
³ Henry Villard wrote of the city in 1856: Milwaukee "was known among German-Americans as *Deutsch-Athen,* and, comparatively speaking, deserved the name." Henry Villard, *Memoirs of Henry Villard* (2 vols., New York, 1904), 1:48.
⁴ Humphrey J. Desmond, "Early Irish Settlers in Milwaukee," *Wisconsin Magazine of History,* 13:369 (June 1930); J. D. B. DeBow, *Statistical View of the United States . . . a Compendium of the Seventh Census* (Washington, 1854), 399.

70

New York countryside. "The people here are principally from New York and the states east of it," wrote Increase Lapham in 1837. "They all possess the enterprising go-ahead spirit of the New Englanders."[5] Of the pioneers of 1833, Albert Fowler had been born in Massachusetts and the Carleys, in New York. Horace Chase and his brother, migrants of the following year, were Vermonters. Burdick and Brown came, by way of Chicago, from New York and Massachusetts respectively, and Byron Kilbourn from Connecticut by way of Ohio. Only George H. Walker is to be identified as a Southerner; and even he, though born in Lynchburg, Virginia, had accompanied his father to Illinois at the age of fourteen.[6] Of the arrivals of 1835 whose birthplace can be traced, the preponderance of New Englanders and New Yorkers lent novelty to the occasional Kentuckian who ventured into the Wisconsin village; and from 1836 forward, the native-American leaders of the community were almost exclusively of New England, New York, and middle Atlantic origin. Physicians, lawyers, merchants, land speculators, and railroad promoters were drawn from the exodus which in the thirties and forties was draining many parts of New England and New York of its vigorous young manhood.

New York's contribution to the growing city justified Charles J. Lynde's reference to it as the "Empire" village of Wisconsin.[7] The Empire State contributed James H. Rogers, Eliphalet Cramer, Joshua Hathaway, Harrison Ludington, Alanson Sweet, Lewis J. Higby, James Kneeland, Increase Lapham, George and William Allen, Edward P. Allis, John M. Stowell, E. P. Bacon, and Edward H. Brodhead; Levi Hubbell, William P. Lynde, and Asahel Finch, lawyers; Doctors Erastus B. Wolcott and William P. Proudfit; and such newspapermen as William E. Cramer, Josiah Noonan, Elisha Starr, and Rufus King. Even the Irish merchant, John Furlong, had spent a

[5] Increase to Darius Lapham, Feb. 25, 1837, Lapham Papers; see also Milwaukie *Sentinel*, Jan. 20, 1844. "New York and New England have contributed the largest proportion of citizens and Germany and Ireland, with few exceptions, the residue of this town." A Milwaukee Sabbath in 1843 reminded a reporter for the New York *Tribune* "of a New England village." Gregory, *History*, 2:1304.

[6] Conard, 1:23.

[7] Charles J. Lynde to John K. Bartlett, M.D., Dec. 19, 1840, Blanchard Harper Papers, Wisconsin Historical Society Library.

considerable time on a New York farm before migrating, by way of Michigan, to Milwaukee. From Maine came Timothy A. Chapman, Abner Kirby, and Daniel Wells; from Vermont, D. A. J. Upham, Henry H. Button, Horace Rublee, Dr. Lemuel W. Weeks, and Jason Downer; and from Massachusetts, William A. Prentiss and Charles T. Bradley. Harvey Birchard and E. Townsend Mix were natives of Connecticut; John Plankinton, of Delaware; James Bonnell and Garret Vliet, of New Jersey; Samuel Marshall, of Pennsylvania; and James B. Martin, of Baltimore, Maryland. Thus early Milwaukee was New York and New England once, twice, or thrice removed, a fact reflected incidentally in the disproportionately large number of graduates of Union College, Schenectady, New York, among the early settlers who had had college training[8] and one which may help to explain the cooperation which prevailed among the small group of men who promoted so many community enterprises in the early years.

In the middle forties Teutonia began to challenge Yankeedom and European migration to transform the tone of what had been predominantly a Yorker-Yankee village; by 1843 a Germanic influence that was to reach its peak by the end of the century had already begun to make itself felt.[9] "Ho! for Wisconsin," proclaimed the Buffalo *Gazette*. "The number of hardy emigrants already arrived and going west, is immense. The Old Country pours in her legions of industrious and frugal husbandmen." By 1850, some 64 percent of the city's population were of foreign birth, and of the total population more than a third was German.[10] The first German immigrants began to appear in 1835,[11] and the remainder of the decade saw

[8] This was true of D. A. J. Upham, Joshua Stark, Eliphalet Cramer, George W. Allen, Robert N. Austin, Edward P. Allis, and William E. Cramer.

[9] By 1890, one-fourth of the inhabitants of Milwaukee were German by birth; more than one-half were of German parentage. By 1910 the German-born population had dropped to one-sixth of the total population, and by 1920 to less than one-tenth. Desmond, "Early Irish Settlers in Milwaukee," *Wis. Mag. of Hist.*, 13:370 (June 1930).

[10] Kate A. Everest, "How Wisconsin Came By Its Large German Element," Wisconsin Historical Society, *Collections*, 12:300 (1892).

[11] According to the Milwaukee *Sentinel*, Oct. 16, 1895, the earliest was Henry Bleyer. See also Koss, *Milwaukee*, 40. Faust asserts that the first German to settle in Milwaukee County was Wilhelm Strothmann. Albert B. Faust, *The German Element in the United States* (2 vols., New York, 1909), 1:470.

THE SOCIAL FABRIC OF THE VILLAGE   73

scattering arrivals, among them a party of German carpenters, who had come at the solicitation of Juneau and Dousman; Matthias Stein, whom Juneau induced to stay;[12] and Louis Trayser, whom the shipbuilder George Barber persuaded to build an inn for his workers: *"Zur Deutschen* Little Tavern."[13] This was a period in which the push of economic, political, and religious circumstance in Germany and the pull of the American environment, settler propaganda, and the competition of western states were compelling a migration of Germans to the North Central section of the United States in numbers that totaled 280,000 by 1850.[14] By the turn of the forties the "torrent of emigration" had begun to swell, and Milwaukee was one of the points of distribution. A few members of a colony of Germans who migrated for religious reasons in 1839 remained in the village when the majority proceeded to take up farmlands near by.[15] By the early forties, 200 to 300 Teutonic migrants were arriving weekly; and soon young Germans from Chicago were visiting Milwaukee to find themselves brides.[16] "One hundred persons, chiefly Germans, landed here yesterday," wrote Increase Lapham to his brother Darius in July 1842.[17] In the summer months of 1843 and 1844 the arrival of 1,000 to 1,400 Germans in a week was not unusual.

Despite the pull of the "emigration fever," it was not an easy journey from Rhenish Prussia, Bavaria, Luxemburg, Baden, or Saxony, regions which supplied the bulk of the Ger-

[12] Gregory, *History*, 2:608.
[13] Koss, *Milwaukee*, 50.
[14] Franz Löher, in his *Geschichte und Zustände der Deutschen in Amerika* (Cincinnati and Leipzig, 1847), argued that since the Irish remained in eastern America or in the cities, and since the native-Americans were scattering through the Far West, the Northwest was destined to become predominantly German. "Germans can remain Germans in America," he wrote. "They can plant the vine on the hills and drink it with happy song and dance. They can have German schools and universities, German literature and art . . . in short they can form a German state, in which the German language is as much the popular and official language as the English is now, and in which the German spirit rules." See Everest, "How Wisconsin Came By Its Large German Element," Wis. Hist. Soc., *Colls.*, 12:306. A book by Carl E. Hasse, published in Grimma in 1841, counseled Germans to go to Wisconsin. Faust, *German Element in the United States*, 1:475n.
[15] Kellogg, "The Story of Wisconsin," *Wis. Mag. of Hist.*, 3:319 (March 1920).
[16] Koss, *Milwaukee*, 114-15.
[17] Increase to Darius Lapham, July 28, 1842, Lapham Papers.

man immigrants of the forties and fifties, or for the Hessians, Württembergers, Swiss, and Austrians who also arrived in considerable numbers in the period from 1848 to 1854.[18] Seasickness, crowded quarters, and poor food harassed them during the five to six weeks of ocean travel before the "endless forest of masts of sailing vessels"[19] in the New York Harbor came in sight. *"Nun danket Alle Gott,"* sang the pioneers, for the moment unmindful of additional hazards to be met before the *Deutsch-Athen* should be reached. Then, acting upon the advice of their countrymen who had gone before, many sought the agent of the *Deutsche Gesellschaft* or the immigration representative from Wisconsin for travel suggestions and for the names of German firms by which their goods could be dispatched to the Wisconsin city. Usually these agents advised against the slow-moving journey by way of the Erie Canal and suggested traveling by steamboat to Albany, from there to Buffalo by rail, and thence to Milwaukee, "partly by steamboat, partly by rail." According to Christian Ficker, the voyage through lakes Erie, Huron, and Michigan took "at least twice as long as to go via New Buffalo and Chicago" and put the traveler "in greater jeopardy of his life than in crossing the ocean." The owner of heavy baggage did well to "turn it over in New York to a forwarding agent" and have it sent as "merchants' goods" directly to Milwaukee, addressed to such firms as Maler and Wend or Greulich and Haertel. This procedure did away with the heavy labor of frequent loading and unloading and saved appreciably in freight charges for excess weight in passenger's goods.[20]

[18] See Kate Everest Levi, "Geographical Origin of German Immigration to Wisconsin," *Wisconsin Historical Society, Collections,* 14:341-93 (1898); Gregory, *History,* 2:618.

[19] "Immigrant Letter [from Gerhard Kremers]," *Wisconsin Magazine of History,* 21:69-71 (September 1937).

[20] "Ficker's Advice to Emigrants," *Wis. Mag. of Hist.,* 25:225-27 (December 1941). In July 1846, the trip by canal from Albany to Buffalo consumed eight days. See "Reminiscences of Arend Jan Brusse on Early Dutch Settlement in Milwaukee," *Wisconsin Magazine of History,* 30:87 (September 1946). In the early forties the journey on the lakes consumed about four and a half days by one of the best steamships. The fare was $14.00, including board. Frederick von Raumer, *America and the American People,* tr. by William W. Turner (New York, 1846), 451.

The experience of the Kremers family was typical of this Teutonic migration to the West. Setting out in 1848, they made an overnight trip by steamer to Albany and at two in the following afternoon boarded a train which brought them, after twenty-nine hours, to Buffalo. Lodging at the *Wilhelm Tell,* run by two of their countrymen, they secured provisions for the four to six-days' trip on the lakes. After a voyage made "well nigh unbearable" by accident, congestion, and cold, they reached Wisconsin at the close of the fourth day, concluding a westward journey which had consumed almost eight days.[21]

By 1843 it was evident that the increasingly numerous German-Americans were going to assume a positive role in the developing village culture. Since 1842, American merchants had been advertising their wares in the German language, and Edward Weisner had been serving as justice of the peace.[22] But the harbor festival of March 22, 1843, gave the Germans their first opportunity to make a showing as a group and in a characteristic fashion. They formed a procession under the leadership of Dr. Franz Huebschmann,[23] the Catholic priest, the evangelical preacher, and others and carried a large banner bearing the inscription: *"Die deutschen Bürger von Milwaukee."*[24] The Fourth of July found them cooperating with the Irish in a celebration in which the American settlers did not participate.[25] In December 1843 they joined newcomers from Ireland in asking the territorial legislature to permit non-naturalized immigrants to vote on the impending question of creating a state government.[26] Huebschmann and John White, the

[21] "Immigrant Letter [Kremers]," *Wis. Mag of Hist.,* 21:72-73 (September 1937).

[22] The census spells his name this way. Koss spells it Wiesner. Koss, *Milwaukee,* 132.

[23] Franz Huebschmann, vigorous champion of Milwaukee's German-Americans, was a native of Weimar. Settling in the city as a physician in 1842, he interested himself in municipal and state politics and became a leader in the political, social, and musical activities of the German element. Faust, *German Element in the United States,* 1:476n.

[24] Koss, *Milwaukee,* 135-36.

[25] *Ibid.,* 145.

[26] According to the organic law of the territory, only citizens of the United States were eligible to vote. Louise P. Kellogg, "The Alien Suffrage Provision in the Constitution of Wisconsin," *Wisconsin Magazine of History,* 1:422 (June 1918).

leader of the Irish element, were chairmen of the meeting; and C. J. Kern and Richard Murphy acted as secretaries for the respective nationalities. Herman Haertel and Dr. F. A. Luening, speaking for their German countrymen, asserted the right of the foreign-born to an equal vote with the American settlers on political matters.[27] More than 1,200 persons signed a petition expressing the newcomers' demands to the territorial legislature; and the latter body, mindful of the foreign vote, responded in January 1844 by extending the suffrage on the question of statehood to all free white male inhabitants above the age of twenty-one who had resided three months in the territory. Opposition to alien voting brought immediate criticism of this measure, and in 1845 the qualification was made increasingly restrictive by requiring six months' residence of all voters and a declaration of intention to become citizens of those who were not already such.[28]

The immigrants' assertion of political equality was in part a reaction to the nativist sentiment then gaining strength, especially among the Whigs in the village, and in part a consequence of the solidarity of opinion and action which followed upon the increasing accumulation of Germans in the urban community. The *Sentinel* decried the tendency to draw "untutored monarchial barbarians out of their legitimate sphere and coddle them with fine things they do not understand."[29] It thus reflected Whig resentment at the affiliation of the newcomers with the Democratic Party, to which the Europeans were drawn, not alone because the title appealed to them and the party welcomed them, but because the Whigs were more inclined to interfere with the living habits of the foreign-born.[30] But in spite of nativist obstruction, the European element,

---

[27] Koss, *Milwaukee*, 151; Wilhelm Hense-Jensen and Ernest Bruncken, *Wisconsin's Deutsch-Amerikaner bis zum Schluss des Neunzehnten Jahrhunderts* (2 vols., Milwaukee, 1900-1902), tr. by Joseph Schafer, chap. 1, p. 7. Dr. Schafer's translation, which omits certain chapters of the original, is in manuscript paged by chapter, in the Wisconsin Historical Society Library. The work will hereafter be cited as Hense-Jensen, Schafer tr., with references to chapter and page of the translated version.

[28] Kellogg, "Alien Suffrage Provision," *Wis. Mag. of Hist.*, 1:422-24 (June 1918).

[29] Bruce, *History*, 1:765.

[30] Koss, *Milwaukee*, 151; Hense-Jensen, Schafer tr., chap. 1, p. 6.

although occasionally at odds among themselves[31] and at the outset timid about expressing their opinions before native-Americans, nevertheless early assumed the right to participate in community life on a basis of equality with the native-born and to transplant their culture in the developing urban environment without interference. In fact, Ficker was constrained in 1853 to advise the new immigrant to "stop being a German and be an American," and to cease comparing "the old and the new fatherland," thus overlooking "the good and wholesome things of America and the doubtful disadvantageous things of Germany."[32]

At a second meeting of the foreign element, held in June 1844, with Huebschmann and White again presiding, a resolution vigorously asserting the rights of foreigners was adopted. The increasing attacks of the *Sentinel* convinced the German settlers of their need of a newspaper, such as the Irish element had in the *Courier*, to provide them with a means of communication and political organization. As a result, Huebschmann collected a fund of $170 to start a publication and enlisted the services of Moritz Schoeffler, who came with journalistic experience from Jefferson City, Missouri, to edit it. The first issue of the *Wiskonsin-Banner*, pioneer German newspaper in the State, appeared on September 7, 1844. Less than two weeks later, the German element organized a torchlight parade to honor the newly arrived territorial governor, N. P. Tallmadge, known to have championed immigrant rights both in Congress and in Michigan. Reflecting the German's enthusiasm for public demonstrations, it was such a celebration as the American-born Milwaukeeans had never seen before. Torches flaming into the night, a German band, an American flag: no wonder Tallmadge was impressed.[33]

By the late fall of 1844, the German Democratic Association was giving unity and direction to the political activities of Milwaukee's German-Americans. The organization proposed " 'to arouse the social consciousness of Germans, to explain and

---

[31] Koss, *Milwaukee,* 167-68.
[32] "Ficker's Advice to Emigrants," *Wis. Mag. of Hist.,* 25:229 (December 1941).
[33] Koss, *Milwaukee,* 152-53, 163-64.

disseminate the principles on which the state governments of the United States rest, and to establish unity and unanimity in political works.'" Huebschmann, a leader in this as in other German-American enterprises, was the president; and his lieutenants were such prominent German citizens as J. Thomssen, J. A. Liebhaber, Friedrich Neukirch, Moritz Schoeffler, G. Fasolt, and H. Niedermann. Matters of both local and national policy were debated although the issue of the State constitution was somewhat overshadowed by that of the municipal charter; pressure was exerted to get a post-office appointment for a fellow-countryman, A. Henry Bielfeld, who ultimately became Milwaukee's first city clerk;[34] and resolutions were passed condemning a Dr. Schaaf who was currently criticizing the Germans in America.[35] This activity discouraged the defection of the German newcomers to the Whig ranks; and in consequence only two German names appeared in the membership of the Clay Club of that year, whereas many Germans belonged to the Hickory Club which supported Polk. A *Freiheitsbaum,* or liberty tree, erected near Haertel's, and the music of a German band, which took part in the celebration following Polk's victory, lent a Teutonic touch to Milwaukee politics in the election of 1844.[36] Early in that year Matthias Stein received the largest number of votes for membership in the board of trustees from the East Ward, and C. W. Schwartz was elected from the West Ward.[37] When Milwaukee County chose its delegates to the State constitutional convention of 1846, Huebschmann, the natural leader of the German element, was included, as was Moritz Schoeffler for the convention of 1847-48. In the deliberations of these bodies, despite pressure from the western part of the State to limit the suffrage to citizens, the efforts of the German delegates led to the enactment of a liberal suffrage qualification allowing the franchise to one-year residents, including white males, twenty-one years of age, who had declared their intention to become citizens.[38]

[34] Bielfeld was born in 1818 at Bremen and came to Milwaukee in 1836.
[35] Hense-Jensen, Schafer tr., chap. 1, p. 10; Koss, *Milwaukee,* 166.
[36] *Ibid.,* 165-66.   [37] Buck, 2:198.
[38] Because of its provisions regarding banking, the constitution proposed in 1846 was rejected by the electorate. The constitution devised by the convention of 1847-48 retained the suffrage provisions proposed in 1846, although

By the middle forties the Teutonic culture was beginning to make its mark on the urban social scene, and the German community, which was to exist in compact self-sufficiency for many years within the American city, was taking shape. The vicinity of Chestnut Street and West Water, on the West side, and that of Division and East Water near the *Grüner Markt,* across the river, comprised a "Little Germany" in the shadow of Yankee Hill. Ludwig's Garden, where the German citizenry danced at night, listened to open-air concerts, and bought cakes, coffee, and beer, began business in 1844. The first German elementary school opened in that year; and the German community assumed a share of civic responsibility in organizing a German fire-fighting force and planning a German military company. Captain August Greulich's[39] firemen enlisted the prominent leaders of the German element, and with the appearance in 1845 of the Washington Guard, in their blue costumes, magnificently ornamented with scarlet braid and topped with military caps, the German society provided the city with additional agents for the maintenance of order.[40] Military Hall, the meeting house of the Washington Guard, became the center of German activities in the city. A German aid club, organized in 1845 to provide sickness and death benefits, afforded a volunteer solution to the problem of relief.[41]

The religious practices of the Fatherland were speedily transplanted in the new society. Many of the German newcomers had migrated to America under the tutelage of their German pastors in the hope of preserving religious practices that were threatened by the state churches in their home localities.[42] One group of Old Lutherans, who arrived in 1843, being

Schoeffler attempted to reduce the period of residence to six months. The German Second Ward endorsed this constitution by a vote of 452 to 8. Hense-Jensen, Schafer tr., chap. 1, pp. 11-16.

[39] August Greulich, born in Baden in 1813, came to America in 1834 and migrated, via Detroit, to Milwaukee in 1840. Early employed as a butcher, he soon became active in politics, serving in the first sessions of the legislature under the constitution. Buck, 3:42-43.

[40] In 1845, Captain George was asked to have his men ready to deal with rumored disturbances at the land office, which, however, did not materialize. Koss, *Milwaukee,* 184, 189, 191.

[41] *Ibid.,* 197.

[42] Louise P. Kellogg, "The Bennett Law in Wisconsin," *Wisconsin Magazine of History,* 2:7-8 (September 1918).

too poor to supply their own minister, appealed to Pastor Krause of Freistadt to supply their congregation. A controversy over his stipend led to a break with the Buffalo Synod and reorganization under Pastor P. Kluegel.[43] German Evangelical communities soon appeared, as well as German Catholic groups whose coming was stimulated in part by the news that Milwaukee had been designated as the center of a new diocese with the Swiss Catholic, John Martin Henni, as the first bishop. A portion of his initial service, on May 5, 1844, was designed especially for German communicants.[44] In a controversy between the Catholics and the Rev. J. J. Miter, of the Congregational Church, reflecting the nativism of the day, the Protestant American clergyman was forced to back down and retract his words.[45] Thus by the middle forties—and some time before the arrival of the Forty-eighters—German-Americans were both a numerous element in the growing city and an identifiable unit in the developing urban culture. Considerations of language, the physical concentration of the urban community, and a natural submission to their political and religious leaders led these former Europeans to reproduce the domestic, religious, and educational practices of the Fatherland in the New World. This concern for the known, however, did not prevent their almost immediate adoption of such institutions as the volunteer fire companies and military organizations that were characteristic features of urban development in the mid-nineteenth-century American Middle West.

Not so numerous as the Germans, but oftentimes politically more vocal, was the Irish ingredient of the frontier village. Unlike the Germans, most of the Irish seem to have sojourned in some other part of the United States before traveling west, some so long as to have become thoroughly Americanized. Many of the early Irish-born arrivals came from Fall River, Massachusetts, between 1839 and 1841, forced to move by industrial depression in that area. Many came from New York and New England and not a few from Michigan, Ohio, Chicago, and St. Louis. Although most of these engaged in humbler pur-

[43] Koss, *Milwaukee*, 138.
[44] Milwaukee *Courier*, May 8, 1844; Gregory, *History*, 2:894.
[45] Koss, *Milwaukee*, 196.

suits, there were among them prominent grocers, merchants, provision dealers, and newspapermen such as Hans Crocker, first editor of the *Sentinel,* Julius P. B. McCabe, **Daniel Fitzsimmons**, and William H. Sullivan, publisher of **the** *Courier* from 1845 to 1847.[46] The predominance of journalists **hints at** the political vigor of the nationality. The Irish were good campaigners, and they knew how to solicit votes. Their collaboration with the Germans in 1843 bolstered their political strength; and as early as 1844 one of their number, Thomas J. Gilbert, was chosen president of the board of village trustees. By that year, too, the Irish-Americans had formed their own military company, known as the Emmett Guards, and had organized a movement for Irish relief. Natives of Ireland were among the representatives of Milwaukee County in the conventions to frame a constitution for the State.[47] Before the close of the village period the arrival of Scotch, Welsh, Swiss, Norwegians, Swedes, and Jews, in small numbers, recalled the polyglot population of the community in aboriginal days.[48] Some of these came specifically to serve the growing urban community; some were employed in the lake service; and others were engaged in temporary pursuits awaiting the accumulation of sufficient funds to permit their migration into the farming region for which Milwaukee was the distributing center.

The early settlers of Milwaukee, whether Yankee or European, came from regions where public-supported elementary education was held in high repute. New England had long boasted free, universal common schools, supported by public taxes; New Yorkers and Pennsylvanians were striving, in the thirties, to adopt the free school plan; and Germany was by this time noted for her progressive advances in elementary education.[49] Yet despite the migrants' awareness of and concern

---

[46] Desmond, "Early Irish Settlers in Milwaukee," *Wis. Mag. of Hist.,* 13:366-67 (June 1930); Milwaukee *Sentinel,* Oct. 16, 1895.

[47] Wallace W. Graham and Garrett M. Fitzgerald (1846); John L. Doran (1847-48).

[48] Milwaukee *Sentinel,* Oct. 16, 1895; Gregory, *History,* 2:627-28, 630; James A. Bryden, "The Scots in Wisconsin," Wisconsin Historical Society, *Proceedings,* 1901, pp. 153-57.

[49] Joseph Schafer, "Origin of Wisconsin's Free School System," *Wisconsin Magazine of History,* 9:28-31 (September 1925).

for "the ideal of the free school,"[50] the frontier environment permitted the realization of but few educational advantages until the close of the village period.[51] A correspondent to the *Sentinel* explained the "wretched condition" of the common schools in 1845 by pointing out that in a population of newcomers, "every consideration, other than that immediately connected with the settlement and permanent establishment of our town as a place of commercial importance" had "been neglected."[52] In 1845 less than a third of the 1,781 children of school age in the village were in school; and of the 584 enjoying educational advantages, meager as they were, 356 were in private schools.[53] There was no public schoolhouse in the East Ward; and what served the purpose in the West was "an old, dilapidated structure, unpainted and half unglazed, standing directly upon the highway, without playground or shade, and not even a retreat for the performance of nature's most private and necessary offices." Textbooks were few and of varied authorship; less than a dollar was appropriated annually per scholar; and teachers were paid little more than ordinary day laborers.[54]

In the absence of adequate community provision for education, parents were forced to engage tutors or patronize private schools.[55] According to the Green Bay *Intelligencer* of June 27, 1835, a "gentleman" was supporting "a school at his own expense";[56] and this was the predominant practice for the succeeding decade. A school district was organized in the fall of 1836 and a school established; but although this was known as a public school, it was not a free school; for parents still had to pay, pro rata, for the instruction of their children.[57] Edward

[50] *Ibid.*, 31.
[51] The *Sentinel* asserted on October 13, 1837, that no subject would be more conducive to "the future happiness and prosperity of the people" than "the adoption of a wise and liberal system of common school education."
[52] Milwaukie *Daily Sentinel,* June 7, 1845.
[53] Report of committee on schools and school systems, Dec. 12, 1845. See *Evening Wisconsin* (Milwaukee), Oct. 15, 1895.
[54] Milwaukie *Daily Sentinel,* June 7, 1845.
[55] *Evening Wisconsin,* Oct. 15, 1895.
[56] Gregory, *History,* 1:59.
[57] Schafer, "Origin of Wisconsin's Free School System," *Wis. Mag. of Hist.*, 9:32-33 (September 1925). Under Michigan territorial law, enacted in 1827, every town having more than fifty families was to support a public school

West was the teacher, an eighteen-year-old Pennsylvanian who had migrated by foot toward the frontier, and who, like most of the early pedagogues, taught school only while looking about for more profitable pursuits.[58] He was paid $50 a month and board.[59] His schoolroom was a store building on Third Street near Poplar. The pupils included "children of all ages, from full-grown youth down to little children," among them the young Kilbourns and Laphams; and in the evening West taught the "rudiments" to older persons. In the course of three terms, he increased his enrollment from forty to seventy. Log benches, a pine table, a few books, a ruler, penknife, and quill pen comprised his scanty equipment; and like most schoolteachers of the period, he had to establish control over his academic domain by physical prowess. An encounter with one of the larger boys, in which an iron fire shovel and a wooden club were weapons, cost the teacher two front teeth but gained him the respect of his pupils.[60] Ministers frequently were the proprietors of the private schools. The young ladies who attended the "select school" established by the Rev. Lemuel Hull in 1841 were charged $3.00 per quarter for the elementary branches, $4.00 for the common English branches, $5.00 for the higher branches, including algebra, Latin, and Greek, $8.00 for piano and organ, $6.00 for French, Italian, and German, $4.00 for drawing and painting, and an additional charge of $2.00 a week for board and 50 cents for laundry. When Hull died in 1842, the school was conducted by his two daughters, both of whom were less than twenty years of age.[61] A considerable number of such private academies appeared in the forties.[62]

and Wisconsin's territorial legislature of 1838-39 put a similar obligation upon every town containing ten families. The county authorities were to tax property for school support; and on occasion the village trustees were given authority to raise money by such levies. There were also meager returns from the school lands. Larson, *Financial and Administrative History*, 20-21.

[58] West ultimately became a surveyor and made a fortune in developing water power near Appleton, Wisconsin.

[59] Gregory, *History*, 2:1151.

[60] A. W. Kellogg, "Recollections of Life in Early Wisconsin," *Wis. Mag. of Hist.*, 7:483 (June 1924).

[61] Gregory, *History*, 2:1163-64.

[62] Louise P. Kellogg, "The Origins of Milwaukee College," *Wisconsin Magazine of History*, 9:388-91 (June 1926).

The close of the village period saw agitation for educational reform which would make free public education a reality. From the middle thirties, occasional individuals had emphasized the need of better educational facilities. The speculative mania distracted Increase Lapham only momentarily from his interest in learning, and as early as August 1836 he wrote Dr. Charles W. Short, requesting a copy of the charter of Transylvania University together with that educator's "views as to any changes that might be made in it to advantage"; for the optimism of the boom days of 1836 inspired the hope that the legislature would establish a college in Milwaukee.[63] The *Sentinel* pointed periodically to the need of better education in a democracy, predicting that "the vote of the most ignorant boy in our streets" would "soon tell as much at the polls as that of the most intelligent man."[64] By 1845 the movement had gathered momentum. In July, the *Sentinel* cited the development of the Chicago schools to Milwaukee's disadvantage: "with but two District School Houses, and one of these in a dilapidated condition, the contrast is striking between our condition and that of our sister city."[65] In October 1845, Rufus King attended a territorial convention which initiated an organization for keeping the question of the common schools alive; and on December 12, pursuant to the request of a public meeting, he joined with E. D. Holton and Francis Randall in pointing out the inadequacies of the existing situation and recommending reforms which would provide more schools, better supervision, uniformity of instruction, and more reliable support.[66]

King and his associates reported that there were "upwards of 1,000 children in the town of Milwaukie" for whose education "no adequate provision" had yet been made, and "but two schoolhouses, one of these hardly deserving of the name." They proposed the creation of a board of school commissioners, elected or appointed from the different districts or wards, with exclusive control over the public schools and the authority to em-

---

[63] I. A. Lapham to Dr. C. W. Short, Aug. 17, 1836, Lapham Papers.
[64] Milwaukie *Daily Sentinel*, June 10, 1845.
[65] *Ibid.*, July 17, 1845.
[66] *Ibid.*, Dec. 17, 1845.

ploy teachers, prescribe texts, determine rate bills, establish a budget, and pay the funds which the trustees should levy.[67] This report became the basis of the educational system provided in the municipal charter of 1846. At the same time, the delegates to the constitutional convention of that year were preparing to incorporate the principle of free education in the first frame of government of the State. The distinguished American educator, Henry Barnard, lecturing both in Milwaukee and before the convention in Madison, made a contribution to this end when he asserted that public schools must be "both good and cheap; good enough to attract the children of the wealthy and educated and cheap enough to be within the reach of the poor and humblest." This principle he regarded as of especial importance because of the "mixed character, varying creeds, conflicting sentiments, and different habits of the several classes" in the population of Wisconsin. As a consequence, both the constitution proposed in 1846 and that adopted in 1848 stipulated that common schools should be as nearly uniform as possible and free to all children.[68] In 1846, Milwaukee had five public schools, one in each of the five wards into which the city had been divided, but they were still housed in rented buildings and church basements.[69] Thus with the achievement of cityhood came a tardy, and not yet wholly satisfactory, realization of democratic educational advantages which both native and foreign leaders had proposed, but which a preoccupation with the more material considerations of city building had delayed.

The orderly development of education was not the only intellectual pursuit retarded by the rise and fall of speculation in town lots in the Wisconsin village. The organization of a lyceum in January 1839 was heralded by the *Sentinel* as evidence that the lakeside community had done "with the insane rage of making fortunes in a day" and had begun to put "a

[67] *Ibid.*

[68] *Constitution of the State of Wisconsin, . . . 1846,* ARTICLE IX, sections 3 and 4; also *Constitution of the State of Wisconsin, 1848,* ARTICLE X, section 3.

[69] Gregory, *History,* 2:1149. For a general historical account of developments in the public-school system of Milwaukee, see *Our Roots Grow Deep, 84th Annual Report* of the Milwaukee Public Schools, 1943.

proper estimate upon the cultivation of the mind and those refinements which necessarily attend it"; but to judge from the recurring difficulties of this pioneer cultural institution, the editor's attitude was largely one of wishful thinking.[70] Members of the lyceum met on Friday evenings to debate such subjects as "Should the Boundary line between Wisconsin and Illinois be established by Congress—as designated in the ordinance of 13th July, 1787?" and "Can any real or supposed grievance arising from national legislation justify the aggrieved State in withdrawing from the Union and establishing a separate sovereignty?"[71] But the lyceum had to rely upon home talent for its speeches and debates; and for this and other reasons it was not easy to sustain support for its programs. A preoccupation with land sales caused its postponement for nearly a month in 1839; and each winter thereafter saw attempts to renew the periodically flagging interest in its activities.[72]

With the improved conditions of the middle forties came somewhat broader opportunities to gratify the cultural urges of village Milwaukee. The first book store was opened in 1842 by Philetus C. Hale, who migrated in that year from Westfield, Massachusetts. In November he instituted a circulating library.[73] In January 1845, the *Sentinel* established a reading room where its exchanges were available to subscribers without charge and to others for "a comparative trifle."[74] As early as 1840, the New York *Mirror*, *Godey's Lady's Book*, and the *Ladies' Confession* were advertised for female readers.[75] The initial interest in art had its practical side, for the portrait painter of the forties performed the function of the photographer of today, and the panorama painter that of the newsreel camera man. In 1842, Samuel M. Brookes was soliciting business as a portrait painter.[76] Bernard I. Durward, a Scottish artist who

[70] Milwaukee *Sentinel*, Jan. 8, 1839.
[71] Increase to Seneca Lapham, Jan. 17, 1840, Lapham Papers; Milwaukee *Advertiser*, Feb. 1, 1840, April 6, 1839.
[72] Milwaukie *Journal*, Nov. 17, 1841. "We are gratified to hear that the Lyceum is about to be revived, and we trust with renewed vigor. There is talent enough in Milwaukie to render the debates interesting."
[73] Buck, 2:121-22.   [74] Milwaukie *Daily Sentinel*, Jan. 23, 1845.
[75] Milwaukee *Sentinel*, July 14, 1840.
[76] Porter Butts, *Art in Wisconsin* (Madison, 1936), 70-71.

arrived in 1845, interested Juneau and Kilbourn in sitting for portraits; and Kilbourn compensated him with a town lot.[77] The village's closest approach to an art museum was the public exhibit of a large painting advertised as the work of Benjamin West and called "Death on a Pale Horse"; but it was not warmly received, despite the comment of the *Commercial Herald*[78] that the subject was "eminently calculated to engross and heighten the moral faculties."

By 1843, "lovers of the Drama," according to the *Courier*, had raised a fund of about $500 to "fit up a suitable room" in Tuffts and Crandall's warehouse as a permanent theater.[79] This was the scene of the performances of Lynn and Powell's Detroit and Chicago Company which had first appeared in the village in late September 1842, playing a week's engagement in a third-floor hall on Third and Chestnut streets. Their original repertoire had included Shakespeare's *The Merchant of Venice* and Schiller's *Wilhelm Tell,* as if to appeal to both Yankee and German audiences; and on their return in 1843 they played *The Stranger, The Lady of the Lake,* and *The Drunkard's Fate.*[80] But theatrical fare was both scanty and haphazard in village Milwaukee; and were the appetite for it strong, or overly particular, the North American Circus; Christy's Minstrels, who were presented in the Military Hall in November 1845; and the occasional performances of a stock company offered it meager satisfaction.[81] Amateur musical performance of considerable merit became available with the arrival of the German immigrants. A quartet consisting of Charles Geisburg, Henry Niedecken, Frederick Schloemilch, and the ubiquitous Huebschmann developed in 1843 into the Beethoven Society. About 300 persons attended their first concert, after which the *Sentinel* quoted the Buffalo *Patriot* as

[77] *Evening Wisconsin,* Oct. 15, 1895.
[78] *Commercial Herald* (Milwaukee), Sept. 4, 1844; Butts, *Art in Wisconsin,* 52-53.
[79] Milwaukee *Courier,* June 14, 1843.
[80] Gregory, *History,* 2:1070.
[81] Milwaukee *Courier,* July 3, 1844; Lillian Krueger, "Social Life in Wisconsin: Pre-Territorial through the Mid-Sixties," *Wisconsin Magazine of History,* 22:412 (June 1939); *Evening Wisconsin,* Oct. 15, 1895.

saying that it was "a good sign in a new country to find a taste for music of a high order."[82]

Lacking much opportunity for professional entertainment, early day Milwaukeeans found opportunities within their own resources to provide a vigorous, if simple, social life characterized by the association of work and play so frequent in frontier and rural communities.[83] The wolf-hunt, which along with horse racing and turkey shooting provided hardy outdoor sport, also served to exterminate the "wolves and other ravenous animals of the vicinity."[84] The dinner or ball was frequently the means of subsidizing a needed urban service. Tea parties, sleigh-rides, sewing societies, lectures, and dances provided most of the social activities for which a busy community could find time.[85] At first the villagers had difficulty in getting fiddlers for their dances; but a Chicago musician was finally secured for a series of twelve cotillion parties attended by about sixty couples in the fall of 1836.[86] At the New Year's Ball of 1841, supper tables "extended twice across the extreme length of the long dining room," and according to the newspaper report, the company was "numerous and brilliant."[87] Holidays were the occasion for celebrations, parades, and dancing parties, especially among the foreign element.[88] By 1843, like most everything else in the village, "society" was flourishing. A St. Patrick's Day celebration commenced with high mass in front of St. Peter's Church, continued with a parade which "marched pretty much all over town," and concluded with dinner at the Cottage Inn.[89] In December there were a "continual string of parties"; dinners with their menus of mock turtle soup, roast turkey, goose, duck, chicken, beef, veal, venison *à la mode,*

---

[82] Milwaukie *Sentinel,* April 26, 1843.

[83] Lillian Krueger, "Social Life in Wisconsin," *Wis. Mag. of Hist.,* 22:160-68 (December 1938).

[84] Milwaukie *Daily Sentinel,* Jan. 20, 1845; Buck, 1:65-66 (rev. ed).

[85] Increase to Darius Lapham, Dec. 9, 1837, Lapham Papers; Reminiscence of Mrs. William P. Lynde, quoted in Gregory, *History,* 2:1274.

[86] *Ibid.,* 1:89-90.

[87] Milwaukee *Advertiser,* Jan. 2, 1841.

[88] The German settlers lost no opportunity to stage a parade, notwithstanding the disapproval of the more sober Yankee element.

[89] Buck, 2:167.

chicken and bird pies, boiled fish, pies and plum pudding, ice cream, and fruit—such as to "make the mouth of an eastern epicure water"; dancing parties; temperance meetings; and religious gatherings "superior to anything that can be started down east." A "perfect jam" attended the Ladies Fair at the Congregational Hall; Caleb Wall's Christmas dinner was so palatable that the guests presented him with a gift; and on New Year's Eve there was the Fireman's Ball at the Cottage Inn for the benefit of the hook and ladder company.[90]

The unquestioned freedom of religious practice of the frontier community resulted in the appearance of no less than a dozen different church organizations during the village period. Congregations were small at first, the ministers itinerant, and the place of worship a home, schoolhouse, or store. Catholic mass was celebrated in the Juneau home probably as early as August 1835,[91] and a priest was regularly stationed in the village by May 1839. Services were conducted in the courthouse until St. Peter's Church could be erected on some lots donated to Father Bonduel by Solomon Juneau; a small frame building was the cathedral in which the Rt. Rev. John M. Henni, bishop of the newly designated diocese of Milwaukee, preached his first sermon on May 5, 1844. As already pointed out, part of the morning service was conducted in German in recognition of the already considerable number of German Catholics in the community. In April 1846 the cornerstone was laid for St. Mary's Church, a special church for German-speaking Catholics; and such was the growth of Catholic communicants as village gave way to city that by the close of 1847 plans had been made and the cornerstone laid for a cathedral of imposing architectural design. Bishop Henni journeyed both to Europe and to Mexico and Cuba soliciting funds, and on July 31, 1853,

[90] Milwaukie *Sentinel*, Dec. 30, 1843. See Milwaukee *Sentinel*, July 14, 1937, for bill of fare.

[91] The Rev. Florimond J. Bonduel is credited with having said the first mass. Father Van den Broek claimed to have visited Milwaukee in 1836 (the best of several disputed dates) where he "formed a missionary station ... and visited it for some years at stated times." For a discussion of the founding of the Catholic Church in Milwaukee, see Peter Leo Johnson, "Milwaukee's First Mass," *Wisconsin Magazine of History*, 27:75-82 (September 1943).

the Cathedral of St. John the Evangelist was formally consecrated.[92]

The itinerant missionary of Methodism in the area was the Rev. John Clark. Riding his circuit of wilderness Wisconsin, he officiated occasionally at the Methodist classes and quarterly meetings held during 1835 and 1836 in the homes of the members.[93] One of Elder Clark's two-day quarterly meetings made a "widespread impression on the town" because of the conversion of a prominent merchant-tailor. The church was legally organized in July 1837; and the members gathered regularly in the carpenter shop of W. A. and L. S. Kellogg, made ready for the meeting "by sweeping out the shavings and placing boards on nail kegs for seats and using the bench for a pulpit."[94] Its construction delayed by the financial collapse of 1837-38, their first church was built in 1841 on a lot donated by Morgan L. Martin; the cost of a new structure built in 1843 was defrayed in part by renting four stores in the basement of the building. In spite of improved facilities, the frontier congregation found it hard to keep a minister. This put a responsibility on the licensed exhorters, two of whom ultimately became traveling preachers.[95]

Other Protestant denominations had similar experiences. The Baptists, whose prayer meetings in 1835 preceded formal organization in November 1836, held their first meetings in homes and in a schoolhouse.[96] Both Congregational and Presbyterian societies appeared as early as 1837. The former soon disintegrated as most of its members moved into the country

[92] Gregory, *History*, 2:842; Peter Leo Johnson, "Unofficial Beginnings of the Milwaukee Catholic Diocese," *Wisconsin Magazine of History*, 23:3 (September 1939). This priest was Father Patrick O'Kelley, whose name is variously spelled in the records; he was succeeded in 1842 by the Rev. Martin Kundig, who arranged the great celebration on St. Patrick's Day, 1843. See also, Annabel D. McArthur, *Religion in Early Milwaukee* (Milwaukee, 1946), 24. This account was prepared under the auspices of the Religious Committee of the Milwaukee Centennial Celebration. The work will hereafter be cited as McArthur.

[93] Gregory, *History*, 2:840; McArthur, 17-19.

[94] A. W. Kellogg, "Recollections of Life in Early Wisconsin," *Wis. Mag. of Hist.*, 7:481, 484 (June 1924).

[95] Gregory, *History*, 2:842; A. W. Kellogg, "Recollections of Life in Early Wisconsin," *Wis. Mag. of Hist.*, 7:485-86 (June 1924).

[96] Gregory, *History*, 2:841.

THE SOCIAL FABRIC OF THE VILLAGE 91

toward Prairieville (Waukesha); but in 1841, dissenters from the Presbyterian Church, finding its organization too strict, asked the Prairieville pastor to organize them into a Congregational Church. The two dozen members found a minister in John J. Miter of Knoxville, Illinois, and on November 7, 1841, began to hold services on the second floor of a store building in which, according to the new pastor, there was "a vending of intoxicating drinks." In May 1843, they began the construction of a church, the major portion of the cost of which was borne by Alanson Sweet.[97] The Presbyterians, meanwhile, had been laboring under difficulties induced in part by the need of a permanent place of worship and by the short tenure of their ministers. Their church edifice, begun in 1841 and dedicated in 1844, was made possible through volunteer effort. James H. Rogers and George Reed donated the brick, William Payne contributed the plastering, and Asahel Finch provided the lath.[98] In a temporary union characteristic of these sects on the frontier, the Milwaukee presbytery united with the Congregational churches of the territory in October 1840 under the name of the Presbyterian and Congregational Convention of Wisconsin, a union from which it did not withdraw until 1851.[99]

Episcopalian services were conducted as early as December 1835 in the home of George D. Dousman. In the following spring, a number of Milwaukeeans, among them Hans Crocker, B. H. Edgerton, William N. Gardner, Joshua Hathaway, and Cyrus Hawley, held regular services in Hawley's office, each in turn acting as lay reader.[100] Following the organization of the parish of St. Paul's in 1838 and the visit of Bishop Kemper in the following year, the Rev. Lemuel Hull held regular services in the courthouse and evening services in the schoolhouse on the West side. He also preached at neighboring settlements and, as has been pointed out, kept a private school for girls. Francis Randall, L. J. Higby, Harrison Ludington, and L. J.

[97] Buck, 2:297; Gregory, *History*, 2:853-56.
[98] Buck, 2:288; McArthur, 31.
[99] Gregory, *History*, 2:850.
[100] *Ibid.*, 2:840-41.

Farwell were among the officers of this church when its permanent edifice was first occupied in 1845.[101] Unitarians began meeting in August 1841 with a Chicago preacher; and a Unitarian Church was organized in 1842 with William Cushing of Cambridge, Massachusetts, as pastor. E. P. Allis, John H. Tweedy, and William H. Metcalf were among its members.[102] In 1841, the first service of the Universalist Church was held in Shepardson's store; a frame building was erected in 1843; and in the following year the congregation secured as pastor the Rev. Clement F. Le Fevre, who had served as a Universalist minister in Troy, Hudson, and New York City, New York, and who was the associate editor of two influential Universalist journals.[103] Lutherans, appearing with the coming of the German migrants, organized their first church, St. Paul's, in 1845, under the auspices of the Buffalo Synod. Differences of opinion in 1846 led a portion of this congregation to form Trinity Lutheran Church, which attached itself to the Missouri Synod. Grace Church, founded by the Rev. John Muhlhaeuser in 1851, was the first organized under the auspices of the Wisconsin Synod in the city. Pastor Muhlhaeuser and his church became famous for their services to the sick and needy of Milwaukee in the fifties. Heinrich Ginal appears to have founded the first Freethinker community in 1845. With the sophistication characteristic of this sect, Ginal aimed to purge Christianity of all its miraculous traditions and to explain the life of Christ as a rational event. He lectured on historical and aesthetic subjects as well as Bible texts. F. Stolze, G. Brosius, and W. Wedemeyer were members of this group. The First Reformed Church of Milwaukee was organized in 1847 to meet the needs of the Hollanders who were inhabiting the *Hollandsche Berg* by the late forties. They called their first pastor in 1850. The first Jewish worship service in Milwaukee was held on Rosh Hashanah, the Jewish New Year, at the home of Henry Newhouse, September 11, 1847. Succeeding New Year services were held at the homes of Isaac Neustadtl (1848) and Nathan

---

[101] *Ibid.*, 2:867-68.
[102] *Ibid.*, 2:863-64; McArthur, 35.
[103] Buck, 2:293-94; McArthur, 37.

Pereles; and the first Jewish congregation was organized in 1850, under the name of Emanu-El.[104]

Fostered by the opportunity for individualistic behavior that prevailed on this frontier, a wide diversity of denominations, nurtured to a large extent on zeal and sacrifice, characterized the village society. Milwaukee was "well off, if a goodly number of religious societies can make it so," wrote a visitor in August 1845, tabulating the existence of "1 Catholic Church, 1 Episcopal, 1 Congregationalist, 1 Presbyterian, 1 Baptist, 1 Methodist, 1 Unitarian, 4 small German congregations of different religious faiths, besides a congregation of German Rationalists who meet every Lord's Day, to glorify the profound and inexplorable mysteries of a sublimated nonsense."[105] Each sect was supported by a small group of the men most prominent in promoting the growth of the community. Unquestioned as an essential ingredient of the developing urban society, the churches carried on, free from interference by the growing municipal community but with an accepted function in its social life. By 1843 to 1845, worship in most of the religious groups had progressed from informal meetings held in members' homes to formal services in buildings specifically designed for the purpose; and as city succeeded village, the formation of additional churches followed the increase and dispersion of population; and improved structures reflected the affluence that attended urban growth.

The variety of lay activities in which the ministers in the village community engaged suggests the predicament in which most professional men found themselves in this generally unspecialized society. If ministers were forced to run boarding schools, so doctors were dentists and druggists as well, and lawyers turned their hands at many trades. Early Milwaukee

[104] Koss, *Milwaukee*, 196-97; McArthur, 39-40, 43, 46-47; Henry S. Lucas, "The First Dutch Settlers in Milwaukee," *Wisconsin Magazine of History*, 30:181 (December 1946). The author is indebted to Rabbi Joseph L. Baron for clarifying the early history of Jewish worship. See the latter's articles on "Milwaukee" and "Wisconsin" in the *Universal Jewish Encyclopedia* (10 vols., New York, 1939-43), 7:565-67; 10:532-36.

[105] Letter of Aug. 28, 1845, in "Wisconsin As Depicted in the Michigan Press," ed. by Sidney Glazer, *Wisconsin Magazine of History*, 27:89 (September 1943).

had more lawyers than the needs required; and yet many, though young, were able men, graduates of New York and New England colleges. Railroad promotion, politics, city offices, newspaper editorships, and land speculation absorbed their attention in the absence of cases to be tried. And undoubtedly the learning of a number of them contributed to the development of order in the community. The early physicians were frequently more interested in town promotion or mill-building than they were in the practice of their professions. The first "doctor" was in reality a blacksmith, the proud possessor of a medicine chest whose contents he applied promiscuously to suffering humanity;[106] and Dr. Enoch Chase, the first educated physician, spent most of his time in real estate, manufacturing, and political ventures. Lewis J. Higby, who came west after having studied medicine in New York, added groceries and dry goods to his stock of drugs; and by 1846 he had abandoned medicine for a career as a commission merchant.[107] Success in politics practically ended Dr. Lucius Barber's career as a physician.[108] The German medic, Huebschmann, devoted much of his time to the political leadership of the German element. King attested this situation in the professions when he wrote in 1845: "Law flourishes here as, strange to say, it does in most newly settled towns. . . . the profession numbers forty-two-or-three members. There are eighteen doctors, but the salubrity of the climate is such that about one-half of them are without patients."[109] Undoubtedly a dearth of business helps to explain why specific professions were frequently abandoned for more diversified pursuits; but more important was the fact that the doctors and lawyers had had the educational background that

[106] Louis F. Frank, *The Medical History of Milwaukee, 1834-1914* (Milwaukee, 1915), xii.

[107] Gregory, *History*, 2:954.

[108] Frank, *Medical History of Milwaukee*, 1.

[109] Albany *Evening Journal*, June 30, 1845. One pioneer wrote: "Our physicians all turn speculators soon after their settlement among us. Very few of them even pretend to practice medicine, the rest are either avowed Speculators and attend to no other business . . . or turn their attention to the culture of the Soil during their leisure hours." Unsigned letter to E. H. Porter, M.D., Dec. 18, 1836, in "Gardner Letters, 1836," *Wisconsin Magazine of History*, 18:82-83 (September 1934).

equipped them for political and economic leadership in the new community, activity for which there were demonstrably lucrative returns. Naturally, as the community matured, more specialization set in and the diversity of pursuits on the part of professional men decreased. It is understandable, too, that under these frontier conditions, the professional skills should have been to some extent dulled. Medical instruments were perforce crude; and qualifications for the practice of law less exacting than in the eastern community.

The social pattern of village Milwaukee was characteristic of that of many another young community of the newly opened Middle West. Compounded of nationality strains that stemmed from both western Europe and eastern America, the society of the young settlement expressed in every aspect of its behavior the self-assured individualism of a people who were responding to impulses born within themselves. Aside from their primary preoccupation with the material aspects of city building, nothing but the lack of physical and professional facilities hampered the variety of their aesthetic, religious, and social experience. Although European and eastern precedent was accepted without hesitation, there was no reluctance to try for improvement. Quality was restricted because of the limitations of the market; but the striking fact is the assurance with which these villagers greeted the opportunity to reproduce the widely varied social fabric of an urban community in this frontier environment and the vigorous self-confidence with which they set about to achieve the task.

CHAPTER 5

The Beginnings of Urban Services

THE task of shaping into urban form a tamarack swamp hemmed in by bluff and forest was at first the self-assumed duty of the speculator-promoters who had caught the vision of a city at the mouth of the Milwaukee River. But even after the village had become a corporate entity the physical development of the community and the services which the citizenry could expect of it were still largely a matter of individual responsibility, especially in an age in which civic accomplishment depended to a great extent upon volunteer response. What the village as a "body corporate and politic" could do was laid down in an act of the Wisconsin legislature concerning the right of communities of 300 or more inhabitants to incorporate,[1] but these powers were few. The president and trustees were authorized to issue ordinances to prevent and remove nuisances, prohibit gambling and other disorderly conduct, curtail the running and indecent exhibition of horses, license public shows, establish markets, open ditches, make available public wells, arrange for pavements and sidewalks, and provide protection against fire. But even these functions could not be performed without the compulsory or voluntary assistance of the local citizenry. Property owners were compelled to pay half the cost of sidewalks in front of their property;[2] and male residents between the ages of twenty-one and sixty had to labor for two days annually (commuted at the rate of $1.00 a day) to keep the public roads, streets, and alleys of the town "in good repair."[3] For fire and police protection

[1] "An act to incorporate the inhabitants of such towns as wish to be incorporated," Dec. 6, 1836, *Wisconsin Territorial Laws*, 1836, [1837, 1838] (Reprint, 1867), 65-70.
[2] *Ibid.*, sec. 5, p. 67.
[3] *Ibid.*, sec. 6, p. 68.

96

the village relied primarily upon the services of volunteers.

Problems connected with the provision of sidewalks, streets, and bridges early demonstrated the physical difficulties involved in transforming wilderness to city, especially at a time when both the equipment to effect such improvements and the tax revenues to pay for them were not readily available.[4] The speculator-promoters were obliged to undertake the first street construction in order to advance the "going appearance" of their respective communities. Juneau and Martin claimed to have expended $4,500 on East Water Street from 1836 to 1840;[5] and Kilbourn spent large sums filling in and grading the swampy portions of the West side. By the early forties the wards took over the responsibility which the hard pressed promoters had earlier shouldered;[6] and in April 1842 management of street work was vested in three commissioners, one for the East Ward and two for the West. Contracts for grading and graveling were let to the lowest bidder; the gravel was to be 6 inches thick at the edge, 12 at the middle.[7] By petitioning the board of trustees, the majority of the lot owners on a given street could compel the construction of sidewalks, for which the owners of lots would pay one-half and the corporation the other half of the expense;[8] but many residents petitioned the trustees for permission to build sidewalks at their own expense.[9]

Throughout the village period the community presented such a scene of scraping, grading, and sidewalk improvement that in 1845 Increase Lapham reported that much of his time was occupied "in the engineering line."[10] Moreover, it was a task that at first was hampered by lack of tools to do the job. As early as November 1835, Juneau contracted with Nelson and Thomas Olin to grade East Water Street, and later he

---

[4] The total revenue of the East Ward, during the period 1837 to 1844, was $21,575.09. Larson, *Financial and Administrative History*, 15.

[5] *Ibid.*, 16.

[6] Solomon Juneau to M. L. Martin, Sept. 20, 1836, Martin Papers.

[7] Larson, *Financial and Administrative History*, 16; Milwaukie *Daily Sentinel*, March 11, 1845.

[8] Milwaukie *Sentinel*, March 2, 1844.

[9] Milwaukie *Daily Sentinel*, March 11, 1845.

[10] Increase Lapham to ——, Sept. 15, 1845, quoted in Milwaukee *Sentinel*, Oct. 16, 1895.

promised to pay them $3,000 for the grading of Wisconsin Street from the river to the lake. However, before they could meet this fundamental urban need, one of the brothers had to return to New York to acquire the carts, plows, scrapers, pickaxes, and other equipment essential to the work. Operations on Wisconsin Street got under way in June 1836 and were completed the following August—a harder job, according to Olin, than any ever done in Milwaukee "for the same money." A depression, 40 feet deep, midway between East Water and Main streets took nearly two weeks to fill, and Van Buren Street "also contained a terrible gulf." There was heavy timber from there to the lake, including some large trees that had to be "grubbed out."[11] Enforcement of the law requiring every male inhabitant to work two days a year on the streets, or pay $2.00 instead, promoted the improvement of the streets, especially with the increase in population; and the commutation fee swelled the meager support from taxes for highway construction.[12] By July 1842, Lapham was able to report that gravel sidewalks which proved "to be very good" extended "nearly the whole length of the town so that it was possible to go out in wet weather without tall boots."[13] By the close of the village period some of these thoroughfares were made of flat limestone, three feet wide," but there was still bitter complaint of the bad state of the sidewalks.[14]

Bridges were of prime importance to a community in which rivers constituted the boundaries between the wards; but, as has already been pointed out, their construction was delayed by the play of politics and sectional rivalry in the developing community. Milwaukee's first bridge was built on the initiative of one of the speculators, when Kilbourn bridged the Menomonee as a means of diverting to the West side the traffic from

[11] Olin, "Reminiscences of Milwaukee in 1835-36," *Wis. Mag. of Hist.*, 13:217-21 (March 1930).

[12] In April 1842, commissioners were appointed to collect a poll tax of $2.00 or compel the male residents to do their street work in lieu of the same. Buck, 2:136.

[13] Milwaukee *Sentinel,* Oct. 16, 1895.

[14] Milwaukie *Sentinel,* March 2, 1844; Milwaukie *Daily Sentinel,* March 11, 1845.

Chicago which terminated at Walker's Point and from there moved to the East side by ferry.[15] Although the county undertook to bridge the Milwaukee in 1840, private individuals continued to provide such thoroughfares as, for example, the "free float bridge between Wisconsin and Spring streets" constructed by James H. Rogers. When it wore out, the editor of the *Sentinel* counseled private individuals who were interested to "look to it."[16] According to Buck, a new float bridge, built by private subscription at Walker's Point, was opened in August 1844. "It rested upon boxes, had a heavy, cumbersome draw, worked by a windlass, the chain from which led to an anchor in the bed of the river."[17] No bridges were built by the corporation during the village period;[18] but in August 1844 a public meeting was held "to see if the trustees would be authorized to loan $2,000 for the purpose of repairing the [county] bridge at Chestnut street."[19]

As already has been indicated, the tardy appearance of federal aid for harbor improvement led private individuals on occasion to take matters into their own hands and even suggest a subscription for the purpose; and for lack of an improved harbor, private initiative found a substitute in the construction of piers.[20] Sewers for the West Ward were being discussed by the board of trustees in March 1845. They were to be 2 feet deep and 2 feet wide in the clear, composed of timber sides and plank bottom and top. With the provision of water left to individual enterprise, most of the citizens depended upon springs and wells for their water supply. In March 1840 the board of trustees granted to Nelson P. Hawks the exclusive privilege of conveying spring water to all persons in the West Ward south of Prairie Street who were "willing and able to pay a reasonable rent therefor." Certain restrictions were placed upon Hawks's operation of this utility. Suitable pipes or conductors were to be brought to Third Street within a year;

---

[15] Larson, *Financial and Administrative History*, 17.
[16] Milwaukie *Sentinel*, April 16, Oct. 26, 1842.
[17] Buck, 2:224.
[18] Larson, *Financial and Administrative History*, 17-18.
[19] Buck, 2:224.
[20] See chapter 2.

disputes over rents were to be settled by arbitration; the government of the ward might buy the works at any time; and firemen were to have the privilege of using the water free of charge in case of fire.[21] Apparently Hawks never took advantage of this opportunity, for what is reputed to be the first waterworks in the city were the pipes constructed of tamarack logs in 1845 by which James H. Rogers conveyed water from Wisconsin Street to the United States Hotel on East Water and Huron streets in the East Ward.[22]

Dangerously vulnerable to fire, like most wood-constructed towns of the forested frontier, early day Milwaukee had to depend on the townsmen themselves for protection against this endemic urban hazard. Although the village ordinances have disappeared, it is possible that colonial precedent prompted a requirement that each householder procure a bucket for fighting fires; for it is recorded that when a fire broke out in Samuel Brown's residence in 1836 there was "a general turning out of villagers with buckets and such other implements of extinguishment as could be mustered." Certainly fire fighting was regarded in the early days as a responsibility of the community as a whole. A volunteer company, made up of some of the most prominent citizens of the village, was formed in 1837, with Benjamin Edgerton as its foreman.[23] Fire Company No. 2, recruited from the German citizenry of the village, was organized on July 19, 1844. Although these volunteers received no pay, they were given such compensatory privileges as exemption from militia duty and, after twelve years, from jury duty. The companies were self-governing, and each one comprised from sixteen to twenty-four men between the ages of eighteen and fifty.[24] The press endeavored to keep both the fire companies and the general public aware of the need for continued vigilance against calamities that were known to fall with "peculiar severity upon all new towns,"[25] and by lurid accounts of local fires reminded the citizens of the dan-

---

[21] Passed March 31, 1840. See Milwaukee *Advertiser*, April 11, 1840.
[22] *Evening Wisconsin* (Milwaukee), Oct. 15, 1895.
[23] Gregory, *History*, 2:791; Andreas, *History of Milwaukee*, 347.
[24] Larson, *Financial and Administrative History*, 22.
[25] Milwaukie *Daily Sentinel*, Nov. 21, 1845.

ger.²⁶ As early as 1837, the *Sentinel* proposed as a further safeguard a committee to "visit every building in the place, and ascertain whether the stores, fireplaces, and chimneys, are constructed in a manner so as not to endanger the property of their neighbors."²⁷ In December 1841, the Milwaukie *Journal* suggested the appointment of fire wardens to marshal the activities of the citizens and organize a bucket line. A disastrous fire early in January 1843 led to a public meeting in which more systematic plans for community participation were proposed.²⁸

The false economy of the trustees, which limited a town of "near eight thousand inhabitants" to only one fire engine— the "Neptune," an old-fashioned goose-neck hand engine imported from Rochester, New York, in 1839—was condemned in 1845 when "the most tremendous conflagration ever witnessed in the western country" destroyed property worth more than $90,000.²⁹ As a result, by the last of November, the expanding village had been provided with "three good Fire Engines, well manned and furnished with the necessary apparatus." But a fire late in that month led the *Sentinel* to press for further reform: "a regularly organized Fire Department," to coordinate the independent activities of the existing three companies, and a good bell to give the alarm.³⁰ The former was provided in the ordinance passed on December 20, 1845, "relating to Fires and to Regulate the Fire Department in the Town of Milwaukie." This empowered the trustees to appoint a chief engineer and assistants, on the democratic recommendation of the fire department, who would direct the strategy at fires, and fire wardens who were to investigate their respective wards for violations of those portions of the ordinance which prohibited the storing of gunpowder without a license and forbade the construction of flimsy dwellings. As a result, the officers of the three companies met with the village trustees

---

[26] Milwaukie *Sentinel*, Dec. 2, 1843; Feb. 24, 1844.
[27] Milwaukee *Sentinel*, Oct. 31, 1837.
[28] Buck, 2:166.
[29] *Evening Wisconsin*, Oct. 15, 1895; Milwaukie *Daily Sentinel*, April 7, 8 1845.
[30] *Ibid.*, Nov. 22, Dec. 1, 1845.

and selected L. H. Cotton as the department's first chief engineer. The Boston uniform was adopted: leather hat, knee-length red flannel frock, and leather belt.[31] The fire companies fulfilled a social as well as a municipal need; and the annual firemen's balls, patterned after the practice of New York, Albany, Rochester, Buffalo, and Detroit, afforded a means of raising funds, through public subscription, to supply relief to disabled firemen. On one such occasion the firemen addressed their appeal to "the owners of property and the businessmen of Milwaukie,"[32] professing to count on the ladies to "create a blaze in the breasts of some of the Firemen which cold water will not quench," and which might "require the assistance of the Hook and Ladder Company to extinguish."[33]

The voluntary efforts of the citizenry also supplied early day Milwaukee with protection against crime and disorder, for there was no urban police in the village period. Although township constable and village marshal were theoretically available for the maintenance of order, the speculator-promoters originally assumed this as well as other municipal responsibilities. According to Juneau, when one of "our Milwaukee Indians" was murdered by two whites in July 1836, the trader-speculator saw to it that they were detected and that a jail was built "for their reception."[34] The murder of a Mr. McNeil, on July 25, 1837, prompted a public meeting, the following day, at which a committee of nine was appointed to "apprehend and bring to punishment" the unknown assailant and "to have full powers as a committee of vigilance" to detect and prosecute offenses against the peace and good order of the community.[35] The meeting went ahead to pledge itself to abolish rumored gambling and to declare it "the duty of every member of the community to make complaint whenever this violation of law shall come within his knowledge."[36] By

[31] *Ibid.*, Dec. 23, 1845.
[32] *Ibid.*, Dec. 19, 1845.
[33] Milwaukie *Sentinel*, Feb. 3, 1844.
[34] Juneau to Martin, July 21, 1836, Martin Papers.
[35] This committee included Samuel Hinman, William A. Prentiss, James H. Rogers, George D. Dousman, D. H. Richards, Samuel Brown, Willard B. Johnson, A. O. T. Breed, and William R. Longstreet.
[36] Milwaukee *Sentinel*, Aug. 1, 1837.

the close of the village period, however, the residents had become skeptical of "self-help" as a means of insuring urban order; and by November 1845 it was recognized that the expanding town could not much longer go without the protection of at least a night watch. Incidents of rowdyism led the *Sentinel* to assert that "if such practices are repeated our citizens will have to guard against them by the establishment of a police."[37] Arguments for the organization of military companies in February 1845 included the assertion that a well-disciplined militia would serve to uphold the supremacy of the laws in the face of civil disturbances.[38]

The trustees attempted to alleviate the most prevalent public nuisance of the rural village by passing ordinances preventing hogs (1840) and cattle (1845) from running in the streets. Owners of vagrant hogs were to be fined $2.00: one dollar to go to the apprehender and the other to the city. If the animals were not claimed within forty-eight hours, the finder could slaughter them.[39] A smallpox epidemic in 1843 led to the organization of a temporary board of health which expended more than $835.61 in the East Ward in that year. Municipal obligations for the preservation of health were met in the following year, however, by the expenditure of only $40.98.[40] Regulations used in Detroit to check the spread of hydrophobia were recommended for Milwaukee in 1845.[41]

Broader action for the municipality was proposed as the village matured toward cityhood. The editor of the *Sentinel* was determined to make the young community face its municipal responsibilities; and in July 1845 he insisted that the urban government should supply a waterworks, build public wharves and docks, compel regularity in the construction of private wharves, improve the streets, and "cleanse and purify" high-

---

[37] Milwaukie *Daily Sentinel*, Nov. 15, 1845.

[38] "Besides the consideration that Milwaukie is to a certain extent a frontier city, and liable in the event of war to foreign invasion, it is like all eastern cities, subject to civil commotions, and the authorities may require prompt interference of a well-disciplined military power to maintain the supremacy of the laws." *Ibid.*, Feb. 6, 1845.

[39] Milwaukee *Advertiser*, Oct. 29, 1840.

[40] Larson, *Financial and Administrative History*, 22.

[41] Milwaukie *Daily Sentinel*, Aug. 22, 1845.

ways, sewers, cellars, vacant lots, and "small water courses" in the interests of the public health.[42] These proposals represented an extension of activity beyond that of the village government to this date, for in the period from 1837 to January 7, 1845, the East Ward, for example, had spent only $22,378.17, the sum being charged to the grading and repairing of streets, the purchase of a fire engine and engine house, the building and maintenance of bridges, health measures during the smallpox epidemic of 1843, and the payment of salaries and miscellaneous bills. The village government had had perforce to deal with municipal emergencies, but further obligations it was reluctant to assume. Demands for relief during the winter of 1845 and 1846 were met by private charity, donation parties, and allotments from the industrial associations.[43] And when it came to measures by which the village could be beautified, this was indeed regarded as an obligation of the individual and quite beyond the realm of municipal responsibility. On April 24, 1845, the editor of the *Sentinel* counseled his readers to plant shade trees, arguing that to have "the beautiful in nature around us" would "give rise to moral emotions" which would counteract "the downward tendencies of city life."

By 1845 it was apparent that the existing village government was incapable both of supplying needed urban services and of preventing such disturbances as the "Bridge War," which occurred in the spring of that year. As early as December 20, 1844, a group of prominent villagers—among them Rogers, acting as presiding officer, D. A. J. Upham, J. E. Arnold, Lindsey Ward, Kilbourn, Huebschmann, Holton, and L. W. Weeks—had participated in a movement to draft a city charter.[44] This first attempt, however, not only met unexpected opposition from the foreign-born but also violated the democratic philosophy of a frontier-conditioned citizenry. In proposing a charter which restricted the suffrage to citizens of the United States, the city-makers had not reckoned with the European

[42] *Ibid.*, July 18, 1845.
[43] *Ibid.*, Jan. 28, Feb. 6, Aug. 22, Oct. 24, Dec. 20, 1845.
[44] Buck, 2:225-26; Milwaukee *Courier*, Dec. 25, 1844; Larson, *Financial and Administrative History*, 24.

element in the village community. When a public meeting was called on January 13, 1845, to pass on the proposed plan, foreign-born objectors made up more than two-thirds of the assemblage. Speaking through the columns of the *Courier*, they called the proscription of the foreign vote "taxation without representation with a vengeance," depriving, as it did, "one half of the citizens" of "a voice in electing their officers or making their laws." Moreover, the proposed three-year term for aldermen was held to place the people's representatives "beyond the reach of public opinion for a time almost equal to an age in older communities."[45] According to the *Sentinel*, however, this attitude of the foreign-born threatened to "strangle in embryo all attempts to improve our condition."[46]

By December 1845 the desire for a more vigorous urban service and for improved fire protection, transportation, and schools intensified the demand for a change from village to city government. Selected in consequence of a public meeting on the subject, Holton, Upham, Arnold, and Captain George were members of a committee whose proposed charter, after some amendment by the trustees, was adopted by a popular referendum on January 5, 1846.[47] Although its suffrage provision, demanding of alien residents a declaration of intention to become citizens, was somewhat less liberal than that which prevailed under the village charter, it nevertheless gave some recognition to the foreign inhabitants of the community and in so doing won the almost unanimous support of the West and South wards for a charter to which the East Ward was by a vote of two to one opposed.[48] Once the charter reached the legislature, the term for aldermen was reduced from three years to one, and the influence of the alien voters was somewhat curtailed by allowing suffrage only to such as had paid taxes, served as firemen, or worked on the roads.[49] Legislative sanction for the new charter was gained by recourse to a bargain

[45] Milwaukee *Courier*, Jan. 27, 1844, quoted in *Evening Wisconsin*, Oct. 15, 1895.
[46] Milwaukie *Daily Sentinel*, Jan. 14, 1845.
[47] Milwaukee *Sentinel*, Oct. 16, 1895.
[48] Larson, *Financial and Administrative History*, 25n.
[49] *Ibid.*, 25.

by which the Prairieville, or Waukesha, delegates consented to support the charter in return for Milwaukee's approval of the division of the county.[50] On January 31, 1846, Milwaukee became a city.

The officers of the municipality were to be a mayor and three aldermen, a justice of the peace, and one constable from each ward, all elected for one year except the justice of the peace who was to serve for two. Other officials, such as the clerk, treasurer, attorney, assessor, and chief engineer of the fire department, were to be appointed by the council; but in the following year most of the appointing power of that body was removed; and the offices were made elective. The mayor was to preside over the council and could vote only in case of a tie.[51] The new city government possessed regulatory powers beyond those of the village, powers similar to the ones granted the mayor and aldermen in the Chicago charter of 1837; but the framers did not succeed in doing away with the sectional autonomy which had plagued the village organization. As a result, Milwaukee's first city government was more a municipal confederation than a real municipality. Each ward continued to be an autonomous corporation, responsible for its own debts and liable for loans for the general improvement of the city only when a majority of its aldermen had voted for them. Each individual ward could sue or be sued, receive legislative permission to undertake improvements on its own initiative, and decide for itself in how far it wished to participate in common municipal activity. It was even with difficulty that fire protection was organized on city rather than ward lines. The chief evil of this situation was the increasing power it gave the aldermen. Ultimately they were authorized to levy special taxes for street, river, and harbor improvements, to borrow money and issue ward bonds for street work, and to provide for building sewers, sidewalks, and the like. Since this work was contracted for by the aldermen and supervised by them, the door was open to graft and ward politics.[52] The wide

[50] H. Russell Austin, *The Milwaukee Story: The Making of an American City* (Milwaukee, 1946), 75.
[51] Larson, *Financial and Administrative History*, 26.
[52] *Ibid.*, 27-28.

powers granted the municipal legislature and the emphasis on a frequently elected officialdom, though not without unfortunate consequences, were consistent with the political philosophy of a community which wanted its government to be quickly responsive to the public will. The ward sectionalism, which prompted the assertion in the 1850's that Milwaukee was not a city "but five villages slightly connected together," was but the heritage left by the river barrier and the speculative rivalries of the thirties to the emerging city.[53]

MILWAUKEE REMAINED a village for less than a decade; yet in that short span of years "the mere skeleton of a frontier settlement" had grown into "a busy, thriving, populous town," and but a handful of men had become 10,000.[54] Basic to such an unprecedented speed of growth were two fundamental factors: a fortunate geographical location and the westward flow of population in the United States. The development of the village was indeed the product of an age of westward movement, as the persistent pressure from the very outset for roads, bridges, canals, railroads, and harbor facilities reveals. Moreover, it was village development at a time and in a region offering large stakes to the real estate agent and speculative financier. In the ubiquitous activities of such figures as Juneau, Kilbourn, Walker, Rogers, and their less active but almost equally important financial backers is seen the prevalence of personal promotion in the town building of the period. It was these speculator-promoters who provided street improvements, built hotels, donated land for churches, and subsidized such harbor development as their lobbying activities failed to achieve. Invariably they were the directors if not the organizers of the canal and railroad companies, the banking and insurance enterprises. They sat on the village board, in the territorial legislature, and among the elders of their respective churches. They were members of the fire department and the vigilance committee. Around them they gathered a group of lesser functionaries in city promotion: newspaper editors,

[53] Larson, "Sectional Elements," Miss. Vall. Hist. Assoc., *Proc.*, 1907-8, 1:126-30.
[54] Milwaukie *Daily Sentinel,* Dec. 2, 1845.

builders, forwarders, and merchants. In a decade of rapid material development interrupted by depression from 1837 to the early forties, the lyceum, the newspaper, the occasional stock company, and the ill-supported elementary school stood feebly for the things of the spirit. As compared with the modern urban community, the village society was relatively unspecialized and self-sufficient; and yet there was a beginning of specialization in merchandising and in processing the raw materials of the hinterland for an outside market. Counteracting the unifying intimacy of the vigorous and simple village life were two potentially divisive factors: a river-dictated geographical sectionalism, of which ward autonomy and jealousy as well as speculator rivalries were the result, and the existence of a relatively self-contained and aggressive foreign element which speedily contributed a European flavor, largely Teutonic, to what in its beginning was predominantly a Yankee settlement. But despite the personal rivalries and nationality conflicts the village emerged into cityhood of one mind as to the potentialities of its growth. As Rufus King predicted, following his initial visit in the summer of 1845, "Milwaukie . . . is destined to be the chief commercial and manufacturing city of this WESTERN EMPIRE."[55] All that was needed, as the *Sentinel* pointed out, was a steadier concern for the good of the whole. "Let us . . . put our shoulders to the wheel," it counseled Milwaukeeans on the eve of cityhood, "and knowing neither party, sect, nor ward, unite in a common effort to advance the common weal."[56]

[55] *Ibid.*, July 14, 1845.
[56] *Ibid.*, Dec. 2, 1845.

PART II

The Expanding City 1846 to 1870

"*Like a gladsome creature in first pantalette, young Milwaukee has gone with a 'hop, skip, and a jump' ... from bank to bank.... Shade trees, neat dwellings, school houses, and churches ... young Irelands and young Germanies—wonderful city not yet entered upon her teens, but already familiar with all languages, her busy population ... being composed of representatives from all the migratory nations upon the earth, and especially from the universal Yankee.*"—Milwaukee Sentinel and Gazette, July 26, 1847.

"*When I first set foot on this soil some thirty years ago, I little thought ... I should behold such a sight as now presents itself. Then the red man was supreme monarch of the place ... but now ... the war whoop ... has given way to the mild councils of civilized ... men; the wigwam is supplanted by massive ... structures; the place of the bark canoe ... filled by hundreds of vessels ... that now annually visit our shores.... Here we behold a city of twelve thousand inhabitants ... when eleven years since the soil was unbroken.*"—Solomon Juneau to the Common Council, April 14, 1847.

CHAPTER 6

The Nationality Background

THE achievement of cityhood at the mouth of the Milwaukee was but the prelude to a sevenfold increase in population which in the succeeding twenty-five years was to transform the overgrown village of 10,000 into a potential metropolis of 71,440 people. In the quarter century that intervened between 1846 and 1870 the city of the speculators' dreams was growing up, with all the ill-coordinated enthusiasm of adolescence. By the close of the sixties the character of the urban scene foreshadowed a new period in the city's life. Observers were then beginning to note a "decidedly metropolitan appearance,"[1] and the mayor was admonishing the citizens "to cast aside the . . . thoughts of the village and to assume the duties and responsibilities of a metropolitan city."[2] But the generation that preceded this change saw the elaboration of many of the social and economic patterns that were ultimately to characterize the mature city.

The expansion of New York and New England still accounted in considerable measure for the American-born residents of adolescent Milwaukee, but between 1850 and 1870 the number of Wisconsin-born residents increased from 13 to 40 percent of the total population. The next most numerously represented states, throughout the period, were New York, Massachusetts, Ohio, and Pennsylvania. In spite of the predominant influence of the native-born ingredient during the first generation of cityhood, transplanted Europeans were actually more numerous in the community until the decade of the sixties. Like the other fast-growing cities of the Great Lakes

[1] Milwaukee *Daily Sentinel,* July 11, 1867.
[2] *Ibid.,* April 21, 1868.

chain, the Wisconsin city drew a large proportion of its population almost directly from Europe; but of all the communities on that water highway to the West, Milwaukee was most conspicuously German. In 1850, some 64 percent of the population were of foreign birth; and nearly two-thirds of that number had been born in Germany. Ireland contributed less than a quarter, and England not many more than a tenth. By 1870, when the total number of foreign-born residents had declined to 47 percent of the city's population, and natives of Great Britain and Ireland to only 8 percent, native-born Germans still constituted a third of the whole.[3] As a result, the coordinate German society within the developing city was in many ways the most distinctive feature of mid-century Milwaukee.

Milwaukee's "German town" was a self-contained and self-conscious community centered in the northwestern part of the city in the Second, Sixth, and Ninth wards. Here the Swedish novelist, Fredrika Bremer, visiting Milwaukee in the fifties, saw "German houses, German inscriptions over the doors or signs, German physiognomies." Here lived large numbers of Germans who never learned English and seldom went beyond the bounds of the German settlement. Banded together "in a clan-like manner," as in many other German communities she visited in the West, they had their own society, working and playing after the fashion of the Fatherland.[4] Most of the German residents were skilled artisans: carpenters, smiths, masons, painters, tailors, shoemakers, saddlers, and the like. Of those listed in the census of 1850, some 1,165 were called craftsmen; 461, laborers; 248, businessmen; and 45, professional men.[5] A chronicler of the city's industry in 1861 reported that "cigars, boots and shoes, furniture, baskets, toys, jewelry, wearing apparel, and innumerable articles of every-day use" were being made in small factories by German artisans and sold to larger houses or peddled through the State. These German-Ameri-

[3] See charts in appendix showing origins of native-born population and percentage of foreign-born persons in population of Milwaukee.

[4] Fredrika Bremer, *The Homes of the New World; Impressions of America* (2 vols., New York, 1854), 1:615-17.

[5] Joseph Schafer, "The Yankee and the Teuton in Wisconsin," *Wisconsin Magazine of History*, 7:151-54 (December 1923).

cans were realizing "a comfortable living," he wrote, and vagrancy among them was comparatively unknown.[6]

Many forces continued to induce the Germanic migration that had begun in the period of Milwaukee's villagehood. The letters of such German-Americans as Franz Neukirch, Herman Kemper, and Ferdinand Goldmann and the writings of Carl E. Hasse, Carl de Haas, Alexander Ziegler, and Theodore Wettstein, as well as those of Increase Lapham, translated into German by Bernhard Domschcke, publicized Wisconsin's favorable climate, fertile soil, liberal franchise, and freedom from public debt.[7] As a result, in many parts of Germany more was known about the Badger State than about an outlying Prussian province.[8] The presence of a German Catholic bishop gave confidence to prospective settlers of that faith, and letters from new arrivals drew relatives and friends still in the homeland with the promise of economic opportunity.[9] In addition, both the city and the State were making a conscious effort during the fifties and sixties to attract German settlers. In 1851, the council appointed one of the aldermen, then in New York, to

[6] Wheeler, *Chronicles of Milwaukee*, 279.

[7] Carl E. Hasse, *Schilderung des Wisconsingebietes in Nordamerika* (Grimma, 1841); Carl de Haas, *Nordamerica, Wisconsin, Calumet: Winke für Auswanderer* (Iserlohn, 1848); Alexander Ziegler, *Skizzen einer Reise durch Nordamerika und Westindien, mit besonderer Berücksichtigung des deutschen Elements, der Auswanderung und der landwirthschaftlichen Verhältnisse in dem neuen Staate Wisconsin* (vol. 2, Dresden and Leipzig, 1848); Theodore Wettstein, *Der Nordamerikanische Freistaat Wisconsin* (Elberfeld, 1851); Increase A. Lapham, *A Geographical and Topographical Description of Wisconsin; with brief sketches of its history, geology, mineralogy, natural history, population, soil, productions, government, antiquities,* . . . (Milwaukee, 1844); Increase A. Lapham, *Wisconsin: its geography and topography, history, geology, and mineralogy* (New York, 1846); Freimund Goldmann, *Freimund Goldmann's Briefe aus Wisconsin in Nord-Amerika. Herausgegeben von Dr. G. Goldmann* (Leipzig, 1849); William Dames, *Wie Sieht Es in Wiskonsin Aus?* (Mörs, 1849); Gustav Richter, *Der Nordamerikanische Freistaat* (Wesel, 1849); Hense-Jensen, Schafer tr., chap. 2, pp. 3-5; Everest, "How Wisconsin Came By Its Large German Element," Wis. Hist. Soc., *Colls.*, 12:314-27.

[8] Hense-Jensen, Schafer tr., chap. 2, p. 2.

[9] Charles F. Heyerman wrote Increase Lapham, February 13, 1854, that German immigration to Wisconsin was greatly influenced by Wettstein's account: "Such a complete description of the country, written and compiled by a man known in a great part of the old country as reliable and honest, will meet better success than a commissioner of emigration" whose reports Germans "consider as being influenced by land speculators." Charles F. Heyerman to Increase

look after the interests of the city and State among the immigrants coming into that port.[10] Beginning in 1852, a State commissioner of immigration, at one time Herman Haertel of Milwaukee, as well as agents of the railroad companies, performed a similar function.[11] In 1859, a group of fifteen prominent Milwaukeeans, perhaps with an eye to swelling the labor supply, proposed the subscription of funds with which to print and circulate throughout Germany "pamphlets and circulars . . . printed in the German language, setting forth the many advantages of our City and State."[12]

Chicago and Milwaukee vied for favor with the migrating horde. Milwaukeeans were concerned over reports, published in Chicago in 1866, that immigrants were mistreated in coming through Milwaukee on their way to the West. At a public meeting held on June 30, 1866, they made plans for the erection of spacious quarters for newcomers and the establishment of a system of education for them which no other city could rival.[13] The press countered Chicago's propaganda with the testimony of the Rev. Chr. Hoistendahl, of Milwaukee, who warned his fellow-Norwegians against the dangers of passing through the Illinois city. In Milwaukee, by contrast, immigrants were "protected by state and city officials," he wrote, "not delayed on their journey here as they are in Chicago," and charged nothing for the transportation of their baggage from boats to cars.[14]

The known sympathy of Milwaukee's German community for the revolutionary movement in the Fatherland was another

Lapham, Feb. 13, 1854, Lapham Papers. According to the Milwaukee *Daily Sentinel,* August 14, 1860: "The news of our abundant crops have [sic] reached Germany, and fired this part of the old world with a desire to come to this land of promise and plenty. We say welcome, thrice welcome to every honest son of Germany. Come with your mines of wealth, come with your love of thrift, come with your strong arms, come with your hatred of tyranny, come with your happy wives and children, sons of the Rhine! There is room enough for you all." Milwaukee *Daily Sentinel,* Aug. 14, 1860.

[10] Milwaukee *Sentinel and Gazette,* Aug. 15, 1851.

[11] John G. Gregory, "Foreign Immigration to Wisconsin," Wisconsin Historical Society, *Proceedings,* 1901, pp. 138-39.

[12] Milwaukee *Daily Sentinel,* June 24, 1859. This was signed by Caleb Wall, L. W. Weeks, August Greulich, M. Metz, J. Schlitz, H. Crocker, J. Rosebeck, P. V. Deuster, W. Finkler, J. S. Fillmore, E. P. Allis, C. T. Melms, F. Neukirch, W. H. Jacobi, and E. Solomon.

[13] *Ibid.,* July 3, 1866.

[14] *Ibid.,* Dec. 29, 1869.

factor which attracted German migrants to the Wisconsin city. As a result, exiled Forty-eighters swelled the existing Teutonic society. The solicitation of funds for such revolutionaries as Dr. Oswald Seidensticker, Ferdinand Freiligrath, and Karl Heinzen had early identified the German element with reform;[15] and Milwaukeeans, regardless of nationality, participated in a public demonstration on April 17, 1848, recognizing the outbreak of revolution in Germany. French, German, and American flags waved in a procession which was led by two brass bands; speeches, presided over by Mayor Kilbourn, were made in several tongues; and the occasion ended with burning a crowned king in effigy.[16] By June, leaders of the German community had organized a *Drei-Cents Verein,* its members pledged to pay 3 cents weekly to the revolutionary cause. Herman Haertel was the treasurer, and two collectors were appointed for each ward. A reactionary pastor, who insisted on reading a prayer for the "all-generous king," lost his job.[17] In 1851 an escort of *chasseurs* and dragoons greeted Gottfried Kinkel when he came to collect funds for the revolutionary movement.[18]

The impact of the Forty-eighters on the developing urban society was chiefly significant for the cultural and intellectual ferment which they stirred up in the already cohesive German community. While many of the most influential leaders of Milwaukee Germandom had migrated before 1848, the *Acht und viersiger* made a contribution in the fields of music, education, and liberal social thought which left a lasting imprint on the urban culture.

Musical expression appears to have been literally spontaneous even with the earliest German migrants; but Hans Balatka, fugitive of the Viennese revolution of 1848, more than any other one man was responsible for the musical pre-eminence of the *Deutsch-Athen.* This Bohemian musician, who came to Milwaukee after a two months' attempt at farming in Washington County, became the focus of the already active interest in music in the German community. In 1849 he organized a

---

[15] Koss, *Milwaukee,* 220-21.
[16] *Ibid.,* 263.
[17] *Ibid.,* 264-65.
[18] *Ibid.,* 347-49; Milwaukee *Daily Sentinel,* Dec. 2, 1851.

male chorus, relying upon an enthusiasm for singing which had been manifested among the Germans by the existence of male quartets on both sides of the river since the early forties.[19] By 1850 the town could boast a string quartet, probably the first to be organized in the West. Chance, modified only by the bent of the German migrants, permitted the assemblage of so skilled a quartet of performers in a frontier community. Concerning its activities, Balatka wrote:

> The four musicians composing it were Dr. Fessel, one of the first in Berlin for a quarter of a century; Dr. Aigner, a fugitive from Austria like myself; a local musician who played the second violin; and myself. It was at the invitation of Dr. Fessel, who had heard that two musicians from Vienna, a viola and a cello, were in town, that we came together. We were not only suspicious, each of the other, but every man thought the other could do nothing. In response to the query, "What shall we play?" it was decided out of compliment to the Austrians, as we were in the majority, to play Haydn's "Emperor Quartet." When the first movement was played through a sigh of relief followed. In the wilderness we had expected nothing.[20]

May 1, 1850, saw the organization of the Milwaukee Musical Society;[21] and by 1856 Henry Villard reported that "good orchestral and vocal music" was more liberally provided in Milwaukee than in any other city in the West.[22]

In developing the Musical Society, Balatka encountered most of the difficulties inherent in the practice of the arts in a frontier community. To be sure, he had the advantage of a well-trained string quartet and the collection of instruments and chamber music which Dr. Christian Fessel had brought to America; but most of the music had to be evolved from piano

---

[19] See J. J. Schlicher, "Hans Balatka and the Milwaukee Musical Society," *Wisconsin Magazine of History*, 27:40-45 (September 1943).

[20] "A Musician's Recollections of Fifty Years," in Chicago *Tribune*, Feb. 24, 1895, quoted in Schlicher, "Hans Balatka and the Milwaukee Musical Society," *Wis. Mag. of Hist.*, 27:42 (September 1943).

[21] See *Der Musikverein von Milwaukee, 1850-1900: Eine Chronik* (Issued by the Musical Society, Milwaukee, 1900).

[22] Villard, *Memoirs*, 1:48-49. According to Villard, the 1848 migration had contributed a "large number of educated and accomplished men" possessed of a marked "love of music and histrionic art."

arrangements; rehearsals were conducted by candlelight; and the performers were decidedly more professional in taste than in performance.[23] Nevertheless at the time of its first concert, on May 25, 1850, the association had an orchestra of 20 instruments and a chorus of as many voices. A Mozart quartet for strings, played by Messrs. Fessel, Aigner, Buderbach, and Balatka in "perfect time and tune, . . . elicited frequent and tumultuous applause."[24] The violin solo of Dr. Fessel and the singing of Mrs. Jacob Mahler, former soprano of the Court opera at Karlsruhe, were highly praised.[25] By 1851 the society had 30 in its orchestra, 78 in its chorus, and an associate membership of 213.[26] The concert of June 28, 1850, served to raise $51.02 for the benefit of European "political fugitives."[27] By the fall of 1869 the society had given more than 185 public performances, in addition to its regular monthly concerts.

The programs of the *Musikverein* bespeak the skill of the director and the taste and appreciation of both performers and public; for they included works of the standard classic repertoire which one would hardly expect to hear in a new community. Haydn's *Creation* was produced in July 1851, with local soloists, a chorus of 100, and an orchestra of 30, using some instruments that were made in Milwaukee.[28] During the first decade of its existence, the group favored by a large margin the works of Mozart and Mendelssohn.[29] In 1853, the society undertook to do an opera, the first to be performed in the Northwest and the second complete performance of Ger-

[23] Membership of the Society in 1853 included 7 professional musicians or teachers of music, 6 doctors, 2 stationers and book dealers, 2 bankers, 3 lawyers, 2 clothing merchants, 3 liquor dealers, 3 carpenters, 4 public officials, 2 engravers, and 1 each of the following: dentist, grocer, commission merchant, clerk, collector, journalist, mason, laborer, coppersmith, secretary, teamster, gluemaker. Schlicher, "Hans Balatka and the Milwaukee Musical Society," *Wis. Mag. of Hist.*, 27:51n (September 1943).
[24] Milwaukee *Daily Sentinel and Gazette*, May 27, 1850.
[25] Schlicher, "Hans Balatka and the Milwaukee Musical Society," *Wis. Mag. of Hist.*, 27:45 (September 1943).
[26] Milwaukee *Sentinel*, July 14, 1937.
[27] Koss, *Milwaukee*, 301; Milwaukee *Daily Sentinel and Gazette*, June 28, July 1, 1850.
[28] Koss, *Milwaukee*, 323.
[29] Schlicher, "Hans Balatka and the Milwaukee Musical Society," *Wis. Mag. of Hist.*, 27:53-54 (September 1943).

man opera in the United States. Balatka chose *Czaar und Zimmermann*, a comic opera by Lörtzing, most important German writer of light opera of the immediate past. He had to write the score from memory.[30] The volunteer services of the members and their wives were responsible for the production of stage settings and costumes. Commenting on a repetition of the opera, the editor of the *Sentinel* wrote: "Altogether the entertainment was choice, and we don't care how often it is repeated. There is nothing so civilizing in its effects as good music, and the community that will patronize and enjoy it can never be a vicious one."[31]

Late in December 1854 a sold-out house greeted a performance of Weber's *Der Freischütz* which was called a "triumph." In 1855, after two months of preparation, the taxing *Norma* of Bellini was presented in a manner "which would have done honor to the New York Academy of Music." The usual local soloists, including Miss Theresa Hintze, Mrs. Emma Mahler, and Messrs. C. Geisberg and A. J. Biederman, sang and acted with skill. To be sure, the critic admitted that "it would be unfair . . . to apply to an amateur performance those strict rules of criticism to which a professional one would be amenable";[32] yet Carl Schurz was of the opinion that the performances were no "better in most of the small capitals of Germany."[33] Flotow's *Alessandro Stradella* was first sung in 1856 and Mozart's *The Magic Flute* in 1858; and within the seven years from 1853 to 1860 a total of fourteen different operas was performed by the society itself or in cooperation with the German theater.[34]

Like most cultural organizations in new communities, the *Musikverein* depended for support more upon popular subscription than upon the box-office receipts from its performances. Its members paid a two-dollar initiation fee and monthly dues

---

[30] Koss, *Milwaukee*, 413, 415.
[31] Milwaukee *Daily Sentinel*, April 13, 1853.
[32] *Ibid.*, Dec. 21, 1854; April 14, 1855.
[33] *Intimate Letters of Carl Schurz, 1841-1869*, tr. and ed. by Joseph Schafer, Wisconsin Historical Society, *Collections*, 30:151 (1928).
[34] Other important musical events in the German community were the organization of Christopher Bach's band, in 1855, the meeting of the Northwestern *Saengerbund* in Milwaukee from June 19 to 22, 1856, and the founding of the Milwaukee *Liedertafel* in July 1858. Schlicher, "Hans Balatka and the Milwaukee

THE NATIONALITY BACKGROUND 119

of 40 cents—"but a moderate tax to pay towards . . . an organization which ministers so largely to the enjoyment of our citizens and which reflects such credit upon our city."[35] It combined recreation for its members with semi-professional accomplishment, from the listener's point of view, and added to those the utilitarian function of performing benefit concerts for many a worthy municipal cause. Balatka himself received no salary during the first five years but was the recipient of such benefit performances.[36]

Hard times after 1857 depleted a treasury that in the booming middle fifties had been well filled; and in 1859 further trouble resulted from factionalism among the members of the German community. This was caused by a controversy over the respective merits of Richard Wagner and the older composers and by the appearance of a musician named Sobolewski under whose direction a short-lived rival to the Musical Society—the Philharmonic Society—took shape.[37] However, the society came upon better days in the sixties, and with the building of the Academy of Music in 1864, as a stock venture, its membership increased from 75 to 600 within a year. The Academy was opened with a performance of Mendelssohn's *Paulus,* on January 31, 1865.[38] In June 1868, Milwaukee was the scene of the Northwestern *Saengerfest,* a musical institution which the German element preserved in the country of their adoption.[39]

In musical ability the German migrants, and not alone the Forty-eighters, admittedly surpassed the American settlers;[40] but their performances gained the enthusiastic support of the American element. Of the 800 spectators at the performance

---

Musical Society," *Wis. Mag. of Hist.,* 27:53 (September 1943); Hense-Jensen, Schafer tr., chap. 3, p. 15; Milwaukee *Daily Sentinel,* June 19, 1856; Gregory, *History,* 2:1092.

[35] Milwaukee *Daily Sentinel,* Dec. 7, 1857.

[36] Schlicher, "Hans Balatka and the Milwaukee Musical Society," *Wis. Mag. of Hist.,* 27:45-46 (September 1943).

[37] J. J. Schlicher, "The Milwaukee Musical Society in Time of Stress," *Wisconsin Magazine of History,* 27:178-93 (December 1943).

[38] Milwaukee *Sentinel,* July 14, 1937; Milwaukee *Daily Sentinel,* Jan. 31, 1865.

[39] *Ibid.,* June 4, 1868. Balatka left Milwaukee for Chicago in October 1860, but returned after the Chicago fire to conduct the Milwaukee Musical Society from November 3, 1871 to April 25, 1873.

[40] *Ibid.,* May 23, 1859.

of *Czaar und Zimmermann*, on April 8, 1853, three-fifths were Germans and two-fifths, Americans.[41] Indeed the common interest in music became a potent factor in forging an ultimate understanding between the native Americans and the German migrants.[42] Certainly the musical traditions of the German residents and the organizational skill and musical interest of the erstwhile farmer Balatka prompted a kind of musical performance in Milwaukee far superior to that of the average new western city and often the equal of musical accomplishment in older parts of the nation.

Amateur theatricals, frequently followed by dancing, laid the foundations for a German legitimate theater which was well established by 1868. The earliest performances were given in February 1850 by the printers and typesetters of the *Banner* and the *Volksfreund;* and shortly thereafter a *Liebhaberverein*, or amateur theatrical association, founded on December 8, 1849, began to give plays by Kotzebue, Strumpf, and others. The admission was a shilling, rough board benches served as seats, and candlesticks provided the only light; but to the German migrants such plays as *Cousin from Bremen* and *The Nightwatchman* by Koerner; *The Deserter, The Sly Widow,* and *The Heritage* by Kotzebue; and Raupach's *The Spirit of the Times* were welcome reminders of the Fatherland in the New World. A local German wrote and produced *The Robber's Revenge* in 1851.[43] The dramatic performances sponsored by Joseph Kurz in the Mozart Hall during 1852 provided the European newcomers with a sort of social center; and to judge from reports of the informality of the audiences, the performances were less appreciated than the dancing which fol-

---

[41] Koss, *Milwaukee*, 415.

[42] Carl Schurz asserted that the cultural interests awakened by the Forty-eighters "very largely bridged over the distance between the native American and the newcomer." Carl Schurz, *The Reminiscences of Carl Schurz* (3 vols., New York, 1907), 245. According to Hense-Jensen, "music was the mediator which gradually made an approach to a good understanding [between German and American] despite the great differences in social views and customs." Hense-Jensen, Schafer tr., chap. 3, p. 13.

[43] Koss, *Milwaukee*, 296, 298-99, 331; Francis Magyar, "The History of the Early Milwaukee German Theatre (1850-1868)," *Wisconsin Magazine of History*, 13:376-77 (June 1930); Hense-Jensen, Schafer tr., chap. 3, p. 10.

lowed. Destruction of the English theater by fire in 1853 supplied added patronage for the German actors; and serious as well as farcical plays were performed twice weekly,[44] the Kurz family continuing to construct the settings and take part in all the performances.[45] In that year, larger quarters in the Market Hall were secured by subscription; the first classical play, Schiller's *Robbers,* was produced;[46] and Raupach's *School of Life* was played before a sold-out audience of 500.[47] Fifty-four plays were given in the following season.[48] With the discovery of a leading lady in Alwine Schindler, a young German actress earning her living as a seamstress in the city, the transition from amateur to professional theater began. Nevertheless the performers still had to be jacks of all trades; and Kurz's successor, one Boetzow from Louisville, served for $24 a month as artistic director, comedian, janitor, handbill carrier, and tailor, to boot.[49] The late fifties and early sixties saw a marked improvement in the literary standard of the productions and in the caliber of the professional actors engaged, among them Alexander Pfeiffer, "at that time the most important German actor in America."[50] With the removal of the theater from the Market Hall in 1863, some decline set in; but despite the increasing competition of the English stage, internal dissension among the players, and the distraction of wartime activities,[51] by October 1868, the legitimate German drama, newly housed in the Stadt Theatre, was filling a respected place in Milwaukee's cultural life.[52]

Forty-eighters were among the prime movers in the organization in 1851 of the Milwaukee *Schulverein,* or educational association, designed to provide instruction in German and a

[44] Magyar, "Early Milwaukee German Theatre," *Wis. Mag. of Hist.,* 13:378 (June 1930).
[45] Koss, *Milwaukee,* 376-77.   [46] Hense-Jensen, Schafer tr., chap. 3, p. 11.
[47] Koss, *Milwaukee,* 410; Milwaukee *Daily Sentinel,* July 15, 16, 1853.
[48] Magyar, "Early Milwaukee German Theatre," *Wis. Mag. of Hist.,* 13:379 (June 1930).
[49] *Ibid.;* Koss, *Milwaukee,* 410.
[50] Hense-Jensen, Schafer tr., chap. 3, p. 10.
[51] Magyar, "Early Milwaukee German Theatre," *Wis. Mag. of Hist.,* 13:385 (June 1930).
[52] Hense-Jensen, Schafer tr., chap. 3, pp. 11-12.

kind of education not then available in either the public or private American schools or in the German Catholic parochial schools. The organizers were Dr. F. A. Luening, Theodore Wettstein, Frederick Fratny, Dr. Aigner, and Vojta Naprstek.[53] The same group founded the German-English Academy shortly thereafter and secured another exile of the revolution, Peter Engelmann, as teacher. In Germany young Engelmann had edited a revolutionary newspaper. Upon migrating to America he had tried his hand at farming in the eastern United States; but once he reached Milwaukee in 1851 he turned to teaching, beginning a career that was to make a significant contribution to the intellectual life of the developing Wisconsin city. The pupils met at first at Engelmann's home; but enrollment soon made necessary a special building.[54] Financial support came in part from benefit festivals given by the ladies of the *Schulverein* and from performances by the dramatic association.[55] The school's enrollment reached a peak in 1865 when it boasted 450 pupils, taught in eleven classes by sixteen teachers.[56] Some of its methods were ultimately adopted in the city system. It was not long before German was taught in the public schools of the German wards; and in 1867 the school board made German a part of the course of instruction in the city system. As a result, by the school year 1870-71, more than 46 percent of the pupils in the schools were studying German.[57] This recognition of a language spoken by more than half the residents of Milwaukee did much to increase the enrollment of children of German families in the public schools, where English was at the same time made available to them. It brought a corresponding decrease in the enrollment in the German private schools.[58]

Three organizations which drew their strength largely from exiles of the German revolution revealed the enthusiasm of

[53] German could be studied only for an extra fee in the public schools; the Catholic parochial schools were distasteful in doctrine to many Forty-eighters. Koss, *Milwaukee*, 331-34.
[54] *Ibid.*, 334-35.
[55] *Ibid.*, 405.
[56] Gregory, *History*, 2:1176.
[57] Patrick Donnelly, "The Milwaukee Public Schools," in *Columbian History of Education in Wisconsin*, ed. by John W. Stearns (Milwaukee, 1893), 458-59.
[58] Bruce, *History*, 1:638.

the Forty-eighters for liberal social thought and identified them with the transcendental trends already active in American society in the Middle Period. These organizations were the *Freie Gemeinde* or Free Congregation, the Society of Free Men, and the Social *Turnverein*.

The moving spirit in the *Freie Gemeinde* was Eduard Schroeter, tenacious opponent of absolute government and exile of the revolutionary movement in Germany. He came to Milwaukee in 1851 at the invitation of a Lutheran-Reformed group which proposed to become a Free Congregation. His first address, delivered on August 8, 1851, enunciated the principles for which the congregation was to stand: opposition to clericalism and official dishonesty, confidence in the authority of the congregation without distinction of sex, and the furtherance of independence and individuality in thought, will, decision, and action.[59] Enthusiastically received by large numbers of the German revolutionaries in the community, Schroeter speeded the growth of the Free Congregation movement and, from November 1851 until the summer of 1853 when he moved to Sauk City, published the *Humanist,* Wisconsin's first religious weekly, in the interest of the cause.[60] The *Verein Freier Maenner,* or Society of Free Men, also anticlerical in tendency, had a similar appeal for the Milwaukee exiles of the German revolution. Organized in January 1853, it proposed the education of its members in religion, politics, and socialism, the development of a library, and the enlargement of scientific instruction in the schools.[61]

The Turner movement provided another refuge for both the retention of the culture of the Fatherland and the perpetuation of the ideals of the Forty-eighters. The Turners, with their creed of liberty, reason, and tolerance—"Free speech, free press, free assembly for discussion of all questions, so that men and women may think unfettered and order their lives by the dictates of conscience"—had played an important part

[59] J. J. Schlicher, "Eduard Schroeter the Humanist," *Wisconsin Magazine of History,* 28:169-76 (December 1944).
[60] *Ibid.,* 176-83.
[61] Koss, *Milwaukee,* 391.

in the abortive revolution.⁶² Interdicted in Germany, they set up their organization in a number of American cities. Milwaukee's first *Turnverein* was a short-lived society organized in 1850 by Eduard Schultz, a political refugee from Baden. A second society, Teutonia, founded in 1852, was of equally short duration. It was left to the Social *Turnverein,* founded on July 17, 1853, and later called the Milwaukee *Turnverein,* to put turning on a permanent basis in the city.⁶³ Its organizer was August Willich, one of the most determined of the Forty-eighters. A former free-troop leader in the revolution, Willich did not reach Milwaukee until 1853. So strong was the appeal of the movement for the liberal-minded Germans in Milwaukee that before the Social *Turnverein* was a year old there it had more than 100 active members;⁶⁴ and for many years the *Turnverein* was "the center of intellectual life for the citizens of Germanic derivation." The practice of the German system of gymnastics, conducted in the open air and later in the society's own building on Fourth Street, and an annual masked ball, first held in 1855, were among the early social activities of the organization. Lectures and debates, in the German tongue, fostered the retention of the language and culture of the Fatherland. Patriotic toward their adopted country, the Turners constituted a company of sharpshooters that participated in the Civil War. Later they developed a gymnastic team, headed by George Brosius, which in 1880 won a world's championship in international competition at Frankfort on the Main, in Germany.⁶⁵

The desire to exert a greater influence on American life in general and on community affairs in particular led to a movement among the Forty-eighters to unite the various liberal organizations of the city and its hinterland. The impetus came from a meeting of the Society of Free Men in July 1853;

---

⁶² See Henry Metzner, *A Brief History of the American Turnerbund* (Pittsburgh, 1924).

⁶³ Hense-Jensen, Schafer tr., chap. 3, p. 17; Koss, *Milwaukee,* 318.

⁶⁴ Schlicher, "Eduard Schroeter," *Wis. Mag. of Hist.,* 28:311n (March 1945); Hense-Jensen, Schafer tr., chap. 3, pp. 17-18; Robert Wild, "Chapters in the History of the Turners," *Wisconsin Magazine of History,* 9:123-33 (December 1925); Koss, *Milwaukee,* 401-402.

⁶⁵ Milwaukee *Sentinel,* July 14, 1937.

and representatives of the three major liberal organizations, the Free Congregation, the Society of Free Men, and the *Turnverein,* joined in issuing the call for a convention. The resulting union was known as the *Bund Freier Menschen,* or Federation of Free People. The chairmen of the five sections of its central committee were drawn with one exception from the most active Forty-eighters: for communication, Loose, Schroeter's successor as speaker of the Free Congregation and publisher of the *Humanist;* for education, Engelmann of the *Schulverein;* for gymnastics, Maerklin, speaker of the *Turnverein;* for art, Balatka of the *Musikverein;* and for support, Schoeffler of the *Banner.* Since its aims were only a recapitulation of those of the member organizations and since it suffered from obstructionism within its own ranks, the federation died a quiet death in the winter of 1854-55. The Free Congregation, torn like the federation with dissension, disintegrated, its remnants merging with the Society of Free Men in May 1854. Vigorous spirits like Balatka and Engelmann soon abandoned this organization, and those who were left ultimately identified themselves with the *Turnverein.*[66]

From these evidences of discord it may be seen that the Teutonic element was not one harmonious unit in the urban society. Despite the self-contained integrity of the German community, implemented as it was by flourishing German drama, music, education, customs, and press,[67] there were many indications in it of the internal friction that so often characterizes newly arrived nationality groups seeking recognition in a strange land. This was manifested, as already has been pointed out, in the factions which developed within the Musical Society and the German theater. It was seen in the tendency of some of the German migrants to resent what they considered an assumption of superiority on the part of the well-educated Forty-eighters,[68] among the Freethinkers themselves on such questions as the payment of salaries to the speakers of the free

[66] Schlicher, "Eduard Schroeter," *Wis. Mag. of Hist.,* 28:312-14 (March 1945).
[67] By 1861 the city had four German daily papers: the *Banner und Volksfreund, Seebote, Atlas,* and *Phoenix*—a number equal to that of the English dailies.
[68] Koss, *Milwaukee,* 278-84.

congregations, and even in the convention of the Federation of Free People where the rivalry of the various newspaper editors for patronage was but one indication of internal strife.[69] These differences approached the point of violence in the relations between the strong-willed Forty-eighters and the conservative followers of the Catholic faith. In this conflict between free thought and priestcraft, the *Freie Gemeinde,* the Sons of Hermann, Schoeffler's *Banner,* Fratny's *Volksfreund,* Schroeter's *Humanist,* and the *Flugblätter* of Vojta Naprstek were lined up against Bishop Henni, the priests, and the *Seebote,* the first issue of which appeared under the editorship of Amand St. Vincent in 1852. September 1853 saw an open declaration by the liberals against the Catholic church and the dominance of the priests and a direct collision of Catholics and Freethinkers over the corpse of a member of the Free Congregation.[70]

With respect to municipal politics, in which the impact of the Germans and Irish was considerable in this period, the Forty-eighters made a contribution in no way comparable to their influence in the cultural field. Franz Huebschmann and August Greulich, the most politically effective Milwaukee Germans of the period, came to America in 1842 and 1834, respectively, and to Milwaukee in the early forties. Greulich was the first member of the German community to be elected to the city council; but he was strongly identified with the Catholic rather than the Freethinking Germans. Among more than fifty German-Americans listed in the 1890's as having made an outstanding contribution to the political and industrial life of the community, not more than three can be identified with the immigration of 1848. It is thus apparent that, contrary to a widespread popular impression, the Forty-eighters were by no means exclusively responsible for the accomplishments of the German element in the city. They undoubtedly strengthened the support for liberal thought and speeded the transmission of improved standards of literature and the arts in the developing urban community. According

---

[69] Schlicher, "Eduard Schroeter," *Wis. Mag. of Hist.,* 28:311-14 (March 1945).
[70] Koss, *Milwaukee,* 313-14, 400, 433.

to Carl Schurz, one of the most distinguished of their number, they were responsible for awakening, more quickly than in any other city in which the German influence was felt, "interests which a majority of the old population had hardly known, but which now attracted general favor."[71] Yet even this was not a contribution of the revolutionary group alone. For example, Theodore Wettstein, one of the founders of the *Musikverein* and a leader in the educational association, arrived previous to the immigration of 1848. Nor was the liberalism of the Forty-eighters a pervasive facet of the Milwaukee-German culture. Karl Heinzen, visiting the Milwaukee Germans in the late sixties, criticized them for losing their liberalism as they prospered in the new land. It pleased him to hear German spoken in the streets; and he admired the city's excellent German school. But the attendance at his lecture was poor; the Roman Catholic church was too much in evidence for his liberal tastes; and he saw little excuse for calling Milwaukee the "German Athens" of America.[72]

Throughout the period of developing cityhood, the American and German communities stood side by side, the institutions of one paralleling those of the other in almost every phase of social life. With their own debating clubs, lodges, music societies, schools, and newspapers, as well as with fire and military companies composed exclusively of Germans, the newcomers contrived a society of their own, not so much on the defensive against the processes of Americanization as indifferent to them.[73] They were slow to intermarry with the Americans;[74] and many of them lived out their lives within the German community, little concerned about developments among the American element. Henry Villard, trying to sell a

[71] Schurz, *Reminiscences*, 2:45-46.

[72] Carl Wittke, *Against the Current: the Life of Karl Heinzen, 1809-1880* (Chicago, 1945), v, vi, 141.

[73] Inventory of German organizations of 1849, in *Daily Wisconsin* (Milwaukee), Dec. 15, 1849, quoted in Gregory, *History*, 2:624. Among the members of the debating club were Luening, Huebschmann, Schoeffler, Fratny, Herzberg, and Prieger. The most popular lodge of the period was the Milwaukee Lodge of the Sons of Hermann, which listed 140 members in 1849.

[74] Schafer, "Yankee and Teuton," *Wis. Mag. of Hist.*, 7:158 (December 1923).

History of American Literature to his countrymen in Milwaukee, reported that they "knew nothing of American literature and did not care much for it. . . . Moreover, their purely German surroundings kept their interest in American affairs at a low point."[75]

Whig nativism or Yankee Puritanism frequently caused a rift between the two groups; and because of the contentious character of the times, violence sometimes resulted. Irishmen predominated among the officers, but Huebschmann was president, of a *Sag Nicht* organization, devised in 1855 to offset the activities of the Know Nothings.[76] A year earlier, a call had appeared in the *Sentinel* for a new military company "composed wholly of Americans to supplement the Milwaukee City Rifles (German) and the Milwaukee City Guards (Irish). According to Buck, this step was motivated by a feeling of uneasiness among the native-born Americans for their personal safety on election days.[77] The "beer question" was a constant cause of difficulty; and the temperance meetings of the Yankee element were on occasion disrupted by German rioters. When the Germans insisted on celebrating a Fourth of July which fell on Sunday, about 1,400 citizens, "both native and foreign-born," urged the council to suppress what they called "Sunday orgies and excesses in Milwaukee."[78] In the same year a native-American member of the *Musikverein* contended that the Sunday evening concerts of the organization —"however attractive and customary these entertainments may be in Germany"—were out of place in Milwaukee.[79] On the other hand, the *Sentinel* remarked upon the "hearty good will" with which those not of German birth participated in the *Mai Fest* which was introduced by the Germans in 1852;[80] and, as has already been pointed out, many Americans gave enthusiastic support to German musical activities. Moreover, the active participation of many of the German-Americans in municipal

[75] Villard, *Memoirs*, 1:48-49.
[76] Buck, 4:110-11.
[77] *Ibid.*, 4:30-31.
[78] Milwaukee *Daily Sentinel*, July 30, Aug. 18, 1852.
[79] *Ibid.*, May 21, 1852.
[80] *Ibid.*, May 20, June 1, 1852.

MILWAUKEE IN 1853

and State politics inevitably integrated their leaders in the developing American community.

In spite of nativist opposition, if not indeed because of it, the German element assumed an ever more confident position in local society as the generation progressed. Their cultural self-assurance was bolstered both by numerical strength and common language[81] and by the conviction that for them the United States was no land of exile but rather a country where "as in Europe the struggle for the highest and holiest interests of humanity is to be fought out," a fight which was the newcomer's as well as the native-American's "interest and right."[82] It was in this spirit that by the time of America's sectional conflict in the sixties many members of the group were making a conscientious, though not always eager, contribution toward preserving the unity of their adopted land. Moreover, their cultural self-confidence was further advanced by the growing prestige of the Fatherland as demonstrated in the Franco-Prussian War. Donations were raised in 1870 to aid Germany, and a mass meeting was held at which Schoeffler, Anneke, Hans Boebel, P. V. Deuster, Haertel, Emil Wallber, and Frederick W. von Cotzhausen were prominent participants,[83] a support for German militarism which revealed the now predominant conservatism of a migrant element once stirred by the liberal appeal of 1848.[84]

By the turn of the seventies the Milwaukee Germans had achieved a society which perpetuated the social flavor of the Fatherland within the already maturing American urban community. It was what Professor Wittke has called "a culturally static *Deutschtum*," having nothing to do with Germany's foreign or political policies, but being "concerned mainly with *Turnvereine*, singing societies, bowling and pinochle clubs, and all those other things which American Germans describe so sentimentally by the all-inclusive term *Gemütlichkeit*."[85]

---

[81] Wittke, *Against the Current*, 284.
[82] Hense-Jensen, Schafer tr., chap. 2, p. 14.
[83] *Ibid.*, chap. 6, p. 18 ff.
[84] See Carl Wittke, "American Germans in Two World Wars," *Wisconsin Magazine of History*, 27:28 (September 1943).
[85] *Ibid.*, 9.

Great jubilation attended the festivities of May 27 to 29, 1871, which celebrated Germany's victory in the Franco-Prussian War. The black, white, and red tricolors of the German Empire, hanging alongside the Stars and Stripes, symbolized in a very real sense the way in which Milwaukee's German town had retained within the frame of loyalty to its new home the culture, customs, and social life of the old.[86]

But there were Irish-Americans as well as German-Americans in the evolving social fabric of urban Milwaukee, and some of them played a more vocal if less constructive role in the development of the city than their Teutonic neighbors. Most numerous among foreign-born Milwaukeeans, after the Germans, they were numerically much less strong and without the difference of language or the intellectual leadership that fostered the growth of a separate German society. Nevertheless, they quickly exerted an influence in municipal politics quite out of proportion to their numbers and swelled the Democratic and Catholic ingredient of the community. John White and Timothy O'Brien were their most aggressive leaders until the middle fifties. White organized and acted as captain of the Irish military company, became sheriff in 1851, and was collector of the port under President Pierce. "Father Tim" O'Brien served as an energetic city marshal and went to the council for many years from the Irish Third Ward. Following 1856, political leadership of the Irish passed to Edward O'Neill, who had come to Milwaukee by way of Vermont in 1850 and who ultimately engaged in the wholesale grocery business with a fellow Irish-American, John Furlong. He served in the State legislature for a number of terms, and was four times elected mayor of Milwaukee. Their common allegiance to the Democratic Party, their common religious faith, in many instances, and their common defense against the nativism of the Yankee Whigs led to cooperation among the Irish and German residents of the young city. To judge from the record there was less friction between the nationalities than among contentious elements within a given group of foreign-born.[87]

[86] Hense-Jensen, Schafer tr., chap. 6, pp. 20-22.
[87] Desmond, "Early Irish Settlers in Milwaukee," *Wis. Mag. of Hist.*, 13:371-72 (June 1930); Buck, 3:276-78, 300-301.

THE NATIONALITY BACKGROUND 131

Still other North European stocks contributed to the social variety of the developing city. In order of numerical strength, after the Germans and Irish, they were as follows: Bohemians, British-Americans, Hollanders, Austrians, and Norwegians.[88] The early history of the Bohemian element, which in 1870 comprised 2 percent of the total population, parallels that of their German neighbors. A sizable migration came as a consequence of the Austrian revolution of 1848, most of the newcomers settling in the Second, or German, Ward. *Lipa,* the first Czech dramatic and singing club, was founded in 1861; and seven years later the *Turnverein Sokol* was organized in the colony.[89] Agitation for a Czech parish dates to 1860 when Catholic Czechs formed a society to collect money to bring annually from the East a priest who could hear confession in the Czech language. In 1865 a permanent Czech Catholic parish was founded.[90] Also associated with the German migration of the mid-century were scattering Poles, a nationality group that was in the succeeding generation to contribute significantly to the development of the urban culture. The first permanent inhabitants of this type came from Posen in 1848; by 1864, there were some thirty families. The formation of a Catholic church in 1863, under the guidance of Father Buczynski, marked the beginning of St. Stanislaus, the first Polish parish. Up to that time the Poles had had to be content with special Polish services in a German parish.[91]

Way station on the water highway from Buffalo to the agrarian Northwest, Milwaukee was to have for many years

[88] For an account of early Dutch settlement in Milwaukee, see "Reminiscences of Arend Jan Brusse," *Wis. Mag. of Hist.,* 30:85-90 (September 1946).

[89] From Anthony Novak, "Ze Zašlých dob" (From Times Past), in *Památník* (Memorial) of the 14th convention of the union of *Český Spolek Podporující Spolky* (Czech Fraternal Association), Milwaukee, 1909, unpaged. This will hereafter be cited as Novak, "Ze Zašlých dob."

[90] *Zlaté Jubileum České Katolické Osady Sv. Jana Nep.* (Golden Jubilee pamphlet of St. John de Nepomuc Church, 1863-1913), (*Rovnost* Press, Milwaukee, 1913).

[91] J. A. Kapmarski, "Dzieje Polaków w Milwaukee, Wisconsin," in *Kuryer Polski* (Milwaukee), June 23, 1938; Wacław Kruszka, *Historya Polska w Ameryce* (13 vols., Milwaukee, 1906), 7:125, 127. According to John Jakusz-Gostomski, "Our First Hundred Years," in *We, the Milwaukee Poles,* compiled by Thaddeus Borun (Milwaukee, 1946), 1, Michael Skupniewicz arrived in Milwaukee in 1846 and spent some time there before removing to a farm in Dodge County.

a peculiar attraction for foreign-born migrants to the United States. As a result, the first generation of cityhood saw the establishment of a Europeanism of which marked suggestions linger even to the present day. Yet in spite of the numerical predominance of the foreign-born until close to 1870, in numbers sufficient to win them respect for their culture and considerable recognition of their political strength, the American-born residents still held the reins of community action in these middle years. For the activities of the "universal Yankee" we must turn our attention to developments in the political and economic spheres.

CHAPTER 7

Local Politics and National Issues

MILWAUKEE was a stronghold of the Democratic Party during the first generation of her cityhood. In every presidential contest the local electorate supported the Democratic candidates with sizable majorities, in spite of the fact that Wisconsin voters, outside of the city, were predominantly Republican from the candidacy of John C. Frémont in 1856 to the election of Cleveland in 1892.[1] Of the sixteen mayors who served the city between 1846 and 1870, only one belonged admittedly to a party other than the traditional Democratic; but some of them, whose Democracy had grown increasingly conservative with the acquisition of property, were elected on a coalition People's Ticket with the aid of Whig or, later, Republican votes. These property-minded Democrats, together with their Whig and Republican sympathizers, lent their support increasingly to movements to curtail the expenditures of the municipal government and limit the unchecked independence of the elected representatives of the urban will. The more frequently dominant "Regular" Democracy, on the other hand, maintained its hold because of its appeal to the foreign-born and because of the popularity of its leaders, as well as its principles, with the working-class ingredient of the community. The *Courier* and, later, the *Daily News* identified the opposition to the Democracy with the "privileged few"; and the foreign-born residents found in the popular, rather than the conservative, party the recognition they desired. The politically

[1] See appendix for a comparison of the presidential vote in Milwaukee County with that of the remainder of the State of Wisconsin, 1848 to 1940. It should be noted that for the election returns in mayoral contests discussed in this chapter it has been necessary to rely on newspaper reports, inasmuch as there appears to be no available official record on the subject.

133

facile Irish, mobilized by G. M. Fitzgerald, Sheriff John White, Ed McGarry, Richard Murphy, Andrew McCormick, and Edward O'Neill, succeeded in elevating two of their countrymen to the mayoralty during the period; and the Germans, under the tutelage of Huebschmann, Schoeffler, Albert Bade, Greulich, and John Rosebeck, exerted an ever more potent balance of power as the years progressed. Both political camps made a play for the German voters; and on occasion they deviated from the traditional Democracy to the advantage of the People's Ticket. But in general the residents of the foreign wards followed the lead of the party mentors with a loyalty that made them important ingredients in the development of the "Regular" Democratic machine.[2]

The political behavior of the young city was manifestly democratic in the general as well as in the partisan sense. This was a generation of rough and tumble politics, heated controversy, and mass meetings that gave violent expression to public sentiments. Annual elections kept the issues of the municipal government constantly before the people; and rotation in office distributed the duties and responsibilities of city management so that from 1848 to 1870 an average of only two aldermen succeeded themselves in each yearly election. As in the village period, the major political offices were frequently held by the commercial and professional leaders of the community; and throughout the period grocers, attorneys, commission merchants, joiners, builders, and land agents were conspicuously represented in the council. However, by the sixties there was increasing representation from the specialized services and trades. The participation of civic-minded citizens in the municipal government did not prevent the development of machine politics or the rise of graft and extravagance in connection with the granting of contracts for city improvement. This situation, as well as the conflict between pressure to develop the expanding community and the objections of the tax-

---

[2] By 1853, Haertel and Huebschmann had received State and Federal appointments, and in 1857 Greulich and O'Neill were the choice of Milwaukee city and county for the State senate. Franz Löher, referring to Milwaukee in 1847, wrote, "Nowhere have the Germans decided so much in politics as here." Conard, 1:80.

payers to the costs of doing so, furnished the issues of most of the municipal campaigns. Toward the close of the period disillusionment with the behavior of the people's representatives prompted the resort to such checks as a bicameral council and a strengthened mayoral veto; and this attitude, as well as an awareness of the increasing complexity of administration, resulted in a tendency in Milwaukee, as in other cities of the nation, to vest responsibility for numerous municipal activities in boards and commissions rather than in the allegedly more corruptible municipal legislature.

Party politics, with the national party labels, attended the first election under the city charter, on April 7, 1846. According to the *Sentinel and Gazette,* the Whigs would have preferred a nonpartisan approach, "as in all previous elections for corporation officers"; but the activities of the Democratic "Milwaukee Regency," which for some weeks had "fanned the flames of political excitement," left them no alternative but to put some opponents to the *"Courier* clique" in the field.[3] The outcome of the election forecast the pattern of politics for the ensuing generation. The Democrats elected all but one of their candidates and polled a majority of 345 for Solomon Juneau over John H. Tweedy, the Whig choice for mayor.[4] Occasional Irish and German names on the Democratic slate and the council's choice of Henry Bielfeld as city clerk suggested the force of the foreign-born ingredient in the dominant party. On April 10, 1846, the board of village trustees turned over the management of the city to the mayor and common council. As many copies of Juneau's inaugural remarks were printed in German as in English.[5]

[3] Milwaukee *Sentinel,* Oct. 16, 1895, quoting *Sentinel and Gazette.* The *Sentinel and Gazette,* which resulted from a merger of the *Sentinel* and the *Daily Gazette,* in 1846, and its successor the Milwaukee *Daily Sentinel* became the champions of Whig and, later, Republican politics in the city. Equally ardent, and somewhat more inflammatory, support for the Democrats was provided by the *Courier* (until 1847), its successor the *Wisconsin,* and, after 1852, the *Daily News,* successor to the *Commercial Advertiser,* which had been started in 1848 as an organ of the "Old Hunker" Democrats. See Gregory, *History,* 2:1005-11.

[4] Milwaukee *Sentinel,* Oct. 16, 1895. Juneau's election was somewhat of a token gesture. He left most of the duties of the office to John B. Smith, the acting mayor.

[5] Milwaukee *Sentinel and Gazette,* April 3, 10, 11, 1846.

A heated controversy over the proposed State constitution influenced municipal politics in 1847 and led to the choice of Horatio N. Wells as the city's second mayor.[6] The divergent reactions to the State constitution proposed in 1846 exhibited the growing cleavage between conservatives and liberals among the local Democrats as well as in the community at large. Its liberal suffrage features[7] won it the foreign vote, but provisions proscribing banks and safeguarding debtors, which were unquestionably distasteful to the Whigs, were more than some of the speculator-promoters, who normally voted in the Democratic column, could bear. Dyed-in-the-wool Democrats like D. A. J. Upham, A. D. Smith, W. P. Lynde, and George H. Walker, as well as such German-American Democrats as Huebschmann, Schoeffler, Haertel, and Liebhaber supported the constitution; but in the opposing camp were such veteran Democrats as Juneau, Kilbourn, Moses Kneeland, John Furlong, and H. N. Wells, as well as Rufus King, John H. Tweedy, and Jonathan E. Arnold, the leaders of Milwaukee's Whigdom.[8] The friends of the constitution, led by the *Courier*, appealed to the "Democracy of Milwaukee—the laborers, the producers—hard-fisted and true-hearted sons of humanity" to support a frame of government which "the interested few" who "live upon the earnings of the masses" were trying to defeat.[9] In the German section of the city, the residents paraded, shouting, "Hurrah for our constitution"; and the inn-keepers served "constitution" and "anti-constitution" beer.[10]

The business-minded opponents of the proposed instrument predicted that, if adopted, it would "wither . . . credit, diminish . . . trade, . . . check our growth." The merchant would see "dealers at the East less willing to sell, and customers at

---

[6] Wells, a native of Vermont, had come to Milwaukee in 1836. A distinguished lawyer, he had an active career in territorial and county politics. Milwaukee *Sentinel*, July 14, 1937.

[7] Huebschmann had been an active delegate to this convention and had secured a provision granting suffrage to foreign males of one year's residence, who had declared their intention of becoming U.S. citizens. Conard, 1:76.

[8] *Ibid*, 1:77-78; Milwaukee *Daily Sentinel and Gazette*, March 8, 1847; Buck, 3:50.

[9] *Ibid.*, 3:48, 58-59.

[10] Koss, *Milwaukee*, 236-38.

home, less able to buy." The forwarder would "find cargoes falling off and freights diminishing." The mechanic would meet with less employment and the laborer with only "an occasional job at the lowest rates."[11] Feeling in the opposing camps became so tense that a collision between two torchlight processions resulted in a free-for-all in which "both sides used their torch sticks for weapons and belabored each other until heads were broken and clothes stripped off."[12] In the long run, the combination of Whigs and Bank Democrats was too strong for the "Simon-pure" Democracy; and the young city spoke out against a fundamental code that threatened the expansion and stability of credit and trade.[13] When the votes were counted, Milwaukee had rejected the ultra-liberal constitution by a vote of 1,437 to 1,148. The only ward to give a majority for the constitution was the German Second. Similar sentiments were expressed in the municipal election of the same year. Horatio N. Wells, a conservative Democrat who had opposed the 1846 constitution, was elected mayor over one of its ardent supporters, George H. Walker. Only in the German Second Ward did Walker receive a majority of the votes.[14]

The consolidation of the Democracy brought the election of Kilbourn over Rufus King for the mayoralty in the following year. The pioneer speculator, along with Fitzgerald, Schoeffler, King, and others, had been named as one of the delegates to a second constitutional convention, held from December 15, 1847, to February 1, 1848. The constitution resulting from its work, shorn of most of the "radical innovations" of the first but retaining a suffrage qualification that pleased the

[11] Milwaukee *Daily Sentinel and Gazette,* April 3, 1847.
[12] A. W. Kellogg, "Recollections of Life in Early Wisconsin," *Wis. Mag. of Hist.,* 8:102-3 (September 1924); Buck, 3:60.
[13] According to the Green Bay *Advocate,* as quoted in the *Daily Sentinel and Gazette,* Milwaukee had "her bank and money traders—more speculators and lawyers than any other place" and was "so situated in reference to the trade abroad, that any laws . . . conflicting with those of other states must materially affect her." "Is it not as clear as sunlight," asks the editor of the Milwaukee paper, "that a constitution which strikes avowedly at credit, which seeks to diminish currency, which makes war on capital, must . . . be the most unsuitable to a new and growing state . . . to build up its cities and villages?" Milwaukee *Daily Sentinel and Gazette,* April 3, 1847.
[14] Buck, 3:61.

foreign-born, won broad endorsement in the city. Even the Second Ward gave it almost unanimous support; and in the city-wide vote on March 18, 1848, it carried by 1,503 to 147.[15] In State and national politics, during this year, the Democrats prospered in Milwaukee, if not in the nation at large. "The heavy German vote of our city, nearly or quite 800 strong, was cast, unbroken, for the so-called 'democratic' ticket," the *Sentinel and Gazette* reported, "and to that vote our Locofoco friends are indebted for their success."[16]

Nativism, the temperance issue, and anti-Catholicism aggravated city politics on the turn of the fifties, without, however, shaking the hold of the Democrats on the municipal government. D. A. J. Upham[17] defeated B. H. Edgerton, People's candidate for mayor, in 1849; and the reelection of Charles Geisberg as city treasurer was in line with what was to become a standard Democratic practice: the allocation of the treasurership to the German wing of the party.[18] Independent tickets were successful in some of the wards; and four aldermen, two constables, and one notary were chosen from German-born Milwaukeeans.[19] The major crisis of Mayor Upham's first term came in connection with a violent reaction on the part of the foreign-born to a temperance law of 1849, in the course of which they broke into the home of John B. Smith, one of the senators responsible for the measure.[20] The enemies of the blue laws staged a meeting on March 11, 1850; and although about a hundred of them were precipitated into the cellar when the floor of the Military Hall collapsed, the assemblage adjourned undaunted to Market Square where they inveighed against the "wooden nutmeg legislators" and the

---

[15] Conard, 1:78; Milwaukee *Daily Sentinel and Gazette*, March 7, 1848.

[16] *Ibid.*, May 9, 1848.

[17] Don A. J. Upham, a native of Virginia, had graduated from Union College and taught mathematics in a New Jersey college before coming to Milwaukee in 1837. There he practiced law and engaged in business, taking an active part in Democratic politics. Milwaukee *Sentinel*, July 14, 1937.

[18] Buck, 3:185; Milwaukee *Sentinel and Gazette*, April 4, 1849.

[19] *Ibid.*, March 29, 1849; Koss, *Milwaukee*, 285.

[20] This law held vendors of intoxicating drinks "pecuniarily responsible for all damages to the community, justly chargeable to such sale or traffic." Buck, 3:190.

"ukases of the Temperance Aristocracy."[21] When the so-called friends of law and order responded with a public demonstration on March 22, the meeting was stormed by opponents of the restrictive measure. Not until near midnight did its organizers gain sufficient control to pass resolutions praising Senator Smith for his efforts on behalf of temperance and warning the foreign element that though they were "welcome to homes amongst us, and to all the rights and immunities of our institutions," they must "refrain from all disorderly and riotous conduct."[22]

In spite of the fact that Mayor Upham had originally endorsed the temperance law, practical politics led him to support its foreign-born opponents in this crisis; and when the Democrats renominated him for mayor in 1850, he won by a vote of 1,981 over Rufus King, for whom the Whigs rallied only 556 supporters, and the much-abused Smith, who polled 385 votes in the interest of law and order on the People's Ticket.[23] In the eyes of the German citizens the election was a defeat for fanaticism,[24] as well as an indication of the political strength of the foreign-born. The reelection of Geisberg for treasurer and the choice of James B. Cross for city attorney revealed important ingredients of the developing Democratic machine. Religious differences were the cause of another civic altercation which took place near the close of Upham's second term. Early in April 1851, a number of Milwaukeeans, presumably Catholics, interrupted the lecture of a Rev. E. Leahy, who styled himself a monk who had renounced Catholicism. The Protestants and the Whig press made the incident an issue of freedom of speech; and as a result of a public meeting on the subject, Leahy was permitted to finish his lectures with 100 special constables and the whole fire department stationed around the church as a guarantee of law and order.[25]

By the spring of 1851, mounting opposition to municipal expenditures fostered the ascendancy of the conservative wing of the local electorate. Loans to railroad companies, coupled

[21] Conard, 1:82.
[22] Buck, 3:241-46.
[23] Conard, 1:83; Buck, 3:194, 248, 253.
[24] Koss, *Milwaukee*, 305.
[25] Buck, 3:334-40.

with outlays incident to the grading of streets and the construction of schools and bridges, had raised the costs of government until the taxpayers and property owners were up in arms, and the municipal debt threatened the financial stability of the city itself.[26] The funding of the debts of the former villages had saddled the city with obligations from the outset; and the expenditures incident to improving a new city, especially since it was possible to issue bonds when two-thirds of the voters consented at a special election, soon increased the figure. Credit loaned to railroads, beginning in 1849, had reached $234,000 by May 1851.[27] Ward expenditures and special assessments added to the burden of the taxpayer and put him at the mercy of aldermen who voted street and wharf improvements for which from two-thirds to all of the cost was charged to the owners of the abutting property.[28] The fact that the wards as well as the city could contract debts—a consequence of the ward sectionalism that was a continuing plague to Milwaukee's urban administration—only compounded the difficulty.

Kilbourn, Sweet, Prentiss, Kneeland, and Walker participated in a meeting of taxpayers which as early as January 1849 proposed charter changes which would limit city taxes and check the enthusiasm of the spendthrift aldermen;[29] but the municipal debt continued to mount until it reached $400,000 in 1851.[30] Meanwhile, in June 1850, the council had authorized a committee to have the charter revised in such a way as to place a check on excessive expenditures and strengthen the city's power to meet its obligations; and before the proposals were published or voted on in the city, Alderman Walker, then a member of the assembly, reported the revision to the State legislature for action.[31] This reputedly high-handed method of instigating charter changes became a political issue; and the city's foreign-born were conspicuous at a meeting at which

[26] See chapter 8 for details.
[27] Larson, *Financial and Administrative History*, 50-51.
[28] *Ibid.*, 32-34.
[29] Milwaukee *Sentinel and Gazette*, Jan. 9, 16, 30, 1849.
[30] Larson, *Financial and Administrative History*, 52.
[31] Milwaukee *Sentinel and Gazette*, Feb. 11, 1851.

the restricting proposals were condemned. They regarded as especially undemocratic the proposed change in the suffrage requirements, by which a year's residence was made a prerequisite for voting; the increased authority granted to the mayor; and the imposition of a second branch of the municipal legislature, admittedly designed to impose a brake on aldermanic action.[32]

When the proposed charter changes were finally submitted to the electorate on May 6, 1851, they were defeated by a decisive majority, with the strongest opposition coming from the predominantly foreign-born Second Ward;[33] but the proponents of reform were generally successful in the municipal election held two weeks later. Joining forces as a People's Ticket, the Whigs and the conservative Democrats elevated Walker to the mayoralty. They were, however, unable to elect German-born August Greulich as treasurer, in spite of the fact that he was supported by a conservative wing of Milwaukee Germanism and its organ, the *Volkshalle*.[34] The opponents of Walker and the "reform council," speaking through the columns of the *Volksfreund*, charged that the pioneer candidate was the speculators' choice and that his election would bring about the surrender to the stockholders of the private obligations by which the railroads had secured their debt to the city. They asserted, also, that Walker was conniving to develop the harbor in the vicinity of his own "hitherto worthless" property and that of other speculators rather than at the "straight-cut" and, moreover, that if he were elected, street grades would be established "as the rich may desire."[35]

Such reactions did not permanently defeat the movement for reform; and charter revision was at last realized by a two to one vote in February 1852.[36] Drafted this time by a popularly elected convention which met in August 1851, the new charter

[32] *Ibid.*, Feb. 8, 1851.
[33] *Ibid.*, May 7, 1851.
[34] Koss, *Milwaukee*, 342.
[35] *Volksfreund*, June 9, 1851, quoted in Milwaukee *Sentinel and Gazette*, June 19, 1851.
[36] The only dissenting ward was the Second, where the charter was opposed by a vote of 353 to 184. Milwaukee *Daily Sentinel and Gazette*, Feb. 3, 1852.

imposed some checks upon the behavior of the council, simplified the administration of municipal finances, and, moving in the direction of an expressed desire to unite the wards "into one city in fact, as they are in interest," centralized the authority of the municipal government by prohibiting the representatives of the individual wards from vetoing acts of the council or negating the vote of the electorate.[37] The provision for an appointive comptroller guaranteed a more efficient supervision of municipal expenditures; and similar economies were expected to result from a regulation holding members of the council personally accountable for ward debts contracted in excess of the amount levied for current ward expenses. The lengthening of the term of half of the councilors to two years was designed to produce a more continuously responsible municipal legislature; but the provision designating them as street commissioners provided an opportunity for continued graft and extravagance.[38]

The conservative coalition, acting through the People's Ticket, retained its control of the mayoralty in the municipal election of 1852. Walker endorsed as his successor Hans Crocker, who had presided over the charter convention of 1851.[39] According to the *Sentinel,* his election marked a victory for "the merchants, mechanics, and business men of our city," and showed what they could accomplish when they stood "together for the honor and welfare of Milwaukee."[40] In his inaugural address, Crocker admonished the council to accept seriously the powers granted it under the new charter and revealed his own philosophy of government in asserting that with respect to street and sidewalk improvements, it was

well known that individuals can at all times perform the work contemplated . . . at . . . much less expense than a corporate body; and in a majority of instances . . . property-holders

---

[37] Milwaukee *Sentinel and Gazette,* July 11, 1851.

[38] Larson, *Financial and Administrative History,* 54-56.

[39] Hans Crocker, a native of Ireland, came to Milwaukee in 1836. He edited the Milwaukee *Advertiser,* served as private secretary to Governor Henry Dodge, sat in the territorial council, and practiced law in the city. Milwaukee *Sentinel,* July 14, 1937.

[40] Milwaukee *Daily Sentinel,* March 1, 3, 1852.

will cheerfully, if due time be allowed, perform the part assigned to them. . . . No city can prosper where her credit is impaired, or where taxation becomes a burthen. They depress industry and enterprize [sic] at home, and discourage immigration and the influx of capital from abroad.[41]

With such a policy of municipal spending, the financial condition of the city naturally improved. In June 1852, the New York *Tribune* was quoting Milwaukee city bonds at 109;[42] and by the end of January 1853, Cicero Comstock, the first comptroller, reported that taxes were being paid and that the financial status of the municipality was good.[43] In February 1853, an amendment to the charter made the offices of city attorney and comptroller annually elective and provided that one railroad commissioner was to be chosen in each ward. The comptroller was to receive $1,500 a year.[44]

Railroad expansion and the reawakened enthusiasm for city improvement which swept the Mississippi Valley in the middle fifties called the tune of municipal politics from 1853 to 1857. Walker owed his reelection in 1853 in part to the continued strength of the conservatives organized again as the People's Ticket, and in part to his support of the pioneer Milwaukee and Mississippi Railroad in a controversy with a proposed Fond du Lac line. The latter allegedly was favored by James Kneeland whom a group of dissenting Democrats put up in opposition to Walker.[45] The *Daily Wisconsin* criticized the condition of the streets and sidewalks under the "economy régime" of the People's Ticket. It held that "a good government consists not in economy merely but rather in that the People obtain the full value of every dollar expended."[46] In spite of this criticism, all of Walker's running

[41] *Ibid.*, March 11, 1852.
[42] Quoted, *ibid.*, June 10, 1852.
[43] *Ibid.*, Jan. 31, 1853.
[44] "An act to amend an act entitled 'An Act to consolidate and amend the Act to incorporate the City of Milwaukee and the several Acts amendatory thereof, Approved February 20th, 1852.' . . . Approved Feb'y 18th, 1853," quoted, *ibid.*, Feb. 24, 1853.
[45] *Ibid.*, March 3, 1853; Buck, 3:429-31.
[46] *Daily Wisconsin* (Milwaukee), March 1, 1853, quoted in Milwaukee *Daily Sentinel*, March 7, 1853.

mates were chosen, including Comstock as comptroller, except the candidate for city marshal, who lost to the veteran Democrat, Tim O'Brien. In his inaugural address, Walker warned the council against loaning the credit of the city to speculative railroad ventures, the support of which would stand in the way of legitimate enterprises.[47]

The question of municipal support for other than the pioneer line of which Walker was one of the directors was the issue that severed the political hold of the People's Ticket and brought into power the more popular wing of the Democracy that was to control the party and the city for most of the ensuing fifteen years. In January 1853, Byron Kilbourn, having broken with the pioneer line, attempted to commit the city to the support of the Milwaukee and La Crosse Railroad. When his proposals were rejected by a meeting dominated by friends of the Milwaukee and Mississippi, Kilbourn turned to the liberal branch of the Democracy and the German Second Ward for aid. Upham, Huebschmann, and A. R. R. Butler were the officers of a meeting at the Market Hall where a loan of the city's credit to the La Crosse road was endorsed.[48] This situation widened the gulf that already existed between the two wings of the Democratic Party. In a hotly contested mayoral campaign in 1854, Kilbourn defeated Walker, the People's Ticket candidate, by a vote of 2,340 to 1,760.[49] Leaders that appealed to the dissident Second Ward and the less conservative, working-class Democracy had achieved a control which they were to retain, with slight interruption, for many years. Kilbourn found it to his advantage to lend his support to these so-called "Regular" Democrats, and his successor, J. B. Cross, following the pioneer speculator's lead, served as mayor for three terms.[50]

The boss of the council during the régime of the "Regular" Democracy was Jackson Hadley, an aggressive party politician

[47] *Ibid.,* March 9, 1853.
[48] Buck, 3:416-17.
[49] Milwaukee *Daily Sentinel,* March 8, 1854; Buck, 4:26, 29.
[50] Cross was a native of Geneva, New York. He came to Milwaukee in 1841. Milwaukee *Sentinel,* July 14, 1937.

LEADING FIGURES OF THE DEVELOPING CITY. Top row: Alexander Mitchell, banker and railroad promoter, and Edward D. Holton, commission merchant. *Middle row:* John Plankinton, pioneer industrialist. *Bottom row:* Rufus King, journalist and civic promoter, and Franz Huebschmann, German physician and political leader.

who was associated with the La Crosse railroad enterprise in which Kilbourn was interested and who built his political machine out of the laborers and contractors who were the chief beneficiaries of the current craze for municipal improvements.[51] With decisions on these matters left to more than a dozen elected and untrained aldermen, graft was inevitable. It was an understatement when Mayor Cross asserted that these officials did not have sufficient "nerve and firmness" to resist the contractors;[52] and collusion among the members of this trade made a joke of the principle of granting contracts to the lowest bidder. Between December 17, 1856, and December 1, 1857, the city's bonded debt was increased by $482,000; and at the beginning of 1858 it stood at nearly $700,000—more than twenty times what it had been seven years earlier. The floating debt, which had accumulated because current expenses and interest were not being paid, had reached $223,000.09 by 1857; and loans to railroad companies aggregated $1,614,000 in the following year. The total indebtedness of $2,500,000 was out of all proportion to the $6,000,000 assessed value of the young city.[53]

The reaction to this debt and to the enormous tax of 1857, greater than that of the five previous years combined, led to disclosures of frightful extravagance and even corruption on the part of the municipal officials. It was shown that "the aldermen and other city officers" had "been interested in and . . .

[51] Jackson Hadley, a native of Livingston County, New York, arrived in Milwaukee in 1844. From the time of his arrival he was one of the city's most influential politicians. A henchman of Kilbourn in connection with the La Crosse and Milwaukee Railroad, he resembled the pioneer speculator in "the ability to plan as well as carry out vast schemes for public improvement as well as for self-aggrandisement." He served on the city council from 1852 to 1858, in the assembly during 1854, 1865, and 1866, and in the senate in 1855 and 1856. He was reelected to the senate in 1866. John H. Tweedy referred to him as an "openly and notoriously corrupt man," and in the opinion of General J. H. Paine he was a "wily demagogue." Buck, 4:253-54, 283.

[52] Milwaukee *Daily Sentinel*, April 23, 1857. Mayor Cross, in his inaugural address of this year, admitted that contracts had been countersigned when there were not sufficient ward revenues to meet the cost and that graveling and paving contracts had recently become so lucrative that "quite a large portion of the laboring community, either as contractors or day laborers," had "turned their attention to that business."

[53] Larson, *Financial and Administrative History*, 72-75.

derived large profits from, contracts for different works of public improvement."⁵⁴ It appeared that Mayor Cross had charged the city $2,600 for offices in 1857, an item of expenditure which had averaged $385 in the earlier fifties. Payments for books and printing had leaped from $588.35 in 1852 to $7,000 in 1857. There had been a similar boost in salaries;⁵⁵ and even the unsalaried aldermen were accumulating fortunes from questionable sources. Comptroller Gardiner reported that the city's creditors frequently never saw bills which the aldermen submitted—at "about double the just amount of the claim so that the faithful public officer might pocket the surplus."⁵⁶ Moreover, bills were frequently presented without specifying the time when or the place where the work was performed, thus "rendering it impossible to ascertain whether it may not be a duplicate of a former account." Cases had come to the comptroller's attention in which bills had been "twice presented and approved by the Local Committee of some of the Wards, for the same identical work done and paid for."⁵⁷

From 1855 to 1857, King of the *Sentinel* attempted to marshal the opposition to the extravagance and corruption of the party in power; but it was not easy to get able men to run for office, and the People's Ticket made little headway against the undisputed majority of the "Regular" Democracy. Cicero Comstock was the People's candidate for mayor in 1855. In 1856 they proposed Daniel Newhall, but when he declined, the reformers had to fall back on the Democratic incumbent, Mayor Cross.⁵⁸ In some of the wards, reformers' caucuses succeeded in nominating worthy men for the ward offices.⁵⁹ In 1857 both parties settled again upon Mayor Cross; but a call for the candidacy of William A. Prentiss, economy-minded alderman from the Seventh Ward, forecast what was to happen in the interests of retrenchment in the following year.⁶⁰

⁵⁴ Milwaukee *Daily Sentinel*, March 23, 1857.
⁵⁵ Larson, *Financial and Administrative History*, 61; Milwaukee *Daily Sentinel*, Jan. 14, 1858.
⁵⁶ *Ibid.*, June 27, 1857.
⁵⁷ E. L'H. Gardiner to Mayor and Common Council, June 22, 1857, *ibid.*, June 27, 1857.
⁵⁸ Buck, 4:74, 147n.
⁵⁹ Milwaukee *Daily Sentinel*, March 29, 1856.
⁶⁰ *Ibid.*, March 27, April 7, 1857.

"Boss" Hadley and the "tax-eating" aldermen were the objects of attack at a series of reform meetings, the first of which was held on November 17, 1857, at Albany Hall. The movement, managed by Tweedy, Huebschmann, and the editor of the *Sentinel*, enlisted the support of both Republicans and Democrats, both native and foreign-born.[61] The Second Ward, usually solidly "Regular," had a political as well as an economic grievance; for in the recent choice of a nominee for governor the Democrats had chosen Cross over Huebschmann.[62] The Albany Hall assemblage condemned the council for destroying the safeguards of the original charter with respect to contracting debts, for issuing bonds in aid of railroads without the security required by law, and for so reducing the credit of the city that its bonds were selling at the rate of 50 cents on the dollar.[63] A committee, composed of Charles K. Watkins, Huebschmann, Crocker, Nathan Pereles, Andrew Mitchell, Comstock, Tweedy, S. B. Davis, and Charles Quentin, was chosen to make a thorough investigation of the city's finances for report at a future meeting.[64]

The Albany Hall movement resulted in the enactment of charter amendments which at last imposed really positive checks upon the independent and self-interested behavior of the municipal council.[65] A bicameral legislature, composed of annually elected aldermen (one from each ward) and biennially chosen councilors (two from each ward), was devised as a means of delaying legislation and checking excessive appropriations. The substitution of three elected street commissioners for the twenty-seven aldermen who formerly acted in that capacity was de-

---

[61] *Ibid.*, Nov. 9, 10, 12, 1857; Buck, 4:222-25.

[62] Ernest Bruncken, "The Political Activity of Wisconsin Germans, 1854-60," Wisconsin Historical Society, *Proceedings*, 1901, p. 201. The strength of the foreign-born element in the urban electorate had been revealed in 1857 when August Greulich and Edward O'Neill, prominent German and Irishman respectively, were sent to the senate from Milwaukee city and county. Buck, 4:187.

[63] *Ibid.*, 4:223-25, 311.

[64] Milwaukee *Daily Sentinel*, Dec. 18, 1857.

[65] Among the amendments proposed in 1856 was one which would have strengthened the hand of the mayor by extending his term to two years and granting him a veto power that would have required a two-thirds vote of the council to override. This type of veto was finally achieved in 1861. *Ibid.*, Jan. 28, 1856; Gregory, *History*, 1:253.

signed to do away with the "plundering schemes" for street improvement which had resulted from the personal interest of the aldermen in the contracts. According to the *Sentinel*, if Alderman Hadley were deprived of his street commissionership he "could no longer muster his little army of graders, officered by his contractors, and march them to Democratic Caucuses to secure his nomination, or to the polls to carry his election, or to Albany Hall to disturb and break up a taxpayers' meeting." Three assessors, chosen by the mayor and council to act for the whole city, were to replace the existing group of assessors elected in the wards, each of whom had tried "to make the best bargain for his own ward" and not infrequently had done "a little business on his own account."[66] The mayor was given a veto, although it could be overridden by a majority of each board. In addition, limits were placed on the amount of annual revenue to be raised, and provisions were made for curtailing salaries and other administrative expenses.[67]

In spite of delaying tactics on the part of Hadley and his henchmen, the proposed amendments were carried to the legislature in time for passage in 1858.[68] The ensuing months saw continued discussion of charter changes and finally a thoroughgoing, committee-drafted revision in the interest of retrenchment, economy, and greater responsibility on the part of the municipal officials.[69] However, its vagueness on the question of debt and the suggestion that it implied repudiation led to its rejection by a large majority in every ward on February 1, 1859.[70] Even the *Sentinel* was opposed on the grounds that the charter was inadequate to the city's needs, loosely put together, no solution of the financial dilemma, and destructive of the interests of the fire department.[71]

The disclosures of the Albany Hall reformers and, more

---

[66] Milwaukee *Daily Sentinel*, March 17, 1858.

[67] The limit on revenue to be raised yearly for city purposes was $175,000. Larson, *Financial and Administrative History*, 79-80; Gregory, *History*, 1:252-54.

[68] See *Wisconsin Session Laws (Local)*, 1858, chap. 117; Milwaukee *Daily Sentinel*, March 11, 1858.

[69] *Ibid.*, March 13, 15, 16, 17, 19, 25, 26, 27, April 2, 19, July 26, 27, 30, Aug. 2, 3, 10, 18, 19, Sept. 15, Nov. 18, Dec. 2, 23, 28, 1858; Jan. 11, 1859.

[70] Buck, 4:303; Larson, *Financial and Administrative History*, 80.

[71] Milwaukee *Daily Sentinel*, Feb. 1, 1859.

importantly, the disaffection of the German voters from the "Regular" Democracy brought momentary victory for the reform, or People's Ticket, in the municipal election of April 6, 1858.[72] William A. Prentiss, whose concern for retrenchment as alderman from the Seventh Ward had kept him in the minority in the "tax-eaters' council," was chosen mayor over A. R. R. Butler by a majority of 1,079;[73] and the People's Ticket for aldermen was victorious in seven of the nine wards.[74] From his position in the council, however, Hadley sniped unceasingly at Prentiss, charging that the mayor had failed to account for money and bonds used in an alleged attempt to resolve the city's financial difficulties and chiding the mayor for his failure to keep his campaign promises. By the close of his term, Prentiss had cleared himself of the charges of malfeasance, but he was unable to report much progress in the direction of financial recovery. In spite of rigid economy, the disrepute of the city's securities in the East and the failure "on the part of a considerable portion of the property owners to meet promptly the heavy tax levy for 1857" had prevented him from retiring much of the legacy of debt which the Cross administration had left him.[75]

In the ensuing municipal election the customary strength of the Democratic machine reasserted itself; as a result, the reformers were turned out, and the "Regular" Democrats returned to power. A ticket which listed John G. Inbusch for mayor and Cicero Comstock for comptroller fell before one headed by Herman L. Page and including, for comptroller, the same E. L'H. Gardiner in whose previous term the value of the city's bonds had fallen to 50 cents on the dollar.[76] The failure of the People's Ticket in this election convinced many of its supporters, who now voted Republican in national politics, that it was time to organize under the Republican banner in municipal politics, as well. "The experiment of 'People's

[72] *Ibid.*, April 7, 1858.
[73] Milwaukee *Sentinel*, July 14, 1937.
[74] Bruncken, "Political Activity of Wisconsin Germans," Wis. Hist. Soc., *Proc.*, 1901, pp. 201-2; Milwaukee *Daily Sentinel*, April 7, 1858.
[75] Buck, 4:280-82, 303-5; Milwaukee *Daily Sentinel*, April 15, 1859.
[76] Buck, 4:309-11.

Tickets,'" commented the *Sentinel,* "has been fully and fairly tried in this city and proved a failure. The Republicans must now organize on a distinctive party platform, as our Democratic friends always do, and trust to the merits of their cause for success."[77]

Although developments in the national scene were drawing a considerable number of Milwaukeeans into the Republican camp, the Wisconsin city was destined never to offer a very congenial environment for the new party. Most of the pioneer founders of the city had been identified with the party of Jefferson, and only on rare occasions did the European element waver in its loyalty to the party that was traditionally pledged to democracy and temperamentally devoid of the temperance tendencies and nativist prejudices of its Whig opponents.[78] Two wings of local opinion were potential recruits for a party in opposition to the Democracy. Many merchants and businessmen were attracted by Whig promises of river and harbor improvements at federal expense; and their support of the Whig position increased as Southern-dominated executives vetoed measures of commercial advantage to the West.[79]

At the same time, the free soil and abolition issues were gaining an increasing audience in the community. Church organizations had begun to express their opposition to slavery as early as 1836. In 1842 Asahel Finch and William P. Lynde aided in the escape of a fugitive slave; and Finch, Holton, and others joined the Territorial Liberty Association, organized in that year. By the late forties Sherman Booth was editing an abolition paper in the city, and friction over the slavery issue had resulted in the establishment of the Free Congregational Church with Holton as a prominent trustee.[80]

The emotions of the abolitionist reformers and the ambitions of improvement-minded commercial promoters thus com-

[77] Milwaukee *Daily Sentinel,* April 9, 1859.

[78] Hense-Jensen asserts that the "Beer Question" largely dictated the choice of political parties, even among well-educated immigrants. More Germans might have joined the antislavery movement if it had not also included the temperance advocates. Hense-Jensen, Schafer tr., chap. 4, pp. 3-4.

[79] Milwaukee *Daily Sentinel and Gazette,* Oct. 28, Nov. 3, 7, 1848.

[80] Gregory, *History,* 2:741-44.

bined to foment sentiments hostile to the South and to the Democratic Party. The issue came to a head in February 1854, when a public meeting, called by King, Kilbourn, Holton, and more than a hundred others, protested the bill permitting slavery in the territories of Kansas and Nebraska. Thousands of citizens signed remonstrances against the "Nebraska Swindle" which were to be forwarded to Washington. The apprehension of a fugitive slave named Glover from the county jail and the arrest of Sherman Booth for abetting the act only added to the excitement.[81] At an ensuing organizational meeting of the Republican Party, held at Madison, July 13, 1854, many Milwaukee Whigs were represented; and it was not long before the wedding of emotion and interest was symbolized in an assertion by the Republican press that a vote for the Republican nominees in 1856 was a vote against "the Nebraska Iniquity, Slavery Extension, the River and Harbor veto, and the general misdoings of the Pierce Administration." In that year a number of Milwaukeeans, headed by Holton, determined to help hold Kansas for freedom. They offered equipment to such volunteers as would make the western trek; and on May 19, 1856, six ox-drawn wagons started out; but interest in their caravan was somewhat diverted to the fire department, which was parading at the same time.[82] In spite of the appeals of the new party and the fact that Republicanism carried the State for Frémont in 1856, nearly three-fourths of the Milwaukee vote went to Buchanan, the Democratic candidate for President. Jackson Hadley, though not elected in the district, was endorsed in Milwaukee by a vote of 6,987 to 2,796 over his opponent for Congress; and the Democrats chose the entire slate of assemblymen and sent August Greulich to the State senate by a vote of 3,572 to 1,168.[83]

Regardless of their efforts, the Republicans found small support among the German voters. The free soil issue was not without appeal for the liberty-loving German, but as early as 1848 Huebschmann and his cohorts had succeeded in identify-

[81] Milwaukee *Daily Sentinel*, Feb. 13, 27, June 8, 1854; Feb. 6, 1855.
[82] Gregory, *History*, 2:764.
[83] Conard, 1:84-85.

ing Cass, the Democratic candidate for President, with the principles of free soil, free vote, and free land, thus keeping most of the Germans on the Democratic side; and many Germans who might have endorsed the free soil movement shunned it because of the connection of many of its members with temperance activities.[84] Few Germans attended the organizational meeting of the Republicans, for the German press had refused to print a notice of the gathering; and some weeks later, Fratny, editor of the *Volksfreund,* described the new party as a "Holy alliance of . . . abolitionists, Whigs, Know-Nothings, Sunday and Cold Water Fanatics, etc."[85] Rufus King of the *Sentinel,* strongest proponent of the new party, made a practical attempt to win the support of the European element when he subsidized a German paper, the *Corsair,* as a Republican antidote to the three Democratic German papers then published in the city. King chose as the editor of the *Corsair* Bernhard Domschcke, a convinced liberal and opponent of slavery, who had come to Milwaukee in 1854. The *Corsair,* first published in October 1854, presented an enlightened view of Republicanism, but it had little attraction for the average German reader.[86]

Through the columns of the *Sentinel,* King tried to convince the Germans that they, too, should support the party that was proposing "to keep open the rich lands of our new territories, to the settlement of the free laborers who came from the Old World to build their homes among us."[87] In the excitement following John Brown's execution in December 1859, a meeting of German citizens resolved that if peaceful means of solving the slavery question should fail, revolutionary ones would "be perfectly justifiable," the blame to rest upon those who "persistently refuse to abolish, by means of reform, an institution that disgraces our century and this republic."[88] But these sentiments and the spirited endorsement of Lincoln's candidacy by some

[84] *Ibid.,* 1:83; Koss, *Milwaukee,* 269.
[85] Hense-Jensen, Schafer tr., chap. 4, p. 8; *Volksfreund,* quoted in Milwaukee *Daily Sentinel,* Sept. 9, 1854.
[86] J. J. Schlicher, "Bernhard Domschcke," *Wisconsin Magazine of History,* 29:325-30 (March 1946).
[87] Milwaukee *Daily Sentinel,* April 10, 1857.
[88] Bruncken, "Political Activity of Wisconsin Germans," Wis. Hist. Soc., *Proc.,* 1901, pp. 207-8. See also Milwaukee *Sentinel,* Jan. 22, April 21, Nov. 9, 1859.

of the Forty-eighters in 1860 were not sufficient to win over their more conservative countrymen, especially the many German Catholics who were suspicious of any cause with which the Freethinking *Acht und vierziger* were identified. As a result, not enough Germans were converted to Republicanism to reverse the normal political reaction; and in spite of a majority for Lincoln in the State at large, almost 58 percent of the Milwaukee vote went to Douglas, his Democratic opponent. The election nevertheless advanced the strength of Republicanism in the city. Four of the nine wards gave a small majority to Lincoln; and the city-wide majority for the Democracy was 901 as against 3,267 in the previous presidential campaign.[89]

The city's most storied tragedy—the "Lady Elgin" disaster —was an indirect consequence of passions excited during the slavery controversy and the presidential campaign of 1860. Members of the Union Guard, recruited from the Democratic Third Ward, found themselves disbanded by the Republican governor and deprived of arms and equipment as a result of their captain's assertion that he would support enforcement of the Fugitive Slave Law. On September 6, they chartered the "Lady Elgin" for an excursion to Chicago in the hope of raising money for equipment as well as to hear the Democratic candidate speak. It was on the return voyage, in the foggy night of September 7-8, that disaster struck. The 400 merrymakers were thrown into panic when a heavily laden lumber schooner thrust its prow into the excursion vessel; about 300 lives were lost with the sinking ship.[90]

The Democrats spared no efforts to win the municipal campaign of 1860, the first in which the opposition abandoned the subterfuge of a People's Ticket and stood openly as the Republican Party.[91] The Republicans made political capital of the

---

[89] Hense-Jensen, Schafer tr., chap. 4, p. 17; see also Joseph Schafer, "Who Elected Lincoln?" *American Historical Review*, 47:51-63 (October 1941); Buck, 4:400.

[90] Quaife, *Lake Michigan*, 256-61; Walter Havighurst, *The Long Ships Passing* (New York, 1942), 67-69.

[91] H. J. Paine, John Ritchie, E. W. Carpenter, John H. Tesch, George G. Houghton, and D. G. Rogers were among the most active of Milwaukee Republicans. In repudiating the resort to a people's movement, they asserted that such tickets were "always controlled and used by disappointed and unworthy aspirants for Democratic nominations." Milwaukee *Sentinel*, March 22, 1860.

official indiscretions of such officeholders as Comptroller Gardiner and City Clerk Lynch, both of whom had been indicted in this year, and of the alleged connection of the Democratic candidate for mayor with the city's excessive loans to railroad companies. They nominated Otis H. Waldo for mayor, Comstock for comptroller, and taking a cue from Democratic Party practices, a prominent German, John H. Tesch, for city treasurer. John Plankinton, Nathan Pereles, and ex-Mayor Prentiss were on their ticket for the municipal legislature. In an effort to win the German vote, the Republican press attempted to foment friction between the Irish and the Germans and asserted that the latter were the catspaws of the Irish in municipal politics.[92]

The Democrats countered with techniques that, throughout the sixties, were to keep Milwaukee "the banner Democratic city of the nation," according to their oft-repeated boast. In mass meetings of Germans and of laboring men, and in the inflammatory columns of the *Daily News,* they whipped up support for a ticket headed by the veteran Democratic wheelhorse, William P. Lynde. In the German wards the Teutonic citizens were exhorted in their own tongue to keep steadfast to the faith plighted in days gone by—before the Republicans had ruined the city's credit. "Let it be remembered," blazoned the *News* in boldface type, "that Otis H. Waldo was the attorney of James H. Rogers," by whose operations as receiver of the Germania Bank, "our German citizens were defrauded of the hard earnings of years." At other meetings, speakers praised the labor wing of the party—"the men of toil"; and one of their own number sought to convince his fellow-workers that laborers received better wages in Democratic than in Republican states. On election day, the *News* urged laboring men to bear in mind that "under Republican management and misrule your wages have been reduced to a mere pittance and you yourself forced to toil for a paltry sum, scarcely sufficient to keep body and soul together."[93] The Democrats also denied their candidate's

[92] *Ibid.,* March 23, 26, April 3, 1860; "German" to editor, *ibid.,* April 3, 1860.
[93] *Daily Milwaukee News,* April 1, 1860.

connection with railroad expenditures, and to counter charges of Democratic corruption they compared the admitted possibility of petty thefts by Democratic city officials with Republican Governor Bashford's $50,000 railroad steal. "Keep it before the People," wrote the editor of the *News*, "that every dollar of our railroad loans were [*sic*] assumed under the advice of men in the opposition," and that "the Republican party is a conglomeration of Aristocrats, nabobs, abolitionists, and know-nothings."[94] This barrage of propaganda kept the city in the Democratic column, but with considerably less than the customary majority. The disaffection of some of the German voters in the Second, Third, and Ninth wards brought a victory for Tesch, the Republican candidate for treasurer, over George G. Dousman; but because of alleged legal obstacles put in his way by the otherwise Democratic city officials it was some time before he could take over the office.[95]

Preoccupation with the problems presented by the Civil War prevented Milwaukee's businessmen from interfering seriously with the Democrats' management of city affairs between 1861 and 1865. A unanimity, which Republicans viewed as the outward sign of machine politics, characterized the conventions at which the Democratic candidates were nominated. The Republicans attempted to induce John Plankinton to run for the mayoralty in 1861; but when he refused for "business reasons," they resorted to selecting what they considered the best men of both parties and ran them on a Union Ticket. This accounted for their endorsement of James S. Brown and Ferdinand Kuehn, Democratic nominees for mayor and comptroller.[96] They favored Tesch over Joseph Phillips for treasurer, predicting that if the latter won, the city funds would be removed from Alexander Mitchell's custody to the Second

[94] *Ibid.*, March 31, April 1, 1860.
[95] Buck, 3:307-8, 308n. William P. Lynde, a native New Yorker, had come to Milwaukee in 1841 after his admission to the New York bar. He had a long career in territorial, state, national, and municipal politics. In his inaugural address he asserted his opposition to excessive expenditures, on the ground that "all taxes in the end come from the laboring classes; that the laboring man bears alone the burden of government." Milwaukee *Free Press*, Aug. 17, 1913.
[96] Milwaukee *Sentinel*, July 14, 1937.

Ward Bank. The results of an unusually quiet election on April 3 were a sweeping victory for the Democrats with all city officers elected and an increased majority in the council.[97]

The "Regular" Democracy triumphed again in 1862 when the pioneer settler Horace Chase was chosen as mayor over William B. Hibbard.[98] More than 250 representative businessmen, including Alexander Mitchell, Lindsey Ward, C. F. Ilsley, William Prentiss, and J. J. Tallmadge, signed the petition urging Hibbard to head a Union Ticket which coupled Tesch, Republican candidate for treasurer, with Democrats Kuehn and La Due for comptroller and city attorney. The *News* won votes for the pioneer Democratic candidate by ambiguously identifying Hibbard with a Captain E. C. Hibbard whose Zouaves had at one time been called out to quell a riot of German citizens. According to the *Sentinel*, "This assertion was made to incense the Germans of the northern wards, and later in the day handbills in German were circulated in these wards, reminding the citizens that W. B. Hibbard charged upon the Germans who were trying to get their just dues from the banks.[99]

A still more "cut and dried" situation prevailed in 1863 and 1864 when the Republicans put no opposition in the field against the dominant Democracy. The election of the ticket headed by Edward O'Neill, in 1863, was a "jug-handle affair—all on one side," to quote the *Sentinel;* and a quiet election on April 5, 1864—without "two parties to make a quarrel"—brought victory for a Democratic ticket that included Abner Kirby for mayor, Kuehn for comptroller, Michael Bodden of the *Seebote* for treasurer, and James G. Jenkins as city attorney. Union men professed to be relatively content with the administrative record of the incumbent Democrats and complained that the right kind of men of their party, who could be elected, refused to make the sacrifice to run. According to the *News*, these developments in the "Banner Democratic City" were evidence that "outside a small circle of politicians influenced

[97] *Daily Milwaukee Press and News,* April 2, 3, 1861; Milwaukee *Sentinel,* March 29, 30, April 1, 2, 1861.

[98] Horace Chase was one of the city's earliest settlers. A native of Vermont, he arrived in Milwaukee in 1834. *Ibid.,* July 14, 1937.

[99] *Ibid.,* March 31, April 1, 2, 3, 1862.

by official patronage, Mr. Lincoln and his policy have no friends in the metropolis of Wisconsin."[100]

This dictum of the *News* was of course a one-sided and partisan interpretation of the reaction of Milwaukee to the American Civil War. From the outset of cityhood, the youthful community had accepted without question its right and its obligation to share the problems of the developing nation. At the same time the presence of so many European newcomers probably limited the enthusiasm and unanimity with which national crises might otherwise have been met. Hardly had cityhood been achieved when the nation's need was felt in connection with the Mexican War. The military companies—both German and American—expressed an eagerness for action,[101] but delay on the part of the War Department in accepting the offer of troops as well as resentments stirred in the controversy over the State constitution ultimately cooled their enthusiasm. A company finally departed on May 2, 1847, escorted to the pier by the Washington Guard, the German riflemen, the mayor, and the common council. Additional recruits were sent in 1847 and 1848; and on the home front a third German company and an artillery company of Americans with Rufus King as captain were formed.[102] Secession, a dozen years later, and the consequent firing on Fort Sumter precipitated a national crisis of immeasurably greater moment on which Milwaukeeans were forced to take a stand.

Sunday duties were forgotten as news came of the Confederate attack on federal property on April 14, 1861; and knots of men gathered anxiously to discuss the reports. On Monday, a mass meeting, presided over by Dr. Weeks, John Nazro, E. H. Brodhead, G. W. Allen, Huebschmann, Allis, Newhall, and other prominent citizens, resolved to support the administration. Four days later the city was festooned with the national colors—"even the windows of the houses in Kilbourntown"

[100] *Ibid.*, March 31, April 1, 3, 5, 7, 8, 1864; *Daily Milwaukee News*, April 2, 6, 1864.

[101] Koss, *Milwaukee*, 223.

[102] See H. W. Bleyer, "Wisconsin in the Mexican War," Milwaukee *Sentinel*, Aug. 13, 1899, and J. L. Loomis, "Captain Quarles Leads Company F to Mexico," *Wisconsin Magazine of History*, 27:170-77 (December 1943).

(the German section); and at the recruiting station in the Light Guard Armory the "anxiety to enlist" was very great.[103] Even the editor of the *Daily Milwaukee Press and News,* who early in April had blamed unsettled economic conditions on Republican policies and later had favored appeasing the Confederacy by compromise, now advocated vigorous prosecution of the war, "once commenced."[104] Within two weeks, seven companies had reported themselves ready for service, among them both American and German military organizations; a home guard, to protect and preserve order in the city, had been formed; funds had been raised for the families of the volunteers; and the women of the community, assuming the national colors in their dress, had begun to sew uniforms for the soldiers. By fall a drive was on for contributions to the national loan—"something as important as the soldier on the Potomac or the Mississippi is doing"—and at 7 3/10 percent interest. Benefits of all kinds, including a bock beer sale which netted $100, swelled the volunteers' fund. Many Milwaukee women threatened to boycott stores employing men eligible for the army; and their daughters promised to forego the attentions of all but Union volunteers.[105] More importantly, they packed boxes of bedding, clothing, vegetables, and fruit, sending them to the front through the auspices of the Wisconsin Aid Society, and gathered at a branch of the United States Sanitary Commission to prepare lint, then used in place of absorbent cotton, roll bandages, and make comfort bags, knit goods, quilts, and blankets for the troops.[106]

Soon Milwaukee manhood was contributing to the preservation of the Union, although not with the most whole-hearted enthusiasm. The first rush of volunteering was short-lived; and as early as the winter of 1861-62 resort was made to the offer of bounties, a method of encouraging enlistment which increased in popularity as quotas multiplied and a draft im-

---

[103] Milwaukee *Daily Sentinel,* April 13, 15, 19, 1861.

[104] *Daily Milwaukee Press and News,* April 12, 14, 17, 19, 21, 1861.

[105] Milwaukee *Daily Sentinel,* April 22, 23, 24, 26, May 20, Aug. 15, Oct. 6, Nov. 19, 1861; Milwaukee *Morning Sentinel,* June 25, Sept. 21, Oct. 2, 1861.

[106] Ethel A. Hurn, *Wisconsin Women in the War between the States* (Wisconsin History Commission, Original Paper no. 6, Madison, 1911), 18-48.

pended. Opposition to the idea of conscription helped the Chamber of Commerce raise a fund of more than $12,000 to provide a new regiment in July 1862; to this amount the members of the chamber and the Merchants' Association added enough to make a $50 bounty available to each volunteer.[107]

In August, Mitchell, Ilsley, and Brodhead were constituted a Central War Committee to collect money to be used in furthering enlistment; but by November there was nothing to do but accept conscription. Rioting in Ozaukee County and an anti-draft parade in Milwaukee on November 8, 1862, caused some apprehension as to the success of this method of raising troops; but on November 19, with the military companies prominently stationed and the roads picketed, the draft proceeded without disturbance.[108]

The draft was still, however, not an inescapable obligation upon Milwaukee's manhood. As it then operated, it was used only in those wards which could fill their quotas in no other way; and because drafted men could furnish a substitute or pay $300 in commutation money, service could still be evaded by raising this amount or by joining draft protective associations which pooled the cost of commutation. Such groups were organized in the various wards and among the workers in certain plants.[109] Some resistance was experienced during enrollment for the draft of 1863; and commenting on an expected riot, Captain Tillepaugh asserted that a large proportion of the predominantly foreign population of the city was and always had been "opposed to the war and the government."[110] In spite of his fears, all was quiet when the draft itself occurred. According to the *Sentinel*, the "utmost good nature prevailed. . . . As the successive drawings were completed it was the

[107] Jerome A. Watrous, ed., *Memoirs of Milwaukee County* (2 vols., Madison, 1909), 1:595. This work will hereafter be cited as Watrous. See also Milwaukee *Daily Sentinel*, July 29, 30, Aug. 9, 11, 12, 13, 1862.

[108] *Ibid.*, Aug. 11, 25, Nov. 10, 1862; Lynn I. Schoonover, A History of the Civil War Draft in Wisconsin, pp. 20-21, unpublished Ph.M. thesis, dated 1915, in the library of the University of Wisconsin. This work will hereafter be cited as Schoonover.

[109] Milwaukee *Daily Sentinel*, Nov. 21, 1862.

[110] *Official Records of the Union and Confederate Armies* (Washington, 1880-1901), quoted in Schoonover, 49.

signal for a cheer on the part of those who had escaped the fortune of the wheel." At the same time the demand for substitutes became so great as to raise the price to $800 in 1864. It was consistent with the prevailing sectionalism of the community that the wards should have collected the money to procure substitutes; and not until 1864 did the city and county pay bounties to encourage enlistment, something which had been begun in Madison in December 1863. Even then city promotion was the excuse for the proposal, since it was claimed that if the city and county paid such bounties, immigration would be drawn to a community that made exemption possible for its residents.[111]

In the election of 1864, Lincoln received less support from Milwaukeeans than he had in 1860. More than two-thirds of the popular vote went to McClellan, the opposition candidate; and in the German wards, especially, there was little enthusiasm for "the great Emancipator." This coolness toward federal policies sprang from several causes. Their lack of understanding of the issues and their remoteness from the national government precluded the development of marked concern in many of the foreign-born newcomers, in view especially of their traditional loyalty to the Democratic Party, their distaste for the curtailment of liberty which the war imposed, and the divisive frictions which kept the urban community separated on the subject. The *Daily Milwaukee News* whipped up partisan antagonism to Lincoln and pointed to federal usurpations as spelling the doom of the Union.[112] And to the machine-dominated opposition of the Democracy was added the desire of the urban community for the restoration of normal commercial intercourse, even at the cost of compromise.

Public sentiment being what it was, it is not surprising that at the news of Appomattox, received on April 10, 1865, the city was "one vast lunacy of joy." According to the press, "all the Fourths of July since 1776 rolled into one were not a comparison." With business suspended, processions filled the

[111] Milwaukee *Daily Sentinel*, Nov. 11, 1863; Schoonover, 67; Milwaukee *Sentinel*, Jan. 23, Feb. 16, 18, 20, 22, 26, 29, March 11, 30, April 1, Aug. 1, 2, 8, Sept. 7, Nov. 18, 1864.

[112] *Daily Milwaukee News*, Nov. 12, 1864.

streets; and more than one effigy of Jefferson Davis hung to a "sour apple tree." Festoons of the national colors decorated the city by day, and bonfires and fireworks brightened it by night. "Every moving thing from street car to poodle dog wore the stars and stripes . . . and not a few took seriously the rumor that the mayor had issued a proclamation compelling every citizen to become drunk before three o'clock on pain of prosecution at the police court in the morning." Through it all, as expressed in both the *Sentinel* and the *News,* was the "promise of peace" and the hope that it might "be greeted in that spirit of patriotism, fraternity, and conciliation which alone can make real peace possible."[113]

Monday's joy was exchanged for Saturday's gloom as dispatches reported the assassination of President Lincoln. Public buildings and private residences were draped in mourning, and flags trimmed with crepe were displayed at half-mast. On Easter Sunday the churches were almost universally shrouded in black and white. A "grandly solemn" procession, in which all the associations of the city participated, took place on April 19, the day of the President's funeral.[114] While this incident tended to win additional support for the Republican Party, political opinion during the later sixties, vigorously interested in national issues, continued to be divided. The *Sentinel* "waved the bloody shirt" and upheld the program of Congressional reconstruction with respect to what it called "the insurrectionary states." On the other hand, the Democratic *Daily News* condemned a situation which made "the will of a political party to the North . . . the supreme law."[115] In national elections a majority of Milwaukeeans continued to support the Democracy, about 60 percent of the voters opposing President Grant in the elections of 1868 and 1872.

In the field of municipal politics, the "Banner Democratic City" ran true to form during the remainder of the sixties,

[113] Milwaukee *Daily Sentinel,* April 11, 1865; *Daily Milwaukee News,* April 11, 1865.
[114] Milwaukee *Daily Sentinel,* April 17, 1865; *Daily Milwaukee News,* April 21, 1865.
[115] Milwaukee *Daily Sentinel,* Oct. 19, Nov. 12, 1866; March 5, 6, 15, 1867; *Daily Milwaukee News,* Nov. 8, 1866.

except when there was dissension within the Democratic ranks. This occurred in April 1865, when J. J. Tallmadge, the People's candidate, defeated Dr. J. J. Orton for the mayoralty in an election in which the Democrats were otherwise victorious. According to the *Sentinel,* Tallmadge was "a pronounced Republican," but the following year saw his reelection at the head of an almost completely victorious Democratic ticket.[116] The most novel feature of the election of 1866 was the participation of Negro voters at the polls. "Some half a dozen voted in the Seventh Ward, 15 or 20 in the Fourth, and one in the Fifth and First," reported the *Sentinel.* "Several voted the democratic ward ticket, but the majority of them voted for the Union nominees whenever a ticket was in the field." No attempt was made to disturb them, but "a few curses followed several of them as they marched up to the polls."[117]

The chief tack of the opposition, between 1867 and 1870, was to concentrate on the undemocratic dictatorship of the Democratic city machine and the alleged inefficiency of its "rubber-stamp" candidates. Against such choices, without hope of success unless there should be "serious dissension in the Democratic ranks," the Republicans brought forward candidates represented as the kind of men you would "have manage your own business."[118] According to the *Sentinel,* the ticket produced by the convention of the "unterrified" in 1867 was the result of a deal between the Irish and the Germans. In spite of Tallmadge's successful record as mayor, O'Neill, a former incumbent, was nominated for that office in return for the choice of G. C. Trumpf and Fred Willmanns for treasurer and comptroller; and amid charges of illegal voting, the Republican candidates, headed by Asahel Finch, fell before what the *Sen-*

[116] Milwaukee *Daily Sentinel,* April 4, 5, 1865; March 14, 30, 31, April 2, 3, 1866; *Daily Milwaukee News,* April 1, 3, 4, 5, 1865; March 25, April 4, 1866. John J. Tallmadge, a native of New York, came to Milwaukee in 1855. After serving as agent of the Western Transportation Company for fifteen years, he engaged in the provisions and packing business. A prominent businessman and civic leader, he was one of the founders of the Milwaukee Chamber of Commerce and its president in 1863-64. Milwaukee *Sentinel,* Oct. 16, 1895; July 14, 1937.

[117] Milwaukee *Daily Sentinel,* April 4, 1866.

[118] *Ibid.,* April 6, 8, 1868. As early as 1860, the Republicans had extolled the virtues of "honest, experienced, and practical business men" as city officials. *Ibid.,* Feb. 18, March 9, 31, 1860.

tinel called the "Corruption-Copperhead-Shillelagh-Kneeland" ticket.[119] The Democrats gained an even more sweeping victory in 1868. The Republicans selected an able slate: John Plankinton, advertised as "one of our oldest and wealthiest citizens"; Peter Van Vechten, "honest, capable, hardworking business man"; John Pritzlaff, "one of our most highly esteemed German citizens—a business man of long standing," and others described as "occupying good positions in the business world." But so decisive was the Democratic landslide returning O'Neill to the mayoralty that the opposition made no nominations in the following year.[120]

The municipal campaign of 1870, though successful for the Democrats, closed the period of undisputed dominance for the Milwaukee Democracy. The city hall ring and the convention by which it forced its candidates upon the electorate were objects of attack. So, too, were its electioneering methods, which for years had involved multiple voting and the lavishing of lager beer upon what the *Sentinel* called "the unterrified, in all their unwashed splendor."[121] A convention which the *Sentinel* described as representing "the ward politicians and little else" nominated Joseph Phillips for mayor and, after a contest between the Germans and the Irish, Jeremiah Quinn for comptroller. The Republicans, gambling on a nonpartisan approach, reverted to what the *News* called the "poor dodge" of a People's Ticket and asserted that the new and costly enterprises then being projected by the city dictated the need of practical businessmen in public office.[122] Phillips' majority of 465 fell far short of the more than 2,000 lead to which the Democrats had been accustomed and approached the more evenly balanced political situation which was to prevail in the succeeding decade.[123]

[119] *Ibid.*, March 29, 30, April 1, 2, 3, 4, 1867; *Daily Milwaukee News*, March 29, April 2, 1867.
[120] Milwaukee *Daily Sentinel*, March 11, 27, April 4, 1868; April 1, 6, 1869; *Daily Milwaukee News*, April 7, 8, 1868.
[121] Milwaukee *Daily Sentinel*, March 11, April 3, 1868.
[122] *Ibid.*, April 2, 4, 1870; *Daily Milwaukee News*, March 31, April 2, 5, 1870.
[123] Milwaukee *Daily Sentinel*, April 6, 1870. Joseph Phillips, a native of Alsace, France, came to Milwaukee in 1842. He engaged in the insurance business and served for two terms as city treasurer before being elected mayor. Milwaukee *Sentinel*, July 14, 1937.

In spite of periodic criticisms by the Republicans of the high taxes, administrative inefficiencies, and extravagances of the Democratic régime, the sixties saw continued improvement in the city's financial situation until by 1869 Mayor O'Neill could contend, without too much opposition, that not a city in the United States could show "so encouraging a financial exhibit" as that of Milwaukee for the past year.[124] An empty municipal treasury in 1861 and a debt of $2,825,850 had prompted the appointment of prominent citizens and members of the council to develop a plan for the restoration of the city's credit. The resulting Readjustment Act, approved by the legislature on March 19, 1861, provided for the funding of the debt on a long-term basis, a task that was delegated to the Public Debt Commission, appointed for a three-year term by the mayor and council. Taxes were to be levied to pay the interest and provide a sinking fund; and it was decreed that the city should incur no debts of any sort until the amount of outstanding readjustment bonds was reduced to $500,000. The city began, also, to gain some returns on the loans to railroads that had caused financial troubles in the fifties. The legislature permitted the Public Debt Commission to dispose of the city's railroad stock; and by April 1866, $890,500 in railroad bonds had been canceled. Of the remaining $723,500, all issues were amply secured except bonds issued in the amount of $100,000 each to the Milwaukee and Superior and the Milwaukee and Beloit companies.[125]

The question of vesting authority in independent boards and commissions, similar to the Public Debt Commission, rather than in the ward councilors, became a major political issue in the sixties. Need for the reform sprang from the fact that within a year after the creation of an elective board of street commissioners, as a result of the Albany Hall reforms, the supervision of streets, gutters, sewers, and the like had been returned to the elected ward councilors. This took place in 1859 with the reversion of power from the Prentiss reform adminis-

---

[124] Milwaukee *Daily Sentinel*, April 1, 1869.
[125] Larson, *Financial and Administrative History*, 81-88.

tration to that of the "Regular" Democracy. The resulting evils were among the reasons leading to a charter convention which sat intermittently from May to October 1867 and which proposed a charter that reflected the increasing maturity of the urban community. The document proposed (1) the separation of the city from the remaining portion of the county, thus consolidating administration in one set of officials rather than two; (2) the abolition of the board of councilors along with the horde of other elective ward officials, thus achieving economy and reducing the sectional autonomy of the various wards; and (3) the vesting of responsibility for public works in an appointive board rather than in the elected ward councilors, thus curtailing inefficiency and graft and making possible a city-wide plan of street-grading and sewerage, something that hitherto had been obstructed by the ever-conflicting interests of the ward-conscious street commissioners.[126]

The opposing political factions responded in characteristic fashion to the proposed charter change. The *Sentinel* and the business interests it represented applauded the curtailment of offices and salaries and the creation of a professional board of public works; but they questioned the wisdom of abolishing the restraints inherent in a bicameral legislature. The office-holding Democrats cited the latter as the reason for their objection to the proposed changes; but according to the *Sentinel* "the real reason for their opposition" was to be found "in the fact that the care of our public works is taken away from them and given to the Board of Public Works, and the profits of contracts, etc., lost to them."[127] In the opinion of the Democratic organ, the *Daily News,* the proposal was a "radical scheme to revolutionize city government and change the location of power" as it was then distributed. "The citizens consider themselves as capable of electing street commissioners who shall transact the necessary business in the several wards," wrote its editor, "as the mayor would be of appointing a board of public works to do the same thing."[128] Considering the influence of

[126] Milwaukee *Daily Sentinel,* May 2, June 4, Oct. 11, 19, 1867.
[127] *Ibid.,* April 4, 1868.
[128] *Daily Milwaukee News,* Feb. 10, 1868.

the *News* and the strength of the party it represented, it is easy to understand why the proposed charter went down to defeat in the municipal election of April 1868.

Proponents of the board of public works continued, however, to press their case. They pointed out the fallacy of saddling the councilors with both legislative and supervisory functions and condemned a system that put elected aldermen at the mercy of "the horde of greedy, unscrupulous contractors" who had "grown fat . . . in the service of the city." "A combination among the contractors gives them the handle end of the poker every time," wrote one prominent tax-payer, "and either the job is let at an exorbitant figure, or else some incompetent man undertakes work that he knows nothing about, because his bid was a dollar lower than that of the man who did know." Advocates of the reform found a telling argument in the assertion that enough money could have been saved in constructing the Huron and Oneida Street bridges to pay the expense of a board of public works for two years, and that enough could have been saved in the construction of the courthouse to keep the board going for ten. These practical examples in the face of the impending construction of expensive public works finally convinced the electorate that it was "better economy and a safer indemnity against abuses to entrust the management of affairs of such magnitude to three capable, honest, experienced business men, chosen for their good qualifications, with a moderate compensation," than to take a chance on annually elected aldermen, who would be "under the constant imputation of petty frauds and speculations upon the ward funds."[129] Finally, in spite of the manifest opposition of the Democratic machine, the April election of 1869 brought the endorsement of a commission which was to have "general control of public buildings, streets, sewers, sidewalks, bridges, wharves, and the like in all parts of the city."[130] The provision

---

[129] D. P. H. to editor, Milwaukee *Daily Sentinel*, April 5, 1869.

[130] The response of the foreign-born to Democratic dictation is revealed in a break-down of ward votes. The only wards in which a majority opposed the board were the Sixth and Ninth (German) and Third (Irish). These three wards tallied nearly two-thirds of the opposition to the board. *Ibid.*, April 7, 1869; Larson, *Financial and Administrative History*, 89.

of a board of public works squared with the prevailing trend in municipal government to allocate administrative authority to quasi-independent agencies in the supposed interest of economy and efficiency. It reflected the current popular disillusionment regarding the capacity of the elected municipal legislators; and, more importantly, it marked a decline in the predominance of the immigrant-implemented "Regular" Democracy in local politics and a further encroachment upon the divisive ward autonomy which had created so many of the financial, administrative, and political problems of the developing city.

CHAPTER 8

When Commerce Was King

COMMERCE was the foundation of Milwaukee's economy during the first generation of cityhood; and upon the expansion of her commercial hinterland and the achievement of railroad connections with it the chances for continuous and stable city growth were early seen to depend. The aftermath of 1837 had demonstrated the fallacy of building towns exclusively on the purchase of "lots in paper Cities and Villages." It became increasingly clear that there would be no sure basis for urban development until "the rich farming section lying west and southwest" filled up, "and the prairies and openings" were "converted into rich and productive farms."[1] By 1850 such settlement had taken place, and the area beyond the city was much more populous than in village days. An average of 45 to 90 people per square mile now dwelt on the lake shore, and in the rest of the territory between the lake and the Mississippi River and south of a line drawn from Green Bay to the northern boundary of Iowa there were 18 to 45. By 1870 the population of the State stood at more than 1,000,000; and increasing numbers in Iowa, Minnesota, and the Dakotas were swelling the city's potential market.[2] The titans of town promotion who had

[1] Milwaukee *Sentinel,* Sept. 12, 1837. "The country back of this is rapidly filling up with actual settlers, who by another year will have farms under a good state of cultivation. . . . Some of the farmers are going very extensively into the business, and it is no uncommon circumstance for one man to have fifty and even an hundred acres ploughed up, preparatory to next year's crops. People generally have turned their attention to the tilling of the land during the present season, and spend their capital in improving their farms, instead of buying lots in paper Cities and Villages; . . . all this has a tendency to increase the growth of our town materially, and as the back country increases in population, so must the town increase."

[2] In 1840 only the southeast corner of the State could boast a population of six to eighteen people per square mile; in the remaining inhabited portion there

managed the land speculation of the village period now turned their attention to making the city the focal point of rail connections with this expanding hinterland. As a result of their efforts, rail connections between Milwaukee and Prairie du Chien were completed on April 15, 1857; and, fulfilling an earlier prediction, the "Iron Horse, starting betimes from the shores of Lake Michigan," slaked "his thirst at eve in the brimming Mississippi."[3] By the close of the sixties, 1,200 miles of railroad ran tributary to the city exclusive of the Lake Shore Railway; an uninterrupted contact with Minneapolis had been achieved;[4] and the individual lines which Milwaukeeans for two decades had promoted and subsidized were consolidated under the control of the Milwaukee and St. Paul Railway Company.[5]

There was more truth than municipal exaggeration in Milwaukee's boast that the city forged "with her own hands and by her own unaided efforts, the Iron Chain" that linked "the shores of the Lakes with the banks of the Mississippi," for local promoters and financiers were primarily responsible for both agitating and accomplishing the railroad connections that were to make Milwaukee the major transportation center of the State.[6] Suggested as early as 1836 by Kilbourn and others, a railroad continued to be proposed in the forties at public meetings in which Ludington, Hathaway, Prentiss, and Rogers took an active part. But many obstacles stood in the way of its realization: sectional rivalries in the territorial legislature; the competitive ambitions of Southport (Kenosha) and Racine; and economic adversities following 1837 and between 1847 and 1853.[7] Even after agrarian pressure compelled the State legislature to incorporate the Milwaukee and Waukesha (later called Milwaukee and Mississippi) Railroad, on February 11,

were but two to six settlers, the population of the whole State totaling little more than 30,000 people. Elmer A. Riley, *The Development of Chicago and Vicinity as a Manufacturing Center Prior to 1880* (Chicago, 1911), 42, 44.

[3] Milwaukee *Daily Sentinel and Gazette*, July 17, 1850.

[4] Milwaukee *Daily Sentinel*, Oct. 16, 1867.

[5] Frederick Merk, *Economic History of Wisconsin during the Civil War Decade* (Madison, 1916), 296.

[6] Milwaukee *Daily Sentinel and Gazette*, Nov. 28, 1849.

[7] *Ibid.*, March 11, Dec. 11, 16, 31, 1846; Jan. 7, 1847.

1847, subscriptions moved slowly; and the business leaders had to force the city to attract its destiny.[8] At a public meeting in February 1849, admittedly designed to rouse Milwaukee "from her apathy and make strenuous exertions to secure the trade of the interior," Tweedy, Kilbourn, James Kneeland, Lemuel Weeks, and Alexander Mitchell were commissioned to devise a plan by which the city might lend from one to three hundred thousand dollars for the promotion of the railroad. On July 19, 1849, by a vote of twelve to one in the council, the city was empowered to subscribe to $100,000 in stock, with the understanding that the money was to be raised by an annual tax of 1 percent on real estate and that the taxpayers were to become stockholders in the road to the amount of the tax they should severally pay. Meanwhile, all the authors of the plan had been chosen directors of the company, with E. D. Holton, E. D. Clinton, Anson Eldred, and E. B. Wolcott, as well; and the everambitious Kilbourn became president.[9]

Many individuals made possible the city's first railroad enterprise. A donation of land provided a place for the terminal; farmers along the line subscribed to stock in sums of $500 to $1,500, to be worked out in clearing and grubbing the right of way; and Kilbourn journeyed East to raise a loan of $250,000, secured by mortgages on the stockholders' property. The reluctance of eastern capitalists to buy these private obligations forced the city to come again to the rescue, itself accepting the farmers' mortgages and issuing municipal bonds which would command a readier market in the East. By 1851, the city's investment in the road stood at $234,000. Thus as a result of the joint efforts of local promoters, farmer beneficiaries, and the city itself, the railroad began to take shape.[10] Once, when the rails were submerged by a storm, Holton and some of the other stockholders got out with crowbars to remedy the dam-

---

[8] Herbert W. Rice, Abstract of doctoral dissertation, "The Early History of the Chicago, Milwaukee and St. Paul Railway Company," in *Abstracts in History IV* (University of Iowa, *Studies in the Social Sciences*, vol. 11, no. 3, Iowa City, 1941), 118.

[9] Milwaukee *Daily Sentinel and Gazette*, Feb. 8, May 11, July 21, 1849.

[10] Milwaukee *Sentinel and Gazette*, April 29, 1850; Milwaukee *Daily Sentinel and Gazette*, June 1, 7, 1850; Gregory, *History*, 1:355; Holton, "Commercial History of Milwaukee," Wis. Hist. Soc., *Colls.*, 4:275-77.

age.[11] At last, on February 25, 1851, frock-coated and crinoline-clad Milwaukeeans in gala mood could board the cars for an excursion to near-by Waukesha; and there, band music and speech making celebrated the achievement of the first link in a network of rails which, more than any other factor, was to give commercial pre-eminence to the Wisconsin metropolis.

The initial success of this pioneer line was the signal for the incorporation of other railroad companies promising profits to the farmer and population and prosperity for the city. The municipal aid given the first road had set a precedent in which the founders of other lines saw potential support; and all that remained to be done was to convince the voting public that further grants of funds should be authorized. The Milwaukee and Watertown Railroad was chartered in the winter of 1851;[12] and in quick succession followed the incorporation of the Green Bay, Milwaukee, and Chicago, or Lake Shore Railroad, which was to connect Milwaukee with Chicago; the Milwaukee and Fond du Lac; the Milwaukee and Horicon; and the La Crosse and Milwaukee. The same local citizens backed most of these enterprises; and mass meetings called by these promoters prepared the public mind to endorse the necessary loans of city credit, now granted on condition that the railway company should pay not only the principal but also all the interest as it came due.[13]

With the multiplication of projected lines came rivalries reminiscent of the ward antagonisms of the village period. This was especially true in the case of a "railroad war" between the Milwaukee and Watertown, subsidized by the backers of the pioneer Milwaukee and Mississippi, and the La Crosse and Milwaukee, a Kilbourn enterprise. By 1850, the West-side promoter had severed his connections with the pioneer road

[11] Milwaukee *Sentinel,* July 14, 1937.
[12] Milwaukee *Sentinel and Gazette,* July 10, Aug. 13, 1851.
[13] Illustrative of the interlocking directorates of these roads is the fact that the promoters of the Milwaukee and Fond du Lac included Eliphalet Cramer, Mitchell, Francis Randall, Edward Brodhead, Lemuel W. Weeks, George H. Walker, John H. Tweedy, J. A. Hoover, Eldred, Kneeland, Crocker, and Wolcott. Directors of the Milwaukee and Mississippi in 1853 included John Catlin, Walker, Tweedy, Kneeland, Eldred, Cramer, Holton, Wolcott, Mitchell, Adam E. Ray, William A. Barstow, Joshua Cobb, Joseph Goodrich, S. C. Hall, and David L. Mills. Milwaukee *Daily Sentinel,* Aug. 25, 30, Sept. 6, 1852; Jan. 21, 1853.

after dissatisfaction with his management had brought a change in the board of directors and the choice of John Catlin of Madison to succeed him as president.[14] The Milwaukeean had then turned to the promotion of a railway to La Crosse only to find that his former associates, the stockholders of the Milwaukee and Watertown, were planning a parallel line in the same direction. When his appeal to a public meeting for the loan of city credit met the opposition of Mitchell, Walker, and J. A. Hoover, all officers or directors of rival railroad lines, he turned, as was earlier related, to the staunchly Democratic Second Ward to champion his cause. After Dr. Huebschmann had explained the issue to his German fellow-citizens there, resolutions were unanimously adopted with three cheers for Kilbourn's La Crosse and Milwaukee.[15] Thereafter, the Second Ward took a personal interest in the La Crosse road and was the only dissenting section when grants of city credit were otherwise enthusiastically extended to new railroad lines. In June 1854, Walker, Crocker, and Mitchell effected a union of the Milwaukee and Mississippi with the Southern Wisconsin Railroad Company, amid promises of aid from the city and its capitalists, merchants, and real estate owners. As we have seen, these railroad rivalries had repercussions in municipal politics; and Kilbourn's success in the mayoral election of 1854 gave him an opportunity to recommend a route for the Watertown road which would not conflict with his La Crosse project.[16]

Meanwhile, the city's promoters had begun to seek federal subsidy for their railroad schemes. At the behest of the board of trade, a committee including Levi Blossom, Holton, Cramer, Kilbourn, and McCrea drafted a memorial asking for land grants from the federal government for all the railroads leading

---

[14] John Watson Cary, *The Organization and History of the Chicago, Milwaukee and St. Paul Railway Company* (Milwaukee, 1893), 8; *Evening Wisconsin* (Milwaukee), Oct. 16, 1895.

[15] Milwaukee *Daily Sentinel*, Sept. 6, 8, 1852; Jan. 5, 1853. The New York Correspondent, writing in the columns of the *Sentinel*, professed to see in the public meetings, "more rivalry, more of a personal feeling of jealousy, than can consist with a true support of the general interest, which should be the supreme motive." He cited the experience of Pennsylvania in counseling against fragmentary expenditures to the detriment of the main line. *Ibid.*, Jan. 21, 1853. This is a reflection of the *Sentinel's* support for the pioneer line.

[16] *Ibid.*, June 8, 24, Oct. 25, 1853; March 15, June 10, 1854.

out of the city. By June 1856 Congress had put lands for railroad promotion at the disposal of the Wisconsin legislature; and Kilbourn moved craftily to win this aid for the La Crosse road. His chief rivals in Wisconsin were the Milwaukee and Watertown, with which the La Crosse Company merged by September 1856, thus uniting Kilbourn, Goodrich, Mitchell, Cramer, and Hibbard as directors of an enterprise eligible for federal benevolence, and the St. Croix and Lake Superior, with which a mutually satisfactory deal was made. More devious methods were needed to outweigh the appeal of a Chicago line, the Chicago, St. Paul, and Fond du Lac. Early in October the federal grant was awarded to the La Crosse and Milwaukee. At this news of victory over their Illinois neighbor, the citizens were jubilant. Bonfires blazed in Market Square and at other points throughout the city, and a torchlight procession, accompanied by detachments from the engine companies, added to the festivity. An investigation in 1858 disclosed that bonds and stocks to the par value of more than $800,000 had been distributed to legislators, the governor, and other key persons, including Rufus King of the *Sentinel,* who accepted a "gratuity" of $10,000 in bonds, Schoeffler of the *Banner,* and S. D. Carpenter of the *Wisconsin Patriot.* This exposé of its activities in combination with bad management ruined the company during the panic of 1857. The road, under receivership, was completed to La Crosse during 1858. Kilbourn seems to have merited the major portion of the blame for both the scandal and the mismanagement, the disclosure of which brought a sorry culmination to the promotional career of the city's most aggressively dynamic speculator-founder.[17]

By the mid-fifties, railroad promotion had assumed the proportions of a mania, a tendency that the State legislature encouraged by extending the ceiling of city indebtedness to make the subsidies possible. A promotional issue of the *Sentinel* described for the benefit of local readers and their correspondents the extensive railroad network that was to connect Milwaukee with the East, tap the city's economic hinterland, and

---

[17] *Ibid.,* Feb. 13, 1854; Sept. 27, 30, Oct. 13, 1856; Gregory, *History,* 1:364. See also John M. Bernd, "The La Crosse and Milwaukee Railroad Land Grant, 1856," *Wisconsin Magazine of History,* 30:141-53 (December 1946).

overcome Chicago's competition for trade; and Lapham's advice to a Swiss correspondent suggests that the efforts to interest investors in the development of rail connections between Milwaukee and the West extended even beyond the boundaries of the United States.[18] He wrote:

> In regard to our railroads, about which you enquire,—I send you the charter, the last year's (1855) report, and some circulars of the "La Crosse and Milwaukee Railroad Company" which of all our roads is the best one to invest capital in just now. The grant of land made by Congress to the state has been conferred upon this company, and is at least sufficient to make the road!
>
> It is therefore the policy of the company to borrow money on the bonds of the company to do the work, reserving the lands until they have been increased greatly in value by the construction of the road. There is not the least doubt but that the stock and bonds are perfectly secure.
>
> The persons at the head of the company are honorable men, and have the business qualifications that will enable them to superintend the work with due economy. The country through which the road passes is studded with villages and the land is rich and productive. A dividend of 5 pr. cent for the last 6 months has just been declared upon the stock of the company, from the earnings of the short portion already completed.
>
> I deem the stock of the company the best that can now be obtained, for the reason above stated that the grant of land will ultimately enable the company to repay the whole amount of it, while the holders will still be the owners of the road.
>
> The earnings of all our roads are such as to enable the several companies to make large dividends.
>
> But there is another mode of investing capital here that is very profitable. Our city has grown up within 20 years from an entire wilderness—it now has a population of about 40,000 souls.
>
> You can readily see how rapidly all real estate must be increasing in value. Many fine fortunes are made here simply by the purchase of real estate which after a year or two may be sold for perhaps double its cost. The constant immigration, the construction of our system of rail roads, and the rapid improvement of

---

[18] *Wisconsin Session Laws (Local)*, 1854, chap. 265; 1865, chap. 164; Milwaukee *Daily Sentinel*, June 20, 1854; Edouard Desor to Increase Lapham, Neuchâtel, Dec. 7, 1856, and Lapham to Desor, Jan. 5, 1857, Lapham Papers.

the farming lands around us all assure us that this increase in the value of real estate will continue for a great number of years.

I shall be happy to take charge (for a small commission) of any funds you or your monied friends may wish to invest here. I can make such references as will be satisfactory.

By July 1857, Milwaukeeans had sunk $100,000 in the Detroit and Milwaukee, a partly amphibious line, which was expected to provide a means of offsetting Chicago's geographical advantage for eastbound trade. Plans were also taking shape for the Milwaukee and Superior, financed under a dubious scheme in which the requisite 5 percent of the $120,000 in stock subscriptions was paid in checks given by the subscribers and entered upon the company's books as cash.[19] By 1858, the city's subsidies to railroads had mounted to $1,614,000.[20]

There were signs, however, that the West in general and Milwaukee in particular had over-extended themselves in railroad promotion. By 1856, the downward tendency in each new issue of bonds threatened the city's reputation; and the companies were beginning to default. In June 1858, stockholders of the Milwaukee and Mississippi complained that no dividends had been paid since January 1857, and that shares were quoted at 15 cents on the dollar in the New York market. In 1858 and 1859, the La Crosse and Horicon companies failed to pay the interest on their bonded debt. In June 1859 it was announced that the La Crosse and Milwaukee had been sold out to its bondholders, who organized as the Milwaukee and Minnesota. Foreclosure of the Milwaukee and Mississippi led to the organization of a new company, the Milwaukee and Prairie du Chien.[21] In spite of these calamities, the press did not curtail its promotional activities, but instead focused attention upon the amphibious Detroit and Milwaukee. On August 31, 1859, the *Sentinel* heralded the arrival of the "Detroit" and the "Milwaukee," first-class ocean steamers which were to traverse the mari-

---

[19] Milwaukee *Daily Sentinel*, July 15, 23, 1857; July 8, 1858.

[20] Ultimately all but two issues of $100,000 each were met by the companies responsible. Larson, *Financial and Administrative History*, 75.

[21] Milwaukee *Daily Sentinel*, May 13, 14, 1856; June 29, 1857; June 12, 1858; Milwaukee *Sentinel*, June 4, 1859; Cary, *History of the Chicago, Milwaukee and St. Paul Railway Company*, 9, 11.

time portion of the line, with the prediction that "a large share of travel to and from the Northwest," which had "hitherto gone by way of Chicago, will henceforth follow the more direct route through Milwaukee, across Lake Michigan and over the Detroit and Milwaukee and Great Western Railways." In the opinion of the editor, it was "clearly the interest of our business men to give this route the bulk of their patronage." Comparative distances between Chicago and Detroit and Milwaukee and Detroit, via the water route, gave further proof that, thanks to the new line, Milwaukee was to be the "Commercial Metropolis of the Great North-west." In view of this promotional enthusiasm, it was a blow to Milwaukee's hopes when winter storms checked the operation of the vessels and the Chicago press could report the failure of "the grand experiment that was to prove that Chicago was outside the line of western trade."[22]

Fortunately for Milwaukee, the experience of the abortive Detroit and Milwaukee was not duplicated by the major tributary lines that ran inland from the city. Through trains began to run between Chicago and Milwaukee early in June 1855; the Milwaukee and Mississippi reached Prairie du Chien on April 15, 1857; and the La Crosse and Milwaukee touched the river one year later, thus directing toward Milwaukee the produce of the increasingly settled Northwest.[23] By September 1858, the grain of Minnesota and northwestern Wisconsin was flowing to La Crosse for transshipment to Milwaukee and the East, thus foreshadowing, long before the closing of the Mississippi by the Confederate government in 1861, the decline of the southern route and the St. Louis market and ensuring the commercial ascendancy of the growing city at the mouth of the Milwaukee. The panic of 1857 threatened this commercial advance chiefly because of the potential advantage to Milwaukee's

[22] Milwaukee *Sentinel*, Aug. 31, Nov. 3, 1859; Chicago *Press and Tribune*, quoted in Milwaukee *Sentinel*, Dec. 5, 1859. A writer in the *Sentinel* contended that the damage sustained by one of the ships was perpetrated by "vile wretches" who plotted its destruction "to kill the route." See also *ibid.*, Dec. 26, 1859.

[23] Until that date, a train left Chicago at 8:30 A.M., arrived in Waukegan at 10:30 A.M., and there connected with stages which arrived at Milwaukee "the same evening." W. H. Stennett, comp., *Yesterday and Today: A History of the Chicago and North Western Railway System* (3d ed., Chicago, 1910), 64; Milwaukee *Daily Sentinel*, April 18, 1857.

rivals in the resulting tendency to consolidate the many fragmentary lines left uncompleted when the depression struck. In the sixties the Chicago and North Western Railway, which had emerged after 1857 from the ruins of the Chicago, St. Paul, and Fond du Lac Railroad, began to amalgamate some of the Wisconsin lines and draw their business to Chicago. At this crisis, Alexander Mitchell became Milwaukee's champion, declaring that the only resource and safety "against the power of the Northwestern was to gather our sticks in one branch and . . . resist its encroachments."[24] The company through which this was accomplished was the Milwaukee and St. Paul Railroad.

The Milwaukee and St. Paul was organized in 1863 to operate the bankrupt La Crosse and Milwaukee. After absorbing the Milwaukee and Watertown and several other defaulting lines, it agreed in 1866 to pool tariffs with the Prairie du Chien, successor to the Milwaukee and Mississippi; and shortly thereafter, through a stock manipulation, it brought the Prairie du Chien under its control. With this development the St. Paul also gained control of the McGregor and Western Railway and looked toward pushing its railroad realm into Minnesota, Iowa, and the Dakotas.[25] A proposed extension of the original Milwaukee and Mississippi to Dubuque promised to make Milwaukee "the virtual eastern terminus of the northern branch of the Pacific Railway."[26] These developments, however, did not entirely allay the fear that the end of consolidation would be a union of the St. Paul with the North Western with the possible result that "the Milwaukee roads, nursed by the city in their infancy, and in behalf of which it had plunged itself deeply into debt, would end by becoming feeders of the Northwestern" and "the proud Cream City . . . the tail to the kite

[24] Merk, *Economic History of Wisconsin during the Civil War,* 296-98; Milwaukee *Daily Sentinel,* Sept. 8, 1858; March 4, 1867.
[25] *Ibid.,* March 4, 1867; Rice, "Early History of the Milwaukee Railway Company" (Univ. of Iowa, *Soc. Sci. Studies,* vol. 11, no. 3), 122; Merk, *Economic History of Wisconsin during the Civil War,* 290-96; William F. Raney, "The Building of Wisconsin Railroads," *Wisconsin Magazine of History,* 19:392-93 (June 1936). See also August W. Derleth, *The Milwaukee Road; Its First Hundred Years* (New York, 1948) for a comprehensive and readable account of the history of the Milwaukee Road.
[26] Milwaukee *Daily Sentinel,* Dec. 14, 1863.

of Chicago."²⁷ At a stormy meeting in March 1867, members of the Chamber of Commerce passed resolutions opposing any consolidation of the two major lines. The two companies were inevitably drawn together in 1868, however, when four directors of the Milwaukee and St. Paul road were elected to the board of the North Western and the president of the North Western was elected to the Milwaukee and St. Paul board; but the choice of Alexander Mitchell as president of the North Western in 1869 helped to quiet fears that Chicago would gain undue advantage from these moves.²⁸ On the eve of the seventies, Milwaukee's railway promoters were turning their attention to lines in northern Wisconsin, the city lending its support to those that could win the endorsement of Mitchell and the St. Paul company. At the same time, the Milwaukee and St. Paul was encroaching upon Chicago's interest in the trade of northern Iowa by the purchase of the Western Union Railroad in 1868-69 and extending its influence into the Northwest in such a way as to make the St. Paul railway "the great wheat route and Milwaukee the wheat market of the Northwest."²⁹

A continuing concern for harbor improvement went hand in hand with the promotion of dependable rail connections between Milwaukee and the interior. Vexed by President Polk's veto of the Harbor and River Bill in 1846, Milwaukeeans joined the businessmen of communities extending from New York through the Northwest in planning the River and Harbor Convention of 1847. A Milwaukeean presided over the preliminary meeting, held in New York; and in the first week in July most of the prominent business leaders of the city, with the exception of Kilbourn, joined delegates from nineteen states and ter-

---

²⁷ Merk, *Economic History of Wisconsin during the Civil War*, 303; Milwaukee *Daily Sentinel*, Feb. 12, 1867. On their part, Chicagoans viewed the Wisconsin consolidation as a threat to the North Western and proposed a direct road from Janesville to La Crosse to offset its effects. *Ibid.*, July 13, 1863.

²⁸ Rice, "Early History of the Milwaukee Railway Company" (Univ. of Iowa, *Soc. Sci. Studies*, vol. 11, no. 3), 122; Milwaukee *Daily Sentinel*, March 4, 1867; Sept. 18, 1869.

²⁹ Gregory, *History*, 1:377, 382. In 1874 the name of the Milwaukee and St. Paul was changed to Chicago, Milwaukee and St. Paul Railway Company, at which time it owned 1,399 miles of railroad in four states. Rice, "Early History of the Milwaukee Railway Company" (Univ. of Iowa, *Soc. Sci. Studies*, vol. 11, no. 3), 123.

ritories at a Chicago convention to demand federal improvement of the harbors of the great inland seas. A public mass meeting had been called in May for the selection of delegates. At the same time the press was urging the widening of Buffalo's harbor and the Erie Canal to facilitate the eastward flow of western produce.[30] Nevertheless, as in the case of the railroads, the municipality ultimately assumed most of the financial responsibility for its harbor development. Improvements in 1847 were financed by an appropriation of $500 from the common council and donations of $1,000 from the merchants, forwarders, and businessmen. In 1852, Congress set aside $15,000 for improvement at the "straight cut," but this proved insufficient and the city was authorized to levy a direct tax for construction. By the time the "straight cut" was completed, the federal government had spent $83,973, the city, $445,971, including the costs of litigation with the contractors.[31]

Familiar names are among the promoters of harbor improvement. A big harbor meeting in 1849 was managed by Holton, King, Kilbourn, Prentiss, C. H. Williams, and D. Merrill; and Kilbourn, Tweedy, Rogers, and Weeks were among the delegates who attended an improvements convention at Port Huron in 1853, in the hope of gaining access to trade which converged upon Grand Haven, Michigan. Acting through the board of trade, Milwaukee's business leaders cooperated with neighboring communities in improving trading conditions on the lakes. In 1855, the board agreed to raise $3,000 to supplement the contributions of other Great Lakes cities in order to improve the St. Clair Flats, obstacle to easy navigation of the lakes. In 1868, Buffalo's board supported the Milwaukee Chamber of Commerce in its request that Congress reimburse the city for the costs that harbor building had incurred.[32]

[30] Milwaukee *Sentinel and Gazette*, Aug. 3, 1846; May 26, 1847; Chicago *Daily Journal*, Aug. 19, 1846; Riley, *Development of Chicago*, 89-90.

[31] Milwaukee *Sentinel and Gazette*, May 26, 1847; Larson, *Financial and Administrative History*, 67; *The Port of Milwaukee: Historical, Descriptive, Prospective*, published by board of harbor commissioners (Milwaukee, 1922), 12.

[32] The Chicago press was critical of Milwaukee's request. Milwaukee *Sentinel and Gazette*, Nov. 20, 1849; Milwaukee *Daily Sentinel*, May 11, 1853; April 5, 1855; July 22, 1867; April 11, 1868.

The completion of the harbor at the "straight cut" in December 1857—"by the liberal and enlightened enterprise of our own people"—was as fortunate for Milwaukee as the attainment of rail connections with the Mississippi in the same year. As a result of the two developments, the city was ready both to receive and forward goods and produce in an eastward flow of trade, which, though inevitable, was greatly hastened by the Civil War.[33] That this flow would reach Milwaukee was assured by the fact that the major shipping companies on the Upper Mississippi had exclusive contracts with the Milwaukee and Prairie du Chien Railroad at Prairie du Chien and with the La Crosse and Milwaukee at La Crosse.[34] Business at the port reflected the expanded commerce. Tonnage regularly using the port increased between 1862 and 1863 from 25,844 to 140,771 and propeller lines serving Milwaukee from five in 1860 to eleven in 1867. Direct shipments of wheat to Europe were begun in 1856; and in 1862, Milwaukee overtook Chicago to become the world's greatest primary export point for wheat.[35] This diversion of commerce from the Mississippi spared Milwaukee the depression of 1861, was responsible for a marked increase in population during the first half of the decade,[36] and greatly quickened her development into one of the major ports on the lakes. However, by the sixties, Milwaukee shippers were threatened by competition resulting from the through overland freight that ran via Chicago from western to eastern cities without the interference of lake closure during the winter months, danger of shipwreck, and, especially, the delays of

[33] Mildred L. Hartsough asserts that the railroads, rather than the Civil War, were the chief single factor in the decline of Mississippi River transportation. *From Canoe to Steel Barge on the Upper Mississippi* (Minneapolis, 1934), 195-96.

[34] Merk, *Economic History of Wisconsin during the Civil War*, 353-54. Through freight from Prairie du Chien increased from 9,960 tons in 1860 to 161,317 in 1865; through freight from La Crosse, from 28,627 tons in 1860 to 89,882 in 1862. Carl R. Fish, "Phases of Economic History of Wisconsin, 1860-70," Wisconsin Historical Society, *Proceedings*, 1908, p. 212.

[35] Merk, *Economic History of Wisconsin during the Civil War*, 380-81; *Port of Milwaukee*, 21; Fish, "Economic History of Wisconsin, 1860-70," Wis. Hist. Soc., *Proc.*, 1908, pp. 212-13.

[36] The population increase of 23 percent between 1860 and 1865 was twice as large as that of the State as a whole. Fish, "Economic History of Wisconsin, 1860-70," Wis. Hist. Soc., *Proc.*, 1908, p. 212.

transfer.[37] A convention of the boards of trade of the important lake cities, held in Chicago in 1869, attempted to meet this competition by reducing rates, improving facilities for storage during the winter months, and effecting savings; but with the increasing development of uninterrupted overland railway transport, access to navigation on the inland seas became a factor of diminishing significance in city growth.

It was to a large extent a "wheat and hog" economy that was served by the rail and lake transport that Milwaukeeans developed between 1846 and 1870; for the city's welfare in those years was pivoted in great measure upon the receipt and exportation of these products of her agricultural hinterland and upon the importation of manufactured goods to meet their producers' needs. Interest was so centered on trade that not until the sixties was there serious consideration of manufacturing as an essential incident in the city's economic life. James Seville recalled that in 1847 "the commercial interests" were the concern of the banks then in existence, and "anyone having sufficient 'nerve' to go into manufacturing" had to "do it on his own resources or 'bust.'" In 1864 the editor of the *Sentinel* asserted that wheat brokerage largely absorbed the capital and attention of the business community, and as late as 1869 the *Daily Herold* printed a communication condemning the city's continued dependence on wheat and the reluctance of bankers to extend credit to any who dealt "in neither wheat nor hogs."[38]

But so long as the farmers of the Northwest had wheat to sell and means to get it to Milwaukee, trade in that commodity was the city's major enterprise. Wheat exports expanded from 213,448 bushels in 1846 to 16,127,838 bushels in 1870, a seventy-fivefold increase. At the same time flour exports increased from 15,756 barrels to 1,225,941. By 1862, Milwaukee had become the largest primary wheat market in the world.[39] In the days be-

[37] The lake was frozen for a period lasting usually from late November to mid-March or April. Buck, 3:486; Merk, *Economic History of Wisconsin during the Civil War*, 383.

[38] Memoir of James Seville, quoted in Gregory, *History*, 1:546; Milwaukee *Sentinel*, Feb. 8, 1864; communication from James G. Hagerman, secretary of the Milwaukee Iron Company, to Milwaukee *Daily Herold,* quoted in Milwaukee *Daily Sentinel,* April 16, 1869.

[39] Milwaukee *Daily Sentinel and Gazette,* Jan. 15, 1847; Whitbeck, *Geography of Southeastern Wisconsin,* 60, 62; Chamber of Commerce, *Report,* 1862, p. 3.

fore the railroads, and even later, farmers hauled their wheat cityward to market and stood with bags untied for the buyers' inspection. Once bargained for, it was hoisted by horsepower into warehouses, like the red structure owned by Alanson Sweet, and stored in bins for future export.[40] With every new mile of railroad, more bushels of wheat flowed into the Milwaukee warehouses; and by the late fifties the cars of the Milwaukee and Mississippi (later the Milwaukee and Prairie du Chien) and the La Crosse and Milwaukee were loaded with grain for the Milwaukee market. At the outset, Chicago buyers were not serious rivals, inasmuch as the Illinois city was 156 miles farther from Prairie du Chien, and Milwaukee's port 90 miles closer to the East.[41] Of the 2,317,000 bushels transported on the Milwaukee and Mississippi in 1858, only 350 bushels went to Chicago. However, after 1859, when the Chicago and North Western Railroad came into control of a line to Fond du Lac, competition on this score set in.

The trade in grain was the source of the fortunes and the occupation of some of the most active leaders in the commercial life of the city. Daniel Newhall was long the most outstanding operator among the pioneers in the grain trade. Taking advantage of conditions in the market following the potato famine in Ireland, he borrowed $300 from Alexander Mitchell in 1846 and invested it in purchases of wheat and flour which ultimately netted him close to $10,000. Abandoning his grocery trade to turn exclusively to grain, he soon gained the reputation of being the largest individual grain dealer in the West. His fleet of twenty sailing vessels—largest on the lakes—carried his produce down the Great Lakes during the season of navigation for shipment via the Erie Canal to eastern markets. At the height of the season he was in the habit of dispatching as much as 15,000 bushels of wheat daily to Buffalo. Collateral activities springing

---

[40] A. W. Kellogg, "Recollections of Life in Early Wisconsin," *Wis. Mag. of Hist.*, 8:95-96 (September 1924).

[41] "Being ninety miles nearer to the eastern terminus of lake navigation than Chicago, the natural current of trade will pass through Milwaukee from the now fertile fields of the vast region north and west of us, rather than be diverted in a detour round the southern end of the lake." Wheeler, *Chronicles of Milwaukee*, 275.

from his commercial operations in the boom years before the panic of 1857 were shipbuilding and real estate. In 1854 he built what was for the time the most spacious warehouse in the Northwest, the Badger Warehouse; the Newhall House, begun in 1856 and completed a year later, was the "show" hotel of the West. Newhall suffered the consequences of over-extended enterprise in 1857. Seriously affected by the drop in grain prices in 1859, he recovered to do an enormous business during the Civil War; but in 1867 he began to experience such reverses as to prompt him to leave the city in 1874 and take up farming in the vicinity of Waukesha.

Other pioneers in the grain trade were George D. Dousman, Alanson Sweet, and Dr. Lemuel W. Weeks; and in time Edward D. Holton, L. J. Higby, Samuel T. Hooker, Henry A. Nichols, Charles J. Kershaw, Lyman F. Hodges, Levi H. Kellogg, Angus Smith, and Philip D. Armour played an active part in making the commission business one of the pivotal pursuits of the lake shore city. From 1864, when he leased the Milwaukee and St. Paul elevator, until 1868, L. J. Higby acceded to Newhall's position as the leading figure in the Milwaukee grain trade.[42]

Many changes took place in the grain trade during the years in which the activities of Newhall and Higby reflected the commercial side of a community whose economy was so vitally affected by the trade in grain. The day of individual purchases from farmer-producers at the outskirts of the city gave way to organized buying through the medium of commercial associations. As a means of systematizing trading procedures a group of commission merchants established the board of trade on March 1, 1849, with E. D. Holton as president. A competitor, the Corn Exchange, soon appeared; but the two merged in 1858 and were chartered as the Chamber of Commerce, an organization of merchants, bankers, and produce dealers designed "to promote just and equitable principles in trade, to discover and correct abuses, and to support such regulations and measures as may advance the prosperity of the Mercantile and Commercial community."[43] In 1857 and 1858 the first

[42] Gregory, *History*, 1:456-59, 466.
[43] *Evening Wisconsin*, Oct. 15, 1895; Milwaukee *Daily Sentinel*, Oct. 22, 1858.

modern grain elevators were built for the reception of wheat in bulk. In the latter year, Higby erected his warehouse and elevator at Chestnut Street, and Angus Smith built an elevator with the almost unprecedented capacity of 50,000 bushels. Not long thereafter, however, the city's storage capacity of 1,750,000 bushels was inadequate to the potential flow of grain. The handling of grain in bulk brought the need of a system of inspection, weighing, and grading. Established in the fall of 1858, this gave Milwaukee wheat an enviably dependable reputation throughout Europe.[44]

During this period of the commission business, trading was not confined to the exchange room of the Chamber of Commerce. Instead, the commission merchants carried on their daily activities at various points in the city. According to John G. Gregory, they assembled in the morning at the Higby Warehouse,

> investigating the consignment books and trading for half an hour. Then they jumped into their buggies and proceeded to the Angus Smith elevator on the Menomonee, and still later to the Kellogg and Strong warehouse, . . . at each of which places the program of the morning was repeated. The hour from twelve to one was devoted to meeting on 'change and the afternoon to settling up trades and attending to correspondence. This, however, did not end the labors of the day, for the universal practice was to pass the evening from seven to ten in the lobby of the Newhall House, carrying on the operations of buying and selling.

Until the existence of an Atlantic cable in 1866, merchants had to depend on the arrival of steamships from abroad for word on European markets. The inauguration of a trading pit in 1870 tended to regularize activities on the exchange.[45] Through the late fifties and sixties, proximity to the ever-expanding wheat fields guaranteed an abundant flow of grain to the Wisconsin city, and the development of modern warehouses and the establishment of a system of grading helped to offset Chicago's superior facilities for the transfer of the grain.[46] But by the middle seventies the attractions of the overland route

---

[44] Gregory, *History*, 1:462, 471; Milwaukee *Daily Sentinel*, Oct. 14, 1858.
[45] Gregory, *History*, 1:463-64.
[46] Milwaukee *Daily Sentinel*, July 22, 1858.

through Chicago, already causing Milwaukeeans alarm by 1866, and the migration of the wheat fields to the Northwest ended Milwaukee's pre-eminence in the wheat trade and brought to a close the era in which trade in this commodity dominated the city's economic life.

The sale of raw materials in Milwaukee or the consignment of goods to forwarders there gave commercial opportunities to the retail merchants of the city. In September 1847, the *Sentinel and Gazette* asserted that since Milwaukee was "the best point to sell, so too, Farmers" would "find it the best point to buy."[47] Some merchants, like Henry Stern and his partner Julius Goll, peddled their goods through the country, making circuits of two or three weeks' duration.[48] The expansion of the hinterland stimulated the enlargement of wholesale houses in the middle fifties. The $65,000 store of Henry Nazro and Company, hardware merchants, promised to be "second to none in the United States." With the lower floor for retail and the upper for wholesale, buyers could inspect "upwards of three acres of iron and hardware under one roof." Among the clerks were men who spoke German, Norwegian, and Welsh.[49]

The twofold concern of the jobbers was to circumvent the competition of the Chicago merchants and to convince the up-country buyers that they no longer needed to travel to New York to replenish their stocks. Trade beyond the limits of Wisconsin was small through 1859, but in 1860 nearly one-half of the freight shipments originating in Milwaukee crossed the inland borders of the State; and Milwaukee merchants succeeded in getting the greater part of the trade of the Northwest which stopped short of New York. As the Chamber of Commerce reported, the merchants were now receiving orders from northern Illinois and Iowa where their agents "have come directly in the path of Chicago, and have succeeded in competing with the trade of that city."[50] By 1863, the Chamber of Commerce as-

[47] Milwaukee *Daily Sentinel and Gazette,* Sept. 13, 1847.
[48] Henry Stern, "The Life Story of a Milwaukee Merchant," *Wisconsin Magazine of History,* 9:69 (September 1925).
[49] Milwaukee *Daily Sentinel,* July 7, 1854.
[50] The Milwaukee merchants had also increased their trade with Wisconsin cities by contributing to railroad projects in the interior. Chamber of Commerce, *Report,* 1860, p. 12.

serted that three-fourths of all the goods consumed in the region west and northwest of the city passed through her jobbers.[51] Railroad promoters enlisted the support of the wholesale merchants in attempting to contest with Chicago and, especially, the Chicago and North Western Railroad the markets of northern Illinois, Iowa, and Minnesota; and Milwaukee's traders were counseled to "scatter their handbills, circulars, and advertisements up and down the Mississippi" and dispatch "some of their shrewdest clerks" to counter the competition of Chicago, St. Louis, Dubuque, Galena, and Cincinnati.[52] In 1861, the leading merchants, headed by John Nazro, undertook systematic promotion of trade in organizing the Milwaukee Merchants' Association (March 5, 1861); and in the following year they sent Captain D. P. Mapes to work up business with Milwaukee in those portions of Wisconsin, Iowa, and Minnesota which were commercially tributary to the city. His salary was raised by individual subscription.[53] The middle sixties were prosperous years for Milwaukee jobbers; but by 1868 the Chamber of Commerce was chiding the wholesalers for permitting the loss of trade to Chicago.[54] The increasing agitation for home manufactures in the sixties tended to discredit and obscure the really predominant role of the merchant jobber during this period in Milwaukee's commercial life.

Milwaukee's hinterland was producing more than wheat for export and a market for the wholesale trade. Whereas Wisconsin farmers had raised slightly more than 30,000 cattle in 1840, nearly 185,000 were raised in 1850; and during the same decade the number of hogs increased from about 51,000 to nearly 160,000.[55] These animals became the basis of two important Milwaukee industries: meat packing and tanning. Packing was

[51] Merk, *Economic History of Wisconsin during the Civil War*, 222.

[52] Milwaukee *Daily Sentinel*, March 17, 1857.

[53] Oliver E. Remey and William G. Bruce, A Half-Century in Business Effort: History of the Merchants and Manufacturers Association covering the period from March 5, 1861, to December 31, 1911 (MS in Milwaukee Public Library, 2 pts.), pt. 1, chap. 2, pp. 7-10. This work will hereafter be cited as Remey and Bruce, A Half-Century in Business Effort.

[54] Chamber of Commerce, *Report*, 1865, p. 3; Milwaukee *Daily Sentinel*, May 18, 1869.

[55] Riley, *Development of Chicago*, 49.

originally a by-product of the commission business, providing a use for the warehouses in the winter months. The commission merchants packed the pork and beef, gaining a small fee for their labor, profit from the sale of salt, saltpeter, and barrels, and in addition their commission for forwarding the product to New York or New Orleans. Ultimately, they began to pay cash for the hogs and cattle, borrowing their money from the representatives of eastern capital who traveled through the West. John Plankinton built his packing business on the foundation of a retail meat market, in which the first year's sales amounted to $12,000. As the surrounding country produced more livestock, he began slaughtering and packing, in partnership from 1850 to 1861 with Frederick Layton, who later formed the meat packing concern of Layton and Company. By 1863, only three establishments of its kind in the United States exceeded Plankinton's business. Ultimately, he made a partner of Philip D. Armour, who had begun a grain, produce, and commission business in Milwaukee in 1859. The latter developed the merchandising side of the business, and the firm profited enormously on Civil War orders for mess pork sold for future delivery at wartime prices. In 1875, Armour moved to Chicago to look after packing interests there. Michael Cudahy, employed by Layton and Company, and by Plankinton and Armour in the sixties, was responsible for the introduction of an ice-storing process which made possible a summer packing term. By 1871, Milwaukee stood fourth among the packing centers of the country.[56]

Hides, abundantly available in the hinterland, and easily accessible hemlock bark were factors responsible for making Milwaukee by 1872 the largest tanning center in the world. The exhaustion of tanbark in Cazenovia, New York, had prompted the removal of George and William Allen to Milwaukee where they set up a leather store in 1846 and a tannery at Two Rivers two years later. In 1847 Guido Pfister opened the Buffalo Leather Company on Market Street Square. Through his store

[56] Rudolf A. Clemen, *The American Livestock and Meat Industry* (New York, 1923), 136-38, 149-54, 164; Whitbeck, *Geography of Southeastern Wisconsin*, 104.

was marketed the leather from the tannery of his friend and fellow-countryman, Fred Vogel. Buying an interest in each other's enterprise in 1849, they became partners in 1853. Trostel and Gallun began producing "Blue Star" harness in 1858. With the stimulation to the leather business attending the Civil War, Milwaukee's nine tanneries, producing leather worth $218,000 in 1855, had become thirty by 1870, with an annual output valued at $2,500,000. In 1868 Pfister and Vogel concentrated their tanneries in one large group of plants in Milwaukee. The contribution of German craftsmen to the development of this Milwaukee industry is seen in the fact that ten of the thirteen tanneries in 1860 were owned by Germans and by 1870, as many as nineteen out of twenty-seven.[57]

German workers and German consumers were at the same time playing a leading role in the development of the product that was ultimately to "make Milwaukee famous." Ministering at first to the demands of the German-American citizenry, the brewing industry had expanded by the late sixties to serve a national market. The Best Brewing Company (later Pabst) was established by members of the Best family who migrated to America in the early forties and in 1844 transplanted in Milwaukee the brewing business they had operated at Mettenheim in Germany. Upon the retirement of Jacob Best, Sr., and his eldest son in the late fifties, management devolved upon Phillip Best. Output increased from 7,270 barrels to more than 100,000 barrels between 1860 and 1873.[58] August Krug's brewery, founded in 1849, produced 400 barrels in its first year. Taken over in 1856 by an employee, Joseph Schlitz, its vats were producing 75,000 barrels annually twenty years later.[59] Valentin Blatz,

[57] Charles E. Schefft, The Tanning Industry in Wisconsin: A History of Its Frontier Origins and Its Development, pp. 16, 23-26, 36-37, 39, MS, M.A. thesis, dated 1938, University of Wisconsin. This work will hereafter be cited as Schefft, Tanning Industry in Wisconsin.

[58] *One Hundred Years of Brewing*, supplement to *The Western Brewer* (H. S. Rich & Company, New York, 1903), 222; Thomas C. Cochran, *The Pabst Brewing Company: The History of an American Business* (New York, 1948), chaps. 1-3. The present spelling of the name of Phillip Best, one among several variations, has been adopted since it is the one most frequently used in legal records.

[59] [Hugo W. Rohde], "Schlitz—The Brewery That Never Stopped Growing," pp. 2-3, reprint from *Beer Distributor* (August 1937).

IT "MADE MILWAUKEE FAMOUS." *Above and left:* Structural evolution of the Schlitz brewery. *Below:* "Beer for Teddy." A shipment of beer to Roosevelt's African expedition put the Milwaukee beverage in the headlines.

Bavarian brewer's son, came to Milwaukee after working in the large breweries of Würzburg, Augsburg, and Munich and found employment as a foreman in a brewery which had been founded by John Braun in 1846. Already possessed of a brewery of his own, upon Braun's death in 1851, Blatz acceded both to the former's widow and to his brewing establishment. Between 1851 and 1868 he increased production from 150 barrels to 15,366.[60] Frederick Miller, fresh from managing a brewery in Württemberg, migrated to America with $10,000 in gold and in 1855 bought the Plank Road Brewery from Charles Best. His first year's production was 300 barrels. First evidence of the export of beer from Milwaukee is found in the figures for 1852 when 645 barrels were shipped.[61] Between 1853 and 1870 the value of malt liquors produced in Milwaukee increased from $169,500 to $706,070.

Considering both the flow of wheat to the port and the normal needs of the urban community it was natural that the milling of flour should early develop in Milwaukee. Propelled by water power, the city's five flour mills produced a total output of 130,000 barrels in 1854. By 1860, the number of mills had increased to fourteen, and as early as 1856 one of the largest mills was equipped with an "immense steam engine." Accelerated production in the mid-sixties made Milwaukee the largest flour-milling city in the West; but by 1871, the flour output of St. Louis exceeded that of the Wisconsin city by nearly a million barrels.[62] The production of clothing and boots and shoes, made in small shops and largely for local consumption, constituted a major industry from the point of view of the value of the product. As a matter of fact, six industries produced commodities worth above $100,000 in the year ending March 1,

[60] *One Hundred Years of Brewing*, 333; Milwaukee *Sentinel*, Jan. 31, 1932; *Industrial History of Milwaukee: the Commercial, Manufacturing and Railway Metropolis of the North-West* (E. E. Barton, publisher, Milwaukee, 1886), 103. This work will hereafter be cited as Barton, *Industrial History of Milwaukee*.

[61] Milwaukee *Sentinel*, Jan. 24, 1932; Milwaukee *Daily Sentinel*, Dec. 30, 1853.

[62] John G. Thompson, *The Rise and Decline of the Wheat Growing Industry in Wisconsin* (University of Wisconsin, Bulletin no. 292, *Economics and Political Science Series*, vol. 5, no. 3, Madison, 1909), 108-9. This work will hereafter be cited as Thompson, *Wheat Growing in Wisconsin*.

1853—the aggregate of which, according to the *Sentinel*, showed "Milwaukee to be no insignificant city in respect to manufactures."[63] Actually, however, production of this sort was carried on in such small units as late as 1860 as to make a factory economy a development of the future. The average flour mill employed five workers in 1860; the average clothing shop, twenty-one; the average tannery, ten; brewery, four; iron foundry, twenty-five; and shoe shop, six.[64] By 1870, the increase in volume of production and in number of workers per establishment suggests the expansion in industrial capacity which had taken place in the sixties and which by 1870 brought Milwaukee to the threshold of her manufacturing era.[65]

Milwaukee's promoters—and especially the press—were eager for the day when the raw materials, now exported, could be turned into manufactured goods within the city itself. Indeed, in the production of leather, packed meat, malt liquors, and flour there was a beginning; but of furniture, agricultural implements, metal products, paint, woolen goods, boots, harness, and stoves the great proportion was imported at "the double costs of . . . unnecessary transportation." The great want was capital, and the major deterrent, the profits attainable in the trafficking trade. As early as 1859 a correspondent to the *Sentinel* suggested as an inducement to the investment of eastern capital "release from tax, of the personal property, employed in manufactories for a series of years."[66] By the mid-fifties the *Sentinel* had begun to publicize the accomplishments of Milwaukee's budding industrialists and to urge local buyers to give "our own mechanics" the preference whenever possible. As the editor wrote, "Every manufactory establishment in our midst is a substantial stone in the temple of the prosperity of our city,

[63] Milwaukee *Daily Sentinel*, March 28, 1853.

[64] *United States Census, Eighth,* 1860, *Manufactures of the United States,* 648-49.

[65] See table showing most productive industries in Milwaukee County, 1852-79, with comparative figures for 1880, drawn from *U. S. Census, Eighth,* 1860, *Manufactures of the U. S.,* 648-49; *United States Census, Ninth,* 1870, vol. 3, *The Statistics of the Wealth and Industry of the United States,* 744; and *United States Census, Tenth,* 1880, *Report on the Manufactures of the United States,* 374-75.

[66] Chamber of Commerce, *Report,* 1871; Milwaukee *Daily Sentinel,* Oct. 12, 1859.

and those who inaugurate such new enterprises are worthy workers on the edifice, and are entitled to the gratitude of the community, even though their motives may be purely for self-aggrandizement."[67] Throughout the sixties the press continued to deplore the folly, in view of possible crop failure, of "relying for our prosperity entirely upon a trafficking business"; to argue that a "thousand dollars invested in a manufacturing establishment is worth more to the city than twenty times the amount engaged in trade"; and to assert that "associated effort" would lay more permanent foundations for prosperity than wheat brokerage could supply. The demands of the Civil War provided a powerful stimulant to manufacturing and by the middle sixties it was evident that Milwaukee was entering her industrial age. January 5, 1863, saw the organization of a manufacturers' association and a visit from members of a similar group in Chicago to pledge cooperation in a program to solicit tax reduction. Active in the meeting were Messrs. Noonan, Allis, Colver, Pfister, and Tracy. The editor of the *Sentinel* pointed out that money was plentiful for investment; he could name "a half dozen dry goods houses alone, a portion of whose profits for the past year, if put into a joint stock enterprise, would suffice to establish a manufactory of . . . coarse woolen goods," and this was "true of other branches of business more or less." All that was needed was "concentration of means in common enterprises."[68]

By the spring of 1866 manufacturing was "commencing on a scale never before attempted." This was especially true in connection with the metal trades; for the extension of railroads and the building of lumber and gristmills in the hinterland as well as the needs of the expanding farmer population created a flourishing local demand for iron products and machinery. As a matter of fact, Milwaukee had had an iron foundry as early as 1840; there were two in 1847 and four in 1859, and edge tools, foundry machinery, boilers, plows, fanning mills, and threshing machinery were being made in 1849. As early as 1853

[67] *Ibid.*, Sept. 22, 23, 24, 26, 28, 1853; May 15, 1862; Jan. 29, 1863; June 10, 1869.
[68] *Ibid.*, May 15, 1862; Jan. 6, 10, 1863; Feb. 8, 1864; Oct. 20, 1866.

ESTABLISHMENTS AND VALUE OF OUTPUT IN MOST

Commodity	Value of Product March 1, 1852, to March 1, 1853	Value of Product Census of 1860 (Mfrs. for 1859)	No. of Establishments (1859)
Boots & Shoes	$103,000	$ 369,932	50
Brick	58,500	129,500	9
Clothing (Men's)	230,000 (all)	515,380	27
Cooperage	45,020	149,521	47
Flour & Meal	311,552	1,883,545	19
Furniture	?	130,705	50
Iron Castings	137,238 (incl. locomotives)	161,000	4
Machinery & Steam Engines	(in above)	242,400	9
Leather	175,304	217,500	9
Liquor (Distilled)	91,584	235,431	15
Liquor (Malt)	169,500	310,130	26
Provisions —Beef & Pork	?	513,820	8
Sash, Door, Blinds	78,800	101,550	11
Soap & Candles	37,000	145,970	9

These figures are all for Milwaukee County.

PRODUCTIVE MILWAUKEE INDUSTRIES, 1852 to 1879

No. of Workers (1859)	Value of Product Census of 1870 (for 1869)	No. of Establishments (1869)	No. of Workers (1869)	Value of Product, Census of 1880 (for 1879)
321	$ 560,579	11	392	$ 554,599
268	213,160	8	314	
556	1,417,962	56	959	3,765,487
161	176,997	56	179	
96	3,914,035	14	182	4,251,150
95	428,020	20	310	
105	1,129,562 (iron, forged & rolled, only)	1	642	5,000,000 (estimate)
114	402,460	7	255	2,252,784
95	(tanned) 799,539	15	238	2,101,195
	(curried) 934,588	14	122	2,219,978
	1,734,127			
42	395,090	5	95	300,509
112	706,070	16	233	4,625,543
60	?	?	?	6,099,486
79	449,422	8	357	557,000
80	213,524	9	39	280,090

between forty-five and fifty hands were employed at Turton and Sercomb's Eagle Foundry, producing engines and mill castings for the surrounding country; another fifty were shaping the millstones which Decker and Seville's Reliance Works exported to Michigan, Iowa, and even California; and wheelbarrows made by A. J. Langworthy's Foundry and Machine Shop were being used in connection with railroad construction.[69]

The most vigorous promoter of heavy industry in the late sixties was Captain E. B. Ward, Detroit capitalist, who joined S. Clement of Chicago, Alexander Mitchell, and others connected with the Milwaukee and St. Paul Railway in incorporating the Milwaukee Iron Company. By 1873 its product was valued at $3,000,000, and it employed a thousand workers. In 1868, Ward urged the citizens to "build up manufactures" and "help themselves to a new life." In 1869 the *Sentinel* reported that an English capitalist was ready to invest $200,000 in two blast furnaces if Milwaukeeans would supply a like sum, and Ward offered to build a smelting works if facilities could be extended.[70] Regardless of war or depression, the press labored constantly in the promotion of manufactures, urging eastern capital to "examine the inducements which Milwaukee offers." In 1868, a correspondent, "Enterprise," urged the citizens "of every grade to unite in one grand effort to regain our prestige. . . . We want more manufacturers," he wrote, "and the way to get them is to let them know that there is a vacuum which it would be for their and our interest to fill." Potential investors, city promoters, and Chamber of Commerce thus continued to whip the city forward, counseling her against putting "all the city's eggs" in the one basket of trade; and as a result of their efforts, by 1872 one-third to one-half of the city's working population was engaged in industry, producing goods to the value of $20,000,000. However, the lack of factories capable of large-scale production made impossible the manufacture in Milwaukee of the typewriter patented by Milwaukeeans Christopher L.

[69] Whitbeck, *Geography of Southeastern Wisconsin*, 112; Milwaukee *Daily Sentinel*, Sept. 22, 23, 24, 1853; March 3, 1866.
[70] Merk, *Economic History of Wisconsin during the Civil War*, 143; Milwaukee *Daily Sentinel*, Oct. 1, 1868; April 19, June 10, 1869.

Sholes, Carlos Glidden, and Samuel Soule in 1868. Invented by Sholes and his associates in 1867, the typewriter was first manufactured on a considerable scale by the firm of E. Remington and Sons, famous gunmakers of Ilion, New York.[71]

The economic depression which had cast its shadow over Milwaukee in the early years of cityhood began to clear in 1853 with the building of railroads and other public works, the increase in migration, and bumper crops for which unprecedented prices could be asked. By the fall of 1855, the streets were blocked with teams, the sidewalks were choked with pedestrians, and Milwaukee, again on the "upper shelf of prosperity," was enjoying the expansive prelude to another collapse. The opening of the Newhall House late in August 1857, challenging "comparisons with the best hotels in New York and Boston," and the construction of James H. Rogers' $60,000 mansion in that year were symbols of the expansion that came to a halt almost at the moment of their completion. By the last of August, business houses were failing in New York and in the following month specie payment was suspended. Although the press ascribed the financial difficulties to an excess of imports and an exclusive dependence on trade in grain, the preoccupation with railroad promotion, already discussed, was a major contributing factor.[72] In 1859 a suggestion of European war stimulated prices; and by the sixties confidence was almost entirely regained. While the panic of 1857 was felt in Wisconsin more than in other parts of the country, Milwaukee was cushioned during the depression of 1861, as has already been pointed out, because of the diversion of trade from the Mississippi. The *Sentinel* reported a "buoyancy and vitality" in commercial pur-

---

[71] Milwaukee *Daily Sentinel and Gazette,* March 6, 1846; May 5, 1849; Milwaukee *Daily Sentinel,* June 22, 1858; April 22, 1868; April 16, 1869; Merk, *Economic History of Wisconsin during the Civil War,* 127. According to an article in the Milwaukee *Daily Sentinel* for December 29, 1868, capital of over $19,000,000 was then employed in manufacturing and industrial activities in the city. For the invention of the typewriter in Milwaukee, see Frederic Heath, "The Typewriter in Wisconsin," *Wisconsin Magazine of History,* 27:263-75 (March 1944). The world's largest collection of typewriters is in the possession of the Milwaukee Public Museum, the gift of Alderman Carl P. Dietz.

[72] Milwaukee *Daily Sentinel,* Nov. 28, 1855; Aug. 21, 1857; May 10, 1858; Oct. 12, 1859; Buck, 4:176-77.

suits which the "suppression of a mighty rebellion" could not impair. The program of promotion—in the fields of railroads, manufacturing, and education—laid down by the editor at the beginning of 1865 showed that there was little relaxation in city development despite the existence of civil war.[73] Moreover, the war itself provided a powerful stimulant to profit-making. Alexander Mitchell's income was listed as $53,071 for 1863; $53,056 for 1864; $77,223 for 1865; $132,000 for 1866; $131,000 for 1867; and $126,000 for 1868. Six Milwaukeeans accumulated more than $30,000 apiece in 1863; seventeen gained that figure or above in 1864. By 1865 the number had dropped to five; for 1866 there were ten; 1867, nine; and 1868, five. Eighty-three persons had incomes of more than $10,000 in 1864; the number fell to forty-eight in the following year. These "solid men" of Milwaukee were predominantly merchants and jobbers, although persons in this kind of business frequently were manufacturers, of a sort, as well. Among them were forty-one wholesale merchants, fourteen manufacturers, three bankers, two lumber dealers, three or four commission merchants, and four warehouse owners. Top incomes were earned by Plankinton, the packer; Lester Sexton, dry goods jobber; Mitchell, banker; John Nazro, hardware jobber; Pfister and Vogel, tanners; James Bonnell, dry goods jobber; and Charles T. Bradley, boot and shoe jobber and manufacturer.[74] One looks in vain for the real estate promoters of an earlier day. The spoils of the sixties went to the railroad financiers, the processors of the raw materials of the hinterland, and the merchants and jobbers whose activities had made Milwaukee by 1870 one of the major commercial marts of the Middle West.

It was in this period of self-confident urban adolescence that young Milwaukee felt most keenly its rivalry with the budding metropolis at the base of the lake. "Which shall be the greatest, Milwaukee or Chicago?" queried a correspondent in an 1847 issue of the Boston *Chronotype*. "On entering a western city, as a first step you are pointed out all the advantages, which it

[73] Milwaukee *Daily Sentinel,* May 2, 1861; Jan. 2, 1865.
[74] For figures on income, see *ibid.,* Aug. 7, 1865; July 31, Aug. 1, 1866; May 25, 1867; May 9, 1868.

has over every other place. In the race of rivalry, Chicago and Milwaukee deserve the premium; separated ninety miles from each other, on the lower part of Lake Michigan, they respectively expect to become the centre of the immense trade which must ultimately belong to this region." The census of 1850 gave Milwaukee hope; she was then more than two-thirds her neighbor's size, and the projected transit route across the lake from Milwaukee to Grand Haven gave promise of by-passing Chicago in the trade flowing to and from the Northwest.[75] By 1860, however, Chicago's growth had left the Wisconsin city half her size, and by another decade only a fourth as large.[76]

In this contest of population, many a subterfuge was devised by each city to discredit the other in the eyes of European immigrants and eastern investors. According to the Chicago *Democrat*, every Milwaukeean constituted himself a "committee of offence and defence, to go forth like some ancient knight-errant to fight the battles of his city." The Chicago newspaper charged that handbills had been circulated along the line of travel from New York giving alarming accounts of cholera in the Illinois city. It printed the following specimen of "gossip" which it accused Milwaukee of hiring writers to contribute to eastern newspapers:

Our next landing was at Chicago. . . . no business was going on; many were leaving the place on account of the pestilence . . . from 20 to 30 dying daily. . . . The thick, greasy water that stands in the streets looks as if it were full of pestilence. . . . It might improve upon further acquaintance, but I could never be made to relish the smell of the place. . . . After leaving . . . , we . . . reached the young and flourishing city of Milwaukee. . . . Its future destiny is not problematical. It is bound to become one of the largest and most delightful cities in the whole country.

The Milwaukee papers countered by asserting that comparisons

---

[75] Quotation from Boston *Chronotype*, in Wheeler, *Chronicles of Milwaukee*, 208; Milwaukee *Daily Sentinel*, April 28, 1859.

[76] Comparative population:

	1840	1850	1860	1870	1880
Chicago	4,470	29,963	109,260	298,977	503,185
Milwaukee	1,712	20,061	45,246	71,440	115,587

United States Census, Fifteenth, 1930, *Population,* 1:280, 1180.

were "odorous" and the Chicago complaint only an attempt to cover that city's behavior in publishing false and discreditable reports on health conditions and population growth in the Wisconsin city.[77]

Trade statistics and the comparative business of their harbors were the basis of inter-city controversy in the forties. "Why is a laden vessel leaving the port of Chicago like a Western Hunter?" asked a correspondent in the *Sentinel and Gazette*, and answered, "Because whenever she takes a 'shute' she hits a Bar." The wheat trade was the symbol of conflict in the fifties. According to the editor of the *Sentinel* in 1859:

> The reasons why Milwaukee can pay a better price for good wheat than can be obtained for it in Chicago are very easily comprehended. It is a well known fact that the great bulk of wheat marketed here is much superior to that which supplies Chicago, coming as a vast deal of the latter does from Central and Southern Illinois. Consequently our market has a better reputation than Chicago, and Milwaukee wheat invariably brings a higher price in Eastern and European markets than Chicago wheat. So much poor spring wheat goes to Chicago, that whenever any good wheat is sent there it becomes absorbed in inferior qualities, and though it might be good enough to pass in Milwaukee as No. 1 club or extra No. 1, at Chicago it is inspected as "standard spring," and sells with the avalanche of dirty stuff that comes under that head at $1.08 to $1.10 while at Milwaukee it would bring $1.14 to $1.20. These are some of the reasons why Milwaukee pays a better price for wheat than her southern neighbor.

By the sixties, the two cities were vying for the markets of the interior, and Milwaukeeans were publicizing correspondence from Rolling Prairie, Wisconsin, in which the writer asserted that despite the conflicting claims of Chicago's agents to the Northwest, trade with Milwaukee was cheaper, easier, and more efficient. Added the writer:

> No man acquainted in Chicago would feel that security and safety that he does in Milwaukee. . . . No quiet country merchant wishes to run the gauntlet of such a set of swindlers and sharpers

---

[77] Milwaukee *Daily Sentinel and Gazette*, Sept. 6, 1850. See also Aug. 26, 1846; Sept. 4, Dec. 4, 1850.

as the police of that city [Chicago] allow to besiege every country man whom they dare approach.[78]

Despite the mutual vilification in which representatives of the two cities indulged, in many ways they were cooperative neighbors. This was apparent in their joint efforts to gain internal improvements from the federal government, in the friendly relations of their respective fire and militia companies which forever were exchanging visits for celebrations, encampments, and parades,[79] and in the joint activities of such organizations as the Young Men's associations of the two cities in making lecturers from the East available to western audiences. The rivalry between the two cities, in addition to attesting the exuberant self-confidence of the expanding West, is chiefly significant as evidence of the bearing of geographical position upon the urban promise of the two competing communities. In a period of waterborne commerce, Milwaukee had a potential advantage with respect to the trade of the developing Northwest. But the increasing emphasis upon overland railroad transport and the elaboration of trunkline connections focusing unquestionably upon the city at the tip of the lake left the Wisconsin city an inevitable, if still assertive, second in the race for urban supremacy in the upper Middle West.

[78] *Ibid.*, Sept. 27, 1848; Milwaukee *Sentinel*, May 21, 24, June 8, Aug. 5, Nov. 9, 1859; Milwaukee *Daily Sentinel*, March 14, 1867; see also April 25, 1867; June 8, 1869. For the development of Milwaukee's chief rival on Lake Michigan, see Bessie L. Pierce's admirable work, *A History of Chicago* (2 vols., New York, 1937, 1940).

[79] Milwaukee *Sentinel and Gazette*, Oct. 18, 1850; Milwaukee *Daily Sentinel*, Sept. 22, 1853; July 8, 1856.

CHAPTER 9

The Pattern of Culture

BY THE sixties, Milwaukee was beginning to exhibit the cultural as well as the commercial attributes of cityhood. A New England visitor, Nathaniel P. Willis, expecting to come upon a settlement of wigwams and wampum, discovered the Wisconsin city in 1860 to be "as smart a little metropolis as you would find anywhere in Massachusetts."[1] Had he analyzed the community, he would have found ample evidence of the commercial specialization that connotes an urban society.[2] On the turn of the sixties the city could boast at least 17 insurance agents; 7 architects and 12 civil engineers; 38 bakeries and 20 confectionery stores; 15 restaurants, 62 private boarding houses, and 42 hotels and taverns; 202 saloons and 36 tobacco and snuff stores; 38 boot and shoe dealers and 52 shoemaker's shops; 49 retail and 15 wholesale dry goods stores, 29 wholesale and retail clothing stores, 27 milliners, 60 tailors, 17 dressmaking establishments, 22 gentlemen's furnishing stores, and 17 dealers in hats and caps; 26 retail drug stores; 18 jewelry stores; 28 wagon shops and 8 carriage makers; 20 cabinet manufacturers, 11 furniture dealers, and 7 lamp and chandelier stores; 64 physicians and surgeons and 10 dentists; 73 lawyers and law firms; and 64 commission merchants, 12 fruit stores (wholesale and retail), 70 retail meat markets, and 224 retail grocers—not to mention the manufactories, hide and leather stores, lumber dealers, machine shops, carpenters, feed stores, livery stables, coal dealers, real estate brokers, house painters, and the like that

[1] Gregory, *History*, 2:1320.
[2] Buck, 4:357-58. See appendix for chart showing distribution of population by selected occupations, 1870 to 1940. The business directories appended to the annual city directories provide a useful classification by trades and professions.

completed the commercial and mercantile inventory of the community.

The young city, with its coordinate German and American communities, was in a stage of transition between the village and the emerging metropolis; and both provincialism and individualism were characteristic of its social life. Individualism was the keynote of the generation; and the citizens, as individuals, more than the force of the community as a social whole, were responsible for the solution of most of the problems which urban living presented. The provincialism was a consequence of both time and place; for although the increase in population made possible somewhat more specialization and professionalism than was true of village days, the standard of living of the community was still conditioned by the distance of the city from New York and the meager industrialism of the age. At the outset of cityhood the east-coast cities were more than fifty hours away by the fastest available route. In 1852 a journey to New York involved traveling to Chicago by boat, boarding the cars of the Michigan Southern for Toledo, and after a series of adventures on plank and railroads, embarking there upon steamers for Buffalo where one connected with "express trains" for the metropolitan centers of the East. By the close of the generation, rail connections were available all the way from Milwaukee to New York, but as late as the middle seventies the trip consumed close to forty-eight hours.[3] The commercial focus of the young city bolstered the provincialism which geography induced, for the interests of the merchant class identified the community as much with the country merchant and the westward-moving farmer as with the city dweller; and in their abundant advertisements for shot guns, pistols, lumber wagons, and ploughs, as well as for white lead, linseed oil, window glass, putty, and

---

[3] In 1869 the Chicago and North Western had three trains daily to Chicago, each traversing the distance in slightly less than four hours; and there was a 3:15 P.M. train out of Chicago that reached New York forty hours later. Sleeping cars ran through to New York without change, but with dining cars a development of the future, travelers had to stop periodically for meals. Edward Hungerford, *Men and Iron* (New York, 1938), 247; Milwaukee *Daily Sentinel*, Sept. 9, 1852; Sept. 10, 1867; Sept. 13, 1869. See "Wisconsin's First Railroad," ed. by Alice E. Smith, *Wisconsin Magazine of History*, 30:336-37 (March 1947).

nails, the newspapers of the period reflected the activities and interests of a community that, almost until the turn of the seventies, was as much concerned with building civilization out of wilderness as with producing the refinements of urban life.

Community self-sufficiency and local fabrication set the keynote of the standard of living in most matters of dress, diet, and household accoutrements. This was an age of "yard goods" in ladies' dress and to a considerable extent that of their husbands. Early in the generation the many advertisements for prints, lawns, delaines, calicoes, cambrics, and striped shirting suggested the home manufacture by which Milwaukee's housewives and their hired seamstresses fashioned the clothing of the generation; and the popularity of such enterprises as the "Fashionable Dress-Making Establishment" of Mrs. R. Patterson, who advertised that she was "ready to execute all orders in Dressmaking in the most fashionable styles," signified that the age of the ready-made dress shop was still to come.[4] Men could purchase cravats, stocks, collars, and gloves at the "Sign of the Golden Hat," but they, too, relied on the local tailors for their suits. The Emporium of Fashion employed the most skillful journeymen tailors and turned out gentlemen's clothes according to the "Simon Pure New York, London, and Paris fashions" from which the garments were "drafted."[5] Occasional advertisements of New York firms listed the "furnishing goods for gentlemen and ladies" that were available on order there;[6] but as late as 1869 "dress goods" rather than ready-made costumes lined the merchants' shelves; and the availability of the sewing machine—in home use by the sixties—and the products of the Milwaukee Hoop Skirt Factory continued to implement a flourishing business for the city's many seamstresses and dressmaking establishments and encourage the domestic production of women's attire.[7]

In the culinary department, Milwaukeeans were no longer completely dependent upon what was produced in their own

[4] Milwaukee *Daily Sentinel and Gazette,* Sept. 9, 1847; Milwaukee *Daily Sentinel,* Sept. 10, 1857.
[5] Milwaukee *Daily Sentinel and Gazette,* Sept. 9, 1847.
[6] *Ibid.*
[7] See advertisements in Milwaukee *Daily Sentinel* for 1867 and 1869.

kitchen gardens and baked in their own kitchens. To be sure, the shelves of the local grocers, both retail and wholesale, were laden with the staple ingredients of such cookery —Rio coffee, Pekin tea, salt, butter, spices, raisins, vinegar, molasses, sardines, and codfish. However, as early as 1847 some of the grocers were advertising the receipt of fresh fruit daily from Buffalo and Cleveland, and the Empire Bakery notified the public that it could furnish "Bread, Crackers, Hard Bread, Cakes, Pastry, etc., . . . at the lowest cash prices." At Peaslee's confectionery there was ice cream "by the glass or gallon" as well as a "mineral fountain" that "gushed forth its delightful beverage."[8] The increase in the number of fruit dealers and bakers by the turn of the sixties relieved Milwaukeeans of an earlier dependence on home cooking and fruit and vegetable gardens; but not until the close of the generation, when the firm of Bickel and Clark was advertising "canned, green, and dried fruits, preserves, Crosse and Blackwell's pickles, olive oils, sauces, and catsups," did they have recourse to the canned goods that were to become an indispensable adjunct to urban living.[9]

During the course of the generation, the "lamp and stove" era was giving way to that of gas illumination and the hot air furnace in household appliances; but furniture, like articles of dress, was in the main produced in the local community. In house heating, the generation was primarily a wood-burning age; popular stoves of the fifties, produced at the local Decker and Seville Reliance Works, were the "Economist," double oven cooking stove; the "Triumph," single oven; the "Radiator," coal stove; and the "Juno Parlor," with its "beautifully ornamented" front, adapted equally "to offices as well as parlors."[10] The "American Air-Tight," an eastern-made cooking stove, could be procured at the "Sign of the Mill Saw." By 1867, Bonnell's was advertising hot air furnaces, and M. M. Leahy could supply gas and steam fittings in all branches, with "particular attention to the heating of public buildings, manu-

[8] Milwaukee *Daily Sentinel and Gazette*, Sept. 9, 1847.
[9] Milwaukee *Daily Sentinel*, Sept. 13, 1869.
[10] *Ibid.*, Sept. 9, 1852.

factories, and private dwellings."¹¹ Local cabinetmakers supplemented the supply of furniture brought by urban migrants to the new community. In 1847, Auchmoody's Cabinet and Chair Manufactory offered bureaus, tables, bedsteads, chairs, ottomans, dressing and toilet tables, cradles, and coffins ("made to order at the shortest notice") for cash, lumber, or country produce; and the Milwaukee Cabinet, Sofa, Chair, and Upholstery Warehouse advertised fashionable furniture in "Elizabethan, Gothic, Louis XV, and plain" designs—the equal of "any made in the city of New York."¹² Twenty years later, the availability of refrigerators, ice-boxes, and water coolers suggested the progress of urban civilization; but the notices of the carriage manufactories, describing their family conveyances, top and open buggies, and the like, are reminders that the community was still in a "horse-drawn" stage.

Milwaukeeans profited from an increasing professionalism in the practice of medicine during the first generation of cityhood; for although many of the doctors took an active interest in city politics and followed hobbies of various types, few of them were the "jacks of all trades" so many had been in the village period.¹³ In spite of the fact that the citizens had access to the services of well-trained physicians, they were still accustomed, as in many other aspects of their existence, to take matters of this sort into their own hands. As a consequence, there was a ready market for the "Private Medical Companion," which could be sent from New York for $1.00, and for such patent remedies as "Anodyne Cordial" for summer complaint, Comstock's sarsaparillas, Dr. Osgood's "Cholagogue," House's "Indian tonic," and "Vegetable Vermifuge" for fever and ague, Scarpa's "Acoustic Oil" for deafness, Dr. Hoofland's "Celebrated German Bitters," and Dr. Thompson's "Patent Pelvic Corset for Afflicted Females."¹⁴ Along with the German immigration of 1848 came a number of distinguished physicians possessed of excellent European training; and at the close of the

¹¹ *Ibid.*, Sept. 10, 1867.
¹² Milwaukee *Daily Sentinel and Gazette*, Sept. 9, 1847.
¹³ See biographies in Frank, *Medical History of Milwaukee*.
¹⁴ Milwaukee *Daily Sentinel and Gazette*, Sept. 9, 1847; Milwaukee *Daily Sentinel*, Sept. 9, 1852; Sept. 9, 1857.

Civil War there was an influx of young, American-trained doctors who had been surgeons in the Union Army.[15] Milwaukee's first woman physician was Dr. Laura J. Ross, who began to practice in the city in 1857.[16]

The work of the Milwaukee City Medical Association, founded on December 11, 1847, and recruited from both Yankee and Teutonic physicians, promoted the professionalism of the group, as did such other organizations as the Medical Society of Milwaukee County (1846), the Medico-Chirurgical Club (1851), the Society of German Physicians (1853), and the Milwaukee Medical and Surgical Club, later Milwaukee Medical Society (1869).[17] By-products of this tendency to organize, in addition to the advancement of professional methods, were the creation of hospitals, the training of nurses, and the improvement of business practices for the doctors, as a result of which a standard fee bill was adopted in December 1868.[18] The appearance of dentists, with their advertisements of "Ethereal Vapor" and "Morton's patent letheon" for those who might "wish to have their teeth extracted without pain," suggested a specialization that was to increase during the generation; and in 1857 Dr. George Capron was advertising himself to be a specialist in diseases of the chest, throat, eye, and ear.[19] St. Mary's Hospital, opened in 1848, under the name of St. John's Infirmary, and the Milwaukee Hospital, founded in 1863, both of them charitable and subscription enterprises, provided a beginning of hospital facilities that were to be greatly multiplied in the next and more fully professionalized generation of cityhood.[20]

Professional music, art, and dramatics of a sort had early supplemented the amateur endeavor of the village period along these lines, but professional expression in the arts remained transient, intermittent, and generally fortuitous in the initial generation of cityhood; for the community had not yet devel-

---

[15] Gregory, *History*, 2:962-69.
[16] *Ibid.*, 2:967.
[17] Frank, *Medical History of Milwaukee*, 108-10; Gregory, *History*, 2:986-87.
[18] *Ibid.*, 2:986; Frank, *Medical History of Milwaukee*, 119-20.
[19] Milwaukee *Daily Sentinel*, Sept. 10, 1857; Milwaukee *Daily Sentinel and Gazette*, Sept. 9, 1847.
[20] Frank, *Medical History of Milwaukee*, 145-48.

oped in taste, wealth, or numbers to the point where cultural advantages could be permanently and continuously available or in such abundance as to permit wide choice. Chicago shared its theatrical fare with Milwaukee in the early years of cityhood.[21] Early in December 1847 a company managed by John B. Rice, which had been performing for several months in the Illinois city, gave a short season of plays after fitting up the Military Hall for a theater.[22] On December 3, "a large and very respectable audience" expressed its "surprise and satisfaction at the neat and comfortable arrangements of the Hall and the unexpected excellence of the Company." The bill included a play entitled *The Wife*, an "amusing farce," "His Last Legs," a comic song by Mr. Merrifield, and the *Cracovienne* by Miss Homer.[23] Rice succeeded in interesting a group of local citizens in providing the city with a theater building; and as a result the press could boast, late in November 1848, that "Milwaukee, though but a two-year-old city," now had a theater. The new edifice had a 39 by 37-foot stage, two rows of boxes capable of accommodating from 450 to 500 persons, and a pit that would hold as many more. A smaller building, attached to the main structure in the rear, provided the Green Room, dressing rooms, and the like.[24] Here, until the theater burned in 1853, repertory or stock companies performed summer and winter seasons lasting variously from one week to seven or eight. At the outset the casts were largely family affairs, inasmuch as two or three couples and their children assumed most of the roles. They usually included, however, a headliner of talent and reputation whom the city's theater-goers took eagerly to their hearts. Among these were Mrs. Mossop (later Mrs. John Drew), Julia Dean (the "Star of the West"), J. H. McVicker, Miss J. M. Davenport, Henrietta Irving, and, in 1868, Edwin Booth.[25] Despite the existence of considerably more Shakespeare in the dramatic diet than would have been available a century later, the less

---

[21] Milwaukee *Sentinel and Gazette,* Nov. 24, 1846.
[22] *Ibid.,* Nov. 27, 1847.
[23] Milwaukee *Daily Sentinel and Gazette,* Dec. 4, 1847.
[24] Milwaukee *Sentinel and Gazette,* Nov. 27, 1848.
[25] An enthusiastic press agent described Julia Dean as without "superior as a tragic actress on the American stage" and as rivaling Mrs. Kean (Ellen Tree), Fanny Kemble, or Mrs. Siddons. *Ibid.,* June 29, 1849.

classic melodrama and the farce were more frequently performed and probably more popular; and serious plays were almost invariably accompanied by a farcical afterpiece. Thus when *Othello* was presented in 1854, it was coupled with *Sam Slick*, *Richard III* with *Angel of the Attic*, and *Macbeth* with *The Lying Valet*.[26]

The new theater was to have opened with *As You Like It* in 1848, but sickness in the cast necessitated the substitution of a less pretentious play, *The Honeymoon*.[27] "Readings from Shakespeare" were announced in 1849, but they drew small crowds;[28] for, according to the *Sentinel's* critic, the public preferred "more modern authors."[29] But J. E. Murdoch was complimented for his performances in *Hamlet, Romeo and Juliet,* and *Othello* in 1850; and large audiences gathered to hear Mrs. Fanny Kemble read from Shakespeare's works in 1856, 1857, and 1868. Opposition to the theater on grounds of Yankee morality had also to be overcome; and press agents were constantly at pains to point out that Mr. Rice's theater was free of the "objectionable accompaniments usual in the Theatre of larger cities."[30]

The intimate identification of player and audience reflected in a sense the provincialism of the local scene; and the enthusiastic welcome accorded the return of such stars as Julia Dean and J. H. McVicker revealed the pleasure of the young com-

[26] A typical stock company repertoire of this period is that of Powell and Dunn's Dramatic Troupe, which gave a series of performances in 1854 with J. P. Adams as star. The bills for succeeding nights included *The Stranger* and *Rough Diamond; Othello* and *Sam Slick; The Iron Chest, or Mysterious Murder* and *Sam Patch in France; Lady of the Lake* and *Nothing Superfluous; Black-eyed Susan* and *Hunter of the Alps; The Firemen of Milwaukee,* a local drama devised especially for the occasion, and *Rough and Ready; Lady of Lyons* and *Perfection; Woman's Rights, Raising the Wind,* and *A Glance at New York; Macbeth* and *Secret; La Tour de Nesle, or Chamber of Death* and *Love Alone Can Fix Him; Richelieu* and *Day After the Wedding; Richard III* and *Angel of the Attic; Pizarro* and *Love, Law, and Physic; Macbeth* and *The Lying Valet; Margaret of Burgundy* and *The Loan of a Lover; The Soldier's Daughter* and *The Spectre Bridegroom;* and a complimentary and farewell benefit to Mr. and Mrs. E. S. Conner to include *Richelieu,* a recitation of Collin's *Ode on the Passions,* and *Personation.* Milwaukee *Daily Sentinel,* Sept. 5 through Oct. 9, 1854.

[27] Milwaukee *Daily Sentinel and Gazette,* Dec. 2, 1848.

[28] *Ibid.,* Aug. 15, 1849; Milwaukee *Daily Sentinel,* Dec. 22, 1857.

[29] Milwaukee *Daily Sentinel and Gazette,* Jan. 15, 1849.

[30] *Ibid.* See also Milwaukee *Sentinel,* Jan. 22, 29, 1857; Milwaukee *Daily Sentinel,* Oct. 20, 1868.

munity in the theatrical entertainment which such actors made available.³¹ The players contributed their services to local causes; and it was the practice of the leading citizens to "tender" a benefit, or complimentary performance, to a popular player before his departure from the city. On the occasion of Mrs. Rice's benefit in April 1850 the invitation was signed by seventy-five of the city's leading citizens, headed by King, Walker, Crocker, and Levi Hubbell.³² Audiences were not always as orderly as the niceties of society dictated, to judge from the number of occasions on which the manager had to reprove them; and from the professions of press agents to the contrary, *double-entendre* and ribaldry must frequently have occurred on the stage.³³ In addition to the stock companies that appealed primarily to those of English speech, there were the earlier mentioned German theater, in which the "utmost propriety" was observed, according to the *Sentinel,* and the "objectionable feature of the 'leg drama' and expressions of double entente . . . guarded against,"³⁴ and a variety of other entertainment such as performances of Christy's Minstrels, the appearance of General Tom Thumb, dime museums, curiosities like Julia Pastrana, the bear woman, and the perennial circuses and menageries.³⁵ A dearth of theatrical fare in the late sixties was broken in June 1869 with the arrival of a company from McVicker and Myers' theater in Chicago. They were scheduled to play *Under the Gaslight,* to be produced with "full scenic effect, a train of cars running across the stage at a terrible rate, a man tied on the track, and everything else necessary to a regular sensational drama." *A Regular Fix* was announced as the afterpiece.³⁶

[31] Milwaukee *Daily Sentinel,* July 5, 1852.
[32] Milwaukee *Sentinel and Gazette,* April 10, 1850. See also Milwaukee *Daily Sentinel,* July 5, Oct. 17, Feb. 14, 1852.
[33] According to the report of the first performance in the new theater, on December 2, 1848, "one or two 'free and easy' individuals in the pit occasioned considerable annoyance by their disorderly behavior. Mr. Rice, however, by a few well-timed words, indicative of his determination to enforce good order in the Theatre, quieted the noise and was warmly applauded." Milwaukee *Sentinel and Gazette,* Dec. 5, 1848.
[34] For German theater see chapter 6; Milwaukee *Daily Sentinel,* Jan. 15, 1869.
[35] *Ibid.,* Oct. 16, 1855.
[36] *Ibid.,* June 14, 1869.

Interest in city promotion as well as the needs of the expanding urban community prompted a demand as early as 1858 for a permanent place of amusement, "open every evening through the year." A good theater, a public lecture room, and concerts or lectures, wrote their advocate, "would attract many persons from the country who would bring their families to enjoy for a short time a city life and who would all leave a sum of money which, in the aggregate, would aid materially not only the hotel keepers but every branch of the retail trade."[37] The close of the sixties saw continued agitation for such permanent places of recreation and amusement where entertainment would have something more than a "chance" or transient character. But in spite of this, public entertainment continued to have a "home-talent" flavor; and professional entertainers of quality were only infrequently available. The sum of professional performances for the last four months of 1869 included gymnastic exercises by John Denier at Quentin Park; four concerts at the Music Hall by Blind Tom, "the Musical Wonder"; the display of a century plant in full bloom; four performances of *Hibernicon*, in which a cast of four persons presented a tour through Ireland; two evenings of Billy Pastor's Great Burlesque Combination; four performances of opera by Parepa Rosa's English Opera Troupe; a concert by Mlle. Carlotta Patti; and two song and dance exhibitions by Charley Gardner and his son, Master Charley. Occasional concerts by the Musical Society, its production of the opera *Fra Diavolo*, the opera *Lurline*, produced by the Philharmonic Society, and *Camille*, presented by members of the Rebecca Lodge, gave amateurs a chance to contribute to the meager entertainment fare; and in addition to the "numbers" on the lecture series of the Young Men's Association there were professional addresses by George Francis Train, Bayard Taylor, and a Doctor O'Brennan, who was listed to speak on "Ireland among the Nations." For the rest of the time, pleasure seekers had to be content with the picnics of the church societies, "social parties" such as those of the Hibernian Benevolent Society and the Mechanics and Blacksmiths Union No. 1, a season of skating at the Skating Rink, or the weekly dances and

[37] *Ibid.*, Sept. 17, 1858.

balls of the many dancing academies that flourished in the city.[38] And even though there was agitation for a wider and more professional selection in the field of entertainment, many of the citizens were content with what prevailed and continued to support what one critic called the "vilest varieties"—negro minstrels, Five Points' dance houses, the "leg drama," and Sunday theaters.[39]

Viewing Milwaukee in 1851, Bishop Henni came to the conclusion that a "taste for art" was "still in its infancy there."[40] Utility and amusement, rather than appreciation, provided the major excuse for painting in a community that did not resist art, but that was neither sufficiently settled nor possessed of enough time or money to subsidize it. Occasional painters like B. I. Durward, the Scotchman, and Henry Vianden, Munich-trained artist, found portrait painting more remunerative than the agricultural pursuits they had hoped to follow in the West;[41] and indeed there was a flourishing market in the city for miniature and portrait painters and for practitioners of the art of daguerreotype and, later, photography. George C. Wood, the proprietor of the Daguerreotype and Phrenological Room, advertised in 1847 that he held himself ready to take, among other portraits, the likeness of a corpse at a moment's warning.[42] The artists labored under difficulties, having to make their own canvas and devise their brushes of broom-straw and horsehair in the early years.[43] Vianden, who exhibited his paintings in the fall of 1849, apparently painted for aesthetic as well as

---

[38] In 1869 there were L. W. Vizay's Dancing Academy, Professor Snow's New York Dancing Academy, and those of Severance and Brother and a Professor Deuchar. *Ibid.*, Aug. 31 to Dec. 31, 1869.

[39] *Ibid.*, Jan. 15, Feb. 5, 1869. A visitor from Iowa blamed Milwaukee's mixed population for the fact that the city lacked first-class places of amusement. He admitted that "the Germans have an extensive theater, which is patronized only by those of their own nationality." *Ibid.*, Dec. 23, 1869.

[40] Peter Leo Johnson, ed., "Letters of the Right Reverend John Martin Henni and the Reverend Anthony Urbanek," *Wisconsin Magazine of History*, 10:79 (September 1926).

[41] Butts, *Art in Wisconsin*, 76-81, 109-14.

[42] Milwaukee *Daily Sentinel and Gazette*, Sept. 9, 1847. In 1857 Brown's Picture Gallery advertised daguerreotypes, photographs, and ambrotypes. Milwaukee *Daily Sentinel*, Sept. 10, 1857.

[43] Butts, *Art in Wisconsin*, 76.

commercial reasons, planting the seeds of a real art movement that was to flower in succeeding years.[44]

The closest approach to a public art museum in the city was the occasional exhibit, for a fee of 25 cents, of such "masterpieces" as "Rossiter's Magnificent Historical Paintings, the Return of the Dove to the Ark, or the Triumph of Faith, and Miriam, the Prophetess, Exulting over the Destruction of Pharaoh's Host," with explanatory lectures,[45] and "Martin's grand and solemn paintings of The Last Judgment, The Great Day of His Wrath, and The Plains of Heaven, covering 200 feet of canvas."[46] The panorama was a substitute for both the art exhibit and the "silent drama" of a later day, and many of them were produced, as well as shown, in Milwaukee. One of the best was Henry Lewis' "Mississippi Panorama": 900 yards of painting, 4 feet in height, unrolling from spool to spool and depicting "faithfully and vividly" the "scenery of the Mississippi, from the City of St. Louis to the Falls of St. Anthony."[47] Panoramas unfolding a replica of the Garden of Eden, with Adam and Eve pictured life size, or of Niagara Falls, Ireland, and the countries of the Continent transported audiences of the fifties out of the relative isolation of the American West. According to advance notices of one of the most popular, "the hurrying clerk, the perfumed dandy, the marvels of New York, the dashing equestrian, the funeral and the festival, dogs and horses, . . . cursing drivers, Turk and Tennesseean, Christian, Chinese—all tribes and tongues who crowd the streets in New York City" could be seen for 25 cents, or $1.00 for parties of five. More than 600 persons attended the opening performance, and during the course of the showing the number of spectators continued to increase.[48]

The opportunity to hear professional musicians was also a matter of chance in mid-nineteenth-century Milwaukee, although good music performed by talented amateurs was almost

[44] *Ibid.*, 101, 108-13.
[45] Milwaukee *Sentinel and Gazette*, July 22, 1851.
[46] Milwaukee *Daily Sentinel*, Sept. 14, 1857. Lotteries provided a popular means for the sale of painting in the late fifties. *Ibid.*, Dec. 24, 1858.
[47] Milwaukee *Sentinel and Gazette*, Oct. 30, 1849.
[48] Milwaukee *Daily Sentinel*, Oct. 10, 1853.

continually available at the concerts of the Milwaukee Musical Society.[49] Occasionally, transient violinists and pianists, of at least professional aspirations, would give concerts in the local churches at which Paganini's "Carnival of Venice" and the airs from Bellini's *Norma* were considerably overworked.[50] For the amateur performer, pianos of the proprietor's own make could be purchased at George F. Ilsley's music store, which opened in the fall of 1847.[51] "Professor" Henry N. Hempsted began to give music lessons in 1849;[52] and in the early fifties he opened a music store where Milwaukeeans could buy such popular sheet music as "Nelly Clyde," "Bonnie Kitty," "Sebastopol Is Taken," "Yankee Girl for Me," "Riverdale Schottische," quadrilles from *Lucia di Lammermoor*, "Maiden Blush Waltzes," and "The Baby Show Polka."[53] In 1850 the press and public showed great interest in Jenny Lind, and some Milwaukeeans journeyed to New York to hear her. An unusual treat for the local community was the concert of the famous violinist, Ole Bull, whose interest in a Norwegian colonization experiment prompted his first visit to Wisconsin. At his initial appearance, in April 1853, he was accompanied by the pianist Maurice Strakosch, his wife, Amalia Patti Strakosch, and her ten-year-old sister, Adelina Patti. Bull's virtuosity in "Carnival of Venice," and the "wee signorina's" startling coloratura so delighted the listeners that an additional concert was arranged for the following evening.[54] The success of return engagements in 1854, 1856, 1857, and 1868 showed the response of Milwaukeeans to fine music when it was available. In November 1853, the New York Italian Opera Company performed the florid works of Bellini; and in 1859 a week of opera in English[55] and two nights of Verdi, featuring Madame Parodi,[56] revealed the popularity of this musical form in the developing urban community.

[49] See chapter 6.
[50] Milwaukee *Daily Sentinel and Gazette*, June 18, 1846.
[51] *Ibid.*, Nov. 16, 1847.
[52] Buck, 3:200.
[53] Milwaukee *Daily Sentinel*, Nov. 27, 1855.
[54] *Ibid.*, April 28, 29, 1853. See Albert O. Barton, "Ole Bull and His Wisconsin Contacts," *Wisconsin Magazine of History*, 7:417-44 (June 1924).
[55] Milwaukee *Sentinel*, July 19, 1859.
[56] *Ibid.*, Dec. 14, 1859.

THE PATTERN OF CULTURE 213

Public lecturers from the East kept Milwaukeeans in touch, at least intermittently, with the intellectual trends of the effervescent forties and fifties. The fads and fancies of the era were the subjects of such lectures as Dr. Houghton's on "Good Health, Bodily Vigor, and Defective Sight"[57] and Mrs. Lucy Stone Blackwell's on "Woman's Rights."[58] It was the burden of Colonel C. D. Robinson's address in 1859 on "The Genius of the West" that the American nation, "though descended from the East, had 'suffered a sea change' and come out an original people with a peculiar and 'manifest destiny' of its own."[59] For reading material there were the newspapers, periodicals such as *Harper's*, *Putnam's*, and *Graham's* magazines and *Godey's Lady's Book*, and the offerings of the circulating libraries and book stores. From the titles listed by the latter, such as *Relics from the Wreck of a Former World*, *The Widow's Walk, or the Mystery of Crime*, *The Miser's Daughter*, and *Mexico and the Military Chieftains*, reading must have filled a need supplied by the movie thriller and the radio drama, a century later.[60] The newspapers carried a quantity of literary filler, but it was seldom of much repute. In the fall of 1846, the *Sentinel and Gazette* was publishing Dickens' *Dombey and Son* as fast as new installments could be brought by steamer;[61] but the German editor, Bernhard Domschcke, concluded in the sixties that Milwaukee newspaper readers were primarily interested in falsified election returns, flattery, gossip, and paper large enough for wrapping material.[62]

In spite of early indifference toward the idea of a public library, voluntary subscription and the interested leadership of

[57] Milwaukee *Daily Sentinel*, Oct. 17, 1853.
[58] *Ibid.*, Nov. 3, 1855.
[59] He cited, as evidence, the "new method of doing almost everything in this new country, the culture of the soil, . . . the schooling of children, . . . the government of the people, . . . and the independence of mind in political, religious, and all other matters." Milwaukee *Sentinel*, Jan. 22, 1859.
[60] Milwaukee *Daily Sentinel and Gazette*, Sept. 9, 1847. Arnold and Wilson announced in 1852 the opening of a "circulating library of nearly a thousand volumes, consisting of the best English and American authors, . . . scarce and interesting works now wholly out of print, [and] . . . translations from many of the continental languages." Milwaukee *Daily Sentinel*, Sept. 9, 1852.
[61] Milwaukee *Sentinel and Gazette*, Dec. 5, 1846.
[62] Milwaukee *Sentinel*, Oct. 16, 1895.

such men as Increase Lapham and Rufus King were responsible for providing the city with library facilities. The only public reading room in 1846 was one connected with the Temperance Club;[63] but in that first year of cityhood an organization of which Leander Comstock was president and Lapham secretary circularized the settled parts of the United States for donations of books toward the establishment of a "permanent Public Library."[64] The desire for a library was a major motive behind the organization of a Young Men's Association, on December 8, 1847. Rufus King was a prime mover, testifying to the usefulness of a similar group with which he had been connected in Albany, New York.[65] After little more than a year of organization, about 120 members had been recruited, some $1,500 had been collected, and a library including 810 volumes and a dozen periodicals was available for use.[66] By 1857 the membership had increased to 404 and the library to nearly 4,000 volumes.[67] In the fall of 1850 the association inaugurated a lecture series, enlisting local ministers, lawyers, and teachers as speakers. One dollar admitted a family for the season, and a single admission could be had for a shilling.[68] Weekly meetings in November 1851 provided an opportunity to debate such subjects as "The Higher Law Doctrine" and "Should the United States ever interfere in foreign affairs on behalf of the people struggling for liberty?"[69] The increasing prosperity of the middle fifties made possible the importation of speakers, through cooperation with the Young Men's Association of Chicago; and under this

[63] Milwaukee *Sentinel and Gazette*, Feb. 16, 18, 1846.
[64] Increase to Darius Lapham, April 1846, Lapham Papers. A. Gray to I. Lapham, June 1, 1846, Lapham Papers, contains a promise to send books.
[65] Milwaukee *Daily Sentinel and Gazette*, Dec. 6, 7, 13, 21, 1847.
[66] Milwaukee *Sentinel and Gazette*, Feb. 17, 1849; "First Annual Report for 1848," in Young Men's Association of the City of Milwaukee, *Constitution, List of Officers, By Laws of the Library and Reading Room, and Catalogue of the Library* (Milwaukee, 1848), iii, iv. See also "Sketch of the History of the Association," in *Catalogue of the Library of the Young Men's Association of the City of Milwaukee* (Milwaukee, 1861), 11-23.
[67] Milwaukee *Daily Sentinel*, Dec. 2, 1857; Lillian Krueger, "Social Life in Wisconsin," *Wis. Mag. of Hist.*, 22:422 (June 1939).
[68] Milwaukee *Sentinel and Gazette*, Nov. 1, 1850. According to the Milwaukee Young Men's Association, *Catalogue*, 1861, p. 14, admission was 10 cents.
[69] Milwaukee *Sentinel and Gazette*, Dec. 1, 8, 1851.

plan, Milwaukeeans had the opportunity to hear George W. Curtis, Horace Mann, Bayard Taylor, Horace Greeley, Ralph Waldo Emerson, James Russell Lowell, Mark Hopkins, Wendell Phillips, Henry Ward Beecher, and many other intellectual leaders of the day.[70]

Cultural benefits of this kind, dependent as they were upon voluntary subscription, were not accomplished without a great deal of promotion on the part of the press and especially of King, of the *Sentinel*.[71] Relating the proposed advantages of the organization to the growth of the city appeared to be the most effective means of stimulating support. In attempting to recruit a list of guarantors for the lecture series among the merchants and businessmen, King asserted that in Albany, Troy, Utica, Chicago, and other localities the reading rooms, libraries, and lectures of the Young Men's Associations were "among the greatest attractions and chiefest boasts of their respective cities."[72] Prospective settlers might choose their residence according to evidence of the city's taste, he later prophesied. "A pretty safe index of the mental advancement or retrogression of a city is the condition of its library corporations."[73] During the prosperous middle fifties, support came with relative ease. In the winter season of 1854, a year in which Horace Greeley and Bayard Taylor proved to be the most popular speakers, the association netted more than $800 on the course, the aggregate receipts being $1,603.28.[74] Financial difficulties following the panic of 1857 curtailed the lecture program for a time;[75] but when Horace Greeley spoke in January 1860, the hall "was

[70] See Record of Directors of the Young Men's Association [Milwaukee], MS in Wisconsin Historical Society Library; also, Lillian Krueger, "Social Life in Wisconsin," *Wis. Mag. of Hist.*, 22:421-25 (June 1939).
[71] Milwaukee *Daily Sentinel*, Dec. 9, 1852; Sept. 21, 1853.
[72] *Ibid.*, Oct. 12, 1853.
[73] *Ibid.*, Dec. 2, 1857.
[74] *Ibid.*, April 4, 1854; Oct. 26, Nov. 12, 26, 1855; May 10, 1856.
[75] *Ibid.*, May 6, 1858; April 27, Nov. 5, 22, 1859. In 1859, the editor of the *Sentinel* pointed out that only 1 percent of the city's 60,000 residents supported "the only Association which sustains a library." *Ibid.*, April 27, 1859. The city would be "turned upside down by a circus or 'nigger-show,'" wrote one friend of the association, but it does not "care a fig for the intellectual." *Ibid.*, Nov. 5, 1859.

crowded to suffocation."[76] By 1867, the association had reached the peak of its influence as a volunteer agency in the promotion of the cultural life of the city. It listed more than 3,000 members, had 10,000 volumes in its library, and reported a successful lecture season for the previous year. In transferring its property to the city in 1878 it provided the nucleus of the public library.[77]

Education was regarded as both a private and a public responsibility in adolescent Milwaukee; and as in the case of other urban services, what the municipality was slow to provide, individuals furnished. At the close of the first year of cityhood 753 students were attending the city's six public schools, and 437 were enrolled in the fourteen select schools and academies then existing in the city. Public and private institutions continued to operate side by side throughout the period; and in spite of marked improvement in the public system during the generation, at its close the comparative enrollment—10,409 in public to 6,409 in private institutions—actually marked a gain for the privately operated schools.[78] These figures, however, by no means represented the total youth of school age in Milwaukee. Throughout the forties and fifties, more young Milwaukeeans between the ages of four and twenty were in no school than were attending either public or private schools; and as late as 1868, fully a third of the youth of school age were totally unschooled. The public schools were under the joint management of the council, which levied taxes, bought sites, and provided buildings, and of a board of commissioners, which actually ran the schools. As in the achievement of library facilities for the city—and numerous other reforms—Rufus King and Increase Lapham were the moving spirits in the early development of Milwaukee's public-school system. King, son of President Charles King of Columbia College and himself a high ranking graduate of West Point,[79] was well equipped to be pres-

[76] *Ibid.*, Jan. 24, 1860.
[77] Gregory, *History*, 2:1078.
[78] "First Annual Report of the Board of School Commissioners," April 15, 1847, published in Milwaukee *Daily Sentinel and Gazette*, April 26, 1847; Milwaukee *Daily Sentinel*, Oct. 16, 1868.
[79] Buck, 4:79-80.

ident of the first city school board, organized on April 14, 1846; and for fifteen years thereafter his enthusiasm, experience, and promotional ability supplied an impetus for public education which the citizens at large were frequently slow to match. Lapham, whose modesty and unpretentiousness belied his national repute as a scientist, and who had already contributed in a scholarly way to an understanding of the resources of Wisconsin, played a pioneer role in the development of both public and private education.

In spite of the Yankee ingredients of the young city and the number of educated men among its citizens, public education made a poor showing in the early years of cityhood. During the first year, the schools were run on the sum of $2,708.03, raised by an assessment of one-fifth of 1 percent on the taxable property of the city. The legislature had authorized the board to charge tuition, but, as the commissioners wrote in their first report,

> It was the desire of the Board to make the Public Schools, as far as possible, Free Schools; to throw open the doors to all, without money and without price; to shut out all distinctions, and to place on the same footing and to treat with strict equality, the children of our city, no matter what the condition, creed, or circumstances of the parents.[80]

Aside from the use of the two buildings then standing in Kilbourntown and Walker's Point, schools were set up wherever rooms were available, as in the basements of the Methodist and Catholic churches, or where they could be hired; and some teachers served for salaries of less than $300 for nine months' work. The schools were crowded with pupils from the time they opened. When King inspected one of them in September 1847, he found 126 children huddled together in a room 24 by 18 feet in size; and there they were being taught without classification as to age or grade. During the first year, the schools were open from June through August, and, after a vacation of

---

[80] "First Annual Report of the Board of School Commissioners," Milwaukee *Daily Sentinel and Gazette*, April 26, 1847. In 1848, Mayor Kilbourn asserted that "the true system . . . almost universally conceded is to make our schools entirely a public charge." Milwaukee *Free Press*, June 23, 1913.

four weeks, from October to early April, with a ten-day holiday in December. By the fifties the school year had been divided into four terms of eleven weeks each, with a fortnight's vacation at the end of each term.[81]

As the increase in population put added pressure on existing facilities, King, Lapham, and their civic-minded colleagues attempted to win public support for the construction of a two-story brick schoolhouse in every ward. Using the columns of the *Sentinel* to amplify the theme expressed in his reports as school commissioner, King continued to propagandize for free public education, pointing to it as a method of welding into a "homogeneous whole" the "large portion of our population . . . made up emigrants from the old world," as a safeguard against the development of a generation of idle and vicious youth,[82] and—perennial argument in promotion—as a means of drawing population to the city. Popular approval was finally achieved for a loan of $15,000, authorized by the legislature, to make the building program possible; and King, Lapham, and Holton were among the members of a five-man committee to supervise construction. The new schoolhouses, built at a cost of about $4,000 apiece, were all ready for occupancy during the school year 1851-52.[83]

The expansive middle fifties brought some progress in public education. An attempt at uniformity in textbooks, after 1847, gave young Milwaukee a somewhat common academic diet drawn from the *Eclectic Readers,* one through five, Town's *Analysis,* Davies' *Arithmetic,* large and small, Wilson's *History of the United States,* and Mitchell's *Geography.* The construction of the new school buildings made possible the classification of the students into three departments—primary, intermediate, and grammar.[84] In 1857, the board decided to organize three high schools; one was opened in the Seventh Ward by January 1858, and the second by the fall of that year. As early as 1846,

---

[81] Milwaukee *Daily Sentinel and Gazette,* Sept. 12, 1846; April 26, July 10, 1847; Milwaukee *Sentinel and Gazette,* April 16, 1851.
[82] *Ibid.,* Sept. 12, Oct. 2, 1846.
[83] Larson, *Financial and Administrative History,* 43-44; Milwaukee *Sentinel and Gazette,* April 30, Aug. 26, 1847; March 6, July 30, 1849; April 16, 1851.
[84] Buck, 3:69; Bruce, *History,* 1:633.

Increase Lapham had donated thirteen acres of land on the West side for the purpose of building such a school; but the project was abandoned when the donor's journey to the eastern states seeking contributions met with only moderate success. In the following year he proposed to appropriate the ground originally planned for a high school to the establishment of a college and reported to his brother that several persons were giving donations of $500, which entitled them to the perpetual right to keep a scholar in the college free of charge. In arranging for the allotment of six such scholarships for himself he may have been thinking of providing higher education for his own family of growing children.[85]

With the expansion of the city and the increase in population came a need for additional buildings and instructors. Between 1852 and 1860, the number of teachers rose from twenty-three to sixty and their salaries, for female and male teachers respectively, from averages of $200 and $500, in 1852, to $300 and $800 in 1860. By 1859 the cost of operating the schools was $70,000, in marked contrast to the $2,700 which had been spent a dozen years earlier.[86] In spite of the ability of many of the teachers in the system during these years, an excess of individualism characterized their teaching methods; and the most marked shortcoming of the educational program was a want of adequate supervision. The legislature authorized the appointment of a superintendent as early as 1852; but visitations from the board of commissioners were an inadequate substitute until 1859 when Rufus King was made the city's first superintendent of schools. King filled this post with distinction, bringing about a decided improvement in the management of the schools; but in 1860 his editorial duties on the *Sentinel* forced him to relinquish the position to Jonathan Ford, in whose term the schools felt the most drastic results of the economic revulsion of the late fifties. From 1858 forward, teachers had complained of below par paychecks, and the board had threatened the closing of the schools unless funds could be provided to meet current expenses.

[85] Conard, 1:157; Milwaukee *Daily Sentinel and Gazette,* May 27, 1847; Kellogg, "Origins of Milwaukee College," *Wis. Mag. of Hist.,* 9:392-93 (June 1926).
[86] Larson, *Financial and Administrative History,* 43, 70-71.

Finally, in 1860, classes were suspended for two months until the council made financial provisions for their continuance. Operating costs were cut from $70,000 to $32,000, sixteen teachers were dropped (although in 1859 there were already sixty-one students to every instructor), and the two high schools were discontinued.[87]

After a period of difficulties during the Civil War years, the superintendency fell to Fenimore C. Pomeroy, who had distinguished himself as a classroom teacher in the Milwaukee system. Pomeroy's incumbency, between 1865 and 1870, brought marked advances for public-school education. He introduced the graded system, with a principal at the head of every school, in place of the departmental structure which had existed to that time. New textbooks were adopted in 1868, among them the perennial McGuffey readers, Goodrich's history of the United States, and the Spencerian copy books. A high school, authorized by the legislature in 1867, was opened in 1868; by the fall of 1869 about 100 students were enrolled and an average daily attendance of 68 was reported. The curriculum included algebra, geometry, surveying, natural philosophy, chemistry, astronomy, physiology, geology, natural history, botany, Greek, Latin, French, German, English analysis, rhetoric, general history, political economy, constitution of the United States, and mental philosophy. By 1870, annual expenditures for public schools had reached $93,000, a figure which represented an increase of from 25 cents to $1.30 in the per capita cost of education during the initial generation of cityhood.

The numerous private and parochial schools, which subsisted on commercial and religious subsidy or private subscription, were patronized by the more affluent families, especially in the First Ward, or by special groups, such as certain German-Americans, who disapproved of some of the practices in the public institutions. Many of these academic enterprises, some

---

[87] See Charles King, "Rufus King: Soldier, Editor, and Statesman," *Wisconsin Magazine of History*, 4:374 (June 1921); Donnelly, "Milwaukee Public Schools," in Stearns, *Columbian History of Education in Wisconsin*, 442; Milwaukee *Sentinel*, July 14, 1937; Bruce, *History*, 1:634. High-school classes were given for a time in some of the wards. Conard, 1:158.

of them short-lived, were established in the village period; but they continued to flourish in the first generation of cityhood, some of them providing the foundations of distinguished institutions of later years. Typical of the private schools of the later forties were the Milwaukee Academy, conducted by Percival C. Millette in 1846, the select school of Mr. and Mrs. E. L. Shannon, on East Water Street, Miss Jones's Ladies Seminary, and Mr. Taylor's and Mrs. Coe's select schools. The Rev. Amasa Buck's Milwaukee Collegiate Institute, which was one of the best of the early private schools, was opened in 1848. Designed to give "a critical, thorough, and extensive education in Literature, Science, and the Useful Arts," by 1850 it boasted a building of its own, 150 students, a telescope, an electric machine, and a cabinet of minerals, sea-shells, and the like, said to be "equal to those of first-class colleges of the United States." The turn of the fifties saw the establishment of the Milwaukee Grammar School (1849), the Spring Street Female Seminary (1850), and Miss M. E. Kendall's select school conducted in the basement of the Baptist Church (1851).[88] Typical of the schools subsidized by religious groups or by the foreign-born were the parochial school, conducted by Mother Caroline and four members of the Sisters of Notre Dame, and the German-English Academy, founded in 1851.[89]

The year 1848, in which Increase Lapham was promoting an abortive college for Milwaukee, saw early developments in the establishment of two of Milwaukee's best-known collegiate institutions. Bishop Henni, while traveling in Belgium, received a gift of $16,000 from the Chevalier J. G. DeBoeye of Antwerp for the establishment of a college of the Jesuits in his diocese. With this he purchased in 1856 what was many years later to be the site of Marquette College.[90] This year, too, marked the beginning of the Milwaukee Female Seminary,

---

[88] Gregory, *History*, 2:1153-54; Watrous, 1:393; Milwaukee *Daily Sentinel*, Sept. 2, 1869; Donnelly, "Milwaukee Public Schools," in Stearns, *Columbian History of Education in Wisconsin*, 460; Larson, *Financial and Administrative History*, 44, 101n, 102; Milwaukee *Daily Sentinel*, Sept. 9, 1852; Kellogg, "Origins of Milwaukee College," 391-92.

[89] See chapter 6; Gregory, *History*, 2:1171-72.

[90] Milwaukee *Sentinel*, July 14, 1937.

which was the ancestor of Milwaukee-Downer College. The foundations of the latter were rooted in the educational renaissance of the transcendental forties, and from its outset it excited the interest of the educational reformers of that ambitious age.

The founder of the Female Seminary was Mrs. William L. Parsons, a former teacher in the Le Roy Seminary of western New York, who had come to Milwaukee when her husband was called there to become minister to the Free Congregational Church. Mrs. Parsons succeeded in attracting to the West as her associate another skilled teacher from New York, Mary Mortimer, who was to play a significant role in the development of the institution. More importantly, she enlisted the interest of Catherine Beecher, educational reformer, in her enterprise; and as a result the school, renamed first the Milwaukee Normal Institute and High School and later the Milwaukee Female College, was the recipient of more than $20,000, accumulated through the efforts of Catherine Beecher, her more famous sister, Harriet Beecher Stowe, and the American Women's Educational Association of New York.[91] When the "gain-absorbed" community delayed in raising a sum of money for a building, a stipulation in Miss Beecher's offer, a committee of women undertook to procure the fund and hounded every "respectable office, counting room, and capitalist" until $2,000 had been collected. The Reverend Mr. Parsons barnstormed eastern pulpits to accumulate a like sum; Catherine Beecher wrote "An Appeal to American Women in Their Own Behalf"; benefit concerts, teas, and dramatic performances made possible the purchase of small articles of furniture; a library and apparatus were the gift of friends in the East; the Ladies' Education Society of Milwaukee raised more than $100; and on occasion the trustees, of whom Increase Lapham was for many years the head,

[91] Kellogg, "Origins of Milwaukee College," *Wis. Mag. of Hist.*, 9:394-400 (June 1926); Forrest Wilson, *Crusader in Crinoline: the Life of Harriet Beecher Stowe* (New York, 1941), 290-91. In the opinion of the trustees, "Milwaukee —our busy, restless, active, enterprising, gain-absorbed Milwaukee," needed pre-eminently "a Female Institution of most commanding influence," an institution which should "create a life-giving atmosphere, and diffuse its purifying and elevating influences over the whole city." "Report of the Trustees of the Milwaukee Female Institute," published in Milwaukee *Sentinel and Gazette*, April 14, 1851.

dug into their pockets to meet a deficit. The curriculum of the school followed Miss Beecher's pattern for woman's education with especial attention to Swedish calisthenics. All but the teacher-training students paid tuition; but few boarded at the college. The enrollment, which had increased from about a hundred in 1852 to 259 in 1859, fell to 60 in the early sixties, a period during which, because of dissension, Miss Beecher had withdrawn her support. With the resumption of the Beecher plan in 1866 and the reappointment of Mary Mortimer to the faculty, the school again began to prosper, a development which was not retarded by the appointment in the early seventies of such prominent and wealthy women as Mrs. William P. Lynde, Mrs. John Nazro, Mrs. Alexander Mitchell, Mrs. W. de L. Love, and Mrs. E. D. Holton to the board of trustees.[92]

An abortive University of Milwaukee, founded in 1855, was a product of the expansive energies that culminated in the panic of 1857. The Rev. Charles Wiley, D.D., was to be the chancellor, and the trustees included Messrs. Kneeland, Eldred, Daggett, William E. Cramer, and others. The chancellor, addressing the trustees on July 31, 1855, asserted that a city destined to hold a pre-eminent position among the cities of the West should have its own university and that if the enterprise of the citizens could be enlisted on behalf of the school they would be contributing not only to "the welfare of their children, and the interests of solid learning," but "to the material prosperity of our favored city, and with it to the value and augmentation of their own private fortunes." In spite of these practical justifications for a collegiate institution, the plans for the University of Milwaukee collapsed with the economic crisis of the late fifties, leaving a free field for the development of the State university in neighboring Madison. The commercial community provided a somewhat more congenial environment for the development of business education. Charles F. Larigo's Mercantile Academy was opened in 1849, the Spencerian College in 1863, and Dr. William Bayer's Commercial College in 1868. The Milwaukee Commercial College was operated by Aaron

[92] Milwaukee *Daily Sentinel*, March 4, 1852; Gregory, *History*, 2:1167.

Baylies, Jr., and Lowell Lincoln from 1856 to 1867.[93]

Milwaukee society of the forties and fifties had the freshness, the exuberance, and the self-possession of youth. Milwaukeeans were gregarious. They loved to organize, and they delighted in a parade. The scarcity of professional entertainment and a relative isolation from the rest of the world resulted in the development of amusements of their own devising. Festivals, holiday celebrations, testimonial dinners, and organization balls and dancing parties were the result. To the boisterous optimism and promotional zeal of the American settlers was added the traditional *Gemütlichkeit* of the German migrants; but the streams of culture from the countries of the Old World and the sections of the New had not yet been reduced to a common pattern by time and urbanism. Each was assertively self-contained, a situation which led on occasion to varying degrees of rivalry and antagonism, but which also lent variety to the social fabric of the developing city. What has already been pointed out with respect to the development of separate cultural institutions among the Milwaukee Germans existed to some extent among the native-born. Native New Yorkers organized the Excelsior Society in 1846; and in the same year the Sons of New England celebrated a Pilgrim's Festival. In January 1849, the Sons of Pennsylvania met for dinner at the American House; in 1850 the Scotch migrants assembled to honor the memory of Robert Burns; and in the following year the Sons of the South gathered to toast "The peculiar institution of the South; if right in the days of Washington, Adams, and Jefferson, it is right at this day."[94]

Political events were the occasion for banquets like the Whigs' "Rough and Ready" supper in honor of "Old Zach," at which "ham, tongue, turkies, chickens, oysters, pheasants, quails, venison, geese, larded rabbits, and larded squirrels" were laid before the guests.[95] Community-wide holiday festivities, upon

---

[93] Milwaukee *Daily Sentinel,* Aug. 3, 1855; Dec. 12, 1856; Gregory, *History,* 2:1179-80.

[94] Milwaukee *Daily Sentinel and Gazette,* Dec. 24, 30, 1846; Jan. 2, 1849; Feb. 7, 1851; Gregory, *History,* 2:744.

[95] Milwaukee *Daily Sentinel and Gazette,* Nov. 25, 1848.

which the Yankee element at first had looked askance, were an early sign of cultural integration. Typical of the celebrations of the Fourth of July was the one of 1848. The military and the fire companies turned out in gala array. The men of Milwaukee Engine Company No. 1 were resplendent in "white shirts and pants, plaid caps, black belts, and red neckcloths"; Neptune Company No. 2 had decorated their engine with bouquets of flowers and wreaths of evergreen. When the procession arrived at the courthouse, the Declaration of Independence was read, and orations were delivered in English and German. Heralded by the salutes of artillery and the chimes of the church bells, the day was ushered out with bonfires, music, and fireworks.[96] Christmas, Washington's birthday, and New Year's Day were the occasion of calls and parties. Every milestone in the community's history—the completion of a railroad or a telegraph cable, the winning of a railroad subsidy, or a presidential election—called for the ringing of bells and the lighting of bonfires. In 1857 the Musical Society sponsored a grand carnival. Cut on a Teutonic pattern, with its masquerade balls, tableaux, and "extermination of the Katzenjammers," it was rather "a stunner to the old settlers of our city, as well as the newcomers from the Eastern States," despite the fact that on the predominantly German committee of arrangements were the names of Rufus King, Dr. J. K. Bartlett, J. S. Fillmore, and others.[97]

The members of the military and fire companies, drawn from some of the most vigorous elements in the local society, took an active part in the civic and social life of the city. The

---

[96] *Ibid.,* July 6, 1848. As an indication of the city's "first citizens" see the officers for the celebration: President, Alanson Sweet; Vice-Presidents: Byron Kilbourn, D. H. Chandler, Alexander Mitchell, George H. Walker, W. W. Brown, Lucas Seaver, S. B. Davis, Charles James, W. E. Cramer, Moritz Schoeffler, S. M. Booth, F. Fratny, James H. Rogers; Orator: Levi Hubbell; Reader of Declaration: William A. J. Fuller; Marshal: Col. Amos Sawyer; Assistant Marshals: Levi Blossom, Charles L. Kane, S. P. Coon, J. S. Fillmore, J. E. Cameron, D. Upham, L. K. Swift, John Bradford, G. B. Boyd, J. A. Liebhaber, and George G. Dousman. Buck, 3:201.
[97] Milwaukee *Daily Sentinel,* Feb. 24, 25, 26, 1857; Aug. 17, 1858. See also Lillian Krueger, "Social Life in Wisconsin," *Wis. Mag. of Hist.,* 22:396-400 (June 1939).

formation of military companies was popular in the middle forties, especially among the foreign-born. Among the groups that could be counted on to lend color to a parade were the Washington Guards and the Milwaukee Dragoons, made up of German citizens who had had military training in Europe, the Montgomery Guards, recruited from the Irish residents, and the native-American City Artillery, organized in 1846 with Rufus King as captain. The press believed in encouraging these uniformed volunteers for the reason that they were "not only ornamental on all occasions of parade, or public celebrations, but at times highly useful as part of the city police." "A pretty sham fight" between cavalry and artillery companies was reported in 1849. Interest in the companies lagged between 1850 and 1855, but in the summer of the latter year, an appeal for subscriptions from the citizenry for a "thoroughly drilled Independent Company," which "would compare favorably with like companies in other cities and which may be needed at any time for the performance of important duties," marked the organization of the Milwaukee Light Guard. Composed wholly of native-born citizens, it drew a distinguished membership and wide popular support. For several years the annual balls of the Light Guard were the most glamorous events on Milwaukee's social calendar.[98] Similarly, the frequent balls given for the benefit of the fire companies combined society for the citizenry with subsidy for a needed urban service. The good-natured rivalries as well as the cooperation and fraternization among the companies of varying nationality helped to promote the fusion and integration of these different elements in the developing community.[99]

The popularity of such amusements as skating, horse-racing, and turkey-shooting was a natural consequence of the rural setting of the developing city as was the prevailing interest, during the early years of cityhood, in outdoor sports frequently

---

[98] Watrous, 1:588-90; Milwaukie *Daily Sentinel*, Feb. 6, 1845; Milwaukee *Sentinel and Gazette*, Oct. 23, Nov. 23, 1849; Milwaukee *Daily Sentinel*, July 16, Nov. 23, 1855; July 16, 1856; Gregory, *History*, 2:813-14; Frederick P. Todd, "Our National Guard: an Introduction to Its History," *Military Affairs*, 5:73-86 (Summer 1941).

[99] Milwaukee *Daily Sentinel*, Aug. 14, 1856.

associated with life on the open frontier. In the winter season, when the absence of navigation more than ever stressed the isolation of the community, skating and sleighing vied with indoor dancing parties for the favor of the city's society. The winter of 1854-55 afforded six weeks of sleighing, "the finest we had enjoyed for the twelve previous years," and this, "with the usual round of balls at Gardner's [sic] Hall, where the votaries of Terpsichore kept time to the music of Father Hess's quadrille band," caused the time to pass rapidly until the first boat arrived from below and spring had come.[100] By the close of the sixties, however, an enthusiasm for organized baseball suggested that outdoor sports were no longer indulged in as spontaneously as in former years. The *Sentinel* endorsed the game as a means of popularizing outdoor exercise and drawing young men away from "the immoral associations . . . of our cities." Milwaukeeans had played cricket and participated in intercity matches in the fifties; but the first baseball club was not organized until April 5, 1860. By 1868 men in all the trades and professions were its patrons, "not even the clergyman, lawyer, doctor, or editor deeming it beneath his dignity to be a member of one of the 'nines' of a favorite club." The Cream City Club held the state championship; but there were three others, one of them, the Monitor, being composed entirely of Germans. The increasing professionalism of the sport was revealed in 1869, when Milwaukeeans were poking fun at the Chicago club for its failure to attract a star player even at an offer of $10,000. In 1870 the Cream City Club defeated the Cincinnati Red Stockings, and in 1878 the Milwaukee club joined the National League. The appearance of the velocipede in 1869 was hailed as a boon for that class of men—"a large one in all cities"—whose business does not necessitate sufficient exercise.[101]

The growing popularity of baseball on the turn of the seventies and the resort to mechanical substitutes for the utilitarian exercise of frontier days were signs of the transition from

---

[100] Buck, 4:67-68.

[101] Milwaukee *Daily Sentinel,* May 14, June 2, Oct. 2, 1852; Aug. 15, 1856; April 6, 1860; April 29, 1868; March 24, Dec. 10, 1869; *Evening Wisconsin* (Milwaukee), Oct. 15, 1895; Buck, 4:381.

village to city in Milwaukee, as were indeed the occasional appearances of such renowned entertainers as Edwin Booth and Ole Bull or of such speakers as Emerson and Beecher; but so long as the amusements of the residents were confined largely to sleigh-riding, home talent concerts, occasional stock company performances, ice cream and strawberry socials, gymnastic exhibitions, and benefit parties for the military and fire companies, the urban society smacked more of a small town than of a city with metropolitan pretentions. A French traveler of the middle sixties saw two or three streets which reminded him of New York; but as for the rest, the spacious extent of the community, its long tree-lined avenues, and the geese frolicking around the tracks of the street railway made it seem "more like a village than a city." Anthony Trollope, visiting Milwaukee in 1861, professed to find there more "beef . . . and book learning" than in a European town; but he was undoubtedly more charitable with respect to the latter than to the former.[102] For although this society was not hostile to the intellectual, the material side of life dominated the culture of the young city, and, as a consequence of the cultural retrogression that frequently characterized the second generation on the frontier, the community was more physically than intellectually urbane.

To be sure, many of the German-American newcomers possessed an advanced appreciation of music and letters, and many Yankees an educated enjoyment of good things when they were offered; but what was available in education and the arts was still a matter of chance; most of the citizens were probably content with second-rate theatrical fare, little interested in art, and unconvinced of the importance of public education; and the community by and large was more concerned with markets than musicals, more impressed with adequate fire houses than adequate school buildings. Increase Lapham and Rufus King spoke the language of the community sufficiently to advance its intellectual standard of living in spite of itself; but less

---

[102] Ernest Duvergier de Hauranne, *Huit Mois en Amérique, Lettres et Notes de Voyage, 1864-1865* (2 vols., Paris, 1866), 1:195-96; Anthony Trollope, *North America* (2 vols., New York, 1862), 1:117.

realistic intellectuals like Bernhard Domschcke labored and despaired. The increase in population and prosperity, as well as advances in industry and science, during the late sixties, began to affect the geographical and spiritual provincialism of the generation; and as a result of a more general conviction that cities could provide superior facilities for enjoying the refinements of life, some Milwaukeeans were heard advocating the development of the parks, schools, concert halls, public libraries, and refined amusements that would make this possible. It was not, however, inconsistent with the spirit of the time, nor with the pattern of the prevailing culture, that the pressure for these improvements should be identified with "a common sense business spirit," and that the proponents of improved facilities for the cultivated and urbane life should argue that "money invested in these enterprises will soon be amply repaid in the growth of the city, and the growth of the city means the prosperity of the inhabitants."[103]

[103] Milwaukee *Daily Sentinel*, April 9, 1868. According to the correspondent, there was "a constant tendency among those who have acquired a competence in this country to drift toward the city and especially the cities that furnish the most facilities for leading a cultivated and pleasant life."

CHAPTER 10

The Extension of Urban Services

AT THE outset of cityhood, Milwaukee, like most of her sister cities of the Great Lakes area, was in what might be called the "subscription stage" of her municipal career. Just as the cultural opportunities available in the city were made possible by the subscriptions of interested citizens, so most of its urban services resulted from the sense of individual responsibility that also had prompted widespread local investment in the railroads and factories that were expected to advance the city's growth.[1] Two or three days' work on the streets, a duty which now could be commuted at the rate of 75 cents a day, was expected of all able-bodied men. Street and sidewalk improvements as well as the eradication of nuisances were to be taken care of individually or charged against the property benefited. The average home had its own provisions for water supply and waste disposal. A city marshal and ward constables, elected by the people, were available to enforce the law; but many citizens undertook to guard their own persons and possessions. Some property owners employed private watchmen, and as late as 1855, when an ordinance was passed compelling all citizens to aid the police if called upon to do so, many residents still resorted to carrying their own weapons.[2] Fire protection was left to companies of volunteers

[1] Bayrd Still, "Patterns of Mid-Nineteenth Century Urbanization in the Middle West," *Mississippi Valley Historical Review*, 28:187-206 (September 1941). Arthur M. Schlesinger, in his "Biography of a Nation of Joiners," *American Historical Review*, 50:10 (October 1944), points out that the nature of city life, which induces the accumulation of people and capital, made it easier to mobilize the voluntary effort and "subscription tendency" which were indigenous in early American thought.

[2] Milwaukee *Sentinel and Gazette*, April 16, 1847; Feb. 6, May 13, 1850; Milwaukee *Daily Sentinel*, Aug. 16, Sept. 7, 1855.

who, on occasion, turned policemen and helped maintain the peace when riot or disorder went beyond the capacity of the mayor or marshal to suppress. By the close of the first generation of cityhood, however, this tradition of municipal "self-help" was giving way to a specialization in urban administration which developments in science and increased wealth encouraged and which the growth of population and its attendant problems made inevitable. Moreover, by that time the suspicions which had long existed between the wards and the nationalities had begun to wane; and the public had less fear that city-wide municipal institutions would come under "political" or "foreign" control.[3] As a result, by 1870, regularized police protection, a semiprofessional fire department, systematic relief organizations, corporate-owned urban transit, and the creation of a city-wide board of public works charged with the development of streets and sewers were but a few indications that corporate enterprise or the municipality itself were beginning to accept a responsibility to do for the community as a whole what hitherto had been accomplished with increasing difficulty by the voluntary efforts and subscriptions of its public-minded citizenry.

Fear of fire as well as of the burglaries and disorders common to lake shore cities prompted pressure for improved police facilities by the turn of the fifties. In April 1850 the *Sentinel* called attention to the inadequacy of a police that consisted of only the marshal, ward constables, and two or three watchmen employed in as many wards. "The watch should be a matter of general city regulation," the editor wrote; "and their number should be increased." On the occasion of riots in the early fifties, the mayor had to call upon the volunteer firemen to guarantee order.[4] Finally, an ordinance, passed in January 1852 and effective only until the following April, provided for fifteen night watchmen to be paid out of the general city fund.

[3] The press was at pains to point out that among the members of the police force were "Irish, Germans, and Americans, Catholics, and Protestants." *Ibid.*, March 28, 1856.
[4] Milwaukee *Sentinel and Gazette*, April 22, 1850; Gregory, *History*, 2:801; Milwaukee *Daily Sentinel*, July 12, 1853.

In addition to arresting violators of the peace, they were to watch for fires and wake the occupants of a burning house, their cry of fire and the number of the ward to be repeated by the other watchmen.[5] A series of thefts, murders, and incendiary fires in 1855 led the newspapers, the board of trade, and the principal property owners and merchants to urge the establishment of police facilities that would provide more continuous protection than was afforded by ward constables or a paid night watch. As a result, a police department was formally established on September 10, 1855.[6] Five Germans, three Irishmen, and four Americans constituted the force—one patrolman for every 3,000 inhabitants. Its first chief was William Beck, a farmer from the neighboring town of Granville who, after migrating from Germany, had become a member of the New York constabulary. The chief, to be appointed by the mayor and council, was to receive $800, later $1,500, a year. Compensation of the policemen, who were appointed by the mayor and chief, rose from $30 a month, at the outset, to $50 a month in the following year.[7] Beck, who contended that it was necessary "to whip a man in a fair fight before you could arrest him," imposed strict standards of discipline on the young patrol; and it speedily brought order to what had been an increasingly unruly community.[8] As early as 1856, when the police were urged to wear their badges conspicuously, there was an attempt to differentiate the representatives of law and order from the other members of the community; but although uniform dress was prescribed as early as 1859, it was apparently not achieved until 1874.[9]

[5] A significant provision of the ordinance was one which decreed a fine of $10 for any policeman who made an arrest without cause or gave a false alarm. "An Ordinance to provide for the organization of a night watch and police," *ibid.*, Jan. 6, 1852.

[6] According to the *Sentinel*, "The City Attorney who drew the Ordinance had several copies from other cities of the best Police Regulations in the country; and after consulting the charter, common law, and common sense, wrote the ordinance as presented." Milwaukee *Daily Sentinel*, Sept. 10, 1855.

[7] *Ibid.*, Aug. 16, Sept. 7, Dec. 6, 1855; Larson, *Financial and Administrative History*, 63. In 1860, the board of trade supplied a $500 bonus for the chief. Milwaukee *Daily Sentinel*, Jan. 14, 1860.

[8] *Ibid.*, Nov. 15, 1855; Jan. 7, 1858.

[9] Gregory, *History*, 2:1123; Milwaukee *Daily Sentinel*, April 21, 1859; "The Milwaukee Police Department," prepared by the Municipal Reference Library (Milwaukee, July 8, 1927), unpaged.

Retrenchment after the panic of 1857 caused a reduction in the department; and, as a result, the inadequacy of police protection was criticized throughout the ensuing decade. In 1865 the *Sentinel* complained that charter limitations accounted for a situation which restricted Milwaukee to one patrolman for every 3,000 inhabitants, whereas the ratio "in nearly every other city of the Union" was one to 1,000. A metropolitan police bill, proposed in 1864, might have given impulse to reform; but it was opposed by the party then in control of the city. Relief came in 1866 when the municipality was authorized to double salaries and increase personnel. By the close of the decade the number of patrolmen was twice what it had been in 1861. The forty-two men on the force represented one to every 1,700 citizens and were such a guarantee of order that Mayor O'Neill could boast in 1869 that Milwaukee was the "most orderly city on the continent."[10]

City growth also brought the substitution of professional fire fighting in the sixties for the volunteer methods that had prevailed in the first years of cityhood. The charter of 1846 had provided for democratically organized fire companies formed of volunteers who should be exempted from highway labor and military duty; but every householder was to have two buckets ready in case of emergency; and during fires, the mayor, aldermen, and citizens in general were expected to lend a hand.[11] The prevalence of the fire hazard kept the question of protection constantly before the council; and the forties and fifties saw repeated criticism of its failure to supply the companies with adequate equipment and to allow them freedom to choose their officers. Destructive fires in the business district led to the ruling that "no *wooden* buildings should be permitted to be erected again in that part of the city" and later to prohibitions upon the deposit of ashes, carrying of fire in the streets, setting off fireworks near buildings, and using unenclosed candles in livery stables. At the same time, regulations were

[10] Milwaukee *Daily Sentinel*, April 20, 30, 1858; April 1, 1864; Nov. 17, 1865; April 21, 1869; Larson, *Financial and Administrative History*, 98.

[11] Gregory, *History*, 2:795; Milwaukee *Daily Sentinel and Gazette*, Dec. 11, 1846; Jan. 22, 1847. At the beginning of cold weather, the "season of fires," fire wardens were obliged to travel their beats seeking out faulty chimneys and other hazards. *Ibid.*, Nov. 15, 1847.

enacted to prevent chimneys, hearths, ovens, boilers, and the like from causing fire.[12]

Throughout the fifties the city's leading businessmen continued to participate actively in the fire-fighting function and the volunteer fire companies to be supported by civic subscription as well as public funds. The roster of a sack company, organized in September 1851, constituted a list of the city's most "solid citizens." On it were Lynde, Prentiss, Mitchell, Blossom, Kilbourn, H. and J. Ludington, Sweet, Rogers, Sexton, Holton, White, Bielfeld, Walker, Lapham, Noonan, James Kneeland, and many others. The members of the company, each vested with the powers of a special constable, were to act as special police at all fires, carrying white canvas sacks and staves and taking charge of exposed property. In 1853, a Chicagoan contrasted the fire departments of the cities in the East with that of Milwaukee where "the best citizens and most respectable business men are members." Through benefit concerts and dances, funds were raised to supplement the city's support of the Ocean, Neptune, and Cataract companies and their disabled members. The report of the department's treasurer for 1851 revealed that the year's donations from individuals and business houses had totaled $1,955, a benefit concert had netted $483.56, initiation fees had brought in $58, and $25 had been paid out for relief. In 1852 the city's contribution to fire protection was $4,409.48; the department paid out about $225 of its funds, retaining the rest to be loaned at interest.[13]

A lack of volunteers in 1852 made it look as if the pay system, to which the city of St. Louis had resorted in 1851, might have to be adopted, and only a campaign for volunteers and the council's promise to act more speedily than in the

[12] Milwaukee *Daily Sentinel and Gazette,* July 16, Aug. 14, 21, 1846; Feb. 27, Nov. 15, 1847; May 18, 1849; Aug. 16, 1850; "An Ordinance for the Prevention of Fire," November 22, 1852, in *Charters and Ordinances of the City of Milwaukee* (Milwaukee, 1857), 460-63. This volume will hereafter be cited as *Charters and Ordinances.*

[13] Milwaukee *Daily Sentinel and Gazette,* Sept. 16, Dec. 17, 1851; "An Ordinance to Organize a Sack Company," September 13, 1851, in Buck, 3:359; Milwaukee *Daily Sentinel,* Jan. 22, 1852; June 18, 1853. Under the half-pay system, the firemen followed their regular vocations during the day and were on duty only at night.

past upon the department's bills for equipment postponed this development. Somewhat later, however, the press was regretting the misplaced liberality of citizens who offered money and distributed brandy and beer by the pailful to the firemen during fires, a generosity which paralyzed the efforts of half of the department at a destructive fire in 1854. But modern invention, as well as the expansion of the city and the lack of zealous recruits, was shortly to bring the volunteer system to an end. The example of other large cities of the West, whose officials were investigating the use of steam fire engines in the late fifties, and the destruction caused by serious fires on the turn of the sixties prompted the purchase of a steam fire engine, costing $3,500, which arrived on November 6, 1861. Christened the "Solomon Juneau," it was escorted to the Newhall House by members of the fire department and a brass band; and there its ability to throw a stream of water 25 feet above the building was soon demonstrated. Since the new engine prevented competition with companies lacking such equipment and required more mechanical training to operate than the average businessman could boast, the advent of the "Solomon Juneau" marked the decline of volunteer fire fighting, a trend which the manpower demands of the Civil War and the increasing size of the city had already begun to bring about. Engine Company No. 1 held its last meeting on April 3, 1863; firemen giving half-time service had been receiving wages since November 1861; and when they were put on full time and full pay in the early seventies the day of the self-governing volunteer department, composed of men of means and influence, was over. Municipal expenditures for fire protection increased from $9,388.69 in 1861 to $45,272.59 in 1870.[14]

Apart from a meager and inadequate tax to support almshouses and furnish medical care for the sick poor, urban relief

[14] *Ibid.,* Nov. 10, 20, 23, 25, Dec. 9, 1852; Jan. 31, 1861; March 4, Aug. 23, Dec. 20, 1862; Larson, *Financial and Administrative History,* 97, 120; Gregory, *History,* 2:1129. Some confusion exists as to when Milwaukee firemen began to assume full-time duties. Gregory sets the date of full-time service at 1868. Larson asserts that a half-pay system was continued until 1874. According to Mrs. Lucile M. Perry, of the Milwaukee Municipal Reference Library, Mayor Seidel, in a series of newspaper articles written in 1928, accepted

in this period of the city's history was supplied through subscription and personal benevolence. Especially during the cessation of navigation there were insistent pleas for community aid, and according to Mayor Upham private enterprise was best equipped to meet the demand. The Ladies' Benevolent Society, headed in 1849 by Mrs. A. D. Smith and Mrs. W. P. Lynde, solicited gifts and organized benefit concerts and donation parties. Late in 1855, the Milwaukee Relief Society, patterned after similar institutions in certain other large cities, was organized to systematize collections. During 1856 its receipts were $1,052.33, of which $1,046.10 was disbursed. The "hard times" following 1857 brought increased demands for relief. Soup-kitchens were subsidized by private gifts, and meal tickets were sold to residents who might wish to offer them to the poor. The managers of the society trusted "to the benevolence of our citizens for the food to be supplied." In January 1858, they were taking care of about 720 individuals; and applicants to the soup house numbered from 200 to 220 daily. An association for the relief of the German poor in the city had been organized in November 1857.[15]

During the sixties, the relief problems normally attending the cessation of navigation were complicated by the destitution of the families of soldiers participating in the Civil War. Each winter saw the organization of a relief society, variously called the Milwaukee Relief Society or the Provident Association. Headed by C. A. Staples, it was designed to do away with street begging and to systematize the collection of funds and the investigation of needy cases through the services of ward committees and two paid agents. Provisions, wood, and small amounts of tea, sugar, soap, and candles were distributed to the poor. Subscriptions, drawn from the Chamber of Commerce and from a canvass of merchants and citizens, netted from $6,000 to $8,000

---

the 1874 date. The existing annual reports of the fire department shed no light on the controversy, but Mrs. Perry cites "An Act to authorize and require the common council of the city of Milwaukee to provide salaries for the engineers, foremen, firemen, drivers and pipe men of the fire department of the city of Milwaukee." This act was approved on March 23, 1871, and was to "be in force from and after its passage." *Wisconsin Session Laws (Local)*, 1871, chap. 445.

[15] Milwaukee *Sentinel and Gazette*, April 12, Nov. 26, 1849; April 5, 1850; Milwaukee *Daily Sentinel*, Nov. 13, 30, Dec. 15, 1857; Jan. 15, 1858.

yearly; and from 350 to 750 families a season were given aid. In addition to this systematic but voluntary city-wide charity, upon which the community as a whole put the responsibility of dispensing its benevolence, other enterprises depended upon subscriptions from the charitable. Among these were the Milwaukee Hospital, founded by Dr. W. A. Passavant in 1863, St. Mary's Hospital, St. Rose's Orphan Asylum, the Milwaukee Orphan Asylum, established by the Ladies' Benevolent Society and partly subsidized by the council, the Home of the Friendless, opened in 1867, the Hebrew Relief Society, founded in the same year, and the Union Bethel Mission societies.[16]

While many community responsibilities were at the outset left to the initiative of volunteers, the corporation did assume some obligations with respect to the physical appearance of the city and the health and welfare of its citizens. In the main, however, this was confined to authorizing action which the citizens were forced to carry out. In this the council was only imitating the practice of the other cities of the Great Lakes area.[17] A major problem during the first generation of cityhood was the grading and construction of the streets and sidewalks needed in a community hewn from the wilderness. Although ward taxes were levied for this work, from two-thirds to three-fourths of the cost was borne by the owners of the property benefited. Planks and bricks were the customary materials for sidewalk construction in the forties, but by the fifties there was agitation for the use of stone rather than wood.[18] By the close of 1852, disillusionment with the continued graveling of East Water Street, the city's "principal business

[16] *Ibid.,* March 9, Sept. 16, 1864; Feb. 2, 1865; Jan. 18, Nov. 12, 1866; Dec. 20, 1867; Milwaukee *Sentinel and Gazette,* Nov. 27, 1849.

[17] See Still, "Urbanization in the Middle West," *Miss. Vall. Hist. Rev.,* 28:191 (September 1941).

[18] The procedure for authorizing the construction of sidewalks was initiated by a petition of three-fourths of the property owners on a given street. The council then passed a resolution directing the completion of the grading and construction of the sidewalks by a given date according to certain specifications and under the direction of the street commissioner. The sidewalks constructed in 1848 were to be "planked 6 feet in width . . . with good 2-inch plank to be laid lengthwise, resting on sleepers 3 x 6 inches every 4 feet and to be well spiked." Milwaukee *Sentinel and Gazette,* July 11, 25, 1848. The *Sentinel and Gazette* reported that a total of three miles of brick sidewalk had been laid during 1849. Nov. 14, 1849.

thoroughfare," brought the suggestion that the street be planked, a method of street improvement that had been "thoroughly tested in Chicago and Cleveland," and was then "undergoing a most successful trial on Third Street" in Milwaukee. The flagstone pavement laid by Guido Pfister and the firm of Sexton and Wing in front of their stores in 1853 provided an example which the press hoped other merchants would emulate. Shortly thereafter, and over the protests of many of the property holders, the council ordered the construction of a costly limestone pavement on East Water Street which promised to be "the most comfortable and durable piece of pavement in the West."[19] A marked increase in projects for street improvement coincided with the aldermen's assumption of the office of street commissioner under the charter of 1852, and in spite of Mayor Cross's counsel of economy, the expenditure of nearly $900,000 for highway purposes was authorized in the expansive middle fifties. This concern for street improvement out of all proportion to other urban services may be explained by the personal interest of members of the council in the contracts, a situation which led to accusations that the aldermen and councilors were improving streets to the advantage of their own property, ordering work done where it was not needed in order to make jobs, and letting contracts on adjoining streets at prices varying from 50 cents to $1.70 per yard. The collapse of 1857 brought street and bridge construction to a halt. Relatively little new work was done in the sixties and then only when the property owners petitioned to have it.[20] Nicholson pavement was laid on East Water Street in the summer of 1863, and shortly thereafter the press began to suggest that the city at large, rather than the lot owners, should bear the expense of improving the principal thoroughfares, since "the city at large" was "benefitted by all

[19] *Ibid.*, May 15, 1850; Milwaukee *Daily Sentinel*, Nov. 26, 1852; June 8, 10, Aug. 18, 1853; Aug. 8, 1854. This pavement was to cost $2.50 per square yard by contrast with the cost of paving in other parts of the city where it was being done for 70 cents. If the work on East Water Street was not accomplished by the owners within twenty-five days, it was to be done under contract, let by the city "chargeable to said lots, as provided by the charter." *Ibid.*, Aug. 18, 1853.

[20] Larson, *Financial and Administrative History*, 45, 47, 68-69, 99.

this traffic and travel." In 1869 the responsibility for street improvement was transferred from the council to the board of public works.[21] The Gas Company held the concession for street lighting in the sixties.

Concern for the cleanliness of the streets was a major consideration behind the proposals for types of pavement which would be durable, clean, less destructive of the health of horses, and at the same time free of the "clattering, banging noise" that, according to the editor, "shocks our nerves during the day and robs us of sleep during the night." Street sprinkling was done on a subscription basis in the early fifties; by the late sixties the primitive methods, wherein the streets were moistened by swinging a huge tin watering pot from side to side, had given way to the barrel on wheels; and the improved rotary sprinkler, in use in Philadelphia, was being suggested.[22] As early as 1856 the council had attempted to prevent citizens from throwing garbage in the streets, but it took police regulations in 1866, requiring householders to keep their cellars and lots clean, to achieve the desired results; and even then it was deemed impossible to compel every housekeeper to keep a waste barrel as was done in some cities of the Union.[23]

Cleanliness of the streets was related less to aesthetic considerations than to a problem which gave the civic officials great concern in the mid-century, and that was the question of public

[21] Milwaukee *Sentinel,* April 14, 1864. Nicholson pavement was constructed of pine blocks saturated with tar. These were covered with a mixture of gravel, sand, and tar. Milwaukee *Daily Sentinel,* March 27, 1867. In the sixties, "sidewalks were repaired at the expense of the ward funds, but new materials used in laying sidewalks or planking streets were paid [for] by the real estate fronting the improvement." Larson, *Financial and Administrative History,* 99.

[22] Milwaukee *Daily Sentinel,* Aug. 13, 1852; Aug. 12, 1853; June 22, 1854; April 12, 1855; Milwaukee *Sentinel,* July 2, Oct. 5, 1867; Sept. 7, 1869. When the owner of the "watering machine" complained that only a few of the merchants were willing to pay him for his labor, the editor of the *Daily Sentinel and Gazette* counseled him to lay the dust only in front of his customers and leave the others dry "so that those who are obligated to trade in dusty stores may see who is to blame for it." August 14, 1852. As late as 1875, streets were to be sprinkled only when lot-owners requested it. Sprinkling of intersections was to be paid for from ward funds. Larson, *Financial and Administrative History,* 117n.

[23] "An Ordinance to prevent nuisances and disorderly practices in the City of Milwaukee," August 18, 1856, *Charters and Ordinances,* 416-18; Milwaukee *Daily Sentinel,* April 19, 1867.

health. For community health was regarded not only as of importance to the individual but also as a major factor in inducing the flow of immigration and business to the city. Hence the city fathers did their best both to protect the citizens against diseases that immigrants might bring and, what was almost more important, to minimize rumors of sickness that would affect the city's reputation abroad. Thus the press was accused of advertising Milwaukee as "a plague-stricken city" when it reported the existence of smallpox in 1846. From the point of view of the citizens, the regulations in the interest of the public health were reluctantly accepted encroachments upon the traditional liberty of the individual. Compulsory vaccination against smallpox in 1847 prompted charges that the measure violated natural rights. According to one of the unsuccessful opponents of the measure in the city council, "A Nero might pass such a law, but it would disgrace a body of freemen to do so." In the years of the dread cholera epidemic, prohibitions were placed on the accumulation of "garbage or filth . . . to poison the atmosphere," a precaution prompted by the theory that cholera was not a contagious but an atmospheric disease, produced by impure air. An elaborate ordinance, passed in September 1846, and substantially repeated in 1855, created a board of health, empowered to investigate the cause of disease, order the removal of nuisances, and provide a pesthouse. Steamship captains and stage drivers were to be fined $50 for bringing into the city passengers who had been sick at the outset of a voyage. Harbor masters were to inspect migrants for contagious diseases; and bystanders were obliged, on pain of fine, to prevent such passengers from landing.[24]

Despite the precaution of cleaning the streets and purifying the gutters with lime, undertaken both by the city and by the citizenry, as an individual responsibility, in the years of heavy migration—1849, 1850, and to some extent in 1854—cholera took a heavy toll. The press was concerned that honest figures

[24] Milwaukee *Daily Sentinel and Gazette*, Aug. 28, Sept. 3, 1846; March 27, 1847; Jan. 24, 1849; "An Ordinance to prevent the introduction and dissemination of contagious diseases and to preserve the health of the city," *ibid.*, Sept. 3, 1846; "An Ordinance to preserve the Health of the City of Milwaukee," June 25, 1855, *Charters and Ordinances*, 477-84.

be given lest rumor magnify the numbers. It took Chicago newspapers to task in 1850 for "shameful" misrepresentation. In 1852 the *Sentinel* was at pains to point out that, slander of eastern editors to the contrary, the city was "distressingly healthy (for the doctors)." The fear of cholera, and later of smallpox, continued during the sixties to be the major motivation for measures enforcing clean-up campaigns and the removal of slaughter houses beyond the city limits. In general, the mayor and council constituted the board of health until the late sixties; but in 1867 the State legislature authorized the appointment of a separate board of health, and Dr. James Johnson became the city's first health officer. This board went systematically to work to abate nuisances and regulate slaughter houses with the result that sanitary improvement was speedily achieved.[25]

By the middle fifties the concern for city health had given rise to agitation for a "thorough system of sewerage for the city." This became imperative with the developing congestion of the business district, where the primitive methods of waste disposal, used in less populous parts of the city, could not be followed. Large sums of money had been expended for wooden sewers in the various wards before adequate consideration was given to the need of a city-wide system. In 1858, a correspondent to the *Sentinel,* apprising Milwaukee of "the results obtained in other cities," came to the conclusion that sewers should be of brick and pottery; that the cost should be assessed against the lots; and that the work could be better done by three commissioners than by the street commissioners of the several wards. In 1863 Mayor O'Neill called attention to the need of sewers, and construction was begun in the Second and Fifth wards; but from complaints made of "the streams of liquid filth" detected on Wisconsin Street in 1865 it appears that reform was slow to be accomplished. By the late sixties most of the citizens were convinced that a "complete and harmonious system" of sewerage "through-

[25] Milwaukee *Sentinel and Gazette,* April 11, July 17, Aug. 31, 1849; Frank, *Medical History of Milwaukee,* 180-81; Milwaukee *Daily Sentinel,* Aug. 10, 1852; March 25, 1869; May 8, June 2, 1866; Gregory, *History,* 2:1137-38; Increase to William Lapham, June 27, July 9, 1849, and Increase to D. Lapham, July 20, 1849, Lapham Papers; Larson, *Financial and Administrative History,* 88-89. Slaughter houses were banned within the city limits as early as 1849.

out the whole city" was needed. In 1866 the legislature created a short-lived sewerage commission; but since this became involved in a political quarrel between the State legislature and the city authorities, the board of public works, created in 1869, was left to develop an adequate disposal system in succeeding years.[26]

In the early years of cityhood, the corporation assumed little responsibility for the aesthetic or recreational side of urban life. The ornamental value of shade trees was recognized as early as 1847, but it was expected that every lot owner would see his duty and plant some. As for parks, although a park or public promenade was suggested as early as 1848, the commercial public gardens of Lackner, Bielfeld, and others and the many unenclosed spaces within the limits of the community were thought sufficient to the need. By the middle sixties, however, less open space for recreation was available, and few grounds within the city remained unoccupied. A proposal for ward parks in 1859 came to nothing; but by the late sixties, the citizens, stimulated by park construction in New York, Cleveland, and Detroit, began to look favorably upon the development of a lake park, "so located as to be accessible to those who cannot afford to go into the country for their recreation." Legislative permission was granted in 1868, and the park was constructed from Division to Biddle streets. Mayor O'Neill's inaugural admonition in 1869 to assume the "duties . . . of a metropolitan city" stressed the need of public parks which would "afford our citizens a place of healthy and innocent recreation." He recommended the acquisition of a rural park and the improvement of single squares within the wards.[27]

Inspired in part by concern for an adequate food and fuel supply and in part by the traditional behavior of older urban

[26] Milwaukee *Daily Sentinel*, Aug. 14, 1856; Dec. 21, 1858; May 31, July 9, 1866; Larson, *Financial and Administrative History*, 113-14. "The first question that puzzles any family of good habits, upon moving into a house in the city, is what to do with the offal that must necessarily accumulate. How the question is finally solved in regard to the fluids may be ascertained any day by one who is curious in such matters. Take almost any street and look into the gutters as you proceed, you will find a little stream trickling down, the stench from which precludes effectually any idea you may be inclined to form that it is pure spring water." Milwaukee *Sentinel*, June 26, 1865.

[27] Milwaukee *Daily Sentinel and Gazette*, Nov. 3, 1847; *Milwaukee Daily Sentinel*, Dec. 18, 1865; July 26, 1867; April 21, 1869; Buck, 3:128-29; 4:368-69.

communities, the city government early attempted to regulate the local economy in ways similar to those which had been employed since colonial times, and indeed even since the Middle Ages, to insure the self-sufficiency of the urban unit. Kilbourn donated land for a public market—thought essential to guarantee a sufficient supply of food, fodder, and firewood for a community in which potential scarcity might breed monopolistic, unsanitary, or fraudulent practices; and the construction of a market house, decided upon by 1847, was completed in 1850 after months of wrangling among the wards. The example of the older cities was followed in the enactment of ordinances compelling vendors of fresh meat, poultry, eggs, butter, lard, fruit, and vegetables to sell their goods at the public market during market hours unless licensed to do otherwise; prohibiting the pitching of quoits, the presence of dogs, and the use of obscene language in the market place; and forbidding the purchase of goods at the market for resale or the forestalling of country producers to buy their goods for the same purpose. Apparently these regulations were not strictly enforced, for by the late sixties there was renewed agitation for more systematic market legislation. A correspondent to the *Sentinel* cited the experience of other large cities where vendors of produce were compelled to observe market restrictions and contended that regulations which appeared to be violations of freedom of trade were necessary to preserve the public from fraud and extortion. It was "an important matter that . . . large cities should be supplied with fresh and wholesome provisions and vegetables," he wrote. Leniency in this respect might breed "disease and ravaging plague." A market ordinance, enacted in October 1869, applied to all markets in the city and authorized thoroughgoing regulation and inspection.[28]

A corollary regulation of urban merchandising led to ordinances enacted in the late forties and early fifties for the supervision of weights and measures in the purchase of boards, bricks,

---

[28] Milwaukee *Journal*, Nov. 16, 1924; *Wisconsin News* (Milwaukee), July 16, 1936; Milwaukee *Daily Sentinel*, Aug. 4, Oct. 21, 1869; "An Ordinance Relating to the First Ward Market, and to License and regulate Butcher's Stalls, Shops and Stands for the sale of Butcher's Meat, Poultry, Game and Fresh Fish," December 2, 1852, *Charters and Ordinances*, 464-65.

coal, casks, hay, flour, tobacco, potash, and salted provisions such as fish—restrictions which in some quarters were opposed as unsound in principle, "whatever the regulations of other cities 'down East' or 'out West.' "[29] In 1859 the farmers in the vicinity opposed as an inequitable tax the weighing charge of 5 cents per load of wood and 25 cents per load of hay—a concession sold by the city to the highest bidder. According to the assize of bread, decreed by ordinance in 1846, the weight of the loaf and the initials of the baker were to be indicated on each loaf of bread.[30]

An attempt to deal with the confusions attending the increase in population led to laws against undue noise, street obstructions, and "speeding." Ordinances were passed in 1846 and 1852 prohibiting the use of bells, cries, drums, and fifes at auctions and disturbances of the peace by runners and solicitors for boats, railroads, or public houses.[31] The citizens were forbidden to clutter the sidewalks with rubbish, lumber, or merchandise or to leave horses unfastened in the streets. One of the first acts of the city council was to ban all "signs, boxes, barrels, barber poles, big pitchers, big hats, big boots, etc." from the curbstones of the sidewalks. Ten years later, in an effort to regulate traffic, it was decreed that horses were not to be driven faster than at a "moderate trot" in the streets or at more than a "walk" at crossings, on penalty of $5.00 for every offense.

[29] Milwaukee *Daily Sentinel*, Dec. 17, 1853; "An Ordinance Relating to the Appointment and Duties of Sealer of Weights and Measures," November 11, 1847, *Charters and Ordinances*, 436-38; "An Ordinance Regulating the sale of Hay and Wood in the First Ward," April 29, 1852, *Charters and Ordinances*, 449-50; "An Ordinance to regulate the sale of Hay and the measuring and selling of Fuel, and to appoint an Inspector of Fuel," December 15, 1853, *Charters and Ordinances*, 472-73. A correspondent to the *Sentinel and Gazette* in 1848 objected to the appointment of a wood inspector. "Whatever the regulations of other cities 'down East' or 'out West,' the measure was unsound in principle," he wrote. It wouldn't effect the end sought, to "lower the price of wood"; and it would lead to inspection of everything else. Letter to the editor, Milwaukee *Sentinel and Gazette*, Nov. 21, 1848.

[30] Milwaukee *Sentinel*, Jan. 4, 1859; "An Ordinance Regulating the Manufacture and Sale of Bread," July 13, 1846, *Charters and Ordinances*, 440-41.

[31] "An Ordinance to regulate the time, place and manner of holding Auctions and Vendues," May 6, 1852, *Charters and Ordinances*, 450-52; Milwaukee *Daily Sentinel and Gazette*, March 7, 1846; see "An Ordinance to regulate and restrain Runners and Solicitors for Boats, Rail Roads, Public Houses or other Establishments," March 20, 1852, *Charters and Ordinances*, 444.

THE EXTENSION OF URBAN SERVICES 245

Apparently the traffic regulations were enforced, for in April 1854, Thomas Dunn was fined $5.00 for driving his horse faster than at a walk on the Spring Street bridge. After the fashion of traffic violators, he asserted: "Well, it's a pretty good way to get a bridge built anyhow, . . . but it's all a poor man can do now to earn oats for his horse." John Bowers, fined a similar sum for reckless driving in 1858, claimed that his horse was a "high-blood English animal" and "no man under the sun" could make him go slow unless he had a mind to. The first appearance of the velocipede or bicycle—hailed in 1869 as heralding a new era in Milwaukee history—brought an additional traffic hazard; but for the time being the new device was given the freedom of the sidewalk.[32]

In spite of prohibitions passed during the village period, the running at large of swine, cattle, and other stray animals and fowls was a continuing reminder of the erstwhile agrarianism of the community. Ordinances were enacted from the year of cityhood forward, but stray animals remained a destructive urban nuisance. Disregarding the complaints of a citizen whose daughter had barely escaped injury from a savage old sow on the corners of Main and Division streets, many Irish residents, supported by Tim O'Brien, the city marshal, demanded the liberty of the streets for their animals. A mass meeting held at the Albany Hall on July 13, 1859, was the first real blast against the cows and hogs; and it was followed by a one-man crusade in which Caleb Wall, city auctioneer, finally shamed the council into correction of the nuisance.[33]

Certain pursuits related to the public welfare were regulated, especially if in the practice of them the reputation of the

[32] Milwaukee *Daily Sentinel and Gazette,* July 20, 1846; "An Ordinance Relating to Streets, Alleys and Side-Walks, and to prevent the obstruction thereof," August 18, 1856, *Charters and Ordinances,* 406-15; Milwaukee *Daily Sentinel,* April 6, 1854; Aug. 26, 1858; Jan. 7, March 4, 1869.

[33] *Ibid.,* June 14, Oct. 14, 1853; May 12, Aug. 31, 1854; "An Ordinance to restrain Horses, Cattle, Sheep, Goats, Dogs, Mules, Jackasses, and other Animals and Fowls, from running at large," August 18, 1856, *Charters and Ordinances,* 418-21; Buck, 4:85, 326-28. On one occasion, Wall offered a set of silver-plated teaspoons for the best poem "on Hogs and Cows running at large and having all the privileges of the sidewalk." Milwaukee *Morning Sentinel,* April 11, 1862. "If we are a city, let us be one," he concluded; "but if we are a country village, so be it " Milwaukee *Sentinel,* June 1, 1861; June 3, 13, 1864.

city were involved. The operation of hackney coaches was controlled as to licenses and rates; and interest in attracting immigrants prompted an ordinance of May 3, 1849, which fixed a maximum charge of 10 cents an article on the goods of passengers landed on the piers of the city. The regulations and restrictions in the interest of urban order were probably variously enforced and did not work as great an interference with the liberty of the individual as their existence on the statute books would imply. Indeed, as has already been suggested, some of the ordinances were undoubtedly enacted more in compliance with charter provisions copied from the constitutional framework of other cities than out of immediate concern for the reform. From the middle fifties forward, however, as the growth of the city made necessary an adjustment to increased population and commercial specialization, there was undoubtedly greater interest in enforcing the restrictions that promised to promote a more orderly community life. Proof of this is found in the statistics of arrests under such headings: for 1854, 238; 1860, 211; 1861, 119; and 1864, 236.[34]

As the community matured, and science and industry offered solutions to its problems which the results of voluntary association could not match, private corporate enterprise began to replace individual subscription in meeting urban needs. This was true in connection with the improvement of facilities for street lighting, a city water supply, and urban transit. By the fall of 1849, George F. Lee of Philadelphia, soliciting stock subscriptions for a proposed local gas works, had convinced Milwaukeeans of the "superior cheapness, convenience, and brilliancy of Gas Lights to all other means of lighting Streets, Stores, and Dwellings"; and the *Sentinel* lent its support by refuting all claims that gas light was "too costly a luxury for so young a city as Milwaukee." Lee's plan gained the approval of the council, but delays forced it to lapse; and it was not until two years later that the work was undertaken by John Lockwood on behalf of the Milwaukee Gas Light Company, chartered on January 3, 1852. Two of the trustees of the new company—

[34] "An Ordinance to regulate Hackney Coaches, Cabs, Drays and Omnibusses," August 29, 1856, *Charters and Ordinances*, 425-31; Buck, 4:72; *Milwaukee Daily Sentinel*, Jan. 4, 1860; Jan. 4, 1861; April 6, 1864.

James H. Rogers and William P. Lynde—had been members of the council while Lee's plan was subject to "delay." Alexander Mitchell became one of the directors and Rogers, president. The company was to build the works and fixtures at its own expense; in return the city was to guarantee it the exclusive right to supply the city with gas illumination for fifteen years at a cost of not more than $2.50 a thousand feet.[35]

Lockwood, who was to figure significantly in the development of Milwaukee's public works, was well equipped to direct the enterprise. He had spent the preceding six years building similar plants in Ohio, Kentucky, and Indiana. A preliminary mishap blew out one side of the gas works, but when the city was lighted for the first time on November 23, 1852, Young's Hall was reported to be a "blaze of light" and there was "brilliant illumination in the streets." By February 1857, seven miles of pipe had been laid, and five more were promised for the ensuing year. Already, the stock, owned principally in Troy, New York, was paying excellent dividends. The complaints of George Dyer in May of 1856 led to the decision that the company, "though a private corporation," was affected with a public interest and must supply gas on demand. Attempts to incorporate a competitive enterprise were quashed in 1857, but in 1858 there was agitation to see that the city and its citizens were getting their money's worth. In 1859 publicity was given to the fact that the city of Philadelphia owned its gas works.[36]

Less successful were the persistent efforts to achieve an adequate water supply by constructing a pumping works that would make drinking water available from the lake. Public cisterns provided no security in case of fire, and both public and private wells were contaminated by sewage. In the business district one had to walk half a mile to find a pump and then risk his health in drinking the water. On the turn of the sixties many families were resorting to the use of rain water filtered from

[35] Milwaukee *Sentinel and Gazette*, Nov. 7, 1849; Feb. 21, 1850; Feb. 3, June 3, 5, 1851; Milwaukee *Daily Sentinel*, Feb. 3, May 22, 1852.

[36] Cincinnati *Commercial*, quoted in Milwaukee *Daily Sentinel*, April 9, 1852; Milwaukee *Daily Sentinel*, Nov. 13, 17, 26, 1852; May 26, 1856; Buck, 3:410; Milwaukee *Sentinel*, Dec. 2, 1856; Feb. 12, 1857; March 16, 1859. According to Buck, "Probably no stock ever owned in Milwaukee . . . ever paid as large returns as . . . this gas stock." Buck, 3:410.

their cisterns. Private capital, organized as the Lake Michigan Hydraulic Company, stood ready to build a pumping plant, if either the citizens or the city would subscribe to a share of the stock. In 1851, Lockwood, acting for the company, negotiated a contract with the city; but since the popular imagination was obsessed at the moment with railroad promotion, the required subsidy of $75,000 failed to materialize.[37] The *Sentinel*, charged by the *Free Democrat* with having a pecuniary interest in the enterprise, continued to agitate, stressing especially the importance of waterworks in time of fire. A second organization, the Milwaukee Hydraulic Company, of which J. H. Rogers was one of the incorporators, carried negotiations to the point where bonds were issued by the council in 1857; but this plan, too, miscarried. During the decade between 1857 and 1867, a number of proposals were put forward in public meetings, but nothing came of them. By 1867, New York, Philadelphia, and Cincinnati capitalists were canvassing the situation; and in the following year the council authorized E. S. Chesbrough, city engineer of Chicago, to make preliminary plans. By 1871, the city's financial situation warranted its undertaking the work, and a board of water commissioners, headed by Alexander Mitchell, began to supervise construction at public expense. City water was available in November 1873.[38]

In the decade of the sixties Milwaukee had its first experience with horse railroads—"as much a necessity for busy and growing cities," according to the editor of the *Sentinel*, "as is a Fire Department, or Gas, or Water Works." Agitation for the new mode of urban transit began in the summer of 1859, when George H. Walker, Dr. L. W. Weeks, W. S. Johnson, F. S. Blodgett, and G. D. Davis petitioned the council for permission to lay tracks and operate the River and Lake Shore City Railway Company through the streets of the First, Third, and

[37] According to the terms of the contract, the company was to have a monopoly for fifteen years, at the expiration of which time the city should buy the works or extend the franchise for an additional ten years. Larson, *Financial and Administrative History*, 108; Milwaukee *Daily Sentinel*, Dec. 14, 25, 1852; June 21, 1860.

[38] *Ibid.*, Jan. 4, Feb. 1, April 9, Dec. 23, 1853; Sept. 4, 1854; June 23, 1857; Aug. 19, Sept. 30, 1867; Jan. 31, 1868; H. P. Bohmann, *Milwaukee Water Works* (Milwaukee, 1935), 4; Larson, *Financial and Administrative History*, 109, 111.

Seventh wards. Opponents of the proposal objected to such a use of the public thoroughfares without exacting a license fee or consulting the owners of adjoining property; but its advocates won their point by asserting that the citizens of Chicago, St. Louis, and Cincinnati were already enjoying this mode of travel, that in Cleveland construction was under way, and that any city without it would be "regarded by travelers as . . . decidedly behind the age." As a result, on May 30, 1860, crowds lined the streets as two blue and buff vehicles, each drawn by four horses, made their first trip from what is now the North Water Street bridge to East Juneau Avenue. Within the year, new rails were added, and the rolling stock was increased.[39]

The plan for the West Side Passenger Railway Company, incorporated in November 1859 for operation in the Second, Fourth, Fifth, Sixth, Eighth, and Ninth wards, collapsed in ward politics; but the success of the original horse-car enterprise led to a wave of petitions for additional companies. Among them were the West Water Street Horse Railway Company and the Cold Spring City Railway Company, whose incorporators included Alexander Mitchell, Hans Crocker, C. D. Davis, E. B. Wolcott, and O. Alexander. The advent of the Civil War prevented these lines from being built. At its close, the council was open-handed in the privileges it granted to John Plankinton, Frederick Layton, Samuel Marshall, and Charles F. Ilsley, when they organized the Milwaukee City Railway Company in 1865; but the enterprise was never financially very successful. In 1866 an increase in fares from 5 to 6 cents was under criticism, and the press was making the practical suggestion that the cars be marked to indicate their destination. A decline in profits in the late sixties led both the Lake Shore and the Milwaukee City companies to sell out their franchises, rights, and properties to Isaac Ellsworth, who ultimately restored the business to a paying basis.[40]

It was the problems presented by the desire for large-scale public works that led, as has already been indicated, to the sub-

[39] Milwaukee *Sentinel*, July 21, Aug. 5, Aug. 27, Oct. 8, 1859; Milwaukee *Daily Sentinel*, Aug. 31, 1860; Milwaukee *Sentinel*, July 14, 1937.
[40] *Ibid.*, Nov. 29, 1859; Jan. 12, 1866; July 14, 1937; Buck, 4:391-92; Milwaukee *Daily Sentinel*, June 12, 18, Aug. 25, 28, 1860; Gregory, *History*, 2:1196-97.

stitution of an appointed administrative board for the untrained, politically chosen, and easily corruptible ward officers who hitherto had managed the development of municipal improvements. The creation of a public debt commission in 1861 began a practice which prompted agitation throughout the ensuing decade to extend the use of administrative boards to other urban problems. The metropolitan police bill, proposed in 1864 but defeated through the play of politics, would have given control of all matters relating to police, fire, and health to a board including the mayor and three other persons appointed by the governor and senate. A short-lived sewerage commission, appointed in 1866, and a separate, mayor-appointed board of health, authorized in 1867, preceded the creation of the board of public works in 1869. This board, to be appointed by the mayor, with the consent of a majority of the council, was given general control over streets, sewers, bridges, sidewalks, wharves, and public buildings in all parts of the city. The replacement of interested ward councilors by presumed specialists marked some advance in municipal administration but it did not do much to overcome the disintegration of the city's administrative organization or to enhance the executive strength of the mayor, the weakness of whose position was to be a continuing characteristic of the city's constitutional structure.[41]

While the realization of a city-wide board of public works was most significant for its promise of an increasingly professionalized and less self-interested approach in the administration of the problems of the emerging metropolis, it was not without meaning as a sign of the long-awaited triumph of the "city" over the "ward" point of view. And there were smaller, but no less suggestive indications of the city's impending metropolitan stature. One was the "never ceasing and ever increasing influx . . . of families from the rural districts," which according to the *Sentinel,* swelled the great mass of young men and women "flocking to learn the tricks and trades of city life." Another was the resort to apartment and boarding house living until the "number of boarders" who could be "stowed away on a given

---

[41] See chapter 7 for the political implications of these developments. See also Larson, *Financial and Administrative History,* 88-89.

area of floor room and the amount of food required to supply a given number of stomachs" were reported to be "cyphered down to the smallest possible point by the genius of boarding house proprietors." And finally, there was evidence that Milwaukee was beginning to feel her age and sense her history. An Old Settlers' Club was founded on July 5, 1869; and late December of that year saw the first annual supper of the Milwaukee Pioneer Club. A toast proposed on this occasion revealed the community's awareness of the accomplishments of the short generation which had brought the metropolis into view:

> Milwaukee City: Here she is. Look at her—her capacious harbor, her yellow brick, her stately elevators, warehouses and stores, and her palatial private residences; the emporium of the state; the greatest wheat market of the continent; the home of industry, social refinement, public order and peace; and all the solid growth of thirty-five years.[42]

THE GENERATION FROM 1846 to the turn of the seventies was a period of transition in Milwaukee's urban life, a period in which a village was accommodating itself to city ways. The community was a bifurcated society throughout the period, in the sense that the populous and self-assertive *Deutsch-Athen*, with its German theater, schools, newspapers, fire and military companies, relief societies, and baseball team, paralleling those of the English-speaking residents, existed coordinately beside the American community within the frame of the developing city. It was a time in which personal promotion was largely responsible for the city's development, and voluntary association and subscription the means of meeting the community's needs. In a sense, this generation was the age of Mitchell, Kilbourn, Rogers, Holton, Huebschmann, and the other vigorous individuals who took a personal responsibility for nurturing and cultivating the city's growth. Alexander Mitchell pushed to corporate magnitude the railroad enterprise whose promotion had been the climax of Kilbourn's speculative career; and his business acumen, together with that of men like Rogers and

[42] Milwaukee *Daily Sentinel*, June 15, 1867; May 16, 1868; Sept. 17, Dec. 23, 1869; Gregory, *History*, 2:1087.

Holton, fostered the commercial and corporate wealth of the community. Huebschmann represented the participation and contribution of transplanted Europeanism at its best, and Rufus King had a hand in every scheme for cultural, industrial, or municipal improvement, using the columns of the *Sentinel* to goad the citizenry to achieve their metropolitan destiny.[43] Men of self-made wealth, the "solid citizens" of this period played an active role in the political and economic life of the expanding city, conscious of their obligation to promote its good as well as aware of the profits to be gained from encouraging its growth.

Fluctuations of the business cycle had significant effect upon the developing community; hence, the boom years of the middle fifties permitted an expansion and accomplishment along all lines, which, together with the timely completion of harbor improvement and railroad connections to the Mississippi, gave Milwaukee an impetus to cityhood which later depression could not check and which only because of its more advantageous geographical position Chicago could surpass. At last, the expansion of both the population and the physical limits of the city resulted in an inevitable trend toward city ways. In the things of the spirit as well as in the management of municipal problems the amateur was beginning to give way to the professional. In the early part of the period the existence of truly professional services was a matter of chance. The artist Vianden, the musician Balatka, the educator Engelmann, and Chief Beck of the police department all had hoped to become farmers; but the growing urban community provided a more congenial outlet for their abilities, and they in turn made a "chance" contribution to the specialization of its society. By the close of the period, the opportunity to gratify the higher tastes was less haphazard than at the outset, and disillusionment with management by the "average man" was prompting a resort to somewhat more specialized and professional administration of municipal government. The need of city-wide improvements and the magnitude

[43] Juneau died in 1856; Rogers and Walker in 1866; Kilbourn in 1870, after his removal to Florida in 1868; and King in 1876. King's municipal activities were curtailed in the early sixties when he left for participation in the Civil War.

of the municipal undertakings of the seventies did much to destroy the ward separatism of the Middle Period. But more important was the fact that a new generation was beginning to identify itself with the city as a whole rather than with one of its formerly "provincial" parts. The "lure of the city" was in the air; the drift to the metropolis was the innovation of the age;[44] and Milwaukee, already benefiting from the advantage of her geographical position, the development of her hinterland, and the ingenuity of her citizenry, was ready to profit from the trend.

[44] See editorials in New York *Daily Tribune,* Feb. 5, 1867; Jan. 25, 1868; Milwaukee *Daily Sentinel,* July 27, 1868.

PART III

The Emerging Metropolis 1870 to 1910

"One of the wonders of the nineteenth century is the growth of American cities. Twenty-eight years ago, Milwaukee was a small, unimportant village, situated on two bluffs and divided by a sluggish river and an almost impenetrable tamarack swamp. Now, on the same ground, stands... the home of a hundred thousand busy people; and in the midst of the whilom tamarack swamp,... the most luxurious hotel west of New York.... On the very spot where thirty years ago the Indians exchanged their furs for trinkets is being built a block of offices at an outlay of over a quarter of a million. In view of what has been done, and with our augmented facilities, what may we not expect in the coming thirty years?"—Correspondent to the Ohio State Journal (Columbus), quoted in the Milwaukee Daily Sentinel, February 3, 1869.

"We cannot all live in cities; yet nearly all seem determined to do so. Millions of acres... solicit cultivation...; yet hundreds of thousands reject this and rush into the cities."—Horace Greeley, in the New York Tribune, February 5, 1867.

CHAPTER 11

Nationality Ingredients

B YRON KILBOURN lived to see the village of his expansive vision become by 1870 a city of more than 70,000 souls. Could he have survived another generation of its history, he would have witnessed an increase in population beyond the limits even of his speculator's dreams. For in the years that intervened between 1870 and 1910, Milwaukee grew in numbers from 71,440 to 373,857. This fivefold increase, while the remainder of the State merely doubled in population, was but a manifestation at the mouth of the Milwaukee of the trek to the city which was the outstanding feature of American social history in the later years of the nineteenth century.[1] In 1871, an editorial in the *Sentinel* insisted that "for the young man in the country" there was no resisting the metropolitan pull. "It draws him like a magnet," it read. "Sooner or later . . . he will be sucked into one of the great centers of life." The 77 percent increase in the eighties convinced the citizenry that Milwaukee was a "metropolitan city"; and for the next two decades similar assertions poured from press, pulpit, and political platform.[2] Writers on the subject of the American metropolis

---

[1] "The census of 1890 revealed another fact which is possibly as deeply significant as the disappearance of the frontier lines. It gave conclusive evidence of the rapid drift of our population toward the city. . . ." Samuel E. Sparling, "The Problem of the Small City in Wisconsin," Milwaukee *Sentinel*, March 4, 1900. Historians have been so preoccupied "with the dispersion of settlers" that they have "given little attention to this countermovement which even more profoundly altered the tissue of American life." Arthur M. Schlesinger, "The City in American History," *Mississippi Valley Historical Review*, 27:58 (June 1940). See appendix for chart comparing total population and sex distribution of Milwaukee and the State of Wisconsin by decades.

[2] Milwaukee *Sentinel*, March 18, 1871; March 16, 1902; March 22, 1904; March 5, 1908; *Evening Wisconsin* (Milwaukee), Sept. 6, 1881; Jan. 26, May 2, 30, July 7, Sept. 7, 1889; April 1, 1900.

257

recognized in Milwaukee a city in the first flush of its urban maturity;[3] and at the celebration of the city's semi-centennial anniversary in 1895, the proud residents boasted that but four cities in the world had grown to Milwaukee's size with equal speed.[4] By 1910, the consciousness of "big cityhood," only dimly sensed on the turn of the seventies, had become an organic reality in the community life. This was attested by the fusion of nationalities, the easing of former ward antagonisms, the increasingly articulate position of urban labor, a vigorous concern for urban crowding, municipal reform, and home rule, and such an assumption of civic social responsibility as to justify Zona Gale's remark that "almost within the last year" Milwaukee had "come to civic self-consciousness."[5]

Natives of the United States made up more than half of the city's population in this period. Wisconsin's contribution increased from 40 percent of the total in 1870 to 61 percent in 1910, and that of New York, Illinois, and Ohio was next most numerous. But in spite of the predominance of native-born residents after 1870, at the outset of her metropolitan era Milwaukee was still to a considerable extent Europe once or twice removed. Forty-seven percent of her population was foreign-born in 1870, and the census of 1890 found her the most "foreign," in this respect, of the twenty-eight largest cities in the United States.[6] By 1910 the essence of Europeanism was diluted to the

[3] See Willard Glazier, *Peculiarities of American Cities* (Philadelphia, 1884); Charles D. Warner, *Studies in the South and West* (New York, 1889); Ernest Ingersoll, "Milwaukee," *Harper's New Monthly Magazine*, 62:702-18 (April 1881); Charles King, "The Cream City," *Cosmopolitan*, 10:549-60 (March 1891); William W. Howard, "The City of Milwaukee," *Harper's Weekly*, 35:538-39 (July 18, 1891); and the translation of Edmund Goes, "Milwaukee: The German City of America," excerpt from *"Ueber Land und Meer,"* in *The Chautauquan*, 27:659-61 (September 1898). See also Bayrd Still, "The Growth of Milwaukee as Recorded by Contemporaries," *Wisconsin Magazine of History*, 21:262-92 (March 1938).

[4] *Evening Wisconsin*, Oct. 15, 1895.

[5] "Milwaukee has been divided by nature into three sections, but the time has gone when the lines which separate them could be regarded as marking the boundaries of submunicipalities, each antagonistic to the others. . . . It is all Milwaukee, a great progressive, homogeneous city, and never before have all sections and all classes been found with more harmony than they are today for its upbuilding and advancement." Milwaukee *Sentinel*, March 5, 1908; Zona Gale, "Milwaukee," *Good Housekeeping*, 50:323 (March 1910).

[6] Goes, "Milwaukee: German City of America," *Chautauquan*, 27:660n (September 1898). See appendix for charts showing origins of native-born popu-

point that the foreign-born constituted only a third of the population; but even at that date more than three-fourths of the total population were classified by the census takers as "foreign white stock." Although a "new" immigration was contributing additional nationality elements to the metropolitan culture during the generation, the Wisconsin city was still predominantly German on the turn of the century. Natives of Germany made up a third of the total population in 1870; and while by 1910 only 17 percent were native-born Germans, more than half of the residents (53.5 percent) were still identified as of Teutonic background. The city's Germanism reached the peak of its intensity during this period, but at the arrival of the twentieth century the processes of urbanization were welding the formerly separate German and American societies of the century before into a fundamentally American community, albeit one in which the flavor and appearance of Teutonism still remained.

Many parts of Milwaukee continued to look like Germany; there were public buildings that might have stood in Strassburg or Nuremberg, ornate residences that were influenced by the German Renaissance, and German faces, German signs, Teutonic speech. The beer gardens and eating places recalled Berlin—from the famous Schlitz Palm Garden, Toser's on East Water, and "Ma" Heiser's, at Jackson Street and Ogden Avenue, to the German boarding houses with their menus of *kalter Aufschnitt* with *Kartoffel Salat* or *Wienerschnitzel* and "German fried."[7] And there was a full round of German amusements: skat, the singing societies, the German theater at the Pabst, and on Sunday afternoons the music of von Suppé and Strauss played by Christopher Bach's orchestra in the West side *Turnhalle*.

The eighties and nineties were years of political and social accomplishment among the German-American element. As has already been indicated, the new generation was made confident by the German victory in the Franco-Prussian War. Bolstered by augmented numbers and increasing wealth, it was less radical

lation listed according to predominance of states of origin and percentage of foreign-born persons in population, listed by predominance of nationality group.

[7] Edna Ferber, *A Peculiar Treasure* (New York, 1938), 132-34.

than that of the Forty-eighters, more assured of its position, and hence readier unconsciously to take on the attributes of Americanism. The pre-eminent Huebschmann died in 1880, and by that time, with Luening, Schoeffler, and Fratny also gone, leadership fell into the hands of a younger group of newspaper men, including P. V. Deuster of the *Seebote* and George Koeppen of the *Germania,* and of the lawyer, Frederick W. von Cotzhausen.[8] In 1882, the German Society, which had been founded two years earlier, asserted the right of German-Americans to greater political recognition; and within two years, one of its leaders, Berlin-born Emil Wallber, had been elected mayor. For the ensuing two decades, the reactions of the city's German voters virtually called the tune of local politics. In campaigning for John C. Koch, who won the mayoralty for the Republicans in 1893 and 1894, the editor of the *Germania* called it a "matter of honor for every German-American to vote for that excellent German John C. Koch. . . . we are confident that the Germandom of the city is conscious of its duty."[9] Koch was a native of Hamburg and his successor, William J. Rauschenberger, had been born in Soldin, Prussia.[10] On the other hand, the Republicans' endorsement in 1890 of a law threatening the German schools of the community alienated enough Lutheran German Republicans to permit the election of the Democrats' mayoral candidate, George W. Peck.

This measure, known as the Bennett Law, had passed the Wisconsin legislature on April 16, 1890. Providing that students must attend school in the district in which they lived and that schools, to conform to the law, must provide elementary instruction in the English language, this legislation threatened many of the agencies which were keeping Milwaukee's Germanism alive. Although German had been offered on an optional basis

[8] Ewald Alfred Arthur Frederick William von Cotzhausen was born at Cambach, near Aix-la-Chapelle, July 21, 1838. Prevented by weak eyesight from becoming an officer in the Prussian navy, he came to Milwaukee in 1856 and was admitted to the bar in 1859. He was counsel for the Milwaukee and Lake Shore Railroad Company and later for the Chicago and North Western. He was a member of the State senate in 1873 and 1874. Gregory, *History,* 2:938.

[9] Quoted in Milwaukee *Sentinel,* June 25, 1893. See *Yearbooks* of the German Society of Milwaukee *(Deutsche Gesellschaft von* Milwaukee), June 1880 to October 1909.

[10] *Ibid.,* July 14, 1937.

in the public schools since the late sixties, where it was taught for three hours per week through eight grades,[11] it was the parochial schools, in which the teachers felt that there was not time in the curriculum for studies in English, that emphasized the continued use of the language upon which the German churches, press, theater, Turner and singing societies, and other institutions were thought to depend. Moreover, the measure was a blow to the freedom and prestige of the European group and one which might be followed, according to their fears, by the complete interdiction of foreign-language studies and religious organizations.[12] United in their opposition, for once the Catholic and Lutheran Germans saw eye to eye; and the religious element, rather than the Freethinking Forty-eighters, stood as the champions of German culture. Of the German press, only the *Freidenker* and the *Arbeiter Zeitung,* which took the stand that the education of youth was the responsibility of the state, were in favor of the bill.[13] Irish support was gained because of the denunciation of the measure by Archbishop Heiss of the Catholic church.[14] Dr. Christian Koerner of Milwaukee headed the predominantly Lutheran Anti-Bennett Law State Central Committee; and he, Rasmus Anderson, and von Cotzhausen were speakers at a rally held in the Turner Hall on June 4, 1890, at which those present resolved to support only such candidates as promised not to interfere with the religious schools. The ensuing State election saw the overwhelming defeat of the Republicans, and, soon after, the Bennett Law was repealed.[15]

As if to symbolize their influence in the city, Milwaukee's German-Americans celebrated German Day on October 6, 1890,

[11] Watrous, 1:393.
[12] Hense-Jensen, Schafer tr., chap. 13, pp. 10-12.
[13] The *Seebote* professed to want ". . . the children of German parents to retain the good old German ways and keep those virtues and qualities which distinguish the German race." William F. Whyte, "The Bennett Law Campaign in Wisconsin," *Wisconsin Magazine of History*, 10:384 (June 1927).
[14] *Ibid.,* 381-82.
[15] Hense-Jensen, Schafer tr., chap. 13, pp. 17-18; Whyte, "Bennett Law Campaign," *Wis. Mag. of Hist.,* 10:390 (June 1927). According to Joseph Schafer, the Bennett Law issue was not the only factor in the Republican defeat of 1890. The Republicans fell everywhere, for one reason because of opposition to the McKinley tariff. Dr. Schafer asserts that the Bennett Law was not primarily a nativistic measure, that it was unnecessary because German children were

commemorating the landing of German migrants with Pastorius some 200 years before. Every German organization participated. The floats representing scenes from German-American history and the procession of 12,000 marchers made a sight such as had not been witnessed since the victory celebration of 1871. Another gala Teutonic occasion occurred when the North American *Turnerbund* held its twenty-sixth *Bundesturnfest* in Milwaukee in July 1893. When the city signalized its semi-centennial anniversary in 1895, Bach's band and the German organizations had prominent places in the parade, and a leading Milwaukee German, General Frederick C. Winkler, was chosen to deliver the oration of the day. Typical of the German-American leadership of the late nineteenth century, Winkler had been born in Germany in 1838 and had come to Milwaukee at the age of six, receiving his education in the German-English Academy. After attaining distinction in the famous "German regiment" during the Civil War, he had become an outstanding member of the Milwaukee bar.[16]

Not until the late nineties did the political assertiveness of the German-American element begin to wane. Then the conservative Lutheran leadership of the Germans, having returned to the Republican fold to support the election of Koch and Rauschenberger, as mayors, was challenged by a younger generation of American-born Germans. Affected perhaps by the national mindedness of the hour, these last were sensitive about their Germanism and critical of their fellow German-Americans who could not speak English fluently or whose manner suggested lack of loyalty to the United States. The defection of this group to the Democratic Party contributed to the defeat of William Geuder and Henry Baumgaertner for the mayoralty in 1900 and 1902; and such was the strength of this point of view that by the latter year the Republicans agreed

learning English on the playground if not in the schoolroom, and that it was ill-advised because it produced "unnecessary social bitterness between classes of citizens equally patriotic and public spirited." Joseph Schafer, "Editorial Comment," *Wisconsin Magazine of History*, 10:455-61 (June 1927). See also discussion of Bennett Law in chapter 12.

[16] Hense-Jensen, Schafer tr., chap. 16, pp. 9-10; Milwaukee *Sentinel*, June 18, 1893; Gregory, *History*, 2-940-41.

that nothing was longer to be gained by advancing German candidates as a means of winning the German vote.[17] Reports conflict as to the warmth with which the Kaiser's brother, Prince Henry of Prussia, was greeted on a visit in 1902;[18] and there were other signs that the strength of Germanism, as such, was beginning to decline. When the European leaders of Pan-Germanism asserted in 1904 that the United States had proved to be "the grave of Germanism," Milwaukee's Teutonic citizens admitted that the German migrant had become American, "not only in law, but in fact—in acts, words, and spirit," part of a "conglomeration of native and foreign elements" which were "crystallizing into one people—prompted by common, national impulses." They nevertheless insisted that the German influence was manifest "at every step in the social, commercial, and political life" of the city, an opinion seconded by the editor of the *Sentinel* when he observed that although the process of Americanization had "involved some relinquishment . . . of German characteristics," such of them as were "not incompatible with a broad, loyal, and paramount Americanism"—for example, "matters of taste and culture, . . . standards of daily living, a liberal view of man's right to the good things and pleasures of life, a knowledge of and pride in the traditions and achievements of the fatherland,"—had been cherished and preserved. If life in the United States had Americanized the German immigrants, he wrote, the latter had "to a perceptible and wholesome degree Germanized" the Americans.

They have taught us, among other good things, some needed lessons in the art of cheerful and pleasurable living. American life was comparatively a hard, prosaic, and sad-colored business before our settlers from the continent helped us dispel the shadow of the too austere Puritan standard of living that brooded over this land of ours. So far from the United States having "proven the grave of German characteristics," it has really proven the fruitful seedfield of some of the best and most gracious German characteristics.[19]

[17] Hense-Jensen, Schafer tr., chap. 17, p. 23.
[18] Milwaukee *Sentinel*, March 5, 1902; William G. Bruce, *I Was Born in America* (Milwaukee, 1937), 193.
[19] Milwaukee *Sentinel*, March 6, 1904.

If there were ultimately a disavowal of Germanism in some quarters, many Milwaukeeans, like von Cotzhausen, had been concerned "to continue in permanent touch with the intellectual life of the Old World," an ambition that was realized to a large extent as a result of the vigorous cultural activities of the German-American group in the last quarter of the century. The Germania Association, organized in the early seventies, was similar to the Young Men's Association of the American element. Possessing a library and lecture rooms in the Opera House, it sponsored lectures by eminent German scholars. At the same time the German theater was reaching the zenith of its accomplishment. Under the leadership of Leon Wachsner, the Stadt Theatre provided a German stock company which was the equal of "any of the stock companies in the provincial cities of Germany" or of "any of the American road companies." The classical German drama as well as the productions of modern German authors, like Lindau, Fulda, or Schoenthan, were produced in a season that ran from the middle of September to the last week in April. Wednesday was subscription night, with 400 seats, at $13.50 to $30.00 a season, subscribed and paid for. This was the fashionable night when one could expect a serious play—something from the classic repertoire or a new work of Ibsen, Shaw, or Wilde—in German. On Sundays and Fridays the fare was lighter, a farce or a musical comedy. Hedwig Beringer and Anna Roithmayr were popular members of the resident company; and among the guest stars were the most famous German actors of the day, including Anna Haverland, Mitterwurzer, Kainz, Agnes Sorma, Emanuel Reicher, and others.[20] Through the seventies the *Musikverein* continued to keep alive the love of German music.

The most continuous channel of Teutonic influence during the period was the German press. Supplementing the *Banner, Volksfreund,* and *Seebote* of the earlier period were the *Herold* and the *Germania.* The combined circulation of the *Germania, Herold,* and *Seebote* totaled, roughly, 92,000 in 1884, when the

[20] Milwaukee *Sentinel,* Feb. 21, 1874; March 20, 1888; Feb. 11, 1894; *Wisconsin News* (Milwaukee), July 16, 1936; Hense-Jensen, Schafer tr., chap. 16, pp. 17-18.

combined circulation of the *Sentinel, Journal,* and *Evening Wisconsin* stood at about half that figure.[21] The *Germania* boasted in 1904 that it stood "second as to paid city circulation and third as to total paid circulation among all Milwaukee newspapers, while exclusive of street sales the *Germania Abend-Post*" was "the first paper in point of home circulation in the city and county of Milwaukee." By 1910, however, the daily issues of the *Germania, Herold,* and *Seebote* totaled about 45,000, while the daily issues of the *Sentinel, Journal,* and *Evening Wisconsin* had climbed to approximately 150,000.[22]

Many forces contributed to the decline of Germanism which these changes in newspaper circulation revealed, thus making inevitable the Americanization of what once was termed the "most German city in the United States." Participation in municipal, state, and national politics speedily identified the newcomers with American life; for, however separate in its social existence, the German community was in no way backward in exerting its political privileges. During the seventies the Milwaukee Germans took an active stand against corruption in national and local politics and against the sumptuary laws passed by the State legislature. Many Germans joined the Liberal Republican movement in 1872; in 1875, under Huebschmann's leadership, they proposed a vigilance committee to "establish surveillance" of the several departments of the city government; and in 1876 mass meetings, "crowded by workingmen and citizens of all classes," spoke out against "municipal rings." The leading German brewers of the city took up the cudgels against the Graham License Law, passed by the State legislature in 1872; and German opposition on this score was in part responsible for the defeat of the Republican candidate for governor in the following year.[23] In their whole-hearted coop-

[21] These figures include daily and weekly issues.
[22] *American Newspaper Directory* (George P. Rowell and Company, New York, 1884), 491-92; *American Newspaper Annual and Directory* (N. W. Ayer and Sons, Philadelphia, 1910), 950-61; *American Newspaper Directory* (1905), 1110. In 1889 Edmund Goes estimated that 50 to 60 percent of the local population had command of the German language. Goes, "Milwaukee: German City of America," *Chautauquan,* 27:661 (September 1898).
[23] Milwaukee *Sentinel,* April 26, 1875; April 19, 1876; Oct. 16, 1895. See also Hense-Jensen, Schafer tr., chaps. 7, 10, and 12.

eration in advancing the city's commerce and industry, the German industrialists related themselves to the developing municipality; thus economic interest and civic promotion as well as the practice of democracy provided a common bond.

Moreover, the urban life which once had fostered such a concentration of Europeans as to retard assimilation now tended to break the resulting cultural solidarity of the German-Americans by promoting class differentiation and social cleavage within the Teutonic element itself. By 1900, according to Ernest Bruncken, one no longer thought of fusing "all groups of Germans from the laborers to the highest of the merchant class and the learned professions into a single social organization."[24] Already the appeal of the Turner societies and such lodges as the Druids and Sons of Hermann had waned for all but the small traders and laborers. For the "upper-class" Germans, the more exclusive entertainment of the home and the club replaced the sociability of picnic, amateur theatrical, and turn hall. Separate celebrations, like that which the Germans held for President Hayes in 1878, were abandoned, and prominent Germans and Americans intermingled in the social activities of the community.

As these changes took place within the German community, its flavor of the Fatherland was tempered by that of an "unmistakably American crust." As early as the turn of the eighties, Ernest Ingersoll remarked the contrast between the "crowds of immigrants . . . fresh from the voyage" and the inhabitants of the West side. The faces were the same, the dress only slightly different; but there was "an entire change, hard to define, in the *sentiment* of all that the late immigrant" said and did. And the increasing predominance of American-born Germans further sped the change. Whereas in 1870, every mature man and woman in the Sixth Ward would have been a native of Germany, by 1900 their children were Americanizing the section, demanding an English newspaper, and even avoiding German customs and the German tongue. In April 1894, the Stadt Theatre began to alternate plays in English with the German

[24] *Ibid.*, chap. 16, p. 3.

MILWAUKEE IN THE EIGHTIES: EAST WATER STREET IN THE DAYS OF THE HORSE CAR

repertoire. Efforts in Philadelphia in 1900 to found a German-American Alliance which would further German interests in America awakened little response in the erstwhile *Deutsch-Athen*. By the turn of the twentieth century, the cohesive and exclusive German community of the middle nineteenth century was gone; the German spirit had penetrated the life of the whole city with its concern for the home, for thrift, and for conservation, its promotion of the brewing industry, and its patronage of the arts. The result was a city with what Zona Gale called the "foreign flavor of a yet genuinely American viand," not less American than New Orleans with its French influence or southern California with that of Spain, yet nevertheless with something of "Nuremberg, and Strassburg and Heidelberg in its veins." By 1910 the *Gesangvereine* were dying out, the English press far outdistanced its German competitors, and World War I, bringing attitudes critical of Germanism, was only over the horizon. In March 1910, the Turner societies honored Christopher Bach's fifty years of service to the city's musical life. His farewell concert, on March 27, might be said to have symbolized the final absorption of the self-conscious *Deutsch-Athen* into the twentieth-century American city.[25]

Milwaukee's Germanism had undergone a metamorphosis by 1910; but already the "new immigration," which by 1907 constituted 81 percent of the total European migration to the United States, was making itself felt in the culture of the Wisconsin city.[26] Promising to become most influential of all the

[25] Ingersoll, "Milwaukee," *Harper's New Monthly Magazine*, 62:717 (April 1881); Hense-Jensen, Schafer tr., chap. 18, pp. 5-6, 10; Milwaukee *Sentinel*, April 6, 1894; March 24, 1910; Gale, "Milwaukee," *Good Housekeeping*, 50:319-21 (March 1910). See Ernest Bruncken, "How Germans Become Americans," Wisconsin Historical Society, *Proceedings*, 1897, pp. 101-22. For a colorful treatment of the character and decline of the German society in Milwaukee, see the following works of Ernest L. Meyer: "Milwaukee Nights—1910," *Capital Times* (Madison), Nov. 17, 20, 25, 29, Dec. 2, 6, 10, 1931; "Twilight of a Golden Age," *American Mercury*, 29:456-64 (August 1933); and *Bucket Boy: a Milwaukee Legend* (New York, 1947).

[26] According to Thomas Čapek, the "old"—or North European—immigration supplied 95 percent of the total until 1883. But by 1907, 81 percent of the total were recruited from Austria, Hungary, Poland, Bohemia, Italy, Portugal, Rumania, Russia, Serbia, and Spain. See Thomas Čapek, *Czechs and Slovaks in the United States Census* (New York, 1939), unpaged.

newcomers were the Poles, who by 1910 were in almost exclusive possession of the southwestern section of the city, including and beyond Mitchell Street, and who inhabited, as well, a district between Brady Street and the Milwaukee River and a fishing community on Jones Island. The old Second Ward was the dwelling place of Czechs and Slovaks; in the Second and Sixth were Russian Jews; and with the scattering of the Irish who formerly occupied the Third Ward the Italians had developed a compact community south of Michigan Street and east of Broadway.[27] The maturing city had seen the dispersion and intermingling of the immigrants of the North European wave; the coordinate communities which now on a much smaller scale replaced the self-contained *Deutsch-Athen* of an earlier day were the colonies of South-European and Slavic newcomers propelled by the "new immigration." Here the church, the native-language press, and the fraternal societies guarded the identity of the nationality group and channeled its influence in the municipal life.

The Polish community could be easily recognized by 1890. When Charles King visited Milwaukee in that year he found that in the southwestern section of the city the "frontiers" of Prussian Pomerania merged into those of Poland. "Fritz" gave place to "Ignatz" in a section where the traveler read "no names but those that end with a sneeze." By 1910 more than 70,000 Poles had joined the some thirty families of the late sixties; seven of the twenty-nine Roman Catholic churches were Polish in their constituency; and the Polish population boasted three free libraries, a hundred Polish societies and organizations, and five Polish newspapers. So prominent had the Polish element become, "during the last two or three decades," that Jerome A. Watrous, writing a history of Milwaukee in 1909, included a special chapter on their growth in the community.[28] Several factors explain the influential position of the Poles by this date. One was their almost universal allegiance to the Catholic

---

[27] Bureau of Labor and Industrial Statistics, State of Wisconsin, *Twelfth Biennial Report*, 1905-6, pp. 315-16.

[28] King, "The Cream City," *Cosmopolitan*, 10:554-56 (March 1891); Gregory, *History*, 2:632; Boleslaus E. Goral, "The Poles in Milwaukee," in Watrous, 1:612-33; W. Kruszka, *Historya Polska w Ameryce*, 7:126.

church, a situation which prompted that institution to promote their social development and political power. Another was the aggressive behavior of the Polish national organizations, whose activities had a wide appeal for a people as yet with few interests outside their nationality group. The Polish press was a natural champion of the advancement of its people, although on occasion it challenged the influence of the church over them; and of no small importance was that quality of personality inherent in most Poles, and fostered by both church and press, which made them tenacious of their nationality and ambitious for political and social recognition of it.[29]

The story of early Polish settlement is largely a chronicle of the expansion of their Catholic parishes.[30] The flow of Polish migrants to America was stimulated in part by the failure of the movement for an independent Poland after the Franco-Prussian War. Many of them settled in the growing cities of the Great Lakes area and Milwaukee was no exception.[31] As has already been related, at first these Polish Catholic newcomers worshiped in German and Czech parishes; but in 1863, with the help of Father Bonaventura Buczynski, St. Stanislaus, an exclusively Polish parish, was formed; and a small church was purchased from a congregation of German Lutherans. In 1872, the parishioners of St. Stanislaus began the construction of an $80,000 church which was finished in 1873; and by 1876 the

[29] Stanislaus Osada, *Prasa i Publicystyka Polska w Ameryce* (Pittsburgh, 1930), 5, asserts that the clergy, the organizations, and the press were the three major forces influencing the general progress of the Polish immigrants in America.

[30] This is well told in Wacław Kruszka's comprehensive history of the Poles in America. W. Kruszka, *Historya Polska w Ameryce*, vols. 7 and 8. See also, discussion of history of Polish parishes by the Rev. Albin C. Waligorski, the Rev. Joseph Swierczynski, the Rev. S. J. Studer, the Rev. Max Adamski, the Rev. John Brzonkała, and the Rev. Arthur Krawczyk in Borun, *We, the Milwaukee Poles*, 3-28.

[31] In 1870 there were 50,000 Poles and ten Polish parishes in the United States. Wisconsin had the most Polish settlements, but Chicago had the largest Polish population. Edmund G. Olszyk, The Polish Press in America, p. 4, MS, M.A. thesis, dated 1939, Marquette University. This work will hereafter be cited as Olszyk, Polish Press. Milwaukee's first permanent Polish inhabitant is said to have been Anthony Kochanek who came from Posen in 1848. August Rudzinski, the tailor, arrived in 1859, and by the middle sixties there were some thirty Polish families in the city. Kapmarski, "*Dzieje Polaków w Milwaukee,*" *Kuryer Polski* (Milwaukee), June 23, 1938; Michael Kruszka, "Forty Thousand Polanders," Milwaukee *Sentinel*, Oct. 16, 1895.

first Polish parochial school, founded in 1867, was serving 450 to 500 pupils. Meanwhile, St. Hedwig's Church, built in 1871, became the center of Polish settlement on the East side. For a time the Poles of this so-called *Kepa* area (or campsite) had attended the St. Stanislaus Church; but because of the difficulties of travel, some forty families, under the guidance of August Rudzinski, undertook to build their own church. As a result of the rush of Polish immigration in the early eighties, the communicants of St. Stanislaus became so numerous that in 1883 those living west of Sixth Avenue formed St. Hyacinth's Church, a development in which Father Gulski played a leading role. The multiplication of Polish parishes and schools solidified the Polish element in the urban culture. To them the congregation was the primary organization of their countrymen, "the Polish church and . . . parochial school the pillar of their language, customs, and . . . nationality."[32]

The reproductive division of St. Stanislaus parish was one manifestation of the increasingly conspicuous position of the Polish population in the city by the middle eighties. Another symbol was the construction at that time of Kosciuszko Hall, center of the activities of the Kosciuszko Guard which August Rudzinski and others had organized in 1874. Pointing up this new prominence was the work of the Polish press. When the first issue of *Krytyka* (The Critic) appeared on November 7, 1885, its publisher Michael Kruszka apostrophized America for the opportunities it gave the Poles to "speak Polish, . . . study it, . . . dress in Polish, . . . wear Polish costumes, . . . express our thoughts freely and boldly, . . . organize Polish civil and military societies, . . . have Polish priests, . . . pray in Polish." The Polish press constituted itself a guardian of these privileges, "our national traditions" and "our faith as well, . . . which no Pole . . . should ever forget" or fail to defend. After an abortive attempt of the editors of *Krytyka* to launch in 1887 the *Dziennik Polski* (Polish Daily), Kruszka started publication

[32] Archbishop Henni opened this church and designated Peter Kończ as pastor. One attraction to Polish migration was the lithographs of St. Stanislaus Church which August Rudzinski had sent to friends and acquaintances in the old country. Gregory, *History*, 2:902; W. Kruszka, *Historya Polska w Ameryce*, 7:131-32, 135, 141-42; M. Kruszka, "Forty Thousand Polanders," *Milwaukee Sentinel*, Oct. 16, 1895.

of the *Kuryer Polski* on June 23, 1888. Down to $125 in resources and knowing that he would have to serve as editor, publisher, reporter, and compositor, Kruszka nevertheless was determined to provide a daily newspaper which would give editorial leadership and expression to the more than 30,000 Poles then in the city. He guaranteed to avoid the controversial issues that had caused the cessation of *Krytyka* and promised that the columns of the *Kuryer* would be given over to "news especially about Poles and Polish matters." "Although at times we may have to engage in controversies," he wrote, "we will strive to express ourselves as politely as possible. In politics and other matters the *Kuryer* will strive to be independent and will take sides only in matters which involve Poles and our national interest."[33]

The *Kuryer* and its vigorous editor played an important part in making this politically ambitious nationality group more effective in a political sense in Milwaukee than in any other American city. From the middle eighties forward, Milwaukee Polish-Americans were always to be found on the roster of State legislators, supervisors, or aldermen. As might have been expected, August Rudzinski was the first among their number to hold public office. In 1878 he was chosen supervisor from the Twelfth Ward. His son Theodore was elected alderman in 1882. Francis Borchardt, captain of the Kosciuszko Guard, was selected for the State assembly in the same year, and in 1893 Michael Kruszka was sent to the State senate. By the nineties the Poles presented such a solid front in the Democratic Party as to hold the balance of power and to cause the Republican press to bemoan the party's inability to bring about a "partition of Poland" in Milwaukee politics. The Polish churches proved to be centers at which Democratic support could be mobilized, and by favors to such organizations clever politicians took advantage of this religious allegiance to gain votes. By 1890 no party dared so to disregard the political strength of the Poles as to fail to place a Polish-American candidate on its ticket, and it became the

[33] W. Kruszka, *Historya Polska w Ameryce*, 7:135; M. Kruszka, "Forty Thousand Polanders," Milwaukee *Sentinel*, Oct. 16, 1895; Goral, "The Poles in Milwaukee," in Watrous, 1:618; Gregory, *History*, 2:828; *Krytyka* (Milwaukee), Nov. 7, 1855; Olszyk, *Polish Press*, 88; *Kuryer Polski*, June 23, 1888.

accepted practice of mayors to appoint a Polish as well as a German secretary to their administrative staffs. The political solidarity of the Polish element was promoted by the fact that most of them had come from the same part of Poland where, in the face of Prussian persecution, they had formed a Polish political party, thereby learning the value of unity and submission to leadership. Thus the political discipline they had learned in the Old World brought advantage to their nationality in the New. In 1890, Michael Kruszka proposed the teaching of the Polish language in the public grade schools, the purchase of Polish books for the libraries, the provision of a Polish translator for the court rooms, and the publication of official notices in Polish. The latter aims were soon gained, but not until 1896 did the school board sanction the introduction of Polish, and even then the advocates of the parochial schools fought the *Kuryer Polski* and the patriotic organizations on the issue.[34]

These national Polish organizations, which had sprung up in the United States in the late nineteenth century, were an additional force lending solidarity to the Polish group. Among them were the Polish Roman Catholic Union, organized in 1873, the Polish National Alliance, organized in 1880, the Polish Women's Alliance of America, organized in 1898, and many another Polish fraternal group, most of them containing an insurance feature. Of the fifty-five societies in 1895, six belonged to the National Alliance and ten to the Catholic Union. Parish units of these organizations served to keep the Polish newcomers in contact with one another. Even the friction among them, as in the case of the conflict between the Union and the Alliance, only heightened a concern for the interests of the nationality group. A controversy between the church and the National Alliance led to the establishment of the *Nowiny Polskie* (Polish News) to counteract the developing anticlericalism of the *Kuryer*.[35]

[34] John W. Tomkiewicz, "Polanders in Wisconsin," *Wisconsin Historical Society, Proceedings,* 1901, p. 152; Stefan Barszczewski, *Polacy w Ameryce* (Warsaw, 1902), 31; W. Kruszka, *Historya Polska w Ameryce,* 7:137; *Kuryer Polski,* June 23, 1938; Goral, "The Poles in Milwaukee," in Watrous, 1:626; Bruce, *Born in America,* 325; M. Kruszka, "Forty Thousand Polanders," Milwaukee *Sentinel,* Oct. 16, 1895.

[35] Olszyk, Polish Press, 11-12; M. Kruszka, "Forty Thousand Polanders," Milwaukee *Sentinel,* Oct. 16, 1895.

The generation from 1870 to 1910 saw many social changes in Milwaukee's Polish population. William George Bruce recalled the travel-stained arrivals of the early seventies nestled near the old Reed Street station "among the boxes, bundles, and bedding of an old-world household." Finding employment in the humbler pursuits, as tailors, saloonkeepers, plasterers, painters, and industrial laborers, they lived a simple life, sending some of their earnings to the Old World and applying most of the remainder to buying lots and building the small one or two-story frame houses which by 1906 dotted the Polish section of the city. The participation of a group of Polish laborers in the strikes of May 1886 brought criticism upon the nationality as a group which the *Sentinel* hastened to soften by pointing out that they were a people easily misled by demagogues and "excitable beyond most other peoples, as witness their violent church troubles here and at Detroit." Shortly after the strike, the Polish element boycotted the members of the Kosciuszko Guard who had attempted to preserve order. So long as the church maintained its hold on the first and second generation Poles, it was the center of the social activities of what was in a sense a Polish village within the city. Singing societies like the *Kalina,* the *Goplana,* and the Harmonia Male Choir reflected the Polanders' love of music and song. Gradually, social differentiation took place. By 1895 there were nineteen Polish building contractors, two lawyers, two physicians, and numerous others engaged in middle-class pursuits. Sixty members of the Polish community were said to be worth from $20,000 to $100,000, among them the successful merchant Ignatz Cerwinski. May 1908 saw the establishment of the *Teatr Polski* (Polish Theater). By 1909, Poles were to be found in almost every kind of business, and in that year the Polish Merchants' and Business Men's Association was organized.[36]

It was not until 1870 that the census credited Bohemia with sending immigrants to the cities of the New World, but

---

[36] Bruce, *Born in America,* 321-22; Bur. of Labor and Ind. Statistics, Wisconsin, *Twelfth Biennial Rept.,* 1905-6, p. 315; Barszczewski, *Polacy w Ameryce,* 26-27; Milwaukee *Sentinel,* May 13, 15, 1886; Goral, "The Poles in Milwaukee," in Watrous, 1:619-21, 630; M. Kruszka, "Forty Thousand Polanders," Milwaukee *Sentinel,* Oct. 16, 1895.

actually, as has already been pointed out, a number of Czechs resided in Milwaukee in the forties. Among these were Nathan Pereles; Isaac Neustadtl; the musician, Hans Balatka; and Vojta Naprstek, book-seller and editor of the *Flugblätter*. The publicity given Wisconsin by Jan Herman, on a visit to his old European home, stimulated migration in the fifties; and many of the newcomers settled in the Second Ward. Czech arrivals of the Middle Period were mainly political refugees; by 1880 economic betterment was the major propellant to migration. As was earlier related, the customary desire of the first generation migrant for church services in his own tongue led to the organization in 1863 of a society to subsidize the annual visit of a Czech priest from the East who would hear confession in the Czech language. By 1865 a Czech Catholic parish had been founded, and shortly thereafter a church was purchased, with a parochial school near by. In the seventies a popular mistrust of the priests combined with the intense individualism of the Czechs to prompt a decline in the support of this church. The Czechs on the South side built a church in 1883. As in the case of the Poles, a Czech press and Czech national lodges supplemented the church in giving vitality to the Czech society within the larger city. The *Turnverein Sokol*, organized in 1868, was one example of the latter, as was the Milwaukee branch of the *Cesky Spolek Podporujici Spolky* (Czech Fraternal Association), organized in 1878. These groups multiplied in the eighties. In 1895, the *Turnverein* Union of *Sokols* and the C. S. P. S. built the Bohemian-American Hall on Twelfth Street which was to become the cultural center of Milwaukee's Czechs and Slovaks. *Lipa,* the first Czech singing and dramatic club, was founded in 1861. A Czech publication *Hospodar* was begun in 1877 under the editorship of Thomas Jiranka; in 1881 its name was changed to *Domacnost* (Hearth). A Czechoslovak benevolent society was formed in 1862, a Czech building and loan group in 1885, and a Czechoslovak fire insurance company in 1898.[37]

---

[37] See *Zlaté Jubileum České Katolické Osady Sv. Jana Nep.* (Golden Jubilee pamphlet of St. John de Nepomuc Church, 1863-1913); Novak, *"Ze Zašlých dob"* (From Times Past); J. J. Vlach, "Our Bohemian Population," Wisconsin Historical Society, *Proceedings,* 1901, pp. 159-62.

Kin to the Czechs, but frequently unwilling to cooperate with them, the Slovaks began to arrive in the city in 1880. Their migration was propelled by their oppression at the hands of the Magyars, their objections to compulsory military training, the lack of fertile land, and Czech reports of the blessings of America. Although they were by experience an agricultural people, their lack of money with which to buy farm lands forced them to settle in the city. Many came without their families, attracted by the demand for labor in the American market, and returned to their native land when what they considered fortunes had been made. Leading families among the Slovak settlers were those of Imrich Kusik, Michael Guzo, and Andrew Firer.[38] Settling close to the Czechs in the old Second Ward, they found employment in the tanneries, foundries, and breweries; some opened saloons and others acted as steamship and travel agents for their migrating fellow-countrymen.[39] Much more predominantly Catholic than the Czechs, the Slovaks early attached themselves to the Czech Catholic Church. As early as 1905, however, the Slovak men of the Knights of St. Mary Lodge established a fund to bring to St. John's, the Czech Church, a priest who could speak Slovak. St. Stephen's parish, which was organized in 1907, was soon reputed to be the largest Slovak congregation in the United States. Such lodges as the Knights of St. Mary, founded in 1890 as a branch of a national Slovakian fraternal organization, served to perpetuate unity among Milwaukee Slovaks. A branch of "Our Lady of Lourdes," the first Catholic Slovak Ladies' Union of America, was formed five years later.[40] Many clashes took place between the Czechs and Slovaks. The tradition of free thought among the Czechs ran counter to the intense Catholicity of the Slovaks; the latter experienced feelings of inferiority beside their western neighbors

[38] Joseph S. Roucek, "The Passing of American Czechoslovaks," *American Journal of Sociology*, 39:612-13 (March 1934); Henry Kusik, Jr., *The Early Slovak Settlers of Milwaukee*, pamphlet of the Ninth Annual Convention of Catholic Slovak Students' Fraternity of America (Milwaukee, August 1930), unpaged.

[39] Memorandum from Helen P. Dressel to author, based on *Milwaukee Slovenský Sborník, 1881-1937*, a collection of facts about Milwaukee Slovaks compiled by Henry Kusik, Jr., and financed by the Slovak Students' League of America (Milwaukee, 1937), and on *Pamätník Strieborného Jubileuma Osady Sv. Štefana, I. Muc.*, 1907-32 (Souvenir Silver Jubilee St. Stephen's Church, Milwaukee, 1932).

[40] Gregory, *History*, 2:635; Kusik, *Early Slovak Settlers of Milwaukee*.

who claimed a closer contact with European civilization. These attitudes explain the tendency of the Czechs and Slovaks to form separate clubs, societies, associations, and churches within the urban community.

The nineties saw the arrival of a considerable number of Hungarians, who, migrating for economic reasons, settled on the lower East side. By 1910, more than 5,000 natives of Hungary were living in Milwaukee. Transplanted into a factory economy from village life, the Hungarian migrants found in the church a substitute for the intimacy they had known in the European village. The nuclei of the Austrian and Hungarian communities were usually boarding houses run by persons of their own nationality. Here the migrants lived under crowded and squalid conditions, awaiting the accumulation of sufficient money to make possible their return to the Old World. Colonies of Greeks, predominantly male, resided in similarly congested conditions in various parts of the city. Most of this group were employed in factory work, while the young men and boys monopolized the boot-blacking trade.[41]

Milwaukee's Italian colony, which numbered 4,685 by 1910, took form in about 1895. Its nucleus was a group of Sicilians who came by way of the Chicago colony and settled among the Irish in the Third Ward. Natives of Palermo, Messina, and Trapani predominated, but, because of the Italian practice of migrating from specific towns rather than general regions, there were settlers from certain localities in south, central, and northern Italy as well. Unable to practice their trades, because of ignorance of the language, and unacquainted with American machinery, the Italian newcomers entered the ranks of common labor, finding employment in the foundries, coal yards, and docks, and as workers on the streets and railroad tracks. Some, with a background as tradesmen, serviced the community as grocers and saloonkeepers; while a few entered the commercial life of the city as wholesale fruit commission merchants. Drawn to America for economic reasons rather than the search for poli-

[41] Mrs. A. L. Banyai and Frank Beleznay, *The Hungarians of the City of Milwaukee, Wisconsin* (Milwaukee, 1929), 2, 9-10; Bur. of Labor and Ind. Statistics, Wisconsin, *Twelfth Biennial Rept.*, 1905-6, p. 317-18.

tical freedom, they, like so many other newcomers of the "new" migration, returned to their native land once they had accumulated money. According to the Italian consul, more than 1,200 Italians left the city after the panic of 1907, and only 50 arrived in the year following it. The Catholic church and numerous lay societies, which provided sickness and death benefits and were recruited from settlers from a given town or province, afforded a social outlet and preserved the integrity of the Italian group. Among such societies were the *Liberta Siciliana, Vespri Siciliani, Cristoforo Colombo, Vittorio Emanuele III, Santa Croce,* and *Tripoli Italiana,* to mention only a few.[42]

The "new" migration added Russian and Hungarian Jews to the Bohemian Hebrew migrants of the pre-Civil War period. German-Jewish families had begun to arrive in the forties, and by 1852 there were at least 50 in the city. This group of newcomers, which included Isaac Neustadtl, Emanuel Shoyer, David Adler, Bernard S. Weil, and Nathan Pereles, contributed to the commercial development of the community, establishing businesses near the city market and living near by. A second wave of Jewish migrants resulted from the anti-Jewish pogroms in Poland and Russia during the early eighties. The first refugees to arrive under the auspices of European committees reached the city on October 13, 1881. When the London Aid Committee sent word in June 1882 that 350 Russian refugees were on their way, the Wisconsin Russian Aid Society called a mass meeting, a Citizens' Aid Committee was formed, and the migrants were received at a reception at which Mayor Stowell spoke. A third migration of Jews began in the early nineties, attracted in part by the prosperity of the immigrants who had preceded them. Milwaukee's Jewish population increased from about 2,500 in 1895 to about 7,000 in 1900. Most of the latecomers settled in the area bounded by Walnut, Chestnut, Third, and Eighth Streets. Content to live in crowded conditions, the newer Jewish arrivals engaged in much humbler pur-

---

[42] G. La Piana, *The Italians in Milwaukee, Wisconsin* (Milwaukee, 1915), 5-8, 10, 64-65; Giovanni E. Schiavo, *The Italians in Chicago* (Chicago, 1928), 21-22; Milwaukee *Journal,* July 22, 1908; Bur. of Labor and Ind. Statistics, Wisconsin, *Twelfth Biennial Rept.,* 1905-6, p. 316.

suits than their fellow Hebrews of the earlier migration.[43]

Generally speaking, at the close of the generation ending in 1910, the colonies of new migrants, unlike the German-American ingredient of the population, remained suspended elements in the urban culture, not yet integrated in it, in many instances transient, predominantly male, and exclusive by preference. Especially was this true of the southern and eastern Europeans who had come to America more for the accumulation of funds than, as in the case of the Poles and Hebrews, to escape political persecution. Conscious of the differences between themselves and the older and already established members of the community, they found satisfaction in church services, lodge meetings, and the security of building and loan organizations recruited from and serving their own people. Of all the newcomers, the Poles made the speediest and most successful bid for recognition and influence in the urban scene. However, the group as a whole was not without effect on the developing metropolis. Forced to accommodate themselves to an urban environment, they supplied workers for heavy industry. Their predominant allegiance to the Catholic church bolstered the influence of that institution in the life of the city; while the very existence of their many undissolved colonies gave a cosmopolitan tone to the urban society which, as the Germans and Irish amalgamated in the social mixture, would otherwise have been lacking. Potential tools of the political machines, living frequently in conditions of overcrowded squalor, they presented some of the new problems with which the evolving metropolis was faced. And the very existence of Czerwinskis, Spicuzzas, Kusiks, Grosses, and Novaks suggested that the nationality pattern of twentieth century Milwaukee was to be even more variegated and complex than that of the combined *Deutsch-Athen* and Yankee town of the nineteenth.

[43] "Jews in Milwaukee" and "Russian Jews," Milwaukee *Sentinel*, Oct. 16, 1895. See also *ibid.*, Dec. 12, 1926, and articles on the Jews of Milwaukee by Julius H. Meyer, *Jewish Encyclopedia* (New York, 1904) and by Joseph L. Baron, *Universal Jewish Encyclopedia*.

CHAPTER 12

The Play of Politics

HARRISON LUDINGTON, almost the last of Milwaukee's "pioneer" mayors, was the city's chief executive during the early seventies. It might have startled "bluff old Hal," as the wealthy lumberman was called, to know that in less than forty years the mayoralty would pass to a soft-voiced wood carver of German ancestry whose inaugural remarks were to praise the workers of the city as "its most valuable asset."[1] Yet in a sense the personalities of these two men symbolize the change that took place in Milwaukee politics between 1870 and 1910. The four decades that intervened between the mayoralties of Ludington and Emil Seidel were to see the working-class of the city become politically articulate and the Milwaukee electorate respond through political action to the problems presented by the pressures of metropolitan life. As early as 1888 the old-line parties were forced to combine in order to prevent the election of a Union Labor candidate who even then would have been chosen but for a split in labor's ranks; and by 1910 the Social Democrats had mobilized sufficient strength from workers and progressives to win the mayoralty, dominate the common council, and make Milwaukee the first large American city to be controlled by Socialism. The concentration of population and the development of large public service corporations raised major political issues; and both realists and reformers, acting through the Municipal League, the Voters' League, and the political parties, attempted by proposals of civil service reform and municipal ownership to overcome the evils of graft, corruption, and profiteering to which the big city gave rise. And to these factors affecting the play of politics must be added the ambitions and

[1] Milwaukee *Sentinel,* April 20, 1910.

animosities of the various nationality elements in the urban electorate — especially German and Polish—and the adaptation of socialist ideology by Victor Berger and others to the immediate and practical problems of the metropolitan scene.

No one political party dominated city politics in the forty years between 1870 and 1910. The predominant Democracy of the Middle Period was a thing of the past, and organizations of Democrats and Republicans, though not always using those names, vied more or less equally for popular support. The Democratic Party, or parties drawing their following from that group, won eleven mayoral campaigns; while the Republicans, mobilized on occasion as the Citizens' Ticket, won an equal number. Candidates of the workingmen triumphed in 1882 and 1910. Generally speaking, the Democrats drew their support from Catholic, Irish, and Polish voters. The Republicans, on the other hand, appealed to the "solid businessman" and the increasingly acclimated and hence increasingly conservative German-American element in the voting population. In federal politics, Milwaukee County remained predominantly Democratic through the presidential contests of the late sixties and seventies, during which time the rest of the State lent the majority of its support to Republican candidates. However, from the election of Garfield in 1880 through the choice of Taft in 1908, Milwaukee County provided Republican majorities, save in 1892 when Cleveland drew five more votes than Harrison. In these years the urban vote more or less paralleled that of the rest of the State. A marked deviation began to appear with the bid of Eugene Debs and the Social Democratic Party for presidential recognition. In 1900, Debs drew more than 7 percent of the vote of Milwaukee County; whereas in the State outside that unit he won little more than half of 1 percent. Four years later Debs's vote was 26 percent of the total in Milwaukee County to less than 3 percent in the rest of the State. This dissimilarity was approximately the same in 1908 and in 1912 when Debs ran second to Woodrow Wilson in the urban county, carrying 30 percent of the vote there to 4 in the remainder of the State of Wisconsin.[2]

[2] See appendix for a comparison of the presidential vote in Milwaukee County with that of the remainder of Wisconsin, 1848 to 1940.

The avoidance of the national party labels in the seventies did not obscure the fact that the Citizens' Ticket drew its support from the businessmen now attached increasingly to the Republican ranks and that the People's Reform Party was the Democracy thinly veiled. Ludington's personal popularity accounted in part for the success of the Citizens' Ticket in electing him mayor in 1871, 1873, 1874, and 1875; but its ascendancy was also the result of the increased national prestige of the Republican Party in the seventies.[3] The identification of this party with the outcome of the Civil War had reduced Democratic majorities; the development of the Milwaukee *Herold* under the management of W. W. Coleman and Bernhard Domschcke had won German support for the Republicans; Henry C. Payne's Young Men's Republican Club, organized in 1872, was exerting an invigorating influence; and the malfeasance of county Democratic officials, coupled with the growing threat of Greenbackism, drew many adherents to the party. Property owners trusted Ludington, himself a "large property-holder," to "exert his executive influence to prevent extravagant expenditure and to lessen the rate of taxation." Indeed, in his first inaugural, the wealthy lumberman had proposed a municipal policy that would "insure . . . reasonable comforts and improvements and encourage at the same time an infusion of that business energy for which all American cities are noted."[4] The withdrawal of Ludington in 1872 gave the Democrats a chance to elect David G. Hooker; and in 1874 they came within 800 votes of returning to office their old stand-by, Edward O'Neill, under the label of the People's Reform Party. The Irish rallied to the support of the latter; while Ludington's victory was attributed in part to the backing of the German element. The Democrats triumphed with small majorities in the next two elections. Ammi R. R. Butler, lawyer, first candidate to be chosen for the two-year term, gained a margin of 343 votes over Caspar Sanger in 1876; and two years later the Democrats found a majority

---

[3] Ludington, born in New York in 1812, had come to Milwaukee in 1838, where he made a fortune in lumber. He resigned during his last term as mayor to become governor of Wisconsin. He died in 1891.

[4] William W. Wight, *Henry Clay Payne: a Life* (Milwaukee, 1907), 24-25, 35, 40-44; Milwaukee *Sentinel*, April 19, 1871; April 1, 1873.

of about 300 from what the *Sentinel* called the "propertyless bummers" of the city for John Black, wholesale liquor dealer and banker.[5]

The opening of the eighties saw the political pendulum swinging sharply in a Republican direction. With the party's opposition to "soft money" to win it support, especially among the German-American element, Milwaukeeans gave majorities to Republican candidates for presidential, congressional, gubernatorial, and county offices. This tide brought to the mayor's office Thomas H. Brown, carriage maker, first native Milwaukeean to hold the office, and resulted in the almost exclusive choice of Republican aldermen, as a consequence of which the council totaled twenty-eight Republican to ten Democratic members. It was a short-lived ascendancy, however; for labor came to the rescue of the Democracy in 1882 when the trades assemblies put forward Democrats John M. Stowell, P. J. Somers, and Henry Smith for mayor, city attorney, and comptroller; and the Democratic Party endorsed their choice. As a result, Stowell defeated Ludington, the Republican candidate, by a vote of 9,635 to 7,321, despite the alleged existence of a fund of $4,000 made up by "prominent manufacturing firms . . . and presented . . . to the Republican executive committee to 'put it where it would do the most good in defeating the Trades Assembly ticket.' " A timely plank in the trades assembly platform was the promise that the police department would be taken out of politics, a proposal then being advanced by the local nonpartisan Civil Service Reform Association which included such civic leaders as G. W. Peckham, Emory McClintock, B. Goldsmith, Henry Mendel, Michael Bodden, and Charles L. Mann.[6]

The Republicans appropriated this proposal in staging a comeback in the ensuing election and in addition chose a

[5] The Democrats had elected O'Neill mayor in 1863, 1867, 1868, and 1869. *Ibid.*, April 9, 1874; April 23, 1878. It should be noted that for the election returns in mayoral contests to 1900, it has been necessary to rely on newspaper reports, inasmuch as no official record appears to be available, save for the elections of 1873 and 1874, for which the vote is stated in the council proceedings. For the contests between 1900 and 1910, the figures were taken from the manuals of the common council for those years.

[6] *Ibid.*, April 7, 1880; April 4, 5, 1882; April 10, 1884; April 4, 1886.

candidate with a strong appeal for the German-American voters. In their city convention of March 1884, they passed resolutions advocating that the terms of office of policemen, firemen, school officials, and teachers should not "depend on the results of each succeeding election but rather upon faithfulness and efficiency in the discharge of their duties."[7] Citing eastern precedents, as had the members of the reform association, they claimed thus to be offering Milwaukeeans what Brooklyn had achieved and what New York was struggling for.[8] Their candidate was German-born Emil Wallber, who had migrated to America as a boy, studied law with Governor Edward Salomon, and served with distinction as city attorney. Wallber's Germanism and his endorsement of civil service reform helped him to win with a sizable majority over Democrat Sam M. Dixon, in spite of the fact that the latter's party had gained the solid support of the Polish element by making them believe that the German candidate, if elected, "would take the crosses off their churches and make turner halls of them all."[9]

In reelecting Wallber two years later on a platform endorsing such progressive measures as civil service reform, public baths and parks, and temperance enforcement, which was as far as the party could go in view of its German constituency, the Republicans claimed to have saved the city from the excesses of "ring rule." All the parties were accused of "bossism" in the elections of this period, and certainly the activities of

[7] Wight, *Henry Clay Payne*, 46.
[8] Milwaukee *Sentinel*, March 31, 1884. The editor of the *Sentinel* wrote: "Everybody recognizes that it is more important to have a reform of this character locally than at Washington, but commonly the hopelessness of getting a party to commit itself to such a reform locally has paralyzed effort. Now that one party has committed itself, taking a position which must win for Milwaukee a widespread respect, it remains for the people to clear the way for the inauguration of the reform." *Ibid.*, March 30, 1884. For years the Republican Party continued to make political capital of their accomplishment in this phase of civil service reform. With each succeeding municipal election the credit due the party was made to loom larger. An editorial in the Milwaukee *Sentinel*, Nov. 9, 1931, read: "Milwaukee's splendid record for law and order is attributable directly to a non-political police force and non-political courts. Milwaukee had these long before the socialist party was anything more than an occasional puff of windy oratory."
[9] Conard, 1:427-28; Milwaukee *Sentinel*, April 2, 1884.

Democrat John A. Hinsey suggest the "boss rule" that plagued city politics in this day. Hinsey exerted a powerful influence over the activities of the Democratic Party and was strongly opposed to civil service reform. When the Democrats and Republicans fused in 1888 to stave off victory for a labor candidate and elected Thomas H. Brown, Republican, as mayor, and George W. Porth, Democrat, as comptroller, Hinsey became the president of a council that included fourteen Republicans, twelve Democrats, and ten laborites.[10]

The narrow margin by which the fusion ticket won the election of 1888 was one of the consequences of the growing strength of labor in local politics during the eighties. Although Democratic votes had helped to secure the mayoralty for the candidate of the trades assemblies in 1882, the outcome of the election nevertheless prompted the editor of the *Freie Presse* to discern the appearance of a new force in local politics: the independent political action of the labor element. In the election of 1884, the force of labor waned; but two years later, in the wake of violent labor disturbance, a real working-class movement swept labor candidates into all the county offices and elected Henry Smith to Congress with sizable pluralities over ex-mayors Thomas H. Brown, Republican, and John Black, Democrat. In the spring of 1887, labor candidates for the judiciary ran 1,500 votes ahead of their fusion opponents in the city, only to be defeated by the township vote; and in the mayoral contest of 1888, the labor candidate would have won in spite of the fusion of the older parties but for the dissension within the ranks of labor itself.[11]

Most of the prominent labor leaders of the city were present at the convention, held on March 20, 1888, which chose Herman Kroeger as the candidate of the Union Labor Party for mayor. There were Robert Schilling, editor of the *Reformer,* Theodore Rudzinski, John Jacques, leader of the cigar makers, Alvord Curtis, Mrs. D. Severance, woman suffragist, Val Blatz, Colin

---

[10] As the editor of the *Sentinel* wrote in 1884: "When [Mayor Wallber] recommends a material increase of the [liquor] license, strict political surveillance of saloons, and a limitation on their number, he takes as advanced ground as a mayor of Milwaukee can reasonably be expected to occupy." *Ibid.,* April 16, 1884; April 4, 1886; April 16, 18, 1888.

[11] Conard, 1:97-98.

Campbell, and A. Bonzel, master workman of the Polonia Assembly. The laborites proposed to recruit a ticket which would include two Germans, one Irishman, and one American. They endorsed the public ownership and management of municipal improvements, the establishment of public baths, taxation in the interests of the small man, and a provision that municipal officers be subject to recall. The success of the old-line parties, they predicted, would "cause an increase in tax-dodging, class legislation, rings, trusts, and other monopolies." In the opinion of a more demanding element among the workers, these proposals did not go sufficiently far. This wing of the laboring group was led by Paul Grottkau, a Chicago Socialist who had moved to Milwaukee to edit the *Arbeiter Zeitung,* successor to the Socialist weekly *Arminia,* and who had exerted a vigorous influence among the foreign-born workers since 1886. Calling themselves the Socialistic Labor Party, the followers of Grottkau advocated a forward-looking twelve-point program which included many of the municipal reforms which the next half century was to see achieved. They recommended paying salaries to aldermen so that men of small means could hold the office and spoils thus be avoided; the abolition of child labor; equal and uniform taxation and municipal confiscation of property falsely assessed; uniform lighting and street cleaning at public expense, in the poor sections as well as the rich; strict factory inspection and safeguards for workers' health; the eight-hour day on public works; the promotion of educational advantages; safeguards to personal liberty and "Sunday freedom"; disposal of industrial waste without injury to the public health; the erection of city meeting halls; the sale of wood and coal to citizens at cost; and the recall of municipal officials. They nominated Colin Campbell for mayor.[12]

This cleavage in the ranks of labor played directly into the hands of the old-line parties whose fusion under the banner of the Citizens' Ticket permitted them to stand "shoulder to shoulder," as the *Sentinel* wrote, "in defense of the sacred rights

[12] Milwaukee *Sentinel,* March 21, 25, 1888. According to the *Sentinel,* the Union Labor Party was "organized in the interests of a class against the rest of the community and is therefore essentially non-American and anti-republican." *Ibid.,* March 23, 1888.

of property, in defense of the homes of thousands of workingmen as well as of capitalists, and against the building up of a class party." Many prominent German-Americans were members of the Citizens' committee, among them F. W. von Cotzhausen, John C. Ludwig, Emil Schandein, Louis Auer, Oscar Altpeter, and Henry J. Baumgaertner. Von Cotzhausen wrote in a call to community action: "If the working class organizes itself as a political party such procedure must have a deadly effect upon the interests of our commonwealth. A popular government is wholly incompatible with class rule, and our citizenry cannot and dare not permit itself to be dictated to or tyrannized over by any element of society—either now or in the future." Similar appeals were made to the Polish population. At a mass meeting held at Kosciuszko Armory on March 26, Max Kucera condemned Socialism as an attempt to destroy in the United States the freedoms the immigrants had come there to seek. Appeals were made to the memories of von Steuben, Pulaski, and Kosciuszko, who were said to have defended principles now at stake. Judge James A. Mallory, chairman of the Citizens' committee, summarized the arguments of the Citizens' Ticket when he said that Kroeger was not fitted for the position; that his election would discredit the city and turn away capital, repeating an argument heard following Stowell's election in 1882; that employment would suffer; and that as a consequence many workers who then owned their homes would stand the chance of losing them. Kroeger's Catholicism won him most of the Catholic vote, but the older, more conservative Poles stood by Brown, the fusion candidate. In the last analysis, it was the split among the laborites themselves that kept the old-line parties in power. The Citizens' candidate received 15,978 votes; Kroeger's 15,033 and the 964 garnered by Campbell and the Socialist group, if combined, would have meant a victory for labor with 19 votes to spare.[13] Thus but for internal friction the labor administration which was not to be realized in Milwaukee until 1910 might have been accomplished a quarter century earlier. To understand the

[13] Hense-Jensen, Schafer tr., chap. 11, p. 13; Milwaukee *Sentinel*, March 27, 29, 31, April 1, 1888. An analysis of the council by party revealed 14 Republicans, 12 Democrats, 10 laborites; by occupation, a variety of pursuits with a

strength which brought labor so close to victory at this point it is necessary to trace the development of the labor movement in the city and examine the background of its effort to exert economic and political control.

Organized labor had asserted itself in Milwaukee as early as 1848 when the journeymen coopers protested against a reduction in pay and the Ship Carpenters' and Caulkers' Association, after a month-long strike, forced the George Barber Shipbuilding Company to reduce the day's work from twelve to ten hours, grant wage increases to skilled workers, and curtail the number of unskilled laborers employed. The late forties and early fifties saw the organization of the cabinetmakers and joiners, the tailors, the cigar makers, and the typesetters, whose typographical union, started in 1854, was the first Milwaukee union to have national affiliation. It was, however, the expanding economic conditions of the Civil War period that prompted the first general adoption of trade unionism in Milwaukee as a means of achieving the ambitions of the working-class. Short-lived and generally successful strikes became a common phenomenon as the workers in various industries formed protective associations between 1863 and 1865 and one or two groups, organized before the war, adopted more vigorous tactics than they had hitherto employed. The resistance of certain skilled mechanics to machine competition was reflected in 1867 when the shoemakers founded the Order of the Knights of St. Crispin on March 7 of that year. A Labor Reform Association, organized in September 1865, gave impetus to the movement for an eight-hour day, and in the municipal election of April 1866 the Eight Hour League nominated candidates for the council in six of the nine wards of the city. The city's first trades assembly, the Milwaukee Labor Reform Assembly, was organized by a number of interested trade unions on October 8, 1869, and it appointed committees to recruit Labor Reform leagues in the various wards. In 1872, labor conditions resulted in strikes in the Wisconsin city on the part of tailors, coopers, cigar makers, printers, trunk makers, pipelayers, coal heavers, bell boys at

total of nine (less than usual) saloonkeepers or representatives of the liquor business; and by nationality, 13 Germans, 7 Americans, 5 Irish, 3 Poles, among the more predominant groups. *Ibid.,* April 16, 1888.

the Newhall House, sailors, brewery workers, shoemakers, and ship carpenters. At this point, labor's advance was checked by the panic of 1873, which also quashed the movement for national organization on the part of the trades assemblies, despite conventions held in Cleveland, in 1873, and in Rochester, New York, in 1874, at which Milwaukee's trades assembly was represented. A trades council coordinated the activities of the unions in the later seventies; and a newly organized trades assembly, which originally represented three unions in 1880, had delegates from nineteen by 1883, by which time, as has been pointed out, it had succeeded, with the help of the Democrats, in elevating John M. Stowell to the office of mayor. As early as 1881, delegates from the Milwaukee organization had joined with representatives from the trades assemblies of Chicago, Indianapolis, Boston, Detroit, St. Louis, Buffalo, New York, Cincinnati, and Cleveland to found the Federation of Organized Trades and Labor Unions of the United States and Canada.[14]

In 1882 it was reported that a number of Milwaukee laborers had been affiliated since the late seventies with the Knights of Labor, an order which had existed secretly in the United States since 1869 but which had not come out in the open until 1878. By 1886 the organization had fifty lodges and a membership of at least 16,000 in the city. The program of the Knights of Labor, as publicized in 1882, was in many ways an urban expression of the program the Populists ultimately endorsed. High among the aims of the organization was the desire to secure to toilers a "proper share of the wealth they create" as well as more leisure and social advantages for the working-class. To achieve this end, they proposed the establishment of bureaus of labor statistics and institutions for cooperative production

[14] Merk, *Economic History of Wisconsin during the Civil War*, 163-64, 179, 179n, 185; John B. Andrews, "Nationalisation (1860-1877)," in John R. Commons, ed., *History of Labour in the United States* (original printing, 2 vols., New York, 1918), 2:77, 159, 162. See also Selig Perlman, "Upheaval and Reorganization (Since 1876)," in Commons, *History of Labour* (orig. print.), 2:321; Bur. of Labor Statistics, Wisconsin, *First Biennial Rept.*, 1883-84, p. 122; Theodore Mueller, Milwaukee Workers, pp. 2, 3, 9, typescript, dated 1937-38, in possession of the writer. This will hereafter be cited as Mueller, Milwaukee Workers. The trades assembly disintegrated in the middle eighties.

and distribution; equality of pay regardless of sex; the abolition of the contract system on public works, child labor under fourteen, and convict labor contracts; the eight-hour day; and such correlative demands as the reservation of the public lands for actual settlers and the establishment of a national circulating medium without the intervention of banking corporations.[15]

Meanwhile, socialistic thought, which encouraged action on the part of the working-class as a unit, was gaining favor with a small group of Milwaukee workers, mainly of recent German origin. Two new sources of socialism, both identified with the Socialist movement coursing through Germany, now supplemented the transcendental socialistic idealism of Milwaukee's pre-Civil War migrants.[16] One was the International Workingmen's Association, founded by Karl Marx in London in 1864, which advocated the promotion of the worker's interests through the organization of trade unions and cooperatives and of which a Milwaukee branch existed in the middle seventies. The other was the program of Ferdinand Lassalle, enunciated in Germany in 1863, which saw in political action alone the road to achievement for the working-class. The eclipse of the trade union movement in the wake of the depression of 1873 put the Lassallean approach in a favored light; and labor parties, drawing their support largely from the younger German element in Milwaukee as elsewhere, began to appear. Among these were the Labor Party of Illinois and the Social Democratic Party of North America, which was founded in the East in 1874. The names of those who adhered to the Milwaukee group, which came out in the open during the Hayes-Tilden campaign of 1876—Joseph Brucker, Gustav Lyser, George Schütz, Alexander Herbold, William Raabe, and F. Oscar Lincke, for example—indicate that Milwaukee Socialism of this period was almost exclusively German. The year 1875 saw the publication of *Der Sozialist,* printed in the German language. In April of that year, on the call of the local Socialists, about 500 workingmen and

[15] Raney, *Wisconsin: A Story of Progress,* 374-75; Milwaukee *Sentinel,* April 15, 1882.
[16] According to Hense-Jensen, "Socialistic activities in the modern sense appeared first in Wisconsin in about the middle seventies." Hense-Jensen, Schafer tr., chap. 11, p. 2.

women gathered at the Stadt Theatre to listen to a "fiery blood[ed]" Socialist organizer from New Haven, Connecticut, who dwelt on the wretched condition of the working-classes and asserted that, being seven-tenths of the voters of the United States, they were in a position to "mould the government to their wishes." His speech was followed by one in German and remarks by Lyser and Brucker, editor of *Der Sozialist*. These two German Socialists were among the leaders of a reform movement in 1876 which took the name of the People's Party and aimed to "inform the people of the corrupt practices of the day." Until every workingman "interested himself in public affairs," asserted Lyser, there would be "government to their disadvantage."[17]

In 1876, delegates of the International, the Labor Party of Illinois, the Social Political Workingmen's Society of Cincinnati, and the Social Democratic Party combined to form the Workingmen's Party of the United States;[18] and the Milwaukee sections of this party formed a Social Democratic ticket with the object of taking part in the spring elections of 1877. They succeeded in polling 1,500 votes and electing two aldermen, two supervisors, and two constables. At this time two Milwaukee newspapers, the German *Sozialist* and the English *Emancipator*, espoused the Lassallean view. Spurred by these successes, the advocates of political action set up a political organization under the name of the Socialist Labor Party in Milwaukee, Cincinnati, and Chicago, the last of which was at that time the "undisputed center of the socialist movement" in the United States, and made nominations in the spring elections of 1878. With the return of prosperity in 1879, the Chicago branch of the party split into factions and dwindled in strength; and though the Milwaukee Socialists published a platform in 1880, they too

[17] Marvin Wachman, *History of the Social Democratic Party of Milwaukee, 1897-1910* (University of Illinois, Studies in the Social Sciences, vol. 28, no. 1, Urbana, 1945), 10. This work will hereafter be cited as Wachman, *Social Democratic Party of Milwaukee*. Perlman, "Upheaval," in Commons, *History of Labour* (orig. print.), 2:204, 206; Hense-Jensen, Schafer tr., chap. 11, p. 3; Milwaukee *Sentinel*, April 20, 1876.

[18] This amalgamation did not realize unity on a program of action; for some of the delegates favored "political" socialism and others endorsed "trade union" socialism. Perlman, "Upheaval," in Commons, *History of Labour* (orig. print.), 2:272.

were adversely affected by the improvement in economic conditions. Even the appearance of two representatives of the Socialist Party of Germany, who addressed large meetings in American cities, including Milwaukee, failed to give needed life to the program of political action.[19] For the moment, the trade union approach was again in the ascendant; and with the trades assemblies' successful promotion of Stowell for the mayoralty in 1882, the philosophy of political action suffered a decline.

By 1886, trade union agitation throughout the United States had assumed the proportions of a real class movement, and Milwaukee presented no exception. Indeed, union organization had made rapid strides in the State at large during the early years of the decade. By 1884, the most potent of all the labor organizations in Milwaukee were the two lodges of the Amalgamated Association of Iron and Steel Workers at Bay View. Strong, too, were the iron moulders, being Number 166 of the Machine Moulders of America, and the Stove and Hollow-Ware Moulders, who had gained a 20 percent raise in wages since their organization. The blacksmiths were about 50 percent organized, and there were active unions among the masons and bricklayers, the typographers, the pressmen, the journeymen plumbers, the boilermakers, the carpenters, the tanners and curriers, the trunkmakers, the hod carriers, the seamen, the musicians, the broommakers, and the coopers. In addition to unions, benevolent societies were organized in some trades as, for example, the Barbers' Benevolent Society and the Brewers' Relief Society. The cigar makers had had a strong organization before 1882, when they numbered about 700; but an unsuccessful strike in 1881-82 reduced their membership. On this occasion, the strike had been sanctioned by the national union and partially financed by it; but when the union refused a compromise settlement in which the five leading manufacturers conceded an advance in wages but not union rules, women and children workers were recruited from New York and cigar makers from Europe in sufficient numbers to doom the strikers to defeat. Two major strikes, that of 1,200 iron and steel workers for

[19] *Ibid.*, 2:273-74, 277, 279, 282, 290-91; Faust, *German Element in the United States,* 2:194; Milwaukee *Sentinel,* April 1, 1880.

higher wages and one of some 25 tanners against a reduction, took place in 1885; but the high point of the movement came in the spring of 1886 when at least forty such disputes, in which thousands of workers were involved, gave the city its first real experience with widespread labor strife.[20]

The issue that precipitated the trouble was the question of the eight-hour day. Proposed for city laborers by Alderman Prentiss, as early as 1866, its general adoption had been recommended in October 1884 by the Federation of Trades, to take place on May 1, 1886. By February of that year, the subject was *"the* topic of conversation," a matter of issue not only between employer and employee but between divergent wings of the working-class itself, especially over the question of whether labor should insist upon eight hours' work at ten hours' pay. This difference of opinion within the ranks of labor, which was to have repercussions two years later in the field of municipal politics, as has already been pointed out, centered around the conflicting appeals of the militantly aggressive Central Labor Union, led by Paul Grottkau, editor of the *Arbeiter Zeitung,* and the somewhat more temporizing approach of the Knights of Labor under the leadership of Robert Schilling, editor of the *Volksblatt.*[21]

The events of the first week of May 1886 were only the Milwaukee phase of labor's nationwide struggle for broader rights—a struggle which in Chicago took the form of the more widely publicized Haymarket bombing.[22] Labor conflicts during the month of April—including an unsuccessful attempt to get the E. P. Allis Company to agree to ten hours' pay for eight hours' work—had taken about 7,000 off their jobs; but by the close of May 1, the number of striking workers had swelled to nearly 12,000.[23] Members of the Central Labor Union predomi-

---

[20] Bur. of Labor Statistics, Wisconsin, *First Biennial Rept.,* 1883-84, pp. 119, 123-34, 140-44; see also Bur. of Labor and Ind. Statistics, Wisconsin, *Second Biennial Rept.,* 1885-86.

[21] *Ibid.,* 314-21.

[22] It was reported in New York on April 30, 1886, that "At Baltimore, Milwaukee, Chicago, and Detroit there is promised a very general demand for the 8-hour day, and in the event of its refusal strikes will follow." Milwaukee *Sentinel,* May 1, 1886.

[23] *Ibid.,* May 2, 1886; Bur. of Labor and Ind. Statistics, Wisconsin, *Second Biennial Rept.,* 1885-86, pp. 321-25, 329.

PERSONALITIES OF THE EARLY METROPOLITAN PERIOD. *Top row*: Edward P. Allis and Frederick Pabst, prominent industrial leaders. *Middle row*: Paul Grottkau, labor organizer, and John I. Beggs, traction manager. *Bottom row*: David G. Rose, "open-town" mayor at turn of century.

nated in a parade which took place the following afternoon. Riding in carriages were delegations from the city's two women's labor organizations, but only one assembly of the Knights of Labor marched. Eight-hour doctrine mingled with socialistic ideology in posters advising the public that labor had come to the crossroads. "Honest workmen will follow the way. Mark the rats. Eight hours." "Capital must come down from its high horse," read another; and a third, suggesting labor's internal strife, attacked the leader of the Knights of Labor in the assertion, "Humbug, your name is Robert." The paraders picnicked at the Milwaukee Garden during the afternoon in good Milwaukee style. There was band music amid decorations in which the American and German national colors were joined; and leaflets and copies of Grottkau's *Arbeiter Zeitung* were circulated. On May 3, as the strike became more general, an additional 4,000 walked out. By order of the Knights of Labor, the remaining brewery workers joined the some 1,200 who had struck for a $10 monthly increase on May 1. Groups of strikers tried to force an entrance into the West Milwaukee car shops and also the Reliance Iron Works which, on the advice of Mayor Wallber, Allis closed.[24]

The conflict progressed to greater violence on May 4, day of the Haymarket bombing in Chicago. The Knights of Labor acquiesced in Mayor Wallber's policy, which recognized the right to strike but promised protection to property and to persons willing to work. The members of the Central Labor Union, however, in a less conciliatory state of mind, marched to the Brand Stove Company factory and forced a shutdown in spite of the fact that the company had just acceded to their employees' demands. Similar tactics, tried at the North Chicago Rolling Mill Company, led to conflict with the militia, which had been called out to preserve order; but no casualties ensued.[25] On the following day, however, a gathering of Polish workers returned to the mills, armed, according to reports, with sticks and

[24] *Ibid.*, 331; Milwaukee *Sentinel*, May 3, 4, 1886.

[25] Five taps of the fire alarm bell had apprised the local militiamen of trouble. The Sheridan Guards, the Light Horse Squadron, and the Lincoln Guards soon put in an appearance. Reinforcements were summoned from Janesville and Beloit. *Ibid.*, May 5, 1886; Mueller, Milwaukee Workers, 12.

knives. When they refused to heed a warning to disperse, according to the official account of the incident, the militia fired; and a number were killed and wounded. On the same day, the police attempted to break up a strikers' meeting at the Milwaukee Garden and ultimately fired upon the crowd without taking life.[26] Within two weeks, thirty-seven offenders had been arrested, including Grottkau; and in the course of a year all had been convicted and forced to pay fines or spend a term in jail.[27]

As a result of this show of force, what the *Sentinel* called the "striking mania" declined. The last of the militia were withdrawn on May 13, and the laborers resumed work at substantially their old wages. The failure of the strikes as a solution of their problems prompted labor to return to politics as a panacea, and in the autumn of 1886 labor candidates were presented with success in both Chicago and Milwaukee. As already has been pointed out, in Milwaukee the People's Party carried the county; and two years later it was only the small minority of Grottkau Socialists which prevented the Union Labor Party from electing Herman Kroeger and defeating the candidate of the fusion ticket to which the old-line parties, in the face of labor's strength, were forced to resort. The developments of 1886 also curtailed the prestige of the Knights of Labor and the Central Labor Union, thus helping to make way for a new national organization, the American Federation of Labor, to which Milwaukee labor gave its support when the Federated Trades Council, organized by the cigar makers', typographical, and moulders' unions, became an affiliate in 1887. By the early nineties, the growth of the unions led to a reported membership of 11,000—almost equal to the peak of 1886. By now, however, the unskilled and semi-skilled workers had left the unions, and the skilled workers had organized as local branches of the international craft unions affiliated with the A. F. of L. By

[26] Milwaukee *Sentinel*, May 5, 6, 1886; Bur. of Labor and Ind. Statistics, Wisconsin, *Second Biennial Rept.*, 1885-86, pp. 337, 340-41; Mueller, *Milwaukee Workers*, 12-13.

[27] Grottkau was sentenced to a year in prison, but a technicality brought his release in six weeks. Hense-Jensen, Schafer tr., chap. 11, p. 9; Mueller, *Milwaukee Workers*, 15.

1904 the Federated Trades Council included sixty locals with 13,000 members.[28]

Most of the blame for the strikes of 1886 was laid upon the Poles and the Socialists, both of which groups were contemporary scapegoats. Actually, however, the smallness of the Grottkau following and its failure to launch a socialistic rival to the Federated Trades Council in the late eighties suggest that the labor agitation of the period was less an indication of the acceptance of socialism by the working class than proof of the growing force of labor in urban life. As yet, socialism carried the taint of "Europeanism," a factor involved in the feud between Grottkau and Schilling, whose conflict, according to Hense-Jensen, symbolized the cleavage "between the Socialists, recruited almost entirely from German labor, and the organized workers of English speech." The popularity of the Union Labor Party lasted longer in Milwaukee than in the other cities of the Middle West; and the adherence of its followers to the creed of urban populism attracted them to the Populist Party, which was to figure in the pattern of politics in the nineties.[29] By 1888, urban labor had become politically articulate in the Wisconsin metropolis; the affiliation of the Federated Trades Council had identified Milwaukee workers with the national organization that was to dominate the labor union picture of the twentieth century; and the programs of the Knights of Labor, the Union Labor Party, and the Socialist organizations had already begun to mark out the policies through which the ideals of the common man as applied to the problems of urban life were to be realized. But for the moment a lack of unity

---

[28] Perlman, "Upheaval," in Commons, *History of Labour* (orig. print.), 2:462-63; Milwaukee *Sentinel*, May 15, 1886; Bur. of Labor and Ind. Statistics, Wisconsin, *Second Biennial Rept.*, 1885-86, p. 338. The similarity of political activity in urban centers at this time is revealed in the fact that there was a similar combination of the old-line parties in Chicago in 1887 but with more positively victorious results. Perlman, "Upheaval," in Commons, *History of Labour* (orig. print.), 2:466. E. Appelhagen was president of the trades council. A charter was granted it by the American Federation of Labor in August 1887. Milwaukee *Journal*, Nov. 16, 1924; Mueller, Milwaukee Workers, 14, 16.

[29] Selig Perlman, History of Socialism in Milwaukee, p. 27, MS, B.A. thesis, dated 1910, University of Wisconsin. This will hereafter be cited as Perlman, Socialism in Milwaukee. Hense-Jensen, Schafer tr., chap. 11, p. 16; Perlman, "Upheaval," in Commons, *History of Labour* (orig. print.), 2:469.

among the workers and contests between the exponents of trade unionism and those favoring political action obstructed the realization of either the economic pressure or the political power which it was labor's ambition to exert. This awaited the identification of labor's program with the socialism and progressivism of a later day—a twentieth-century progressivism and a socialism modified in both form and nationality through contact with the developing metropolitan scene.

The rapprochement between the trade unionists and the Socialists, the political ambitions of the divergent nationality groups, and an increasing concern for municipal reform set the pattern of politics of the nineties. Milwaukee was the most European of America's large cities at the beginning of that decade; and every election gave increasing evidence of the influence of the German and Polish elements in the voting population. It was because of this Europeanism that the Bennett Law, threatening the parochial school, figured so prominently in the municipal elections of 1890. The Republicans straddled the issue, and endorsed "the right of the State to make and enforce suitable legislation to secure compulsory education, including the acquirement of reading and writing in the language of the country." At the same time they affirmed as sacred the "rights of worship according to individual preferences."[30] The Democrats, after some hesitation, came out categorically against the Bennett Law and demanded its repeal. Mindful of their Polish support, they chose Roman Czerwinski, a prominent Polish merchant and captain of the Kosciuszko Guard, for comptroller, and, having already gratified the Germans, coupled him with George W. Peck, an American rather than a German candidate for mayor. "There is nothing more pleasant in the world than to have people happy," asserted the author of *Peck's Bad Boy*, in an acceptance speech that was full of quips and jollity. "Let the public schools in our state be the best in the Union," he said, "and let the schools that are maintained by private societies bring up children in religion without being molested." The church authorities spared no effort to defeat

[30] Conard, 1:98; Milwaukee *Sentinel*, March 23, 1890. See also Bennett Law discussion, chapter 11, pp. 260-61.

the Bennett Law candidate, soliciting the support of all Catholic and Lutheran voters through visits from their priests and pastors. The participation of about 80 percent of the registered voters was in part made possible by the coincidence of Archbishop Heiss's funeral and election day, a situation which permitted Catholic workers to take time off for the funeral and at the same time support the church at the polls. Peck's plurality of more than 4,000 represented a landslide over Brown, the Republican stand-by, and N. S. Murphey, candidate of the Citizens' Ticket; and according to the *Seebote*, the outcome proved that the foreign-born were not to be "robbed of the dear speech in which our mothers taught us our first songs. The German language shall be maintained in America." The resulting board of aldermen contained nineteen Germans, six Irishmen, five Americans, five Poles, and one member of Scandinavian descent.[31]

The "happy mayor" did not remain long in office. On November 17, 1890, he resigned to assume the governorship. He was succeeded by Peter J. Somers who served as acting mayor from December 1890 to April 1892 and was elected in his own right in the spring election of that year. The opposing Republicans saw their best chance of victory in an all-out appeal to the predominant Germanism of the city, a technique on which they were to rely for more than a decade. In Paul Bechtner, native of Stuttgart, they found a candidate whose German-Americanism could be emphasized. He was a "thorough American," asserted his backers, but at the same time a "thorough German—proud of his native land" and of "her poets, scientists, musicians, . . . artists, and . . . customs." He had

[31] Peck, a native of New York, had been brought to Wisconsin at the age of three. He served as a newspaper editor and chief of police at La Crosse, Wisconsin. Milwaukee *Sentinel,* July 14, 1937; March 25, 30, April 2, 6, 1890; Kellogg, "Bennett Law in Wisconsin," *Wis. Mag. of Hist.,* 2:20-22 (September 1918). The occupational composition of this council was as follows: 6 saloon-keepers, 2 collectors for breweries, 2 lawyers, 2 coal dealers, 2 hardware merchants, 2 grading contractors, 2 implement manufacturers, 2 real estate agents, 1 telegraph operator, 1 plumber, 1 mason, 1 locomotive engineer, 1 building contractor, 1 meat merchant, 1 ice dealer, 1 insurance agent, 1 barber, 1 laborer, 1 commission merchant, 1 candy manufacturer, 1 tinsmith, 1 bank teller, and 1 bookkeeper.

"always taken an active part in German society life," was a former president of the Germania Society, director and secretary of a German immigrant aid society, a member of the *Deutsche Gesellschaft*, the *Journalisten Verein*, and the Milwaukee *Turnverein*, and had been one of the most active promoters of the German Day celebration.[32] Somers' victory, with a vote of about 20,000 to Bechtner's 17,000, showed that while a number of German-Americans had returned to the Republican fold, many were still grateful to the Democrats for the repeal of the Bennett Law.[33] A more important cause of Democratic success, however, was the solidarity of the Polish vote, as exhibited in their overwhelming support of Somers in the 14th Ward and in the Polish precincts of the 18th. Nor did Republican politicians foresee a chance to effect a political "partition of Poland" among this nationality so long as the Catholic church and parochial school continued their current hold.[34]

The key position of the Poles in municipal politics was further demonstrated in the special election of 1893, made necessary by the resignation of Mayor Somers in favor of a Congressional career. Again the Republicans employed the tactic that had so nearly succeeded in 1892 and, as we have already seen, nominated a prominent German-American, John C. Koch,

[32] Bruce, *History*, 1:453; Milwaukee *Sentinel*, March 13, 1892.

[33] This law was repealed at the legislative session of 1891. As Henry C. Payne said: "For the repeal of the Bennett law, the Lutherans have given the Democrats a United States Senator, a governor and state officers, two mayors in the city of Milwaukee, and all that goes with it." *Ibid.*, April 7, 1892.

[34] In the Polish 14th Ward and the two Polish precincts of the 18th Ward, Somers received 2,297 votes to Bechtner's 235. According to the *Sentinel:* "At present, the Polish voters hold a balance of power, even without the Irish voters. . . . The most of the Irish-Americans are Democrats, and they vote with a good deal of solidarity, but the exceptions are increasing; and anyhow the number of the Irish is so small now that they are hardly to be considered. The Germans, with the exception of the German Catholics, do not vote solidly as a group in ordinary times. The native Americans are divided between the two parties. The fact that the native-born Americans and the German-Americans do not form a solid group in politics gives to the Poles the balance of power that will soon make them by far the most important element in our politics." The *Herold* contended that the "solidity of this Polish and Irish vote" resulted from obedience to directions from a source which the individual accepts as authoritative and superior to his own judgment." *Ibid.*, April 6, 9, 1892; quotation from *Herold, ibid.*, April 8, 1892.

a native of Hamburg, Germany. The *Germania* asserted that the German citizens of Milwaukee had "repeatedly expressed the wish that a German might again be placed at the head of the most German city of the United States" and with "that excellent German John C. Koch running for mayor" exhorted "the Germandom" of the city to be "conscious of its duty."[35] In hoping to elevate Garrett Dunck to the mayoralty the Democrats had not reckoned with the Poles. Somers' appointments had ignored this politically ambitious people, especially the desire of one of their number, Martin Schubert, to be commissioner of public works. Two others, Peter Pawinski and Ignatz Czerwinski, professed to have been slighted in the choice of federal appointees. At a mass meeting of Polish citizens held at St. Hyacinth's Hall, their leaders aired their objections to being regarded "as so many cattle, useful only for piling up Democratic majorities." Their determination to give the Democrats a "practical lesson" by staying away from the polls resulted in such a decrease in the vote of the Polish wards as to permit a Republican victory by a vote of 11,689 to 8,420.[36]

Political developments of the middle nineties reflected a conscious response to the movement for municipal reform that was sweeping an increasingly urbanized nation. The focal point of the movement was the Municipal League, organized in the early nineties. Its president, John A. Butler, who represented the city at the "first great convention of the National Municipal League," held in Cleveland in May 1895, reported that its work was "being prosecuted on a definite plan, and that it had probably determined the character of the next state election." Bending its efforts toward divorcing municipal government from partisan politics, by April 1895 the league had pushed through the Wisconsin legislature a law creating a nonpartisan city service commission with powers

[35] *Germania*, quoted in Milwaukee *Sentinel*, June 25, 1893. The *Rundschau*, a paper printed in Chicago in the German language, Democratic in politics and an organ of the German Lutheran Church, endorsed Koch's candidacy by saying, "We ... heartily desire his success next Saturday, and hope that none of our people will fail to give him their votes." Quoted, *ibid*.

[36] *Ibid*., June 22, 23, 24, 25, 1893.

over the other branches of government similar to those granted the existing fire and police commission. The commission was organized on June 20, 1895, with Joshua Stark as president. Charles E. Monroe, the first chief examiner, was succeeded shortly by Carl H. Doerflinger, a liberal German-American and one-time editor of the *Freidenker,* a Turner organ. Despite the opposition of the political jobbers, the commission had removed 1,300 laborers from the influence of ward politics by 1897 and was without question promoting greater efficiency in municipal government.[37] The Municipal League also stimulated discussion of municipal issues and in 1896 inspired the organization of nonpartisan Good Government clubs to recommend suitable candidates in the various wards. The West Side Literary Club devoted its meetings of January 23, 1896, to a discussion of "what has been . . . attempted in the interest of better municipal government for Milwaukee." Butler read a paper on the policies and aims of the Municipal League; and on the discussion topic, "Needed Reform in Municipal Affairs," remarks were heard on the subject of "The Ethics of Municipal Reform," "Citizens' Movements as Factors in Municipal Reform," and "Ward Clubs." During the same month the newspapers reported lectures on city government by Amos P. Wilder, John Johnston, Frank Hoyt, James G. Flanders, and Joseph V. Quarles, most of whom cited European practices in municipal government as models for the United States.[38]

In view of this persistent interest, the political parties were forced to mount the band wagon of municipal and civil service

[37] *Ibid.,* May 30, 1895; *Wisconsin Session Laws,* 1895, chap. 313, "An act to regulate the civil service of cities"; Board of City Service Commissioners of Milwaukee, *Fifth Annual Report,* 1900, p. 39; *Wisconsin News* (Milwaukee), Aug. 14, 1896; Oct. 27, 1897; *Chicago Record,* Nov. 20, 1896; Milwaukee *Sentinel,* July 18, Nov. 21, 1897.

[38] *Ibid.,* Jan. 26, Feb. 2, March 4, 1896; *Evening Wisconsin* (Milwaukee), Jan. 3, 18, 31, 1896. Mrs. Helen M. Gougar called Toronto the model city of America. Wilder asserted that Berlin was better and less expensively governed than American cities and that the British Local Government Board provided a model for state boards of municipal supervision. Since there was a tendency to view civil service reform as a European importation, its early acceptance in Milwaukee may be explained by the fact that Milwaukee had fewer prejudices against foreign practices in this period than many American cities: "We should not be too conceited to learn what we can in regard to practical business administration

reform in the elections of 1894 and 1896. In the former year, the executive committee of the Municipal League distributed 10,000 circulars, in which the friends of reform were urged to greater activity at the primaries, and catechized all candidates on their support of municipal purity, especially with respect to the extension of the civil service system.[39] The Republicans, in renominating Mayor Koch, gave hearty support to "the doctrine of municipal reform in the broadest and fullest sense" and recalled "with pride," as they had in 1892, the fact that the fire and police departments had been taken out of party politics by the Republican Party. The Democrats nominated Herman Fehr for mayor and, to remedy recent oversights, again named Roman Czerwinski, prominent Pole, as candidate for comptroller. Dissension among the Poles and between the Catholics and the American Protective Association tended to confuse party allegiances. The labor vote, which had joined hands with the People's Party in 1892 to present John Stippick, president of the Federated Trades Council, for mayor on a workers' ticket, now rallied under the banner of the Cooperative Labor Party. After trying to nominate such prominent figures of the labor wing as Henry Smith, Victor Berger, and Frank J. Weber, president of the Federated Trades Council, the Cooperative Labor ticket finally settled upon John Ulrich, elementary school principal, as their candidate. Scoring the injection of religious issues "to draw the attention of the working people from the main question which is bread and butter," this group, too, gave strong endorsement to civil service reform in a platform that was decidedly socialistic. The outcome of the election was a Republican sweep which recalled their victory in 1880 and suggested the influence of the panic of 1893 upon political change. Koch won some 24,053 votes to 18,815 for Fehr. The Cooperative Labor candidate ran a poor third. The Republicans gained full control of all branches of the city

in governmental affairs from nations and communities who have already paid their tuition for one thousand to two thousand years of experience." Bd. of City Service Commissioners, Milwaukee, *Fourth Ann. Rept.*, 1898, p. 36.

[39] Milwaukee *Sentinel*, March 30, 1894. The executive committee of the Municipal League included Frederick von Cotzhausen, W. P. McLaren, E. J. Lindsay, C. W. Norris, William J. Anderson, J. E. Friend, Edward K. West, and John A. Butler.

government save the board of public works whose appointive terms had not expired.[40]

Efforts to divorce national issues from municipal politics and an increasing concern for some of the practical issues of urban government characterized the election of 1896. The Populists, presenting Henry Smith for the mayoralty, advocated public control of all public utilities; city ownership of street-car lines, gas works, electric light plants, and telephones; the abolition of the contract system on public works; free textbooks; the construction of public works to alleviate unemployment; public pawn shops; and the curtailment of tax-dodging. The Democrats demanded a comprehensive plan of street care and improvements, the abolition of tax-dodging by the street railways, in which they said the Republicans had acquiesced, a reduction in water rates, and prohibitions on the improper use of money in elections. Their candidate, Glenway Maxon, together with Populists Smith and Robert Schilling, attested their support of municipal reform in a meeting held under the auspices of the Municipal League on April 2. Again the Republicans nominated a German-American, this time a cordage manufacturer, William Rauschenberger, native of Soldin, Prussia; again they took credit for existing accomplishments in the field of civil service reform. Their candidate, true to Republican philosophy, confirmed his faith in "improvement by private enterprise and competition in street railways, telephone service, gas and electric lighting" but advocated that all franchises granted in the future should contain provisions favorable to the city's acquisition of the plant. The triumph of Republican individualism was a forecast of what the party was to accomplish in national politics in the fall. Rauschenberger won 17,917 votes to 15,377 for the Democrat. But the 9,121 Populist votes suggested that urban labor was a force to be reckoned with as soon as continuity of party action by this group could be achieved.[41]

[40] Milwaukee *Sentinel*, March 20, 24, 27, April 3, 4, 1894; Wachman, *Social Democratic Party of Milwaukee*, 13.

[41] Milwaukee *Sentinel*, March 17, 19, 21, 29, April 3, 8, 1896. The resulting council was made up of twenty-six Republicans, fifteen Democrats, and one Populist. The most numerously represented occupations were as follows: 8 contractors, 7 real estate and insurance agents, 6 saloonkeepers, 2 grocers, 2

The campaign of 1898 at last saw the emergence of a party capable of maintaining the continuity necessary for political action on the part of the working-class. In spite of the fact that labor groups had advanced candidates on a variety of tickets, no party had as yet been able to weld together effectively the predominantly German adherents of socialistic thought and the advocates of trade unionism who had shunned party allegiance in general and developed the movement independently of socialist ideology. Socialism had still to be identified with the practical problems of the American city and so divested of the taint of European radicalism as to win the American trade union movement to its philosophy of political organization. This was to be the work of Victor Berger, a Milwaukee schoolteacher, born in Austria-Hungary, who in 1892 took over Grottkau's *Arbeiter Zeitung* and transformed it into the daily *Wisconsin Vorwärts*.[42]

Berger set about to adapt scientific socialism to the American environment. This meant a closer integration with the labor movement, less emphasis on the revolutionary aims of socialism, and a repudiation of the program of the Socialist Labor Party and its leader Daniel De Leon, who had carried on a campaign against the trade unions. Berger's support of the Cooperative Labor Ticket in 1894 and of the People's Party in 1896 put socialism in a good light with labor. Meanwhile he was carrying on a personal crusade to gain adherents to the cause. He found an able lieutenant in Frederic Heath, Milwaukee liberal, who had helped to start the Milwaukee Ethical Society in 1895 and who had been associated with the

butchers. The difficulties inherent in the short-lived attempt to ally the labor groups with the essentially agrarian Populist Party are discussed in J. M. Klotsche, "The 'United Front' Populists," *Wisconsin Magazine of History*, 20:375-83 (June 1937).

[42] Victor L. Berger was born in Nieder-Rehbach, Austria-Hungary, February 28, 1860. He attended the gymnasium and the universities of Budapest and Vienna. His parents having lost their fortune, he emigrated with them to the United States. Going West, he engaged in odd jobs of all sorts, including cattle punching, but soon returned to New York, where he learned the trade of metal polishing. Not long after, he took up teaching and came to Milwaukee, where he became prominently associated with the Turner movement. In December 1892, he resigned from the Turner Normal School in Milwaukee to devote his attention to Socialist politics. Frederic Heath, *A Brief History of Socialism in America* (Terre Haute, Ind., 1900), 107.

Liberal Club, sometimes referred to as the "crank's paradise." Visiting Eugene Debs in the Woodstock, Illinois, county jail, Berger won the support of the head of the Railway Brotherhood and began a friendship which soon bore fruit when Debs, Heath, and Berger formed the Social Democratic Party in June 1897. The "Americanism" of the new party was revealed in its executive board, which included, in addition to Debs, Berger, and Heath, Jesse Cox and Seymour Stedman. Its platform identified it with trade unionism and populism; and its ranks were soon augmented by a dissident group from the ever-volatile Socialist Labor Party.[43] Berger's appeal to the trade unions won his party the overwhelming support of the Federated Trades Council by 1899;[44] and although neither the unions nor the party exerted control over the other, such were the common interests of their membership that by 1910 "the result for which the Socialists had been striving—to make their party the political arm of the trade union movement"—had been achieved.[45]

The Social Democrats made their debut in city politics when large-scale municipal undertakings were before the public; and their first essay did not get them far against the old-line parties. Robert Meister, a machinist at the Vilter Manufacturing Company, was their candidate for mayor in 1898. Campaign meetings brought forward Debs and Stedman as speakers; and money was raised to bring back Grottkau, who was then residing in San Francisco. Addressing a gathering at the Kosciuszko Armory, Debs asserted that "Socialists all over the country were interested in the Milwaukee campaign, for it was the first appearance of the Social Democracy in politics." Their platform

[43] July 29, 1901, saw the formation of the Socialist Party of America, but the Milwaukee branch of the party continued to be called Social Democrats. Selig Perlman and Philip Taft, *Labor Movements*, vol. 4 of John R. Commons, *History of Labor in the United States* (augmented to 4 vols., New York, 1935), 222, 225-29.

[44] Perlman, Socialism in Milwaukee, 46.

[45] "A kind of 'interlocking directorate' existed between the movements. . . . With few exceptions, the secretaries, business agents, and executive officers of the unions were active members of the Social Democratic party. Berger, Heath, Brockhausen, Weber, Berner, Melms, Coleman, Elsner, and Strehlow are only a few of the names of outstanding trade-unionists who were victorious at the polls under the Social-Democratic banner." Wachman, *Social Democratic Party of Milwaukee*, 39, 40.

reflected the pragmatism of Berger's politics; it was compounded of the demands by which the labor parties of the preceding generation had marked out a program congenial to the needs of the urban common man. Thus it included municipal control as soon as possible of all public utilities, the employment of union labor at an eight-hour day for city work, public work for the unemployed, fair taxation of large corporations, free legal and medical service for the needy, additional public baths, free school books, condemnation of slum habitations injurious to the public health, half-holidays for workers on election days, and the provision of at least one symphony concert a month at a nominal fee.[46] When the returns were in, the Social Democrats had mustered only 5 percent of the total vote.[47]

The meagerness of this vote is to be explained in part by the fact that the Democratic platform competed for the support of the progressive element among the voters and at the same time advanced a candidate whose drawing power was to that date unexcelled in the history of Milwaukee politics. Municipal ownership of public utilities was the key issue of the campaign. Robert Schilling, still refusing to cooperate with the liberal wing of labor, promised the Democrats the Populist vote if they would endorse the Populist program, which was in many

[46] Milwaukee *Sentinel*, March 27, April 2, 1898; Perlman, Socialism in Milwaukee, 45; Wachman, *Social Democratic Party of Milwaukee*, 23. Grottkau spoke in part as follows at a meeting on March 26, 1898, held in the West Side turn hall:

"I understand very well that all the rich people will vote for Mr. Geuder. He belongs to their class, and is personally an honest man. But he belongs to the class that exploits labor and makes money out of the marrow of working children. Rose or Smith would do the same if they had a tinware factory; therefore a wage worker who would vote for Geuder would show poor taste and lack of common sense. He would simply be proud of his chains. But the Democrats, or rather the Popocrats, have the audacity to talk in their platform about cleaning out the lobby of the city hall, and then put up for Mayor one of the most notorious lobbyists ever known in Madison. A man not only a capitalist, but one whose business it is to defend capitalists by all kinds of tricky practises. If a working man vote for such a man, it is not only a sign of his stupidity but it is putting a premium on corruption. I hope no working man in the city will be led to such a criminal blunder, in spite of Smith, Schilling, and men of that caliber." Milwaukee *Sentinel*, March 27, 1898.

[47] The vote was insignificant in all but the German (Ninth, Tenth, 19th, 20th, and 21st) wards. Wachman, *Social Democratic Party of Milwaukee*, 24; Milwaukee *Sentinel*, April 6, 1898.

ways similar to that of the Social Democrats. It included the municipal ownership of all public utilities, uniform rates for water, gas, light, etc., the abolition of the contract system, free textbooks, home rule, the consolidation of city and county government, a more perfect civil service, and a revision of the city charter to provide for initiative and referendum. There was consequently a Populist flavor in the resulting Democratic platform, especially in the party's support of municipal control and ownership of public utilities and in its condemnation of the Republican Party as the tool of the "street car monopoly" and "garbage ring."[48] The candidate of the "Popocrats" was David G. Rose, a political chameleon who was destined on five occasions to gain the mayorship for the Democratic Party. At the moment, this dashing and eloquent campaigner, who before long was to prove that he could be "all things to all men," was focusing his appealing attentions on the "poor workingman."[49]

With customary concern for the German-American vote, the Republicans nominated William Geuder, product of the Engelmann school and the German-English Academy. Their endorsement of municipal ownership stopped with support of a municipal garbage plant; in their opinion the city was not financially ready to engage in other such enterprises. Rose, however, was able to convince a good many voters that the conservative Geuder was the tool of the street car interests. The Republican candidate might be honest, he asserted, but if so he was "buried in a monopolistic cemetery." The election of April 5, 1898, brought a landslide for Rose and the Democrats. Rose received 26,219 votes to 18,207 for Geuder and 2,444 for the Social Democrat. The combination of Democrats and Populists lacked by one member a two-thirds control of the council. Sensing the current municipal trend, the retiring council voted unanimously on March 17 for a municipally owned garbage plant.[50]

[48] "Therefore, in the interest of the public morality and good government, we favor, when the condition of the city's finances warrant, municipal control and ownership of all public utilities, and the immediate erection of a municipal plant." *Ibid.,* March 5, 15, 1898.
[49] Rose was born in 1856, in Darlington, Wisconsin. Twice elected mayor of Darlington, he came to Milwaukee in 1886 where he undertook the practice of law. Bruce, *Born in America,* 107, 223; Milwaukee *Sentinel,* July 14, 1937.
[50] *Ibid.,* March 3, 8, 15, 16, 18, April 6, 1898.

Little time elapsed before Mayor Rose revealed his opposition to civil service reform by attacks upon the city service commission and the Municipal League. He soon showed, too, the emptiness of the promises on the subject of the regulation of corporations and the municipal ownership of public utilities by which he had won so many progressive and Populist votes. Cooperating with the organized efforts of the aldermen who supported the street railway company, whose control over the Republican candidate he had condemned two years earlier, he now lent his support to a street railway ordinance which gave excessive privileges to the company—"a ten year extension of franchises, gifts of streets and bridges, immunity from paving between the tracks, assurance of freedom from competition," —so shameless an action, according to the Chicago *Tribune,* "in the face of the protests of the people," as to bring Milwaukee "universal notoriety." To sugar-coat these concessions he stressed the merit of the 4-cent commutation fare useful for four and a half hours during the day, promised by the company, and had distributed among the voters leather cases for the proposed commutation tickets, decorated with a sprig of rose bush and the adage, "A penny saved is a penny earned." By 1900, the Populists, refusing to go along with the Democrats so long as they supported Rose, joined the Municipal League in condemning the street railway franchise and nominated Theodore Fritz for mayor. The Republicans, again following their practice of choosing German-Americans, nominated Henry J. Baumgaertner on a platform which was viewed as opposing the street railway monopoly and favoring public ownership of public utilities as soon as the city was financially capable of taking the step.[51] The Social Democrats proposed Frederic F. Heath for mayor and came forward on essentially the same platform they had proposed in 1898, but this time with even a closer tie-up with the trades unions. Of the 147 delegates at their February 12 convention, 37 were from various branches of the party, 43 from the wards, and 67 from the trades unions. Beyond the proposals of their 1898 platform they now advocated a

---

[51] *Ibid.,* Dec. 16, 1899; Jan. 7, March 3, 16, 20, 1900; Chicago *Tribune,* March 22, 1900. As a member of the council in 1888, Baumgaertner had advocated a municipal electric lighting plant. Milwaukee *Sentinel,* Feb. 25, 1900.

public crematory; public comfort stations; shower baths in factories; the sale at cost by the city of coal, wood, ice, and pure milk for babies; and membership in trade unions by all members of the party. The Federated Trades Council endorsed the ticket and established a campaign committee. The Socialist Labor Party nominated Alwin Flechsig. The assertion of its leader, Richard Koeppel, that it stood "upon the ground of scientific, revolutionary socialism and uncompromising class struggle" was a dig at the temporizing program of Berger socialism.[52]

Mayor Rose's turn-about on the street car issue did not prevent his election in this campaign, but it was by a plurality greatly reduced from what he had mustered two years earlier. His magnificent campaigning style stood him in good stead; his gifts to certain Polish churches helped to account for widespread support in the 14th and 18th as well as the Third, or Irish, Ward;[53] and his advocacy of "a wide-open town" drew him support from the liquor interests. He benefited, as well, from the dissension which the street railway company was said to have fomented within the Republican ranks. Seven of the twelve street railway aldermen were reelected and five defeated. The lineup in the council was a tie between the Democrats on the one hand and on the other the Populists and Republicans combined. In his inaugural address, Rose flayed civil service reform as "a hypocritical pretense." Not that he wanted to practice the spoils system, he said, but he thought department heads should have the privilege of naming their own subordinates and that nothing could be gained by extending the principles of

[52] Frederic Heath, born in Milwaukee in 1864, as a young man engaged in art and journalistic work. In 1891 he took charge of the Milwaukee *Sentinel*'s art department. He became a Socialist in the early nineties, participated in the meeting that inaugurated the Social Democratic Party, and helped formulate its platform. Heath, *Brief History of Socialism*, 113; Milwaukee *Sentinel*, Feb. 13, 15, 1900; Frederic Heath, A Call to Arms, unpaged, typescript of an address delivered before the Socialist Party State Convention in Milwaukee, June 1940, in possession of Milwaukee County Historical Society.

[53] According to the *Sentinel*, Democratic politics were discussed from the pulpits of five Polish Catholic churches on the Sunday morning preceding the election. Rose's contributions were announced; and at two churches, sample ballots, "all duly marked for the Democratic nominees," were distributed. Milwaukee *Sentinel*, April 2, 1900.

civil service to municipal affairs.⁵⁴

La Follette Progressivism worked to Mayor Rose's advantage in the election of 1902. The conservative Republicans, abandoning a German-American nominee for the first time in a decade, nominated Charles H. Anson and resurrected the campaign argument which gave the Republicans credit for divorcing the police and fire departments from municipal politics. The La Follette clubs proposed the Republican stand-by of the eighties, Thomas H. Brown, and promised the expulsion of corruption from the city hall, the abolition of political protection for gambling and prostitution, and municipal ownership of public utilities. For the Democrats, "All-the-time-Rosy" was a candidate with manifold appeal. He opened his speaking campaign on dress parade, wearing a "Prince Albert coat" and "immaculate shirt front"; the next day he was "in his working clothes haranguing the workingmen in the Menomonee valley." Posters bearing letters six feet high attested his interest in "Personal Liberty and Up to Date Administration." In nominating Peter Pawinski for comptroller, the Democrats cast their customary bait for the Polish-American vote. The Social Democrats advanced Howard Tuttle, a scene painter and union organizer, for mayor, and stressed the obligation of the trade unions to effect social reform through wise use of the ballot. Seeking to win the support of other nationalities than the Germans, they circulated political literature among the Italians of the Third Ward and distributed to the Poles a Polish translation of the writings of a Catholic priest from Louisville which countered some of the objections of the Polish priests to socialism. Again Debs and Stedman came from Chicago to boost the Socialist cause. The latter expounded socialism and referred to the mayor as "Dave Roach"; Debs warned the Social Democrats that the eyes of the country were upon Milwaukee—"the center of Socialism, the Paris of America." The election returns showed that support for the Social Democrats had increased from about 2,500 in the election of 1900 to close to 8,500. But again it was a Rose year. According to the *Sentinel,* his plurality of about 8,000 was the result of a deal by which the La Follette

⁵⁴ *Ibid.,* April 4, 18, 1900.

men voted for Rose in order to gain Democratic support for the Progressive candidate for circuit judge.[55]

More than seventy grand jury indictments against aldermen and supervisors in 1903 revealed the extent to which graft and corruption had infected Milwaukee politics by the turn of the century, in spite of the current concern for municipal reform. A former alderman of the Fourth Ward was charged with agreeing to accept a bribe of $3,000 for securing the passage of a street-car franchise on Eighth Street, an alderman from the Third Ward with receiving a total of $750 in connection with the passage of a naphtha lighting contract, and the city building inspector with taking a bribe of $1,500. There were revelations of gross mismanagement in the House of Correction, and aldermen were accused of receiving gifts of as much as $500 for licenses for illicit gambling houses. These and other disclosures involving the solicitation and acceptance of bribes in return for liquor licenses and side-track and bay-window privileges came as a result of a movement which had been developing since 1901. In 1903 a mass meeting of reformers, called by the Milwaukee *Turnverein,* led to the appointment of a Citizens' Committee of Ten; and this group prepared the way for grand jury indictments by which the long-needed municipal housecleaning got under way. Early in 1904 a group of the city's leading businessmen organized the Voters' League, patterned on the Municipal Voters' League of Chicago, which had had notable success in ridding the common council there of corrupt elements. Funds for the work of the Milwaukee Voters' League were subscribed by the members themselves or solicited from friends. The resulting ward organization endorsed candidates who were listed in the local newspapers shortly before the April elections in 1904.[56]

[55] *Ibid.,* March 12, 14, 15, 18, 21, 1902; *Social Democratic Herald* (Milwaukee), Dec. 13, 1902; Austin, *The Milwaukee Story,* 162; Wachman, *Social Democratic Party of Milwaukee,* 42-43. The discrepancy between Anson's vote and that of Judge Warren D. Tarrant would seem to substantiate this interpretation. Milwaukee *Sentinel,* April 2, 1902.

[56] *Ibid.,* Jan. 31, March 16, 17, 22, 1904; Wachman, *Social Democratic Party of Milwaukee,* 46; Duane Mowry, "The Reign of Graft in Milwaukee," *The Arena,* 34:589-93 (December 1905); Ovid B. Blix, Milwaukee Voters' League, Resumé of Its Activities during Its Existence, 1904-1925, unpaged, typescript in possession of Milwaukee Municipal Reference Library.

Municipal graft was the issue of this campaign; and in an atmosphere friendly to reform, the candidates of the Progressive Republican and Social Democratic parties were the beneficiaries of the recent grand jury action. The Republicans, influenced by the La Follette wing of the party, nominated Guy D. Goff, condemning graft as the "canker at the root of Milwaukee's welfare" and blaming the Democrats for fastening upon the city "the brigade of grafters which now have Milwaukee by the throat." Henry F. Cochems, Progressive Republican, asserted that as a result of Rose's manipulation of bids from dummy companies the city was paying $2.30 per yard for asphalt pavements where other cities paid $1.56. The Social Democrats, scenting a possible victory, presented their trump card by nominating Victor Berger. Again Debs and Stedman appeared as campaign speakers; and Edmund T. Melms organized the famous bundle brigade by which Social Democratic literature in seven languages was distributed from house to house. With reform in the air and Rose's unsavory practices to provide spectacular campaign arguments, Berger was confident of success. Pitting his record as a student of municipal socialism and city administration against Rose's "studies" in how to "save $150,000 out of a salary of $4,000 a year," he predicted that his supporters would "march by the thousands and ten thousands and give the city of Milwaukee the most thorough socialistic house-cleaning that any city in the United States ever had."[57] But Rose had two tricks up his sleeve with which to counter the Social Democratic ace. One was his appeal for the Polish Catholics and their opposition in principle to socialism. The other was his play for Republican votes by convincing conservatives that a vote for Goff was a vote for Berger and control of the city by the Federated Trades Council. As a result of these tactics, Rose gained his fourth mandate as mayor.[58]

The novel feature of the contest, however, was the signal gains of the Social Democracy, won not only through organization but because of the current urge for municipal reform. In

[57] Milwaukee *Sentinel*, March 22, 24, 26, April 2, 3, 1904; Wachman, *Social Democratic Party of Milwaukee*, 54; Heath, A Call to Arms, unpaged. The Socialist Labor Party accused Berger of insincerity and put their own ticket in the field. Milwaukee *Sentinel*, April 3, 1904.

[58] *Ibid.*, April 4, 1904.

spite of the fact that they " 'treated' no voters . . . corrupted no elector," they nearly doubled their vote of two years before in garnering 15,056 votes for Berger to 17,598 for Goff and 23,515 for Rose. Nine Social Democratic aldermen, among them Emil Seidel and Frederic Heath, were chosen by the predominantly German wards. The editor of the *Sentinel* touched the chief significance of the outcome when he wrote: "The enormous increase in the vote of the social democratic party indicates that a new element has come upon the field to assertively dispute the right of the democrats and republicans to dominate the politics of the city of Milwaukee." The vote was of importance, too, in the evolution of the Social Democratic Party itself. For with the realization that they could carry the city elections, Berger's party moved one step further in the direction of opportunistic realism. Having already made themselves acceptable to the trade unionists, they now prepared to appeal to that wing of liberal business and professional men to whom the graft within the old-line parties was unpalatable. To accomplish this they set aside the plank in their platform which condemned the grant of franchises to privately-owned public utility corporations and substituted for it one demanding special guarantees from corporations applying for city franchises. A concern for the practical problems of the municipality increasingly overshadowed "the purely socialistic part of their program." Once the party had turned this corner in its political evolution, the Socialist victory of 1910 was already coming into view.[59]

The increasing desire for purity in municipal politics, a split between Mayor Rose and William George Bruce within the Democratic ranks, disaffection among the Polish voters, and the novel campaign tactics of the Republicans' spectacular candidate, Sherburn M. Becker, combined in 1906 to break Mayor Rose's winning spell. Progressivism was the point at issue between the aspiring Democrats, and in his bid for nomination Bruce advocated city promotion, the curtailment of tax evasion, the closing of gambling houses and stall saloons, the develop-

[59] *Daily News* (Milwaukee), quoted in Wachman, *Social Democratic Party of Milwaukee*, 54; Milwaukee *Sentinel*, April 6, 7, 1904; Perlman, Socialism in Milwaukee, 3-4.

ment of a playground program, and attempts to hold the utilities in line. Profiting from the support of La Follette Republicans and Social Democrats, he came within 1,200 votes of wresting the nomination from the incumbent Democratic mayor.[60] Rose, having bested what he termed this combination of Socialists and "half-breeds," based his chances for reelection on a platform which advocated "the immediate establishment of a municipal lighting plant, to be owned and operated by the city," and "liberty in individual conduct, consistent with good order and good morals." But charges that the veteran mayor had spent more time at an Arizona silver mine than in his office and a personal scandal in which his name was linked with that of a former Milwaukee woman retarded his chances of victory, as did the fact that the Poles failed in the primary to secure representation on the Democratic slate.[61]

In Sherburn M. Becker, the twenty-nine-year-old son of a Milwaukee financier, the Republicans advanced a candidate whose campaign antics attracted national publicity. Early in the contest he engaged W. F. Hooker as a press agent to publish a *Bulletin* which contained "pointed paragraphs" from Becker's speeches. The organization of the Young Men's Sherburn M. Becker Club, with a membership of between 3,500 and 5,000, reflected the candidate's appeal to youth. Becker himself conducted a vigorous campaign, speaking nightly at club meetings and social gatherings and devoting much of his time to the Polish wards. One feature to attract attention was the offer of a barrel of flour to the woman who would phrase the best answer to the question: "Why should Sherburn Becker be elected mayor?" "Fresh Red Blood is needed in the Chief Office of the City Administration" was Becker's appeal to "Young Men! First Voters! Work for, shout for, vote for Becker, not controlled by Bosses or Corporations but by the People." To counter this, Rose accused his Republican opponent of being bred of a corporation father, nursed on corporation milk, and reared on corporation

---

[60] The vote, with two precincts missing, was Rose, 14,845; Bruce, 13,688. Milwaukee *Sentinel*, March 4, 11, 14, 21, 1906.

[61] Father Gulski, pastor of St. Hyacinth's Church, pointed out, however, that much less could be expected from the Republicans than from the Democrats. *Ibid.*, March 20, 22, April 1, 1906.

wealth. But Becker's youthful enthusiasm and self-confident wit were a match for the political manipulation and campaign oratory of the older politician. When Rose accused Becker of having been born with a silver spoon in his mouth, Becker retorted that "Mayor Rose may not have been born with a silver spoon in his mouth, but I think he was born with a tin horn in his mouth, and he has been tooting it ever since."[62]

"A better, not a greater Milwaukee" was the campaign pledge of the Social Democrats in offering William A. Arnold as candidate for mayor. With a platform softened so as not to alienate the progressive business and professional voter, they continued to temper with political realism their former class-conscious attitude. On the persistently important question of municipal ownership, they proposed that the city should "secure the ownership and management of all public service enterprises as far as the state laws will allow." Where this should be impossible, no franchise was to be granted unless it was agreed that the entire property should revert to the city without compensation after a given period, that rolling stock and trackage be kept in good order, that the city receive a certain yearly revenue from the company for the franchise, that the eight-hour day and trade unions be recognized by the company, and that every franchise be subject to referendum. The customary outside speakers—"slang whangers," the *Sentinel* called them—were imported from Chicago to help the Socialists[63] swell the strength of a party which, according to this most outspoken journalistic opponent of socialism, was putting the city increasingly in bad repute. Nevertheless, when the votes were counted on election day, the Socialists appeared to have suffered less than the Democrats from the appeal of the ebullient Becker. Becker was the winner, with a plurality of about 1,518 over

[62] *Ibid.*, March 9, 20, 21, 28, 29, 1906.
[63] According to the *Sentinel* for April 2, "Impresario Berger's imported socialistic slangwhangers from Chicago continue to abuse and belabor this 'darkest Milwaukee' of ours, its morals, its manners, its citizenship, and its non-socialist candidates. Orator Mills, of Chicago, for instance, was in great force and form last Saturday night, and his whirlwind finish of billingsgate at the expense of this poor old town was enough to make even Citizen Berger wince." *Ibid.*, March 21, April 2, 1906; Perlman, Socialism in Milwaukee, 54-55.

Rose that progressivism within the Democracy and the disaffection of the Poles in the 14th and 18th wards help to explain. But the Social Democrats had virtually maintained the strength which Berger had shown two years earlier in gaining 25 percent of the total vote; and the election of five aldermen to increase their number in the council to eleven brought them one step nearer the day when they could dominate the city hall.[64]

By 1908, the chief lines of defense against the Social Democratic threat had taken shape. A proportionately larger number of seats in the council was put at the disposal of the old-line parties by a change in the city charter in 1907 which reduced the number of aldermen from forty-six to thirty-five and provided for the election of twelve of them from the city at large rather than from the individual wards. In a number of wards—the Fifth, 11th, and 12th—the conservatives settled upon a common candidate to oppose the Socialists. In addition, the *Sentinel* continued to raise the "red bogey" by asserting that Milwaukee could not afford "the reputation of a red flag town." The Republicans, while appreciating Mayor Becker's ambition to give the city "a thoroughly business administration; . . . a full dollar's value for every dollar of their money expended," had tired of the young mayor's effervescent exhibitionism and eccentric behavior. This had included an automobile trip from Milwaukee to the New York city hall in his crimson "Red Devil" Pope-Toledo touring car and a personal—and somewhat destructive—crusade against the clocks and signs on Wisconsin Avenue. In presenting Thomas J. Pringle as their candidate for mayor, they promised the city a business administration. Rose, once more the Democratic standard bearer, pointed to the accomplishments of his four terms as mayor, ridiculed the opponents of an "open town," and tried to draw the labor vote from the Social Democrats by charging that Emil Seidel, the Socialist candidate, and Frank Weber employed non-union labor and that Victor Berger was abandoning the common people in buying Lake Drive property.[65] Without changing their platform of

[64] Milwaukee *Sentinel*, March 31, April 4, 1906.
[65] Blix, Milwaukee Voters' League, unpaged. Milwaukee *Sentinel*, April 18, 1906; March 24, 27, April 4, 21, 1908; July 14, 1937.

"realistic socialism," the Social Democrats asserted their party to be "the American expression of the international movement of modern wage-workers for better food, better houses, sufficient sleep, more leisure, more education, and more culture." The effectiveness of Rose's organization and his promise of an "open town" restored him to the mayoralty for a fifth term; but Seidel, the Socialist, ran second and only 3,000 votes behind the winner. It appeared that a number of La Follette Republicans had at the last moment supported the Socialists' choice.[66]

The steady, persistent campaigning of the Social Democrats, the workmanlike accomplishments of their representatives in the council, and their appeal to an increasingly wider reform-minded constituency bore fruit in the election of 1910. Emil Seidel, the Social Democratic candidate, received a plurality of more than 7,000—the largest given a Milwaukee mayor to that date. The party elected seven aldermen at large—all that were up for election, carried sixteen of the twenty-three wards, and gained a working majority in the council, which in the ensuing term would comprise twenty-one Social Democrats, ten Democrats, and four Republicans. Although the Democrats continued to be strong in the Third, Fourth, and 18th wards, Socialists made large gains in the Polish 14th, where literature in Polish was distributed, including a Polish newspaper, *Naprzod* (Forward), established in November 1909.[67] Of the new members of the council, fully eighteen represented trades which required physical exertion. The platform of the victors included the oft-repeated promises which, because of the progressivism of the times, the old-line parties were just beginning to endorse. Home rule; initiative, referendum, and recall; the ownership and control of public service corporations; equitable taxation; the establishment of a public works department; the eight-hour day on city work; free textbooks; a municipal ice

[66] *Ibid.*, April 8, 10, 1908.
[67] According to Wachman, the Social-Democratic aldermen won a respected reputation during the first decade of the century. "Nearly all the proposals that attracted serious public attention . . . emanated from this minority. The Socialist membership alone came to the meetings with definite policies agreed upon, with arguments prepared on pending measures, together with complete and accurate information as to the progress of municipal business." Wachman, *Social Democratic Party of Milwaukee*, 62-63, 71; Milwaukee *Sentinel*, April 6, 1910.

plant; the public sale of coal, wood, and stone; better housing; a park system; and free medical care for the poor—these were the tenets of the urban populism which the Social Democrats, and the labor parties before them, had enunciated since the late nineteenth century. As Berger said, it was a platform "built on the basis of modern international socialism, but localized to meet the needs of Milwaukee and the conditions under which we are now living."[68] A factor of no small importance in the Socialist success was their smooth-running political machine, directed by such capable leaders as Victor and Meta Berger, Elizabeth Thomas, C. B. Whitnall, Edmund Melms, Daniel Hoan, Frederic Heath, Carl Dietz, Carl D. Thompson, and Emil Seidel. Berger and Seidel were an effective vote-getting combination, the former compelling, incisive, carefully articulate, and politically shrewd; the latter small, soft-voiced, and modest, but possessed of an appealing intelligence, earnestness, and zeal. During this campaign, Melms's famous volunteer bundle brigade distributed more than 750,000 pieces of literature.[69]

The most outspoken opposition to Seidel's candidacy had come from J. M. Beffel, the Republican choice for mayor. The essence of his opposition was not to the Socialist platform, from which indeed the Republicans had drawn a good many ideas, but to the idea of socialism itself.[70] Raising the bogey of "red flaggery," he asserted that the "news, flashed over the country . . . that 'Socialists Carry Milwaukee' would do more mischief

[68] *Ibid.*, March 30, April 7, 1910. See *ibid.*, April 19, 1910, for Berger's statement of party aims.

[69] Berger was elected to the council in 1910, but in the fall he was chosen for Congress. Melms, a former baseball player, knew the language of the man in the street. "The Voice of the People" had a wide appeal to Milwaukeeans and a circulation greater than all the regular papers. There was a page in Polish for the Polish section, in German for the Germans. Bundles of the publication were distributed to key points—usually taverns run by Socialists—and from there distributed from house to house by volunteers. Milwaukee *Journal*, May 12, 1940; Bruce, *Born in America*, 224.

[70] The Republicans endorsed equitable taxation, the restriction of taxes to the 14-mill limit, the extension of the civil service, reasonable control of the social evil, elimination of the white slave traffic, regulation rather than prohibition of the saloon, the beautification of the city through eliminating smoke and noise, a reasonable amount of home rule, a fair deal from the public service corporations, more sanitary housing, a fair trial for civil service employees before dismissal, and the initiative, referendum, and recall. Milwaukee *Sentinel*, March 11, 22, 24, 1910.

in a day than our associations to promote and advance the city industrially could undo in a year." On one occasion he described Seidel as a "nice gentleman," coming before the people "in a peaceful, purring way like a cat, but beneath are the sharp claws [of] Victor L. Berger," the real candidate behind Seidel, hulking, to choose another figure, "like a leviathan beside a sprat." The Democrats, too, endorsed municipal lighting, home rule, and the principles of initiative, referendum, and recall. They nominated Vincenz J. Schoenecker, who, not unmindful of the popular reaction to Mayor Rose's derelictions from duty, promised to devote his entire time to the office and to provide an efficient business administration. Like Beffel, he condemned the Social Democrats as "inexperienced, visionary agitators," and queried, "Can Milwaukee afford to be the first city to adopt Socialism?"[71]

For the moment, at least, a plurality of the electorate appeared to think the city could. Seidel's vote was 27,608; Schoenecker's, 20,530; while Beffel ran a poor third with 11,346. To the jubilant Berger, the outcome marked the real conversion of a people at last "saturated with Socialist doctrine";[72] and Seidel predicted that the "intelligent working classes in Milwaukee" would thereafter always "insist on having the controlling voice in the management of municipal affairs." Time was soon to prove such interpretations to be wrong; and in the light of later events the returns of 1910 appear less indicative of the voters' saturation with socialism than of the peak of their exasperation with the existing incompetence, not to say corruption, of the old-line parties. For a decade, individual Socialists had been proving their capacity in city office; and, as many civic leaders observed, the "time had gone by when Victor Berger and Emil Seidel" could "be used as bugaboos."[73] Under such circumstances, many voters who were by no means Socialists,

[71] *Ibid.*, March 24, 25, 26, 29, April 1, 4, 1910.

[72] Frederic C. Howe, "Milwaukee, a Socialist City," *Outlook*, 95:417 (June 25, 1910).

[73] For the outcome of the election, see Milwaukee *Sentinel*, April 6, 1910. For popular reactions, see undated clipping from Milwaukee *Journal*, in Duke University Socialist Collection, Duke University Library. The *Journal* commented, as later quoted in issue of May 12, 1940: "The result was inevitable all through the years Milwaukee has been misruled. Big business has manipulated municipal government to serve its own purpose and has winked at or abetted

but who were disillusioned with the record of the veteran parties, were increasingly less hesitant to support the Social Democratic ticket. Thus the Socialists, steadily strengthened by their mobilization of the working-class vote, were in a position to profit from the current surge of municipal progressivism which drew its support from reform-minded business and professional men as well as from members of a skillfully endoctrinated labor group.[74] The platforms of all the parties showed their eagerness to meet the implications of this trend; but the Social Democrats were able to capitalize upon it most successfully because at a time when the old-line parties were in disrepute they had become a respected third party in a position to wield an effective balance of power. That the leadership of the older parties was not unaware of the means by which to redress this balance was seen in the *Sentinel's* significant forecast of April 6, 1910: "The victory Tuesday means beyond a question that two years hence both the old parties will have to unite in order to have any chance to oust the social democrats from the City hall. This was admitted by politicians Tuesday night after they had read the returns."[75]

From 1870 to 1910, the development of politics in the emerging metropolis presented Milwaukee with a procession of municipal executives that included the propertied Ludington, the progressive Brown, bait for the German-American vote like Koch and Rauschenberger, a corporation-controlled demagogue, and an intellectual champion of the workingman. By the twentieth century, the idea of limited municipal action

things detrimental to the material interests of the city." Joseph Uihlein, manager of the Schlitz brewery, interpreted the vote as "more clearly an endorsement of Mr. Berger and his excellent associates than an endorsement of Social-Democratic principles."

[74] According to the New York *Tribune,* 7,000 Republicans and 4,000 Democrats voted the Socialist ticket, a drift from the regular parties which it explained by saying that the people of Milwaukee had "grown accustomed to radicalism." Quoted in Milwaukee *Sentinel,* April 11, 1910.

[75] Trials of the persons indicted for municipal corruption continued through 1909. Austin, *The Milwaukee Story,* 164; Milwaukee *Sentinel,* April 6, 1910. A day or two before the election, Seidel defined the expected sources of his support: "First, the workingmen, who are united for us as never before, because they see in social democracy their only hope for the future. Second, the professional class because of their intelligence. And lastly many business men . . . , because of the trend of economic conditions, and the ruthless competition of the trusts." *Ibid.,* April 3, 1910.

was being replaced by a concept which implied broad social service on the part of the municipality. The progress of reform from improvement of the civil service to support for municipal ownership reflects a transition in the popular mind which in part accounts for the popularity of a qualified and "Yankeefied" socialism at the close of the period. The almost continuous existence of a workers' party, given effective continuity from the close of the nineties as a result of the organizational skill of Victor Berger, kept political attention focused on the pressing problems of metropolitan living as they affected the rank and file of the urban populace; and it was concern for these problems which really gave vitality to the various, ever-present, and often factious Socialist groups which tried throughout the period to exert political power. The ultimate assumption of control by the Social Democrats in 1910 was more a political than a social incident. To be sure, it marked a victory for the industrial workers, who, with the growth of the city, had become increasingly articulate as a class; but the victory was primarily that of a political party which by 1910 had developed a broad appeal for the voting public. By that date the Social Democrats were well established and organized, with a platform adapted to the realities of American labor organization and metropolitan life, and in a position to hold the balance of power against two fairly evenly matched opponents. The prevailing Germanism of the city reduced the resistance of the electorate to socialistic ideas and terminology; and both the progressivism of the age and the corruption of the hour gave the tempered socialism of the program an appeal for voters outside the working-class. Thus both the nature of the party and the character of the electorate account for the most significant political trend of the generation in the Wisconsin city and explain why the Socialist Party, though originally stronger in Chicago than in the Wisconsin metropolis, came into power in Milwaukee before it did elsewhere in the large cities of the nation.

CHAPTER 13

Industrial Foundations

THE growth of manufacturing was the most significant development in the economic life of the Wisconsin metropolis between 1870 and 1910; for during that forty-year period industry gradually overshadowed trade and commerce, without replacing it, as a fundamental bulwark of the city's economic structure.[1] The annual value of manufactured products increased more than tenfold during the period, forging ahead consistently from an output valued at $18,798,122 in 1869 to $43,473,812 in 1879, $97,503,951 in 1889, $123,786,449 in 1899, and $208,323,630 in 1909. The last of these decades saw the most remarkable industrial growth in the history of the city, as in the nation at large, to date. The percentage of increase in the gross value of manufactured products was 88 percent from 1899 to 1909, a gain for the ten-year period almost equal to the increase in the entire sixty years preceding. Old and established lines continued to expand at an almost phenomenal rate, and new industries grew large in a single decade.[2] On the other hand, while some departments of trade and commerce continued to flourish, in others there was an actual decline. For example, shipments of wheat from Milwaukee, which totaled 22,681,020 bushels in 1875, had fallen by

[1] See statement of veteran secretary of Chamber of Commerce, William J. Langson, in Chamber of Commerce, *Report*, 1904, p. 27.
[2] The basis of these figures is not altogether consistent. The figure for 1869 is for Milwaukee County. Industries conducted by less than three establishments were not reported by the U.S. Census. Whitbeck, *Geography of Southeastern Wisconsin*, 87, 90-93. See also *United States Census, Ninth*, 1870, vol. 3, *Statistics of Wealth and Industry of the U. S.*, 744; *United States Census, Tenth*, 1880, *Rept. on Manufactures of the U. S.*, 374-75; *United States Census, Thirteenth*, 1910, vol. 8, *Manufactures, 1909*, p. 115. See appendix for chart showing persons and capital employed in industrial pursuits in Milwaukee, 1860-1939.

1880 to less than 10,000,000 bushels and a decade later failed to reach 2,000,000.[3] By the close of the period, Milwaukeeans, reversing a long-held conviction, regarded manufacturing rather than commerce as the surest safeguard of civic stability.

This economic revolution was in part a result of the industrial specialization which the growth and development of the city's hinterland made possible; it was induced by the expansion of the local consumer market, the advent of potential workers, and the increase of investable capital which attended the rise of the metropolis; it was stimulated by improved and extended transportation facilities which made it possible to supply the demand of the West for manufactured goods and the East with commodities fabricated from western raw materials; it came about, as well, as a response to a conscious effort to promote the city's growth. Editors of 1870, pondering the meaning of the census of that year, came to the conclusion that manufacturing was the major cause of urban development, that while commerce could make a city, manufacturing alone could keep it great.[4] The Chamber of Commerce asserted in 1871 that in addition to the commercial advantages which the city offered it supplied a potential "home market for more than four times the quantity of articles [now] manufactured here"; and the burden of Mayor Ludington's inaugural admonitions against high taxes was his argument that "Manufactures we must have, if we would prosper."[5] To the vast loans of credit for railroads and harbor improvement which had supported the commercial pre-eminence achieved in the preceding period, the corporate entity was now to add a vigorous promotion of manufacturing as a stimulus to city growth.

The decade from 1870 to 1880 saw substantial if not rapid advance in types of manufacturing which had begun to take

[3] Whitbeck, *Geography of Southeastern Wisconsin*, 62.

[4] The editor of the *Sentinel* wrote: "Another fact shown by the Massachusetts census (and one which the people of Milwaukee will do well to ponder) is the great advantage resulting from the introduction of manufactures. Numerous instances of large and rapid growth find their explanations in this." Milwaukee *Sentinel*, Oct. 22, 1870.

[5] Whitbeck, *Geography of Southeastern Wisconsin*, 89; Milwaukee *Sentinel*, April 19, 1871.

shape in the preceding decade. The lack of banking capital and skilled labor and the continued preference of local capitalists for subsidies to railroads rather than for investments to develop territories opened up by them still retarded somewhat the growth of industry.[6] By 1877, however, the inhibiting effects of the panic of 1873—which had not seriously affected the city—had disappeared; and factories, rolling mills, and blast furnaces were in a flourishing condition. Calculations made at the close of the decade revealed that during the seventies the lines of manufacturing which produced goods valued at over $2,000,000 had increased from one to seven.[7] The eighties ushered in an expansion which led the editor of the *Evening Wisconsin* (Milwaukee) to write: "All the signs tend to confirm the flattering prediction often made that Milwaukee is to become *the* manufacturing metropolis of the West." Capital formerly loaned on wheat receipts was flowing into manufacturing channels. Per capita bank deposits increased from $67 in 1871, to $120 in 1881, and $132 ten years later. Resident capitalists as well as those from the interior of the State with money to lend were looking for investments in industry. Real estate agencies were swamped with requests for manufacturing sites and residences for mechanics who had been "attracted from all parts of the country by hearing Milwaukee spoken of as a manufacturing city and a good place in which to obtain work." According to the *Evening Wisconsin*, the city's manufacturing interests were "expanding like a green bay-tree, and the amount of population which [was] pouring into the South Side, where most of the manufactories [were] being established [was] a marvel to the oldest citizens."[8]

[6] President West, of the Chamber of Commerce, counseled in 1872 that the city ought to spend more effort bringing manufactures to the city than on building railroads through every hamlet in the country. "The people of the West," he said, "seem to think that their salvation depends upon overrunning and settling the whole country in the present decade. Overrunning a country is not developing it, and should we go a little slower and fill in better as we go, and reserve a little of our new territory for the enterprise of the next generation it might be just as well for the future of the country." *Ibid.*, April 9, 1872.
[7] Whitbeck, *Geography of Southeastern Wisconsin*, 89.
[8] *Evening Wisconsin* (Milwaukee), Nov. 10, 21, 29, 1881; William J. Anderson and Julius Bleyer, ed., *Milwaukee's Great Industries* (Milwaukee, 1892), 70-72.

With the general commercial depression of 1883 came a setback for industry, and marked activity in manufacturing establishments was not again noted until 1889; but by 1892 the progress of manufacturing was such as to convince observers that the city's future depended upon industry, that the time was past when "Western towns" could "rest content . . . upon purely commercial pursuits."[9] This trend was seriously interrupted by the panic of 1893 which, unlike that of twenty years earlier, hit Milwaukee with great severity. Five banks were forced to close; and though no bad failures occurred among the manufacturing plants, work was suspended and wages were reduced.[10] The gradual resumption of manufacturing in 1895 brought a reassertion of the claim that "the prosperity of Milwaukee and its future growth" were "dependent in a large measure upon the success of its manufacturing industries."

Business in 1897 was better than in the preceding year, which had been beset by election uncertainties. Labor was more generally employed, and some factories were working to the limit. A flood of foreign orders for heavy machinery swelled profits in 1898; and in 1899 the plants were taxed beyond their capacity.[11] In 1902 the total volume of production exceeded $200,000,000;[12] and by 1904 few observers doubted that industry was more important than commerce to the economic health of the community[13]—an opinion that gained strength during the remainder of the decade as annual

[9] Chamber of Commerce, *Report*, 1889-90, p. 27; *ibid.*, 1892, p. 42; Anderson and Bleyer, *Milwaukee's Great Industries*, 200.

[10] The Plankinton Bank closed, June 1, 1893; the Commercial Bank, July 19; the South Side Savings Bank and the Milwaukee National Bank, July 22; and the Milwaukee Marine and Fire Insurance Company Bank, July 25. Three of the five were able to resume business without loss to the depositors. Gregory, *History*, 2:1212; Chamber of Commerce, *Report*, 1893, p. 31; *ibid.*, 1895, p. 36.

[11] *Ibid.*, 1896, p. 41; *ibid.*, 1897, p. 30; *ibid.*, 1898, p. 36; *ibid.*, 1899, p. 29.

[12] "Employment of labor is essential to growth in population," continued the writer. "Labor is the great wealth producer. Upon its fruits all branches of trade depend for success. When a city of 300,000 population produces over $200,000,000 worth of manufactured products in a year as the results of the labor of 72,998 of its inhabitants, who receive over $36,000,000 in wages during the year, the secret of the general prosperity of that city and of its substantial growth in every important regard is clearly revealed." Milwaukee *Sentinel*, Jan. 1, 1902; Chamber of Commerce, *Report*, 1903, p. 28.

[13] *Ibid.*, 1904, p. 30.

output climbed by 1909 to double the figure of ten years before.[14] The last half of the decade saw an almost phenomenal expansion, when there was a 37 percent increase in wage earners, as contrasted with the 5 percent increase from 1899 to 1904, and a 51 percent increase in value of output as compared to a 25 percent increase in the first half of the decade. "Hands employed" in the major industrial pursuits in 1870, exclusive of the packing industry, totaled 4,352. By 1880 the number, including packing workers, had jumped to 13,782; by 1899 the total of "persons engaged" stood at 45,297; and in 1909, at 68,933. In 1879 per capita production of manufactures approximated $165 in value; by 1909 the figure had risen to $550. Moreover, the consolidation of management already being noted in the sixties continued to prevail. According to a Chamber of Commerce figure, the number of firms increased only 2 percent between 1870 and 1880; while "hands employed" increased 147 percent. Whereas the number of establishments increased only 24 percent between 1899 and 1909, there was just short of a 50 percent increase during that period in the number of persons engaged in factory work.[15]

The increasing interest in manufacturing did not mean that trade and commerce ceased to figure significantly in the urban economy. As a matter of fact, the development of manufacturing served in a sense to augment the city's commerce. But as in the case of the traffic in wheat, activity in some lines of trade reached its peak early in the period and declined thereafter. In the early seventies Milwaukee ranked

[14] Milwaukee suffered comparatively little from the financial disturbance of 1907-8. The banks experienced no loss, although deposits fell off somewhat. To safeguard themselves the banks followed the eastern practice of giving out clearing-house certificates, thus saving their currency for an emergency which fortunately failed to materialize. The first decade of the twentieth century saw marked industrial development throughout the nation. The gross value of manufactured products increased 80 percent during the decade in the nation at large; for Milwaukee the increase was 88 percent. Watrous, 1:574; Whitbeck, *Geography of Southeastern Wisconsin*, 92.

[15] *United States Census, Thirteenth*, 1910, vol. 8, *Manufactures, 1909*, p. 115; *United States Census, Ninth*, 1870, vol. 3, *Statistics of Wealth and Industry of the U. S.*, 744; *United States Census, Tenth*, 1880, *Rept. on Manufactures of the U. S.*, 374-75; *Milwaukee Sentinel*, April 13, 1886. For a tabulation of these figures, see appendix for chart showing persons and capital employed in industrial pursuits in Milwaukee, 1860 to 1939.

as the largest primary wheat market in the world. The high point in the trade was attained in 1873 when, of the some 32,500,000 bushels of grain handled, 28,457,000 bushels were wheat. In the later seventies, poor crops began to reduce imports; and by the eighties changed conditions in the region of supply diminished the flow. With the extension of railroads and the westward movement of population, Wisconsin wheatgrowers had difficulty in competing with producers who were cultivating cheaper and more fertile lands. Great increases in wheat imports from Russia and India combined with the product of the Middle Border to keep the price of wheat at a persistently low level. In consequence, from 1890 to 1910 the per capita yield for the entire State declined 37 percent, as Wisconsin farmers, and especially those in the immediate vicinity of Milwaukee, turned from the production of wheat to such specialties as dairying and cheese making.[16]

Moreover, dangerous rivals were attracting the supply that formerly flowed to the Wisconsin metropolis. The "milling-in-transit" privilege, by which wheat was stopped at a given point en route, manufactured into flour, and then moved to its destination at the original rates, gave the smaller cities of the State a relative advantage over Milwaukee; and with the movement of the wheat fields north and west, Minneapolis and Duluth competed for a supply that formerly made its way southward. By 1881, it was recognized that the prosperity of the city was no longer dependent on wheat; and by 1886 the city's primacy in the wheat trade had become a memory.[17] Compensation for the decline in this field was found, for a time, in increased activity in the production of flour and, more permanently, in the trade in coarse grains, produced in the vicinity to meet the need of the malting and brewing, as well as the milling, industries. By the nineties, receipts of these grains were such as to approach the imports of the seventies; and in 1910 more than 48,000,000 bushels were received.[18]

[16] Milwaukee *Sentinel*, April 24, 1873; Jan. 1, 1921; Thompson, *Wheat Growing in Wisconsin*, 82-102.
[17] *Ibid.*, 105-10; Chamber of Commerce, *Report*, 1881, p. 24; *ibid.*, 1886, p. 29.
[18] Thompson, *Wheat Growing in Wisconsin*, 111; Whitbeck, *Geography of Southeastern Wisconsin*, 62.

Dealings in grain in this period were carried on largely at the Chamber of Commerce where, according to Secretary William J. Langson, the first trading pit was inaugurated in 1870. This was the scene of the sometimes boisterous practices that came to characterize activities on the Exchange. "Piking" and "pounding the market," dealing on margin, and attempts to "corner" were a few of the speculative maneuvers which lent excitement and uncertainty to the produce business. In 1875 Peter McGeoch and Nelson Van Kirk, finding themselves possessed of an abundance of wheat in a year when harvests were heavy, attempted to corner the market in order to prevent a drop in prices. This they might have done but for the fact that the St. Paul Railway issued wheat receipts not only for the grain that was in their Milwaukee elevators but also for wheat as much as 250 miles away on cars en route for the city. McGeoch later made up for his losses on this deal when in 1878 unexpectedly poor crops brought him and John Plankinton high profit on wheat that dealers expected them to have to sell "short." In 1883-84 another titan among the traders, William Young, and his brother, Alexander M. Young, attempted to corner wheat; but a bountiful harvest in the latter year frustrated their plans and sent the speculators "to the wall."[19] Few fortunes were made and kept in these speculative operations, but behind the scenes in these as well as in so many other financial enterprises of the period was evidence of the profit-making activities of the city's most prominent financier and banker, Alexander Mitchell.

Unlike the traffic in wheat, the decline in which was offset only in part by the trade in coarse grains, the wholesalers' business experienced continuous expansion, a development which the extension of railroad lines in the seventies tended to stimulate. By 1873, ten lines of railroad, with fourteen branches, radiated from the city. Four years later, connections were completed with Ashland on Lake Superior; and the establishment of a line of steamers from Milwaukee to Ludington, Michigan,

---

[19] Gregory, *History*, 1:482-83, 485. A year-by-year account of the commercial development of Milwaukee is to be found in the annual statements of the trade and commerce of the city compiled for the Chamber of Commerce by William J. Langson, its secretary from the middle sixties until 1908.

linked the city with trunk line railroads leading to the eastern coast. Commerce, retarded with the depression of 1883 and the years following, had picked up by 1891, when the general volume of trade exceeded that of any former year. In 1899, the Chamber of Commerce reported that jobbers' and merchants' sales had reached a new high; and in 1901 the business of the wholesale trading concerns had passed the $300,000,000 mark when manufactured products, though developing at comparatively greater speed, still aggregated in annual value little more than $200,000,000. By 1907 the wholesale business approximated $442,414,742; and the increased trade in coarse grains, extended lake tonnage, and expansion of banking attested the continued commercial advance of the first decade of the new century.[20]

The rapidly expanding manufactures, like the industries in the other cities of the Central states, had their foundations, as already has been pointed out, in the raw materials supplied by the farms and forests of the State and its neighbors.[21] This was especially true of flour milling, meat packing, tanning, and brewing, and even of the iron and steel industry, which relied upon a supply of iron mined in Wisconsin, augmented by ore from the Lake Superior region. These five locally supported industries were consistently predominant in the period from 1870 to 1910, save for the fact that the clothing industry was among the leaders in 1870 and that flour milling had reached the peak of its importance by the close of the first decade of the twentieth century. Flour production in the city increased relatively steadily from 1870 to 1892 during which time the annual production in barrels increased from 530,049 to 2,117,009. A new process of milling, introduced by 1874, might have permitted Milwaukee's production to exceed that of her rival, St. Louis, had it not been that the production of wheat in the immediate vicinity was falling off and that the opening of the Northwest made Minneapolis a more natural milling center. Nevertheless, the period from 1889 to 1892 saw a 50 percent

[20] Chamber of Commerce, *Report,* 1873, p. 18; *ibid.,* 1877, p. 19; *ibid.,* 1899, p. 29; Milwaukee *Sentinel,* Jan. 1, 1902; Watrous, 1:581.
[21] See chapter 8.

increase in flour production. Minneapolis, however, now constituted so serious a threat that the Milwaukee Chamber of Commerce was forced to go before the Interstate Commerce Commission in 1897 in an attempt to curtail discriminatory collusion between Minneapolis millers and the railroads. By 1909 Milwaukee still ranked as the third city of the nation in the value of flour manufactured, but at that date her output was less than 70 percent of what it had been in 1892, and in 1915 it attained less than a third of that figure.[22]

The advance of the brewing industry provides a more convincing barometer of the truly remarkable increase of manufacturing in the urban economy during these years. A twenty-sixfold expansion raised the annual output from 142,000 barrels in 1871 to 3,700,000 in 1910. On the turn of the nineties, heyday of the city's Germandom, brewing was the city's first industry; and while other kinds of production ultimately replaced it as "the central pillar in the temple of Milwaukee's advancement," the industry experienced consistent growth for many years. This was to a considerable extent the result of broadened financial foundations, new processes of manufacture, the exploitation of wider markets, and recourse to high-powered techniques of advertising.[23]

New names are associated with the financial expansion and reorganization of the brewing firms in the post-Civil War era. The association of Captain Frederick Pabst with the Best Brewing Company in the early sixties provided this firm with the leadership of one of Milwaukee's most dynamic business personalities. Having migrated from Germany at the age of twelve, young Pabst worked his way from cook's assistant and cabin boy to the captaincy of one of the lake vessels of the Goodrich line. In 1864, at the age of twenty-eight, he became a partner of Phillip Best, whose daughter he had married some years earlier; and with Best's retirement in 1866 he became responsible for

[22] Thompson, *Wheat Growing in Wisconsin*, 109-11; Whitbeck, *Geography of Southeastern Wisconsin*, 100-101.
[23] See Chamber of Commerce, *Report*, 1918; Anderson and Bleyer, *Milwaukee's Great Industries*, 166; *One Hundred Years of Brewing, passim*; Herman Schlüter, *The Brewing Industry and the Brewery Workers Movement in America* (Cincinnati, 1910).

the management of the brewery together with another of Best's sons-in-law, Emil Schandein. As business was extended within the boundaries of other states it became expedient to relieve these partners of individual responsibility; and incorporation as the Phillip Best Brewing Company was the result in 1873, with a capitalization of $300,000 that stood at $4,000,000 by the close of the eighties and by 1892, at ten. The Best Company, whose name was changed to Pabst in 1889, following the death of Schandein, made tremendous forward strides in the period from 1873 to 1893, at which time an output of more than a million barrels made Pabst the nation's first producer. The output of the Schlitz Company surpassed that of Pabst in 1902, a supremacy it maintained until the prohibition era.[24]

The name of Uihlein figured prominently in the evolution of the Joseph Schlitz Brewing Company, which was organized with a capitalization of $200,000 in 1874. August Uihlein, born of a family of Bavarian brewers, had come to America at the age of nine, received his education at Engelmann's German-English School, and early found employment in the brewery of his uncle Krug. Upon the latter's death this fell into the hands of Joseph Schlitz. Soon Uihlein and his brothers were holding responsible positions in the Schlitz Company; on Schlitz's death by shipwreck in 1875 they came into control of the business. Henry became president and Alfred, the brewmaster; but August, owning the majority of the stock, ruled by common consent under the unassuming title of "secretary and treasurer." As in the case of Pabst's widely ramified enterprises, the financial foundations of the Schlitz Company were doubly secured by investments in real estate and banking and insurance operations. The Schlitz Brewing Company was capitalized at $12,000,000 in 1903.[25] The Blatz brewing interests were in-

[24] Barton, *Industrial History of Milwaukee*, 114. See also Milwaukee *Sentinel*, Jan. 10, 1932. For an intensive study of the financial development and business operations of one of the brewing companies in this period, see Cochran, *The Pabst Brewing Company*, chaps. 4-9. Professor Cochran finds the explanation of Pabst's accomplishments of these years in the company's flexible, efficient management, its traditionally skilled labor, its progressive technology as exhibited in the introduction of new mechanical methods, its well-calculated plant expansion, the successful acquisition of the business of two large competitors, aggressive sales promotion, and the personal promotion of Captain Fred Pabst.

[25] Barton, *Industrial History of Milwaukee*, 125; Milwaukee *Sentinel*, Jan. 17, 1932.

corporated in 1889 as the Val Blatz Brewing Company with a capitalization of $2,000,000. In 1891, Valentin Blatz sold out to a group of London financiers known in brewing circles as "the English syndicate." On the death of Frederick Miller in 1888, responsibility for his brewery, then having a capacity of 80,000 barrels a year, fell to his sons Ernest and Fred who reorganized it, put up new buildings, and increased the output. The Gettelman Company took shape in 1877 when Adam Gettelman applied his name to a brewery, founded in 1854, which his wife had inherited.[26]

Part of the progress of the industry is to be explained by innovations in method which the brewers were quick to institute. Milwaukee's brewers were professionals, many of them schooled in the European traditions of the trade. In 1883 William J. Uihlein, assistant superintendent of the Schlitz Company, brought the first yeast culture apparatus from Denmark to the United States. By the end of the seventies the larger companies were expanding physical facilities: building great elevators —to which the barley was carried by wagon; huge tanks—where the grain was soaked preparatory to sprouting on the malting floor; refrigeration plants, first installed by Pabst in 1878, which cooled the brew once the wort had been boiled with hops; and cavernous underground vats for storing the liquor until it became lager beer. Improved bottling facilities were installed in the later seventies to accommodate this new method of marketing the brew. At Schlitz a crude bottle-washing apparatus was operated by young women, after which the beer was pumped from kegs and the bottles corked, wired, labeled, and packed in barrels preparatory to horse-drawn delivery. The Pabst plant began to bottle beer in 1875; by the early eighties the bows of blue ribbon then being attached by hand to the bottles of its "Select" beer were setting a precedent which led to the adoption of the "Blue Ribbon" trade name in the later nineties. In 1890, when the capacity of the Pabst plant had reached 700,000 barrels, Captain Pabst built "the largest bottling plant in the country" with "the first underground beer pipe line from the cellars to the bottle house." The same year saw the Miller Company installing electric lights. By the middle eighties the

[26] *One Hundred Years of Brewing*, 333; Milwaukee *Sentinel*, Jan. 24, 31, 1932.

plants were becoming increasingly conscious of the bearing of scientific knowledge on the brewing process. Trained chemists were attached to their staffs; and innovations such as the Schlitz brown bottle resulted from their scientific study of such problems as the effect of light on beer.[27]

But annual sales of Milwaukee beer could not have increased from 108,842 barrels in 1870 to 1,809,066 barrels twenty years later had it not been for the zeal with which its promoters widened the market for the product and the ingenuity with which they advertised it. Promotion was the keynote of Pabst's great period of expansion from 1873 to 1893; and by the close of the period the company was expending as much as $69,000 annually on this newly developing marketing technique. Determining to capture the urban market for his "Blue Ribbon" product and identify it with people and places of taste, Captain Pabst established fashionable outlets for the exclusive sale of his brew not only in Milwaukee but in Chicago, San Francisco, Minneapolis, and especially in New York. Here he established the Pabst Hotel, a hostelry for bachelors at Times Square, a restaurant and theater at Columbus Circle, a pavilion called Pabst's Loop at Concy Island, and what was at its opening in 1900 the largest restaurant in America, the Pabst Harlem located near Eighth Avenue at 125th. He employed matinee idols to visit bars, buy beer for "the house," and drink to the health of Captain Fred Pabst, "Milwaukee's greatest beer brewer." At his instigation, signs, plastered on dead walls and wagon tops or hung from street cars, fore and aft, proclaimed, "Milwaukee beer is famous—Pabst has made it so." By curious coincidence or promotional ingenuity, Admiral Peary found a Pabst bottle near the North Pole. Schlitz advertising men were equally resourceful. A reward of 3,600 bottles of Schlitz to Admiral Dewey and his men for the capture of Manila led to an order for sixty-seven carloads of the brew for the Philip-

[27] Interview with Hugo W. Rohde, chief chemist, Jos. Schlitz Brewing Company, September 1941; Gustave G. Pabst, "The Brewing Industry in Milwaukee," in Anderson and Bleyer, *Milwaukee's Great Industries*, 161-67; "The Story That Malt Told," *ibid.*, 169-73; "Pabst, A Blue Ribbon Champion," *Modern Brewery Age*, 29 (August 1941); letter to author from G. R. Holtz, Advertising Department, Miller Brewing Company, Aug. 19, 1941.

pines. Schlitz beer went to Africa with Theodore Roosevelt; nine bottles were found in the stomach of a dead whale. From Europe to the Orient advertising tricks and by-words caused the product to be known. It was perhaps only by inadvertence that two such slogans served to publicize Milwaukee, too; but the result was such as to make the association of the product with the city traditional. "The beer that made Milwaukee famous"—the particularly effective advertising line which the Schlitz Company purchased for $5,000 from a smaller brewing concern, became the subject of a controversy between Schlitz and Pabst advertising men in 1898. As a result, the Pabst Company ultimately relinquished their original slogan because of its similarity to the more famous one to which Schlitz had a prior claim.[28]

In 1880, at the opening of the decade of great manufacturing expansion, meat packing was the city's first industry in point of value of goods produced. Seven packing establishments had an output valued at more than $6,000,000. As early as 1871 Milwaukee had become the nation's fourth largest packing city and almost the exclusive slaughtering and packing center for the State of Wisconsin.[29] Packing was confined principally to hogs; and the fate of the industry depended in large measure on the supply of those animals in the State. The Chamber of Commerce reported in 1877 and 1878 that a decline in prices due to the magnitude of the hog crop, especially in the latter year, had reduced the packers' profits. Reports of 1890, 1897 and 1898, and 1907 revealed that in these years packing progressively exceeded previous records. For the season ending February 28, 1898, the receipts of live hogs by railroad reached a total of 1,019,980, of which 1,002,044 were killed and packed in the city. The general use of refrigeration from the middle seventies forward made possible year-round activity in this pursuit. One of the leading firms of the period was Plankinton and Armour, which was dissolved in 1884 and reorganized

[28] Anderson and Bleyer, *Milwaukee's Great Industries,* 164; Milwaukee *Journal,* May 30, 1930; Milwaukee *Sentinel,* Jan. 10, 17, Feb. 7, 1932.
[29] Ninety percent of the hogs packed in Wisconsin in 1874 were slaughtered in Milwaukee. Whitbeck, *Geography of Southeastern Wisconsin,* 104.

under the name of John Plankinton and Company, with a new partner in the person of Patrick Cudahy. When John Plankinton retired from active business in 1888, the firm came under the control of the Cudahy brothers, who in 1893 moved their plant to Cudahy at the southern outskirts of the city. The Layton Company continued to do business on a large scale; and the Peter McGeoch Company, a new Plankinton Packing Company (1894), and the Bodden Packing Company were among the other firms which kept the industry among the city's four largest between 1880 and 1910.[30]

The decade of manufacturing advance saw a 400 percent growth in the tanning business and rewon for Milwaukee in 1890 a distinction the city had enjoyed in the early seventies: that of being the world's largest producer of plain tanned leather. Between 1880 and 1909 the annual value of the city's leather output increased from $2,101,195 to $27,484,000. Proximity to raw materials and expansion of the source of supply through the development of railroads help to explain the increased activity of these years. Receipts of hides increased from 117,255 in 1870 to 266,818 in 1880, 622,456 in 1890, 1,277,927 in 1900, and 1,765,840 in 1910. It was the result, too, of access to wider markets—in the eastern and southern states—and of innovations in method and management. The keynote in management was consolidation of control, a tendency early revealed in the incorporation of the Pfister and Vogel Company in 1872 and in predictions from the press in 1873 that with the demand for manufacturing sites along the river, "a general consolidation of like interests will . . . result, . . . by which more service would be performed with less expense (for buildings, machinery, insurance, etc.) than heretofore." The consequence of this trend was that whereas the average production rate quadrupled during the eighties the number of tanneries dropped from about twenty-seven to fourteen. Markets were broadened, and by the early twentieth century Pfister and Vogel had five tanneries together with marketing branches in Boston, New York, London, Northampton, Paris, and Milan. The search for

[30] Chamber of Commerce, *Report*, 1876, p. 13; *ibid.*, 1877, p. 17; *ibid.*, 1878, p. 18; *ibid.*, 1890, p. 34; *ibid.*, 1897, p. 37; *ibid.*, 1898, p. 35; *ibid.*, 1907, p. 36; Whitbeck, *Geography of Southeastern Wisconsin*, 105.

a new supply of hides led to tapping South American and European markets with a consequent appearance of combines of tanners and packers from the middle nineties forward. The trend toward consolidation of control in this industry was reflected in the $80,000,000 capitalization of the United States Leather Company in 1893.[31]

Meanwhile, innovations in methods of manufacture tended to concentrate tanning activities in the city. With the development of larger units of production and the resultant increase in capital, recourse was had to mechanical methods which shortened the process of tanning heavy hides from three years to eight months. The use of tannin extract, extensively after 1890, made the industry less dependent on the rapidly diminishing supply of tanbark; and with the substitution of the chemical, which could be imported by rail or boat, there was less reason for maintaining tanneries in the forested inland areas. Following the panic of 1893 the leather industry experienced a decline; and although some improvement began after 1895, not until 1905 had conditions returned to normal. A temporary setback occurred at the time of the panic of 1907.[32]

The city's geographical position and the needs and products of her hinterland made it natural that the iron and steel industry should early develop into one of the five major enterprises in the industrial life of the Wisconsin metropolis. The cities of the Great Lakes were the logical meeting place of iron ore, cheaply transported from the Iron Ridge and Lake Superior regions, and soft coal or coke, brought at low cost from Pennsylvania. Blast furnaces, steel works and rolling mills, and foundries and machine shops fashioned the rails, farm implements, and lumbering tools essential to the spread of civilization into the West, and with the rise of cities there was a demand for the heavy machinery necessary to the operation of large public works.

The six blast furnaces and two rolling mills of the Milwaukee Iron Company (Bay View works), established in 1866 as one of the constituent members of the Wisconsin Iron Com-

[31] *Ibid.*, 90, 109; Gregory, *History*, 1:537; Schefft, Tanning Industry in Wisconsin, appendix. See also *ibid.*, 40, 42, 67, 76.
[32] *Ibid.*, 48, 76.

pany, were producing 45,000 tons of railroad iron in the early seventies. More than 1,000 workers operated the puddle rolls, rail train, Burden squeezers, shears, straighteners, punches, and slotters which turned out the equipment needed by the multiplying railroads of the West. About 62,000 tons of ore were consumed annually, of which a third came from Escanaba in the company's own vessels, the rest by way of the Milwaukee and St. Paul Railway from Iron Ridge, where two-fifths of the iron mines were company owned. By 1873 the original capital of $250,000 had been increased to $1,500,000 in addition to $750,000 of cash capital used in the business.[33]

Upon the death of Captain E. B. Ward, prime mover in the industry, a reorganization brought into control J. J. Hagerman, as president, John H. Van Dyke, secretary, and Alexander Mitchell, treasurer. Financial difficulties after 1873 led to a reorganization by which in 1878 the Bay View works came into the possession of the North Chicago Rolling Mill Company which also leased the Minerva Furnace, the city's other major smelting plant. By 1885 this company was employing 1,500 men at $2.50 to $6.00 a day at the Bay View plant. It operated on a capital of more than $5,000,000 and owned plants at Milwaukee, North Chicago, and South Chicago. On this foundation was built the Illinois Steel Company which was organized in 1889 with a capital of $50,000,000 and which operated plants at Milwaukee, North and South Chicago, Joliet, Illinois, and the Union Steel Company's works at Chicago.[34]

The nature of iron-working enterprise tended to confine the pursuit originally to a small number of establishments, despite the comparatively great value of the output. The census of 1880 had reported two iron and steel establishments only; but the capital invested was listed as $1,300,000 and the annual value of the product, nearly $5,000,000. By the census of 1890, the iron and steel works reported a product valued at $7,410,213, which represented 83 percent of the output of this industry for the State as a whole. Shortly before the opening of

[33] *Wiley's American Iron Trade Manual* (New York, 1874), 178-79; Whitbeck, *Geography of Southeastern Wisconsin*, 113.

[34] Gregory, *History*, 1:555-56; Whitbeck, *Geography of Southeastern Wisconsin*, 114; Barton, *Industrial History of Milwaukee*, 58; Riley, *Development of Chicago*, 108.

the new century, iron and steel production in Milwaukee was affected by the tendency toward consolidation then prevailing throughout the nation. The stock of the Illinois Steel Company was purchased by the Federal Steel Company, which was acquiring many of the steel-producing facilities of the Great Lakes area together with the rail and lake transport connections on which distribution depended. In 1901 the Federal Steel Company became a part of the United States Steel Corporation, which in the first year of its existence accounted for "45% of the pig iron production of the country, 65% of the steel production, and 51% of the finished rolled products."[35]

The decade of the seventies also saw marked advances in another branch of the city's metal trades—the foundries and machine shops, whose annual output increased in value from $402,480 to $2,252,784 in these years. By 1889 the forty-four establishments engaged in this business were producing annually goods valued at $5,568,445; and by 1900 the figure stood at $14,495,362, making this for the moment the city's "first industry" in value of goods produced. By 1909 the value of foundry and machine-shop products was listed as $18,146,000. The increasing demand for the products of foundries and machine shops was in itself an index of the expanding industrial development of the community. Local industry required machines, millstones, engines, and pumps; and fast-growing inland cities duplicated the demand. Of the firms which arose to fill this need, the most outstanding was the Reliance Iron Works, an establishment which had grown out of the millstone factory founded by Decker and Seville in 1847 and which had come into the possession of E. P. Allis and others as a result of the financial revulsion ten years later. In 1860 Allis took over the concern himself and between that date and his death in 1889 he converted a business amounting to only $31,000 into an enterprise reporting an annual production averaging more than $3,000,000 a year.[36]

[35] *United States Census, Tenth,* 1880, *Rept. on Manufactures of the U. S.,* 374-75; Bur. of Labor and Ind. Statistics, Wisconsin, *Eleventh Biennial Rept.,* 1903-4, p. 363; E. D. McCallum, *The Iron and Steel Industry in the United States* (London, 1931), 118, 121.

[36] *United States Census, Ninth,* 1870, vol. 3, *Statistics of Wealth and Industry of the U.S.,* 744; *United States Census, Tenth,* 1880, *Rept. on Manufactures of the*

The secret of Allis' success was his ability to anticipate the mechanical needs of his market and to engage specialists capable of developing machinery to meet those needs. In 1869, when the city of Milwaukee was projecting a water system, he succeeded in underbidding all competitors to obtain a contract for the piping, although at the moment he had no machinery for making the pipe. He then went ahead to build the pumps and engines for the service.[37] To meet the demands of the locality for grist and sawmill machinery, he early specialized in the production of sawmill equipment and millstones. In 1873 the millstone department of the company had fifty men engaged solely in dressing stones. In 1876 Allis enlisted the services of W. D. Gray with whose assistance he introduced to America the roller system of grinding flour. By 1878 the Allis plant had built and installed the first all-roller flour mill in America for C. C. Washburn of Minneapolis, a step which led to the introduction of the roller system in all the large milling centers with a consequent stimulation to the business of the Reliance Works. In 1873, Allis had employed George M. Hinkley, sawmill expert; and developments started in that line of production. In 1885, the company installed the first band sawmill for the Jump River Lumber Company of Prentice, Wisconsin. The first all-iron band sawmill was placed on the market by the Allis Company in 1889; and in 1896 they produced the first successful electrically driven sawmill for a California company. In 1877 Allis brought to Milwaukee Edwin Reynolds, an employee of the famous Corliss Steam Engine Company of Providence, Rhode Island. In the fortunate choice of Reynolds, Allis procured an engineer who could design and build the great engines and power plants for mines, lumber mills, and public works which were becoming the specialty of the Allis organization in the nineties and

U.S., 374-75; Whitbeck, *Geography of Southeastern Wisconsin*, 91; Bur. of Labor and Ind. Statistics, Wisconsin, *Eleventh Biennial Rept.*, 1903-4, **p. 362;** Conard, 2:316; *Dictionary of American Biography*, 1:220; *United States Census, Thirteenth*, 1910, vol. 9, *Manufactures, 1909*, p. 1354.

[37] *Dictionary of American Biography*, 1:219-20. In 1869, Allis purchased the Bay State Iron Works of Watson and Goodnow, operating them as a branch. Gregory, *History*, 1:551.

INDUSTRIAL FOUNDATIONS   339

which permitted it increasingly to serve a national market.[38]

By the turn of the century, the expansion of the plant had dwarfed the equipment of thirty years earlier, but in the seventies Milwaukeeans pointed to the 18 power iron lathes, 2 hand lathes, 4 power wood lathes, 7 iron planers, 4 wood planing machines, 2 gig saws, 2 shaping machines, 8 stationary and 2 portable drill machines, 1 gear cutter, 2 milling machines, 1 slotting machine, 2 iron boring mills, 1 cutting-off machine, 3 bolt cutters, 1 iron punch, 2 steam hammers, 15 hand power cranes, 1 20-ton traveling crane, 4 rotary blowers, 5 cupolas, 5 boilers, and 5 steam engines as symbols of the industrial promise of the developing metropolis. When the twentieth century arrived, in this as in the other major industries of the city, production sought a national if not an international market, and company organization manifested the current trend toward financial consolidation. A reorganization of 1890 transformed Edward P. Allis & Company into the Edward P. Allis Company; and in 1901 it was one of four firms which consolidated to form the Allis-Chalmers Company. These included in addition to the Milwaukee company the Fraser and Chalmers Company of Chicago, specialists in mining and metallurgical machinery, pumps, and air compressors; the Gates Iron Works of Chicago, manufacturers of rock-crushing, cement, and mining machinery; and the Dickson Manufacturing Company, of Scranton, Pennsylvania, producers of Corliss engines and special machinery. With the completion of this merger, Allis-Chalmers' annual business exceeded $10,000,000. The company was employing 5,000 men in five plants and had branch offices in ten American cities and four outside the United States. In 1905 the Allis-Chalmers Company built the first "Manhattan Type" Angle Compound Corliss engine, one of twenty-four units ultimately produced for the New York subway system. The ability of the western city so to supply the nation's great Atlantic Coast metropolis might be said to mark the coming of age of Milwaukee's industrial economy.[39]

[38] *Pioneer Power: A Story of the Growth and Development of Allis-Chalmers Manufacturing Company* (Milwaukee, 1942), 16-18, 27-29; Conard, 2:317; Gregory, *History*, 1:552-53.

[39] *Wiley's American Iron Trade Manual*, 170; *Eighty-Eight Years of Progress,*

Meanwhile in the early eighties other small concerns were laying the foundations of later accomplishment in the machine and foundry field. A stock company known as Filer and Stowell was incorporated in 1880 on foundations laid by John Stowell when he established a small machine shop in the late fifties and in 1867 entered into partnership with Delos L. Filer for the production of sawmills and mill machinery. January 1880 saw the founding of the Geuder and Paeschke Manufacturing Company; while the machine and pattern shop of Alonzo Pawling and Henry Harnischfeger, opened early in the decade, was the birthplace of the Harnischfeger Corporation, which ultimately specialized in the manufacture of cranes. By 1908 railroad equipment and supplies constituted a manufacturing interest of great importance. Four shops with an invested capital of more than $10,000,000 were employing 7,400 men annually in this pursuit.[40]

The increasing industrialization of the urban community brought social consequences elsewhere described. Physically, the migration of industry to the outskirts of the city tended to disperse population in that direction and, incidentally, to deprive the city government of an important source of tax revenue. The decade of the nineties saw a greater increase in industrial production in the county as a whole than within the city limits, the increase for the county approximating 45 percent and that for the city only 34.2 percent. The value of manufactures in the county, outside the city limits, increased nearly tenfold during the decade. Moreover, the influx of immigrant workers recruited to meet the factories' needs led to the crowded conditions in urban housing which characterized the metropolitan society on the turn of the century. At one time or another the major industries experienced labor difficulties, but on the whole relations between capital and labor were harmonious.[41] As has been pointed out, the most serious

booklet issued by Allis-Chalmers Manufacturing Company (Milwaukee, Jan. 19, 1935), 37; *Pioneer Power: Story of Allis-Chalmers*, 41.
[40] Conard, 2:321-22; Gregory, *History*, 1:559-60; Watrous, 1:578.
[41] Bur. of Labor and Ind. Statistics, Wisconsin, *Eleventh Biennial Rept.*, 1903-4, p. 361. "Our labor difficulties have been of comparatively small moment, and readily adjusted. It is to be hoped that the same conciliatory spirit

crisis—a phase of a national contagion—came in 1886. The brewery workers struck in 1888, and in 1892, some 2,000 tannery workers began a six months' strike. John M. Stowell and E. P. Allis experienced marked success in their relations with labor. The existence of the Allis Mutual Aid Society tended to win the latter the confidence of his employees. Stowell frequently expressed his faith in the worker. "If I and my brethren of the manufacturing fraternity have the right to counsel (combine if you please) together," he wrote in 1882, "to establish adequate and uniform prices of our fabrics, shall we deny the same right to the men to put a price on their labor which is such a factor in the product?"[42]

The interests of the industrial tycoons of metropolitan Milwaukee, like those of the commercial leaders of the midcentury, were interrelated and bound together in many a commercial and financial undertaking—along the lines of banking, railroad promotion, real estate, and insurance—in the economic life of the city. Most of these businessmen reinvested their earnings in the expansion of their own plants or found use for them in other local enterprises. The Second Ward Savings Bank passed virtually into the hands of the brewers, with Joseph Schlitz, William H. Jacobs, Phillip Best, and Valentin Blatz in control. Ultimately Pabst and Schandein acquired Best's interests, as did August Uihlein that of Schlitz. Uihlein later took over the Pabst and Schandein stock; and at the time of the bank's merger with the First Wisconsin National it was popularly known as the "Uihlein Bank." Captain Pabst had taken the lead in organizing the Wisconsin National Bank, capitalized at a million dollars, in 1892. The brewing interests, especially, also made extensive real estate investments, especially in the construction of theaters and hotels. The activities of the Pabst Company along this line made it the largest property owner in Milwaukee in the nineties. Captain Pabst also became interested in the development of a traction line which ultimately became a subsidiary

which has obtained between employer and employee in the past will continue." Milwaukee *Sentinel*, April 15, 1900.

[42] Schefft, Tanning Industry in Wisconsin, 76; Milwaukee *Sentinel*, April 14, 1882.

of the Milwaukee Electric Railway and Light Company. Intermarriage among the wealthy increased holdings and doubled fortunes which were used in many ways to underwrite the social and economic development of the community, a contribution that came more through the promotion of industrial activity conducive to the prosperity of the city than by direct gift. However, such encouragement of the cultural life of the city as that of the great packers Layton and Plankinton, already referred to, should not be forgotten. And Ernest Miller, prominent brewer, bequeathed $2,500,000 to charity.[43] Although this generation of industrialists took an active part in organizations for the commercial promotion of the city, they were increasingly reluctant to hold public office for which they would have to make a political campaign. This trend was to become even more apparent in the twentieth century, when the commercial and professional leaders, unlike their prototypes who served personally in fire department and city council in the early years of village and cityhood, were content to influence the conduct of the government indirectly through serving on the boards of such citizens' groups as organized charities, the City Club, or the Citizens' Governmental Research Bureau.

Other factors beside the promotional ingenuity of the industrialists themselves speeded the industrial advances of the generation under discussion. One of these was the continued effort to make new markets available through the extension of transportation facilities. By 1873 the Chamber of Commerce was boasting that ten distinct lines of railroads radiated from the city, making Milwaukee the terminus for 4,000 miles of

---

[43] *Ibid.,* Jan. 31, 1932. Considerable detail on the relation of the Pabst interests to the developing community is to be found in Cochran, *The Pabst Brewing Company*, especially in chapter 10. Regarding their contribution, Professor Cochran writes: "Wealthy Americans of this period did not in general regard it as their duty to give large sums for the private promotion of the pursuits that their fathers had had little chance to appreciate or enjoy. The day of heavily endowed colleges, museums, and foundations had not yet dawned. The reinvestment of capital in business was generally regarded as more socially valuable and morally righteous than was the encouragement of 'nonproductive,' aesthetic, or intellectual pursuits. The Pabsts seem fairly typical, in these respects, of the business leaders of the rapidly developing Middle West."

railroad highway. "With one exception," read the report, "no other city on the continent enjoys more extended or ample lines of communication." A fleet of 120 vessels of all classes, with an aggregate tonnage of 23,276 tons, was at that time owned and registered at the port. The intervening years saw improvements in rail and lake communication until by 1908 it was asserted that Milwaukee was served, directly or indirectly, by more than 50,000 miles of rail connections. According to the 1908 yearbook of the Merchants' and Manufacturers' Association, the city was a terminal point for three railroad lines—the Chicago, Milwaukee and St. Paul, the Chicago and North Western, and the Wisconsin Central, the tracks of which extended north, west, and south from the city for a total of 17,000 miles. Moreover, the Pere Marquette and Grand Trunk systems carried goods from Milwaukee to their lines by way of large steel car-ferry boats, each with a capacity for carrying thirty freight cars loaded or empty at all seasons of the year. In addition to this, twelve regular break-bulk steamers plied to and from the port during the season of navigation. Owned and operated by the Pennsylvania, Lackawanna, Erie, and other large Eastern railroad systems, these vessels gave Milwaukee shippers a connection with the rail lines of such companies in the East. From the nineties forward, there was a marked expansion of lake commerce; and by 1908 plans were under way to improve it through the development of a turning basin.[44]

It was probably the recognition of what rail connections meant for city growth that at last quieted the long-cherished ambitions of the Wisconsin city to surpass in metropolitan stature her enterprising and aggressive neighbor at the base of the lake. In spite of both the aspirations and the pretensions of an earlier day, there was no combating the realities of geography and modern railroad engineering. C. J. Kershaw, speaking before the Chamber of Commerce in 1872, admitted that Milwaukee was "not Chicago," but asserted that, after all, there were "few cities" like the Illinois metropolis. "Still," he continued, "if Milwaukee be not Chicago, Milwaukee has

[44] Chamber of Commerce, *Report,* 1873, pp. 15, 17; Watrous, 1:583-85.

grown at a rate surpassed by a very limited number of cities in this whole Union." At the same time, Milwaukeeans lost no opportunity to glory in their city's primacy as a wheat market and to resist attempts on the part of the Chicago press to belittle or misrepresent her position in this respect. It was a blow to the city's pride when, in advocating an eighty-five-minute train between Chicago and Milwaukee, the Chicago *Journal of Commerce* referred to the latter as "the delightful suburb north of us," a slur which real estate promoters of the city had not forgotten as late as 1881.[45] By 1889, however, Milwaukeeans were willing to admit that there could be "but one Chicago" and to congratulate the Illinois city on her growth, "not only because we are honestly proud of her and glory in her progress, but because we are all in due degree sharers of the prosperity she enjoys." Nevertheless, despite the fact that Milwaukeeans had by the eighties resigned themselves to a second-place position in the race for metropolitan prominence, there continued to be occasional outcroppings of the old rivalry that had once sprung from the conviction that the Wisconsin metropolis could be the "Queen City of the West."[46]

Another potent factor contributing to both the industrial and commercial expansion of the generation was the promotional efforts of organized business interests; and although the development of manufacturing in the city coincided with a trend in that direction in the nation at large it is doubtful whether without such cooperative promotion accomplishment could have been nearly as great as it proved to be. As a contemporary wrote, associations of this sort were "a powerful element in promoting the welfare of the cities where they

[45] Milwaukee *Sentinel*, Feb. 4, April 6, 11, 1871; April 8, 9, 1872; April 15, 1873; April 10, Sept. 16, 1876; April 15, 1878; Jan. 5, 1881. "Our capitalists and real estate owners should some evening stand at either one of the bridges spanning the river and connecting the South and North Sides of the city at 6 o'clock and see the people returning from work. They then could better appreciate that Milwaukee is no longer a suburb of Chicago." *Evening Wisconsin*, Nov. 21, 1881.

[46] *Ibid.*, June 6, July 16, 1889; June 13, 1896. The editor contended that Chicago merchants were turning business away from Milwaukee by asserting, after the street railway strike in the Wisconsin city, that Milwaukee was not a safe place in which to trade.

exist."[47] In the course of the period from 1870 to 1910, the Chamber of Commerce, the Merchants' Association, the Association for the Advancement of Milwaukee, the Citizens' Business League, and the Jobbers' and Manufacturers' Association provided a continuous and powerful stimulus to the economic expansion of the urban community.

At the beginning of the seventies, the Chamber of Commerce, which had been transformed from the Corn Exchange in 1858, undertook to "make known the commercial advantages" of the city and to "secure the cooperation of those most largely interested in extending . . . commercial and manufacturing facilities." A committee on Commerce and Manufactures was established, and a fund of $860 was raised from the dues paid by members who joined the association in response to the new movement. This committee, under the chairmanship of O. H. Waldo, prevented the impending bankruptcy of the Newhall House, the commercial travelers' hotel, and undertook negotiations to establish direct railroad connections with northwestern Wisconsin and the water power of the upper Fox River. In this it reflected the faith of the chamber in the formula of the railroad and an extended commerce as the key to metropolitan growth. As one of the officers expressed it, "a few great cities" were putting forth mighty efforts to draw to themselves all the trade and commerce of the country"; and Milwaukee had "entered the lists, and already proved that she can neither be left out of the fight nor vanquished." At the same time, an interest in promoting manufactures led to the publication in 1871 of a list of the city's advantages for that purpose which included reference to fifteen miles of dockage on the finest bay of the lakes, water power, railroad facilities "nearly equal to those of Chicago," cheap land along the waterfront, low building costs, low taxes and a virtual freedom from municipal debt,

[47] *Ibid.*, April 30, 1881. In the yearbook of the Merchants' and Manufacturers' Association for 1908 it was asserted that American cities had found "that the enterprise and energy of individuals can be considerably augmented by co-operation of commercial, industrial, and professional factors. There are opportunities for promotion of local interests in every community—opportunities which cannot be fostered by single individuals on the one hand, nor by the municipal government on the other." Watrous, 1:578-79.

a labor supply 15 percent cheaper than that of Chicago, and the city's frugal, industrious, and productive German population. A year later the chamber chose a prominent industrialist as vice-president and heard him assert that since pig iron could be cheaply produced in the city, Wisconsin's "pigs of iron should be no less familiar [to the nation] than pigs of another kind." In 1873, the editor of the *Sentinel* proclaimed it to be the duty of the "Chamber, the city government, and every individual" who had "the interest of Milwaukee at heart to encourage and promote their [sic] growth by every legitimate and honest means in their power." In April 1874, it was reported that the chamber had increased from 338 to 445 members in the past year. During the middle eighties it concentrated on improving conditions in the commission trade between Milwaukee and New York.[48]

Meanwhile, the Merchants' Association was playing a similar role. By 1880 the 20 firms which had formed the organization in 1861 had become 101; by the middle nineties there were about 350 members. The toasts proposed at their annual banquets, held from 1878 through 1888, suggest the commercial focus of their interest. At the original banquet, on May 9, 1878, speakers toasted "The Merchants' Association," "The Chamber of Commerce," "The Banking Interests of the City of Milwaukee," "The Railroad Interests of Milwaukee," "The Mercantile Interests," and "The Press and the City of Milwaukee." The association attempted to advance the city's growth by such moves as that of 1876 when it voted to send three members to New York "to induce capital to come to Milwaukee and engage in the wholesale dry goods business," and by its promotion of railroad construction in 1879. Also throughout the period it kept its eye on national, state, and local politics and legislation affecting the commercial development of the metropolis.[49]

---

[48] Board of Directors of Chamber of Commerce, *Report*, carried in Milwaukee *Daily Sentinel*, April 12, 1870; Chamber of Commerce, *Report*, 1871, quoted in Whitbeck, *Geography of Southeastern Wisconsin*, 88; Milwaukee *Sentinel*, April 9, 1872; April 15, 1873; April 24, 1874; April 14, 1884.

[49] Conard, 1:285; Remey and Bruce, A Half-Century in Business Effort, pt. 1, chap. 1, p. 8; chap. 2, pp. 14-17; chap. 3, p. 12. In 1878, the association was agitating for repeal of a federal bankruptcy measure and also engaging in a

In 1879, the Merchants' Association joined with the Chamber of Commerce and the city council to organize an industrial exposition patterned after the Centennial Exposition which had been held in Philadelphia three years earlier. The committee representing the three organizations was made up of some of the most active promoters of the city's commercial and industrial growth. It included Charles G. Stark, John S. Ricker, Henry M. Mendel, J. A. Roundy, E. P. Matthews, G. W. Allen, John Black, William P. McLaren, David Ferguson, C. T. Bradley, William H. Jacobs, Elias Friend, H. S. Mack, E. P. Allis, Valentin Blatz, E. H. Brodhead, and Robert Hill. The Milwaukee Industrial Exposition Association was incorporated in the winter of 1880. Its first officers included John Plankinton, Fred Pabst, John R. Goodrich, Charles G. Stark, and Charles L. Pierce. Among the other business leaders who took an active part in this promotional enterprise were A. W. Rich, J. C. Iversen, August Uihlein, August Stirn, John Johnston, William Frankfurth, Isaac Ellsworth, Sebastian Brand, and Frederick C. Winkler; but many men of lesser note made their contribution to the capital stock of $300,000 through the purchase of shares at $10 each. The resulting building, of "modified Queen Anne . . . architecture, in which Norman and Gothic elements" were blended, was considered "magnificent" in its day. The exposition, opened in September 1881, was pronounced the best held in the country since the one in Philadelphia. Repeated annually for twenty-one years, it not only attracted the attention of the surrounding community to the industrial accomplishments of the city but, in addition, was a financial success. The final exposition was held in 1902, when its function was being wrested from it by the State Fair. On June 4, 1905, the exposition building was destroyed by fire, and four years later—September 21, 1909—the Auditorium, destined to be the gathering place of millions of future convention-goers, was opened on its site.[50]

controversy over the appointment of the local fire chief. In 1881, it was opposing State legislation against adulteration of food as detrimental to the commercial interests of the city and State. Remey and Bruce, A Half-Century in Business Effort, pt. 1, chap. 2, pp. 15-17.

[50] Milwaukee *Sentinel*, April 30, 1933; Conard, 2:295-96; Gregory, *History*, 1:495-506; Bruce, *Born in America*, 148.

At the same time, the city's promoters were employing other methods to acquaint the commercial hinterland with the benefits of the Milwaukee trade. As early as 1862, Captain D. P. Mapes was hired to visit communities tributary to Milwaukee in southwestern Wisconsin, Iowa, and Minnesota; and in 1878, trade excursions were begun. In June, 108 of Milwaukee's leading businessmen, including E. P. Allis and T. A. Chapman, visited cities in Wisconsin and Minnesota. Bach's band played, and speakers, among them the popular clergyman Dr. John Fulton, lauded the flourishing metropolis as a center of trade. These trips became annual undertakings and were carried on for several years with great success. A relaxation of the practice by 1886 led the Merchants' Association to assert that "Our merchants remain too much at home" and to recommend that committees of five or more representative merchants adopt the practice of making periodic visits to the larger cities, within a radius of 150 to 200 miles, whose trade was tributary to Milwaukee.[51]

The growing interest in the development of manufacturing as well as commerce was reflected in March 1888 in agitation for a "central bureau of information" for city promotion, similar to one then existing in Kansas City, and in the establishment of an advisory committee "for the commercial and general welfare of the city of Milwaukee."[52] The former enlisted the support of the Bankers' Association, the Chamber of Commerce, the newspapers, many clubs, the German-American societies, and the real estate interests of the community. Out of the recommendations of the advisory committee grew the Association for the Advancement of Milwaukee. Anything that would advance the city's interests was to be within the realm of the advancement association's work, but its primary concern was "to advertise to the world the advantages which the city had to offer to manufacturers seeking new locations." As a writer in the *Evening Wisconsin* phrased contemporary sentiment:

[51] Bruce, *History*, 1:393-94; *Evening Wisconsin*, Feb. 2, 1886.
[52] Milwaukee *Sentinel*, March 28, 1888. Members of the committee were John R. Goodrich, B. B. Hopkins, John Johnston, E. P. Allis, Elias Friend, E. H. Brodhead, and William Plankinton. Anderson and Bleyer, *Milwaukee's Great Industries*, xiii-xiv.

INDUSTRIAL FOUNDATIONS   349

It is not enough to sit in a comfortable counting-room and write a letter now and then inviting some enterprise to come . . . ; the manufactories should be urged to come; we should go out and "compel them to come in." Thus other manufacturing cities are doing with results profitable to themselves. . . . There must be tangible money inducement which hitherto Milwaukee has been unable to offer through lack of specific organization to this end.

Free rents for a period, free sites, and local subscription of capital were suggested as the bait Milwaukeeans should offer industry if the city were to fulfill its destiny as "the manufacturing metropolis of our boundless West."[53]

After the first nine months of its activity, Curt M. Treat, the secretary of the organization, was able to make a good report. Additional capital had been mobilized to help the Cream City Glass Company to resume operations; the Moore Manufacturing Company, the Midland Mazea Milling Company, and a "score of other manufactories" had been brought in; and answers had been written to hundreds of letters "seeking information relative to facilities afforded as a location for industries of different kinds." Personal subscriptions in the amount of $5,400 in 1888, $6,025 in 1889, and $1,850 in 1890, not all of which was collected, subsidized this promotion.[54] In 1890, C. C. Rogers, the new secretary, and B. M. Weil were instrumental in negotiating the establishment in Milwaukee of a western branch of the Troy Stove Works of Troy, New York. The Fuller-Warren Stove Company was organized, considerable stock being subscribed by Milwaukee capitalists; and this was but the beginning of activities for the procurement of industries that continued for several years.[55]

William W. Howard, writing in *Harper's Weekly* in July 1891, commented upon the recent movement to Milwaukee of manufacturers from other parts of the country and commended the association's efforts to resume the advertisement of Milwau-

[53] *Evening Wisconsin,* July 16, 1889; Anderson and Bleyer, *Milwaukee's Great Industries,* xiii.

[54] According to the *Sentinel,* the advancement of the city's industrial destiny awaited only the "modest assistance which every business man and citizen can with reason be expected to give." Milwaukee *Sentinel,* Jan. 9, 1889; *Evening Wisconsin,* Jan. 9, 1889; Anderson and Bleyer, *Milwaukee's Great Industries,* xvi, xvii, xix.

[55] *Ibid.,* xviii.

kee in the East.[56] Along with the other promotional organizations the advancement association was responsible for securing for Milwaukee the twenty-third National Encampment of the G.A.R., held in the city in August 1889, as well as conventions of many other societies.[57] In that year, A. W. Rich proposed to implement the work of the association by creating a fund, through stock subscription, to be invested at the discretion of a board of officers in any promising and businesslike manufacturing enterprise that should seek to establish itself in Milwaukee. This was not to be a donation but an investment for profit to piece out the capitalization of firms needing "additional funds for larger and more remunerative operations." Although the advancement association approved the plan, legal barriers caused abandonment of the project. The association itself was absorbed after several years by its parent organization, the Merchants' Association, and its work thereafter was done by one of the departments of the Merchants' and Manufacturers' Association.[58]

Promotional activities in the city at the opening of the twentieth century centered around the work of the Merchants' and Manufacturers' Association and its foster organization, the Jobbers' and Manufacturers' Association. The former grew out of a consolidation in 1894 of the Merchants' Association and the Manufacturers' Club, the latter having been organized in the early nineties to supply information, loan money to worthy projects, and promote the interests of the city's manufacturers in the State legislature. The first meeting of the new association was held on May 18, 1894. The appointment of a paid secretary led to an increase in membership of from 670 to 871 during 1903. The association's activities ran the gamut of the promotional enterprises that had characterized such organ-

[56] W. W. Howard, "The City of Milwaukee," *Harper's Weekly*, 35:538 (July 18, 1891).

[57] *Evening Wisconsin*, March 4, 24, June 2, July 13, 14, 16, 19, 22, 24, 1886; Jan. 9, 1889.

[58] *Ibid.*, June 5, 1889; Anderson and Bleyer, *Milwaukee's Great Industries*, xx; Gregory, *History*, 1:507. In January 1891 it was proposed that the Merchants' and Advancement associations, now composed of virtually the same people, be united, and that a full-time secretary, to be paid $5,000 or more yearly, be procured, a responsibility which the city itself might assume. Milwaukee *Daily Journal*, Jan. 12, 1891.

izations since the sixties. Better freight rates and improved transportation facilities were secured from the established railroads, and discriminations in favor of Minneapolis were brought to the attention of the Interstate Commerce Commission. In 1896 money was raised to bring the Baptist Young Peoples' Convention to the city and in the following year, the National Educational Association. In 1897, the association began to subsidize excursions of country merchants to the city. As time went on, its auxiliary organization, the Jobbers' and Manufacturers' Association, formally organized in 1901, induced the country merchants, by low railroad fares, to visit the city; by 1902, upwards of 70,000 circulars publicizing the merchants' excursions had been distributed throughout the Northwest.[59]

At the same time, the merchants continued their semi-annual visits to the city's commercial hinterland. There was no doubt, according to the *Sentinel*, that "these annual invasions into an ever-widening field of commercial possibilities" had "done Milwaukee good." With an itinerary that lay across southern Minnesota and reached as far as Sioux Falls, South Dakota, the spring trip of 1908 touched the territory of a dangerous northern rival. A special train was furnished by the Chicago, Milwaukee and St. Paul Railway. Stops were made at all the sizable towns along the way; at each, speakers extolled the city's advantages for trade; and the Merchants' and Manufacturers' octet sang. To these excursions was credited an increase of almost 100 percent in the wholesale business of the city during the course of the decade. Meanwhile the association continued with considerable success to devote time and effort to inducing manufacturers to locate in Milwaukee.[60] It was in line with the current expansion of civic responsibility that when William George Bruce became secretary of the society in 1907 he endeavored to widen its scope "from a purely commercial body

---

[59] *Ibid.*, Jan. 7, 1891; Remey and Bruce, *A Half-Century in Business Effort*, pt. 1, chap. 2, pp. 29-30; Bruce, *Born in America*, 100. A Commercial Club attained some prominence during 1889 to 1893.

[60] Milwaukee *Sentinel*, March 20, 1908; Watrous, 1:581. For the development of Milwaukee's chief rival in the Northwest, see Mildred L. Hartsough, *The Twin Cities as a Metropolitan Market* (Research Publications of the University of Minnesota, *Studies in the Social Sciences*, no. 18, Minneapolis, 1925).

to one that contemplated the civic and social progress of the community as well." In 1897 there was organized a Citizens' Business League, the object of which was to make a "systematic canvass" to bring conventions to the city, encourage pilgrimages of businessmen and merchants, and stimulate tourist travel. It carried on its work for eleven years, during which period it induced nearly a thousand conventions to meet in the city. Its functions were later assumed by the Association of Commerce.[61]

While organized effort was undoubtedly the most important factor in inducing the commercial and industrial growth of the city, the citizens, in both their individual and corporate capacity, did their part, and the newspapers never let them forget the existing need. As early as 1872 the president of the Chamber of Commerce asserted that the municipality itself must take the responsibility of city promotion. Its citizens needed to "cultivate the talent of brag," he said, "and whether at home or abroad . . . boast of Milwaukee, her beauty, her order, her growing trade, commerce, and manufactures." Property-minded citizens like Mayor Ludington continued to believe that low taxes would constitute the best attraction to population and industry. The increase in taxes from 21.22 mills on the dollar in 1870 to 28.43 mills in 1874 led him to assert in 1875, "Our city is now at a point in her prosperity and development where oppressive taxation alone can retard her progress."[62] On the other hand, this period saw less pressure for the subsidy of railroads as an aid to urban growth than did the period prior to the Civil War. Concern at this time was rather to achieve the abolition of rates which discriminated against the city's business interests. However, by 1906, Bruce was reverting to the old cry. "Milwaukee must be placed on the railroad map," he asserted, advocating that the mayor invite every railroad that had "a bona fide proposition to enter the city."[63]

[61] As a standard for accomplishment he asserted that "all conditions making for the health and comfort and the educational and moral progress of the people, in themselves wield a wholesome influence on the material advancement of the community." Bruce, *Born in America*, 163-64; Milwaukee *Sentinel*, Jan. 1, 1902; Watrous, 1:581; Gregory, *History*, 1:507-8.

[62] Milwaukee *Sentinel*, April 8, 1872; April 20, 1875. The tax was reduced to 25.64 mills in 1876. *Ibid.*, April 18, 1876.

[63] Letter, William George Bruce to author, Feb. 18, 1948.

The *Evening Wisconsin* labored to get the individual citizens to take even small investments in firms considering location in the city. It was a "dire necessity," wrote the editor in 1881, "to make Milwaukee more conspicuous and render it more attractive to outsiders and to induce them to select it for a permanent place of settlement." The decision of the Beloit Reaper Works to move to the city was said to have been influenced by Edward Barber, real estate dealer, who drove the agent of the company "over the Cream City and pointed out to him her many advantages." When the Whitehill Sewing Machine Company decided to locate in Milwaukee rather than Chicago "on account of the greater cheapness of labor and of building sites and material," leading Milwaukee capitalists rallied to the cause and agreed to raise $150,000, the city's quota of the stock.[64] From the late seventies forward there was a large output of promotional literature advertising the city. Among such items were Charles B. Harger: *Milwaukee Illustrated: Its Trade, Commerce, Manufacturing Interests, and Advantages as a Residence City* (1877); E. E. Barton, publisher: *Industrial History of Milwaukee, the Commercial, Manufacturing, and Railway Metropolis of the North-West* (1886); *Milwaukee's Great Industries*, published by the Advancement Association (1892); *Milwaukee: One Hundred Photogravures*, issued by the Milwaukee Real Estate Board (1892); *Milwaukee of Today: The Cream City of the Lakes* (1892); *Milwaukee the Beautiful* (1900); *Milwaukee Illustrated* (1901); *Milwaukee, a Bright Spot*, prepared by the Citizens' Business League (1902); and *Pictorial Milwaukee* (1904).[65]

[64] *Evening Wisconsin*, Jan. 7, March 26, Nov. 2, 1881.
[65] Other pictorial pamphlets and brochures descriptive of the city included *Along Grand Avenue* (1889), 17 pp.; *Along Prospect Avenue* (1889), 16 pp.; C. N. Caspar and Company, *Souvenir Album of the Cream City* (1902); Association for the Advancement of Milwaukee, *Souvenir* (1888), 20 plates; Caspar and Zahn, *City of Milwaukee* (1886); Silas Chapman, publisher, *In and Around Milwaukee* (1885), 44 pp. and maps; *City of Milwaukee*, a souvenir of the 24th Saengerfest, Milwaukee (1886); *Book of Milwaukee*, published by *Evening Wisconsin* (1901), 136 pp.; R. G. Frackelton, *Milwaukee Guide, 1896–97*, 160 pp.; Knell Publishing Company, *In and Around Milwaukee* (1904); Merchants' and Manufacturers' Association, *An Account of the Mercantile and Industrial Interests* (1903), 86 pp.; J. C. Miller, publisher, *Milwaukee, The Cream City* (1891), 96 pp.; Carnival Association, *Milwaukee and Its Commercial Industries* (1899); Milwaukee Real Estate Board, *Milwaukee, 100 Photogravures* (1892); Milwaukee

In no department of its life during the period from 1870 to 1910 was Milwaukee more the mirror of what was going on at the same time in the nation than in its economic development. The union of manufacturing with commerce as the economic basis of urban prosperity paralleled a trend that was currently characteristic of the United States as a whole. This was nowhere better symbolized than in the twofold interest of the Merchants' and Manufacturers' Association both in excursions to develop the wholesale trade and in the mobilization of capital to subsidize the establishment of factories in the city. It was revealed, too, in the dual interest in these respects of such a prominent industrialist as E. P. Allis and so successful a merchant as T. A. Chapman. With respect to the organizational evolution of the manufacturing enterprises, here again the experience of Milwaukee industry duplicated what was happening on the national scene. The incorporation of stock companies for brewing, tanning, and packing was the order of the day in the earlier seventies. Great increases in capitalization were uniformly true by the nineties, and at the advent of the new century, national consolidation, represented in the activities of such organizations as the United States Leather Company and the United States Steel Corporation, was binding Milwaukee industry more tightly than ever into the industrial fabric of the nation as a whole. So, too, the increasing diversification of Milwaukee's industries and the efforts of her industrialists to find a world market and to combine small producing units into a few large establishments approximated a pattern true of industrial activity elsewhere.

As in an earlier period promotion was a major factor in inducing commercial and industrial advance and, by conse-

Sentinel, publisher, *An Illustrated Description of Milwaukee* (1890); *Milwaukee Souvenir* (1877), 76 pp.; Milwaukee *Evening Wisconsin*, Souvenir Edition, *1891* (views, etc.); Milwaukee *Sentinel*, publisher, *Milwaukee Fifty-Three Years Ago* (1893); *Milwaukee of Today (Its Growth, Commerce, Manufactures, Financial Interest, etc.)* (Milwaukee, 1893), 240 pp.; Andrew Morrison, editor, *The City of Milwaukee* (1888), 143 pp.; *Picturesque Milwaukee: A Guide through the Cream City and Its Suburbs* (1901); *Pictorial Milwaukee: a Souvenir Album of the Cream City* (1902); W. H. Ranstead and Company, publishers, *Milwaukee in 1860*, 64 pp.; Yenowine and Pick, publishers, *Milwaukee, the Beautiful* (1900); G. H. Yenowine, publisher, *Milwaukee Illustrated Annual*, 1891-92, 1892-93.

quence, city growth; but in this generation a concern for manufacturing overshadowed that for real estate and railroads; and while individuals still took an active part in furthering the interests of the community, an increasingly prominent role in promotion was played by the organized business associations. Industrial titans like Allis, Plankinton, Pabst, the Uihleins, Becker, and Mitchell replaced the Kilbourns, Rogers, and Holtons of the earlier period as key figures in the economic life of the city; but of no little importance in advancing the community's developing economic stature were the growing group of industrial workers who manned the machines, the rank and file of small investors who helped to make their purchase possible, and the many newspaper editors and public-minded citizens whose identification of their welfare with that of the city and their loyalty to it caused them to agitate and support the economic expansion of the metropolis.[66]

[66] In discussing the great increase in industrial activity in April 1900, a writer in the Milwaukee *Sentinel* asserted: "In most cases the investments are made by Milwaukee capitalists. . . . In some cases, however, the industrial growth is the result of the incoming of capital from sources outside the city." Milwaukee *Sentinel*, April 15, 1900.

CHAPTER 14

Signs of a Municipal Conscience

THE platform pledges by which the political parties attempted to "sell" their candidates to the public in the forty years between 1870 and 1910 reveal the changing concept of municipal responsibility that accompanied the growth of the Wisconsin metropolis. At the opening of the generation the municipality was making only the initial moves toward providing a safe water supply and sewage disposal; police and health protection was still inadequate; firemen were serving on half pay; and the negative policy of the city's officialdom was exhibited in its promises to "lower . . . taxes," avoid "costly public improvements," and follow a "policy of strict economy and retrenchment."[1] By 1910, the expenditures of the fire, police, and health departments had increased manyfold; the existence of public waterworks, parks, and natatoria reflected a deepened concern for the welfare of the citizens; the accomplishments of science and industry were overcoming the inconveniences of urban living; and a party committed to a significantly expanded concept of urban service was about to assume control of the municipal government. These gains were not accomplished without the pressure of journalists and reformers, resort to the experience of other cities both in America and abroad, the competing play of political parties for popular support, and in some instances the existence of critical situations—prompted by the force of the expanding metropolis—

[1] According to Larson, "In 1871 the city had no waterworks, practically no paved streets, and only the beginnings of a sewerage system; the fire department was on half pay, the police force was inadequate, and the health department enjoyed little more than a nominal existence." Larson, *Financial and Administrative History*, 132. See also Mayor Harrison Ludington's inaugural remarks, April 20, 1875, in Milwaukee *Sentinel*, April 29, 1875.

which made action necessary. But when Zona Gale observed in 1910 that "almost within the last year" Milwaukee had "come to civic self-consciousness" she was testifying to a municipal maturity of which the achievements of the generation in the realm of urban services were the most positive sign.[2]

Although the constantly expanding population brought demands for added police protection, good order prevailed, generally speaking, throughout the period, and conditions foreshadowed the banner reputation the city was to win on this score in the twentieth century. In spite of the existence of a police force of only 42 members, or one for every 1,700 citizens, life and property, according to Mayor O'Neill's valedictory remarks in 1870, were at that date "more secure in Milwaukee than in any other city on the continent of equal or greater size" —and this at half the per capita cost for the same service in six of the principal cities of the nation. Twenty-five years later, Milwaukee continued to "hold the reputation of being one of the best policed cities in the country." The crime record of 1906 revealed that to Chicago's 22 murders, Milwaukee had 1, and 6 burglaries to Chicago's 840. It looked, as Mayor Rose said, as if "the larger Milwaukee gets, the better she gets." The growth of population prompted the addition of 25 patrolmen in 1874, making a total force of 67; and by 1888 the system comprised 2 lieutenants, 10 detectives, 150 patrolmen, and 11 traffic officers, plus 3 horse-drawn patrol wagons: all told, 1 member for every 1,100 Milwaukeeans. Newspaper references to the facilities of other cities, such as to Albany—"a smaller city with 118 men to our 59 and 5 stations to our one"—served to hasten additions to the force. Increases in per capita costs were from 55 cents in 1868 to 90 cents in 1888, $1.13 in 1899, and about $1.61 by 1910.[3]

Until the passage of the act creating the board of fire and police commissioners in 1885, by which the merit system was applied to the service, the police department was the football

[2] Gale, "Milwaukee," *Good Housekeeping*, 50:323 (March 1910).
[3] Milwaukee *Daily Sentinel*, April 20, 1870; Jan. 28, 1871; Milwaukee *Sentinel*, Feb. 17, 1876; April 22, 1896; March 11, 1906; "The Milwaukee Police Department," MS in Milwaukee Municipal Reference Library, unpaged; Larson, *Financial and Administrative History*, 121, 164.

of politics. Despite his good record, Chief William Beck was dropped from the force three times for political reasons. Beck, the Granville farmer of German birth who had been selected as the city's first chief of police because of his experience on the New York police force, served in this capacity from 1855 to 1862, from 1863 to 1878, and from 1880 to 1882. In the intervening periods, mayoral ambitions to build the police force into a political machine resulted in a succession of short-term incumbents. The consequent laxness in police protection contributed to the reform realized in 1885. Thereafter, the term of the chief depended on good behavior, and as a result the department was to have but two different leaders in the ensuing half century. Applicants for the force had to be from twenty-five to thirty-five years of age, stand at least 5 feet, 9 inches in height, weigh 150 pounds, and pass oral, written, and physical examinations. German-born John T. Janssen began a thirty-three-year term as chief of police in 1888. With the grip of party politics shaken from the force, the new chief—operating at times almost as a law unto himself—instituted reforms which on the whole improved the efficiency and discipline of the Milwaukee department. A relentless opponent of professional crime, Janssen was tolerant of many of the activities that made Milwaukee an "open town" on the turn of the century; and before he resigned in 1921 the corruptibility of many of his underlings was not without question.[4]

As in the case of the police force, the increase in population necessitated the expansion of fire fighting facilities. Last vestiges of the volunteer method of fire fighting, employed in the preceding generation, appear to have been abandoned when in 1871 a full-time paid fire service was authorized. The department grew from 53 firemen in 1870 to 119 in 1885. Per capita costs increased from 40 cents in 1868 to $1.25 some twenty years

[4] *Evening Wisconsin* (Milwaukee), Oct. 15, 1895; Milwaukee *Journal*, April 2, 1933; Milwaukee *Sentinel*, July 14, 1937; Daniel W. Hoan, *City Government: The Record of the Milwaukee Experiment* (New York, 1936), 198-206. The roster of chiefs included Col. W. S. Johnson, 1861-62; Herman L. Page, 1862-63; Daniel Kennedy, 1878-80; Robert Wasson, 1882-84; Lemuel Ellsworth, 1884-85; Florian J. Ries, 1885-88. For fire and police commission, see *Wisconsin Session Laws*, 1885, chap. 378.

later and reached more than $2.00 by the close of the first decade of the new century — expenditures which, per capita, were consistently greater than for police protection. Improved apparatus increased the efficiency of the department. A fire alarm telegraph was in operation by the close of 1869; sliding poles supplemented stairways in the fire houses, and electric attachments on the stall doors speeded the readying of horses and equipment in time of fire. A water tower, put in operation in 1888, met a need created by the increased height of buildings, the first fireboat was placed in service in 1889, and a Mitchell roadster, purchased in 1907 for the use of the chief engineer, became the fire department's first piece of motorized equipment. The careless and often faulty building construction incident to rapid urban development created a serious fire hazard and prompted agitation for precautionary measures in the form of adequate building regulations. Severe loss of life and property resulted from the burning of the Newhall House in 1883; and in the great fire in the Third Ward, nine years later, property worth $5,000,000 was destroyed, and 1,893 people were left homeless. Improved building inspection followed from the action of a citizens' committee formed as a result of the Third Ward fire; but the council was reluctant to take effective action; and not until the advent of the Socialist administration was a detailed inspection code worked out.[5]

Public-school facilities, like fire and police protection, had to expand with the physical growth of the city. By the late eighties Milwaukee needed three times the school equipment of 1870; the 22 schools of 1871 had increased to 37 in 1888 and the number of teachers, from 145 to 484. Expenditures for public schools grew from $112,811.09 in 1871 to $696,266.38 in 1890 and $1,072,882.82 in 1904. Although the population increased little more than fivefold from 1870 to 1910, school expenditures augmented at a rate twice that great in the course of the generation. The gradual multiplication of educational services showed an increasing concern for the needs of children and young people in an industrial society. Kindergarten educa-

[5] Larson, *Financial and Administrative History*, 120, 164; see "Fire Department Clippings," in Milwaukee Municipal Reference Library; Conard, 2:270-79.

tion was made available in 1878; evening classes on the elementary level in 1880 and on the high-school level ten years later; elementary and high-school summer sessions in 1892; a technical high school with day and evening classes in 1907; classes for the deaf in 1885, for the blind in 1907, and for the anemic and defective of speech in 1909. Free textbooks were provided in 1897; school lunches in 1904; and at this period also a program of free lectures for adults.[6]

The construction of streets and bridges presented a perennial problem to the rapidly growing city. The total of twenty-five bridges in 1874 had become about forty by 1888, the new ones having been built at an average cost of $34,000. The early seventies saw great activity in the addition of new streets and the grading and graveling of old ones. A marked extension of street construction resulted from the passage in 1873 of a law permitting the council to order street work without previous petition of the property owners in the locality concerned. In that year the city could boast only 57 miles of improved streets; but this figure had grown to nearly 220 miles by 1889. To 1872, little more than a beginning had been made in paving business streets that were to be given ever heavier wear as the city grew into a metropolis. Some paving had been done in 1854 on and near Wisconsin Street and in 1861 on Grand Avenue and West Water Street. From 1872 forward, however, paving became an important subject of discussion and experiment. In 1873, Mayor Ludington advised the council to inquire into the "best material used for street pavements in older cities"; and in the spring of 1878 the council instigated a thoroughgoing investigation of the city's 223 miles of streets, with resulting recommendations which exhibited no little comprehension of the problems of traffic and street improvement raised by rapid urban growth. The committee found that of the 75 miles of thoroughfares which might be called "improved," 16 were paved with wooden blocks, a mile and a quarter of which had been prepared by the Thilmany process; a quarter mile had been improved with

[6] Larson, *Financial and Administrative History*, 118-19, 151-52, 164; Citizens' Governmental Research Bureau of Milwaukee, *Growth of Milwaukee's City Governmental Activities, 1846 to 1947, Inclusive* (dittoed, Milwaukee, 1948).

URBAN SERVICES OF THE LATER NINETEENTH CENTURY:
Guardians of life and property in the early metropolitan period. *Above:*
Policemen at attention in front of the West Side Police Station in 1875.
Below: City firemen in action in the days of horse-drawn equipment.

Telford macadam, poorly laid; and the rest were "graveled." Correspondence with city engineers and other officials in Buffalo, Cleveland, Fort Wayne, the District of Columbia, and Chicago had revealed a preference for stone pavement and a general criticism of wooden blocks.

As a result of their studies the committee recommended that experiments be made with Medina sandstone and Telford macadam; that the pressure of traffic on Grand Avenue be relieved by extending and paving Canal Street; that the city purchase a steam road roller for the purpose of improving the Telford construction; and that so long as wooden pavement continued to be laid because of its quietness, relative cheapness, and ease of repair, an ordinance regulating the width of tires for heavily loaded vehicles be passed and enforced.[7] In spite of these recommendations as well as persistent mayoral admonitions on the subject of false economy, Milwaukee remained a city of wooden pavements until virtually the end of the century. In 1893, after studying the experience of Buffalo and Washington, D.C., a beginning was made with asphalt pavement, at a cost of $70,000 a mile; but of the 60 miles of paved streets in 1896, 55 were still paved with wood. After considerable agitation, a law was passed late in 1896 providing that henceforward streets would be paved with granite blocks, brick, or asphalt laid upon a concrete foundation.[8] Contracts for undertakings of this magnitude gave rise to opportunities for graft. As already pointed out, it was charged during the mayoral campaign of 1904 that as a result of Mayor Rose's manipulation of bids from dummy companies Milwaukee was paying $2.30 a yard for asphalt pavement that cost other cities only $1.56.

Police and fire protection, schools, and public thoroughfares were by now without question the city's charge, but in the matter of other urban services there was controversy as to which

[7] Larson, *Financial and Administrative History*, 115, 118; Milwaukee *Sentinel*, April 30, 1873; April 9, 1878.

[8] Larson, *Financial and Administrative History*, 148; *Evening Wisconsin*, Dec. 12, 1896. See also Milwaukee *Sentinel*, April 18, 1894. Originally a large part of the cost of paving was levied upon the abutting lots; but as the more expensive improvements were undertaken the municipality had to shoulder a larger share. Larson, *Financial and Administrative History*, 116-17.

should be the responsibility of the municipality and which could best remain in the hands of private enterprise. Mid-century plans for the provision of waterworks by private companies had failed to materialize. Negotiations with private contractors such as John Lockwood and the firm of Hubbard and Converse of Boston during the fifties and sixties had been without results; and it became apparent that if the legal obstacles to municipal investment in such undertakings could be overcome, the city itself would have to provide a water system. As Mayor Phillips said in 1870, "Wells and springs do not meet the community's immediate needs; an abundant supply of good pure water is a great desideratum for any city, and no city containing the population of Milwaukee should be without it."[9]

Upon the authorization of the legislature in 1868 the council employed E. S. Chesbrough, Chicago engineer, to report plans for water and sewerage systems. A reduction of liabilities sufficient to warrant new indebtedness occurred in 1870, whereupon the city was authorized to create a board of water commissioners and begin construction. Distinguished Milwaukeeans served gratuitously on the board, which included Alexander Mitchell, John Plankinton, Fred Pabst, Edward O'Neill, Guido Pfister, E. H. Brodhead, George Burnham, Matthew Keenan, secretary, and David Ferguson, treasurer. Keenan and Moses Lane, city engineer, toured the cities of the Atlantic coast for the purpose of studying their waterworks; and on their return they recommended that construction be started immediately on the basis of one of Chesbrough's plans. The first plant was completed on October 24, 1873; and shortly thereafter the works began to furnish water.[10] When the system was turned over to the board of public works in June 1875, its cost had reached $1,900,000 —40 percent more than the estimates of 1871. As Mayor Ludington declared, the completion of the waterworks marked "an epoch in the history of our city"; for with their construction the

[9] Milwaukee *Daily Sentinel,* April 20, 1870.
[10] This plant was composed of a pumping station on the lake, two pumping engines of 8,000,000-gallon capacity, an intake extending into the lake for a distance of 2,100 feet in 18 feet of water, a standpipe and reservoir of 21,000,000-gallon capacity, and fifty miles of distributing mains. Barton, *Industrial History of Milwaukee,* 39-40; Bohmann, *Milwaukee Water Works,* 4.

municipality was committed to supplying a commodity indispensable to the very existence of metropolitan life, a fact driven home in 1881 when a temporary shortage of water emphasized the dependence of the urban community in this respect for purposes of drinking and cooking, fire protection, sanitation, industrial uses, and the like. During the eighties and nineties the pressure of increasing population compelled the enlargement and expansion of the water supply system at great cost and effort; and by the close of the century there was a growing concern over the contamination of the city water with garbage and sewage, a problem which had not been resolved by 1910.[11]

The problem of disposing of the human and industrial waste of an increasingly crowded community constituted one of the major "growing pains" of urbanization and one for which Milwaukee found no satisfactory solution until more than forty years of trial and error had transpired. The independent practice of the wards in constructing underground conduits to carry sewage to the rivers and thence to the lake was by 1871 making the rivers a menace to the public health. In 1869 the board of public works advised the establishment of a complete plan of sewerage for the entire city; and two years later a commission of three engineers was appointed to "aid in devising a scheme for abating the river nuisance." The latter group recommended a system of intercepting sewers by which the waste, exclusive of storm water, instead of being discharged into the rivers, would be conveyed to a pumping station on Jones Island from whence it could be carried into the lake. Meanwhile, Health Commissioner James Johnson was consulting the experience of European and eastern American cities on the problem. Nothing was done about these suggestions until 1880, although by January 1, 1879, the mileage in sewers had increased to 93½, consisting in part of small brick conduits, in part of 18-inch pipes. With the increase in population during the early eighties, the situation had to be faced. On legislative order, the intercepting sewer was completed at a cost of $346,750 in 1886; and when

[11] Larson, *Financial and Administrative History*, 111; Bohmann, *Milwaukee Water Works*, 6, 8; Milwaukee *Sentinel*, April 20, 1875; *Evening Wisconsin*, July 19, 1881; Aug. 18, 25, Sept. 25, 1896.

this failed to solve all the difficulties, a flushing tunnel was constructed two years later at a cost of $240,744.88. By this time the total mileage in sewers had increased to 165, built at a cost of $2,116,127.93, of which sum the owners of abutting property must have paid about two-thirds. It soon appeared, however, that efforts to purify the river only putrified the lake, from which the city's water supply was drawn. A new commission, authorized in 1909 to study this question, proposed a system of intercepting sewers which would conduct the waste to a sewage plant in Bay View from whence, after partial treatment, it could be conveyed to the bottom of the lake. This recommendation did not bear fruit until the creation of the city sewerage commission in 1913.[12]

The city had been forced by necessity to furnish water and to provide a sewerage system, but opinion divided much more sharply on the question of whether it should engage in the business of garbage disposal. In this it would be undertaking a service which, more easily than in the case of the provision of water and sewerage facilities, could be performed by private contractors; and any solution of the issue was tied up with the increasingly controversial problem of municipal competition with private enterprise. Nevertheless, the bearing of the garbage question upon the public health made civic interference more readily justified than in the case of some other activities. As urbanization had enveloped the family chickenyard, traditional outlet for garbage disposal, city dwellers had contracted with private collectors who used the garbage to feed their hogs. The council's ban on the possession of these animals within most of the city limits curtailed this method of disposal; and in 1878 the city undertook the responsibility for garbage collection, its negotiations with a private contractor marking the beginning of a series of expedients by which the city handled the problem until a municipally owned garbage crematory was realized in 1903. The first contractor charged the city $3,120 for the service; by 1881 it was costing nearly $10,000, being performed by

[12] Milwaukee *Sentinel*, April 20, 1870; April 9, 1872; April 12, 1878; Gregory, *History*, 2:1142-43; Barton, *Industrial History of Milwaukee*, 41; Larson, *Financial and Administrative History*, 115-41.

farmers who made two trips daily, carrying the garbage to their farms.[13] When the neighboring towns refused the right of passage to these collectors, the garbage was transported down the river on barges for disposal in the lake; and, later, resort was had to burning which, since the method was applied within the city, raised a storm of protest. Every method of disposal provoked complications; but Milwaukee was not alone in her difficulties, for when Health Commissioner U. O. B. Wingate returned from the Kansas City convention of the American Public Health Association in October 1891 he reported that "the garbage problem was without doubt the most important subject which came up for discussion, . . . one which is occupying the attention of almost every board of health in the country."[14]

The middle nineties saw widespread support for a garbage crematory owned and operated by the city—one "fully able to convert into grease and fertilizer the maximum amount of garbage from a city of 275,000." The only misgivings, according to one writer, sprang from the city's need of going into the grease and fertilizer business, in which it would be too much to expect a success equal to that achieved by private individuals. Both Democrats and Social Democrats endorsed the proposal; and even many Republicans were willing to support public ownership of a project which, like the waterworks and sewerage system, had as its object "not convenience, but health." Even before the landslide for the "Popocrats" in April 1898 the council had sensed the public trend and on March 17 voted unanimously for a municipally owned plant. The issuance of $80,000 in bonds was authorized for the purpose, and the plant was put into operation about April 1, 1903.[15]

The attempt to achieve municipally owned street lighting facilities ran into more powerful commercial and political

[13] Regularized collection was beset with many annoyances. The citizens grumbled because garbage was not collected daily, but often showed their lack of cooperation by mixing ashes with their garbage and placing poisonous disinfectants in the refuse pending its collection.

[14] *Evening Wisconsin*, July 9, 1886; Milwaukee *Journal*, April 20, May 18, June 3, 10, 19, 20, 23, 24, July 8, 13, 16, 22, 31, Aug. 17, 18, Oct. 12, 26, Dec. 15, 1891.

[15] *Evening Wisconsin*, Dec. 14, 1896; Milwaukee *Sentinel*, March 4, 18, 1898; Larson, *Financial and Administrative History*, 150.

opposition than did the question of municipally managed garbage disposal. Until the 1880's gas had been the standard means of street illumination, a none too satisfactory method considering the laxness of the lamplighters employed by the Gas Light Company.[16] An investigation in 1871 revealed a total of 395 unlighted lamps during the month of January. Experiments with the arc light in 1878 and Edison's development of the incandescent lamp in 1879 gave promise of more adequate illumination, at least for the business district; and on the evening of April 5, 1880, curious crowds gathered at the Newhall House to see two electric lamps giving forth "a brilliancy equal to one thousand candles." The one above the main entrance, "although surrounded by a ground glass globe, lighted the street, so much so, as to admit of reading finely printed matter without difficulty." The other was sufficient to illuminate the Newhall House office. The electricity was generated by a Weston Dynamo Machine in the basement of the hotel.[17]

The officers of the gas company belittled the new invention, condemning "Tom Edison's promises" as a "giant humbug" and conjuring up so many dangers to users of the "incandescent carbons" that the *Evening Wisconsin* satirically accused them of contending that electricity would induce fire and electrocution, attract thunderstorms, spoil food, damage fabrics, cause freckles, reduce "the standing of boardinghouse hash," and show up "everybody by night." In spite of obstructionism from the investors in gas illumination, C. H. Haskins, the promoter of the new enterprise, succeeded in introducing electric lighting in several East Water Street stores;[18] and by the close of 1881 he had determined to install enough machinery to run 200 lights and bid for lighting the city streets. For more than a quarter century thereafter, various companies supplied electric street illumination on contract from the city, among them the Badger Illuminating Company, the Edison Electric Illuminating Com-

---

[16] In 1851 the municipality had contracted with the Milwaukee Gas Light Company to provide illumination for the city. Gregory, *History*, 2:1194-95.

[17] *Evening Wisconsin*, Feb. 6, 1871; Milwaukee *Sentinel*, April 6, 1880.

[18] The user was charged from 80 cents to $1.00 per night for each lamp. According to the promoter, the cost of the lamp equalled that of 12 gas jets, but it produced 25 times as much light. *Evening Wisconsin*, May 11, Dec. 1, 21, 1881.

pany, and the Milwaukee Light and Power Company, which received its franchise in 1890. By February of the latter year plans for a $600,000 municipal lighting plant had been submitted to the board of public works; and by the late nineties a majority of the residents appeared to favor a municipal lighting plant, on the theory that it would reduce rates. But conservative opinion continued to oppose its construction with the argument that the city had neither the right nor the financial resources to engage in this kind of manufacturing.[19] Public resentment at paying $145 to $150 a light for service which Chicago, with city control, obtained for $65 and the disclosure, some years later, that the annual bill for gas, gasoline, and electric street illumination exceeded $250,000 prompted the electorate in 1904 to sustain a proposal to issue $500,000 in bonds for constructing a municipal lighting plant.[20] Upon the expiration of the contract with the Milwaukee Electric Railway and Light Company in 1905, the council rejected the company's offer to reduce rates to $65 a light and prepared to establish a municipal plant, going so far as to sell a portion of the bonds to purchase a site and in March 1907 authorizing an issue of $150,000 for the erection of the plant. It had not, however, reckoned with the legal obstacles which the interested parties could set in the path of accomplishment. A short-lived lighting commission, similar to the one that supervised the building of the waterworks, was dispersed on the ground that it had no legal existence; and in 1910 the supreme court upheld an injunction which had been brought in 1907 by Thomas J. Neacy preventing the sale of the proposed bonds. William C. Quarles, of the firm of Quarles, Spence, and Quarles, counsel for Neacy, won his case on the argument that whereas the law had authorized the sale of bonds only for the erection of a municipal plant, the vote authorizing the bond issue had been

[19] *Ibid.*, Dec. 1, 1881; Anderson and Bleyer, *Milwaukee's Great Industries,* 104; Leora M. Howard, Changes in Home Life in Milwaukee from 1865 to 1900, p. 28, MS, M.A. thesis, dated 1923, University of Wisconsin. This work will hereafter be cited as Leora Howard, Home Life in Milwaukee. See also Bruce, *History,* 1:197; Milwaukee *Sentinel,* March 4, 6, 1898.

[20] At this point in his career, Judge Rose, later mayor, scoffed at charges that municipal ownership paved the way for communism and asserted that the city could manage its lighting efficiently at a cost of only $65 a light. *Evening Wisconsin,* Oct. 17, 1891.

taken on the erection and maintenance of the plant, as well. Fundamentally, the decision upheld the contention that, as Neacy put it, there was no excuse for the city "to engage in an industrial proposition of this kind." The inaugural promises of Mayor Seidel in 1910 included action looking toward the acquisition of a municipal lighting plant—for which, according to the new mayor, "the people of Milwaukee had for 15 years expressed desire."[21]

Along with the controversy over municipal street lighting went discussion of another urban service in which the ultimate use of electricity was involved—the question of urban transit. With the extension of population had come a need of improved facilities for transportation from one part of the city to the other. Indeed, the physical limits of the city's growth appeared by the sixties to be dependent upon the speed with which businessmen could get from home to work. From 1860 forward, horse-car companies had supplied this need. By 1882, three companies, using improved cars—about 16 feet long, with seven windows to the side—monopolized the business within their own particular territories. The Milwaukee City Railway Company represented the consolidation in the hands of Isaac Ellsworth and others (in 1869) of the two original companies, property that was later sold to a group headed by Peter McGeoch.[22] The other companies of the middle eighties were the West Side Street Railway Company, which was incorporated in 1874 and came under the control of Washington Becker two years later, and the Cream City Street Railway line, incorporated in 1876. The Milwaukee City Railway Company operated fourteen and one-half miles of track; the Cream City, thirteen and one-half; and the West Side Railway, five. Together they owned 610 horses and mules and employed 200 men. Rattan covered seats ran lengthwise of the improved cars, the 5-cent fare was dropped in a slot at each window from which it jingled downward to the front,

[21] Larson, *Financial and Administrative History*, 149; Milwaukee *Sentinel*, April 20, 27, 1910.

[22] These were the River and Lake Shore Street Railway, which ran its first car in 1860, and the Milwaukee City Railway Company, founded by John Plankinton, Frederick Layton, Samuel Marshall, W. S. Johnson, and Charles F. Ilsley in 1865. *Ibid.*, July 14, 1937; Gregory, *History*, 2:1196.

light was furnished by a big oil lamp which hung below a large vent in the ceiling, and for heat there was either a coal stove or hay spread over the floor in which passengers could bury their feet. Thin bars of iron laid on top of long strips of wood constituted the rails; and when the car slipped off the track, as it frequently did, the driver had to call upon the male passengers to lend a hand, and everyone got out and helped lift the car back on the track.[23]

By the middle eighties, the pressure of the expanding metropolis was compelling more extensive and speedier transit facilities; and by 1890, the first electric trolley had challenged the "muly-jog" of the horse car, which took an hour to go from one side of the city to the other and in bad weather half a day. In 1886, the *Evening Wisconsin* reminded the community that Milwaukee was "no longer a village" and urged the council to charter companies that were "ready to take the franchises and build the roads." A company which enlisted the interest of John A. Hinsey, president of the council, projected a cable car line, but before it was completed Washington Becker of the West Side Street Railway Company had proved the merits of electric motive power in successful experiments on the Wells Street line.[24]

As in the proposal of electricity for street lighting, the discussion of electric trolleys aroused popular apprehensions regarding the use of the "dangerous stuff." Lightning was electricity, it was said, and the thought "of burying the horrid stuff down to travel by . . . was really too much. Everybody would be killed, and Milwaukee be turned into a regular angel factory." The *Evening Wisconsin* printed gruesome accounts of accidents sustained from contact with electric wires and predicted that "if the electric street railway system, with its overhead wires, proves as dangerous in Milwaukee as it has done in Cleveland, the public will regret that they were not content with horse cars." April 3, 1890, nevertheless saw the public operation of the city's first electric street car. Curious spectators drew back

[23] Milwaukee *Sentinel*, July 14, 1937; Gregory, *History*, 2:1197-98; Milwaukee *Journal*, Nov. 16, 1932.
[24] *Evening Wisconsin*, April 3, 1886.

as the application of the trolley to the wire drew a shower of bluish-red sparks; and horses pranced and snorted as this mechanically propelled vehicle of the West Side Street Railway Company made two trips along Wells Street. By April 7, however, the electric cars were running in good order, and the "passing of the horse car" was in sight. The managers of the Hinsey line, foreseeing the new developments, gained permission to use their franchise for electric rather than cable propulsion and changed the name of their enterprise to the Milwaukee Electric Railway Company. By late 1889, the Cream City line began to transform its road into an electric line.[25]

In spite of earlier misgivings as to safety, the realization of electrified urban transit facilities was to have far-reaching effects upon suburban growth and business operations, as well as upon the convenience of urban life. A correspondent to the Milwaukee *Daily Journal,* on September 12, 1891, thanked "divine providence" for providing "electricity as a mode of transit. . . ." He wrote:

Now a person can make a date with the reasonable certainty of getting there within the time. But when the old mu-ly, mu-ly, mu-ly jog was in force, parents living on the east side would kiss their little ones with tender solicitude before starting out for the West, and vice versa, for like men who go out in ships, the length of their absence was uncertain, to say the least of it. Now you may leave the Northwestern station at any time you please, slide through the city like a grease pig through a lasso, touch the limit and return to your starting point in less than an hour.[26]

But if the electric trolley extended the influence of the city over a wider metropolitan area, the monetary backing essential to its development involved this fundamental urban service in the manipulations of national finance. This was a consequence both of the trend toward consolidation which characterized industrial activity in the late nineteenth century and of the fact that municipal activities offered a promising field of investment for the eastern capital that was seeking western outlets in the period previous to the panic of 1893.

[25] Milwaukee *Journal,* Sept. 12, 1891; *Evening Wisconsin,* Nov. 25, 26, 1889; Milwaukee *Sentinel,* April 4, 7, 10, 1890.
[26] Milwaukee *Journal,* Sept. 12, 1891.

By the turn of the nineties, Walter G. Oakman of New York had become president of the Milwaukee City Railroad Company which Ellsworth had sold to McGeoch in 1881; and thanks to the efforts of Henry C. Payne, Henry Villard's North American Company, a New York corporation, was induced to take large holdings, which Payne represented, in the Milwaukee street railway system. In December 1890, Villard and his associates gained control of and merged the Cream City and the Milwaukee City Railroad companies to form the Milwaukee Street Railway Company. Of this, Villard became president and Payne, vice-president. On September 29, 1891, the stock of the West Side Street Railway Company was transferred to the North American Company in the interest of the Milwaukee Street Railway Company; and by January 29, 1894, this company had absorbed all the strictly city transit lines, as well as the Badger Illuminating Company and the Edison Electric Illuminating Company. Payne served as president from 1892 to 1895. In the latter year, the Central Trust Company of New York, to whom the property had been mortgaged in January 1894, foreclosed; and Payne and George R. Sheldon were appointed as receivers. The resulting financial tangle was resolved with the organization on January 29, 1896, of the Milwaukee Electric Railway and Light Company. William N. Cromwell of New York became president and Payne, vice-president. Shortly thereafter, John I. Beggs, experienced in managing power plants in the East, was sent from New York to make a survey of the street railway system. He remained to become general manager of the company and to play a dynamic role both in extending transit facilities to the suburban limits of the city and in acquiring lines that expanded the power of the company and the economic hinterland of the growing metropolis, as well. In May 1896, shortly before Beggs's assumption of the managership, the Amalgamated Street Railway Employees demanded recognition of their union and a 1-cent increase over the 19 cents an hour which they were receiving. When the company refused to negotiate, a strike ensued which tied up the service for several weeks. The company barricaded its property and brought in hundreds of strikebreakers. Against these there was strong public sentiment. Grocers and butchers refused their patronage so that the company had to import food from Chicago; and Payne was the object of intense hatred. The strike terminated in favor of the company, which refused to rehire the most active participants.[27]

In an environment increasingly favorable to municipal ownership and regulation, the monopolistic activities of the Railway and Light Company made it assume the same "monstrous" proportions which had characterized the railroads in the eyes of the Grangers some years earlier. As early as 1886, an editorial writer in the *Evening Wisconsin* had applied the Granger principle to the street railway in asserting that

> the time for the people or the officers of the city to permit corporations to dictate upon what terms street-car passengers will be carried, or to render such service as they choose with sole reference to their private profits and no reference to public convenience is passed [*sic*]. Milwaukee is no longer a struggling, dependent village, but an independent metropolis.

The mid-nineties saw much agitation for municipal ownership of the utility; and if not ownership, at least regulation. But it was early apparent that in dealing with the power company the public had met a formidable adversary and one that was capable of presenting an almost universally effective case in the courts.[28] When, in June 1896, the council adopted an ordinance requiring the company to sell tickets at the rate of six for a quarter and twenty-five for $1.00, injunctions sought by the company and the Central Trust Company of New York were upheld in the Circuit Court of the United States, eastern district of Wisconsin, on the ground that the proposed rates were unreasonable and that the power of a municipality to regulate street railway fares was limited by the popular need of lower rates and the reasonableness of the terms. Similarly, when controversy arose

---

[27] Wight, *Henry Clay Payne*, 56-63; Gregory, *History*, 2:1200, 1202-4; Milwaukee *Sentinel*, July 14, 1937.

[28] *Evening Wisconsin*, June 24, 1886; July 6, 14, Nov. 28, 1896. Dr. Albert Shaw, editor of *Review of Reviews*, was impressed in studying the relations between German cities and quasi-public supply corporations "with a sense of the first-class legal, financial and technical ability that the city is always able to command, while American contracts always impress one with the unlimited astuteness and ability of the gentlemen representing the private corporations." Milwaukee *Sentinel*, March 15, 1898.

as to whether the street-car company could re-lay tracks on a right of way that had been temporarily abandoned by it, the Supreme Court reversed the injunction against the company upheld in the lower court and found in favor of the company on all points.[29]

The fact that the corporation was obliged to seek from the council a franchise for its use of the streets gave the municipality its one effective weapon; and of this the city took advantage when in the spring of 1898 the power company sought an extension of its franchise so as to give it freedom from competition for a period of years. At this juncture a proposed new company offered to pay the city $25,000 for the right to operate a rival line, on which it planned to charge a 4-cent fare. With the city now in a position to play the new company against the old, Payne's organization was forced to offer a bonus of $50,000 and as a further consideration to promise "to sell tickets, six for 25 cents or 25 for a dollar, good . . . in the city from 5:30 to 7 o'clock a.m. and from 5:30 to 6:30 p.m. and also to continue the . . . transfer system." The public was convinced, however, that the company could afford to offer a 4-cent fare at all times and believed that this was the moment for the council to press the concession. The Municipal League issued 14,000 bulletins warning the voters against being misled by propositions which had only the appearance of generosity and demanded further concessions on the part of the corporation. In addition to an original payment they demanded an annual division of the company's profits with the city, inspection of its books by the municipality, reduction of fares to 4 cents with a further reduction whenever circumstances should warrant, improvements in service by which payment of fare should guarantee a seat, and at the expiration of the franchises of the present company their reversion to the city.[30] In the summer of 1899 negotiations be-

---

[29] Milwaukee Electric Railway and Light Company v. the City of Milwaukee; Central Trust Company of New York v. the City of Milwaukee (87 Federal Reporter 577); Wright v. Milwaukee Electric Railway and Light Company (95 Wisconsin 29, 36 L.R.A. 47); Milwaukee Electric Railway and Light Company v. the City of Milwaukee (95 Wisconsin 42, 36 L.R.A. 45); Wight, *Henry Clay Payne*, 65, 67.

[30] The League asserted that "low long-ride fares are in the interest . . . of outlying real estate, and the moral influence of leading the working population

tween representatives of the city and the company, represented by Villard, Cromwell, Charles W. Wetmore, Sheldon, Payne, Benjamin K. Miller, Jr., Charles F. Pfister, and Beggs, led to the preparation of a compromise ordinance, but one which gave small comfort to the municipal reformers. The company conceded passes to policemen, firemen, and health officers; consented to furnish the city with electric power to operate its draw bridges; and agreed not only to extend the hours during which the 4-cent commutation ticket could be used but to permit its use throughout the day after January 1, 1905. Moreover, it was understood that the railway company was to pave and keep in good repair the roadway between the tracks and one foot outside each rail. In return for these concessions, however, the company gained a substantial victory on the fundamental issue of the 5-cent fare. According to the resulting ordinance, it was protected in a fare of not to exceed 5 cents, as well as in the other privileges of its franchises, until December 31, 1934; and it obtained rights with respect to a Maryland Avenue franchise which it at one time had agreed to abandon.[31]

Strong protests came from members of the Municipal League, from proponents of municipal ownership, and from affected lot owners. At a mass meeting of business and workingmen held at the West Side Turn Hall on December 15 it was asserted that far from insuring a 4-cent fare the proposed ordinance gave "exclusive franchises" which would "prevent competition and make lower fares in the future impossible." In spite of outspoken opposition, Mayor Rose, who apparently had experienced a change of heart on the evils of corporations, and a majority of his council proceeded in great haste to pass the ordinance. They refused to listen to suggestions that action await the decision of the citizens in the approaching municipal election; and in the council meeting of December 18, all efforts to amend the ordinance to meet popular demands were summarily quashed by a vote of twenty-five to seventeen.[32]

away from the central parts of town is exceedingly important and will become more so as the city grows." Milwaukee *Sentinel*, March 11, 12, 15, 1898.

[31] Ordinance Authorizing the Milwaukee Electric Railway and Light Company to construct, maintain, and operate street railways . . . passed . . . January 2, 1900; Wight, *Henry Clay Payne*, 71; Milwaukee *Sentinel*, Dec. 19, 1899.

[32] *Ibid.*, Dec. 16, 19, 1899.

By the time the ordinance came up for final action on January 2, 1900, the mayor, council, and city clerk had been enjoined from signing it on the ground that steps in its adoption had not complied with terms of the city charter. But friends of the measure were eager. Assured by the corporation's counsel that the injunction was void, twenty-five of the forty-two aldermen signed it; and Mayor Rose was there to add his signature lest further interferences arise. According to the Chicago *Record*, "the doors of the council chamber were closed and guarded, in order that the aldermen might not be interfered with in the execution of the plan. Mayor Rose was on hand to sign the ordinance as soon as it was passed for fear that some new manifestation of popular indignation might prevent the delivery of the goods to the Payne-Pfister crowd who stood in waiting to receive them."[33] Accusations of bribery were speedily made, but no proof was ever presented. The most serious charge against the mayor and council was their impetuous and uncompromising determination to pass the measure in defiance of injunction and on the eve of a municipal election when haste was manifestly of so much greater advantage to the corporation than to the public. Its behavior in the street-car issue showed the city government of Milwaukee to be no less amenable to the pressure of the interests than other municipal governments of the period whose activities were giving American city politics a black eye at the advent of the new century. The outcome of the controversy furthered the movement for municipal reform and especially for a popular referendum on the acts of the municipal legislature. As the Chicago *Record* put it, the experience of Milwaukee pointed "to the referendum as the only sure and effective means of preventing spoliation of cities by franchise grabbers."[34]

[33] Chicago *Record*, quoted, *ibid.*, Jan. 5, 1900. Chief of Police John T. Janssen later refused council members an explanation of who was responsible for the presence of the policemen who had restrained spectators at the meeting. *Ibid.*, Dec. 27, 31, 1899; Jan. 3, 18, Feb. 27, 1900; Wight, *Henry Clay Payne*, 67-71.

[34] Quoted in Milwaukee *Sentinel*, Jan. 5, 1900. This controversy, with references to the personalities and issues only thinly veiled, forms the plot of *The Autocrats* (1901), a novel by Charles K. Lush. The cheaper fares in parts of Chicago, Detroit, and Toronto and the Indianapolis street car contract, guaranteeing a 4-cent fare at all hours and many additional concessions, gave the reformers grounds for disappointment at the Milwaukee ordinance. Milwaukee

The controversy over municipal ownership of the lighting plant and the objections to the high-handed behavior of the council in the matter of the street-car ordinance gave weight to agitation in the early twentieth century to square the city charter more effectively with the realities of city life. At the outset of this generation the city was still subject to the charter of 1852 in its amended form. In 1874, however, the common council drew up a new charter without consulting the electorate; and after its enactment into law by the State legislature it became the charter under which, subject to amendment, the city was operating as late as 1940. This charter on the whole strengthened the power of the council. It abandoned the two-chamber system which had been adopted in 1858, as a result of the Albany Hall movement, and provided for a unicameral council of thirty-nine aldermen, chosen for three-year terms, one member annually from each of thirteen wards.[35] The authority of the council was increased with respect to taxation and expenditures; but at the same time the new charter recognized the prevailing trend to vest authority in the administrative boards which, since the sixties, had been given duties formerly performed by the council. Its liberal expenditures during the seventies prompted a movement as a result of which the taxing power of the council was severely limited in 1881; and in 1887 the number of aldermen was reduced to two per ward and their term from three to two years. In 1878 the board of health was abolished, and its power was conferred on a health commissioner appointed by the mayor and council. To the already considerable number of boards were added the nonpartisan board of fire and police commissioners in 1885, the board of park commissioners in 1889, and the city service commission in 1895.[36]

Moreover, like other maturing cities, Milwaukee became increasingly restive at the control exerted by the State legisla-

Sentinel, Dec. 16, 1899. In 1909 the city of Cleveland negotiated a franchise providing for a 3-cent fare with an additional cent for transfer, thereby obtaining what was thought to amount to "municipal operation" of the system. *Ibid.*, March 16, 1916.

[35] Larson, *Financial and Administrative History*, 104-5. See also Milwaukee *Sentinel*, Jan. 15, 16, 24, 28, 29, 31, Feb. 2, 3, 5, 1874.

[36] Larson. *Financial and Administrative History*, 106-7.

ture over the city's internal affairs. From the middle eighties forward, it sought to free itself from the interference of rural-minded legislators who not only failed to comprehend the problems of the urban community but who were frequently swayed by the arguments of minority interests within the developing city. The consequences of this subjection to outside authority had been demonstrated at the arrival of the eighties when a serious curtailment of municipal activity resulted from legislative limitations on the city tax rate enacted at the insistence of the Tax League, the Committee of 100, and other opponents of municipal spending. Early in 1887, the council memorialized the legislature for the purpose of attaining a general act that would give cities control over their own financial and other matters; but this bore little fruit, although in 1892 a constitutional amendment restricted the legislature to the passage of general, rather than special laws, for cities of several classes. However, inasmuch as Milwaukee was the only urban community in its class, the city was still subject to what amounted to special legislation. In 1896, Mayor Rauschenberger asserted that Milwaukee had "grown to be too large a city to be hampered by state laws passed without the knowledge and consent of her common council and citizens" and proposed, as a partial corrective, the passage of a general law, in imitation of one just enacted by the New York legislature, requiring that "before any act [involving a city] becomes a law it shall first be submitted to the mayor and common council and published in the official paper of such city." In 1902, the council carried the issue of home rule for cities in their local affairs to the other municipalities of the State; and finally, in 1907, cities of the first class, meaning Milwaukee, were authorized to hold a charter convention for the purpose of preparing a comprehensive home rule charter to be presented to the succeeding legislature.[37]

The ensuing attempt at charter revision, in 1908, was vitalized by the current concern for municipal reform. Here was the long-awaited chance, according to Victor Berger, to establish the

[37] *Ibid.*, 125; Milwaukee *Sentinel*, April 22, 1876; "History of the Milwaukee City Charter," MS in Milwaukee Municipal Reference Library, 1-2. See also, Citizens' Bureau of Milwaukee, *A New Charter* (Milwaukee, 1924).

principle of home rule and majority rule, block graft, and meet "the needs of a modern, great city." Prior to the election of delegates, chosen so as to represent each of the major political parties, meetings of such organizations as the Merchants' and Manufacturers' Association provided an opportunity to discuss the issues involved; and as the election day approached, the *Sentinel* urged the voters to exercise their "sacred civic function" and make certain that every delegate "bear the mark of ability and integrity" and "be a man who enters upon his work with the single purpose of serving the whole people to the best of his ability." Mayor Rose, however, viewed the whole scheme as an attempt of the Social Democrats to engraft their "doctrines upon the fundamental law"; and when it appeared that the Republicans and Social Democrats were going to control the convention, he declared the gathering unconstitutional—"a voluntary association with no legal status," denied it the use of the city hall, and succeeded in getting the finance committee of the council to refuse funds for its support. In spite of these objections, the religious and civic societies stood firmly behind the movement. On June 3 the convention was endorsed by the Federation of Civic Societies which represented twenty-eight different civic and commercial bodies—all the leading ones except the Chamber of Commerce; and the convention went ahead to frame a charter which embodied the home rule principle. This the State senate passed; but its defeat by the assembly in 1909 postponed for a time the realization of the reform. As early as 1882, Mayor Stowell had proposed city-county consolidation, an idea that was gaining acceptance in the East and one which was to be agitated more vigorously as the twentieth century progressed.[38]

The city that wanted home rule was already developing satellite communities of its own; for the generation between 1870 and 1910 saw the first conscious recognition of suburban development in the Milwaukee area. As late as the middle seventies many people in referring to suburban places had in mind

[38] Milwaukee *Journal*, May 19, 21, 22, 25, 29, June 1, 4, 6, 1908; Milwaukee *Sentinel*, April 19, 1882; March 22, 1908; "History of the Milwaukee City Charter," 2.

the summer resorts outside the city limits; but by the middle eighties there existed a clear distinction in the popular mind between the "downtown" area and the outlying residential districts. The promoters of the street railways took the credit for suburban growth when they asserted in 1876 that "the scores of new buildings going up in the outskirts of the city" showed that once transportation facilities were available businessmen were not slow to take advantage of the opportunity to have "a clean, healthful home away from the noise and din of the business portion of the metropolis." The suburban thrust not only enveloped communities that originally had had a social and economic life of their own but also encouraged the creation of new outlying settlements to accommodate the surplus industrial or residential population of the city. For example, the village of Humboldt, which had been laid out in 1851 because of water-power facilities on the west side of the river at Mechanicsville, was quickly swallowed up by the expanding metropolis.[39] Oak Creek, settled by pioneers from Massachusetts in 1835, was subjected to the developmental activities of the South Milwaukee Company in the early nineties; in 1891 the name of its post office was changed to South Milwaukee, and shortly thereafter construction began on the factories that speedily were moved into the once pioneer community. The Milwaukee Street Railway Company extended its tracks there in 1896; and in that year South Milwaukee was incorporated as a city. The nucleus of present-day Wauwatosa had existed as Hart's Mill since the middle thirties. With the development of the street railway, the once remote settlement became an attractive residential community for people who worked in Milwaukee and West Allis. In 1886 it was being advertised as "the most attractive suburb of Milwaukee," with its fine churches, street lights, transit facilities, and freedom from saloons and heavy industry.[40]

On the other hand, the pressure of population and expanding industry led to the development of new communities beyond the limits of the city where property owners hoped to find relief either from the annoyances of life in the congested central city

[39] *Evening Wisconsin*, Aug. 5, 1876; Jan. 30, 1886; Buck, 3:314-15.
[40] Gregory, *History*, 2:1227-29, 1236-40; *Evening Wisconsin*, July 26, 1886.

or from the interferences and controls imposed by its maturing government upon industrial pursuits. Shorewood, on the north lake shore, speedily became a select residential district; and by 1892 realtors were grading streets and projecting a residential community still farther north at the resort spot known as Whitefish Bay, a residential enterprise which the panic of 1893 made for the time abortive. A station on the North Western railroad at North Greenfield became the focus of the industrial community of West Allis. Here the Edward P. Allis Company, seeking room for expansion with adequate transportation facilities, bought 100 acres of land at $250 an acre and stimulated the growth of a community which soon attracted other industries. Property owners and real estate interests saw to it that the needed transportation was realized. West Allis was incorporated in May 1902; and 200 houses had been constructed before the community was a year old. It became a city in 1906. Rolling mills, established in 1867 in Bay View, provided the nucleus of a settlement which was at that date distant from Milwaukee. As late as 1880, when the expanding city was reaching toward it, Bay View was still opposed to annexation. Less than ten years later, however, upon the petition of a majority of its residents, it became the 17th Ward of the city. Cudahy was founded in the early nineties when Patrick Cudahy moved his packing establishment into the open spaces northeast of South Milwaukee in anticipation of municipal legislation curtailing packing activities in the city. Other manufacturers followed; and their employees moved also, to be near their work. The village was incorporated in 1895 and the city in 1906. The *Evening Wisconsin*'s department of "Suburban Items," which in 1896 included "personals" from South Milwaukee, North Greenfield, Soldiers' Home, Cudahy, Wauwatosa, Whitefish Bay, and Bay View, reflected the identification of the metropolis with the communities on the rim of the central city. But if the metropolis was exerting a centripetal pull upon the neighboring settlements, a centrifugal force was operating at the same time to disperse the population of the central city in their direction. In 1880, some 34 percent of the city's population were living within a mile of the business center at the corner of present

Third Street and Wisconsin Avenue; by 1900, less than 17 percent resided in that zone. On the other hand, whereas in 1880 only 17.4 percent inhabited the more remote zone three miles from the business district, by 1900 nearly 31 percent were dwelling there.[41]

Although the aesthetic and recreational services of the municipality hardly more than suggested in the early part of the period what was to be achieved along that line after the turn of the century, they too were affected by the metropolitan trend. A nationwide interest in free public libraries coincided with financial difficulties suffered during the seventies by the Young Men's Association, then the private guarantors of the community's library facilities.[42] The association's lecture courses had subsidized the library project; and as their popularity waned between 1867 and 1877, the society incurred a deficit of nearly $1,400. The want of private support at last caused the city to undertake the obligation of providing public library service. On February 7, 1878, the legislature established the Public Library; in the following month it authorized the transfer to the city of the association's collection of some 9,958 volumes, together with numerous pamphlets and magazines; and in due time direction was assumed by a board of trustees, made up of four citizens at first named in the law but ultimately to be elected for three-year terms by the board; three aldermen to be selected by the mayor; the president of the school board; and the superintendent of schools.[43] In May 1880 the library, then comprising about 15,000 volumes, was moved from rooms in the Academy of Music Building to quarters in the Library Block, which John Plankinton had built with an eye to this

[41] Gregory, *History*, 2:1226, 1230-36; *Evening Wisconsin*, July 11, 1896; McClellan and Junkersfeld, Inc., *Report on Transportation in the Milwaukee Metropolitan District to the Transportation Survey Committee of Milwaukee* (vol. 1, text; vol. 2, appendix containing maps, graphs, and charts, New York, 1928), 2:5.

[42] See chapter 9.

[43] The first board of trustees of the Public Library included Matthew Keenan, John Johnston, Gustave C. Trumpff, and William Frankfurth, citizens at large; G. E. Weiss, W. E. Kittredge, and Thomas H. Brown, aldermen; Joshua Stark, president of the school board, and James MacAlister, superintendent of schools. Conard, 2:292; see Theresa H. West, "Milwaukee Public Library," in Stearns, *Columbian History of Education in Wisconsin*, 422-27.

particular use. In 1890 the council approved the purchase of a site for a library and museum on the northeast corner of Grand Avenue and Ninth Street and three years later appropriated funds with which to erect the building. After many delays and discouragements this structure was completed at a cost of nearly $630,000 in 1898. Meanwhile, the library had already recognized the needs of the expanding metropolis by establishing sub-stations in remote sections of the community. Like the library, the museum went through an evolution from private to public support. On the foundation of the specimens collected by Peter Engelmann for his teaching at the German-English Academy, a group of twenty-one Milwaukeeans established the Engelmann Museum of Natural History. During 1881 and 1882 negotiations were accomplished by which the holdings of this organization were transferred to the city to be held in trust and the museum supported by a general tax. In 1882 the collection was moved to rooms especially provided for it in the Exposition Building to remain there until it was housed in the new library and museum building.[44]

Shortly after the Exposition Building had been projected and the library and museum taken under public auspices there began to be agitation for a "public bath and swimming institution free to the masses." "A public bath is a promotion of public health," wrote "Res Publica" to the Milwaukee *Sentinel*. "A public library, a public museum, an art museum, an exposition building, a large skating rink, and a public bath—what city can compare with this?" Two years later Mayor Wallber advocated such a public bath along with a proposal for the establishment of public parks. Bids for the natatorium were taken in 1889; and in the following year more than $25,000 was spent on this public institution, which was opened on February 14, 1890. The provision of a public library, museum, natatorium, and parks marked a halfway station on the road of expanding urban services which extended from the public schools and fire and police protection of the mid-century to the free medical care, municipal social centers, municipal

[44] Larson, *Financial and Administrative History*, 146-47; Conard, 2:292-94.

symphony concerts, and public sale of coal, wood, ice, and pure milk proposed by the Social Democrats and other reformers by 1910.[45]

Not until about 1890 did Milwaukeeans remedy their backwardness in providing the citizenry with parks. At that date the municipality owned slightly more than seventy acres of park lands, all but twenty-five of which had been donated by public-spirited citizens.[46] An ordinance establishing a park commission in 1875 was repealed the following year as a result of concern as to whether the city was large enough to "demand public places in each ward." As late as 1889, conservatives called the proposed expenditure of $600,000 for park purposes "out of the question until municipal revenues are materially increased." They asserted that Milwaukee was a "residence park without a park," in small need of an extensive "breathing spot." Although Mayor Wallber had suggested the need of parks as early as 1886, it was not until the turn of the nineties that the city undertook a systematic treatment of the park problem. By this date a number of prominent citizens had become convinced of the need of "healthy breathing spots"—similar to London's Hyde Park, the *Bois de Boulogne* of Paris, Berlin's *Tiergarten,* and the *Prater* of Vienna—the "lungs of those great cities," as Christian Wahl expressed it. They undertook to secure the passage of a law enabling the city to develop a complete park system, an ambition which was realized when a bill was passed in 1889 providing for the expenditure of $100,000 and establishing a board of park commissioners. To this board, which had its first meeting on June 16, 1889, a number of the leading proponents of the park movement were appointed, among them Wahl, president, John Bentley, Calvin E. Lewis, Charles Manegold, Jr., and Louis Auer. The legislature having remedied in 1891 the provision that all the parks must be purchased within the city limits, suitable places were found within the bounds of the county to provide for Lake,

[45] Milwaukee *Sentinel,* April 21, 1884; April 21, 1886; *Evening Wisconsin,* Jan. 29, 1889; Larson, *Financial and Administrative History,* 164.

[46] At the opening of 1890 the city could boast only eleven squares and small parks, the most pretentious of them being Kilbourn Park, Juneau Park, the Flushing Tunnel Park, and the Waterworks Park. Conard, 1:300-301; *Evening Wisconsin,* Nov. 3, 1906.

Washington, Mitchell, Kosciuszko, and Humboldt parks.[47]

For advice on the landscaping of Lake and Washington parks the commissioners turned to Frederick Law Olmsted, creator of Central Park in New York. By 1894 one could rent boats on the park lagoons; and a gift of seven deer by Louis Auer and Gustave Pabst, a year earlier, became the nucleus of the Washington Park zoo. By the middle nineties the recreation-loving Milwaukee community began to discover its park system. Facilities for reaching the parks by electric trolley were improved; and free concerts furnished by the Milwaukee Electric Railway and Light Company at Lake and Washington parks attracted many visitors. The estimated attendance at the parks during the year exceeded a million. The broadened interest in the park problem during the mid-nineties was but one indication of the awakened municipal conscience which was to encourage a marked expansion of the services of the urban community in the ensuing progressive era. As Christian Wahl wrote, if one would but visit "the stifling alleys of any great city . . ." he would "appreciate that the task of providing a great town with beautiful parks is one of the most grateful in the world; but it also becomes a duty."[48]

The mid-nineties saw, too, a deepened concern over urban health. An epidemic of smallpox during 1894 and 1895—the seventh in the city's history—called attention to the hazards of urban congestion with respect to communicable disease; and by 1896 editorial opinion was drawing upon the experience of New York, London, and other large cities to point out the importance of insuring sanitation in street cars, abolishing the river nuisance, maintaining clean streets and alleys, and inspecting milk and bakery products in the interest of the public health. The current support for publicly induced sanitation

[47] Save for Mitchell Park these parks were not given their present names at once, in the hope that "some affluent citizen might, by gift or testamentary remembrance, earn the right to have his name associated with this system." Milwaukee *Sentinel,* Jan. 23, 1876; April 20, 1886; *Evening Wisconsin,* Jan. 29, 1889; Christian Wahl, "Public Park System of the City," in Conard, 1:300; Larson, *Financial and Administrative History,* 143-44; *Wisconsin News* (Milwaukee), July 16, 1936; Conard, 1:301, 306.

[48] *Ibid.,* 1:302, 306; *Wisconsin News,* July 16, 1932.

revealed a popular attitude quite different from that against which the health commissioners of the seventies labored in an attempt to insure a healthful community. From the middle fifties until 1867, the mayor and council had served as a board of health for the city, but in the latter year the legislature authorized the appointment of the board of health for the city of Milwaukee. Dr. James Johnson, who served as president of the board from 1867 to 1877, strove manfully for compulsory vaccination, but he was ahead of his time,[49] as was Dr. O. W. Wight, who served as health commissioner from 1878 to 1881. When this versatile figure, at once attorney, master of arts, and doctor of medicine, undertook a one-man crusade to remove filth and garbage from the city streets and achieve a safe milk supply by a personal inspection of 227 dairies, he met a languid response from the citizenry. His efforts to bring about a regular dairy inspection through the passage of a milk ordinance aroused such violent opposition that he postponed its consideration; and not until 1887 did the council provide by ordinance for the inspection of milk and dairy farms. Until then local housewives were content to purchase milk from vendors who filled their pitchers from open milk cans. Small wonder that the general death rate in 1880 more than doubled what it was to be fifty years later. An average of more than twenty persons died annually for every thousand in the population during the seventies; and because of the terrific toll of death among the city's children, the average length of life in 1880 was eighteen years by contrast with more than fifty-two years about a half century later.[50]

But attitudes were changing by the middle nineties. In 1893 the legislature authorized the establishment of an office

[49] The city's first board of health, consisting of the mayor and five physicians, was created in 1846; a second board was formed July 15, 1850; and the mayor and council constituted the board in 1855, 1856, and 1857. Bruce, *History*, 1:477; *Evening Wisconsin*, Jan. 11, 18, March 18, June 9, 15, 1896; Gregory, *History*, 2:1137-38.

[50] Dr. Wight made two voluminous reports, published as Commission of Health of Milwaukee, *First Annual Report*, 1879 (Milwaukee, 1879) and Health Commissioner of Milwaukee, *Second Annual Report*, 1880 (Milwaukee, 1880). See Commissioner of Health (Milwaukee), *37th Annual Report*, 1913, p. 191. He resigned in 1881 to become health commissioner of Detroit. Dr. Robert Martin was health commissioner from 1881 to 1890.

of vital statistics in the department of health; and records, compiled by professionally trained men, became the basis of future preventive activities. Laboratory analysis was started in the same year. Health Commissioners Wingate (1890 to 1894) and Dr. Walter Kempster (1894 to 1898) kept in touch with innovations in public sanitation in the other metropolitan centers of the nation; and progress in the development of sanitary precautions resulted. Antitoxin for diphtheria, supplied free to needy families, proved an effective means of decreasing the death rate in 1896. General food inspection was authorized in 1901, the inspection of maternity hospitals in 1903, and the licensing of milk vendors by 1906. Milwaukee club women followed the example of Philadelphia and Chicago in securing the passage of an antispitting ordinance in 1904. Street cars and public buildings were now forbidden territory for the indulgence of this traditionally American habit. Mrs. R. C. Reinertsen was given credit for the passage of the ordinance that thus defended sweeping skirts from contamination. Milwaukee club women would not hesitate, she said, to resort to several expedients proposed for effecting compliance with the new regulation. One of the most novel provided that every club woman should "carry a little silver bell to be rung at every offender, so that the man who dares to transgress will be greeted by a veritable chorus of bells at every expectoration."[51] Public concern over the prevalence of tuberculosis in the urban community led to the passage of an ordinance for the maintenance of tuberculosis hospitals in 1907, to agitation in the following year which resulted in tuberculin tests for cows from which the city's milk supply was drawn, and to provisions for the medical inspection of school children and the maintenance of school nurses in 1909. In the following year, Dr. G. A. Bading, who served as health commissioner from 1906 to 1910, proposed the licensing of all places where food was manufactured, commercially prepared, or offered for sale, advocated better care of the streets as a means of overcoming the "dust evil," reported that some 11,000 school

[51] Milwaukee *Sentinel*, April 22, 1896; March 11, 1904. Dr. F. M. Schulz was health commissioner from 1898 to 1906. *Official Program Commemorating Wisconsin's 100th Anniversary as a Territory* (Milwaukee, 1936), 34.

children had been vaccinated in 1909, and recommended that medical inspection of school children be extended to the parochial schools. Among the planks of the platform on which the Social Democratic Party came into control of the city in 1910 was one which advocated improved hospitals and free medical care for the poor; and once in office the Seidel administration undertook a health department project which in one year reduced the death rate by 50 percent in one underprivileged district and provided a lesson in municipal health and sanitation to the urban community as a whole.[52]

While the municipality was assuming an increasing responsibility for the health of the urban dweller, it was also exhibiting an interest in community beauty and order. Although the cleanliness of the streets was a matter of civic interest from the middle seventies, for more than a decade the motivation was more economic than aesthetic or social. Urging the removal of ash barrels from the front of residential property in 1886, the *Sentinel* asserted:

> The impression made upon strangers by the streets of a city has very much to do with its prosperity, a favorable impression leading to an increase of population and capital. The value of real estate in a neighborhood depends much upon the cleanliness of the householders and the absence of unsightly ash barrels and slop buckets.

The enthusiasm for park development in the early nineties resulted in a plan, in 1892, for Newberry Boulevard—a street from Lake Park to River Park bordered by ornamental shade trees; but not until the twentieth century was there a real movement to achieve "the city beautiful." A conference of club women held on February 21, 1900, resulted in the organization of a central committee to undertake work in town improvement. Mrs. George Ide, vigorous promoter of city beautification, was made chairman of a committee[53] which was to include representatives from nine woman's clubs, among

[52] Milwaukee *Sentinel*, March 30, 1910; Robert E. Nye, History of the Socialist Party of Wisconsin (Paper submitted at University of Wisconsin Summer Session, July 1935), MS in Wisconsin Historical Society Library, 18.

[53] On December 20, 1899, Mrs. Ide addressed the College Endowment Association on "The Influence of Commercialism on the Beauty of Cities." Milwaukee *Sentinel*, April 25, 1886; Dec. 21, 1899; *Wisconsin News*, July 16, 1936.

them the Woman's Club, the Milwaukee College Endowment Association, the Ladies' Art and Science Class, the Social Economics, the M.W.K., the Woman's School Alliance, the Public School Art League, and the South Side Woman's Club. Addressing the meeting, John A. Butler, head of the Municipal League, said:

You women can really accomplish more in the line of civic improvement than four times as many men. Men are often prevented from participation in reforms which they endorse at heart because of the injury that such participation might do their business interests. But women are practically free and independent and with them lies the creation of the right public sentiment.

The central committee intended to establish communication with groups interested in town improvement elsewhere and turned its initial attention toward clearing the streets of waste paper and doing away with objectionable billboards.[54]

A more lasting contribution to civic beauty was to follow from the suggestions of A. C. Clas and a small group of Milwaukeeans who were attempting to turn civic attention to European remedies for the congestion and ugliness of the modern city. In public addresses, newspaper articles, and letters Clas advocated the appointment of a commission to plan coordinated parks and boulevards. In 1905, Mayor Rose lent his support to the proposals, pointing to the work that had been done "on similar lines in other American cities." But a reluctant council delayed its decision until April 1, 1907, when it authorized the appointment of a metropolitan park commission of eleven members. Chosen by the mayor in the following July, the group was ultimately empowered to undertake planning in the broad sense of the term. Although the idea of comprehensive zoning was still in the future, the commission aimed to provide residence areas apart from the commercial and factory zones; and indeed there already existed an ordinance, passed in September 1902, which regulated the height of buildings with respect to the width of the street. The

[54] On this score, Butler reminded the crusaders that the law protected a man in the inartistic defacement of his own property so long as he did not offend the moral sense. Milwaukee *Sentinel*, Feb. 22, 1900.

movement for improving the appearance of the city gained momentum in March 1908 when the president of the Art Commission of New York, speaking on "Civic Beauty" under the auspices of the Citizens' Business League, suggested a program for beautifying the city; and a month later, the *Sentinel* endorsed a movement to achieve "Milwaukee the Beautiful." At the insistence of the members of the Citizens' Business League and the Outdoor Art Association, a Chicago landscape architect was called in to suggest methods of beautifying the river front. The *Sentinel* repeated its practice of conducting a contest to encourage the cleaning up of unsightly back yards; and Mayor Rose promised that the city would "undertake to see that the property in the rear of the buildings along the docks" was cleaned up and that everything which was "offensive either to the eye or health" would be removed.[55]

The concentration of population in the city presented Milwaukee with a housing problem somewhat different from the tenement evil with which many American cities of the period were faced. While an inspection of 1905 revealed that "no definite tenement district" existed, many observers believed that the city's basement dwelling places fostered worse conditions than the tenements of other metropolitan centers. Many lots held two houses, one in back of the other, their basement and first floor rooms almost totally devoid of air and light. Recently arrived immigrants occupied these squalid quarters, the inhabitants frequently sleeping in shifts, with day and night workers using the same beds.[56] Although reform of these conditions was agitated as early as 1904, in connection with the crusade against tuberculosis, the situation was not improved as late as 1910, when the field secretary of the charity organization of the Russell Sage Foundation described Milwaukee as "one of the worst cities in its control of the housing problem." Contending that greater numbers of people were crowded into

[55] City Planning Commission of the City of Milwaukee, *Preliminary Reports*, November 1911, p. 4; Bruce, *History*, 1:488; Milwaukee *Sentinel*, March 21, April 25, 26, 1908.
[56] Bur. of Labor and Ind. Statistics, Wisconsin, *Twelfth Biennial Rept.*, 1905-6, pp. 289-90, 297.

small floor space with less light there than in "any other city," he blamed the congested dwellings for the prevalence of tuberculosis, chronic rheumatism, and juvenile delinquency, as well. His recommendations, made before numerous civic organizations, focused attention upon the need of creating conditions where children would "have green grass to play on, instead of the filth and dirt of the streets."[57] Such sentiments were echoed by civic leaders like William George Bruce, who as early as 1906 had called attention to the fact that the growth of population had absorbed the vacant lots formerly available to children for exercise and play and reported the practice of the larger cities of Germany where "suitable plots of ground" had been provided for this purpose. By the middle of the decade the South Side Woman's Club had agitated the provision of playgrounds in six of the city's public parks. The current trend toward municipal recreation facilities for the citizenry was further advanced in 1908 when the members of the North Side Civic League requested that the city's school buildings be converted in the evenings and on Sundays to such civic purposes as free night schools, reading rooms, and social centers, a proposal repeated in 1910 by the City Club when it endorsed the experience of Rochester, New York, in organizing similar civic activities. Some supervised playgrounds were provided in 1907, and a beginning was made with community centers in 1909.[58]

The expanding concept of municipal responsibility for urban health, beauty, and order naturally involved some curtailment of individual liberty. City dwellers had early become accustomed to subordinating individualism to community good in connection with fire protection, quarantine of contagious diseases, and the restriction and segregation of public nuisances.

[57] Milwaukee *Sentinel*, March 25, 1910. A writer in the Milwaukee *Sentinel* asserted in 1904 the necessity of getting rid of the basement living room. "How can you fight tuberculosis in the basement?" he asked. "What moral standards can be expected of a large family which lives in one or two rooms and is ready to admit boarders in the family circle? . . . In many instances the basement living room is much more like a stable where the family herds together like cattle." *Ibid.*, March 19, 1904. McLean spoke at the University Club on "The Helter-Skelter and the Planned City." *Ibid.*, March 27, 1910.

[58] *Ibid.*, March 9, 14, 1906; Milwaukee *Journal*, May 23, 1908.

But the development of the metropolis brought new restrictions on its members. The liberties of bicyclists became a political issue in 1896. The *Sentinel* proposed that riding on sidewalks should be prohibited, that cyclists should be required to use a warning bell and a lighted lamp at night, and that they should be limited to a moderate speed in the city's busy thoroughfares. Despite the fact that some of the devotees of the new fad tried to prevent the passage of a regulatory ordinance, it was accomplished in the summer of 1896, only to prompt proposals for regulating the speed of trolley cars so long as the streets were full of cyclists.[59] In 1902 the council passed an ordinance to regulate the use and speed of automobiles, specifying a fine of one to five dollars or a jail sentence of not to exceed ninety days for infringement of the law. In 1904 the council passed an antismoke measure which was designed to prohibit plants from emitting dense black smoke and which provided for a smoke inspector; and in 1908, Health Commissioner Bading, decrying the effect of city noises on the nerves of city dwellers, proposed that steps be taken to "limit unnecessary noises."[60] In March 1910 the Republicans came out in favor of "a Milwaukee beautiful; the enforcement of the smoke ordinance; the suppression of unusual and unnecessary noises; and the establishment and maintenance of comfort stations in proper places throughout the city."[61]

A fivefold increase in population, between 1870 and 1910, was not the only sign that Milwaukee was maturing into a metropolis. Worries over a water supply, a sewerage system,

[59] According to the *Sentinel*, "The question of regulating and defining the relations between wheelmen and pedestrians or vehicles" had "occupied the attention of the authorities in most of our large cities." Milwaukee *Sentinel*, March 23, April 19, July 2, 1896; *Evening Wisconsin*, July 6, 1896.

[60] Milwaukee *Sentinel*, March 8, 1904; Milwaukee *Journal*, Aug. 20, 1908. This recalls agitation in 1876 to curtail the noise of the engine whistles of the vessels on the river—"an uproar beyond all the other noises of the city combined." "We have ordinances regulating nearly every business carried on in the city, and that in a way generally intended to promote the health and convenience of the people, and the general prosperity. Hackmen may stand only in certain streets, the venders of things consumed in the household are subjected to regulations; there is an ordinance relating to the awnings over shop doors and windows; incautious individuals who imbibe too freely . . . are . . . dragged before . . . the law. . . . All this is proper." *Evening Wisconsin*, June 3, 1876.

[61] Milwaukee *Sentinel*, March 24, 1910.

the disposal of garbage, and the provision of parks; controversies over municipal ownership in the field of public utilities; and charges of graft and corruption in connection with urban construction and street improvement—these were the "growing pains" of urbanization out of which metropolitan maturity was achieved. In reacting to these problems of the urban drift, the traditional conservatism of the community prevailed. Food inspection was resisted in the seventies as were municipal ownership and regulation of public utilities some decades later. As has been pointed out, modern types of pavement were tardily provided; and the transit system was less extensive in the middle eighties than in most cities of Milwaukee's size. As late as 1906 park development was far behind what similar cities had accomplished, and the housing situation as late as 1910 was the subject of serious reproof. Yet for over a decade many Milwaukeeans had been taking these problems seriously. The civic conscience very definitely began to prick in the middle nineties—a development with which the welling up of municipal reform and the rise of the Social Democratic Party both coincided. The period 1893 to 1896 saw greater and more varied expenditures for heavy public works than had any period of equal length before; and it was a foregone conclusion that municipal funds rather than the volunteer donations of prominent citizens would meet the cost.[62] More and more, expenditures for public improvements were charged to the municipal corporation, less to the specific beneficiaries or owners of abutting property. And by the first decade of the twentieth century the expansion of urban services was such as to give evidence of what the Republican candidate for mayor in 1910 called "a decided awakening of the city conscience."[63]

A number of factors were responsible for this achievement. One was the pressure of the expanding city and a popular

[62] Larson, *Financial and Administrative History*, 152. In 1873 when there arose the question of building the North Street bridge, certain leading citizens offered to donate from $500 to $1,000 to make up whatever deficiency might exist in connection with the project. Pledges were made by Edward O'Neill, John Nazro, Alexander Mitchell, Levi Blossom, Guido Pfister, E. Mariner, and others. Milwaukee *Daily Sentinel*, April 5, 1873.

[63] Milwaukee *Sentinel*, March 24, 1910.

awareness of impending metropolitanism, the "manifest destiny" of the metropolis, so to speak. Waterworks were supported in the early seventies on the ground that they were a necessity in a densely populated community; and the extension of transit facilities was later argued for the same reason. It was the opinion of an editorial writer in 1889 that the practice of leaving ash boxes on business streets should be opposed by people who had "the city's growth toward metropolitanism in view." In 1896, the *Sentinel* asserted: "Milwaukee has long passed the experimental stage of existence. She has no excuse for the continuance of slipshod practices characteristic of that stage. Milwaukee is a great city."[64] City promoters argued for improvements as a means of stimulating the growth of population.[65] But on and beyond these material considerations, Milwaukeeans increasingly viewed the city as a social entity which had an obligation to its members, an obligation which should be fulfilled, to be sure, in the most practical and expedient fashion. According to the *Sentinel* in 1892, the people of the city had

formed a chartered corporation for a definite purpose, to make community existence tolerable, perhaps beautiful, by the making and care of streets, by the building and support of schools, by the providing of pure water and the keeping of the air we breathe from contamination, by the prevention of the spread of contagious diseases, and so on.

From this point of view, the "doing of anything directly by the municipal government that now needs the consent of the municipal government for others to do" followed naturally and as a practical consequence of community organization.[66] The pressing realities of urbanism thus lent expediency to an increasingly social philosophy of municipal government and laid the foundations for the program on which the Social Democrats came into power in 1910.

[64] *Ibid.*, Nov. 20, 1889; Nov. 30, 1896.
[65] President West of the Chamber of Commerce asserted in 1872 that the city government "must not, in the guise of economy, be too parsimonious" if an impulse were "to be given to the growth and business of Milwaukee." *Ibid.*, April 9, 1872.
[66] *Ibid.*, Feb. 21, March 30, 1892.

In devising ways to meet the obligations of the municipality, its representatives had ready recourse to the experience of other cities, both in America and abroad. This was true in the case of almost every improvement of the period. City officials investigated the paving methods of neighboring cities, toured the East to study waterworks and gain ideas for garbage and sewage disposal, and cited the park and playground enterprises of European and American cities. A manager, experienced with transit systems in the East, developed the street railway system; the designer of Central Park, New York, was consulted on park improvement. New York's legislation on home rule, Cleveland's experience with electric railroads, Philadelphia's antispitting ordinance, and English and German sanitary legislation contributed to the pattern of Milwaukee's urban regulations. Certainly there was nothing provincial in the city's solution of its municipal needs. To the influence of other urban communities, and of reformers from them who visited the city, must be added the efforts of the public-spirited citizens whose funds or whose vision propelled the city toward the realization of broader social goals. The newspapers, as in an earlier period, played a significant suggestive role. The *Evening Wisconsin,* the *Sentinel,* and the Milwaukee *Journal* took turns crusading for municipal improvement and reform. Toward the close of the period the *Sentinel* was speaking strongly for Republican conservatism; but none of the three was really obstructionist. The political parties, too, exerted an influence, especially the Social Democrats, whose aggressive and well-planned activities in the council during the first decade of the twentieth century "to a great extent determined the economic"—and social—"policies of the older parties." By 1910 all the parties were vying to advance proposals which would "make for the uplift of the whole city."[67] The organized efforts of the municipal reformers kept the idea of improvement before the public, until the average urban dweller began to be concerned about and interested in what the municipality could do. This educative process bore

[67] Larson, *Financial and Administrative History,* 157; see also Republican campaign argument in Milwaukee *Sentinel,* March 24, 1910.

fruit in 1910 when all the political parties endorsed a concept of urban service which would have found few supporters forty years earlier and when the voters elected the candidate who promised to go farthest in this direction, "in accord with the trend of civilization . . . toward a great city with a free, independent civic spirit," a city which would take positive and vigorous action in securing and improving the urban dweller's way of life.[68]

[68] Inaugural remarks, quoted, *ibid.,* April 20, 1910. Victor Berger said: "We want suggestions from householders, civic societies—everybody. No one need feel that he is butting in." Unidentified clipping, in Duke University Socialist Collection.

CHAPTER 15

The Metropolitan Mold

JOURNALISTS of the seventies found an explanation for the prevailing "lure of the city" in the social and cultural attributes of urban life: luxurious houses, famous pictures, prima donnas, popular preachers, the theater, the emporiums of art and fashion—"the pomp and pride of life." In the city, wrote the editor of the *Sentinel* in March 1871, one could "shop better, . . . dress more fashionably, . . . give parties more conveniently, . . . get better concerts, and see more sights";[1] and to judge from a survey of the social scene in Milwaukee between 1870 and 1910 what he said was to a considerable extent true. The city dweller did have more access to the conveniences of living: a broader selection of food, clothing, and furniture; recourse to churches and educational institutions that were increasingly adapted to individual differences and desires; an opportunity to obtain specialized services from the professions; and an ever-widening choice of recreation and entertainment.

Milwaukeeans of the period were a home-loving people, whether they were the long-established residents whose mansions on tree-shaded Prospect Avenue were patterned after castles on the Rhine or the East European newcomers whose small, two-story dwellings on the South side were symbols for them of the economic opportunity of the New World.[2] As in the case of most of the large new cities of the Middle West,

---

[1] Milwaukee *Sentinel*, March 18, 1871. A writer for the *Evening Wisconsin* (Milwaukee) spoke in similar vein: Considering the advantage of gas, electric lights, sewerage, good streets, parks, and amusements, "as a general thing the comforts are infinitely greater in the large cities." July 24, 1886.

[2] "Almost every family has its own little home." King, "The Cream City," *Cosmopolitan*, 10:556 (March 1891).

Milwaukee of the eighties had no residential architecture peculiar to itself. As Ernest Ingersoll wrote in 1881: "These men and women are New York and New England transplanted. . . . They have brought with them the mingled customs of all the Atlantic centres of civilization, and have fitted them together to suit the new exigencies of the Northwest."³ Nevertheless, visitors were impressed with the spacious grounds that surrounded most of the private residences in the finer parts of the city and with the abundance of shade trees which softened the effect of the often too garishly ornamental "gingerbread" decoration of the period. The ornately decorated balconies and railings of the Victorian "mansion"—products of cast-iron work and the power scroll saw—attested the contribution of a new-found industrialism to architectural design; while the multiplication of apartments or "flats," as they were called, was the builder's solution to the ever-increasing concentration of population in the urban scene. One of the most admired of these, the Grand Avenue Flats, as advertised in a feature article in the *Evening Wisconsin* for February 18, 1886, contained thirty-six suites and boasted elevators, electric bells, steam heat, a chute for garbage and ashes from each apartment, speaking tubes, and a drying room for laundry on the top floor. According to the editor, their construction, with expected rents of $400 to $800 yearly, was "a venture based on faith in the future growth of the city."

Within the residence, as outside, the tendency of the pretentious seventies and ornate eighties was to make furniture and decoration appear to be something other than what they really were. Living rooms were a confusion of whatnots, stands, and fancy tables, vying for attention with statuary, ornamental bric-a-brac, and pictures. For the small apartment, which began to replace the roomy dwellings of an earlier day, industrial ingenuity provided such household equipment as a multiple-

---

³ Ingersoll, "Milwaukee," *Harper's New Monthly Mag.*, 62:712 (April 1881). The Emil Schandein home was the work of an American architect who had been sent to Germany to design the owner a home in the "architecture of a modernized castle palace on the banks of the Rhine." George Yenowine, "A Western Mansion," *Cosmopolitan*, 10:414-15 (February 1891).

duty parlor bedstead which could serve at pleasure as bookcase, dressing table, wardrobe, sideboard, or desk. As wood became scarce, and coal transportable, coal-burning hot-air furnaces, advertised as early as 1871, began to replace the stoves of the preceding wood-burning era.[4] Bathrooms were coming into general use by the middle seventies; and labor-saving devices such as washing machines were placed on the market. Advertisements for canned fruits and vegetables, appearing in the early seventies, suggested, as did the notice of a steam laundry in 1875, that commercial and industrial responses to the demands of a populous urban market were making life easier, if less self-sufficient, for Milwaukee housekeepers. The increasing availability of commercially canned foods foretold the passing of the kitchen garden, as reflected in the advertisement of Savage and Son—Cash Grocers and Meat Market, in 1885: "Ten cents will buy either [sic] of the following articles: 3-lb. can table Peaches, 3-lb. can Tomatoes, 2-lb. can Corn, 2-lb. can Lima Beans, 2-lb. can String or Wax Beans, 2-lb. pkg. Rolled Oats or Wheat, best brand, 2½ lb. bag Self-rising Buckwheat." As yet, however, there were few references to the widely distributed packaged products which were ultimately to cast the urban dweller's dietary habits into a national mold. Advertisements for Dr. Price's and Royal Baking Powder and for certain brands of meat sauces appeared in the eighties. Gail Borden Eagle Brand condensed milk was advertised in the middle nineties; and by 1900 readers were urged to purchase Jell-O, Lea and Perrin's sauce, Martha Washington baking powder, Uneeda Biscuit, and Jap Rose and Ivory soap.[5] This period saw, too, the development of the telephone as a household as well as a commercial convenience. Charles H. Haskins became the local representative of the National Bell Telephone Com-

[4] Leora Howard, Home Life in Milwaukee, 22, 27. Anti-clinker coal was advertised in 1875.

[5] According to Henry M. Mendel, who discussed the grocery jobbing business in 1892, the business of canning vegetables was in its infancy in the early eighties, and the ante bellum grocery stock had been confined to "sugars, coffees, syrups, spices, fish, dried fruit, and a few manufactured articles such as tobacco and soap." In 1880, Dixon's Cash Grocery House was advertising canned fruits, vegetables, fish, soups, etc. Business in these commodities had increased very greatly by 1890. Anderson and Bleyer, *Milwaukee's Great Industries*, 123-26; Milwaukee *Sentinel*, Nov. 25, 1880; Nov. 26, 1885; July 14, 1937.

pany in 1879. A switchboard was operating in the city as early as 1877; but the first formally organized telephone exchange dates to May 10, 1879. By 1881, there were at least 600 subscribers; fifteen years later the number had increased to 3,000. Boys, who chased up and down in front of the switchboard to make connections, were the telephone operators of this early period.[6]

The decreasing self-sufficiency of the urban household and the growing specialization in urban merchandising were manifested in the appearance of chain and department stores which catered to the increasingly varied categories of urban purchasers as well as to the multiplying variety of their desires. Without a doubt, as the editor wrote, one could "shop better" in the city. Turpin and Company's "Great 5, 10 and 25 cent Store," established in Milwaukee in 1884, was one of seven nationwide branches.[7] At the other extreme of the purchasing scale was the fast-developing "department store" where, according to the editor, one could engage in "shopping in its sublimated sense." When T. A. Chapman and Company, built on a merchandising firm founded in 1857, moved into its new establishment in the early seventies, the event was heralded as "another instance of Milwaukee's metropolitan development."[8] It was something new for Milwaukeeans to be able to select "a yard of Chantilly from twenty different patterns," and it was no less an indication of the new potentialities of the market when the proprietors could ask $150 for "dinner costumes in Worth's best manner" and advertise "black Llama polonaises as fine as thread," for $50, embroidered walking jackets of cashmere, and shawls anywhere from $1.00 apiece to $500. It was claimed

[6] *Ibid.*, July 14, 1937. Among the Milwaukeeans who invested in the telephone enterprise were E. H. Brodhead, Henry C. Payne, Charles Pfister, Charles G. Stark, D. L. Wells, and H. F. Whitcomb. See also, Harry Barsantee, "The History and Development of the Telephone in Wisconsin," *Wisconsin Magazine of History*, 10:150-63 (December 1926).

[7] Barton, *Industrial History of Milwaukee*, 164. A local branch of the Great Atlantic and Pacific Tea Company was operating before 1882. Milwaukee *Journal*, Nov. 16, 1932.

[8] *Milwaukee of Today* (Phoenix Publishing Company, Milwaukee, 1892), 87. A. W. Rich and Company, founded in 1867, James Morgan's, established in 1874, and Espenhain's were among the most prominent of the "dry goods" stores which catered to both the retail and wholesale trade. Barton, *Industrial History of Milwaukee*, 123, 178.

that the store was "stocked from basement to dome with the same variety of goods at the same prices which [New York's] A. T. Stewart himself offers"; among its departments were those for "gentlemen's furnishings, a ladies ditto, cloak and dressmaking rooms, a counter for the sale of jewelry and toilet articles, and an immense department lined with mirrors and crowded with ready-made costumes." At the parasol counter could be found "3,000 sunshades of every style and price from the baby's blue silk canopy at 75 cents to small umbrellas with gold or ivory handles, for $12.00." The eighties saw the addition of other establishments of the department store type. Gimbel Brothers came in 1888, taking over the site of the Harris Brothers Fair and promising an "active store" like those "in other great cities." A variant of the department store was that of Julius Simons at Grand Avenue and Fourth Street where the departments were leased out by the owner to a number of different merchants. Stone Brothers of Chicago had the jewelry and leather goods concession and the Herzfeld-Phillipson Company, several other departments. Ultimately Nat Stone and Carl Herzfeld bought out Simons and together founded the Boston Store. The development of Schuster's department store at North Third and West Garfield streets was a response to the geographical expansion of the metropolitan market. Typical of other specialized services for the urban consumer was Mrs. C. B. Kessler's New York Hair Store, the parlors of which were "stocked throughout with a full line of hair goods" and where in 1885 there were "two skillful artists," who dressed "ladies' hair in any style desired."[9]

With the growth of the city came more numerous opportunities for the professional entertainment that urban dwellers expect of the metropolis. Instead of the infrequent and intermittent performances of an earlier period, which left the spectator little or no selection of professional entertainment, Milwaukee's amusement and theatrical bill of fare now began

[9] A. T. Stewart operated the largest retail store in the world, an eight-story building covering an entire block in New York City. *Dictionary of American Biography*, 18:4; Milwaukee *Sentinel*, April 7, 1875; Oct. 16, 1895; Milwaukee *Journal*, Nov. 16, 1932; Barton, *Industrial History of Milwaukee*, 217.

to offer something to suit nearly everybody's taste and the continuous provision of it. By the seventies such entertainments were increasing in number, and from the middle eighties forward there was available a choice of amusement nightly. The Grand Opera House, built by Jacob and Herman Nunnemacher in 1871, joined the Academy of Music as the scene of most of the better performances. The Davidson Theatre was opened in 1890; and by the end of the century a number of smaller houses had been added, including the Alhambra, which opened in 1893. The theatrical offerings were, however, more continuously available than consistently meritorious. Actors of reputation, with their New York companies, made periodic visits. Edwin Booth, Lawrence Barrett, Richard Mansfield, Mary Anderson, E. H. Sothern, Modjeska, and Sarah Bernhardt represented the English stage with as much distinction as did the famous exponents of the German drama brought by the German theater. But on the whole, the English theater was not enthusiastically received in Milwaukee. Edwin Booth, Lawrence Barrett, and Richard Mansfield had unpleasant experiences in the city. When Sarah Bernhardt presented *La Tosca* and *Cleopatra*, in March 1892, the audience, unlike the performance, did not come up to the reviewer's expectations; "there was little clapping—not much—and the audience put on its wraps and hustled homeward." Ten years later, the agent of a theatrical syndicate asserted that Milwaukee was "the poorest theatrical city in the United States."[10]

More frequently present in the procession of entertainment that passed across the stages of the Academy of Music and the Grand Opera House were stock companies like those of Katie Putnam, Maggie Mitchell, Bartley Campbell, and J. H. McVicker, engaged by the week to play such favorites as *Fanchon the Cricket, A Celebrated Case, Little Barefoot,* and *The Pearl of Savoy*. Added to these were minstrel performers; pantomime troupes like those of Morris or the Jee Brothers in such shows as the ever-popular *Humpty Dumpty Abroad;* and "gorgeous spectacles" like that of the Undine Combination. Engagements

---

[10] See chapter 11 for discussion of the German theater. *Evening Wisconsin,* Oct. 15, 1895; Milwaukee *Sentinel,* March 9, 1892; April 9, 1902.

at the Grand Opera House during September and October 1881, each running for a week, included the Original Madison Square Company in *Hazel Kirke;* Sol Smith Russell in *Edgewood Folks;* John McCullough, tragedian; Mitchell's Pleasure Party in *Our Goblins;* Professor Hermann, the "Great Prestidigitator"; and Rice's Surprise Party in a repertoire of light comic opera. Admission prices were 25, 50, and 75 cents, and $1.00. By the opening of the new century, New York productions, like those of DeWolf Hopper and his company in *Panjandrum* and E. H. Sothern and Julia Marlowe in Shakespearean repertoire, usually ran for three nights and a matinee. In April 1898, the amusement seeker could choose among the following offerings on a single night: Jolly Nelly McHenry playing in *A Night in New York* at the Davidson; the "funny farce comedy," *The Prodigal Father,* at the Bijou; Agnes Sorma, German tragedienne, playing *The Doll's House* at the Pabst; the nightly concert by Clauder's Solo Sextette at the Schlitz Palm Garden; roller skating at the Exposition; or twelve acts of vaudeville at the Alhambra.[11]

The "John B. Rice" of this period was Jacob Litt. This impresario endorsed the theory that city dwellers as well as visitors to the city "expect more or less in the line of amusements"; and this he undertook to provide for every level of the urban society. In addition to leasing the Academy of Music, which he had redecorated so as to provide "four elegantly constructed proscenium boxes . . . designed to represent Moorish pagodas," he managed the summer theater at Schlitz Park and the Dime Museum which stood opposite the Plankinton House. Open daily, with hourly performances from one to ten o'clock in the evening, the latter offered to as many as 3,000 spectators a day such curiosities as "The Frog Child, London Middle-Age Boy Giant; Ritter's Swiss Warblers and Harp Players; Burt Barton, the Human Salamander; Dr. Casanovia, Who Cuts Up a Man before the Audience; the Montezuma Flatheads; Barnum's Fiji Cannibals; and Maggie Minott the Midget." By the late nineties, Litt was managing the Bijou Opera House

[11] *Ibid.,* April 2, 1874; April 4, 8, 1876; April 4, 1878; April 8, 1894; April 10, 1898; see theatrical bill reproduced in *Wisconsin News* (Milwaukee), July 16, 1936.

where stock company shows were offered for 25 cents admission. Burlesque, too, was popular in this gay decade. Ada Ray's English Girls played a week at the Peoples' Theatre in 1894; later the popular house for this type of entertainment was the Star Theatre. There one could see the Gay Masqueraders' Burlesque Show (10 to 30 cents admission; front rows 50 cents), the City Club Company, and the Daintee Paree Burlesquers. The Majestic Theatre opened in April 1908 with vaudeville performances of the Orpheum circuit. Moving pictures were available shortly after the turn of the century, one of the earliest being shown in 1905 at the Theatorium, on the corner of Second Street and Wisconsin Avenue.[12]

Other popular pastimes bore more noticeably the stamp of the prevailing Germanism of the populace. The taverns and pleasure resorts were symbols of a type and era of entertainment which prohibition and the prejudices of World War I were ultimately to bring to a close. The spacious Schlitz Palm Garden, with its broad-domed ceiling and huge fringing potted palms, was nightly the haunt of "Society" and on Sunday afternoons of family groups, come to listen to Arthur Pryor's or Bohumir Kryl's bands. Some of the most famous saloons were the gathering places of the politicians: Weber and Stuber's, with its excellent free lunch of suckling pig or stuffed Watertown goose, where Democratic leaders gathered after council meetings; the Plankinton and Pfister bars, which drew their political followings from the patronage of Mayor David S. Rose and Charles F. Pfister, respectively; and Joe Kalt's, which was a center for the La Follettites. Others catered specifically to Milwaukee's Germandom. "Ma" Heiser's, on the corner of Ogden and Jackson, with its back room reference library, became a center for the discussion of problems affecting the German residents. After-theater audiences from the German theater gathered at the Forst Keller, remodeled from church to rathskeller, to hear Viennese airs played by a string orchestra and listen to the songs of visiting German opera stars. Golden Rhine

[12] Barton, *Industrial History of Milwaukee*, 194; Milwaukee *Sentinel*, April 4, 1884; April 8, 1894; April 17, 1900; April 9, 1902; April 7, 1904; April 4, 1906; Milwaukee *Journal*, Oct. 22, 1922; Feb. 4, 1923.

wines and fine sherries, served amid surroundings that recalled the Fatherland, were available at Herman Toser's *Wein Stube*.

Private parks and pleasure resorts compensated in part for the lack of the public parks for which municipal reformers were agitating in the eighties and nineties. The expansion of population had swallowed the Milwaukee Garden into the center of the city by 1885, but its dance pavilion, bowling alley, and shooting gallery were still popular with the German residents. National Park, at the corner of National and Washington avenues, boasted a race track, artificial lake, deer park, baseball and cricket fields, and roller coaster. Schlitz Park, which the Schlitz Brewing Company had equipped with theater, menagerie, and fountains in 1879, was the scene of summer opera. On the outskirts of the city, the Whitefish Bay resort, with its picturesque umbrella stands and quaint, toadstool-shaped tables, could be reached by bicycle or horse and buggy along the lake shore or via the "Bloomer Girl," a popular excursion steamer, on the lake.[13]

The "vicarious exercise" of a city people, baseball and boxing, drew increasing interest as the century wore to a close. Local baseball was early identified with the national organization of the sport. By 1878 the Cream City Club was a member of the National League, which had been organized two years earlier; but it dropped out after that year because of the poor patronage that attended a last-place finish. In succeeding years the club was affiliated with the Union and Western leagues; and it later became a charter member of the junior major league, the American, which was founded in Milwaukee in 1900. Connie Mack, who had managed the Milwaukee club in 1897, 1898, and 1899, piloted it to a second-place finish in the American League contest of 1900; but with his shift to Philadelphia, the Milwaukeeans finished in last place in 1901. This marked the final appearance of a Milwaukee team in the major leagues; for the club became a charter member of the American Association when that loop was formed in 1902, an

---

[13] Barton, *Industrial History of Milwaukee*, 142, 153; Milwaukee *Sentinel*, July 14, 1937.

THE METROPOLITAN MOLD 405

affiliation which it was to maintain for many years. Prize fighting in the city dates to the late seventies; and during the decade which followed, John L. Sullivan, Billy Madden, and others gave exhibitions at the old Slensby Theatre on Plankinton Avenue. During the nineties, as bare knuckles gave way to the skin-tight gloves and later to those of two and three ounces, Sullivan, Jim Corbett, Bob Fitzsimmons, Tommy Ryan, Dan Creedon, Jack McAuliffe, and other pugilistic celebrities gave exhibitions in the city or appeared in melodrama.[14] Golf, the ultimate response to the city dweller's urge for outdoor exercise, made its appearance in Milwaukee in the fall of 1894. First enthusiasts were Grant Fitch, J. H. Tweedy, and J. K. Ilsley, who had played the game at the Old Chicago Golf Club in November of that year. The Milwaukee Country Club, located in what is now the heart of Shorewood, was formally opened on June 28, 1895; and a six-hole course was laid out. The first golf tournament in the city was held in 1900. By 1912 an eighteen-hole course on the Milwaukee River had been established. A correlative development which provided outdoor recreation for the city dweller was the growing popularity of the motor car. The first automobile to be operated in Milwaukee was driven by George L. Odenbrett, on May 18, 1899. By 1906, advertisements for automobiles were appearing frequently in the newspapers. In that year the Buick and the Winton could be had for $2,500; the Cleveland and the Merkel, for $3,500; Ramblers brought from $1,750 to $2,500; and in the "low price field" there were the Wayne at $1,250 and the Maxwell runabout at $780. The organization of the Aero Club on March 2, 1908, reflected an awakening interest in aeronautics which was stimulated by the aerial exploits of such

[14] For information on the history of baseball in the city the author is indebted to City Treasurer Joseph J. Krueger. See also *Dictionary of American History*, 1:165-66; *Evening Wisconsin*, Jan. 12, 1886; June 3, 1889; and, for considerably fuller treatment, Oct. 15, 1895. "Something beautiful to behold is the clinging faith of Milwaukeeans in the ability of their league baseball team to play winning games of ball," commented a writer in the *Evening Wisconsin* in June 1889. "The boys have made a pretty consistent record of losses thus far since the league season opened, but there is hardly a baseball enthusiast in the city who does not expect to see them 'get their grip' after a while and come out as pennant winners."

barnstorming aviators as Art Hoxey, who performed at the State Fair in 1910.[15]

Musical performances, in this period as in village days, provided Milwaukeeans with both recreation and entertainment. The more abundant and increasingly professional offerings attracted by a metropolitan market only expanded the opportunities to enjoy good music which the earlier period had made available; and musical performance of a high standard, blending the amateur performer and almost professional accomplishment, continued to be in large measure a folk expression in Milwaukee life. The Musical Society, by the late sixties the leading musical organization of the West, remained the symbol of the tradition of fine musical performance which the German element had contributed to the urban culture. Now, under a succession of able leaders, including Reinhard Schmelz, Hans Balatka, who had returned momentarily to the scene of earlier triumphs of conductorship, William Mickler, and Eugen Luening, it presented Milwaukee listeners with distinguished programs. A production of *Fra Diavolo* in 1869, with Clara Huck, reflected a developing interest in opera. When Auber's *Masaniello* was performed for the re-opening of the Academy of Music in 1872, all the parts were taken by members of the society. Mickler's contribution as director was to develop the orchestra to the point where it undertook Liszt's *Les Préludes,* Brahms's *First Symphony,* and Beethoven's *Ninth.* In 1875, the society celebrated its twenty-fifth birthday with well over 200 monthly concerts to its credit. Typical was the 234th concert at which the program included two scenes from Max Bruch's *Odysseus* sung by a sextet with mixed chorus and orchestra, two numbers by a promising young violinist recently from the Leipsig Conservatory, a brilliant performance of Liszt's *Hungarian Rhapsody* and a Chopin *Impromptu* by a Miss Rukeyser, a well-blended Dudley Buck quartet, Speidel's *"Waldestrost"* sung by the male chorus, and two overtures performed "without accident," according to the reviewer, by an orchestra of "rather modest proportions."[16]

[15] Milwaukee *Sentinel,* April 1, 1906; July 14, 1937; Milwaukee *Journal,* Nov. 16, 1924; Bruce, *History,* 1:189.
[16] Conard, 2:108-10; Milwaukee *Sentinel,* April 8, 1876.

The German element, however, had no corner on either musical talent or interest. By the early seventies a group of Milwaukeeans, barred from participation in the activities of the Musical Society for lack of the German language, organized the Philharmonic Society and under the leadership of a Professor Abel presented Flotow's *Martha* at the occasion of the opening of Nunnemacher's Grand Opera House on August 17, 1871. Although the Philharmonic Society was short-lived, it became the musical progenitor of the Arion Club and Cecilian Choir, which after the middle seventies represented the interest of the English element in musical performance of high quality. Recruited from local performers, the Arion Club was never as locally self-sufficient as the German Musical Society. Its first concert was given under the direction of A. G. Faville, on February 20, 1877; but shortly thereafter leadership fell to William L. Tomlins, director of the Apollo Club of Chicago, under whose guidance the emphasis of the organization leaned toward the presentation of oratorios. In 1879 the club presented Haydn's *Creation* and in the following year the *Elijah*. In 1884 it began the sponsorship of an annual musical festival. Theodore Thomas' orchestra from Chicago and distinguished soloists from Germany were imported for the occasion. In 1878, the singing section of the German Free Thinkers Society organized the *Liederkranz*.[17]

The vigor of Milwaukee's musical taste and interest gained national recognition in the middle eighties when the city was chosen for the meeting of the National North American *Saengerbund*, which took place in July 1886. City promoters saw in this an opportunity to advertise the city; and John Plankinton's offer of $1,000 to subsidize a world-wide competition for a prize cantata reflected the support of the city's industrialists in encouraging promotional ventures of this kind. About $85,000 was spent in preparation, and the citizens of the city contributed $200,000 to a guarantee fund. The finished product revealed that however much the city was eager for self-advertisement its musical reputation was no empty boast. Approximately 1,200 voices were assembled from the various

[17] Conard, 2:109, 111-13.

local musical organizations for the mixed chorus which sang on the first evening. On another occasion, a chorus of 1,000 children performed. Seven concerts in all were given with an orchestra of 120 pieces and a group of soloists that included Lilli Lehmann, Marianne Brandt, and others. German composers came to direct their own works. As might have been expected, the Musical Society distinguished itself; but the Arion Club male chorus, singing under the direction of Tomlins, showed that Americans as well as Germans had high standards in song. Thus by the middle nineties both German and American performance had demonstrated the musical pre-eminence of the Wisconsin metropolis. By 1893 there had developed a serious movement for a permanent symphony orchestra. Two years later Henry Mendel, president of the Musical Society, was seeking a "wealthy lover of the art of music" who would follow the example of Frederick Layton and "enrich the city with what is a need as vital as the Art Gallery—a high grade permanent orchestra."[18] That this project failed of realization may be in part a paradoxical consequence of the unusually high level of musical taste and performance achieved by the community prior to the existence of sufficient industrial wealth to subsidize a great orchestra. By the time such funds were available, amateur and semiprofessional organizations had already proved their capacity to fill the need. Moreover, by the time a subsidy might have been supplied, the periodic visits of Theodore Thomas' orchestra of Chicago had pre-empted the market for a symphony orchestra that would satisfy the Wisconsin city's already well-developed musical taste. More in spirit with the achievement of fine musical performance as a folk expression in Milwaukee life was the proposal of the Social Democrats in 1910 that the municipality provide the people of the city with symphony concerts at low cost.

Throughout the period, musicians of national repute supplemented local talent in making good music available in the metropolis. Maretzek's Italian Opera Company, with Pauline Lucca as its star, was popular, as were such vocalists as Anna

[18] *Ibid.*, 2:114-16, 120.

THE METROPOLITAN MOLD 409

Louise Cary, Christine Nilsson, and Clara Louise Kellogg. Performances of the works of Verdi, Mozart, Gounod, and Wagner, sung by artists who had performed a winter season in New Orleans, were an admired feature of summer entertainment at Schlitz Park. Recitals by Ernestine Schumann-Heink and Johanna Gadski and performances by the Henry W. Savage Opera Company and by Theodore Thomas' orchestra of Chicago, with Frederick Stock conducting, in 1906, indicate that by the close of the period Milwaukee's music lovers were drawing top-class musical talent to the city. With the visit of the Metropolitan Opera Company of New York, in 1910, presenting a season which introduced Caruso, Emmy Destinn, and Louise Homer in *Aida*, Milwaukee was providing musical opportunities not only for its citizens but for its suburban and rural cultural hinterland as well.[19]

Opportunities for the appreciation of painting as an aesthetic and emotional medium awaited, much more than in the case of music, the growth of urban population and the patronage of industrial wealth. One critic, reporting that this form of expression "languished" in Milwaukee in 1876, explained the "rather dubious existence of art in the West" by asserting that the people were "too busy in acquiring a plentiful of the 'Almighty dollar' to devote much time to the cultivation of that particular branch of art embraced within the limits of painting and pictures."[20] In the early seventies a number of business and professional men made an abortive attempt to revive a movement for an Academy of Fine Arts which had been conceived in the forties. But art still found a primarily utilitarian expression in the work of the portrait painters and in the education of young ladies at Milwaukee College, where the department of aesthetics announced in 1867-68 the existence of facilities for systematic training in drawing and painting. Progress in art appreciation was stim-

[19] King, "The Cream City," *Cosmopolitan*, 10:559 (March 1891); Milwaukee *Sentinel*, April 4, 1906; April 19, 21, 1910.
[20] *Evening Wisconsin*, May 6, 1876. The development of an appreciation for music was different, he thought; there the taste was "elevated and perfected under a process that is entertaining in the highest degree . . . ; one improved himself very much as the lover of walking takes healthful exercise without knowing it."

ulated, however, by the leisure-time interests of a group of Milwaukee women and by an industrial enterprise which in the middle eighties brought a colony of German artists to the growing metropolis. About fifty women took a vigorous interest in the Ladies Art and Science Class which was conducted weekly by Charles S. Farrar during the late seventies. Even earlier—in connection with the Soldiers' Home Fair in 1865— Mrs. Lydia Ely and others had organized what was Wisconsin's first public art exhibition; in 1879, Mrs. Ely, a vigorous crusader for art appreciation, exhibited most of the painting and sculpture then owned in the city; and as director of the art department for the Industrial Expositions of 1881 and following, she developed what have been called "for the time and place truly colossal art shows." Enthusiasm for these exhibits led to the founding of the Milwaukee Museum of Fine Arts and, as interest in this waned, to the organization of the Milwaukee Art Association by Mrs. Susan Frackleton, reputed for her work in the field of ceramic painting. However, these were movements without a wide appeal; the public preferred cheap machine-made paintings to the work of local artists; and in 1881 an artist's agent named Storney listed Milwaukee as one of the two cities in the country in which he presented art goods "without hope."[21]

Further stimulating art activity in the city was the arrival of a group of German panorama painters whose presence made Milwaukee a sort of Hollywood, between 1885 and 1888, for the production of the panoramic representations that were the "motion pictures" of that day. The artists had been recruited in Germany in 1883 by an agent of the enterprise; and Milwaukee was selected as a congenial place of residence for them. A large panorama studio was built near the corner of Fifth and Wells, and here the European artists produced the huge canvases, depicting such scenes as the battles of Mission Ridge and Atlanta, Christ's Entry into Jerusalem, and the Crucifixion, which ultimately were exhibited in the principal cities of the Middle West. The twenty German-trained artists were under

[21] Conard, 2:87; Butts, *Art in Wisconsin,* 127-28, 130-31; *Evening Wisconsin,* Nov. 19, 1881.

the direction of F. W. Heine and August Lohr; but the most distinguished member of the group was Richard Lorenz, who had joined the panoramists as a specialist in the painting of horses. Once his attention had been drawn to the opportunities of the American West as a subject for the canvas, he became, next to Remington, the foremost painter of western genre. He was the first teacher of Louis Mayer, Alexander Mueller, and George Raab, who were ultimately to stand high on the list of local artists.[22]

The presence of the German panoramists augmented a Teutonic influence already operating to turn artistic expression and interest in Milwaukee away from the utilitarian and factual and toward the interpretive and aesthetic. Henry Vianden had been sowing the seeds of a real art movement since his arrival in 1849, and, what was more remarkable, living by the profession. Teaching such promising young Milwaukeeans as Robert Koehler, Carl Marr, Frank Enders, and Robert Schade, he transmitted to them the "Düsseldorf approach," which conceived of art as an interpreter rather than a reporter of nature. Vianden's growing influence, bolstered by the presence of the German panoramists, now made Milwaukee art masculine and German.[23] Whether or not there was as yet among the citizenry any widespread aesthetic appreciation of painting, there now were industrial and urban conditions which made possible the gathering together of artists of like mind and the establishment of art schools. Wealthy manufacturers now bought the paintings displayed at the industrial and other expositions—the sales aggregated $18,000 early in the Exposition of 1895; in 1888 Frederick Layton, prominent packer, presented a building, thirty-eight paintings valued at $50,000, and an endowment fund of $100,000 in patronage of art; and the wealthy brewers sponsored artists and art schools. The ensuing years, however, saw little encouragement of local artists; for the wealthy residents wanted the work of "painters of reputation"; and the

[22] Conard, 2:85; Butts, *Art in Wisconsin*, 136, 180, 182.

[23] *Ibid.*, 110-12, 136. It is significant that both Vianden and Lorenz prompted the return of most of their students to Munich or Weimar for study. Some, like Carl Marr, became primarily German artists. Others, like Koehler and Mayer, returned to the United States to exert an influence in the development of American art.

Layton Gallery grew only slowly in spite of its auspicious beginnings.[24] Nevertheless by the nineties, to the folk art of portraiture and the finishing-school decoration of an earlier period had been added the professional production, the patronage, and the public exhibition of painting which only a metropolitan society could support. And such had been the cultural development of the city by the end of the century that one of its native sons, Louis Mayer, could have had his first training between 1888 and 1891 with Otto Von Ernst and Richard Lorenz, in his home city, have gone thence to Munich and Paris, and by 1900 have returned to Milwaukee to write weekly art critiques for three Milwaukee newspapers and become the leading spirit in organizing in 1901 the Society of Milwaukee Artists, parent of the Milwaukee Art Association and later the Milwaukee Art Institute. Mayer was the father of the proposal that led to the creation of the Municipal Art Commission, and he served as its first secretary.[25]

From a study of occupational density in these years it is apparent that the last quarter of the century was a period of transition, in the developing Wisconsin metropolis, from a stage of urban society centering around the home to one focused on the factory and the machine. Thus, as the period progressed, there was a considerable decrease in the number of dressmakers, seamstresses, tailors, blacksmiths, and household servants, per 1,000 in the population, and a corollary increase in the number of persons engaged in retailing and the number of women employed in industry. At the same time the wider availability of specialized service which a city civilization affords became evident both in the appearance of increased specialization in the professions and developments in education which adapted method and facilities to the individual differences of the students involved. In the field of medicine, highly trained practitioners were replacing the jacks-of-all-trades of an earlier

[24] *Evening Wisconsin,* Oct. 15, 1895; Bruce, *History,* 1:691; *Wisconsin News,* July 16, 1936. Edward J. Steichen said of Milwaukee in 1910: "For a city the size of Milwaukee, you have a wonderful art gallery, and it is too bad that it does not grow more. The fact that it does not grow shows a lethargy on the part of the people." Milwaukee *Sentinel,* March 30, 1910.

[25] Butts, *Art in Wisconsin,* 184.

period. Although the late fifties had seen the appearance of a specialist in women's and children's diseases, it was not until the seventies and eighties that medical specialists became numerous. The number of surgeons increased steadily from the sixties forward. In 1870 came Dr. E. W. Bartlett, specializing in diseases of the eyes and ears; in 1871, Dr. Julia Ford, pulmonary diseases and the diseases of women; in 1877, Dr. G. C. Dermott, maladies of the eyes and ears; in 1883, Dr. Nehemiah Dodge, nervous and mental diseases, and Dr. Alden B. Farnham, disorders of the nose and throat; in 1888, Dr. W. F. Miller, nervous diseases; and in 1891, Dr. Edgar A. Neyman, eye, ear, nose, and throat. By the seventies Milwaukee-born physicians who had had the advantage of broad professional education at the medical schools of Europe, the East, or the Middle West were beginning to return to the home town to practice. For example, Dr. Byron H. Kilbourn, who had been born in Milwaukee in 1840 and educated at Yale and at Rush and Louisville Medical colleges, came back to Milwaukee to practice in 1881. Establishing an office in the same year was Dr. William Meyer, born in Milwaukee in 1856 and educated at the Philadelphia College of Pharmacy and Rush Medical College. The number of Milwaukee-born doctors increased rapidly after 1879.

Similar developments were taking place in the field of dentistry. Rarely now, as in an earlier generation, were doctor and dentist combined in the same person. Some of the dentists of the seventies and eighties were graduates of dental schools; others had learned their profession by the apprentice method. Many had practiced elsewhere before setting up offices in Milwaukee. The increasingly professional attitude of both physicians and dentists was reflected in the rise of organizations to promote higher professional standards. The Odontological Society was organized August 25, 1878, with Dr. Arthur Holbrook as president. The physicians established similar groups. An abortive organization under the leadership of Dr. Nicholas Senn took shape in 1885. The Wisconsin College of Physicians and Surgeons was opened in October 1893, and in the following year, the Milwaukee Medical College, which had been incorporated in 1893. The latter had departments of medicine, dentistry, and pharmacy. In 1907 it became affiliated with Marquette University, which also took over the College of Physicians and Surgeons in 1913.[26]

Education, too, was affected by the tendency toward specialization which the growth of the metropolis made possible. Prior to the administration of F. C. Lau, who became superintendent of schools in 1871, few teachers in the Milwaukee schools had had professional training. In the early seventies, Superintendent Lau added to the high school a normal department which did much to improve the standard of instruction in the elementary schools. In 1872, special teachers for art and music were added to the teaching staff. An impulse for kindergarten education was provided by James MacAlister, who, succeeding Lau in 1874, was convinced that the existing course of study was not meeting the needs of children under six years of age. Incorporated by Peter Engelmann in the program of the German-English Academy as early as 1873, by 1881 kindergarten education was provided in the city schools; and ten years later more was paid annually in salaries to kindergarten teachers than had been paid to the entire teaching staff in the Milwaukee schools in 1861-62. Under the superintendency of William E. Anderson, who served from 1883 to 1892, provision was made for the education of deaf mutes. By the eighties the city was large enough to prompt the concern of the Phonological Institute for children of the community who were hard of hearing. In 1885, the small private school which it supported became a charge of the city school system, on the basis of a subsidy by the State. A room was provided in the primary building on the corner of Seventh and Prairie streets; and Paul Binner, who had specialized in the education of the deaf in the East and in Europe, became the teacher. Children employed in industry during the day constituted a third group of pupils to become the subject of special attention. Beginning in 1880, elementary

[26] For a more extended discussion of the age, sex, and occupational characteristics of the generation, 1870 to 1910, as well as comparisons on these scores with the generation that followed, see chapter 16. See also, chart, in appendix, showing distribution of population of Milwaukee by selected occupations, 1870 to 1940. Frank, *Medical History of Milwaukee*, 37-38, 48-50; 56, 64, 68-69, 76, 80; Andreas, *History of Milwaukee*, 1034-38; Gregory, *History*, 1:1000-1003.

education for boys was provided three nights a week, and for girls, on two. The original plan of charging a small fee for books, slates, and stationery was abandoned when it became apparent that this practice was causing a decrease in enrollment. In 1897 the evening schools were discontinued. This came about in part for lack of good teachers, when the pay was but $2.00 a night, and because the children who worked were frequently too tired to study in the evening. In 1907, a School of Trades, conducted under the auspices of the Merchants' and Manufacturers' Association, became a part of the school system, subject to support from taxation. Mechanical drawing, machine design, plumbing, and pattern making were in the course of study. It has been said that this was "the first instance in the history of education in America where such an institution" was made "a part of the public school system."[27]

The evolution of public-school administration during this generation was to parallel the trend from ward autonomy to municipal integration which characterized developments in the sphere of civic management. At the close of the sixties, the efficiency of the school system was hampered by the same ward separatism that hindered municipal unity, but in 1868-69 the school board condemned the prevailing lack of uniformity and recommended that the city "be divided into school districts without regard to ward lines." Nevertheless, ward individualism continued into the seventies, even though in 1875 the buildings were given district numbers in place of names. The adoption of uniform textbooks in 1868 was a unifying influence as was the central high school, which was opened in the same year. By 1910 city growth had necessitated the erection of four high schools, one for each "side" of the city. The late eighties and early nineties saw the construction of East, South, and West Division high schools; and North Division was occupied in 1906. By 1907, a total of 2,407 pupils was enrolled in the city's high schools; and there were at that date

[27] Donnelly, "Milwaukee Public Schools," in Stearns, *Columbian History of Education in Wisconsin,* 447, 451-52, 454-56; Gregory, *History,* 2:1155-56; Bruce, *History,* 1:637-38; Watrous, 1:413.

91 teachers. Although the physical resources of the school system were severely taxed by population increases during the period, there nevertheless was a high percentage of truancy among the children who should have been enrolled in the city schools. Laws of 1879 and 1891 requiring that children between seven and thirteen or fourteen be kept in school at least part of the day were loosely enforced. But the schools were crowded anyway, so much so that by the late nineties resort was made to barracks and movable schoolhouses. However, as late as 1910, only 58 percent of the residents of the city between six and twenty years of age were attending school. During the superintendency of G. W. Peckham (1892 to 1896), one of the most distinguished figures in local public education, the school system came within the purview of the organized municipal reform movements of the hour. A Women's School Alliance promoted the improvement of sanitary conditions in the school buildings, and a People's Institute advocated opportunities for study by adults. Compulsory attendance was widely discussed, and there was pressure for additional buildings. In 1895, Mrs. S. S. Merrill became the first woman to be elected to the school board.[28]

Facilities for higher education were enlarged during the period in the opening of Marquette College and the expansion of Milwaukee-Downer. A charter for Marquette College had been obtained in 1864; but not until 1881 was the college formally opened, at last realizing Bishop Henni's dream of a Jesuit college for the Wisconsin city. In 1887 the degree of bachelor of arts was awarded to the first class of five students. By 1905, the traditional Jesuit curriculum of the seven-year college had been adapted to the American plan of eight-year high-school and college education; and through the generosity of Robert A. Johnston, a prominent Catholic merchant of the city, the college department was removed to a site at 12th and Wisconsin Avenue, where, in 1907, Johnston Hall was ready for occupancy with all the latest features of college architecture, including science laboratories, library, and chapel. In the same year, after

[28] *Ibid.*, 1:393, 395-96, 399-400, 405, 409, 413-14; Gregory, *History*, 2:1157; *United States Census, Thirteenth,* 1910, *Abstract, Statistics of Population, Agriculture,* . . . , 231; Milwaukee *Sentinel,* April 1, 1896.

the Milwaukee Medical College had asked for affiliation with Marquette, the legislature granted university rights to the school with authority to grant degrees in the colleges which ultimately were to be developed. A law school and college of applied science and engineering were opened in 1908. In the following year Marquette instituted the first summer session ever offered by a Catholic university in the United States; and in 1910 came affiliation with the Wisconsin Conservatory of Music and the inauguration of the Robert A. Johnston College of Economics.[29] Concordia College, an Evangelical Lutheran school, was established in 1881. In 1895, the resources of Milwaukee College were combined with those of Downer College of Fox Lake and the president of the latter, Miss Ellen C. Sabin, became president of the institution henceforward to be known as Milwaukee-Downer College.

Milwaukee College, to which the Milwaukee Female College had succeeded in 1876, had been experiencing difficulties since the death of Catherine Beecher, benefactress of the latter institution. As has been pointed out earlier, Mary Mortimer directed the school from about 1853 to 1857. The Misses Mary and Caroline E. Chapin were in charge from 1857 to 1863. Professor S. S. Sherman, one of the trustees, took over in the latter year and restored the institution to financial solvency by 1866, when Miss Mortimer was recalled. When Mary Mortimer retired in 1874, the school had a faculty of four. On her advice, Professor Charles Farrar, of the Vassar College faculty, was put in charge of the institution with full responsibility for keeping it financially stable; but discouragement over the lack of an endowment prompted him to resign in 1889. However, the accomplishments of the Milwaukee College Endowment Association, organized during the incumbency of his successor, Charles F. Kingsley, and the union in 1895 with Downer College, to which Jason M. Downer had left a fortune in 1883, brightened the financial prospects of the institution. Under the vigorous presidency of Miss Sabin the academic scope and physical equipment of the college were greatly enlarged. A

[29] *Ibid.*, July 14, 1937; R. N. Hamilton, *Brief History of Marquette University* (mimeographed, Milwaukee, 1944), 4-9.

new campus on the outskirts of the city near the lake shore was occupied in 1899; and by 1906 there were 356 students and 32 instructors. Miss Sabin's philosophy of education reflected the contemporary concern for a realistic program of higher education for women. "The steadfast policy of this college," she wrote, "has been to try to meet the needs of its locality, and always to understand and meet the essential requirements in the education of women."[30] In 1901, the Wisconsin Federation of Women's Clubs voted $10,000 to the institution for the establishment of a two-year diploma course for the education of home economics teachers—first course of its kind in the country.[31]

Milwaukee had early made a bid for one of the teacher training institutions for which the Wisconsin legislature had allotted funds in 1865. Despite the city's offer of an improved site and $31,000 to be paid over a five-year period, the regents saw fit to locate the first normal schools at Platteville, Whitewater, Oshkosh, and River Falls. In 1880, the legislators forced the regents to establish such a school in Milwaukee, in return for which the city was to supply a site and building worth $50,000. The city turned over property on Wells Street between 18th and 19th streets and in 1885 provided a building valued at $53,000; the legislature authorized an annual appropriation of $10,000. The school opened in the fall of 1885 with a faculty of seven and 46 students. The model school had originally only the first four grades, but by the end of the year these had expanded to eight, and in 1892 it was agreed that the city schools

[30] The endowment association soon raised $75,000, of which sum Edward D. Holton donated $37,000. Miss Louise R. Upton served as head of the institution from 1893 to 1895. Gregory, *History*, 2:1167-69; Watrous, 1:425.

[31] Milwaukee *Sentinel*, July 14, 1937. Miss Sabin's educational creed is reflected in the following: "We are not indifferent to academic traditions or to the experiences of other colleges, but we have not simply adopted for ourselves the curricula of men's colleges, or made some other woman's college of reputation our pattern and guide. . . . We have constantly protected and emphasized sound academic studies, and we would allow nothing to impair the cultural disciplines of the languages and literature, the social sciences, pure science, and philosophy. . . . We further believe that woman's education should prepare a woman for women's chief vocation, and that the science and art of home-making, which is a business most complex and most significant, should form a recognized part of her training for life. We believe that music, . . . the principles of art, appreciation of beauty, and taste are essential to a well-rounded education." Gregory, *History*, 2:1169-70.

should be used for practice teaching. By 1910, the faculty had increased to thirty-four, and the introduction of a special two-year course for kindergarten teachers marked the beginning of a professional specialization that was to be greatly extended in the ensuing decade. Increases in enrollment necessitated enlargements of the original structure and ultimate removal to new quarters at the northern outskirts of the city on Downer Avenue. The new building was occupied in September 1909, at which date 510 students were enrolled.[32]

The church was affected in a number of ways by the metropolitan expansion of the generation that bridged the nineteenth and twentieth centuries. The advent of the "new" immigration toward the end of the period bolstered the Catholicism that the recent European origin of earlier migrants had already made predominant. As the city extended its limits, offspring of the original churches of all denominations, existing at first as missions, served the outlying neighborhoods. The parent organizations, pressed by the encroachment of business districts, built new and costly edifices that reflected the increased wealth and security of their communicants. The specialization increasingly apparent in other aspects of the urban society found expression in the establishment of churches that ministered exclusively to German, Norwegian, Swedish, and colored worshipers. And organizations like the Young Men's and Young Women's Christian associations labored to fill a social need and to meet a social problem aggravated by the friendlessness of city life.

The Europeanism of the Wisconsin metropolis dictated the denominational complexion of the community during the generation. Throughout the period, the Roman Catholic church claimed more supporters than any other; and the Lutheran bodies were second in strength. According to the Ninth Census, more than a third of the church members of Milwaukee County in 1870 were Catholics; between a sixth and a seventh were Lutherans. By 1890, Roman Catholics numbered 52 percent of the city's church members, and by 1906 they accounted for 65 percent. On the other hand, while Lutherans increased from 15 percent of the total county church membership in 1870 to

---

[32] Marian Silveus, History of Milwaukee State Teachers College, pp. 1-27, *passim*, typescript, dated 1941, in possession of Milwaukee State Teachers College.

28 percent of the total city membership in 1890, by 1906 their numbers had declined to 20 percent of the total—a trend reflecting both the intense Germanism of the eighties and nineties and the more predominantly Catholic character of the "new" migration at the turn of the century. Methodists made up 12 percent of the county church membership in 1870; but they were less than 4 percent of the city's communicants in 1890 and only 2.5 percent in 1906. A similar decline in comparative strength was characteristic of the other early-established Protestant churches of the village period until by 1906, membership in the Baptist Church was 1.5 percent of the total, in the Congregational Church, 1.1 percent, in the Presbyterian Church, 1.6 percent, and in the Protestant Episcopal Church, 1.8 percent. Prominent among the new sects to appear during the generation was Christian Science. The first Christian Science Association in the West was organized in Milwaukee in October 1884; the first church was organized in 1889, and a second had been incorporated by the close of the century.[33]

The phenomenal drift to the city in the eighties led to the establishment of no less than eleven new Catholic churches in contrast to the half dozen which were organized in each of the other decades of the generation. Leadership during the eighties was centered in Archbishop Michael Heiss. In 1881 he succeeded Archbishop Henni, German "Patriarch of the West," whose career, stretching back to the middle forties, was crowned in 1875 with the elevation of the city to an archdiocese. The church of the Gesu, dedicated in 1896 at Grand Avenue and Twelfth Street, was said in 1909 to be the "finest and largest edifice in the city." At that time Milwaukee had about thirty-three Catholic churches and a number of missions. Like the Catholic church, the Lutheran church drew its support largely from the European element in the urban society. Owing allegiance to five different synods, these churches, with few exceptions, conducted their services in German and found their mem-

[33] Percentages of church membership were derived from *United States Census, Ninth,* 1870, vol. 1, *The Statistics of the Population of the United States,* . . . , 560; *United States Census, Eleventh,* 1890, *Report on Statistics of Churches in the United States,* 94-95, 98-99; Bureau of the Census, *Special Reports, Religious Bodies, 1906* (2 pts., Washington, 1910), pt. 1, pp. 380-407, *passim.* See also, Watrous, 1:374.

bership largely among the German residents of the city. The pioneer Lutheran churches, St. Paul's and Trinity, were building handsome new church structures in the seventies. Already their concern for the religious needs of the more remote sections of the growing city had prompted the establishment of missions which became the foundations of more permanent religious offspring. Trinity's offshoots were St. Stephen's on the South side and Immanuel on the North. Immanuel in turn had fathered Zion and Nazareth churches by the middle nineties. As has already been pointed out, the period from 1870 to 1890 was one of marked expansion for this sect. The most significant trend of the decade that followed was an anglicizing movement, which took shape in the nineties with the work of the Rev. William K. Frick, whose slogan was "The Faith of the Fathers in the Language of the Children." His mission, founded in the fall of 1889, fostered a movement which resulted in the establishment of no less than six English Lutheran churches by 1910.[34]

If the census figures can be trusted, Methodism in the Milwaukee area declined between 1870 and 1910. Methodist membership in Milwaukee County dropped from 3,835 in 1870 to 2,980 in 1908. Concern for the laggard growth of Methodism in comparison with its progress in other cities prompted a movement between 1881 and 1883 which resulted in the formation in the latter year of the Milwaukee City Mission and Church Extension Society of the Methodist Episcopal Church, legally incorporated in March 1890 as the Milwaukee Missionary Society of the Methodist Episcopal Church. So stimulated, Methodist membership increased during the eighties at a rate exceeding the rate of increase of urban population in those years. The establishment of mission Sunday schools and Saturday sewing classes produced new churches in outlying and suburban areas. For example, meetings held in 1889 in a store on the West side led in 1891 to the organization of Epworth Church; and the Mitchell Heights Mission Sunday School, established in 1889 as an offshoot of the Summerfield Church, gave way in 1890 to an independent church which ultimately

[34] *Ibid.*, 1:339-40, 350, 352; Conard, 2:152-60, 215-17, 220; Paul H. Roth, *Story of the English Evangelical Lutheran Synod of the Northwest* (n.p., 1941), 22-23.

became the Oakland Avenue Church. Similarly, the assignment in 1891 of a pastor to North Milwaukee by the City Missionary Society led to the foundation in 1893 of a fully organized suburban Methodist Church, of which there were six by 1895. Meanwhile, as in the case of the other denominations, old church structures were giving way to new and finer ones. The Methodist Church at Grand Avenue and Fifth Street dedicated a new structure in 1871 and in 1893 improved its property so that it was valued at $66,000. In 1892, the South Side Society dedicated a new church. Such was the specialization by nationality that in 1895 there were eleven English-speaking, six German-speaking, and one Norwegian-speaking Methodist churches. In 1908 the cornerstone was laid for a Swedish Methodist Episcopal Church.[35]

Similar developments took place in the evolution of the other Protestant churches during the period. The division of the original St. Paul's parish and the creation of city missions swelled the number of Protestant Episcopal churches. For example, in 1892 and 1893, St. Paul's commenced a mission on the East side which became St. Mark's Church; and St. James's, an early offspring of St. Paul's, established a mission which became St. Andrew's on the West side. By the end of the period, in about 1909, there were nine Episcopal churches in the county and four organized and three unorganized missions. The Rev. E. P. Wright, employed as a city missionary, held services in many of the public institutions of the city. In 1874, St. James's Church was rebuilt at a cost of $40,000. As early as 1857, a colony of Baptists from the First Baptist Church established a second church on the West side of the river; in 1875 a similar colonization resulted in the organization of the South Baptist Church. A local mission conducted by this church led to the creation of Immanuel Baptist Church in 1889. In 1892 certain members of the South-side church extended the work of the denomination to Bay View where services were held in the Odd

[35] Watrous, 1:357-58; Conard, 2:200-203, 205-6, 208-9. Itinerant German Methodist ministers preached from house to house in 1846 until a society was organized. The first German Methodist Episcopal church was dedicated in 1848. It had sixty members by the end of the year.

Fellows Hall and a church organized. Pushed by business development, the West-side church moved to 17th and Wells in the middle eighties and erected a large new building; while in 1889, the First Baptist Church completed a new church structure at a cost of $60,000. German Baptist services existed as early as 1854. In 1890 the First Scandinavian Baptist Church was organized; and by the close of the first decade of the twentieth century there were two churches for colored Baptists. Paralleling the Methodist organization for denominational promotion in the eighties was the Milwaukee Baptist Church Union, organized on April 6, 1885, for the purpose of promoting the interests of the church and establishing missions and mission Bible Schools.[36]

Congregationalism kept pace with her sister sects in supplying churches for the outlying areas, as well as in ministering to the needs of the various nationalities in the city. Pilgrim Congregational Church, an offshoot of the Grand Avenue Church, was designed in 1887 to meet the demand for a church in the western limits of the city, and in time there existed Welsh, Swedish, and German as well as suburban Congregational churches. The Grand Avenue Church built a splendid new edifice in 1888 at a cost of $38,000, and the Hanover Street Church dedicated a new structure in 1892. In 1889, under the pastorate of Judson Titsworth, the First, or Plymouth, Congregational Church erected a structure costing $54,061 with a pipe organ valued at $8,400. A reunion of the adherents of Old and New School Presbyterianism on December 7, 1870, led to the creation of Immanuel Presbyterian Church; its edifice, dedicated in 1875, together with grounds and pipe organ, was valued at $200,000, in marked contrast to the original structure of the Old School Presbyterians, which had cost $720 at the time of its dedication in 1849. Taking a vigorous interest in the extension of city mission work, the parishioners of Immanuel were largely responsible for the building of three additional churches: Grace, Bethany, and Westminster. In the seventies they built a mission in the First Ward where a Sunday school, sewing

[36] Watrous, 1:348, 369; Conard, 2:180, 183-84, 223-28.

school, and prayer meetings were conducted, sustained for a time by volunteer effort. They subsidized, too, the work of the Bethany Mission on the South side. In 1890, the Westminster Society was incorporated on the East side. In the same year, a German Presbyterian Mission was established at the corner of Thirteenth and Harmon streets; and a year later, in 1891, the First German Presbyterian Church was organized.[37] Additional opportunities for worship in this period were provided by the Evangelical Association, the Evangelical Church, Seventh Day Adventists, Christians, Unitarians, Universalists, the Jewish Church, and four Spiritualist congregations. In 1869, some thirty-five members seceded from the congregation B'ne Jeshurun (which had been formed from a merger of two earlier Jewish congregations in 1856) and founded the first Reform temple in Wisconsin, resolving, significantly for a people whose mother tongue was German, to hold all their services in the English language. This congregation ultimately outgrew its temple on the corner of North Broadway and East State Street and in the twentieth century moved to a location on Kenwood Boulevard. The great wave of East Europeans of Jewish faith after 1881 led to the organization of as many as five new orthodox congregations between 1884 and 1906.[38]

The program of the churches reflected their desire to counter the reputedly deleterious influences of urban life. Many of them recognized their social service functions; in building its new structure in 1889, Plymouth Congregational Church offered an example of what was known as an "institutional" church and provided rooms "devoted to practical use in all the various ways in which the Christian church may minister to the service of humanity . . . parlors, lecture rooms, school rooms, . . . reading room, . . . a large recreation room, rooms for boys' clubs, evening classes." But there were organizations designed more specifically to meet the social needs to which a city civiliza-

---

[37] *Ibid.*, 2:187-88, 191-94, 210-12. A group of Hollanders had sustained since the late fifties what ultimately was known as Perseverance Presbyterian Church. In 1859 or 1860, a short-lived First German Presbyterian Church had been established.

[38] See Watrous, 1:375-78; McArthur, 44; Wisconsin Jewish Chronicle, *The Jewish Community Blue Book of Milwaukee and Wisconsin, and Supplement* (Milwaukee, 1924), 31-39.

tion gave rise. After somewhat interrupted activity dating from as early as March 14, 1855, the Young Men's Christian Association underwent a reorganization on December 22, 1876, from which day its permanent existence dates. Mid-day prayer meetings, relief work, and open-air gospel gatherings were undertaken almost immediately; boys' work was inaugurated in 1881; a railroad branch with recreation rooms was organized in January 1883; and in 1887 a new building with gymnasium facilities was occupied. It was the avowed purpose of the Y.M.C.A.—with gymnasium and reading room—to provide the change, diversion, and company needed in leisure hours by "young men who are strangers and come to our large city with no acquaintance and subject to no active influence for good." At the coffee house, next to the association building, meals at 10 cents or under were served to thousands of persons each month. After the middle seventies, there existed a German Branch of the Young Men's Christian Association, but in 1893 this was amalgamated with the central association.[39]

The Young Women's Christian Association, organized in September 1892, grew out of a desire to aid girls whom the expansion of urban industry was drawing to the city and to counter the hazards presented by such areas as Milwaukee's notorious "River Street" to unattached young women in the community. Procuring down-town rooms and engaging as secretary Miss Emily P. Dunlap of the Moody Bible Institute, this organization provided recreation and companionship for the young women employed in offices, stores, schools, and factories. Groups of their members met the trains to extend a friendly hand to newcomers seeking employment in the metropolis. A Noon-rest provided a place for an economical lunch and

[39] There is considerable conflict in the dates given in the standard histories for the founding of the Y.M.C.A. in Milwaukee. From a contemporary report in the *Sentinel*, it is clear that such a society was organized on March 14, 1855, presumably the first in the city. London was the scene of the original organization of the Y.M.C.A., on June 6, 1844; and the movement first appeared in America when associations were founded almost simultaneously in Boston and Montreal, in 1851. Milwaukee's society was interrupted during the Civil War but started again in November 1864, after which it apparently had relatively continuous existence until 1876, when incorporation took place. Milwaukee *Sentinel*, March 14, 1855; Conard, 2:210-11, 251-58; Watrous, 1:378-79.

relaxation. Additional services of the organization included classes in stenography, millinery, and physical culture; an employment bureau; a social and cultural program; and the recommendation of safe boarding houses at reasonable prices. In June 1893, rooms were procured in the heart of the factory district on the South side; and three years later a summer camp was founded at which girls could spend their vacations for only $2.75 a week. The philanthropy of Elizabeth Plankinton made possible a building in which lodging could be provided within the salary limits of the working girl.[40]

Meanwhile, Mrs. Henry Whitcomb was calling attention to the problem of juvenile delinquency in the city. Following what had been done in Massachusetts and New York, she and her associates in this reform established in the late eighties a boys' club which within a decade had a paid superintendent and was conducting a vacation school designed to keep boys off the streets in the summer. Mrs. Whitcomb's studies of farm schools, begun in 1898, had borne fruit by 1908 in the establishment of the Niel Norris Farm. The creation of a juvenile court in 1901 was in large measure the result of her investigation of juvenile crime and of her agitation in February 1900 for such a court for juvenile delinquents as the one set up in Chicago in the previous year. By the close of the generation, the People's Pulpit, the Salvation Army, and the Volunteers of America existed as additional agencies specifically designed to exert a morally healthful influence upon the urban society.[41]

"River Street" was the symbol of the sorry side of the metropolis which these agencies were designed to combat; and if tradition can be trusted, saloons, gambling dens, and houses of prostitution did an almost unbridled business in some parts of the city in the nineties and during Mayor Rose's "open town" era on the turn of the century. "Stall saloons," where couples could meet in privacy, day or night, were the object of the reformers' attack as were the rooms for poker, faro, and roulette above such famous establishments as the Marble Hall, popular whiskey bar, and Weber and Stuber's restaurant. Brothel-

---

[40] Conard, 2:259-62; Watrous, 1:379; Milwaukee *Sentinel*, July 14, 1937.
[41] Gregory, *History*, 2:1042-50; Watrous, 1:379.

infested River Street was as notorious as San Francisco's Barbary Coast. Here there were houses for every social level, from the bawdy Red Star and John Radke's, low in the social scale, to the "fashionable" resorts of such "shady ladies" as Jeanette Hampton and Kitty Williams. The latter's elaborately decorated establishment was said to have forty-two rooms, among them a Roman room with "sunken floor, splashing fountains, and marble baths," a Japanese room, a Moorish room, and one in Louis XIV style with a raised dais and ornate golden throne. In the days of "Anything Goes Rosy" the reformers found little support from the municipal administration, but after his last term a crusade led by District Attorney Winfred C. Zabel cleaned up this disreputable district, and the council even authorized a change in name which replaced "River" Street with the more enlightened "Edison."[42]

If the city was producing a seamy society with which the religious associations were inspired to deal, it was also fostering the kind that is spelled with a "capital S." This development became apparent in the eighties with the publication in 1884 of the first volume of the *Milwaukee Society Blue Book and Family Directory*, purporting to offer "the society people of the Cream City" a reliable list of the leading families. From a number of the "leading society ladies," so-called "visiting-lists" had been obtained, and stated "reception days" specified. Slightly more than 800 names, including some from Racine and Kenosha, appeared upon the pages; to judge from the addresses most frequently given, "Society" resided especially on Grand Avenue, Marshall Street, Prospect Avenue, Cass, Jefferson, Astor, and Jackson streets. The *Elite Directory* of 1891-92 professed to be more than "a mere Society Blue Book." It listed "several thousand well-known and well-to-do Milwaukeeans," together with a club list and a section on etiquette. In 1894, with "much dubitation" and after "many solicitations" the Elite Directory Company began the publication of a *Milwaukee Blue Book of Selected Names* which was published periodically for more than a decade.[43]

[42] Austin, *The Milwaukee Story*, 164-66.
[43] *Milwaukee Society Blue Book and Family Directory, 1884-1885* (Milwaukee, 1884), 1:7-8; *Milwaukee Elite Directory: Society and Club Lists, 1891-1892* (Mil-

Symbol of the new society was the exclusive Cotillion Club which was organized in 1887. Among its members were the debutantes of the season, the Misses Ida Eliot, Alice Bradley, and Agnes and Hedwig Wahl, and the beaux of the moment: William O. Goodrich, James K. and Spencer Ilsley, Grant Fitch, John W. Mariner, George H. Russell, William P. Miller, Robert B. Tweedy, and Otto Falk. The Prospect Avenue "Society" extended itself in these days. The square stone Petit house boasted the first private ballroom in the city. The Gustave Pabsts, L. J. Petits, and William Mariners maintained "four-in-hands" that outshone the victorias, surreys, and broughams of the other Milwaukee gentry. The Petits were the last of the old guard to relinquish coach and footmen. The first butler in Milwaukee "Society" was employed by the Charles Colbys who built the house later occupied by the College Women's Club on Prospect Avenue. New Year's Day receptions were among the most resplendent occasions of winter seasons that were dull without seven or eight large formal balls. At such affairs, according to contemporary accounts, "hostesses of the late nineties received their guests all afternoon and evening . . . in full formal attire." Truly, as the editor wrote in 1871, one could "give parties more conveniently" in the city. The rise of what passed for an exclusive "Society" added additional social groupings to a community on which size, a geographically-induced ward sectionalism, and nationality loyalties had already exerted a divisive influence. Writing *The Autocrats,* a novel based on his observations of Milwaukee social life in 1901, Charles K. Lush asserted: "A city is made up of circles, or groups, great and small, divisions and sub-divisions, the members of which have apparently little in common, whose mode of life is dissimilar, and who really know as little of each other as do Hottentots and Esquimaux."[44]

The social differentiation to which the novelist referred was primarily the consequence of the increase in population which

waukee, 1890—), 3; *Milwaukee Blue Book of Selected Names . . . 1894* (Milwaukee, 1894). These *Blue Books* were published in 1894, 1895-96, 1897-98, 1899-1900, 1901-2, 1903-4, 1905-6, and 1908-9. The last-named listed 17,500 names; the *Directory* for 1891-92 listed about 2,400.

[44] Milwaukee *Sentinel,* March 18, 1871; Sept. 14, 1937; Charles K. Lush, *The Autocrats* (New York, 1901), 99.

brought the metropolis about; but it was intensified by the differences in economic status to which current developments in urban industry gave rise. Indeed it was the development of industry and the application of mechanical invention to problems presented by the rapid accumulation of people that more than anything else dictated the social pattern of metropolitan Milwaukee at the beginning of the twentieth century. Specialization was the most characteristic quality of the metropolitan mold, a specialization in this instance conditioned by the industrial developments of the day. Mechanical ingenuity plus specialization in tasks formerly performed exclusively in the home was responsible for the conveniences of apartment "flats," canned food products, commercial laundries, and department stores. The magnitude of the metropolitan market permitted an increase of specialization in professional services, educational opportunities, and provisions for religious preference beyond what the younger and less populous city had provided; but here, as in the increase in the professional performance of music and the drama, the existence of industrial wealth assisted in making the specialization possible. Numbers, more than any other force, induced the geographical expansion of the community and the multiplication of educational and religious institutions to meet the needs of the outlying and even suburban settlements; but mechanical invention and industrial capital were responsible for the utilities that made possible the identification of this expanded population with the city itself. The inevitable consequences of specialization were a social differentiation and a loss of individual self-sufficiency which were increasingly characteristic of the metropolitan scene. To be sure, the differentiation resulting from economic causes had the wholesome consequence of tending to erase or cut across lines of cleavage that in an earlier period nationality differences had created. Thus, for example, East-side "Society" was recruited from the Wahls and Pabsts as well as the Fitches and Ilsleys, and trade union strength was drawn from workers of Yankee as well as Teutonic background. Nevertheless, by the turn of the century the social dependence, impersonality, and even corruption of city life were beginning to be recognized and even feared. Enthusiasts for the city continued to extol the "infinitely greater" comforts of life in the metropolis. But some there were who, like the novelist in 1901, were asking:

Who shall fathom the vast and deep mystery of a city? . . . this wilderness of brick and mortar, . . . ? . . . From the liberty of the country swarm men and women to a new bondage, to be warped and twisted by the fierce heat of competition—competition for all things, for the very air they breathe. . . . The city is the Dark Continent of this century, into the depths of which have gone many explorers, each returning with but a fragment of knowledge; none with the whole truth.[45]

[45] *Evening Wisconsin*, July 24, 1886; Lush, *The Autocrats*, 291.

PART IV

The Mature Metropolis 1910 to 1940

"In the nineteenth century local government was regarded as a sort of glorified policeman whose function was the protection of property and the maintenance of law and order. The vast increase in urban concentration of population has created new and complex problems, and today the average citizen demands services that were entirely unknown a few years ago. A municipality is no longer a mere policeman, but a public servant that must be responsive to the immediate, fast-changing, and rapidly-increasing needs of the citizenry."—Daniel W. Hoan, in City Government: The Record of the Milwaukee Experiment (1936).

"I don't know of another large American city that sets more good examples in the administration of justice and the thrifty management of its affairs. Milwaukee has character and a conscience that makes its character function."—James O'Donnell Bennett, in the Chicago *Tribune,* June 17, 1930.

CHAPTER 16

The Structure of Society

THE generation from 1910 to 1940 saw the realization of mature cityhood at the mouth of the Milwaukee. On the foundation of city builders' dreams and speculators' ambitions there stood by 1940 a metropolis which could count 587,472 persons within the city limits and nearly half again as many in the wider area over which its metropolitan influence held sway. But there had been more than physical growth in the short century from the day when some 1,500 Milwaukeeans had combined to form the consolidated village; for by the 1930's the expanded city of more than half a million people had established such a record for public safety, fire and health protection, and municipal solvency and order as both to attest its maturity as an urban community and to make it in these respects the envy of its metropolitan neighbors at home and abroad.[1]

By 1910, the torrent of population which had been moving cityward since 1870 had begun to abate. In the seventies and eighties decennial increases had reached 60 to 70 percent, but after 1910 no decade added as much as 30 percent. In the generation between 1910 and 1940, annexation swelled the physical area of the city from twenty-two to forty-four square miles; yet during the thirties the increase of residents within these doubled boundaries fell as low as 1.6 percent; and for the first time since 1860, the population of the State as a whole actually grew at a greater rate than did the population within the city limits of Milwaukee.[2] The competitive lure of near-by residential sub-

[1] *Annual Report to the Citizens of Milwaukee, 1939* (Milwaukee, 1940), 6; see *Milwaukee's World-Wide Fame—Why?* (pamphlet, Milwaukee, 1932), for comments of American and European press on Milwaukee.

[2] The state-wide increase from 1930 to 1940 was 6.8 percent. The Milwaukee metropolitan district increased 6.3 percent and the area within it, outside the

urbs, a decline in the birth rate, and the depressed economy of the thirties combined to retard the growth of the central city and arrest a trend that had characterized the first 100 years of Milwaukee's municipal career.

In sex distribution, twentieth-century Milwaukee continued to exhibit the appeal of the city for women. At every census count between 1840 and 1940, the proportion of women in the population of Milwaukee was greater than in the population of Wisconsin as a whole. Whereas men always outnumbered women in the State at large, in Milwaukee, after the first few years of city building, the sexes were closely matched; and at the censuses of 1860, 1870, 1890, 1900, and 1940, women were slightly in the majority.[3] The increasing over-all age of twentieth-century Milwaukeeans reflected both the current decline in the size of the family, partially induced by war and depression, and the nationally-recognized accomplishments of the city's health and safety programs. Between 1912 and 1940, the birth rate declined from 27.9 to 17.4 births per 1,000 in the population; and a rate of only 14.5, the lowest in the city's history, coincided with the depressed economic conditions of 1933.[4] At the same time, the period saw such progress in public health and safety that the average age of death, which had stood at 18.1 years in 1880, had advanced to almost 27.6 in 1900, to 38.7 in 1920, and to 58.4 in 1940. By the latter date, considering only persons over five years of age, the average age of death for men was 60.8 and for women, 64.6.[5]

city of Milwaukee, 22.8 percent. Fox Point increased 148.9 percent; Whitefish Bay, 80 percent; Pewaukee, 26.7 percent; Wauwatosa, 31 percent; West Milwaukee, 20.2 percent; Shorewood, 12.6 percent; and Waukesha, 12 percent. See appendix for chart comparing total population and sex distribution of Milwaukee and the State of Wisconsin by decades, 1840 to 1940. Arthur M. Werba and John L. Grunwald, *Making Milwaukee Mightier: a Record of Annexation and Consolidation* (Milwaukee, 1929), 78; *United States Census, Sixteenth*, 1940, *Population*, 1:1176.

[3] See appendix for chart showing total population and sex distribution of Milwaukee and the State of Wisconsin by decades, 1840 to 1940.

[4] The birth rate for 1914 was 29.4; 1918, 26.2; 1922, 22.2; 1924, 24.1; 1928, 22.3; 1932, 16.5; 1936, 15.9; and 1940, 17.4. *Municipal Government and Activities of the City of Milwaukee for 1924* (Milwaukee, 1925), 96; *ibid. . . . 1928* (Milwaukee, 1929), 80; *Milwaukee, 1937* (Milwaukee, 1938), 64; *Milwaukee's Progress in 1940* (Milwaukee, 1941), 116.

[5] *Municipal Activities of Milwaukee for 1932* (Milwaukee, 1933), 94; *Milwaukee's Progress in 1940*, p. 43.

The consequence of this increase in birth and decrease in death was to amplify the proportionate influence of age and experience in the social and political activities of the community. Youths in the age category of five through nineteen constituted 26.7 percent of the community in 1840; 31.1 percent (five to eighteen-year-olds) in 1870, 28.7 percent in 1910, and only 22.6 percent by 1940. The middle-age group, from twenty through forty-four, made up an estimated 49 percent of village Milwaukee; an estimated 38.3 percent (eighteen to forty-five-year olds) in 1870; 43.2 percent in 1910; and 41.9 percent in 1940. In the older-age category, including persons from forty-five through seventy-five and older, the percentage increased from 5.4 percent in 1840 and an estimated 14 percent in 1870 to as much as 17.8 percent in 1910 and 28.7 percent in 1940. Thus by the latter date, Milwaukeeans of forty-five and over were more than five times as numerous, proportionately, as they had been a hundred years earlier. By comparison with the State as a whole, where the rural influence was more strongly felt, persons in the age category from twenty to fifty were consistently more numerous, proportionately, in Milwaukee than in the State as a whole, throughout the century, 1840 to 1940. Conversely, the State showed a greater proportion of youths and elderly persons than was true of its most populous city.[6]

The occupational patterns of twentieth-century Milwaukee mirror the growing mechanization and specialization of the urban economy, the expansion of municipal services, and the wider employment of women in gainful pursuits which characterized both city and nation as the community approached its centennial of cityhood. As a consequence of the increasing use of machines—for transportation, in the tasks of housekeeping, and for the production of ready-made clothes and hats—there was progressively less call for the blacksmiths, livery-stable workers, dressmakers, seamstresses, tailors, milliners, and household servants who had been necessary to the urban and domestic economy of the late nineteenth century. This fact is strikingly revealed in occupational density figures compiled from the

[6] For the basis of these figures, see appendix for charts comparing the age distribution in the population of Milwaukee and the State of Wisconsin for selected decades between 1840 and 1940.

census for the period 1870 to 1940. From 1870 through 1910, the city made use of between 3 and 4 blacksmiths per 1,000 persons in the population. By 1920, this figure had dropped to less than 3, and in 1940 it stood at less than 1. Laundresses decreased in number from 4 per 1,000 in 1900 to less than 1 in 1940. In 1880 there were nearly 30 dressmakers, tailors, and milliners per 1,000; but such was the influence of the "ready-to-wear" industries that between 1910 and 1940 the number of seamstresses, not employed in factories, declined from nearly 10 per 1,000 to 1.5; tailors from 4.9 to 1.2; and milliners from 3.4 to .2. The marked reduction in the proportionate number of servants, waiters, waitresses, and housekeepers (from 42 per 1,000 in 1870 to 21 in 1910 and 17 in 1940) followed from the decreasing size of the home and the wider application of labor-saving devices therein.

At the same time, the multiplying use of the automobile, the telephone, and the typewriter swelled the number of garage mechanics, telephone operators (1.2 per 1,000 in 1900 to 2.6 per 1,000 in 1940), and stenographers (4.1 per 1,000 in 1900 to 13.8 per 1,000 in 1940) essential to these new developments in the urban scene. The last two fields provided increasing opportunity for the employment of women. More men than women served as telephone operators in 1900; but by 1940 women outnumbered men by a total of 1,437 to 73. A similar trend prevailed in stenography, bookkeeping, and accounting. In 1900 there were only 3 women to every 1 male stenographer; but by 1940 the ratio was 20 women to 1 man. Male bookkeepers predominated by a ratio of 3 to 1 in 1900, but forty years later twice as many women as men were so employed.[7]

Throughout the period, between 40 and 50 percent of the city's labor force was employed in manufacturing; but to judge from figures compiled by the census under the heading of persons ten years and older in selected industries, women were taking an increasing proportion of the available jobs in this field. In 1870, about 17 percent of the persons employed in the industries selected were women. By 1910, women held 24

[7] For the sources upon which these figures are based and a discussion of the hazards in relying too heavily thereon, see footnote to chart, in appendix, showing distribution of population of Milwaukee by selected occupations, 1870

MILWAUKEE IN 1938: AIR-AGE VIEW OF THE MODERN METROPOLIS

THE STRUCTURE OF SOCIETY 437

percent of the jobs and by 1940, more than 29 percent. Women in these selected industries represented 5.5 percent of the total population in 1870, but during the first forty years of the twentieth century such female workers constituted from 10 to 11 percent of the residents of the city. Whereas the heavier industries enlisted almost no women prior to 1900, by 1920 they were employed in the manufacture of iron and steel products and by 1930 in the production of automobiles. However, the pursuits most dependent on women workers continued to be the clothing and textile industries, leather production, telephone and telegraph communication, hotel, restaurant, boarding house, and other types of personal and domestic service, and such professional and semiprofessional activities as teaching, nursing, stenography, and clerking. The increased employment of women in activities outside the home, as well as the bobbed hair which they began to effect in the twenties, stimulated the barbering, hairdressing, and manicuring trades. Less than 1 person per 1,000 was employed in such pursuits in 1870; and of the total of 67, only 1 was a woman. By 1910, nearly 3 persons per 1,000 were so employed, but men still outnumbered women 4 to 1. The census of 1930 reflected the tonsorial revolution of the twenties; by 1940, nearly 4 persons per 1,000 were required

to 1940. The following chart shows the distribution of employment in industries in the city having the greatest number of employees in 1940:

Industry	No. of Employees in City—1940	Percent of Total Employees
Retail Trade	38,229	17.9
Manufacture of Machinery	20,733	9.8
Professional & Related Services	17,449	8.2
Personal Services	14,948	7.0
Manufacture of Iron & Steel & their products	12,766	6.0
Transportation	11,148	5.3
Manufacture of Food & Kindred Products	9,798	4.6
Finance, Insurance, and Real Estate	5,937	4.2
Construction	8,919	4.2
Government	8,276	3.9

William L. Slayton, *Milwaukee's Labor Force* (mimeographed, Milwaukee, 1944), 34-35. The city directories provide an index to shifts in occupations. For example, 26 auto repair establishments were listed in 1910; 105 in 1920; 185 in 1930; and 308 in 1940.

to groom and beautify the residents of Milwaukee, and of the total so occupied there were 1,233 women to 971 men.[8]

The continued specialization of the urban economy, already manifest in the late nineteenth-century city, found expression in the census listing of actors, showmen, and architects, after 1900, of which there were less than 1 per 1,000 in the population, and in the multiplication of dentists and nurses. A per capita increase in schoolteachers, from 5 per 1,000 during the period from 1870 to 1910 to between 6 and 7 thereafter, and in policemen, from 1.3 per 1,000 in 1910 to 2.1 in 1940, indicated the expanding role of urban service in community life, as well as the increased attendance in the public schools. In the practice of the standard professions, however, the period 1870 to 1940 saw surprisingly little variation in the number of practitioners per 1,000 residents. The ratio of lawyers stood at 1.5 in both 1870 and 1940, with almost no change in proportionate number in between. The proportion of physicians and surgeons was almost similarly unchanged, the decennial ratio per 1,000 fluctuating only between 1.2 and 1.5 in the seven decades. The same was generally true of musicians and music teachers; artists, sculptors, and art teachers; journalists and writers; and clergymen. The ratio of ministers to 1,000 residents was .95 in 1870, .8 in 1900, and .8 in 1940. These figures suggest the hypothesis that once the community had achieved the status of a large city, the proportion of practitioners of the standard professions reached a level which thereafter prevailed. The only noticeable change in the professional picture was the increased number of women employed in such pursuits. The 1940 census listed 18 women lawyers, 14 women clergymen, 43 women physicians, 9 women dentists, and 72 women journalists and writers.[9]

[8] *United States Census, Ninth,* 1870, vol. 1, *Population,* 789; *United States Census, Thirteenth,* 1910, *Population, Occupation Statistics,* 4:565-66; *United States Census, Fourteenth,* 1920, *Population, Occupations,* 4:1140-44; *United States Census, Fifteenth,* 1930, *Population,* vol. 3, pt. 2, p. 1345; *ibid., Population, Occupation by States,* 4:1771-73; *United States Census, Sixteenth,* 1940, *Population,* vol. 2, pt. 7, p. 685; *ibid., Population,* vol. 3, pt. 5, pp. 981-83.

[9] For the sources on which these figures are based and a discussion of the hazards in using them, see footnote to chart, in appendix, showing distribution of population of Milwaukee by selected occupations, 1870 to 1940.

The generation from 1910 to 1940 saw fewer of Milwaukee's youth in the labor force and more of them in the schoolroom than ever before in the city's history. Between 1910 and 1940 the percentage of young people of school age registered in school increased from 58 to about 87 percent. In the first decade of the period, public-school enrollment swelled more than 48 percent while the city's population was growing less than half as fast; and although the peak of the increase had been reached by 1926, by 1930 more than 98 percent of the children between seven and fifteen were in the classroom, as were nearly 88 percent of those sixteen and seventeen and nearly 24 percent of those in the eighteen to twenty age group. By the close of the thirties, Milwaukee's youth were staying in school twice as long as they had in 1877, and the daily attendance at the schools was ten times what it had been in that year.[10]

Several factors account for this expanded interest in education. Technological developments in industry decreased to some extent the demand for children in the labor force; but more importantly, State legislation, prompted by a progressive concern for child welfare, was responsible for keeping young people in school longer than otherwise might have been the case. Thus, between 1911 and 1935 the age for compulsory full-time attendance for youth not high-school graduates was lifted, successively, from thirteen to eighteen years of age. Moreover, during the economic depression of the thirties, young people were attracted to academic activities for want of other occupation, a situation reflected especially in the phenomenal growth in high-school enrollment; and from the outset of the generation the development of part-time vocational education and improved facilities for the physically handicapped gave the schools an appeal for increasingly numerous special groups.[11]

The Wisconsin legislature provided for a system of part-time

[10] *United States Census, Thirteenth,* 1910, *Population,* 1:1113; *United States Census, Fifteenth,* 1930, *Population,* vol. 3, pt. 2, p. 1333; *Municipal Activities of Milwaukee for 1935* (Milwaukee, 1936), 110; *ibid. . . . 1936* (Milwaukee, 1937), 82; *Milwaukee, 1937,* p. 51; Milwaukee Board of School Directors, *Proceedings,* July 1, 1939-June 30, 1940, p. 36.

[11] *Municipal Government and Activities of the City of Milwaukee for 1927* (Milwaukee, 1928), 50; *Municipal Activities of Milwaukee for 1933* (Milwaukee, 1934), 116; *ibid. . . . 1936,* p. 84.

vocational education in 1911. The law required half-time attendance at vocational school of boys and girls fourteen and fifteen years of age who lacked the equivalent of a high-school education and who were regularly employed in a useful occupation at home or elsewhere. Youths aged sixteen or seventeen were to attend eight hours a week.[12] In 1912, Milwaukee began pioneering activities, which, under the directorship of Dr. Robert L. Cooley for more than a quarter of a century, were to make the school a model in the field of vocational education.[13] Starting with an annual budget of $3,500, in 1912, and a total enrollment at the year's end of 2,242, the school expanded until it listed at its twenty-fifth anniversary, in 1937-38, an enrollment of 34,037 and a budget of $1,266,835. Early in 1923, the school was moved from its scattered, rented quarters to a six-story, 158-room, $2,000,000 building on Seventh and Prairie streets, equipped, among other items, with printing presses, electrical shops, apparatus for a steel foundry, materials for the study of household arts, and the paraphernalia of a complete business college. A $1,500,000 addition, completed in 1929, provided space for an auditorium and pipe organ and permitted the introduction by the late thirties of courses in air conditioning, the operation of Diesel engines, beauty culture, and meat merchandising. On the turn of the war-minded forties, the school had become a great training center for industrial war, with classes operating on a twenty-four hour schedule and a ground course in aviation designed to further America's preparedness in the air.[14]

These changes in curriculum reflect the progress of an institution which had begun its career as a continuation school for sixth- and seventh-graders, and which practical Milwaukeeans had at first justified on the theory that "neglect of the thousands

[12] This was for the period the regular schools were in session.
[13] The local board of vocational education was made up of two employers of labor, two employees (not superintendents or foremen), all appointed by the school board, and the superintendent of schools, ex-officio.
[14] *Municipal Government and Activities . . . 1927*, p. 50; *Milwaukee Civic News: 1938* (Milwaukee, 1939), 14; *Municipal Government and Activities of the City of Milwaukee for 1922* (Milwaukee, 1923), 61; *ibid. . . . 1929* (Milwaukee, 1930), 73; *Municipal Activities of Milwaukee for 1931* (Milwaukee, 1932), 146; *Milwaukee, 1937*, p. 53; *Milwaukee's Progress in 1940*, p. 61.

... of young people who go into industry at an early age is bad for business if it serves to develop the kind of people who are not able to buy the goods manufactured in our factories." As time went on, and as more and more of Milwaukee's youth stayed longer in the neighborhood schools, or found themselves without employment, the clientele of the vocational school changed from juveniles to adults.[15] With this change came an expanded concept of the social role of the school. Not only was it determined to make certain that "young people who drop out . . . to go to work shall not become mere robots tied to machines," but it desired to bridge the gap from school to jobs which, in the thirties, were none too easy to find and to "serve not only the vocational needs but the more complete life needs of the many thousand adults of the city." The popularity of its trade-finding classes and those of its 150 courses which met the needs of a predominantly high-school-trained clientele attested the accomplishment of these goals, as did the fact that by 1940, six-sevenths of its 34,000 students, about equally divided between men and women, were attending the school of their own free will.[16]

Improved facilities for training the physically handicapped further swelled the numbers for which the Milwaukee school system was responsible. To the Paul Binner School for the deaf, in operation since the late nineteenth century, there were added classes for the blind, provided for by the legislature in 1907 and first operated in the Cass Street School. Open-air classes for children inclined to tuberculosis and classes in speech correction, both instituted in 1909, met the needs of children with correctible difficulties. Pre-vocational schools, or junior trade schools, served the boys and girls whose interests leaned toward manual rather than academic activities; and a cooperative plan

[15] In 1913, almost a third of its students were sixth-graders. By 1934, this was true of only 2 percent of the boys and 1 percent of the girls enrolled. By November 1939, approximately 63 percent were high-school graduates, and 55 percent were between nineteen and twenty-five years old. *Municipal Government and Activities . . . 1927*, p. 50; *Milwaukee Civic News: 1938*, p. 14; *Annual Report . . . 1939*, p. 88.

[16] *Municipal Activities . . . 1931*, p. 146; *Municipal Government and Activities . . . 1928*, p. 59; *Municipal Activities . . . 1932*, p. 134; *Milwaukee's Progress in 1940*, p. 61.

was approved in 1924 for developing a mental clinic for the problem school child. The opening in 1940 of the Frederick J. Gaenslen School for crippled children, with its therapeutic pool, sun deck, and rest room for heart cases, expanded facilities for combining normal education and therapy and further realized the school board's aim to provide equal opportunities "for children who by reason of some physical defect or abnormality are misfits in the regular classroom."[17]

The shortage of classroom space was the most critical problem facing the Milwaukee School Board during the generation, and, as a consequence, from the middle twenties until the depth of the depressed thirties, large-scale expansion of the city's educational plant took place, its character dictated by the swelling high-school enrollment and the movement of population from the center to outlying portions of the city. In the first decade of the generation, high-school registration increased 135 percent by contrast with a 40 percent gain in the elementary schools. In the decade of the twenties, the increase in the high-school grades approximated 274 percent; and while the gain in this group of students was smaller each year after 1931, by 1939 the high-school enrollment was more than 10,000 beyond what it had been ten years earlier. At the same time, the declining birth rate brought a reduction of 7,500 in the elementary-school enrollment during the thirties and made it possible to close two of the elementary schools and distribute their pupils to other buildings.[18]

Fourteen new buildings were erected in the dozen years following 1910, but still there were complaints of overcrowding. By 1923, nearly 3,500 pupils were housed in barracks, more than 6,000 were restricted to a half-time schedule, and many others were reciting in assembly rooms and basements. In that year,

[17] Some crippled children had been enrolled in the Lapham Park School since 1928. Milwaukee *Journal*, Sept. 6, 1934; Dec. 23, 1939; *Municipal Government and Activities . . . 1924*, pp. 65-66; *Milwaukee, 1937*, p. 52; *Milwaukee Civic News: 1938*, p. 14; *Milwaukee's Progress in 1940*, p. 59.
[18] The increase in the first six grades had been only 16.1 percent during the decade of the twenties. High-school graduates numbered 4,500 in 1937, by contrast with the nine graduated in 1877. *Municipal Government and Activities . . . 1922*, p. 59; *Municipal Activities . . . 1933*, p. 113; *ibid*. . . . *1934* (Milwaukee, 1935), 103; *Milwaukee, 1937*, p. 51; *Annual Report . . . 1939*, p. 85.

THE STRUCTURE OF SOCIETY 443

a $6,600,000 building program, providing for thirteen new schools and additions to four old ones, was recommended by a committee appointed in 1922. And in 1924 the school board authorized an experimental plan for rotating classes in such a way as to give a full day's instruction to students formerly on a half-time schedule. By the middle twenties the building program began to show results; but since the thronging school population continued to exceed construction, a revised program calling for expenditures of more than $11,000,000 was approved by popular referendum in 1928; and by the close of this expansive decade, the construction of twenty-seven new buildings was in sight. For the first time in years no new school was opened in improvised barracks in 1931; and by the year's end the school board could list 8 high schools, 5 junior high schools, 2 technical high schools, 4 junior technical high schools, and 86 elementary schools, in marked contrast to the total of 6 public high schools, 2 trade schools, and 63 elementary schools available ten years earlier. During the early years of the depression of the thirties, the school board was the largest contributor to the city's building program, and federal funds helped finance some construction, including that of the $2,400,000 Pulaski High School. Nevertheless, in spite of recurring congestion, the scope of building activities had to be reduced during the later years of the depression until, by 1940, repair only, and no new construction, was listed. A sharp decline in public-school enrollment on the turn of the forties was the only sign of relief in an otherwise still critical situation.[19]

The generation presented academic problems as well as problems of construction, to Milwaukee's popularly chosen school board and to its school administration, which was under the superintendency of Milton C. Potter, for more than a quar-

[19] The 81,447 pupils enrolled in the public schools in 1940, while numerous by comparison with the 41,633 enrolled in the public schools in 1910, nevertheless represented a decrease of 9,430 under the preceding year. *Municipal Government and Activities . . . 1922*, pp. 57, 59; *ibid. . . . 1923* (Milwaukee, 1924), 66; *ibid. . . . 1924*, pp. 66-67; *ibid. . . . 1925* (Milwaukee, 1926), 58; *ibid. . . . 1926* (Milwaukee, 1927), 60; *ibid. . . . 1927*, pp. 48-49; *ibid. . . . 1928*, pp. 56-57; *ibid. . . . 1929*, p. 71; *Municipal Activities . . . 1931*, p. 142; *ibid. . . . 1936*, p. 82; *Milwaukee, 1937*, p. 52; *Milwaukee's Progress in 1940*, pp. 59-60; Milwaukee Bd. of School Directors, *Proc.*, July 5, 1910 - June 30, 1911, p. 7.

ter century, after January 1914. In this field they acted with more deliberate conservatism than in the development of the physical plant, a policy which the Milwaukee *Journal* endorsed when it commended the board in 1932 for avoiding "all the frills that some cities have adopted."[20] However, by comparison with its content in the preceding generation the curriculum was considerably expanded in the direction of character education, the development of leisure-time activities, health improvement, and training for citizenship—changes reflecting the policy that "training children to live as social beings now is more valid than training for the remote future."[21] By the early twenties, deference was being paid the current endorsement of the project method, socialized recitation, individualization of instruction, departmentalization, and educational measurements. The ex-

[20] "Milwaukee has not made so many experiments in secondary education as some cities. It has not run off after this or that idea which someone proposed. It has stayed closely to the best practices as sanctioned by slow development and national studies made by this type of education. . . . Today other cities are simplifying their courses . . . coming back to the Milwaukee point of view." Milwaukee *Journal,* May 21, 1932.

[21] Some indication of the change in the content of the educational program is seen in the following comparison of the time distribution for studies in the third and eighth grades for 1910 and 1940:

	1910			*1940*	
	3rd	*8th (B)*		*3rd*	*8th*
Reading and Lit.	300	100	Reading and Lit.	300	150
Language	125	200	Language	250	150
Spelling	100	50	Spelling	80	80
Writing	100	20	Writing	75	80
History of U.S.		125	History and Cit'ship	70	170
Geography	50	140	Geog., Nature Study	100	100
Calisthenics	50	50	Organized Play &		
German	150	175	Physical Education	120	120
Arithmetic	150	200	Arithmetic	125	200
Music	75	75	Music	75	75
Drawing	75	75	Drawing	75	80
Manual Training	60	90	Construction &		
			Industrial Arts	75	90
Special Help	150	150	Individual Help	150	150
Optional	15	—	Optional	75	175
Recess	125	75	Recess	125	75
Opening & General	150	150	Health Instruction	30	30
Total minutes	1,675	1,675	Total minutes	1,725	1,725

Manual of the Milwaukee Public Schools, 1910-11, p. 21; *ibid., 1939-40,* p. 18; *Milwaukee's Progress in 1940,* p. 59.

pansion of the junior high-school program gained qualified endorsement in 1928; but in the following year the board postponed definite action on the question of providing nursery schools. The depression brought the expansion of a life advisement program as well as what some members of the board considered undue emphasis on industrial education. On the eve of American participation in World War II, the industrial arts courses were standardized so as to conform more fully to the needs of industry, and the course in eighth-grade geography was revised to emphasize Americanism. Meanwhile, there was improved cooperation both among teachers and with parents, through such organizations as the Teachers Cooperative Council and the Milwaukee City Council of Parent-Teacher Associations. While practices in the public schools did not achieve for Milwaukee the position of leadership attained in connection with the city's vocational and adult education programs during the generation, the real advance in educational resources found tangible measurement in many ways. High professional standards, with respect to training, tenure, and salary schedule, prevailed in the teaching staff. Extensive facilities were provided for educating the physically handicapped. And such was the over-all expansion of the educational program that total expenditures for educational purposes increased from $923,728.72 in 1905 to more than $12,000,000 in 1932, and to as much as $9,931,915 in 1939, and that the per capita cost of instruction, based on average daily attendance, was raised from $4.05, in 1846-47, to $116.04, for the first six grades, and $131.38, for the upper six grades, in 1939.[22]

[22] The per capita cost of education increased as follows: 1846-47: $4.05; 1869-70: $13.77; 1890-91: $21.21; 1904-5: $26.59; 1922: $66.76 (elementary), $134.73 (high school); 1931: $146.10; 1939: $116.04 (lower six grades), $131.38 (upper six grades). The salaries of elementary school teachers increased from a range of about $585 to $1,040, in 1909, to a range of $1,400 to $2,400 in 1940. The salaries of high-school instructors increased from a range of about $910 to $1,950 in 1909, to a range of $1,400 to $3,300 in 1940. These figures do not apply to some types of assistants, special teachers, principals, or other administrators. *Manual of the Milwaukee Public Schools, 1913-14,* issued January 1914, pp. 12-13; Milwaukee Bd. of School Directors, *Proc.,* July 1, 1939-June 30, 1940, p. 285; Larson, *Financial and Administrative History,* 173; *Municipal Government and Activities . . . 1922,* pp. 59-60; *ibid. . . . 1926,* p. 60; *ibid. . . . 1928,* p. 57; *ibid. . . . 1929,* p. 71; *Municipal Activities of the City of*

Because of the large Catholic and Lutheran population of the city, private and parochial schools continued throughout the period to draw a good many students. Nevertheless, the percentage of Milwaukee school children attending such schools decreased from 60 percent in 1910 to 39 percent in 1939. Parochial-school enrollment was heaviest in the predominantly Roman Catholic Polish wards. In 1910, nearly three-fourths of the children of the 14th Ward were attending church schools; and by 1940, the wards in which private or parochial schools served nearly half or more of the school population were the First, Eighth, 11th, 12th, 13th, 14th, 16th, 19th, 21st, and 24th —most of them strongly Polish in constituency.[23]

The development of higher education in Milwaukee during the period 1910 to 1940 was characterized primarily by greatly increased enrollment and the expansion of facilities for professional training. The former was in part a consequence of the augmented desire for college education that followed World War I and of the demand, during the depression of the thirties, for college instruction that could be had without leaving home. The latter followed from the peculiar adaptability of the urban community, because of its clinical resources and opportunities for part-time employment, to study in the professional fields, especially since the State University at Madison had pre-empted a predominant position in liberal arts study and research. Counting enrollment in the summer sessions which Marquette established in 1909, the number of students at the Catholic university ranged from 886 in 1910 to 3,091 in 1920, 5,012 in 1930, and 4,951 in 1940. At the State Teachers College (Milwaukee Normal until 1927), enrollment, exclusive of summer sessions, increased from 510 in 1909-10 to 1,874 in 1922-23, 1,535 in 1932-33, and 1,588 in 1939-40. The student population of Milwaukee-Downer increased by nearly 50 percent; and a

Milwaukee for 1930 (Milwaukee, 1931), 75; *Municipal Activities . . . 1931*, p. 143; *ibid. . . . 1932*, p. 129; *ibid. . . . 1933*, p. 112; *Milwaukee, 1937*, p. 51; *Annual Report . . . 1939*, p. 86; *Milwaukee's Progress in 1940*, pp. 59, 86.

[23] Milwaukee Bd. of School Directors, *Proc.*, July 5, 1910-June 30, 1911, p. 7; *ibid.*, July 1, 1939-June 30, 1940, p. 36. In 1921 there were 41 Catholic private or parochial schools to 29 Lutheran, and 15 other. *Municipal Government and Activities of the City of Milwaukee for 1921* (Milwaukee, 1922), 5.

small number of evening classes offered at the Milwaukee Extension Center of the University of Wisconsin in 1910 had grown by 1939 into a junior college providing a full two-year credit program in both Letters and Science and Engineering to as many as 738 regular-credit day-school students. Enrollment more than doubled at Mount Mary College, a Catholic girl's school which was moved from Prairie du Chien to Milwaukee in 1929; and Concordia, a preparatory school for Lutheran ministers and teachers, reported 241 students in 1939.

At Marquette, the development of professional schools, which had begun with the acquisition of university status in 1907, went on apace. By 1916, the Robert A. Johnston School of Economics had become the College of Business Administration, and the courses dealing with news writing had been expanded into the College of Journalism. The growth of the School of Medicine and the Dental School after 1913 was such as to warrant enlarged facilities, including the largest dental clinic of any such school in the country. By 1925 Marquette was setting standards for dental training and turning out a large proportion of the dentists of the State. Graduate instruction at the university was begun in 1922. A similar professional specialization, together with a lengthening of the course of study, characterized the training of teachers at the Milwaukee Normal School after 1910. By 1916, the curriculum included departments of art and music, rural education, and the teaching of the deaf, in addition to special courses for primary, grammar-grade, and high-school teachers and administrators, as well. A shortlived excursion into the field of liberal arts training, begun in 1911, was terminated in 1923 over the protests of President Carroll G. Pearse and many members of the local community, when nationwide discussion of the role of normal-school training led the regents to order the discontinuance of the college courses. With the accession of Frank E. Baker to the presidency in that year, emphasis reverted to the training of teachers; and additional professional specialization and elevated standards of admission and graduation followed, the latter made possible in part by the increased appeal of the college for local residents of college age during the depression years. By 1927 most of the courses had been lengthened to four years, and the institution had been transformed, by legislative fiat, from normal school to teachers college. By 1938 national recognition attested its leadership in the field of teacher training. At Milwaukee-Downer, where Lucia R. Briggs succeeded President Sabin in 1921, increasing emphasis was placed on the development of a four-year liberal arts program. Here, too, the concern for professional specialization led to the establishment during World War I of a department of occupational therapy, which developed to such an extent that by 1931 the college could become the first institution in the country to offer a major leading to a degree in that field. Training at the University Extension was frankly pointed toward meeting the needs of young Milwaukeeans who found it impossible to attend the University at Madison during their first two years and of workers in the city who desired to advance their education through evening study. The Milwaukee School of Engineering, established in 1903, developed its curriculum during the period to include specialized training in such fields as electrical engineering, radio, refrigeration, heating, air conditioning, and welding. By 1921, more than 2,000 students were enrolled in its home study, residence, and evening classes.[24]

Other forces, in addition to the greatly broadened base of popular education, were conditioning the development of twentieth-century Milwaukee. Chain-store merchandising was standardizing the local taste as well as shaping it to the nation's mold. By 1932, "A. and P." stores, in the city since the eighties, were 140 strong; there were Woolworth and Kresge stores in the most populous neighborhood centers; and by 1925 the Walgreen Company had begun the purchase of local drug chains which ultimately placed that ubiquitous urban institution in about

[24] For the data in these paragraphs the author is grateful for information supplied by Dean M. G. Barnett of Marquette University, G. A. Parkinson, Director of the Milwaukee Extension Division of the University of Wisconsin, J. M. Klotsche, President of the State Teachers College, Mrs. Russell E. Jupp, Director of Public Relations, Milwaukee-Downer College, the Dean of Mount Mary College, and G. Murphy, Director of Public Relations, Milwaukee School of Engineering. Excellent accounts of the history of two of the institutions are Silveus, History of Milwaukee State Teachers College, and Hamilton, *Brief History of Marquette University.*

twenty localities in the greater Milwaukee area by 1940.[25] In addition, the widespread utilization of such innovations of the preceding generation as the motor car, the telephone, and motion-picture entertainment was not only widening the outlook of the citizenry but further identifying it with national trends. Automobiles increased in number from 3,608 in 1913 to 161,671 by 1940—or, from 1 for every 103 to 1 for less than 4 residents of the city.[26] In 1940, subscribers to Alexander Graham Bell's invention totaled more than 170,000 in the city and its suburbs by contrast with the 3,000 telephones used in the city in 1896.[27] Motion pictures, first exhibited shortly after the arrival of the century, were by 1914 providing residents in all corners of the city with identical entertainment, making of the downtown cinema and the neighborhood "movie house" the channels of common fashions, common habits, and an increasingly common point of view. In January 1914, serial installments of the thriller *The Adventures of Kathlyn*, starring Kathlyn Williams —"who risks her life time after time with lions, leopards, tigers and other . . . beasts, with nothing between her and death but her wonderful magnetism and dauntless will," could be seen at the Princess, Columbia, Silver City, Gem, Avenian, Mozart, Apollo, Liberty, Iris, and Fern theatres. *The Birth of a Nation* was showing for 25 cents to a dollar at the Davidson Theatre in 1915; and for a smaller sum, there were movies starring Marguerite Clark, Douglas Fairbanks, and Francis X. Bushman and Beverly Bayne. In 1918 the Butterfly, the Toy, and the Orpheum were advertising such favorites as Mary Pickford in the war-inspired *The Little American*, Fatty Arbuckle in *The Bell Boy*, Charlie Chaplin in *A Dog's Life*, and William S. Hart, king of the two-gun western heroes, in *The Bargain*. By the early twenties, Rudolph Valentino had set the stamp of *The Sheik*

[25] Milwaukee *Journal*, Nov. 30, 1927; July 15, 1928; Nov. 16, 1932; *Wright's Milwaukee City Directory, 1940*, p. 1221. The development of A. and P. supermarkets led to a decline in the number of these groceries by 1940. Five J. C. Penney stores were established in various parts of the city between 1928 and 1937. The first Sears, Roebuck store appeared in 1927. William G. Bruce, *Builders of Milwaukee* (Milwaukee, 1946), 74-75.

[26] In 1916, the assessors discovered that the number of automobiles exceeded the number of horses owned in the city. *Evening Wisconsin* (Milwaukee), Aug. 29, 1916; *Municipal Activities . . . 1933*, p. 9; *Milwaukee's Progress in 1940*, p. 115.

[27] *Ibid.*, 116; Gregory, *History*, 2:1205.

upon local mores; and the Wisconsin Theatre, which opened with great fanfare in March 1924 as "Milwaukee's newest monument to civic progress," emerged resplendently as the prototype of the metropolitan movie palaces. In such theaters, Milwaukeeans, young or old, rich or poor, suburbanites and rural visitors alike, could enjoy the ever available "movie," from Clara Bow's *It,* Greta Garbo's *Flesh and the Devil,* and Walt Disney's *Mickey Mouse* of the late twenties to *Gone with the Wind* and the "Road" series of Hope, Crosby, and Lamour as the threadbare thirties approached the wartime forties. The revolutionizing innovation of sound film was introduced to Milwaukee on September 3, 1927, when a "talkie" entitled *When a Man Loves* was shown at the Garden Theatre; and by 1940 greater Milwaukee had some eight downtown and sixty-three outlying theaters where carbon-copy substitutes for the spoken drama, musical play, and burlesque of a half century earlier could be seen and heard.[28]

If the motion picture exerted a unifying influence on the developing metropolitan culture, this was ultimately even more true of the radio, which first excited interest in Milwaukee in the early twenties. The city's initial broadcasting station was WAAK, inaugurated in 1921 by Gimbel's department store. Live talent, including actors from the stock company that was playing at the Davidson Theatre, was alternated with phonograph recordings to provide the entertainment for Milwaukee's earphone-equipped radio listeners. In 1927, WTMJ was established, transformed from WHAD, a Marquette University experimental station in which the Milwaukee *Journal* had invested in 1925. Programs were originally offered only a few nights a week, when dance music from the Wisconsin Roof Ballroom and stage shows from the Wisconsin Theatre were put on the air. The A.T. and T., later N.B.C., sent its first chain program to Milwaukee on January 1, 1927, when the *Victor Hour* was broadcast. By 1930, in spite of the absence of daytime "soap operas," radio programs were accessible to Milwaukee listeners from 7:00 A.M. until late in the evening, offering such network

[28] Milwaukee *Journal,* Jan. 12, 1914; June 18, 1916; March 31, 1918; March 29, 1924; Aug. 1, 1940; Austin, *The Milwaukee Story,* 188.

favorites as the *Yeast-Foamers,* Jessica Dragonette on the *City Service Program,* the *Voice of Firestone,* the *Palmolive Hour, Floyd Gibbons—Headline Hunter,* and *Amos 'n Andy.* By 1940, with the widely increased use of the radio and several Milwaukee stations, as well as Chicago outlets, from which to choose, the opinion, culture, and comedy of the nation at large were available in almost every Milwaukee living room at a turn of the dial.[29]

The development of the radio and the motion picture, together with the proximity of the city to Chicago, prevented thrifty twentieth-century Milwaukee from becoming as extensive a market for professional music and the drama as might otherwise have been the case. Actors and musicians of distinction touched Milwaukee only "on tour," and the entertainment they provided continued to be only infrequently available to Milwaukee audiences. Until World War I, German drama was available at the Pabst, and for some time thereafter seasons of stock were played at the Davidson; but beyond this, theatergoers had to await the long-separated few-night stands of such famous players as Maude Adams, George Arliss, E. H. Sothern, Ethel Barrymore, and Katherine Cornell. In spite of the fact that Milwaukee had cradled the "little theater" movement in the United States, when Mrs. Laura Sherry founded the Wisconsin Players in 1909, an attempt to establish a nonprofit civic theater came to nothing in 1928.[30] For professional music, too, Milwaukeeans were largely dependent on visiting performers. As anti-German sentiments stilled the *Maennerchor* and *Liederkranz,* the Arion Music Club, with its annual *Messiah,* the *Freie Gemeinde* Chorus, and the *A Cappella* Chorus, founded in 1895, alone carried on the tradition of the *Deutsch-Athen* where nearly everybody sang. Increasingly a satellite of Chicago in the musical realm, Milwaukee patronized the Chicago Grand Opera Company, which starred such artists as Mary Garden and

[29] In the early thirties the radio proved to be such a competitor for the movies that the most important radio programs were broadcast during intermissions at the motion picture theaters. Milwaukee *Journal,* February 1930, *passim;* Jan. 6, 1933; July 25, 1937 (a feature edition on WTMJ); Aug. 20, 1940; Austin, *The Milwaukee Story,* 188.

[30] Milwaukee *Sentinel,* Nov. 15, 1928; Milwaukee *Journal,* April 18, 1947.

Rosa Raisa, and subscribed eagerly to the annual seasons of symphonic music played in Milwaukee by the Chicago Symphony Orchestra. Concert bureaus, such as those of G. H. Moeller, Marion Andrews, and Margaret Rice, introduced world-famous artists to Milwaukeeans on a subscription-series basis. Efforts to found a local symphony orchestra gained only intermittent encouragement and no really permanent backing. The most promising ventures in this field were the Milwaukee Civic Orchestra, organized in 1921, which enjoyed several successful seasons with Carl Eppert as conductor, and the Milwaukee Philharmonic Orchestra, which existed in the early thirties under the leadership of Frank Waller.[31]

As a matter of fact, the entertainment interests characteristic of Milwaukeeans, as a whole, were perhaps best revealed in the enthusiasm with which the community supported the outdoor concerts and festivals held throughout the summer in the city's parks and along its well-kept waterfront. Thousands attended the open-air concerts which had been held in the parks since the turn of the century. Sunday afternoon concerts, inaugurated in Lake and Riverside parks in 1899 and subsidized by private donation, proved to be so popular that in 1913 the park board appropriated a fixed sum and charged Joseph Clauder and Christopher Bach, veteran band leaders, with developing the program. After 1918, the concerts were given by the Park Board Band; and by the thirties, when economic conditions curtailed the number of their concerts, it was customary to present several performances of light opera. The Temple of Music bandshell in Washington Park, a gift of Emil Blatz dedicated in 1938, provided an outdoor setting in which thousands could hear a series of distinguished artists; and the annual lake front midsummer festival, with its tableaux and fireworks, was drawing a million and a quarter spectators by 1940. Whether it be an indication of its thrifty conservatism and unsophisticated simplicity or a heritage of its festival-loving and folk-participating past, it was in outdoor recreation, open-air concerts, family entertainment, and lake shore celebrations rather than in con-

[31] *Evening Wisconsin*, Jan. 8, 1912; Milwaukee *Journal*, March 21, 1920; Oct. 22, 1922; May 15, 1927; March 13, 1932.

THE STRUCTURE OF SOCIETY   453

tinuously available and professionally organized music or drama that the cultural tastes of mid-twentieth-century Milwaukee were expressed.[32]

Although by 1940 the *Deutsch-Athen* was largely a matter of memory, at the outset of the generation the flavor of Europeanism was still one of the most pervasive characteristics of the urban social scene. The number of foreign-born had diminished to 30 percent of the population by 1910, but more than 3 out of every 4 Milwaukeeans at that date had at least one parent born outside the United States. By 1940, the percentage of foreign-born white persons in the urban community had dropped to less than 15, and the foreign white stock to slightly less than half the total population; but more than 20 percent of the residents still spoke German; Polish and Italian were taught in the city schools as well as French, Spanish, and German; and when it came to taking the 1940 census in one two-by-five-block area which housed forty nationalities and two extra culture groups, in the heart of the city, a census taker was needed, according to a *Journal* reporter, who could "use six languages and smile in several more." To the increasingly large proportion of native-born persons who comprised the population between 1910 and 1940, the State of Wisconsin was by far the largest contributor, with neighboring Illinois and Michigan consistently next in line throughout the period. New York gave the fourth largest contribution in 1910 and 1920, but by 1930 near-by Iowa and Minnesota had crowded out the State from which so large an ingredient of the city's population had originally come.[33]

---

[32] Austin, *The Milwaukee Story*, 198; *Milwaukee's Progress in 1940*, p. 48; Bruce, *History*, 1:678-79.

[33] Between 1930 and 1940, the percentage of German stock fell from 44.9 percent to 40.7 percent of the total foreign stock in the city, while the percentage of Polish stock increased from 18.3 percent to 19.6 percent. For figures expanding these conclusions, see charts in appendix showing origins of native-born population of Milwaukee, listed according to predominance of states of origin, and percentage of foreign-born persons in population of Milwaukee, 1850 to 1940, listed in the order of predominance of nationality groups by decade. See also, Milwaukee *Journal*, May 1, 1933; June 16, 1940; Richard S. Davis, "Milwaukee, Old Lady Thrift," in Robert S. Allen, ed., *Our Fair City* (New York, 1947), 202; *United States Census, Thirteenth*, 1910, *Population*, 1:913; *United States Census, Sixteenth*, 1940, *Population—Nativity and Parentage of the White Population, Country of Origin of the Foreign Stock*, 78.

Germans constituted the most predominant foreign stock throughout the generation, with Poles gaining proportionately in second place and Austrians and Russians next in order; but the colonies of foreign-born southern and eastern Europeans, who now outnumbered the foreign-born from northern Europe, made Milwaukee a veritable patchwork of nationalities by the turn of the twenties. By 1920, the 15th, 20th, 22nd, and 25th wards were predominantly German, as were portions of the 18th. Americans prevailed in the 19th Ward and part of the 18th. The south half of the Ninth Ward was peopled by Hollanders, while Bohemians monopolized the remainder of this ward and a portion of the Tenth between North Avenue and Vine. In the Sixth and Tenth wards there was a large Jewish community. An area in the First, 13th, and 21st wards bounded by Newhall, Bartlett, Ogden, Jackson, Reservoir, Third, Meinecke, 12th, Burleigh, Holton, and Brattle; a Jones Island group; and portions of the Eighth, 12th, 14th, 17th, and 24th wards on the South side were the centers of Poland in Milwaukee. A colony of Slavs inhabited the Second Ward around Seventh Street; there was one of Greeks in the Fourth Ward, where a community of Austro-Hungarians also resided; Italians shared the Third Ward with the Greeks and constituted a section of the 17th near the rolling mills; and a block of Austro-Hungarians lent variety to the predominantly Irish 16th ward. Slovenians could be found in the Fifth, Seventh, and 22nd wards; Scotch in the 17th, and Scandinavians principally in the 17th and 23rd. The original locale of Milwaukee's Negro population, which comprised only 996 persons in the entire county in 1910, lay between West State and West Walnut streets. The northward migration of Negroes during and following World War I had more than doubled the number of colored residents by 1920, and by 1939 most of them lived in the Sixth and Tenth wards.[34]

Apart from some movement prompted by this colored invasion of the Sixth and Tenth wards, the foreign-born continued by 1940 to inhabit generally the colonies in which they had re-

[34] These data were compiled from information gathered by the Associated Charities, July 1918. See also Milwaukee *Journal*, Nov. 26, 1939.

sided twenty years earlier. Most of the newer arrivals, such as the Italians, Mexicans, and Greeks, stayed in the low-cost areas adjacent to the central business district; and only as a measure of affluence was achieved, did they move to outlying sections of the city. On the whole, it was a slow process. The one major exception to this practice, on the part of relative newcomers, was the behavior of the Poles, whose passion for land ownership led them to purchase homes among their own countrymen in the more outlying Polish communities of the city. And here they remained by the turn of the forties, still recent enough arrivals to prefer life among their own people to the movement and intermingling which was increasingly characteristic of the older German stock by that date.[35]

The Europeanism of its people complicated the reactions of Milwaukee to World War I—primarily because of the long-recognized Germanism of its citizenry, but also because of the identification of Socialism with opposition to the war and because of the existence within the city of such nationality groups as the Czechs and Poles, who on occasion fought the battles of their countrymen in the local wards. Considering the known sympathies of Milwaukee Germans for the Fatherland, it was not unnatural that superpatriots should look for something suspicious in a city where more than 50 percent of the population had German names and where there were a flourishing German press, German clubs, schools, and restaurants, and a distinguished German theater which the Milwaukee *Journal* was complimenting in April 1914 for its production in German of Shaw's *Pygmalion*.[36] The focus of the prevailing pro-German sentiment was the National German-American Alliance, an organization of American origin, which had been founded in Pennsylvania in 1901 to promote the interests of the German element in the country, and which claimed 37,000 Wisconsinites among its some 2,000,000 members in 1914. With the outbreak of the war, the Alliance made no secret of its sympathy for the

[35] These observations are based on data plotted from 1940 census returns by Professor Philip H. Person of the faculty of the University of Wisconsin Extension in Milwaukee.

[36] The daily *Germania Herold* (Milwaukee) had a circulation of 24,000 in 1914 and the weekly *Germania* (Milwaukee), 100,000. Milwaukee *Journal*, Jan. 14, March 28, April 1, 1914.

Central Powers. Dr. Leo Stern, one of the assistant superintendents of the Milwaukee public schools and president of the Wisconsin Alliance, organized an impressive demonstration at which resolutions were passed appealing to the American press to "throw off the yoke which the English-monopolized news service has placed upon it." Dr. Bernhard Dernburg defended Germany's invasion of Belgium before a large gathering in Milwaukee on December 11, 1914. The Wisconsin Alliance raised money by selling pictures of Wilhelm II and Franz Josef, and nearly 175,000 Milwaukeeans attended a bazaar held for seven days during the first week of March 1916, at which a fund of about $150,000 was raised for the German, Austrian, and Hungarian war sufferers of Europe. Mrs. Gustave Pabst, Mrs. Meta Berger, and Mrs. Louis Auer presided over booths in "Old Heidelberg"; and Miss Paula Uihlein, "in quaint gown and attractive hair dressing" received visitors in the Biedermeyer Garden, where "pretty nurses with German 'army officers' danced in the enclosure . . . and Biedermeyer girls floated about with men in evening clothes."[37]

When German sympathizers in the city began to protest against the nation's foreign policy—criticizing loans to the Triple Entente and accusing President Wilson of favoring Britain in connection with Germany's submarine warfare,[38] the

[37] Clifton J. Child, *The German-Americans in Politics* (Madison, 1939), asserts that in spite of the fact that the German-American Alliance became violently pro-German after 1914, it did not owe its rise to any guidance from Germany, but was "the product of peculiarly American conditions." 2-4, 7, 20-21, 26-27, 30; Milwaukee *Journal*, March 1, 3, 1916. Francis Hackett, in "How Milwaukee Takes the War," was of the opinion that Milwaukee was "pro-German on the whole." He thought that combustion was not likely, however, for Milwaukee's Germans were "not desirous of German victory at any cost." *New Republic*, 3:272-73 (July 17, 1915). Ernest Bruncken, a prominent Milwaukee German, wrote in December 1914: "It is surely little enough that we Americans of German birth or descent can do if we contribute mere money, although that is also needed. From the standpoint of American citizens we ought to be profoundly sorry that we are unable to take part in the tremendous sacrifices which are being made by the German people for the preservation and welfare, first of their own country, and, as a consequence, of all mankind." Child, *German-Americans in Politics*, 40.

[38] The German-American press called the loan of 1915 a "conspiracy against the welfare of our people." *Ibid.*, 60. The *Free Press* (Milwaukee) said Great Britain could "rob us of ships, of trade, of cargoes," but "the lovesick grandfather in the White House" would not "venture further than an apologetic admonition." Later it attributed the sinking of the "Lusitania" to an internal explosion. Milwaukee *Journal*, Feb. 10, 1916.

Milwaukee *Journal* took up the cudgels for American policy and so promoted the national cause at the expense of the pro-German point of view that in 1919 it was awarded the Pulitzer medal for what the committee considered "the most disinterested and meritorious public service rendered by any American newspaper" during the previous year. Not only did it condemn the pro-German policies of such newspapers as the *Free Press* and the *Germania,* but it labored, by printing testimonials from loyal German-Americans, to show that in spite of the fact that the great body of citizens of German origin "naturally sympathized" with Germany as against her enemies, most of them, "instead of following those who mouth disloyalty," stood "heart and soul with America."[39] In its editorial policy it undermined the anti-Wilsonian influence of the German-American press and opposed the formation of a Wisconsin branch of the German-American conference to take political action as German-Americans in national affairs. Publishing a serial on a hypothetical invasion of America, it advocated a policy of preparedness; and its efforts contributed to the plurality of 6,000 by which Milwaukee endorsed the reelection of President Wilson in November 1916, a vote which its editors interpreted as vindicating the city and proving it to be a real "American community."[40]

As friction between Germany and the United States increased, the Alliance labored strenuously for the preservation of peace and advised Wisconsin senators of an informal referendum which was said to show a vote of 300 to one against involvement in the war. But "America first" sentiment prevailed when preparations for a German-Austrian relief bazaar were abandoned in February; and at a mass meeting of 7,000 citizens, held in

[39] Beside Gyula de Pekar's assertion that "the German-Americans of Chicago . . . remain German even in Chicago," it set President Wilson's avowal: "A man who thinks of himself as belonging to a particular national group in America has not yet become an American; and the man who goes among you to trade upon your nationality is no worthy son to live under the Stars and Stripes." *Ibid.,* Nov. 16, 1932; Jan. 9, 18, 24, Feb. 14, 16, 17, March 4, April 13, 22, 1916.

[40] The Alliance was identified with the Republican Party in 1916. *Ibid.,* Feb. 10, March 2, April 6, June 3, Oct. 14, Nov. 8, 1916; Child, *German-Americans in Politics,* 137. The *Journal* organized a preparedness parade in which more than 28,250 persons participated on July 15, 1916. Milwaukee *Journal,* June 22, 23, July 14, 16, 1916.

the Auditorium on March 17, strong assertions of patriotism countered the charges of disloyalty which had been leveled at the city in the nation's press.[41] Once war was declared, the city rallied conscientiously to the nation's need. The Milwaukee County Council of Defense, organized on April 30, 1917, undertook to mobilize the community for war, securing the cooperation of local agencies in promoting the health and efficiency of the population, assisting industrial and commercial groups in facilitating their transition to a war economy, and planning programs for recruiting the men, money, and materials needed in the struggle. Milwaukee was the first large city to complete its registration under the selective service law; and although volunteering lagged and a few Italian anarchists resisted the draft, the Wisconsin metropolis contributed its full quota of fighting men. Large quantities of fish, potatoes, beans, and rice, sold at the public markets by the Food Bureau of the Council of Defense, helped to reduce the cost of living for the needy families of the city. What was probably the nation's first "war bread" resulted from experiments made by the Domestic Economy Committee of the Council and Milwaukee's wholesale bakers. Put on the market in July 1917, it ultimately effected savings of 25 to 50 percent in wheat content. A campaign was conducted to help housewives prepare better food from the standpoint of nutrition, and instruction was given in food and clothing conservation.

Thanks to the activities of the Fuel Bureau, wartime Milwaukee had less trouble with heating than most American cities. Emergency stations were opened where small quantities of coal could be bought at prices no higher than those asked by dealers for large orders. Through the encouragement of the Agricultural Bureau, more than 1,000 vacant lots were put into cultivation, and 11,000 children were enrolled in the U.S. School Garden Army. The child welfare division and rent profiteering committee of the Social Service Bureau were only two agencies of the some 212 wartime committees, aggregating 1,000 persons, by which every phase of the social, industrial, and commercial

[41] Child, *German-Americans in Politics*, 161-62; Milwaukee *Journal*, Feb. 9, 22, March 4, 7, 13, 15, 17, 18, 1917.

life of the city was regimented, largely on a voluntary basis, in the interest of prosecuting the war. Women made an important contribution to the conduct of local campaigns through the Women's Ward and District organization and in the work of the American Red Cross.

Officially recognized as early as June 29, 1916, Milwaukee's Red Cross chapter had raised money for a base hospital by the date of America's declaration of war. In June 1917 it was able to exceed by 50 percent its quota for the First War Fund, and thereafter it made a distinctive contribution to the war effort— in its Canteen Department, which served refreshments at troop trains passing through the city; in its preparation of medical supplies and clothing; in its home service department, which lent assistance to the families of men in the service; and in the nursing aid which it provided during the influenza epidemic which struck more than 18,000 persons and took a toll of 1,108 deaths in 1918. Meanwhile, the city not only was filling war contracts to the value of more than $50,000,000 but also was consistently going "over the top" in subscribing money to finance the war. With popular enthusiasm stimulated by posters, publicity, and parades, each successive loan drive elicited a better response. More than a hundred units participated in a great parade staged at the opening of the Third Liberty Loan drive in April 1918; among the five blocks of student marchers were 500 from West Division High School, carrying red, white, and blue streamers and posters bearing such legends as "Buy a bond and bury boastful Bill," "Your mite makes might," "If you don't come across, Willy will," and "Every quarter, every dollar, helps to make the Kaiser holler." By such community appeals, a total of more than $122,000,000 was raised during the course of the war.[42]

In spite of these manifestations of cooperation, many Milwaukeeans continued to be critical of America's participation in

[42] For over-all reports of wartime activity, see Milwaukee County Council of Defense, *Milwaukee, Twenty Months of War-Time Service* (Milwaukee, January 1, 1919), and American Red Cross, *The War History of the Milwaukee Chapter, 1916-19* (Milwaukee, 1920). See also Milwaukee *Journal*, May 7, 18, June 5, 1917; April 13, Nov. 11, 1918; Austin, *The Milwaukee Story*, 178, 181. Austin sets the figure raised by bond sales at $145,384,000. *Ibid.*, 179.

the conflict. The Socialists, already suspect as pro-German, endorsed the St. Louis platform of the party, which accused the capitalist class of forcing the war upon the nation against its will. In due time their newspaper, the *Leader,* was deprived of its mailing privilege and Berger, its editor, attacked as disloyal.[43] Milwaukee had also a branch of the People's Council, whose national leaders were Louis P. Lochner, Jane Addams, and Norman Thomas, and whose program, defending freedom of speech, stood for an early and general democratic peace. This group issued a publication called *Facts,* which bolstered the opposition of local pacifists and Socialists to the war. Condemning this obstructionism, as it did the alleged disloyalty of the German-language press, the *Journal* continued its apparently sincere attempt to thwart the opponents of the nation's war effort; but whether or not inspired by the newspaper's activities, in some Milwaukeeans patriotism boiled over into bigotry, with consequences that were to prove fatal to some of the best fruits of Milwaukee's prewar German culture.[44]

The Wisconsin Loyalty Legion, which held its first meeting in Milwaukee on March 22, 1918, took upon itself the task of ferreting out disloyalty and apathy toward the Allied cause. It urged the boycotting of the German press, opposed the teaching of other than the English language in the graded schools, and called upon the Attorney General of the United States to indict the framers of the city platform of the Milwaukee Socialists, which both affirmed opposition to capitalistic wars and demanded that the government negotiate a speedy peace "without forcible annexations or indemnities" and one in which all nations should "determine their own destiny." Its members participated in the "collection committees" that on occasion coerced

[43] The Socialists affirmed their willingness to obey all laws, but pledged themselves "to fight the efforts of any administration . . . to destroy our established liberties of whatever nature." On March 7, 1921, the Supreme Court handed down a decision upholding the Postmaster General's wartime treatment of the *Leader* (Milwaukee) on the ground that its articles constituted "a willful attempt to cause disloyalty" and "obstruct recruiting and enlistment." Charges against Berger were dropped in 1922 and 1923. Karen Falk, Public Opinion in Wisconsin during the World War, pp. 63, 67-73, 110, MS, M.A. thesis, dated 1941, University of Wisconsin. This will hereafter be cited as Falk, Public Opinion. See also Milwaukee *Journal,* April 8, 1917.

[44] A *Journal* editor wrote on June 15, 1917: "There is disloyalty here, . . . a tireless and determined effort here inimical to America, . . . but it has been

Milwaukee workmen or farmers in the vicinity into buying unwanted Liberty bonds. If what the committee considered a "fair share" were not subscribed, yellow placards were posted advising the world that "the occupant of these premises has refused to take his just share of Liberty Bonds."[45] While audiences were thronging to see a sensational motion picture entitled *The Kaiser*—"*the Beast of Berlin*," Milwaukee's far-famed German theater dropped into disrepute. Early in the war a presentation of *Wilhelm Tell* had to be abandoned when a mob of "patriots" set up a machine gun in front of the playhouse; and later on, when the nearly destitute actors attempted to stage a German comedy at the *Freie Gemeinde Hall,* the sheriff had to disperse a uniformed mob which professed its determination to "break up this Hun show." In April 1918, it was announced that no German-language performances would be given in the season of 1918-1919.[46]

The boycotting and condemning of people who spoke German or bore German names led at least 250 persons to Americanize their names in the first four months of the war; and before long, the *Deutscher* Club had become the Wisconsin Club, on the petition of its members, and the pupils of the German-English Academy had agreed among themselves to "foreswear the use of the present name of the institution for the period of the war, and call their school hereafter the Milwaukee Academy."[47] The *Germania* Bank became the Commercial National, the German-American Bank, the American National, and the *Germania* Building, shorn of the statue of *"Germania,"* was rechristened the Brumder Building. Even familiar German foods appeared under new names, as "Bismarcks" became "American beauties" and "sauerkraut," "liberty cabbage." By

---

curbed. It has been fought, it has been exposed to public gaze, and for the time at least it stands baffled and defeated." See also *ibid.,* June 19, July 15, Dec. 11, 13, 14, 17, 1917; May 21, 1918; Falk, Public Opinion, 110-13.

[45] *Ibid.,* 103, 110; Charles D. Stewart, "Prussianizing Wisconsin," *The Atlantic Monthly,* 123:99-105 (January 1919) ; Milwaukee *Journal,* April 16, 1918; Jan. 5, 15, 1919; Oscar Ameringer, *If You Don't Weaken: the Autobiography of Oscar Ameringer* (New York, 1940), 329.

[46] *Ibid.,* 336; Milwaukee *Journal,* April 21, 24, 1918.

[47] "It is not because we are opposed to the German language or the German people," said Rudolph Vogel, "but because of the unpleasantness that now goes with the name." *Ibid.,* July 29, Nov. 24, 1917; March 8, 1918.

August 1918 the *Journal* had won its campaign to remove compulsory foreign-language instruction from the elementary schools. In the face of resolutions from the *Musikverein, Liederkranz, Maennerchor,* and *Turnverein,* urging continuance of the study, and of a reluctant school board, desirous of gradual reduction so that German teachers could find new positions, the vigilant newspaper argued that in such "a melting pot of races" as Milwaukee, children should "imbibe Americanism and only Americanism." In January 1919, it announced the resignation of Stern, the assistant superintendent of schools who had championed the German-American Alliance, and reported that between 1916 and 1918 the number of pupils studying German in the grades had declined from 30,000 to 400 and the number of teachers from 200 to one. In June 1919 the teaching of German was to be completely discontinued in the elementary schools.[48]

After the "false alarm" of November 6, news of the real Armistice routed Milwaukeeans from their beds at 2:00 A.M. on November 11, 1918. Sirens rent the night with joyous shrieks, and by 3:00 A.M. Grand Avenue was alive with the celebrating throng. By daybreak Henry Wehr's bar was lined two deep, several women placing their feet on the rail, and, according to report, "taking 'theirs' in the true spirit of democracy." Chorus girls from the Gayety Theatre, accompanied by a band from the Randolph Hotel, paraded on Grand Avenue singing the "Star Spangled Banner." Representatives of Milwaukee's "Little Italy" waved American and Italian flags, and as early as 2:30 in the morning a crowd of Czechs and Slovaks with cowbells and horns had marched downtown. As the day wore on, organized parades from the city's factories reached the business district; and the three Schuster stores closed for the day "in Honor of the Triumph of Democracy." Most of

[48] The *Journal* endorsed the teaching of foreign languages in high school and college, but opposed their study in the grades on the premise that teaching German "to immature children in public schools" has "long been abused and perverted and devoted to a campaign of foreignism dangerous to America." *Ibid.,* June 8, July 31, Sept. 14, Dec. 19, 1917; Feb. 2, 4, Aug. 8, Sept. 26, 1918; Jan. 12, June 3, 1919; Bruce, *Born in America,* 295. In the fall of 1936, the public schools started offering the three foreign languages predominating in Milwaukee (German, Polish, and Italian), when parents of at least thirty seventh- or eighth-graders asked for the instruction. *Municipal Activities . . . 1936,* p. 81.

Milwaukee's German-Americans rejoiced, too. In spite of their reluctance to see the United States participate in the war and in spite of the mixed loyalties evoked as the country of their adoption warred with the land of their birth, men and women of German lineage had been among the foremost in responding to the nation's wartime needs. As Samuel Hopkins Adams said, the community had "as sound cause to be proud of the best of its Germans" as it had "to be ashamed of the worst of them." Nevertheless, whether they realized it or not, the wartime emotions had debased the prestige of Milwaukee's prewar Germanism to such an extent as to make its revival well nigh impossible; and speeding this as it had so many other changes in American life, the war hastened a development which the increasing assimilation of Milwaukee Germans, since the peak of their influence on the turn of the century, had already foreshadowed. There was something prophetic for the local scene as well as for the nation in the words of the *Journal's* Armistice Day editorial: "The war has shaken the world to its very foundations. The old world has gone forever. A new world is here today."[49]

Fifteen years later, as Hitler's brand of German ambition loomed on the world horizon, a unit of the Friends of New Germany, which ultimately became the German-American *Volksbund,* appeared in Milwaukee, shortly after the organization of the former in New York in 1933. Led by German migrants of the postwar period, among them George Froboese, their policies followed the *Führer's* anti-Semitic and anti-Communist "party line." In 1937 these pro-Nazis organized Camp Hindenburg on the Milwaukee River, near Grafton, where uniformed youth drilled under German commands and gave the Nazi salute. Their swastika-decorated public assemblies, held in the Milwaukee Auditorium, during the middle thirties, were frequently picketed by liberals and Communist sympathizers; but the most determined opponents of Hitlerism in Mil-

[49] Samuel H. Adams, "Invaded America," *Everybody's Magazine,* 38:33 (January 1918); Milwaukee *Journal,* Nov. 11, 12, 1918. See also I. L. Lenroot, "War Loyalty of Wisconsin," *Forum,* 59:695-702 (January 1918); Carl Wittke, "German-Americans and the World War," Ohio State Archaeological and Historical Society, *Collections,* vol. 5 (1936) ; and Edward H. Heth, *Some We Loved* (Boston 1935), the theme of which is the transformation of Milwaukee from a city that had distinction, because it was German, to a commonplace American city.

waukee were Germans themselves—the members of the Wisconsin Federation of German-American Societies, organized in 1932 by Bernard Hoffmann, who, like Froboese, had migrated from Germany to Milwaukee in the period following World War I. Froboese and his pro-Nazi cohorts never succeeded in infiltrating and thus controlling this group as they attempted to do, and by 1939 the supremacy of the Federation—pledged to promote the economic and cultural interests of Germans "as Americans in our new homeland America"—was assured when its members took over the bundist-operated Camp Hindenburg and changed its name to Camp Carl Schurz.[50] But the relative indifference of most of Milwaukee's Teutonic stock to these conflicts over developments in the New Germany revealed the extent to which Milwaukee Germanism had been diffused in the two decades following the war. The predominantly rugged North European physique and ruddy complexions of its people, as well as the Teutonic names on billboards and storefronts which greeted the visitor from the moment he approached the city, still reflected on the turn of the forties the almost indelible Germanism of the urban culture; but Milwaukee school children no longer sang *Die Wacht am Rhein* and *Deutschland über Alles,* the German theater, Martini's, and the Schlitz Palm Garden were no more, and Mader's cookery and the Rhenish ornamentation of the Pabst Building and the city hall remained among the few tangible reminders of that facet of the urban culture which lent Milwaukee its greatest distinction in the era preceding World War I.

That conflict, which contributed to the thinning of the city's Germanism, enhanced the prestige of those nationality groups in the urban culture whose homelands had been the beneficiaries of the war that was to "make the world safe for democracy." This was especially true of the Polish element, which in the postwar years progressed increasingly toward a position of influence in the city reminiscent of that of the German-American ingredient in the late nineteenth century. By 1939, Milwaukee was the seventh largest Polish center in America, and its Polish-American population, approximating 120,000 people, was play-

[50] Milwaukee *Journal,* July 14, 1940.

REPRESENTATIVE CITIZENS OF TWENTIETH-CENTURY MILWAUKEE. *Top row:* Frank J. Weber, trade union leader, and Otto H. Falk, prominent industrialist. *Middle row:* William George Bruce, civic promoter, and Michael Kruszka, Polish journalist. *Bottom row:* Victor Berger, Socialist editor and political leader.

ing a vigorous and generally self-conscious role in the developing metropolitan life. The quarter century preceding World War I found Milwaukee's Poles torn by a controversy which centered around the activities of the Catholic Church, focus of the Polish-American community since its earliest appearance in the city. Involved in the issue were the question of the teaching of Polish in the public schools, which threatened the appeal of parochial education; the demand for popular representation in the administration of parochial property; and the desire to attain equal rights for the Polish clergy in the Catholic hierarchy. Lined up in favor of the program were Michael and Waclaw Kruszka, the *Kuryer Polski,* and their followers; opposing it with equal zeal and invective were the clergy, the Catholic hierarchy, and their supporting press. The climax came in 1912 when the *Kuryer* was blacklisted by the church and the faithful forbidden to read it. Although the controversy subsided after the outbreak of World War I, when the Polish community turned unitedly to aid the rebirth of its homeland, it was not without significant results. In 1909 the school board authorized the teaching of Polish in the public schools. And added consequences were the expansion of the Polish National Church in the city and the founding of the Federation of Poles in America, organized by Kruszka when he failed to win the support of the Polish National Alliance.[51]

The swelling consciousness of Polish nationality following World War I served not only to unify a people whom diversity of national background and a traditionally independent spirit had torn apart but also to strengthen all the Polish cultural institutions of the city. The Roman Catholic Church carved out at least seven new parishes in the twenties; and the towering St. Josaphat's, further beautified under the pastorate of the Very Rev. Felix Baran, became the first Polish basilica in America, on November 18, 1928. Units of the great fraternal organizations multiplied;[52] and out of a committee, created in 1928 to

[51] According to the census, there were 56,895 persons native to Poland or with one or both parents born in Poland in the city in 1940. J. A. Kapmarski, "The *Kuryer Polski,*" in Borun, *We, the Milwaukee Poles,* 53-56; Olszyk, *Polish Press,* 35, 38, 40. Michael Kruszka died a few days after Poland's restoration. Managership of the *Kuryer* ultimately went to Colonel Peter Piasecki.
[52] See chapter 11.

commemorate the tenth anniversary of the liberation of Poland, grew the Casimir Pulaski Council, a representative body designed to coordinate the activities of some 106 Polish groups and societies in the community. National recognition of Milwaukee's Polish organizations came in 1931 when Francis X. Swietlik, dean of the Marquette Law School after 1934, was chosen as censor of the Polish National Alliance. Council No. 1 of the Polish Women's Alliance was organized in Milwaukee in 1911; and from 1910 forward, *The Polish Woman's Voice* was published in the city under the editorship of Mrs. Mary O. Kryszak.[53] The Polish Theater continued its activity in the postwar era, ultimately contributing talent to Polish programs on the city's radio stations; and the Polish Opera Club, recruited from the Polish choirs of the city, carried on an ambitious, if not always financially successful, operatic enterprise during the early and middle twenties. They began with Balfe's *Bohemian Girl,* translated into Polish by a retired nun, and continued with the works of Flotow, Verdi, Oscar Strauss, and Moniuszko, the production of whose *Halka* marked its first complete performance in the United States. Of the last work, which the club also performed in Chicago, a critic there wrote: "What an example to us Americans. Hats off to Polish Milwaukee!"[54]

The boom times of the later twenties greatly increased the affluence of the Polish element of Milwaukee, a development which led some of the second-generation residents to lose interest in and even repudiate their Old World background. While the prosperity lasted, home ownership multiplied in the Polish-American wards; small business expanded; real estate agents and building contractors flourished; the Polish banks prospered; and by 1924, Fons and Company, a pioneer real estate and building and loan firm, had achieved a capitalization of $500,000.[55] But the early thirties brought a sorry sequel. With the economic

[53] See articles in Borun, *We, the Milwaukee Poles,* 17, 29-38, 191, 193. Carl Glazewski, "History of Pulaski Council," *ibid.,* 59-61; Thaddeus Borun, "Polish Organizations in Milwaukee," *ibid.,* 167.
[54] Milwaukee *Journal,* Dec. 9, 1939; Stasia Pokora, "The Polish Theatre in Milwaukee," in Borun, *We, the Milwaukee Poles,* 97; A. J. Lukaszewski, "The Polish Opera Club," *ibid.,* 94-95.
[55] *Ibid.,* 236-39.

collapse, which arrived before the Polish community had had time to achieve an economic stability comparable to that of the older nationality groups, came forfeiture of homes and an invasion of the Polish business community by chain stores and other foreign-owned enterprise. In part by way of compensation, many members of the Polish community now increased their efforts to expand the appreciation of their native culture and to exert even greater influence in the political and administrative life of the city—ambitions vigorously forwarded by the Polish-language press.[56] Out of an appearance of Polish youth in connection with an international festival on the lake front in 1930 grew the Polish Fine Arts Club, which later sponsored such activities as a "Polish Month" and a symphony concert in 1938 conducted by Jerzy Bojanowski. Similar activities were sponsored by the Josef Conrad Club at Marquette University. At the insistence of the Poles, the teaching of their language became a part of the Milwaukee high-school curriculum in 1934. Two years earlier, the study had been introduced at the Milwaukee Center of the University of Wisconsin, and soon thereafter fourteen different courses in Polish language, literature, civilization, and history were available there.[57]

It was in the realm of politics, however, that the Poles made their most positive mark upon the developing urban community. These accomplishments resulted in part from their solidarity, as fostered by press and church, and in part from their tendency to find in the distinctions of public office a compensation for lack of recognition in the economic and financial sphere. Throughout the period 1910 to 1940, the Poles continued to hold the balance of power in municipal politics which they had begun to wield in the late nineteenth century; and because of their numbers and their activity on election day, it came to be recognized that, in order to be elected, candidates chosen

[56] See *Kuryer Polski* (Milwaukee), June 23, 1938.
[57] Stasia Pokora, "The Polish Fine Arts Club," in Borun, *We, the Milwaukee Poles,* 81; Szymon St. Deptuła, "The Department of Polish at the Milwaukee Center of the University of Wisconsin, 1932-1946," *ibid.,* 145-51. See also, Bernard C. Wiczynski, "Contributions by Polish-Americans in the Field of Education in Wisconsin," *ibid.,* 79-80. Polish was taught in the seventh and eighth grades, after 1936, when thirty parents petitioned for the study.

on a city-wide basis must be acceptable to the Poles. At least five, and at times eight, of the city's wards could be counted upon to send Polish-Americans to the city council. From the day that Roman Czerwinski was elected as comptroller in 1890, Polish-Americans had a virtual corner on this important political office, a post that was held by Louis M. Kotecki from 1912 to 1933. Both Mayor Hoan and his successor, Mayor Zeidler, chose Polish secretaries; Polish support was an important factor in the latter's election in 1940; and during the course of the generation Milwaukeeans of Polish extraction were increasingly found in such key municipal positions as chief of police and commissioner of public works. The predominance of workingmen among the Poles inclined the group most consistently to the Democratic Party, their coolness toward the Socialists being motivated by both the attitude of the church and the Socialists' opposition to fighting the battles of Poland in World War I. President Wilson's espousal of the Polish cause won him a virtual landslide in the Polish wards in 1916; and the appeal of Franklin D. Roosevelt as a friend of labor prompted such unanimity in the Polish vote as to effect the election of Thaddeus F. Wasielewski to the House of Representatives in 1938.[58]

Hitler's attack on Poland fostered an almost unprecedented unity of spirit among the outspokenly individualistic, and frequently litigious, Polish population of the city. But in spite of the nationalizing influence of this assault upon their reborn homeland, social and economic forces operating upon the community and the Polish-American members of it were inevitably integrating this nationality-conscious group into the life of the larger city. To the horror of the older generation, English was heard increasingly from Polish-Catholic pulpits; and while the old-timers still thought politically in terms of choosing Poles, as such, on election day, political responses among the youth depended increasingly upon economic and social conditions rather than upon considerations of nationality. Moreover, the appearance of Polish banking institutions, large in-

[58] John C. Kleczka was elected to the House in 1918 and 1920. Wallace E. Maciejewski, "Our Role in Municipal Affairs," *ibid.*, 71-72; Clement Zablocki,

dustrial enterprises like the Maynard Electric Steel Casting Company, owned by the Wabiszewski family, and dozens of Polish-American attorneys, physicians, dentists, and architects suggested a developing economic stratification which, as in the experience of the German-Americans, promised ultimately to identify the Milwaukee Poles with groups that cut across nationality lines. By the forties, the Sears, Roebuck, Goldblatt, J. C. Penney, Woolworth, and Walgreen stores which intermingled in the Mitchell Street area with the offices of the *Nowiny Polskie*, the Modjeska movie theater, and Fons and Company's National Savings and Loan reflected the evolution of Polish Milwaukee under the very shadow of the twin spires of St. Stanislaus and within sight of the brilliant dome of St. Josaphat's basilica. But ward solidarity and church allegiance were still strong, and the Polish element was still young enough and aggressive enough to force the stamp of its distinctive culture upon the metropolitan scene. It is not without significance that one of the best planned and executed contributions to the city's centennial in 1946 was a handsome volume entitled *We, the Milwaukee Poles* and that the conductor of Milwaukee's celebrated "Music under the Stars," after 1941, was Jerzy Bojanowski, a Chicago Pole.[59]

As in the case of the Poles, the period from 1910 to 1940 saw an increased assimilation of the many other—especially South European—strains which the turn of the century had added to Milwaukee's urban populace. The movement to create Czechoslovakia, between 1916 and 1918, unified Czechs and Slovaks who up to that time had developed separately the churches, fraternal organizations, and building and loan associations which facilitated the adjustment of first-generation mi-

"Our People in State Government," *ibid.*, 77; John Jakusz-Gostomski, "The Democratic Party and Polish-Americans," *ibid.*, 289-90.

[59] As late as 1946, Szymon Deptuła wrote, "The American Poles, unlike the Jews or the Germans, are not as yet, by and large, college conscious. Car, church, cinema, and home-conscious, yes; book—rarely." This will come, he implies, once the Poles become "economically secure and sure of their status in the new world." *Ibid.*, 150-51. Shortly after Hitler's attack on Poland, the Milwaukee Poles organized a Polish Relief Committee on which all the prominent Polish groups were represented. *Ibid.*, 2. See tribute to Polish pioneers by B. Snella, "Our Pioneers," *ibid.*, 57, 58.

grants to the New World.⁶⁰ However, once the new republic had become a reality, antagonisms based on the political, economic, and religious problems of the homeland led to heated controversy among Milwaukee Czechs and Slovaks, as did differences springing from the fact that the local Czechs assimilated more readily and were less subject to control by the church, whereas the Slovaks were inclined to subordinate loyalty to the culture group to allegiance to their Catholic faith. By contrast with the almost exclusive use of the native language in the Slovak church, by the middle twenties the Czechs had only one service in the Old-World tongue. The encouragement of cultural nationalism by various agencies in the city during the thirties lent support to the Bohemian *Sokols* and to such institutions as Mrs. Capek Novak's Saturday school, which, since early in the century, had sought to foster an appreciation of the European culture and bridge the gap that often alienates foreign-born parents from their children. From 1930 forward, the Slovaks participated in an annual Slovak Day; and 1937 saw the organization of the Federation of Milwaukee Slovak Societies to coordinate the activities of the more than fifty Slovak groups in the city.⁶¹

Many of greater Milwaukee's more than 20,000 Italians moved during the course of the generation from the Third to the First Ward, Bay View, and other suburbs. Their migration to the city flourished between 1900 and 1924; and in the hilarious, prohibition-checked twenties they lent color to the "wide open" Third Ward where "gin, dago red . . . and plain 'moon' were sold . . . to all comers, . . . where food meant spaghetti or ravioli, and where the diamonds and furs of the rich gleamed among the soiled garments of labor." Organizations like the Italian Civic Association fostered such nationality solidarity as prevailed in this group. Little class distinction existed among the Hungarian population of the city,

---

⁶⁰ The Milwaukee *Journal* for April 21, 1918, carried the announcement of a projected "monster demonstration of the Czechoslovak, Polish, Serbian, Croatian, and Russian peoples of Milwaukee" to "'demonstrate that Milwaukeeans are not all Prokaiserites and Prussianists.'" The Czechoslovak committee initiating the movement for the mass meeting was affiliated with the Free Bohemia League.

⁶¹ Milwaukee *Journal*, April 3, 1928; May 6, 1935; March 14, 1936.

THE STRUCTURE OF SOCIETY 471

united by its fraternal and benevolent societies, its Hungarian Reform Church, and its soccer teams. Restaurants, soft-drink parlors, confectionery and fruit stores, and groceries occupied the attentions of Milwaukee's Greeks whose social life was oriented around the Greek Orthodox Catholic Church and such societies as the American Hellenic Educational and Protective Association, the Greek-American Protective Association, and the Hellenic-American Republican Club. And to the more numerous Russians, Italians, Jugoslavs, Hungarians, and Czechoslovaks must be added the Armenian rug dealers, French war brides, Syrian Masons, and Mexican tannery and steel workers who lent the variety of their nationality to the heterogeneous urban scene. An important force in promoting the wholesome assimilation of Milwaukee's foreign-born population was the International Institute, organized in 1923, whose aim was to develop leadership among the foreign-born and promote appreciation of them through acquainting other Americans with the contribution of their culture. Classes for immigrants, as well as folk festivals, furthered this end, as did the activities of the city's adult education program. The latter conducted citizenship classes and, after 1931, sponsored an annual *Harvest Festival of Many Lands,* a pageant featuring the costumes, songs, and dances of as many as thirty-two of the city's nationality groups.[62]

The northward movement of Negroes during and after World War I did not swell the colored population of Milwaukee as much as it did that of some of the other cities of the Middle West. Between 1910 and 1920, Milwaukee's Negro population doubled; it tripled during the twenties and increased 18 percent in the thirties; but by 1940, Milwaukee still had a smaller proportion of nonwhites than twenty-two of the twenty-five largest cities of the nation. Milwaukee's Negro community, which totaled 8,821 in 1940, dwelt almost exclusively within the square mile bounded by West Wright, West Kilbourn, North Third, and North Twelfth streets on the northern and western outskirts of the city's business dis-

[62] *Ibid.,* March 27, 30, April 2, 4, 1928; March 10-13, 21, 1936; *Municipal Activities . . . 1933,* p. 115.

trict. The depressed thirties, which curtailed the flow of Negro migration, stimulated the enterprise of this group by encouraging former wage earners to strike out for themselves in small merchandising, personal services, and the ice, coal, and junk business. A People's Cooperative Store was opened in 1936. West Walnut Street was the main thoroughfare of Milwaukee's "Little Harlem," with its variety of Negro-operated businesses: groceries, barber shops, saloons, drug stores, tailor shops, beauty parlors, and a Negro motion picture theater. In 1939 there were 10 Negro physicians, 5 lawyers, and 5 dentists, and a Negro Chamber of Commerce and Business Men's League. Five major churches, including 2 Methodist, 2 Baptist, and 1 Catholic, ministered to the religious needs of this people, as well as 12 storefront tabernacles, such as "Heaven at Hand," "Heavenly Spirits," and the like. A Negro newspaper, *The Wisconsin Enterprise Blade,* was founded in 1916. Of prime significance in advancing the social welfare of the Negro community was the Urban League, founded in 1919 as one of the branches of a national organization. By 1939 it was providing free employment service, a day nursery, health education, a music department, and classes in Negro history, art, and drama.[63]

The nationality background of the community goes far to explain the religious complexion of twentieth-century Milwaukee. The continuing preponderance of Poles and Germans kept the city predominantly Catholic and strongly Lutheran throughout the period 1910 to 1940. According to the census of religious bodies in 1936, Roman Catholics totaled 175,087; Lutherans, 70,729; and Jewish congregants, 29,600. The combined membership of the reformed Protestant churches, such as the Baptists, Congregationalists, Methodists, Presbyterians, and Protestant Episcopalians, did not exceed 25,000. Proportionately speaking, Milwaukeeans, like most Americans of the period, appeared to be increasingly desirous of affiliating with the church as the generation progressed. Church members

[63] Milwaukee *Journal,* Nov. 26, 1939. See also *Milwaukee's Negro Community,* prepared by Mrs. Paula Lynagh, Citizens' Governmental Research Bureau of Milwaukee (Milwaukee, 1946), i, 1, 4, 33.

ARCHITECTURAL CONTRASTS. *Left:* Cottage Inn, hostelry of the village period. *Below:* Hotel Schroeder, skyscraper hotel of the twentieth-century metropolis.

counted in 1916 represented 44 percent of the 1920 population, while those counted in 1936 made up 54 percent of the residents enumerated in the census of 1940. Between 1916 and 1936, Lutheranism and Presbyterianism, on a more restricted scale, showed the most marked expansion, both denominations growing at a rate considerably in excess of that of the population of the city as a whole. Many churches saw their attendance increase during the depression years; but some of the wealthier congregations fell off at that time, their members refusing to participate for want of ability to pay their customary assessments. Generally speaking, the prevailing increase in membership was not accompanied by an equivalent interest in attending service or bearing the other responsibilities of church association. Because of the mobility of the urban population, the Protestant churches, whose appeal frequently depended as much upon the congeniality of the congregation or the popularity of the minister as upon the obligation to worship, suffered more than the Catholic churches in this respect.[64]

The religious life of the maturing metropolis was characterized by a decided liberalization of practices in most of the churches and an increasing spirit of cooperation among the various denominations. For example, the generation saw a marked relaxation of the sternness with which Baptists, Methodists, and Presbyterians had viewed dancing, card playing, and Sunday pleasures. Among Jewish communicants, the appeal of the reform and conservative congregations made inroads upon the still predominantly orthodox groups. English found increasing use in Polish, Czech, and German Catholic pulpits; and Lutheranism moved far away from the German forms of speech and liturgy which had characterized its worship on the turn of the twentieth century. The institution of union services on the part of certain congregations—such as on Good Friday, Easter, and Thanksgiving—attested the growth of more cordial relationships among the denominations, al-

[64] Bureau of Census, *Religious Bodies, 1916* (Washington, 1919), pt. 1, p. 438; Bureau of Census, *Religious Bodies, 1926* (Washington, 1930), pt. 1, pp. 468-69; Bureau of Census, *Religious Bodies, 1936* (Washington, 1941), pt. 1, pp. 584-85. Variations in the bases upon which the various churches report their membership prompt caution in interpreting the figures.

though the Catholic and certain Lutheran clergy found it less easy to cooperate in these enterprises.[65] And within the various sects, there was a lowering of the barriers which formerly had resulted in intra-denominational friction.[66] Moreover, the churches, without exception, addressed themselves increasingly to the social welfare of the urban community and the world at large. The sermon subjects in the reformed Protestant churches dealt ever more frequently with concrete social issues;[67] and while Lutheranism deviated little from its emphasis on preaching the gospel, through its commissions and its Lutheran Welfare Society it guided its laymen in wholesome community action. The activities of the Jewish congregations reflected their consciousness of the social welfare responsibility of the church; and in many phases of its work Catholicism showed itself to be wide awake to the opportunity to serve the urban community. Its Catholic youth organization and social work program were pointed toward the needs of the developing metropolis as well as the expansion of the church; and in the realization of its goals it continued to exert a political influence of no inconsiderable scope in the municipal life.

By the turn of the air-minded forties, both the physical and social patterns of the Wisconsin metropolis had taken shapes unlike those of thirty years before. Trolley buses were beginning to replace street cars, and air travel to challenge automobiles and trains. The competition of readily accessible

[65] For the opening day of the Mid-Summer Festival in July 1936, a community religious service, under the direction of the Rev. E. LeRoy Dakin, prominent Baptist minister, featured music by the Salvation Army Band and the United Choirs of the Colored Churches of Milwaukee and addresses on "The Value of Religion to the Community" by ministers of the Jewish, Lutheran, and Roman Catholic faiths. *Official Program, Milwaukee Mid-Summer Festival, 1936,* p. 37.

[66] For example, the dissatisfaction of the Lutheran laity with the divided church prompted a movement to lower the barriers on questions of church practice between the clergy of the more conservative Lutheran Synodical Conference of North America and those of the American Lutheran Conference and United Lutheran Church in America. The period also saw increased harmony among the orthodox and liberal Jewish rabbis in spite of ritualistic differences.

[67] The Milwaukee Federation of Churches published a report in March 1913 stating that the cost of living required a minimum wage for women of at least $8.90 per week. Mueller, *Milwaukee Workers,* 19.

suburbs as places of residence had left the business district rimmed with dilapidated flats and run-down wooden dwellings. Youth hurried to school rather than to the factory, and housewives went about their mechanized housekeeping to the accompaniment of a broadcast concert. Towering new structures on Wisconsin Avenue were the most outspoken signs of the break with the nineteenth century; but as the soaring shaft of the Mariner Building all but locked shadows with the massive, classic lines of the Public Library and Museum and as the Old-World spires and cupolas of the city hall stood up to the clean-cut bulk of the trimly modern Bankers Building, the face of the business district itself revealed the continued hold of the old and the staid resistance to the new which were traditionally, if paradoxically, characteristic of socially progressive Milwaukee.[68]

[68] The growth of Milwaukee had not been sufficiently rapid by 1940 to permit the rebuilding of its fundamentally one-street business thoroughfare along consistently modern lines. The expansion of the later twenties resulted in the addition of a number of structures built in strict adherence to the principles of modern architecture and reflecting the westward migration of the example of New York's "set-back" trend in skyscraper architecture. The Mariner Tower, Schroeder Hotel, Warner Theater Building, Bankers Building, and Milwaukee Gas Light Company, designed by Eschweiler and Eschweiler, Milwaukee architects, exhibit a clean-cut line and lack of overhang and classic ornamentation which contrast strangely with the top-heavy stone-block reminders of the ornate eighties and the classic temple style of such structures as the Library, the Wells Building, and the Northwestern Mutual Life. Most daringly modern in design was the A. O. Smith Building with its stone, aluminum, and glass exterior. Gas stations and plastic storefronts began to reflect the architectural trends of the early thirties; but few residences in traditionally conservative Milwaukee showed interest in the modern style. See Milwaukee *Journal*, Sept. 27, 1932.

CHAPTER 17

The Economic Base

IF IT was the Europeanism of Milwaukee that lent the city distinction in the nineteenth century, industrialism was its prevailing feature in the twentieth; for Milwaukee, from 1910 to 1940, was increasingly a manufacturing center, despite its rural overtones. Its industrialism was less apparent to the sight than to the smell, for although the once pale-colored bricks of the Cream City had weathered to a dingy hue, the twentieth-century metropolis was no smoke-filled Pittsburgh; and because of the dispersion of its industries and retail marketing centers, the odors of packing plant and malt house more than the concentration of smoke stacks and ovens attested the comparatively high percentage of the population engaged in manufacturing pursuits.[1] Regardless of appearance, the censuses of 1910 and 1920 showed that more than 50 percent of the city's labor force was employed in manufacturing; and although the retrenchment of the thirties had reduced the proportion so employed to slightly less than 40 percent by 1940, the city remained one of the most intensively industrial communities of the nation.[2] The per capita value of manufactured output in the city, which had stood at $165 in 1879, increased from $550 to $745 between 1909 and 1939; and

[1] Proof of the wide distribution of industries in the Milwaukee metropolitan district is the fact that of the total number of persons employed in 1926, only 40 percent worked in the central business district. McClellan and Junkersfeld, Inc., *Report on Transportation in the Milwaukee Metropolitan District*, 1:52.

[2] By comparison with more than twenty of the largest cities of the United States, Milwaukee showed the fourth largest concentration in industry in 1919, second largest in 1929, and fourth largest in 1939. Robert Filtzer and William L. Slayton, *Manufacturing in Milwaukee and 22 Metropolitan Cities, 1919, 1929, 1939* (mimeographed study, Milwaukee Land Commission, 1944), 8. See also Slayton, *Milwaukee's Labor Force*, 12, 48.

counting the industrial establishments outside the city limits, the 1940 figure reached close to $778.[3]

The rapid industrial advance of the first decade of the century was not maintained between 1910 and 1914. In the latter year, production was hampered both because of uncertainty as to federal regulation of business and because of the outbreak of the war in Europe. But wartime orders proved a bonanza to Milwaukee's factory owners, and during the second half of the decade, the value of manufactured commodities increased 158 percent in contrast with the 7.5 percent increase of the preceding five years. In 1917, the Chamber of Commerce reported that the value of finished products had for the first time exceeded a half-billion dollars; and in 1918 the city's workers received the largest returns in industrial Milwaukee's history. Iron, steel, and heavy machinery were in tremendous demand; but the war brought greatly increased calls for motor vehicles, packed meat, and leather products, as well. Even the breweries and malt houses shared for the moment in the prosperity, having gained access to South American markets formerly supplied by Germany. The wagon manufacturers—victims of the age—alone showed decreasing returns; and as if to compensate for their decline, a Ford Motor Company assembling plant, valued at $6,500,000, was erected in the city in 1916.[4]

With the signing of the Armistice came a momentary reduction in orders; but the inflated demands and inordinately high prices of the postwar era stimulated industry to such an extent that in March 1920 "the percentage of business failures to the total number of firms in business" was at the lowest point in fifty years. The high cost of living was the unhappy side of the picture; and as rents soared and living expenses more than doubled their prewar peak, there arose a mass protest against the "H.C.L." Ten men and women of the Mil-

[3] Whitbeck, *Geography of Southeastern Wisconsin*, 92; *United States Census, Sixteenth*, 1940, *Manufactures, 1939*, 3:1082-83.
[4] Chamber of Commerce, *Report*, 1914-15, pp. 41-42; Milwaukee *Sentinel*, Jan. 1, 1915; Jan. 1, 1916; Jan. 1, 1919; Whitbeck, *Geography of Southeastern Wisconsin*, 94-95; Chamber of Commerce, *Report*, 1916-17, pp. 74-75.

478 MILWAUKEE: THE HISTORY OF A CITY

waukee State Normal School faculty determined to wear overalls and gingham dresses until the end of the year; the Federated Women's Clubs organized a fair price committee; and the Council of Jewish Women and the Home Economics and Citizenship Study clubs sponsored a high cost of living mass meeting at the Public Museum.[5] But before long, collapses in silk, hides, wool, cotton, and other raw materials foretold the end of an unhealthy state of business; and the midyear brought a reaction from which the city was only beginning to recover in 1922. Nationwide prohibition contributed to the brewers' decline in 1920; and in the following year iron and steel production fell off by 58 percent, wood products by 48 percent, motor vehicles by 43 percent, and leather by 41 percent. To add to the difficulty, the export market decreased 43 percent in monetary value. Fortunately, the inevitable upturn in industrial activity was not too long delayed; and by the close of 1922, R. E. Wright, commercial analyst of the First Wisconsin National Bank, reported a 6.4 percent increase in manufacturing returns—"a sedate prosperity," he wrote, "dressed in a sensible economic garb rather than an illusive and elusive phantom of frenzied finance."[6]

After a slowdown toward the end of 1923, the steadily expanding value of the city's industrial output heralded what a report for 1928 called "the greatest advance ever made in the growth and progress of Milwaukee." That expansive year saw the expenditure of $44,000,000 for new buildings, three-fifths of it in residential construction. March employment hit a five-year high. The value of manufactured products stood at $1,053,472,000 whence it had climbed from $789,519,605 in 1922. Prosperity soared even higher in 1929, when some 569 new firms were organized, and the worth of manufactures showed a $100,000,000 gain. Black Thursday—October 24, 1929—punctured the bubble; but its deflation was more gradual —if ultimately more complete—in Milwaukee than in many industrial areas of the nation. Unlike the motor industry and

[5] Milwaukee *Journal*, March 16, 23, April 3, 21, 1920.
[6] Milwaukee *Sentinel*, Jan. 1, 1921; Jan. 1, 1922; Jan. 1, 1923; Chamber of Commerce, *Report*, 1922-23, p. 59.

its branches, heavy machine manufacture was at first little affected; and, as the *Sentinel* reported on January 1, 1930: "The receding tendency of general business has been considerably less sharp in Milwaukee than elsewhere." A federal survey showing that production was still higher in Milwaukee than in many other American cities brought thousands of job-hunters there seeking the employment that eluded them elsewhere. By March 1930, some 51 percent of the unskilled and 15 percent of the skilled laborers applying for work at the public employment office were from outside the city. But by the close of the year, the municipal administration was forced to admit that Milwaukee was facing "the worst business depression in its history." More people were "out of employment and living on charitable doles, both private and public," than ever before in the city's career.[7]

If the Wisconsin city had been the envy of other American communities in 1930 and 1931—for the diversified industries and thrifty citizens that allegedly cushioned its collapse—conditions on the turn of 1932-1933 reached depths which no one could admire. By this date it was clear that Milwaukee had actually been hit harder than almost any other industrial community in the nation. By 1933, the number of wage earners employed had dropped to 66,010, a decline of 75 percent from the 1929 total of 117,658; and less than 50 percent of the general property taxes levied could be collected. The city's number-one industry, the iron, steel, and heavy machinery division of the metal trades, was suffering from lack of purchasing power on the part of the railroads, the depressed farmer, and the consuming public generally. The total year's expenditures for building approximated but 12½ percent of the average annual cost of construction for the past twenty years.[8]

[7] *Ibid.*, 1923-24, p. 53; *ibid.*, 1924-25, p. 48; *ibid.*, 1925-26, pp. 47-48; *Municipal Government and Activities . . . 1923*, p. 11; *ibid. . . . 1928*, p. 9; *ibid. . . . 1929*, p. 4; Milwaukee *Journal*, Nov. 16, 1924; March 5, 1928; Milwaukee *Sentinel*, Jan. 1, 1926; Jan. 1, 1930; Austin, *The Milwaukee Story*, 191; *Municipal Activities . . . 1930*, pp. 11, 72.

[8] A study comparing the Milwaukee industrial area with Cincinnati, San Francisco, Rochester, Minneapolis, and Buffalo showed that Milwaukee had the greatest decrease in number of wage earners from 1929 to 1933. See Board of Public Land Commissioners, *A Study on Milwaukee's Economic Base* (in process),

The condition of the depressed community began to improve somewhat by the close of 1933, doctored by the federal relief program and the legalization of 3.2 percent beer. By October 1933, the pay-roll index stood at 53.4 as compared with 34.1 in October 1932 and 27.7 in March 1933. In the following year, department store sales increased by more than 10 percent; more people paid their taxes and restored their telephones; business failures showed a 45 percent decrease as compared to 1933; marriage licenses multiplied; and even the expanding birth rate reflected the upturn in the business cycle. A 100 percent increase in building construction in 1935 indicated that recovery was continuing; and by the year's end, the index of employment in the production of both durable and non-durable goods reached the highest level attained since 1930. Increased earnings and a sharp advance in building activity in 1936, together with industrial mergers and refinancing and a huge expansion in the breweries, prompted the *Sentinel* to assert that Milwaukee's industry and commerce had thrown away "their crutches and walked out of the depression sick room" at last. A serious recession, which prevailed from August 1937 to September 1938, brought drastic lay-offs in the automotive, farm implements, and heavy machines group and threatened the gains of recent years; but by 1939, the community appeared to be back on the road to recovery, and marked increases in factory employment on the turn of the forties suggested that a period of war-invoked prosperity was at hand. In spite of these gains, the 1939 Census of Manufactures could not hide the industrial setback of the decade; and in reporting an output worth only $437,444,671, by comparison with the $700,760,456 of ten years earlier, it was the first decennial census in the city's history to show an industrial decline.[9]

10, 15; Milwaukee *Sentinel*, Dec. 31, 1932; Dec. 30, 1933; *Municipal Activities* . . . *1933*, pp. 78, 103; *ibid*. . . . *1936*, p. 40; *Milwaukee Civic News: 1938*, p. 10. In the field of wholesale trade, Milwaukee felt the depression later than did the State or nation, but recovery was slower in the Wisconsin city, and as late as 1939, Milwaukee had not recovered to the extent the State and nation had. Carl H. Quast, *Wholesale Trade in the Milwaukee Area* (mimeographed study, Board of Public Land Commissioners, Milwaukee, 1947), 17.

[9] Factory employment in 1940 increased by 10,000 over the 1939 figure. Milwaukee *Sentinel*, Dec. 30, 1933; Dec. 31, 1934; Jan. 1, 1937; Milwaukee *Journal*, Dec. 31, 1934; Dec. 31, 1937; Dec. 31, 1938; Dec. 31, 1939; *Municipal Activities* . . .

The depressed decade had demonstrated, as never before, the vulnerability of the urban community in time of economic storm; and but for the relief that the government supplied, the community would have been hard put to weather the distress. The relief load—handled as a county function—soared from aid to less than 1,000 families in January 1930 to support for approximately 140,000 people—one person in five of the population—in April 1933; and as late as 1939, it was estimated that one in every five families in Milwaukee County was still receiving some form of public aid. Before 1933, the local community shouldered the problem of relief for the unemployed. Since the facilities of the Rescue Mission were inadequate to the sudden influx of unemployed single men in the winter of 1929-30, Mayor Hoan transformed a vacant armory into a food kitchen and dining room and with the cooperation of merchants and others fed the daily bread line. To prevent a recurrence of this depression phenomenon, organized relief, through the activities of a Committee on the Homeless, was instituted in the following year. Although the county handled direct relief, the city council attempted to promote activities that would minimize the need for its provision, continuing to do so as long as money lasted. It considered projects for which R.F.C. loans could be obtained; and heeding the recommendation of President Hoover's Unemployment Committee, it appropriated money for use on public works and directed that all available balances be put at the disposal of the departments which "could provide the most work for the most men." Under this plan, more than 12,000 unemployed men were certified during 1931 for at least one ten-day shift at 60 cents an hour, to be spent in "pick-and-shovel" work on the city's parks and playgrounds. The council's special committee on unemployment worked with a citizens' volunteer group to place the unemployed with largest families on the city list and attempted to connect workers with odd jobs through the use of cards dis-

1934, pp. 40-41, 68, 99-100; *ibid.* . . . *1935*, pp. 30, 64, 94, 107; *ibid.* . . . *1936*, pp. 6, 43; *Milwaukee, 1937*, p. 50; *Milwaukee Civic News: 1938*, pp. 6, 14; *Annual Report . . . 1939*, p. 81; *Milwaukee's Progress in 1940*, p. 108. See appendix for chart showing trends in persons and capital employed in industrial pursuits in Milwaukee, 1860 to 1939.

tributed by the milkmen of the community. In addition, the county and the city benefited from emergency State legislation which brought the Milwaukee area $1,642,860.50 for relief in 1932.[10]

The weight of the relief burden was to a large extent removed from the common council in 1933 when the federal government assumed the responsibility under the New Deal; and the inauguration of public works projects late in September helped to offset the continuing downward spiral of industrial employment. The expanded role of the federal government in this respect had come in part as a result of pressures exerted by the United States Conference of Mayors, at the original instigation of Milwaukee's Mayor Hoan, pressure which brought $300,000,000 for direct relief to municipalities early in 1933 and hastened the decision of Congress to provide $400,000,000 for civil works projects when the $3,300,000,000 public works program of the New Deal was slow to materialize. A common council committee of fifteen was appointed to act on the proposed plans for which federal aid was to be sought. In due time, P.W.A. programs for the construction of miles of sewers and streets, a $4,600,000 water purification plant, two low-cost housing developments (Parklawn and Greendale), and several school buildings were under way. Sewer and street construction and repair activities, under W.P.A., effected vital improvements that the depressed municipality was unable to carry out. For example, in 1936 a maximum force of 3,500 men worked on 174 miles of streets, oiling 88 miles, macadamizing 6, and laying bricks on 2. Six of the city's 7 miles of creosoted block were replaced with asphalt pavement. In 1937, more than 6 miles of sewers were laid under W.P.A. direction by contrast with less than 1 mile constructed under city contract. Other federal agencies, such as the C.W.A. and F.E.R.A., subsidized work which long had been delayed for want of funds.

[10] According to Mayor Hoan, Milwaukee was "the first large community to provide made work for those on relief who volunteered for it and to pay cash wages therefor." To persons wholly dependent on relief, the county supplied cash, food, fuel, light, gas, and rent. The average allowance for a totally dependent family was about $50 a month. Hoan, *City Government*, 311-12, 321; Milwaukee *Journal*, Dec. 31, 1939; *Municipal Activities* . . . *1930*, p. 73; *ibid*. . . . *1931*, pp. 18, 31-32; *ibid*. . . . *1932*, pp. 20, 22.

The city's park and playground program was advanced ten to fifteen years ahead of schedule; municipal buildings were renovated and repaired; and modern lighting, improved casing, and new decorations made the Museum more attractive and serviceable to the public. Outstanding among the scores of more specialized activities were the W.P.A. sewing project, where 750 workers, organized as a mass-production garment factory, fabricated clothing for the public institutions of Wisconsin; a toy-lending headquarters, which repaired and circulated more than 40,000 toys; a newspaper digesting and microfilming enterprise, which helped preserve the valuable journalistic record of the city's history; and a handicraft project, in which more than 1,000 workers were engaged in making rugs, draperies, and book bindings for the tax-supported institutions of the State. In spite of these accomplishments, the traditional conservatism of the common council and its concern for economy prevented it from appropriating the funds which would have brought federal aid for the construction of such large community structures as a stadium or auditorium, facilities which a number of cities obtained in connection with the work relief program.[11]

The peak year for emergency relief expenditures came in 1936 when nearly $26,000,000 was received in the county for social security benefits, soldier's relief, aid to transients, general relief under the Department of Public Assistance, C.C.C. camps, C.W.A., and other federal works programs. At that date, some 44,589 cases were certified for direct and work relief on the Milwaukee County relief rolls. Department of Public Assistance relief expenditures dropped from more than $14,000,000 in 1935 to less than $5,000,000 in 1936; while expenditures under the Federal Works program increased from two to eighteen million dollars in these years. During 1938, nearly 5,000 persons left their W.P.A. jobs to return to industry; but by the year's end 23,057 men and 2,464 women—the breadwinner in one of every five families in the county—remained on W.P.A. employment. New rules laid down for W.P.A., now

[11] *Ibid.* . . . *1933*, pp. 22, 24, 28, 110-11; *ibid.* . . . *1934*, pp. 24, 53, 55, 57-58, 110; *ibid.* . . . *1935*, p. 38; *ibid.* . . . *1936*, pp. 68, 77, 82; *Milwaukee, 1937*, pp. 20, 40; *Milwaukee Civic News: 1938*, p. 10; Milwaukee *Journal*, Dec. 31, 1939.

called the Works Projects instead of Works Progress Administration, in 1939 tightened the qualifications for relief and transformed its administration from a job program, run simply to give the unemployed a chance to earn money, to a work program for the needy. These new regulations, coupled with improved business conditions in the city, led to a marked decrease in the number employed by W.P.A. during 1940. The actual numbers employed varied from 6,750 in February to 3,850 in June.[12]

The economic calamities of the thirties called attention to the concentration on heavy industry in the city's economy and the signal dependence of the community on the welfare of such enterprises as the manufacture of machinery, iron and steel, automobiles, and automotive equipment. By 1910, clothing and flour—important products of nineteenth-century manufacture—had given way to the four major items of twentieth-century production: iron and steel products, leather, meat, and malt liquors (until the twenties). From 1913 forward, the iron and steel industry was consistently the leader. World War I provided a powerful stimulant to the metal trades; and after a slump in 1921, they forged ahead with tremendous comparative gains. Between 1923 and 1929, the metal trades group rose 68 percent in dollar value and increased in volume of production from 37 to 48 percent of the total manufactures in the city. Not only did the industry respond to the expanded domestic demand for automobiles, agricultural machinery, and heavy durable goods that characterized the prosperous twenties, but it increased its exports to foreign markets from 50 to 100 percent. By 1940, more than 46 percent of the men employed in the city's factories were engaged in the production of iron and steel products or machines; and more than half of the total employment in manufacturing in the county was associated

[12] According to a tabulation prepared by Mrs. Paula Lynagh, of the Citizens' Bureau of Milwaukee, relief expenditures, including social security aids, etc., for Milwaukee County totaled $236,115 in 1923; $628,433 in 1929; $20,714,997 in 1934; $25,921,691 in 1936; and $21,557,811 in 1937. By the close of 1939, it was estimated that relief costs to the owner of a $7,500 home would be $65 in taxes for relief, pensions, and W.P.A. contributions. In 1928 such taxes would not have exceeded $13.65. Milwaukee *Journal,* Dec. 31, 1938; Dec. 31, 1939. See also *Milwaukee's Progress in 1940,* p. 51.

THE ECONOMIC BASE 485

with the production of machinery, iron and steel, automobiles, and automotive equipment. Leather and leather products and food and kindred products accounted for an additional 24 percent of manufacturing employment in Milwaukee County in 1940.[13]

The crisis of the thirties exhibited not only the high industrial intensity of metropolitan Milwaukee but also a quality of the community which sprang from its concentration on the production of heavy durable goods—its high sensitivity to economic changes in the nation as a whole. Between 1919 and 1940, employment fluctuated more violently in Milwaukee than in most of the large cities of the United States. In periods of expanding economic activity—such as in 1929, 1935, 1937, and 1940—conditions in the Milwaukee area improved more rapidly and extensively than in the United States as a whole. Conversely, in periods of contraction, Milwaukee suffered more intensely than most of her metropolitan neighbors. Thus, Milwaukee County, between 1927 and 1933, experienced the most serious setback of any of 37 major industrial counties; and its decline in the ten-year period from 1929 to 1939 was more severe than that of such comparable communities as Cincinnati, San Francisco, Rochester, Minneapolis, and Buffalo.[14]

[13] Whitbeck, *Geography of Southeastern Wisconsin*, 97; Milwaukee *Sentinel*, Jan. 1, 1930; Board of Public Land Commissioners, *Milwaukee's Economic Base*, 6; Slayton, *Milwaukee's Labor Force*, 26.

[14] The fluctuation in employment in Milwaukee County is revealed in the following figures, using employment in 1927 as the index number 100:

Year	Number	Index Number	Year	Number	Index Number
1919	106,137	99.1	1935	82,795	77.3
1927	107,128	100.	1937	97,686	91.2
1929	117,658	109.8	1939	80,255	74.9
1931	79,906	74.6	1940	88,316*	82.4
1933	66,010	61.6			

*Adjusted to *Census of Manufacturers* figures.
Board of Public Land Commissioners, *Milwaukee's Economic Base*, 10, 12, 15-16. See also William L. Slayton and Robert L. Filtzer, *Manufacturing in the Milwaukee Industrial Area Compared to Five Comparable Industrial Areas: 1929, 1931, 1933, 1935, 1937, 1939* (mimeographed study, Board of Public Land Commissioners, Milwaukee, 1944); William L. Slayton, *Manufacturing in Milwaukee City, Milwaukee County, the Milwaukee Industrial Area, Wisconsin, the East North Central Division, and the United States, 1919 through 1939* (mimeographed study, Board of Public Land Commissioners, Milwaukee, 1944); Richard S. Dewey, *Comparative Economic Sensitivity of Thirty-four Cities with Special Reference to Milwaukee* (mimeographed study, Milwaukee County Regional Planning Department, 1945).

Just as the over-all industrial development of twentieth-century Milwaukee was subject to economic trends in the world at large, so each industry group was conditioned by the changing tastes, demands, and business practices in the wider nation. Regardless of the world-wide scope of their commercial operations between 1910 and 1940, Milwaukee's major industries continued to be those which in pioneer days had been based on the raw materials and local needs of the city's immediate geographical hinterland. The heavy metal trades, originally dependent upon iron mined in Wisconsin and ore from the Lake Superior region, now, however, drew their raw materials from everywhere and marketed their products around the globe. By 1920, at least 200 plants in the region were turning out products manufactured of iron and steel. The Allis-Chalmers Manufacturing Company, largest industrial enterprise in the community, produced a widely diversified line of agricultural, electrical, and industrial machinery and equipment, ranging from small stock items to especially designed hydraulic turbines priced at more than $1,000,000. Employing about 6,000 workers in 1920, its labor force varied from 6,800 ten years later to 4,200 in 1932; 17,700 in 1937; 14,500 in 1939; and 16,900 in 1940. Approximate sales in these years fluctuated from $13,200,000 in 1933 to $87,000,000 in 1940. But the West Allis plant was only one of many huge enterprises in the metal trades field. By 1930, the A. O. Smith Corporation was assessed at $9,450,000; International Harvester at $6,085,000; Cutler-Hammer at $3,098,000; the Harley-Davidson Motor Company at $2,848,000; Seaman Body Corporation at $2,444,000; and the Falk Corporation at $2,256,000—to mention only those firms engaged in the metal trades within the municipal limits of Milwaukee whose 1930 assessment exceeded $2,000,000.[15]

In the first decade of the period, packed meat, leather, and malt liquors marched in that order at some distance behind iron and steel in the parade of production; but at the approach of

[15] Whitbeck, *Geography of Southeastern Wisconsin*, 115; Chamber of Commerce, *Report*, 1913, p. 42; Milwaukee *Journal*, Nov. 16, 1924; Milwaukee *Sentinel*, Jan. 1, 1921; Jan. 1, 1922; Jan. 1, 1926; Jan. 1, 1930; Bruce, *Builders of Milwaukee*, 66; Slayton, *Milwaukee's Labor Force*, 26, 34-35; Allis-Chalmers Manufacturing Company, *Prospectus*, March 31, 1944, pp. 5-7; Gregory, *History*, 1:563.

the twenties, motor vehicles had nosed out beverages to achieve fourth place in 1919, third place in 1920, and second in 1922, a position which the industry maintained for most of the period thereafter. Boots and shoes and knit goods began to assume some prominence in the twenties; and as the product of the breweries disappeared from the "Big Ten" list of industries, candy and confectionery found a place. A newcomer among the first ten after 1920 was gasoline and oil. By 1940, iron and steel, machinery, and automotive equipment were far in the lead; but malt liquors, leather products, packed meat, textiles, and chemicals still held a prominent place in the industrial picture.[16] Like the metal trades, the other leading manufactures had, in the main, evolved from the industries of the pioneer community; and in many of them, despite the wide dispersion of investment inherent in corporate ownership, management remained in the hands of descendants of the original founders.[17]

The evolution of Milwaukee's major industries during the period from 1910 to 1940 followed the patterns of industrial behavior which already had become apparent by the turn of the twentieth century.[18] Of foremost importance was the continuing consolidation of ownership and units of production within a given industry. While in most instances the number of firms decreased, the number of employees per firm, the capital invested, the properties, local or distant, acquired, and the value of the product multiplied. For example, while capital invested in industry increased 11 percent in the period from 1920 to 1926, the number of firms increased only 8 percent; yet the value of the product increased about 38 percent and

---

[16] See Milwaukee *Sentinel* annual trade reviews published January 1, yearly. See also *United States Census, Thirteenth*, 1910, vol. 9, *Manufactures, 1909*, pp. 1360-61; *United States Census, Fourteenth*, 1920, vol. 9, *Manufactures*, 1646-47; *United States Census, Fifteenth*, 1930, *Manufactures*, 3:562; *United States Census, Sixteenth*, 1940, *Manufactures, 1939*, 3:1098-1100.

[17] This was especially true of the brewing industry. For example, as late as 1940, the Miller Brewing Company remained a closed corporation, no portion of its stock having ever been made available for public sale. History of the Miller Brewing Company, p. 5, typescript, dated Aug. 19, 1941, in letter to author from G. R. Holtz, Advertising Department, Miller Brewing Company. This will hereafter be cited as History of the Miller Brewing Company.

[18] See chapter 13.

the number of persons employed, 29 percent. In the brewing industry the number of firms decreased from ten to nine between 1909 and 1939; but the value of the commodity more than doubled. Establishments producing bread and bakery goods fell from 318 in 1909 to 213 in 1939; but the value of the product more than tripled. The experience of typical, but widely different, industries in the Milwaukee area further illustrates this trend.[19]

For example, the Allis-Chalmers empire took shape during the period as the result of the successive acquisition of properties which by 1935 covered nearly 500 acres throughout the United States and Canada. When the Allis-Chalmers Company was reorganized in 1913, as the Allis-Chalmers Manufacturing Company, the new president was Otto H. Falk, a native Milwaukeean recently retired from the United States Army as a brigadier general. Falk's interest in farming and his genius for organizing mass production led to marked expansion of the company's tractor division, which constituted only one branch of activities that extended also to the production of sawmill, flour mill, and mining machinery; engines and condensors; centrifugal pumps; hydraulic and steam turbines; and scores of other mechanical products. Between 1924 and 1931, machine and assembly shops at Springfield, Illinois, La Porte, Indiana, La Crosse, Wisconsin, Pittsburgh, and Boston were added to the Allis-Chalmers domain, some of them, such as the La Crosse Plow Company and the Advance-Rumely Company of La Porte, themselves pioneer farm-machinery firms of the Middle West. Allis-Chalmers Rumely, Ltd., owned warehouses, office buildings, and other properties in several Canadian cities. From 1935 to 1939, the foreign business of the company approximated 10 percent of its total sales.[20]

A similar chain of acquisition was responsible for bringing

[19] McClellan and Junkersfeld, Inc., *Report on Transportation in the Milwaukee Metropolitan District*, 1:52; *United States Census, Thirteenth*, 1910, vol. 9, *Manufactures, 1909*, pp. 1360-61; *United States Census, Sixteenth*, 1940, *Manufactures, 1939*, 3:1098-1100.

[20] *Pioneer Power: Story of Allis-Chalmers*, 80-90; Allis-Chalmers, *Prospectus*, 9-10; Allis-Chalmers, *Eighty-Eight Years of Progress*, 39. See also Allis-Chalmers Manufacturing Company, *Annual Reports* and *Annual Reviews*.

CHANGES IN THE HEAVY METAL TRADES. *Left:* Allis Company foundry in late nineteenth century. *Below:* Heavy installation in a modern plant.

under one head all the electric utility properties in the Milwaukee area. The Wisconsin Electric Power Company, which ultimately possessed this monopoly, stemmed in part from an earlier utility, the Milwaukee Electric Railway and Light Company. In 1896 the latter had succeeded to the property and business of the Milwaukee Street Railway Company, which by the early nineties had consolidated some eight small city railroad and illuminating concerns. In 1919 the Milwaukee Electric Railway and Light Company purchased all the operating properties of the Milwaukee Light, Heat, and Traction Company, which from time to time since its incorporation in 1896 had acquired most of the railway and electric utility properties in the suburban communities and rural area surrounding Milwaukee. In addition, during the period 1896 to 1938, the Electric Company acquired a dozen other utility concerns operating in the city and its suburbs and incorporated all its holdings into a single unit furnishing power and transportation services to Milwaukee and its environs. In October 1938, the Electric Company purchased the stock of the Wisconsin Electric Power Company, from which it had leased the Lakeside Generating Station, merged itself into this holding, and assumed its name. Employing approximately 2,000 workers, the Wisconsin Electric Power Company by 1940 was furnishing electric service to Milwaukee and most of southeastern Wisconsin. Its subsidiary, the Milwaukee Electric Railway and Transport Company, was operating virtually all the street-railway, trackless-trolley and motorbus business in the city of Milwaukee as well as suburban and interurban railroads and intercity bus lines in the surrounding area. Executives of the utility who exerted a dominant influence in the industrial life of twentieth-century Milwaukee were John I. Beggs, who guided the destinies of the company from 1902 to 1911 and again from 1920 to 1925, and his successor, Sylvester B. Way, who was serving as president at the time of his death in 1946. The million-dollar merger of the Pabst Company and the Premier Malt Products Company in 1932, to combine brewing properties in Milwaukee and Peoria, provided another example of the consolidating trend. And in quite a different field, a complex series of consolidations and mergers, during the late twenties and early thirties, forwarded the development of the First Wisconsin National, the city's largest bank.[21]

In addition to consolidation, both local and national in scope, an expanded appeal to a nationwide consumer market further characterized the development of the city's major industries. This was especially true in connection with the product which already had "made Milwaukee famous." At the outset of the generation—in about 1911—the Schlitz brewery embarked upon a modern advertising campaign reminiscent of Captain Pabst's efforts to sell his product in the nineties. The post-prohibition period saw even more intensive efforts in this direction. Early in February 1937, Schlitz began a campaign of full-color advertising in thirteen large magazines, designed to reach four out of every five homes in the United States. Publicity appeared in 500 city newspapers during the summer, twenty-four-sheet bill postings were displayed in 500 cities, and the *Schlitz Palm Garden of the Air* carried the message to the nation's radio listeners. A similarly extensive advertising campaign acquainted the American public with the merits of the "Blue Ribbon" product; and the Pabst network of sales organization covered the country. By the early forties, Allis-Chalmers maintained offices in sixty-one cities of the United States and six abroad for the sale of its general machine products and thirty-four domestic and ten foreign offices for the sale of tractors, farm and road machinery, and the like.[22]

While advertising and marketing methods were being brought up to date, there came also a progressive modernization in the methods of production, as the skill of engineers and chemists, no less than business technicians, was applied to speeding and improving the output of Milwaukee's factories. Building plans as well as assembly lines exhibited the streamlined approach of the day; and the clean-cut stone, aluminum,

[21] Bruce, *Builders of Milwaukee*, 33-37, 51-52; "Pabst, A Blue Ribbon Champion," *Modern Brewery Age*, 29 (August 1941).
[22] [Rohde], "Schlitz—the Brewery That Never Stopped Growing," p. 11, reprint from *Beer Distributor* (August 1937); "Pabst, A Blue Ribbon Champion," *Modern Brewery Age*, 32, 35 (August 1941); Allis-Chalmers, *Prospectus*, 6.

and glass exterior of the A. O. Smith research building, completed in 1930, marked it as the most daring example of modern architecture in the city. Similarly functional construction characterized the $2,000,000 addition to the Schlitz Company's brewery, which was opened in 1937. The development of new and intricate machinery in the post-prohibition era revolutionized the old style of brewing. Glass-lined, steel storage tanks replaced the copper kettles and wooden tanks of the nineteenth century. Scientifically diffused light and new style automatic germinating drums improved the malting process. Monster grain dryers and 400-ton ice machines dwarfed earlier apparatus of this type; and new mechanical casing equipment made it possible to insert twenty-four bottles at a time into cardboard cases without resort to manual labor. Comprehensive conveyor systems, in this as in the other major industries, symbolized the substitution of mechanical for human power; and outside the breweries motor tractors replaced the rumbling, horse-drawn wagons of an earlier day.[23]

The brewing industry, also better than any other of the city's manufactures, exhibits the extent to which the industrial evolution of metropolitan Milwaukee was conditioned by changes in law and popular practice during the period 1910 to 1940. Despite its association with the *Gemütlichkeit* of the Wisconsin city, beer, more than the other major items of production, was vulnerable to attack on social grounds. This was increasingly apparent during the reform-minded "progressive era"; and as early as 1916 some of the city's promoters were at pains to point out that in one census year only—that of 1889—had brewing constituted Milwaukee's largest industry, and that "in 1915 not more than one-twentieth of all the goods produced . . . was beer." As state after state "went dry" in 1916, the Wisconsin Brewers' Association became sufficiently alarmed to propose cleaning up the saloon business in the city as a means of quieting criticisms by the Anti-Saloon League; but more than the forces of reform was spelling the indus-

[23] "Beer and the Fame of Milwaukee," in *Official Program, Milwaukee Mid-Summer Festival, 1936*, pp. 20-21, 27; [Rohde], "Schlitz—the Brewery That Never Stopped Growing," pp. 2-11, reprint from *Beer Distributor* (August 1937).

try's momentary doom. World War I presented a more essential need for the grain from which the beverage was made; and when it was disclosed that such German brewers as Joseph Uihlein, Gustave Pabst, and members of the Miller family had supported Arthur Brisbane's purchase of the Washington *Times,* as a means of fighting prohibition, the industry was accused of subsidizing German propaganda and obstructing the nation's war effort. The brewers' allegedly disloyal behavior was the subject of a Senate investigation ordered in September 1918, and a month later, President Wilson signed a bill prohibiting the manufacture of intoxicating beverages after May 1, 1919, and their sale after the first of the following July.[24]

This reform-fostered and war-invoked legislation dealt the brewers a drastic blow. By 1912—less than fifty years after the industry had reported an annual output of 69,000 barrels—production had been boosted to 4,182,000. By 1918 the total had declined to 2,217,000 barrels; but the product still represented a value of $35,000,000 and jobs not only for approximately 6,000 brewery workers but also for the employees of the city's some 1,900 saloons. Russell Austin's *The Milwaukee Story* describes the funeral of John Barleycorn, held in the city shortly before the day when liquor sales were scheduled to close:

> On June 21, 1919 . . . twenty-some sad faced Milwaukeeans . . . gathered at the . . . Weis liquor dispensary . . . to hold a funeral. In a back room overlooking the Milwaukee river a specially made coffin containing the "earthly remains of Mr. John Barleycorn" rested upon a bier lighted by bourbon bottle candelabra. Floral tributes were tastefully arranged in beer mugs around the casket. . . . The pallbearers bore the weighted casket to the river, dropped it in, and tossed after it numerous empty bottles and the firm's cash register for good measure.

Equally indicative of Milwaukee's sentiments was the comment of August Kahlo, retiring saloonkeeper, who posted a

[24] According to the Milwaukee *Journal,* four out of five of the saloons in the city were owned or controlled by the brewers. Milwaukee *Journal,* April 2, 14, Dec. 13, 1916; Nov. 22, 1918. C. A. Miller of the Miller Brewing Company frankly admitted that his family contributed to Brisbane for the purpose of "saving our business," but denied any connection with German propaganda. *Evening Wisconsin* (Milwaukee), July 15, Sept. 20, 1918.

placard reading: "The First of July Is the Last of August." National prohibition, arriving on January 16, 1920, was greeted in Milwaukee without ceremony or celebration; and only six citizens took leave of liquor so violently as to require the attentions of the police. By 1921 the value of beverages produced in the city had dropped from $35,000,000, the 1918 figure, to less than $2,600,000; and by the close of the twenties the number of employees stood at 512 as compared to 3,217 in 1910.[25]

Many Milwaukeeans found their adjustment to prohibition in the bootlegger, the "speak-easy," and home brew. But the former producers turned to the manufacture of such legally acceptable commodities as cheese, malt, chocolate candy, chewing gum, and near beer. The Miller brewery turned out a cereal beverage bearing the "High Life" label; and all the leading breweries produced millions of pounds of malt syrups yearly. A Schlitz advertisement in 1928 contrasts strangely with earlier and more succinct publicity for the contents of the "brown bottle": "Schlitz—Flavored Malt Syrup. The name Schlitz on the label gives you the same absolute assurance of purity and confidence in malt syrup as the name 'Sterling' . . . on silver. For Better Bread and Finer Candy—Schlitz—Milwaukee." The relegalization of beer—on April 7, 1933—brought the promise of prosperity regained. Fifty thousand spectators milled around the breweries on the eve of the new day; and when 12:01 A.M. arrived, there was dancing in the streets, factory and tugboat whistles blew, and an American Legion band at the Schlitz brewery blared out, "Happy Days Are Here Again." The city's breweries, with plans for expansion already under way, had 15,000,000 bottles of beer ready for shipment across the nation, as the signal struck; and by the end of the year, sales had mounted to $30,000,000; nearly $10,000,000 had been spent in reconditioning plants, and more than 8,000 workers had been returned to brewery and allied pay rolls. Produc-

[25] Whitbeck, *Geography of Southeastern Wisconsin*, 103; Milwaukee *Journal*, Nov. 17, 22, Dec. 1, 1918; April 7, 1933; Oct. 25, 1936; Milwaukee *Sentinel*, Dec. 31, 1932; *Evening Wisconsin*, July 15, 1918; *Wisconsin News* (Milwaukee), Jan. 21, June 30, 1919; Chamber of Commerce, *Report*, 1918-19, p. 65; *ibid.*, 1921-22, p. 56; Austin, *The Milwaukee Story*, 185; "Beer and the Fame of Milwaukee," *Mid-Summer Festival Program, 1936*, p. 21.

tion mounted as the thirties progressed. In June of 1936, Pabst reported the best month in its history; and Schlitz, Blatz, and Miller were making shipments of unprecedented size. In 1936 and 1937, the major breweries undertook costly plant expansion, until by 1940 the total value of brewery property in the city approached $20,000,000. By that date, their comeback had restored the industry to a position on the "Big Ten" list; and the output of the city's nine brewing establishments, valued at nearly $40,000,000, exceeded by 10 percent the value of production in pre-prohibition days.[26]

The tanning industry, too, was the victim of changing needs and tastes, for it was as much stimulated by the demands of World War I as it was later depressed by social habits that greatly minimized the use of leather goods. The years between 1909 and 1912 brought the period of soundest prosperity to an industry that as early as 1890 had given Milwaukee first rank for the production of plain, tanned leather. The approach of war swelled the call for leather goods. The year 1916 saw a $10,000,000 increase in output; and by 1919 the value of the tannery product reached an all-time high of $60,000,000. Thereafter, the industry experienced a progressive decline. Seventeen establishments produced goods worth about $47,000,000 in 1924; by 1929, fourteen firms reported a $20,000,000 output; and a decade later, the product of the ten tanneries within the city limits was valued at only $16,818,235. The manufacture of boots and shoes expanded at a phenomenal rate between 1909 and 1919, as did the production of leather gloves and mittens in somewhat less degree; but twenty years later the value of the output in these fields also had declined. A number of factors, in addition to the cessation of the wartime demands, brought about the contraction of tanning operations. With the increased use of the automobile, and the ever more sedentary character of

[26] History of the Miller Brewing Company, 4; souvenir booklet for the Diamond Jubilee of the *Turnvereine*, Milwaukee, June 2-3, 1928; "Beer and the Fame of Milwaukee," *Mid-Summer Festival Program, 1936*, p. 21; "Pabst, A Blue Ribbon Champion," *Modern Brewery Age*, 29 (August 1941); Austin, *The Milwaukee Story*, 192; Milwaukee *Sentinel*, Dec. 30, 1933; Dec. 31, 1935; Jan. 1, 1937; Milwaukee *Journal*, April 7, 1933; Nov. 17, 1935; Oct. 25, 1936; April 7, 1938. According to the various censuses of manufactures, the output of malt liquors was valued at $19,643,242 in 1909; $22,509,127 in 1919; and $39,754,531 in 1939.

modern living, shoes wore longer and lighter footwear better served the popular need. The virtual disappearance of horse-drawn transportation reduced the call for harness and buggy leather; while the expanded use of electric motors affected the market for leather belting on machines. Fashion made inroads, too, as rubber-soled sport shoes and low-cut cloth models replaced the high-topped shoes and leather boots of earlier days. Manipulations of the hide market by the packing interests, as well as serious competition from foreign countries in the middle twenties, further complicated the tanners' problems. These conditions, together with revolutionary changes in methods of production, greatly reduced the physical size as well as the volume of output of the city's tanneries. By 1940, the Pfister and Vogel plant was only a fraction the size of the gigantic structure operated between 1890 and 1920; and the value of the output of the major tanning firms had declined from $54,007,415 in 1919 (an era of high prices) to $16,818,235. In spite of this reduction, the tanneries remained among the city's wealthiest, as well as oldest, industries. In 1930, the Pfister and Vogel Leather Company was assessed at $4,125,000; A. O. Trostel and Sons Company, at $1,847,000; and A. F. Gallun and Sons, at $1,473,000.[27]

Flour milling was another of Milwaukee's pioneer industries to suffer a twentieth-century decline. Although the peak of flour production was reached in 1892, when more than 2,000,000 barrels of flour were ground in the city's mills, by 1910 its manufacture still ranked high on the list of major industries. Between 1910 and 1919, however, production dropped from 1,318,565 to 584,883 barrels. By the latter date, the city's four mills were not grinding enough flour for local consumption; and after 1920 flour milling was no longer listed among the city's ten most prominent industries. The decline, in this instance, was not the consequence of changes in law or public taste, but rather of the northward movement of the grain supply, as a result of which new milling centers sprang up closer

[27] Gregory, *History*, 1:537-38, 563; Whitbeck, *Geography of Southeastern Wisconsin*, 110; Milwaukee *Sentinel*, Jan. 1, 1926; Jan. 1, 1930; Schefft, Tanning Industry in Wisconsin, 79-91.

to the source or the raw grain by-passed Milwaukee as it was shipped eastward via the Great Lakes for milling at Buffalo or on the Atlantic coast. Fluctuating fashion led, however, to the rise as well as the decline of industrial pursuits. Pre-eminent in this respect was the phenomenal growth of the automotive and related industries, a consequence of popular desires reflected in the forty-fivefold increase in motorcar ownership in Milwaukee between 1913 and 1940. The emergence of the production of gasoline and oil as major industries in the twenties was related to this trend. Fashion, too, was responsible for demands which lifted knit goods and hosiery from tenth to fifth place on the "Big Ten" list between 1909 and 1928. In 1930, the Phoenix Hosiery Company was assessed at $4,071,000—one of the most highly valued properties within the city limits; and Holeproof Hosiery was valued at $2,597,000.[28]

A final characteristic of Milwaukee's industrialism during the generation was the increasing recognition of collective bargaining in the relations between management and labor, with the result that during the thirty-year period under discussion wages climbed from lower-than-average to higher-than-average levels and what had been an open-shop town before 1930 had become by 1940 one of the most solidly organized labor centers in the United States.[29] Organized labor was able to do little more than hold its own in the first decade of the century, and by 1913 it was numerically no stronger than it had been in 1904, when the Federated Trades Council numbered sixty locals and

[28] Whitbeck, *Geography of Southeastern Wisconsin*, 101; Milwaukee *Journal*, Dec. 31, 1939; Milwaukee *Sentinel*, Jan. 1, 1930; Gregory, *History*, 1:563.

[29] The following table, drawn from figures in Filtzer and Slayton, *Manufacturing in Milwaukee and 22 Metropolitan Cities*, 9, reveals employment and wages in industrial concerns within the city from 1909 to 1939:

	1909	1919	1929	1939
Total Employees	72,171	99,913	112,948	72,854
Salaried Employees	7,959	15,691	18,075	11,182
Percent of Total Employees	11.3	15.7	16.0	15.4
Wage Earners	64,212	84,222	94,873	61,672
Percent of Total Employees	88.7	84.3	84.0	84.6
Percent of Wage Earners to Total Population	17.0	18.5	16.5	10.5
Average Real Salary		$1,417	$2,877	$3,316
Average Real Wage		$ 770	$1,513	$1,786

13,000 members.[30] By the close of the decade, however, the influence of labor unionists in the local Socialist Party and the force of labor leaders such as Frank J. Weber in the legislature at Madison were showing results. State laws were passed providing for workmen's compensation and governing the employment of women and children in industry; and one of the early acts of Mayor Seidel's administration was the organization of a permanent Citizens' Committee on Unemployment, in 1911, so constituted as to represent the city, the county, the industrialists, and organized labor. Labor became more aggressive with the outbreak of World War I; and as wages failed to keep pace with doubled living costs, strikes multiplied. Although they involved no considerable number of workers, they rose in number from thirteen in 1914 to fifty-four, four years later. By 1918, membership in the Federated Trades Council had increased to 20,000, about 80 percent skilled workers.[31]

The postwar depression and ensuing prosperity of the later twenties quieted the labor movement in the period from 1920 to 1930. Marked reductions in wages in 1921, an unsavory reputation gained because of the activities of I.W.W., communist, and anarchist groups, and a drive for the open shop, launched by industry under the direction of the National Association of Manufacturers, helped to crush the assertiveness which labor had exhibited in 1919. By the mid-twenties, wages as well as profits began to climb, and labor made little complaint. Between 1927 and the end of 1930 there were as few as seven strikes, and these involved a total of only 647 workers. However, with the economic revolution of the thirties—when the per capita weekly factory wage dropped 51 percent from its 1929 figure—industrial Milwaukee felt the force of the worker as never before in its history; and by the close of the decade, about a quarter of the residents of the industrial area were identified with organized labor in one or another form.[32]

[30] The Building Trades Council, originally organized separately, joined the Federated Trades Council in 1907, but the strength it added was offset by the consequences of the panic of that year which temporarily reduced union membership by half. Mueller, Milwaukee Workers, 16, 20.
[31] *Ibid.,* 19-21; Hoan, *City Government,* 307.
[32] Theodore Mueller, The Growth of Labor in Milwaukee, pp. 37-39, type-

Both the depression and the New Deal were responsible for labor's new militancy in the thirties. Layoffs and reductions in hours and wages created the unrest and insecurity which gave organization an increasing appeal for the worker. The New Deal legislation not only endorsed the principle of collective bargaining but in providing relief for the unemployed made it possible for more workers to go out on strike. The psychology of the depression era was conducive to violence; and as such techniques brought success, they were more frequently used. And the organizational ambitions of labor itself, once they had the encouragement of government, prompted a show of strength in the developing movement. As a result, union locals began to appear in the early thirties in shops that formerly had been open, and strikes soon ensued. In 1934 there were at least 107, involving more than 27,000 workers; and in no year thereafter did labor fail to exhibit its force in the industrial life of the city.[33]

The outstanding industrial dispute of strike-bound 1934— when even the pupils of the Dover Street grade school struck for no homework and shorter hours—was a conflict between three unions and the Milwaukee Electric Railway and Light Company. This struggle was precipitated by the company's refusal to comply with an order of the National Labor Relations Board finding it guilty of union discrimination and directing the reinstatement of thirteen discharged employees. The strike began on June 26 and continued until June 29 when the company came to terms, promising to rehire the discharged workers as well as all strikers and recognizing the A. F. of L. unions, after years of resistance, as bargaining agencies. The violence connected with the strike recalled a previous conflict won by the company in 1896, when cars had been stoned, passengers egged, and a motorman shot. This time, riots at the carbarns resulted

script, dated 1937-38, in possession of the writer. This will hereafter be cited as Mueller, The Growth of Labor; Mueller, Milwaukee Workers, 21, 23.

[33] Milwaukee *Journal*, Dec. 31, 1934; Mueller, The Growth of Labor, 42-44. The pay-roll index, using 1925 as a base of 100, stood at 107.6 in August 1929, at 27.6 in July 1932 (a drop of 74 percent from 1929), and at 77.5 in August 1935 (still under 1929 by 28 percent). The per capita weekly factory wage fell from $29.03 in October 1929, to $14.21 in March 1933, and stood at $20.88 in August 1935. Milwaukee *Journal*, Oct. 20, 1935.

in broken windows and damaged equipment; cars were obstructed in the streets until, on the twenty-ninth, business in the city was paralyzed for want of car or bus service; and on the third night, a demonstration at the Lakeside power plant eventuated in the death of a strike sympathizer who was said to have come in contact with high voltage apparatus in smashing a window with an iron bar. Following this tragedy, President Way of the Electric Company agreed for the first time to meet the union leaders and ultimately acceded to their demands.[34]

While the Electric Company conflict gave labor its most spectacular victory in 1934, strikes, as many as eight running at a time, won comparable victories in other industries. Practically every strike brought an increase of from 5 to 10 percent in wages, as well as other benefits. Most of the settlements resulted from compromise; and while the closed shop was rarely achieved, nearly every strike gained union recognition. Once this was obtained, labor hoped that complete unionization would follow. In other industries, strikes were avoided as employers submitted to unionization, agreed to recognize legally created union bargaining committees, and made other concessions to their employees. By the close of the year, the number of strikes had dwindled, and the enforced cooperation between labor and management gave promise that industrial peace was in sight. The only strike in progress at the year's end was that of the employees of the Boston Store—the nation's first big department store strike and the "first large white collar workers' strike of the New Deal." The Federated Trades Council looked back upon the year as marking the resurrection of the A. F. of L. as a collective bargaining agency. An increase of 35,000 had brought its total membership to between fifty and sixty thousand.[35]

The strike wave ebbed in the years immediately following 1934. The outstanding conflict of 1935, which saw a total of only 31 strikes, was the beginning of the seventeen-month-long strike

[34] Mueller, Milwaukee Workers, 17, 24-25; Milwaukee *Journal,* June 26, 27, 29, 1934. A sixteen-hour strike of street-car workers, on New Year's Day, 1919, had been quickly arbitrated with wage increases of from four to seven cents an hour. *Ibid.,* June 26, 1934.
[35] *Ibid.,* Aug. 2, Dec. 31, 1934; Mueller, Milwaukee Workers, 25.

of employees at the Lindemann-Hoverson Manufacturing Company. Clashes between pickets and the police, in the course of this controversy, led the council to pass the Boncel Act, a measure which permitted the mayor and the chief of police to close an industrial plant when in the opinion of a committee of three employers, three workers, and three clergymen the strike threatened the public safety. Employers attacked the measure as an unconstitutional attempt to force upon them the principle of collective bargaining, and such was their influence that the newly elected common council of 1936 repealed the ordinance, over the opposition of Mayor Hoan, before it had ever been used or its legality tested in the courts. February 1936 saw the beginning of a seven-month strike of professional workers at the Hearst-owned *Wisconsin News,* which gained wage increases, a reduction in hours, and recognition for the American Newspaper Guild. The refusal of employers to comply with the Wagner Act led to the outbreak of a new wave of strikes in 1937—including the new "sit-down" technique first used at the Wrigley Restaurant and Seaman Body plant in April; but the strikes began to taper off during the last half of the year, a trend which continued through the close of the thirties.[36]

The strikes of 1937 revealed the organizing accomplishments of a new wing of the labor movement—the Committee for Industrial Organization, which, since the 1935 meeting of the American Federation, had professed its intention to organize all workers, regardless of trade unions, along industrial lines. The C.I.O. began its organizational drive in Milwaukee in the summer of 1936; and despite the opposition of the Federated Trades Council, by 1937 it had won the support of the workers in the Allis-Chalmers and Seaman Body factories as well as in such hitherto little organized plants as the Bucyrus Erie Company, the Harnischfeger Corporation, the Heil Company, Harley-Davidson, Briggs and Stratton, and A. O. Smith. It was in some of these plants that the major strikes of 1937 oc-

[36] Milwaukee *Journal,* Dec. 29, 1935; Dec. 31, 1937; Dec. 29, 1940; Mueller, Milwaukee Workers, 26, 28-29; *Municipal Activities . . . 1935,* p. 21; *ibid. . . . 1936,* p. 19.

curred. In July 1937, seventy C.I.O. unions formed the Milwaukee County Industrial Union Council. A series of antilabor measures passed by the Wisconsin legislature in 1939 offset to some extent labor's gains of the later thirties; but in spite of this reactionary trend the close of the thirties found Milwaukee labor, if somewhat disunited, at least solidly organized. Organization among the truck drivers had expanded from two weak locals in 1930 to nine, 12,000 members strong, in 1939. The Allis-Chalmers Industrial Union numbered 6,500; most of the other heavy industries were equally well organized; and a majority of the workers of the community—including professional, skilled, and unskilled types—were identified with some branch of organized labor. Thanks to the economic realities of the age, the sympathetic legislation of the New Deal, and the organization of the unorganized, which had resulted from the competition between the American Federation and the C.I.O., by the close of the thirties the Milwaukee labor movement appeared at last to have achieved a position of abiding strength and influence in the city's industrial life.[37]

The commercial development of Milwaukee during the period failed to keep pace with the city's industrial advance. As early as 1904, the secretary of the Chamber of Commerce admitted that the growth of manufactures had "perhaps overshadowed without diminishing" Milwaukee's "commercial importance"; and from that date forward not only were proportionately larger gains made in manufacturing than in commercial activity but a greater proportion of the population was engaged in industrial rather than in commercial pursuits. Commercial activity, as measured in the total tonnage of freight receipts and shipments, increased generally from 1901 to 1916, in spite of setbacks in 1908, 1911, and 1915. During these years, the total tonnage handled advanced from 10,072,466 to 23,377,150 short tons. Activity declined in 1921, as it did in industry, and even in 1929, the tonnage only slightly exceeded the 1916 level, to reach 23,873,387. A precipitous decline in the early thirties reduced the tonnage handled to 11,129,844; and although some

[37] Mueller, Milwaukee Workers, 26-27, 30, 33; Milwaukee *Journal*, June 27, 1937; Dec. 31, 1939.

recovery ensued, the total of 14,438,964 tons in 1939 was still below the figure for 1906. The average annual volume of rail and waterborne freight was practically the same for the second and third decades of the century, but the thirties brought a 28 percent decline in the average annual figure. Between 1901 and 1915, the railroads handled about three-fifths of this tonnage; and from then to 1930, they took care of more than two-thirds of it; but during the thirties their share was again reduced to three-fifths or one-half. By the close of the period, motor trucks were beginning to impose serious competition for both lake and rail lines.[38]

As in preceding generations, Milwaukee's commerce was compounded primarily of raw materials brought in from the city's westward hinterland for reworking or shipment to the East, fuel and metal imported for its factories or those of its hinterland, and manufactured commodities designed for retail or wholesale distribution in Milwaukee or the surrounding area. During the course of the generation each of these streams of commerce was to be in some measure curtailed. The 1916 peak in commercial activity was in part the result of the boost given the grain trade by World War I. Receipts of grain leaped from 48,355,914 bushels in 1910 to 76,654,300 in 1914, stood at 86,522,686 in 1916, and were as high as 76,905,019 in 1918. From that point, receipts declined steadily to a low of 20,109,515 bushels in 1932, recovering only to between thirty-six and forty-six million bushels in 1938 and 1939. Shipments of grain also reached an all-time high during the early years of the war when they rose from 29,515,846 bushels, in 1910, to 55,441,130 bushels in 1914 and 59,345,254 bushels in 1916. They, too, struck the low point of the century (10,332,769 bushels) in 1932 and in their recovery by the late thirties fluctuated annually between only fourteen and twenty-six million bushels. The trade in wheat, which during the seventies had lent fame to Milwaukee's

[38] Chamber of Commerce, *Report*, 1904, p. 27; *Annual Report . . . 1939*, p. 77; *United States Census, Sixteenth*, 1940, *Manufactures, 1939*, 3:1082-83; Milwaukee Grain and Stock Exchange, *Report*, 1939-40, p. 68; see graph on total lake and rail freight tonnage in Citizens' Bureau of Milwaukee, *The Lake Front in Milwaukee County* (Milwaukee, 1940), 17; Board of Public Land Commissioners, *Milwaukee's Economic Base*, 2.

export market, was approaching a more strictly local consumptive basis by 1913; and as the wartime demand appeared, oats became the number-one commodity for both receipt and shipment, with corn and barley next in line. The latter, because of its use in the brewing industry, had been the leader from 1890 to 1913. Corn was predominant in the grain trade of the early and late twenties; but by the thirties, with the relegalization of beer, barley receipts rose in record quantity until a peak of 29,323,117 bushels was received in 1936. By the late thirties, trade in that commodity, which alone represented two-thirds of the intake in 1936, was bolstering the currently unsteady grain market.[39]

In spite of the upswing in industrial activity by 1929, the grain trade never recovered the position it had held on the turn of the twenties. The railroad strike in 1922 and the generally congested transportation situation presented difficulties early in the decade. Competitive freight rates caused a diversion of the trade northward to Duluth or southward to the Gulf ports; and Chicago interests tried to obstruct the realization of transit privileges promised by the major railroads. From time to time, poor crops curtailed receipts, especially during the severe droughts of the thirties. And from the late twenties, when the threatening McNary-Haugen bill was vetoed by President Coolidge, there was always the fear of federal regulation of the trade and interference with exchange activities. Conditions improved considerably in 1938, but receipts for 1939 fell 21 percent short of the figure for the preceding year, a development brought on by the entrance of the federal government into cash grain operations as warehouseman and merchandiser. According to E. S. Terry, president of the Exchange, the "compulsory storing of corn in Mr. Wallace's 'tin cans,' adjacent to the production area, instead of utilizing the adequately available storage provided by country and terminal facilities," had almost completely eliminated "the commission merchant as a factor in the process of

[39] These statistics are drawn from Milwaukee Grain and Stock Exchange, *Report,* 1939-40, pp. 33, 35-36. Wheat shipments averaged about 23,000,000 bushels annually in the middle 1870's; during the second decade of the twentieth century shipments averaged about 5,000,000 bushels annually. See Chamber of Commerce, *Report,* 1913-14, pp. 39-40.

normal grain marketing" and "just about wrecked what was left of the general grain business."[40] Federal curtailment as well as popular criticism of its activities was reflected in the decreasing membership of the long-flourishing Chamber of Commerce, the name of which was changed to the more accurately descriptive Milwaukee Grain and Stock Exchange on June 10, 1931. Membership declined from 605 in 1910 to 158 in 1938-39. A securities market had been added in March 1931.[41]

As the traffic in grain declined, the handling of other commodities to some extent took its place. The expansion of industry on the turn of the century swelled the demand for coal, which was readily transported from Lake Erie ports to Milwaukee. Before 1890, coal receipts did not exceed a million tons a year; but by 1910, imports of the fuel reached 5,000,000 tons; and from then to 1939, coal represented, almost consistently, two-thirds of the city's waterborne commerce. An annual average of between 4,500,000 and 4,800,000 tons was maintained between 1910 and 1929; but during the thirties receipts fell to an average of 3,952,235 tons; and the 3,509,852 tons received in 1940 confirmed what appeared to be a permanent decline in the traffic. This was the result not only of the somewhat less vigorous industrial activity in Milwaukee itself but also of the loss of markets in the competitive area west and northwest of the city, the more efficient use of coal by industry, and the increasing resort to electricity and petroleum products as a source of power. Between 1929 and 1938, coal constituted 63 percent of the tonnage at the lake front, grain 5.5 percent, and other commodities 31.5 percent. Among the other commodities which by 1939 made up Milwaukee's commerce by lake and rail were wool from Idaho, canned goods from Wisconsin and its

[40] According to Terry, "About the only branch of the business that has escaped, in some measure, the withering hand of the bureaucrats, is the malting industry." Chamber of Commerce, *Report*, 1922-23, pp. 28, 66; *ibid.*, 1923-24, p. 27; *ibid.*, 1924-25, p. 55; *ibid.*, 1925-26, pp. 26-27; *ibid.*, 1926-27, pp. 25, 28; *ibid.*, 1927-28, p. 26; *ibid.*, 1929-30, p. 21; *ibid.*, 1930-31, pp. 19-20; *Municipal Activities . . . 1934*, p. 71; Milwaukee Grain and Stock Exchange, *Report*, 1934-35, p. 24; *ibid.*, 1936-37, p. 18; *ibid.*, 1937-38, pp. 18-19; *ibid.*, 1938-39, p. 15; *ibid.*, 1939-40, pp. 15-17.

[41] *Milwaukee Sentinel*, Jan. 1, 1921; *Wisconsin News*, July 16, 1936; Chamber of Commerce, *Report*, 1910-11, p. 38; *ibid.*, 1930-31, p. 20; Milwaukee Grain and Stock Exchange, *Report*, 1938-39, p. 16.

westerly neighbors, meat from Nebraska and Iowa, and flour from the Twin Cities. By lake came steel from Gary and South Chicago for the city's heavy industries and, after the early twenties, automobiles from the Lake Erie ports. Petroleum products were newcomers to Milwaukee's commerce in the middle thirties. The first oil tanker arrived in April 1936; and by 1940, petroleum receipts netted 125,067 tons. And added to these basic products were packaged goods and manufactured articles from all over the world. Less than 1 percent of the tonnage of foreign commerce handled on the Great Lakes between 1920 and 1939 stopped at Milwaukee; but 45 ocean vessels docked there in 1939, nearly double the number that used the port the year before.[42]

To urban promoters who continued to regard expanded transportation as the key to city growth, the further exploitation of the maritime potentialities of Milwaukee offered a remaining hope. Rail facilities could not be expanded unless the city built them; the accomplishments of aerial transport were still remote. For these reasons, the promotional drive that in the nineteenth century had pushed Milwaukee's railroads to completion now was turned toward building up the city's port. In the years that followed Kilbourn's efforts to achieve a "straight cut" to the lake, the city had spent nearly $2,000,000 and the federal government about $2,500,000 more to improve the outlets of the three streams that constituted the city's inner harbor. Along the improved arms of the Milwaukee River, the Menomonee Valley, the Kinnickinnic Bay and Creek, and along the adjoining canals and slips, lay the dock facilities of Milwaukee's private commercial and industrial firms. But twentieth-century promoters envisioned a municipal port in which the principal water traffic would be located in an outer harbor under the protection of a federal breakwater, thus leaving the then-congested inner harbor for the use of small vessels and barges. On the frontage north of the entrance, piers and warehouses would accommodate passengers and local

[42] Citizens' Bureau, *The Lake Front*, 30-31, 39; Milwaukee *Journal*, Dec. 31, 1939; Chamber of Commerce, *Report*, 1922-23, p. 66; *Municipal Activities . . . 1936*, p. 75; *Annual Report . . . 1939*, p. 76; *Milwaukee's Progress in 1940*, pp. 69, 115.

package freight. South of the entrance were to be built a public wharf and warehouse, dry dock, shipyards, car-ferry slips, and the grain elevators and coal and ore docks for transshipping freight by rail. A publicly owned belt-line was to connect the outer harbor with the railroads of the city. Predicated on the hope of lake-to-ocean transport and on an expansion of commerce comparable to that of the prewar years, Milwaukee's twentieth-century port development was a promotional dream worthy of the best its nineteenth-century city builders could have offered.[43]

By 1920, comprehensive plans had been completed, based on the council's approval in 1909 of a report recommending the purchase of Jones Island as the site for the city's development of an outer harbor. This was to be protected by a breakwater which, in 1922, the federal government agreed to build on condition that the land between Wisconsin and Russell avenues would be dedicated to harbor purposes. Years of negotiation ensued before it was possible to remove the claims of the picturesque fisher folk and the Illinois Steel Company, then in possession of the island. In 1926 the company agreed to exchange the southern portion, together with its claim to the Kinnickinnic basin, in return for made land onto which the city would move its property. In 1938, however, this contract was abandoned when the company, regarding the plant as obsolete, sold the entire property to the city for $2,744,000. Meanwhile, construction of the new harbor facilities got under way. The federal government completed the $5,600,000 protective breakwater in October 1929. June 9 of the same year saw the opening of the municipal car-ferry terminal, which had been begun in 1927, and which now provided direct rail connections with the East without going through the congested Chicago railroad area. The municipal open dock terminal was ready for service in July 1929. Construction continued apace during 1931 and 1932; and the following year saw the completion of a $1,800,000 program which included the construction of South

[43] Whitbeck, *Geography of Southeastern Wisconsin*, 68-71; War Department report entitled, "The Port of Milwaukee, Wisconsin," in Citizens' Bureau, *The Lake Front*, 24.

Pier and South Slip No. 1, Transit Shed No. 1, and a municipal mooring basin, as well as extensive dredging, track building, and road making. As in the case of other municipal improvements, marine construction was retarded with the continuation of the depression into the middle thirties; the transfer of terminals from the river to the outer harbor was slow; and as late as 1939 most of the commerce was still handled in the inner harbor. By the close of that year, Milwaukee had seventy-six docks—sixty-seven private and nine public—for transportation purposes; and the city, under the jurisdiction of its board of harbor commissioners, had completed permanent municipal harbor facilities costing $5,500,000. Contracts for the future purchases of land, with interest charges, promised to bring the cost of the harbor to more than $10,000,000, exclusive of earlier expenditures for harbor improvement.[44]

The board of harbor commissioners, originally the harbor commission, had become by the thirties one of the most vigorous promotional agencies in the community. The commission was first formally organized in November 1911; and its function remained advisory to the city council until a reorganization in 1920, which empowered the board to award contracts for construction and gave it jurisdiction over publicly owned docks. Dynamic leadership was for many years provided by William George Bruce, who served as the commission's president for more than a third of a century. Through the efforts of the

[44] Among the arguments for a municipal port advanced between 1909 and 1920 were (1) that Milwaukee's waterborne commerce had increased 260 percent during the 25 years preceding the war; (2) that increased transportation facilities were necessary to maintain parity with Chicago; (3) that the inner harbor not only could not be expanded but also contributed to the congestion of the city's business district by necessitating the frequent raising of bridges, and (4) that the city, rather than individuals, was alone capable of working out a comprehensive plan. Bruce, *History*, 1:290, 312; Citizens' Bureau, *The Lake Front*, 22-23. The Illinois Steel Company held to a price of $3,500,000 for its property for nine years, but finally reduced the figure when the city obtained P.W.A. funds to fulfill the contract. *Municipal Government and Activities . . . 1925*, p. 31; *ibid. . . . 1927*, p. 29; *ibid. . . . 1929*, p. 43; *Milwaukee Civic News: 1938*, pp. 1, 12. See also *Municipal Government and Activities . . . 1922*, p. 32; *ibid. . . . 1924*, p. 36; *ibid. . . . 1927*, p. 29; *ibid. . . . 1928*, p. 31; *ibid. . . . 1929*, pp. 42-43; *Municipal Activities . . . 1932*, pp. 77, 79; *ibid. . . . 1933*, p. 68; *Milwaukee, 1937*, p. 48; *Annual Report . . . 1939*, p. 78; Citizens' Bureau, *The Lake Front*, 15, 25-27. See also publications of the Board of Harbor Commissioners, *The Port of Milwaukee* (Milwaukee, 1922, 1928, 1933, 1940, 1942).

commissioners, studies were compiled of the best harbor practices throughout the nation, the public was made conscious of the harbor problem, discriminatory practices of Atlantic steamship companies were thwarted, Chicago's diversion of the lake water was challenged, and the claims of the municipality were effectively presented before the Rivers and Harbors Committee of Congress. In 1938, the commission convinced federal legislators that the navigable channels of the inner harbor should be dredged at national cost; but the appropriation was vetoed by President Roosevelt in the interests of conserving funds for national defense. The commission also championed proposals for a Great Lakes-St. Lawrence Seaway which held the promise of making Milwaukee an ocean port.[45]

Meanwhile, two other agencies were taking aggressive action to promote the city's commercial and industrial advance. The transportation committee of the Chamber of Commerce (later the Milwaukee Grain and Stock Exchange) sought to secure railroad rates conducive to the flow of goods to and from Milwaukee and to challenge the encroachments of rival transportation centers. The Association of Commerce, which dates to December 10, 1917, carried on the work of the Merchants' and Manufacturers' Association, laboring to locate new industries in the city, publicize the products of local manufacture, and attract business to the doors of Milwaukee merchants. Industrial expositions, trade excursions, and the distribution of a stream of booklets and brochures, outlining the advantages of the city for industry, contributed to this end. Under the auspices of the industries committee of the association, Milwaukee businessmen visited the headquarters offices of various companies to extend a personal invitation to locate in the city, a phase of the association's work which was greatly amplified after 1927 when a fully staffed division took over the function and extended its activities to include efforts to promote a community-wide adjustment to the problems which faced Milwaukee industry in the thirties. From August 1921, the association's publication

[45] Bruce, *History*, 1:296-97, 315-18; Bruce, *Born in America*, 170-85; *Municipal Activities . . . 1936*, p. 74; *Milwaukee Civic News: 1938*, p. 12; *Annual Report . . . 1939*, p. 75; Citizens' Bureau, *The Lake Front*, 32-33.

Milwaukee, "A Magazine for Her Business Leaders," served as a promotional trade journal for the city's commercial interests. In 1923, this monthly publication was replaced by a weekly official bulletin ultimately entitled *Milwaukee Commerce*. The convention bureau of the association carried on activities as a result of which the city fulfilled its late nineteenth-century promise of becoming a mecca of convention-goers. By 1940, it was estimated that conventions brought an additional 110,000 people to the city annually, visitors who spent close to $5,000,000 in the area.[46]

Organized action to achieve the deepening of existing channels to the sea took shape in 1919, with the founding of the Great Lakes-Tidewater Association. Almost immediately the city's promoters envisioned Milwaukee as "a seaport and manufacturing center combined—the Manchester of the Middle West." According to a writer in the *Journal*:

As Manchester rose in rank as a commercial metropolis, when the sea was brought to her door, by a marvelously constructed ship canal, so will Milwaukee acquire added prestige as a producing and shipping port when the Great Lakes are linked to the Atlantic Ocean in such a way that steamships from every part of the world will be able to reach the piers and wharves on Jones Island and along the lake front north of the harbor entrance.

However, the improvements to bring the Atlantic 1,500 miles inland were slow to appear. The opening of the new Welland Canal in 1931 provided a channel, 30 feet deep, through which Great Lakes shipping could reach the ports of Lake Ontario; but the 14-foot channels of the St. Lawrence River still obstructed heavy sea-going transit. By 1940, the seaway was still an unrealized and controversial New Deal enterprise.[47]

Despite the promoters' dreams, their hopes for a marked expansion of waterborne commerce had not been realized by

[46] Memoranda to author from Charles G. Crabb and Carl H. Nuesse, Milwaukee Association of Commerce. See *Milwaukee*, monthly publication of the Association of Commerce, August 1921 through April 1923, and *Milwaukee, Official Bulletin of the Milwaukee Association of Commerce*, later titled *Milwaukee Commerce*, May 5, 1923, to date.

[47] Havighurst, *The Long Ships Passing*, 271-72; Milwaukee *Journal*, April 11, 1920; Dec. 31, 1939.

1940. The tremendous gains of the period from 1895 to 1913 were not repeated in the postwar years. The total inbound and outbound tonnage dropped from 8,875,231 tons in 1913 to 5,760,596 in 1920. A 49 percent increase thereafter brought the figure to 8,564,863 tons by 1929; but by 1939 it had fallen again to 6,329,802. Between 1929 and 1938, the average annual tonnage of the Milwaukee Harbor, which ranked tenth in this respect on the Great Lakes, was little more than a sixth the size of the tonnage handled in the Duluth-Superior Harbor and about three-fifths the size of that handled at Chicago. In the value of the traffic, however, because of the worth of the car-ferry traffic, the Milwaukee port ranked fourth, almost equaling the value of goods handled at the Duluth-Superior Harbor and exceeding by more than $100,000,000 the value of the goods handled at Chicago. Nevertheless, even in terms of value, the decade of the thirties found Milwaukee's share of Great Lakes commerce on the decline. According to a study prepared by the Citizens' Bureau, a comparison of the average annual commerce for the twenties and thirties showed that, in the latter decade, the "value of the Great Lakes traffic had decreased 19.8 percent, while the value of Milwaukee's waterborne commerce decreased 30 percent. In 1923, Milwaukee had 30.1 percent of the total value of the Great Lakes commerce; in 1938 Milwaukee's share amounted to only 15.8 percent."[48]

By 1939, the brightest hope of the Milwaukee port—short of the still desired but still unrealized seaway—lay in the expansion of the car-ferry traffic. Between 1929 and 1938 this activity accounted for 57 percent of the value of Milwaukee's waterborne commerce, though it represented only 25 percent of the total tonnage of the port; and in 1939, when 19,346 cars moved through the municipal car-ferry terminal, the Pere Marquette line was building a $2,000,000 streamlined car ferry, the largest on the lakes, for the Milwaukee service. Like some of the ill-fated lake-rail schemes of the nineteenth century, the car-ferry traffic intrigued Milwaukee's promotional imagination in no small measure because it met the long-sought need for speedy eastward connections that would by-pass the larger railroad

[48] Citizens' Bureau, *The Lake Front*, 18, 20-21, 30.

THE ECONOMIC BASE 511

terminal at the base of the lake. Two new regular lake services, both from the ocean, were inaugurated in the middle and later thirties. One was provided by a line of motor ships that plied up and down the Atlantic coast and reached the Great Lakes through the Hudson River and the New York State barge canal. The other was a European service operated by the Norwegian Fjell line, established in 1933, and the Dutch Oranje, which functioned for a time in the late thirties.[49]

In their quest for speedy communications with the outside world, Milwaukeeans did not neglect aviation, newest travel medium of the age. A few aerial enthusiasts were flying in the city as early as 1908, and in May of 1912, a sixteen-year-old stunt flyer delivered the Milwaukee *Journal* to Waukesha, Oconomowoc, and Watertown by air; but aviation was still in its "teens" when city promoters pointed to its bearing on civic advancement. Proclaiming that "the day of aerial transportation" was "at the door," a writer in the *Wisconsin News* for May 22, 1919, urged the city to acquire and equip a suitable landing field so that it could take advantage of air-mail developments then being forwarded in Washington, D.C. Propellers and other aeroplane parts were already being manufactured in the city, he explained, and forehanded action "to provide a public aviation field with hangars, landing place, and adjacent factory sites" would pave the way for the "development of the aeroplane industry" in the city. This, and other requests, prompted the County Park Commission, over the protests of the farmers in the vicinity, to open Milwaukee's first public airport, at Currie Park, in 1919. In the following year, several air-minded citizens were selected as members of an Air Service Committee of the Milwaukee Association of Commerce, which ultimately grew into a bureau whose full-time efforts were devoted to furthering Milwaukee's position and progress in airline transportation.[50]

[49] *Ibid.*, 20; *Annual Report . . . 1939*, p. 77; Milwaukee *Journal*, Dec. 31, 1939; *Milwaukee's Progress in 1940*, p. 69.
[50] Controlled power flight was first demonstrated by the Wright brothers on December 17, 1903. The United States Army pioneered the air mail on May 15, 1918. John T. McCoy and Bayrd Still, eds., *The Official Pictorial History of the AAF* (Historical Office of the Army Air Forces, New York, 1947), 21, 49. See also, Milwaukee *Journal*, Dec. 8, 1927; *Wisconsin News*, May 22, 1919; Milwaukee *Journal*, May 10, 1931; Sept. 15, 1940.

Air-mail service was inaugurated in the city on June 7, 1926; and thirteen months later, on July 5, 1927, a Stinson *Detroiter,* operated by Northwest Airways, Incorporated, carried the first air passengers from the Wisconsin city to Chicago. The plane arrived five hours late, due to difficulties in take off, but it made the trip from Milwaukee to the Illinois city in less than an hour and a half. In December 1928, airline service was inaugurated between Milwaukee and Green Bay, for a $15 fare; and by 1930 the city was a port of call for the daily service of the Northwest Airways between Chicago and the Twin Cities and for planes of the Kohler Aviation Corporation, which flew three times daily to Muskegon and Grand Rapids. Ten years later, transport planes of the Pennsylvania Airlines made three trips daily to and from Milwaukee as they crossed Lake Michigan to Detroit and Washington; and planes of the Northwest Airlines stopped at the Wisconsin city five times daily each way on their flights from Chicago to the Twin Cities and Seattle.[51]

Meanwhile, improved landing facilities had been provided. In 1926, the County Park Commission purchased a site along East Layton and South Howell avenues which Thomas F. Hamilton, of the Hamilton Aero Manufacturing Company, was using as an airport. Territory was added, and with million-dollar improvements in the thirties, some of them subsidized by W.P.A., the county airport came to be regarded as one of the best in the country. In 1927, the city established an emergency landing field on Lake Michigan at the entrance to the inner harbor and named it Maitland Field after the local aviator who co-piloted the first plane to fly the Pacific from California to Hawaii. This field, abandoned in 1930, was operated as a seadrome after 1937. Activities at the city's airports did much to foster air-mindedness among Milwaukee's youth; but this was greatly furthered by the encouragement to aeronautical training on the eve of World War II. The National Youth Administration, the School of Engineering, the Catholic Youth Organization, the University of Wisconsin Extension, and the Y.M.C.A. all offered aerial training opportunities in 1939, almost a year before the government announced its extensive civilian

[51] Milwaukee *Journal,* June 7, 1926; July 5, 6, Nov. 16, 1927; Dec. 6, 1928; May 10, 1931; Sept. 15, 1940.

aviation training program. By 1940, Milwaukee and its suburbs had 250 licensed pilots; and its airport, considered as one of the twelve major civilian flying fields in the United States, had been selected as an air base for the United States National Guard.[52]

Despite the expansion of the city's sky and seaports during the generation, the bulk of the freight and passenger traffic was still carried on the three steam railroads and two electric express lines that operated in and out of the city. The most spectacular development in railroading was the race for speed between the two major steam lines, which resulted in achieving virtual commuter service between Milwaukee and Chicago by the middle thirties. In the spring of 1935, both the North Western and the Milwaukee roads introduced streamlined, Diesel-powered trains which traversed the distance from Chicago to the Twin Cities in six and a half hours, instead of nearly ten, and cut the 85-mile run from Milwaukee to Chicago from 105 to 75 minutes. With a comparable speed-up in service to the East, Milwaukeeans could board a train at noon and be in New York in time for the start of the next day's business. For months, the North Western's saffron "400" and the sleek silver-and-orange-streaked "Hiawatha" of the Milwaukee Road put on a daily show as they flashed through the countryside at 80 to 100 miles an hour; but more significant was the announcement early in 1935 that travel between Chicago and Milwaukee would be put on a commuter's basis with the largest fleet of high-speed trains to operate between two metropolitan centers in the United States.[53]

The most important consequence of these developments in air and rail communication was the extent to which, in a practical sense, they increased the proximity of Milwaukee to Chicago, thus amplifying the influence of an already fundamental geographic factor in the social and economic history of

[52] In 1940 a resolution was pending before the county board which ultimately resulted in naming the airport Mitchell Field, in honor of Milwaukeean Brigadier General William Mitchell (grandson of Alexander Mitchell) whose enthusiasm for air power had resulted in a court martial when he criticized Army and Navy officials for failure to develop America's air strength. *Ibid.*, June 16, Sept. 15, 1940; *Municipal Government and Activities . . . 1927*, p. 5.

[53] Of the freight tonnage moved in and out of Milwaukee between 1910 and 1940, an average of 39 percent went by water and 61 percent by rail. Trucks carried an increasing, but unknown, proportion. Citizens' Bureau, *The Lake Front*, 15-16; Milwaukee *Journal*, Jan. 2, 18, March 13, April 3, 1935; Oct. 25, 1936.

the city. The ever easier access to the Illinois metropolis not only drew Milwaukee into the cultural orbit of the larger city but also permitted the dominance of the latter in the financial and commercial sphere, as well. Just as many of the raw materials of Milwaukee's northwest hinterland, which once flowed to the Wisconsin city, were increasingly drawn to the more accessible Twin Cities and the better located Duluth-Superior port,[54] so, in a day of speedy communication, Chicago's more highly specialized wholesale, and even retail, market drew buyers formerly impressed by the trade excursions or local wares of Milwaukee's merchants. This contraction of the city's sphere of commercial influence was a significant factor in slowing the recovery of the community in the post-depression thirties. It also checked the growth of Milwaukee as a wholesale trading center and curtailed the expansion of its central business district—a trend already retarded by the wide dispersion of marketing centers in outlying areas of the community.[55] But more than that, it furthered the development of the Wisconsin metropolis into what by 1940 it had become: an industrial workshop, whose commerce supplied its factories with raw materials and fuel, whose retail and wholesale merchants and professional personnel provided both industry and residents with their needs, and whose tree-lined streets and landscaped lake front reflected the concern of a fundamentally worker-minded citizenry for a substantial, agreeable, and well-ordered way of life.[56]

[54] Between 1929 and 1938, the Duluth-Superior Harbor outclassed the Milwaukee Harbor in both volume and value of tonnage. Citizens' Bureau, *The Lake Front*, 18, 21.

[55] The number of Milwaukeeans employed in wholesale trade declined by 16.9 percent between 1929 and 1939, whereas there was a gain of 2.3 percent in the nation at large. Between 1935 and 1939, Chicago held to its position of second rank for wholesale sales, Minneapolis-St. Paul held to its seventh rank, but Milwaukee declined on this score from nineteenth to twenty-second place. A study of wholesale activities in the Milwaukee area showed that by the forties local industry and local retailers were the best market for the wholesale trade. Quast, *Wholesale Trade in the Milwaukee Area*, 3, 7, 17, 25. The McClellan and Junkersfeld report of the late twenties described the central business district of Milwaukee as "less extensive and less developed than in most other American cities of approximately the same population, but on the other hand its decentralization into outlying business districts has been carried considerably further." 1:41.

[56] The Milwaukee *Journal* explained the record-breaking retail sales of April 1916 by "the fact that many thousands of Milwaukee workmen have recently had their wages advanced, thus increasing their buying ability very materially." Milwaukee *Journal*, May 3, 1916.

CHAPTER 18

Politics and Urban Maturity

POLITICAL and administrative developments in Milwaukee between 1910 and 1940 reflect the vitality of what the reformers called the city's "civic conscience." By the opening of the generation, the political temper of the community was already remarkably responsive to the currents of municipal reform which were beginning to prick the nation's sensibilities in this regard; and by 1940 the scope and character of its municipal activities and the efficiency and honesty with which they were administered had won Milwaukee a reputation for progressive government which few cities of the nation could enjoy. This accomplishment was no doubt accelerated by the reforming zeal and idealism of the Social Democrats whose elevation to short-lived power at the opening of the period manifested a local protest in the interests of municipal reform. It was encouraged in no small degree by the continued vigilance of the Socialist minority and the continuity of capable executive leadership which resulted from the long-time incumbency of their party member, Daniel Hoan, as mayor. But in view of the dominant position of the common council in the city's governmental structure and the preponderance of Nonpartisans in that body throughout most of the period, it is apparent that no one political group had a monopoly on the will to realize good government for the community and that the achievements of the generation sprang in large measure from those qualities in the rank and file of the citizenry, reflected in the officialdom of the city as a whole, which inclined them to orderly civic behavior and won their support for realistic and progressive solutions to the urban problems of their time.

As already has been pointed out, the Socialist administration of 1910 came into office with a mandate for reform not only from the workingmen of the community but from disillusioned progressives drawn from the old-line parties as well. Piloted by party members Seidel as mayor, Carl P. Dietz as comptroller, Charles B. Whitnall as treasurer, and Daniel W. Hoan as city attorney[1] and fortified by a clear majority on the city and county boards, the Socialists set about, with all the crusading enthusiasm of their cause and of the hour, to achieve good government and progressive democracy for the Wisconsin city. Before a fusion of the old-line parties, two years later, succeeded in denying them the plurality which had brought the newcomers originally to power, the Socialist administration had done much to redeem the municipal government from the graft, deficit financing, and subservience to special interests which had characterized local administration under the Rose régime. Convinced that municipalities as well as corporations should have the benefit of expert advice, the new administration created a bureau of economy and efficiency—the only one of its kind in the country maintained by a city government—and called upon Professor John R. Commons of the University of Wisconsin to direct its work. The common council was soon enacting its voluminous recommendations into law, consolidating and reorganizing departments, in the interest of economy, installing techniques of cost accounting, and expanding the services of the municipality to the rank and file of the community. With spe-

[1] Emil Seidel, born of German parents in Ashland, Pennsylvania, in 1864, had come to Milwaukee in 1869. His term as mayor was preceded and followed by terms as alderman (1904-8, 1909-10, 1916-20, 1932-36). Daniel Hoan was born in Waukesha, Wisconsin, on March 12, 1881, the son of a pump and horseshoe maker. He attended public school in Waukesha until he was fourteen, after which he worked as a cook in restaurants and hotels until he earned enough money to enroll in the University of Wisconsin from which he graduated in 1905, a major in political science and president of the Senior Class. The restaurant business in Chicago paid his way through Kent Law School; and two years of service in the law office of Seymour Stedman strengthened an interest in socialism which he had acquired in the late nineties. In due time Victor Berger prevailed upon him to locate in Milwaukee; and there, as attorney for the Wisconsin Federation of Labor, he drafted the first state workmen's compensation bill, parent of the act passed by the Wisconsin legislature in 1910. His friend Paul Gauer deflected him from a judicial career by urging him to accept the Socialist nomination for city attorney in 1910; and after serving in this capacity for six years, he began what was to be nearly a quarter century of service as the city's chief executive. Chicago *Tribune*, July 27, 1930; Milwaukee *Journal*, March 10, 1940; Milwaukee *Sentinel*, July 14, 1937.

cial concern for public health, it adopted a program which included improved sanitary facilities and inspection in the city's factories, the abolition of the public drinking cup, construction of at least one public comfort station, improved resources for isolating contagious diseases, and municipal backing for the campaign against infant mortality which formerly had been privately subsidized. An experimental project in sanitation and health education cut the death rate in a test area by 50 percent in one year. Street flushing machinery was purchased, and rubbish cans and wastepaper boxes were installed in an attempt to free the streets of filth.

The lack of a three-fourths majority in the council prevented the Socialists from abolishing the contract method of street improvement and from purchasing materials so that the city could do its own paving; but their substitution of one commissioner for the former four-man board of public works resulted in a worthwhile concentration of responsibility and a consequent reduction in the costs of asphalt paving. Although the members of the "Asphalt Ring" contended with some reason that durability was being sacrificed to economy, changes in asphalt specifications reduced the price from $1.75 to 40 cents per square yard and brought about a more genuine competition for street improvement contracts. Moreover, contractors were made to realize that they could no longer default on city work. Eight administrative ordinances forced a reformation in the street railway service, with requirements for the inspection, disinfection, ventilation, and better cleaning of cars, the regulation of speed, and expanded facilities at rush hours. Meanwhile, the twenty-nine-year-old city attorney and the able young lawyers he had gathered around him were enforcing, for the first time, the franchise which required the street railway company to pay the costs of paving not only between the rails but one foot outside, thus saving the taxpayers thousands of dollars. Land, housing, and harbor commissions were appointed; and in their activities, as in the city planning and river beautification programs of City Treasurer Whitnall and the building ordinances developed by Building Inspector Carl F. Ringer, emphasis was placed upon a regulated use of private property in the interest of the public good. For the first time in many years, the city administration refused applications for "bay-window" permits, thereby preventing the encroachment of buildings into the area needed for the public highways.

Concern for the standard of living of the city's workers led to the enactment of a minimum wage and union scale for all employees of the city and the founding of a permanent committee on unemployment to represent labor, industry, the city, and the county. Proceeding on the principle that "wholesome recreation and relaxation" are the "best antidote for vice," the Socialists encouraged the expansion of the public concert program and the use of the public schools for social, civic, and neighborhood clubs. An attempt was made to close disreputable saloons and gambling places; and in the interests of cleaner politics, a law was secured which regulated registration and elections and gave each party representation among the officials at the polls. In these matters of regulation, as well as in curtailing privileges formerly enjoyed by special interests, the new administration experienced greater success than in its attempt to achieve the number-one aim of the Socialist program—municipal ownership. Bills permitting the city to engage in plumbing activities and to establish municipal lodging-, ice-, and slaughterhouses were indefinitely postponed by the combined opposition of the old-line parties in the State legislature. The realization of the Seidel program was obstructed not only by the city's dependence upon the legislative will, but by the fact that the franchises of the street railway and gas companies had years to run, the city's expenditures had almost reached the legal limitations on its debt, and the assessment machinery was in the hands of a commissioner holding over from the Rose régime. Nevertheless, the most honest of their critics agreed that the newcomers had undertaken and at least partially carried out a constructive municipal program—one which, to the surprise of many, seemed to subordinate "business considerations to human welfare" without subjecting "human welfare to economic theory."

As a matter of fact, there were areas of administration in which the Socialists were vulnerable to attack from an electorate which adjusted with difficulty to the idea that the working-class party was in power. To begin with, an excess of reforming zeal had resulted in promises of more than could be actually accomplished by the close of one two-year term. Moreover, performance did not always meet expectations; for despite the mayor's willingness to appoint experts regardless of party affiliation, salaries were not sufficient to attract the best men; and the consequent choice of inexperienced Socialists led on occasion to official blunders. As incompetent men began to be appointed, the number of city employees increased, giving rise to charges that the mayor was flouting civil service reform. The administration was accused of multiplying the costs of government, of making purchases without calling for bids, and of refusing to submit the proposal of a million-dollar park to popular referendum. Advocates of nonpartisanship in municipal politics complained that the Socialist majority in the council blindly obeyed the dictates of party leadership emanating from secret sessions held in the party headquarters in Brisbane Hall. Property holders dreaded the "tax ferrets" that the administration attempted to employ. And there was always the underlying threat of its proposed public ownership of utilities to mobilize a powerful opposition to the continuance of the Socialist régime.[2]

In a sense, however, it was the successes as much as the shortcomings of the Seidel administration which curtailed its tenure in the city hall. For with good government restored, many of the independent voters who had supported the Socialists in 1910 returned to a former party allegiance, not wholly without suspicion of the almost fanatical class consciousness which on occasion manifested itself in the party whose crusade for good government they had been willing to endorse. More importantly,

[2] Emil Seidel, *What We Have Done in Milwaukee,* pamphlet issued by the National Office of the Socialist Party (Chicago, n.d.); Hoan, *City Government,* 89-95, 307-11; Social-Democratic Party, *Municipal Campaign Book* (Milwaukee, 1912), 34-38, 40-47, 207-8; Social-Democratic Party, *Municipal Campaign Book* (Milwaukee, 1913), 10-15; Milwaukee *Journal,* March 29, 1912; Milwaukee *Leader,* March 5, 1912; John Collier, "The Experiment in Milwaukee: What Socialism has accomplished and where it has failed after a year's trial in Wisconsin's chief city," *Harper's Weekly,* 55:11 (August 12, 1911); John R. Commons, *Eighteen Months' Work* (Milwaukee Bureau of Economy and Efficiency, Bulletin no. 19, Milwaukee, 1912).

by that date nonpartisanship, which some reformers had been urging since 1908, had provided a formula by which the opponents of Socialism could prevent a further repetition of the Socialist victory of 1910. Like "good government," "nonpartisanship" was in the idiom of municipal reform; and the partisan dictation of Brisbane Hall could be painted as boss rule in proletarian guise. Dr. George Kleinschmidt, resigning from the Socialist Party in January 1912, argued that Socialism was nothing short of "an attempt to leash together all the wage-workers in the country, subdue them all to the iron will of a few bosses, and lead them on in political onslaught upon capital and political positions." Good government groups like the Westminster Civic League and the City Club endorsed the nonpartisan approach; while the Milwaukee *Journal,* its most vocal champion, cited the adoption of the principle in Boston, Pittsburgh, and other American cities and explained that what looked like fusion of the old-line parties to defeat Socialism was actually an expedient forced upon the "citizens of high character, Republicans and Democrats alike," because of the defeat of a nonpartisan bill, at the hands of the Socialists, in the last session of the legislature. The resulting coalition of Democrats and Republicans in the mayoral campaign of 1912 reduced the Socialists' proportion of the total vote from 47 percent, the 1910 figure, to 40.6 percent and elevated former Health Commissioner Gerhard Bading to the mayoralty with a council in which the Nonpartisans held a majority of fifteen seats. The *Leader* contended that the Nonpartisans had won by "fusing everybody crooked with everybody ignorant" and that thereafter the old parties must remain " 'nonpartisan,' that is to say 'all-partisan' against the Socialists"; but regardless of the motives involved, the new technique of victory was assured when the nonpartisan bill passed the State legislature and was signed by the governor on May 6, 1912. As a result of the operation of this law, party designations were removed from the primary ballots, and final election for a given office was made from the two candidates receiving the highest vote in the primary. This law was extolled by the City Club, the *Journal,* and the other proponents of nonpartisanship as a victory for majority rule;

but it also operated to destroy the leverage enjoyed by the Socialists as a third party and tended to encourage the combination of non-Socialist voters, of whatever party affiliation, against Socialist candidates in ensuing elections.[3]

In spite of the effectiveness of fusion, the Socialist vote continued to grow; and as a consequence, succeeding mayoral campaigns brought the fundamental antagonism toward Socialism more clearly into the open. Inspired by the ever-vigilant Berger and aided by the energies of the bundle brigade and the Milwaukee *Leader*, the Socialists raised their proportion of the total vote to 43.5 percent in 1914, although Bading again defeated Seidel by a vote of 37,673 to 29,122. Hoan, having had a four-year term in which to establish himself as city attorney, alone of the Socialists hung on to a major city office, in spite of strong opposition from the Electric Company which advised the public that if "Bull were electricity," Hoan would "be a power house." Backed by the Nonpartisans, Bading stood on a record of efficiency in administration, respect for civil service, durable paving, and support for such reforms as pure drinking water, the scientific treatment of sewage, child welfare, home rule, and privately supported administrative research. The Socialists continued to score the principle of nonpartisanship, arguing that no poor man could be elected "without the aid of a political party" unless he accepted "aid from the moneyed interests." They accused the Bading administration of extravagance and of concentrating power in the hands "of small commissions made up mostly of men of wealth"; and they reiterated their determination to "work for the municipal ownership of

[3] Gerhard A. Bading was born in 1870, a native of Milwaukee. He was graduated from Rush Medical College, Chicago, before beginning the practice of medicine in the Wisconsin city. Milwaukee *Sentinel*, July 14, 1937. The Nonpartisan candidates were selected by a conference of representatives of the Democratic and Republican organizations. Albert J. Nock, "Socialism in Milwaukee," *The Outlook*, 107:608-12 (July 11, 1914); Milwaukee *Journal*, Jan. 8, 12, 16, 24, 25, 26, 27, 29, Feb. 3, 8, March 5, 11, 16, 19, 25, 29, 30, April 3, 5, 8, May 4, 7, 1912; Jack D. Grace, A History of the Milwaukee *Leader* taking the treatment of the important news stories and policies of the paper from its inception on Dec. 7, 1911, to America's entrance into the World War on April 6, 1917, pp. 27, 38, MS, B.A. thesis in Journalism, dated 1932, Marquette University. The results of mayoralty contests used in this chapter were taken from the biennial reports of the board of election commissioners.

the gas, electric lighting, and street railway service," to be carried out "as far as the people authorize and the courts and financial condition of the city . . . permit." Said Seidel:

What we stand for is the ownership by the workers of those public enterprises which pay dividends. Capital lets us have the schools to run because they pay no profits. It lets us have the streets because they pay no profits. But when it comes to the ownership of an enterprise like the street railway, it says we must not have that, because it is one of the public enterprises which is profitable. And that is what the Socialists will change. We will own the things that pay a profit, and that will solve this problem of high taxation we hear so much about.

Such argument bolstered Bading's contention that the issue was one of "Americanism against Socialism," and led him to oppose the advance of the opposition in the campaign of 1916 by urging the voters to bar "Socialism, with all its heresies and un-American ideas" as they had in the past two years "and send out word to the people of the United States—yea, even to the world—that Milwaukee will never again allow the Red Flag to replace the Stars and Stripes on the . . . City Hall."[4]

The elevation of the Socialist city attorney to the mayoralty in that year was proof, however, that the "red flag" bogie carried less weight with the electorate than the promise of needed reform. Hoan was a "doer"; his backers claimed that as city attorney he had "wrested thirteen million dollars worth of concessions out of the public utilities, . . . won several track depression cases, and reduced the rates of gas, light, power, street railway, and telephone" services. Beside such accomplishments, Mayor Bading's record provided scant appeal. He had vetoed a proposed eight-hour

[4] Among the Nonpartisan slogans during the 1916 campaign were "Either Socialism or the American government must perish" (Milwaukee *Sentinel*, April 3, 1916) and "Join the nearest anti-Red club, young man" (*Evening Wisconsin* [Milwaukee], March 29, 1916). According to the *Journal*, there was "just one way to avert the menace of Socialism in Milwaukee and that is to make nonpartisan city government all that good government should be and thus intrench it strongly in the confidence of the people." Milwaukee *Journal*, April 10, 1914. See also *ibid.*, Jan. 5, 19, 20, March 16, 18, 19, 25, 26, 28, 31, April 1, 3, 4, 9, 20, 1914; Milwaukee *Free Press*, Jan. 21, 1914; Hoan, *City Government*, 73; Bd. of City Service Commissioners, Milwaukee, *18th Ann. Rept.*, 1913, p. 33; Joseph P. Harris, "Mayor Daniel W. Hoan of Milwaukee," *New Leader* (New York), Oct. 19, 1929.

MILWAUKEE'S FIRST SOCIALIST MAYORS. *Above, right:* Daniel W. Hoan, veteran city executive at the close of his twenty-four-year mayoral career. *Above, left:* Hoan, campaigning, in 1916. *Right:* Emil Seidel, Milwaukee's initial Socialist mayor, in office from 1910 to 1912.

workday ordinance, progress had been delayed on the new water intake tunnel, and there was evidence of collusion with the Electric Company and the "Asphalt Ring" to the city's harm. Moreover, Hoan undoubtedly benefited from dissension within the ranks of the Nonpartisans when City Treasurer J. P. Carney contested Bading's nomination by asserting that it was time "the working people" had a "working man in the mayor's chair," albeit one who would not be controlled by Brisbane Hall. Sparked by their vigorous candidate, the Socialist organization stepped up its efforts; and the forthright young city attorney, carrying his campaign to factory audiences, countered the flag analogy of Nonpartisan propaganda by asserting that "the main issue of this campaign is whether the flag of the street car company will float over the City Hall instead of the Stars and Stripes left there by Emil Seidel, former Socialist mayor." The election returns showed that for the second time the voters had put their faith in a Socialist executive; but on this occasion he approached the mayorship with all the other major city offices, as well as twenty-six of the thirty-seven positions on the common council, in the hands of the Nonpartisan opposition. In the first of what in time were to total seven inaugural addresses, the new mayor affirmed his support of a municipal lighting plant, harbor improvement, comprehensive city planning, a pure water supply through the construction of filtration and sewage disposal facilities, a minimum wage for the city's workers, charter reform, open and honest city service, full competition on city contracts, and centralized purchasing of city supplies. "Ours is a city of liberal and progressive-minded people," he said, "and it behooves us to administer the affairs of government in the spirit of her citizenship."[5]

In the ensuing two campaigns, the rangy executive main-

[5] Chicago *Tribune*, July 27, 1930; Harris, "Mayor Daniel W. Hoan of Milwaukee," *New Leader*, Oct. 19, 1929; Milwaukee *Journal*, March 8, 14, 20, 21, April 5, 18, 24, 1916. Hoan declared that he had positive proof that the Electric Company had discharged men for not voting for Mayor Bading at the primary and asserted that the people of Toronto paid only 3 cents for an amount of electricity for which Milwaukeeans were charged 11. The Milwaukee *Leader* claimed that by electing Hoan and the eleven Socialist aldermen the city had been saved from the local railway company's designs to take $2,000,000 a year in added fares and nullify the referendum vote favoring municipal lighting. "Mayor Hoan!" it wrote, "It sounds good. The city hall won't be such a bad

tained a growing, but still precarious, lead over his Nonpartisan opponents. He defeated Percy Braman in 1918, by a vote of 37,485 to 35,396, and another aspiring city attorney, Clifton Williams, in 1920, by a vote of 40,530 to 37,205. In both contests, the mayor's chances were potentially imperiled by the Socialists' stand on World War I; but in each election the party gained one additional member of the council until by 1920, with 14 Socialists to 17 Nonpartisans, the majority of the latter was whittled down to 3. According to the analysis of the election in the Milwaukee *Journal* on April 9, 1920, the growth in the Socialist vote since 1908 had "not only absorbed the entire increase in the vote cast in Milwaukee since that time," but had taken "an additional 4,081 from the ranks of those who were voting against the Socialist candidates twelve years ago."

Most of the leaders of Milwaukee Socialism supported the St. Louis platform of the party, which opposed the war as one "which the capitalist class is forcing upon this nation against its will"; and in spite of Mayor Hoan's opposition to it, the stand of the party gave the Voters' League a long-awaited excuse to withhold its recommendation of Socialist candidates in 1918. An order indicting Berger and four other Socialists for violation of the Espionage Act was issued ten days before the primaries of 1918, and not long thereafter the mayor was ousted from the chairmanship of the administrative committee of the County Council of Defense. This action followed from his open support of the Socialist city platform which, along with its endorsement of public ownership of utilities, city planning, harbor improvement, and public health and economy, blamed the capitalist class of the nation for America's involvement in the war and proposed that the profiteers should pay the costs of the struggle. The *Journal,* hewing to its wartime patriotic line, contended that the municipal contest was no longer a question of the economic doctrines of the Social Democrats but "solely one of support or desertion of the nation in its hour of peril—a struggle between the forces of Americanism, as centered behind Mr. Braman's

place to wait for an Oakland-Delaware car as it was when it couldn't be told from the Public Service building on Sycamore street." Milwaukee *Leader,* March 31, 1916; *ibid.,* April 5, 7, 1916. The vote in this campaign was Hoan, 33,863; Bading, 32,206.

candidacy, and anti-Americanism, as represented in the Milwaukee Socialist party platform upon which Mr. Hoan is a candidate for reelection." The incumbent mayor nevertheless gained over his 1916 vote in a large majority of the wards, a victory which his defeated opponent interpreted as showing that "Milwaukeeans of pro-German tendencies" desired "to register their opposition to the national administration for putting the United States into the war." The Polish vote alone was adversely affected by the mayor's antiwar stand; in the strongly Polish 14th Ward, he received less than half the votes he had won there two years earlier.[6]

The loyalty issue continued to figure in the municipal election of 1920. The Voters' League, while recognizing the service of the Socialists as a "watchful minority," nevertheless condemned them for "attempting to discredit and destroy American institutions, . . . encouraging the I.W.W., the Bolsheviki, and other revolutionary agencies, . . . opposing the purchase of Liberty bonds by the city and county of Milwaukee, . . . refusing greetings to General Pershing," failing to extend an invitation "to the official representatives of Belgium, an allied nation," and following the dictation of a party machine "in every instance where party principles or policies were involved." Clifton Williams, the chief Nonpartisan contender, contested Mayor Hoan's incumbency on the ground that government in the city hall had been deadlocked for the past four years. Urging the electors to "Vote for Milwaukee," he identified the Socialists with internationalism and accused the mayor of being more concerned about conditions outside the city than within. But Hoan could point to the material progress of the city since his assumption of the office; his welcome for the returning soldiers swelled his popularity; the Poles began to drift back into the Socialist

[6] Mayor Hoan stood by the party's opposition to war profiteering when he vetoed a resolution providing for the purchase of $500,000 in Liberty bonds on the grounds that the council had not provided for redeeming the bonds "from the profits made by persons or business organizations where profits are in excess of those made before the war." The Nonpartisan majority in the council was not sufficient to override the veto. Edmund G. Olszyk, History of the Milwaukee Leader, pp. 29, 35-37, MS, M.S. thesis, dated 1933, Marquette University. This will hereafter be cited as Olszyk, History of the Milwaukee Leader; Milwaukee Leader, March 7, 1918; Milwaukee Journal, Jan. 4, March 3, 4, 7, 10, 12, 13, 14, 15, 17, 20, 21, 25, 27, 28, April 2, 16, 29, 1918.

column; and although the party was not strong enough to elect comptroller or treasurer or provide him with a majority in the council, the Socialist mayor held on.[7]

Hoan's popularity continued to increase from the mid-twenties to the mid-thirties, with the result that during this decade he pushed aside his Nonpartisan rivals with ever larger majorities. The reappearance of David Rose as the Nonpartisan candidate in 1924 won Hoan a more general support than might otherwise have been the case; for with the threat of another Rose régime, the better elements of the community rallied behind the existing administration to prevent a return of the "good old days." Promising to reduce taxes and "bring back a little life to Milwaukee," "All-the-time-Rosy" nosed ahead of Hoan in the primaries, whereupon the forces of decency, including the group that originally had backed Dr. Ralph Elmergreen for mayor, many newly enfranchised women, and the Protestant clergy, mobilized a vote that returned Mayor Hoan to the city hall by a majority of nearly 17,000. The church federation instructed its affiliated pastors "to urge their congregations to vote conscientiously and with an eye to the moral issues of the campaign"; and such clergymen as Dr. Charles H. Beale of the Grand Avenue Congregational Church and the Rev. Holmes Whitmore, dean of St. Paul's Episcopal Church, came out openly for the incumbent mayor. Once the election was over, Mrs. Allan J. Roberts, president of the Wisconsin branch of the Women's International League for Peace and Freedom, complimented the churches "upon the manner in which they measured up to their civic obligation"; and Mrs. C. G. Junkerman, president of the Milwaukee Woman's Club, gave women the credit for putting the election over not as "an issue of one party or another," but as "an issue of moral character." Rose's support came from the downtown wards, the Polish 14th, and the conservative 18th. Manifesting the bigotry which had characterized his campaign and for which the early twenties were noto-

---

[7] It was when Hoan was criticized for his indifference to the impending visit of the King of Belgium that he uttered the much publicized statement: "To hell with the King; I am for the common man." Harris, "Mayor Daniel W. Hoan of Milwaukee," *New Leader*, Oct. 19, 1929; Olszyk, History of the Milwaukee *Leader*, **62-63**; Milwaukee *Journal*, March 13, 17, 28, April 1, 5, 7, 8, 9, 1920.

rious, the former mayor attributed his defeat to "a rabble of pulpit hypocrites, character defilers, red-card Socialists, and a small section of the Mühlenberg Society still worshipping their kaiser."[8]

By the prosperous late twenties, many of the mayor's former opponents appeared to prefer him to the less promising candidates presented by the Nonpartisan opposition. "Milwaukee has had pretty good government for some years and seems to like it," wrote the formerly critical *Journal*. "Mayor Hoan gets a good deal of credit for this. The city has rather got into the habit of reelecting him." In spite of the mayor's loyalty to the Socialist Party, his repeated insistence on the importance of party backing (which, after all, contributed significantly to his political success), and his endorsement of municipal ownership, there was an appeal for the solid business element of the community in his graft-free administration, with its achievement of municipal solvency and community safety and order, and in his vigorous promotion of such commercial projects as harbor improvement and the St. Lawrence Seaway. If his was a "sewer Socialism," as party members outside Milwaukee insisted, it was Socialism suffused with an "Association of Commerce" appeal, as well. Even his somewhat tentative excursions into the realm of municipal ownership and operation caused more approval than alarm. The inauguration of a competing municipal stone quarry reduced the price of crushed rock for paving, and the establishment of a municipal repair shop halved expenditures for pavement repairs. A municipal street lighting distribution system, achieved over the opposition of the Nonpartisan aldermen, reduced the cost of brighter lights from $65 to $39 per lamp, while the threat of a municipally operated power plant brought a reduction in both public and private electric lighting bills. Municipal harbor facilities promised to stimulate the city's commerce; and only the lack of two-thirds support in the council prevented the municipal marketing of "a small amount of gasoline regularly so that profiteering and

[8] Dr. Ralph Elmergreen had sought the nomination on a platform of "cleanliness and principle." "You will either go forward with me," he declared, "stand still with the present administration, or go backward to the days of 1900 to 1910." *Ibid.*, March 2, 8, 9, 10, 12, 13, 15, 16, 19, 20, 23, 24, 25, 26, 27, 31, April 3, 1924.

holdup prices could be abated." (Municipal investment in the Garden Homes project, which was begun in 1921 and finished in 1923, resulted in the construction of more than a hundred workingmen's homes, at an alleged saving of $1,500 per dwelling, and made Milwaukee the first city in the United States to sponsor such a low-cost, cooperative housing enterprise.) In addition, forward strides had been made in the fields of education, public health, city planning and zoning, and community recreation; and centralized purchasing, improved budgeting, and financial planning had brought Milwaukee "closer to a cash basis than any other large city in the country." Such accomplishments, together with the political advantages resulting from his previous tenure of the office and the prevailing prosperity of the period, explain the majority of more than 18,000 by which Hoan defeated Sheriff Charles Schallitz in 1928.[9]

What prosperous times had done to cement the mayor's hold on the urban electorate the community's first reactions to depression continued. In the year of the Roosevelt landslide in national politics, the Socialists not only returned the incumbent mayor with a majority of 45,000 over Nonpartisan J. P. Carney but, with the election of John W. Mudroch as city treasurer and Max Raskin as city attorney, won three of the four major city offices. Moreover, the election of 12 Socialists and 2 independent Nonpartisans interested in union labor and municipal ownership gave promise of Socialist control of the council. The mayor's dynamic attack on the depression at the turn of the thirties had won him national recognition and increased local acclaim; disclosures of faulty sewer construction had shaken popular confidence in the Nonpartisans' support of the contract system for city improvements; and the discovery of questionable

[9] *Municipal Government and Activities . . . 1921*, pp. 8, 10; *ibid. . . . 1923*, p. 12; *Milwaukee Leader*, March 2, 1928. On occasion Mayor Hoan attested his support of "collective ownership and the brotherhood of man," but in his campaign arguments he was inclined to emphasize such practical matters as "a maximum of public achievement at lowest possible cost," assistance to the unemployed, improved standards of municipal finance, city planning and zoning "for home protection," support of harbor development and the deep waterways project, promotion of transportation, consolidation of units of local government, and the continued reiteration of the slogan, "a better, bigger, and brighter city." See *Milwaukee Journal*, March 3, 1932.

practices in the office of City Treasurer John I. Drew had led the *Journal* to shift its support to Mudroch. The new council, with Socialist Paul Gauer, the mayor's erstwhile secretary, as president, made a grist of Socialist appointments and proceeded to consider an ambitious social and economic program which included municipal banking, city marketing, especially of milk and fuel, the six-hour day for city employees, which the mayor hoped would be generally adopted as a means of overcoming unemployment, and steps in the direction of municipal ownership of public utilities.[10]

However, before the council had traveled far in this second excursion toward the "Cooperative Commonwealth" its attention was diverted to immediate problems of tax delinquency, unemployment, and labor strife. The mayor weathered a movement for recall in 1933, instigated by real estate and taxpayers' groups; but his sympathetic treatment of strikes and especially his support of the Boncel ordinance, permitting the closing of strikebound industries, began to alienate business interests that formerly had approved his régime. At this juncture, the opponents of municipal ownership redoubled their efforts, with the result that in 1936 the voters rejected by a vote of 107,941 to 81,440 a proposal that the city acquire the property of the Electric Railway Company within the municipal limits. And other forces, in addition to the prolonged depression, were operating to weaken the mayor's and the Socialists' hold. The

[10] Olszyk, History of the Milwaukee *Leader*, 113-18, 142-46; *Municipal Activities . . . 1931*, pp. 19, 24; *ibid. . . . 1932*, pp. 23, 27, 29; "1932 Municipal Platform of Socialist Party of Milwaukee," in Hoan, *City Government*, 333-38; Milwaukee *Journal*, March 3, 4, 5, 6, 16, 31, April 1, 6, 7, 8, 10, 19, 20, 26, 1932. Alderman Carney challenged the sincerity of Hoan's Socialist promises. "What has he done all these years he has been mayor?" he asked. "What has he done to bring down street car fares, telephone, and gas rates? He has been mayor since 1916 and he has the effrontery to tell you that he is fighting the utilities and the big bankers. It's all campaign bunk and he knows it. The truth is that the utility and bank magnates understand Dan. You talk to them and they will tell you that Dan talks a bit wild to fool the boobs at election time, but the rest of the time he is all right. Not only that, the big bankers and other rich men dig down in their pockets and contribute to his campaign fund." *Ibid.*, March 11, 1932. Previous to the municipal election, thirty delegates of the Communist-sponsored Unemployment Council of Milwaukee condemned the mayor for his failure to accomplish public ownership and accused him of having "betrayed the working class and aided the capitalists." *Ibid.*, March 1, 1932.

appeal of the New Deal drew off voters who originally had strengthened Socialism; while a new and more opportunistic leadership within the ranks of organized labor deprived the Socialist Party of its formerly dependable trade union support. Intraparty friction made more serious inroads on the strength of the organization than would similar disputes in the older parties; and such practices as its requirement that elected officials sign resignations deposited with the party subjected it to charges of being "Red" or "foreign." In the mayoral campaign of 1936, Hoan's record on the question of municipal solvency carried less weight with many voters than charges that his avowed support of collective ownership, "the cousin of communism," threatened to make Milwaukee a "laboratory for testing . . . Karl Marx's theories, with our citizens as guinea pigs." When the votes were counted, the Socialist Party had suffered a drastic blow. Hoan's majority over Nonpartisan Joseph J. Shinners had been reduced to less than 15,000, not a third of the majority he had garnered four years earlier. City Attorney Max Raskin was snowed under; and with six incumbent Socialist aldermen swept out of office—including Frank Boncel and veteran Socialist Paul Gauer—the Nonpartisans were restored to dependable control of the common council.[11]

Increasing conflict between the mayor and council, after 1936, foreshadowed the Nonpartisan victory of 1940, which brought the mild-mannered socialism of Hoan's twenty-four-year incumbency to a close. The waning influence of the veteran executive was exhibited when the new council speedily repealed the Boncel ordinance and assumed the power of filling vacancies in the common council. This encroachment on the mayor's

[11] *Municipal Activities . . . 1934*, p. 24; Chicago *Daily News*, Aug. 30, 1933; Milwaukee *Leader*, April 30, 1933; *Municipal Activities . . . 1935*, pp. 19, 22; *ibid. . . . 1936*, pp. 19-20; Milwaukee *Journal*, March 1, 2, 3, 5, 6, 8, 9, 12, 14, 18, 27, 30, 31, April 1, 8, 9, 1936. See Frederick I. Olson, "In the Days of Berger and Seidel," an interpretation of the history of Milwaukee Socialism, in Milwaukee *Journal*, July 9, 1947, and Frederick I. Olson, The Milwaukee Socialist Party, 1897-1941, MS, Ph.D. thesis, in progress, Harvard University. In presidential politics, the largest number of voters in Milwaukee County supported Wilson in 1912 and 1916, Harding in 1920, La Follette in 1924, Smith in 1928, and Roosevelt, by large majorities, in 1932 (65.6 percent), 1936 (74.6 percent), and 1940 (59.8 percent). See appendix for a comparison of the presidential vote in Milwaukee County with that of the remainder of the State of Wisconsin, 1848 to 1940.

authority had been denied the council by popular referendum in 1929; but a similar ordinance, passed over the mayor's veto in 1936, was approved by the electorate in the following year. In 1937, the mayor rejected seven measures of the council, five of which were passed over his veto; in 1938 he contested the council's stand on the public housing issue; and by 1939, council confirmation of appointments became increasingly difficult to obtain. In Carl Zeidler, youthful city attorney, the Nonpartisans found a candidate whose buoyant optimism and appealing vocal gifts matched the rugged forthrightness and challenging platform style of the older candidate. Encouragement of business and reduction of taxes were at the heart of the Nonpartisan offensive, as its proponent urged his supporters to pull "this town" out of the "Socialist lethargy that scares away business, keeps our men unemployed, denies our youth a chance for jobs." The incumbent mayor exhibited strength in the primaries; but after a display of campaign showmanship that recalled the spectacular tactics of Sherburn Becker a generation earlier, his youthful opponent, making exceptional gains in all the predominantly Polish wards, carried the election by a vote of 111,957 to 99,798.

Whatever were to be the achievements of the new régime, with its motto of "Hats off to the past, coats off to the future," Zeidler's inauguration on April 16, 1940, brought to a close an era in Milwaukee politics unified in no small degree by the personality of Daniel Hoan and the ideals and objectives of the party from which he drew his original support. Not that Hoan or his vigilant, if rarely dominant, colleagues were alone responsible for the widely recognized accomplishments of the Wisconsin city during the three decades between 1910 and 1940, nor that with the accession of the new mayor such accomplishment was bound to cease. But to the outside world, Hoan, the Socialist, was the symbol of early twentieth-century Milwaukee; and his reputation for honest, vigorous, and democratic municipal administration, as well as his outspoken championship of his workingman constituency—qualities which kept him in office rather in spite of than because of his connection with Socialism—identified the veteran mayor, more than any other one person, with the forward strides of the Wisconsin city in its adjustment to the problems of the maturing metropolitan scene.[12]

But the accomplishments of the Hoan régime, attested by the fifteen red, gold, and blue awards for fire prevention, health, and traffic safety which decorated the Auditorium on the day of his successor's inauguration, had come about not alone because of the executive leadership of the outgoing mayor. To be sure, the social ideals of the party he represented, the integrity of his administration, and the cumulative effect of his appointing power had a bearing on the results; yet in the exercise of the latter he was subject to the check of a predominantly Nonpartisan common council. Thus, as a result, job-experienced elective or appointed officials from Nonpartisan ranks, as well as the civil service personnel on whom the work of many a municipal office devolved, contributed significantly to the city's achievements in the administrative field. Of no small importance was the continuity of service—of both elected and appointed officeholders—which characterized Milwaukee's municipal administration in these years, a situation not only in marked contrast to the frequent turnover in officialdom which prevailed in the early years of cityhood but one which reflected the increasing emphasis on specialization in municipal administration as well as in other phases of twentieth-century urban life. Not only did the mayor serve for a quarter century, but there was a more than 50 percent holdover in council membership with

[12] According to John M. Pfiffner, Hoan was "largely responsible for administrative coordination in Milwaukee," a coordination "accomplished through the example of a great democrat and humanitarian who believes that somehow people will take the right action if they get together and talk it out." See *Municipal Administration* (New York, 1940), 32-34. Wrote Richard S. Davis in "Milwaukee, Old Lady Thrift," contained in Allen, *Our Fair City,* "It was during Hoan's long régime that the tradition of clean city government became so well established that an immense amount of slippery inside work, plus general civic apathy, would now be needed to change it." pp. 194-95. See also, *Milwaukee, 1937,* p. 16; *Milwaukee Civic News: 1938,* pp. 2-3; *Annual Report . . . 1939,* p. 18; Austin, *The Milwaukee Story,* 199-200; Milwaukee *Journal,* April 8, 1936; March 1, 3, 8, 10, 28, April 3, 16, 1940. Carl Zeidler was born in Milwaukee in 1908. After attending the public schools of the city, he was graduated from the Marquette University Law School in 1931. An active member of numerous local lodges, clubs, and singing societies, he served as city attorney for three-and-a-half years, and in 1939 received five civic awards for service to the community. He was lost in action during World War II. *Ibid.,* March 10, 1940. His brother, Frank P. Zeidler, a Socialist, was elected mayor of Milwaukee by a large majority in April 1948.

each succeeding election after the first decade of the period, except in 1928; and on two occasions the percentage of holdovers mounted to 75. Four of the aldermen elected in 1936 had served twenty years or more, and the death of Cornelius L. Corcoran in February of that year closed a career of forty-three years as alderman. The same was true in the case of appointed personnel. For most of the period between 1910 and 1940 but two different fire chiefs and chiefs of police directed these important services; the same health commissioner served from 1925 to 1940; and save for a short interlude, the commissioner of public works remained in office from 1922 to 1940. It was estimated in 1935 that two-thirds of the incumbent "key" personnel had held their jobs for at least ten years; and many of them had acceded to their positions after long periods of preparatory service as subordinates in the same department. That such long-term appointed personnel were on the whole men of capacity may have been one of the fortunate consequences following from the necessity, in these years of bipartisan administration, of seeking an appointee whom both the Socialist mayor and the Nonpartisan council would approve.

Many of the fiscal and budgetary reforms instituted during the twenty-year tenure of Nonpartisan Comptroller Louis M. Kotecki were the work of his deputy, William H. Wendt, who had served in the office since 1911, and of James Barr, who qualified as chief clerk, by examination, in 1912. Wendt succeeded Kotecki when charges of malfeasance in office led to the latter's suicide in 1933. Barr, a law school graduate, gained his early experience with the Wisconsin Tax Commission and the United States Census Bureau. He became secretary of the board of estimates in 1918 and deputy comptroller in 1933. Charles Brand, who left the office of city clerk in 1932, had been fifty-two years in the city's service. Dr. George C. Ruhland, who was appointed health commissioner in 1914, had joined the health department as a bacteriologist in 1906. For want of council confirmation of a Socialist successor, he remained in office until his resignation in 1924; and in the following year Mayor Hoan agreed to the appointment of Nonpartisan Dr. John P. Koehler, a graduate of Marquette Medical School, who had joined the health department as deputy commissioner in 1918. Under his leadership, Milwaukee was to gain recognition as the healthiest large city in the United States. The twenty-year administration of Thomas A. Clancy, as fire chief, was followed from 1925 to 1945 by that of Peter J. Steinkellner, who had joined the department in 1912. In appointing Steinkellner, Mayor Hoan defied the wishes of the Nonpartisan majority in the council and prevailed upon the mayor-controlled fire and police commission to inject "young blood" and proved leadership into the department by appointing Socialist Steinkellner over the heads of nine men with longer records of service.

Hoan continued to put promise of leadership ahead of either party or seniority rights in recommending Nonpartisan Jacob G. Laubenheimer as chief of police in 1921. The new appointee had joined the force more than a quarter of a century earlier, during the régime of his predecessor, "Czar" John T. Janssen, who held the position for thirty-three years; and he was to give aggressive leadership to the department until his death in 1936. Lack of council confirmation prevented Hoan's appointment of a qualified engineer as commissioner of public works until he chose Roland E. Stoelting, a friend of the mayor's who was regarded as a Nonpartisan. Stoelting had entered the city service in 1911, as an engineer in the department of public works. Socialist David N. McKeith, his deputy, had been employed by the city since 1895. Henry P. Bohmann, who joined the water department as a bookkeeper in 1892, carried on an eminently successful career as superintendent of the waterworks from 1912 to 1940. Tax Commissioner Louis A. Arnold, who held the office from 1912 to 1914 and again from 1922 to 1938, was the first of Hoan's appointments to receive council confirmation and then only when three insurgent Nonpartisans voted with the Socialists to make the selection possible. A similar insurgency in 1927, this time on the part of three Polish Nonpartisans, aided Hoan in ousting Building Inspector W. D. Harper, after a seven-year effort to gain confirmation of an appointee who would respect the zoning laws, and led to the appointment of Leon M. Gurda, a Polish architect, neutral in politics, to the position. Other exponents of career service in

POLITICS AND URBAN MATURITY 535

municipal administration, all in office as late as 1940, were Charles B. Bennett, city planning engineer since 1926, who joined the city service in 1915 as a rodman in the engineer's office; Herbert W. Cornell and Ovid B. Blix, long-time incumbents in the city service commission; James L. Ferebee, chief engineer of the sewerage commission, who entered the city service in 1914; and Joseph W. Nicholson, city purchasing agent, who was attached to the central board of purchases through civil service examination in 1918.[13]

But agitation from outside, as well as activity within the city hall, fostered the achievements which brought Milwaukee fame. In the years following 1910, numerous citizens organizations carried forward the work of the reformers of the nineties, attempting to guide the municipality in the direction of more effective service to its people.[14] The emphasis in some of these groups was primarily political, in the interest of bringing about the election of public officials sympathetic to the members' social and political points of view. Thus the Voters' League, which published the voting record of incumbent aldermen during its period of activity from 1904 to 1925, focused attention upon securing the election of candidates reflecting the organization's increasingly conservative ideas. The avowed aim of the Good Government League, established in 1919, was "to decide on the most effective method for getting out the non-Socialist vote"; and while the Voters' Council, organized at the Milwaukee Athletic Club in 1932, claimed to be without political bias and recommended Socialists as well as Nonpartisans, Mayor Hoan denounced it as "a political shell game" that would be "knocked unconscious on election day."[15]

[13] For a discussion of administrative personnel in Milwaukee, see Norman N. Gill, "Career Personnel in Six Large Cities," *Public Management*, 17:260-63 (September 1935) and Career Personnel as Exemplified by Milwaukee City Officials, *passim*, unpublished MS, dated 1934, in the Milwaukee Municipal Reference Library. "Milwaukee, unquestionably one of the best-governed cities in the United States, has as qualified a set of administrators as are to be found in any municipality in this country. The relationship between this generalization, if conceded, and the long tenure in office of practically all present incumbents of important administrative posts cannot be termed accidental." *Ibid.*, 21-22.
[14] See chapter 12, p. 299 and following.
[15] Though avowedly nonpartisan, the Voters' League endorsed few Socialists in its twenty-year career. Milwaukee *Leader*, Oct. 19, 1925; Jan. 25, 1926; Milwau-

On the other hand, the City Club, founded in 1909 "by a small group of men interested in promoting civic welfare," worked throughout the period to advance a broad program for the social, civic, and economic betterment of Greater Milwaukee without such specific attention as the former groups to the selection of candidates for municipal office. Its standing committees, which dealt with such subjects as city charter, city planning, civil service, juvenile court, public health, and public utilities, attempted to reach workable solutions for the problems confronting the city and county governments; and by petitions and appearances before State and local legislative groups the club aided official bodies in carrying these solutions out. As early as 1912, it professed to be providing Milwaukee with "an organized civic conscience"; and by 1922 it had taken an active part in promoting the civic center, the zoning ordinance, home rule, centralized control of municipal finances, the provision of funds for public school extension, adequate salaries for teachers, an improved health program, and many other reforms. According to its secretary, the club regarded itself the guardian of the public interest, striving "to create and construct as well as to stand watch and ward." A somewhat similar role was played by the Milwaukee County League of Women Voters, founded in 1920, and by the Milwaukee Woman's Club, which developed from the East Side Suffrage Association in 1916. The former studied municipal problems, queried candidates at election time, and sponsored such improvements as a housing authority and more effective smoke regulation in the city. The latter took an active stand on questions of local import, not hesitating to express itself on controversial issues. The Women's Court and Civic Conference of Milwaukee, founded in 1922, became the channel of organized civic action for some thirty women's groups, including the suburban women's clubs, the College Women's Club, the Council of Jewish Women, the Women's International League for Peace and Freedom, and the women's organizations of the local church. A similar coordinating agency for the men's service clubs of the community

kee *Sentinel,* March 23, 1919; Milwaukee *Journal,* Oct. 18, 1925; Feb. 15, 16, March 11, 14, 1932.

was the Milwaukee Civic Alliance, organized in 1920, and made up of the president, secretary, and two delegates from each of twenty-two service clubs of Milwaukee and its suburbs. Through its resolutions, Greater Milwaukee's Civitans, Cooperatives, Cosmopolitans, Gyros, Kiwanians, Lions, Optimists, and Rotarians, as well as members of its Business Men's, City, and Exchange clubs, the Milwaukee Advertising Club, the Milwaukee Real Estate Board, the Milwaukee Round Table, and the Junior Chamber of Commerce, endorsed or opposed propositions of local concern. Influence toward a more specialized end was exerted by the Milwaukee Harbor and Rivers Association, organized in 1915 to represent the interests of owners of property located on Milwaukee's rivers; the Milwaukee Real Estate Board; affiliates of both the Wisconsin Taxpayers Alliance (1932) and the Wisconsin Citizens Public Expenditure Survey (1939); and the Affiliated Taxpayers Committee, representing the Association of Commerce, the Milwaukee Real Estate Board, the Savings and Loan League of Wisconsin, and the Association of Building Owners and Managers. The last-mentioned committee had been organized in 1938 with the avowed purpose of militantly demanding "all practical economies in Milwaukee City and County Governments consistent with ability of citizens to pay the tax bill."[16]

Both civic economy and municipal improvement were goals of the Citizens' Bureau (later called the Citizens' Governmental Research Bureau), a non-governmental counterpart of the Bureau of Economy and Efficiency, an agency established by the Socialist administration in 1910. When the victorious Nonpartisans abandoned the Socialist agency two years later, the City Club proposed the organization of an independent research bureau. Funds were raised to subsidize an investigation of the city government by a representative of the New York Bureau of Municipal Research; and in 1913 the local bureau was organized to carry out the resulting suggestions. Support for its

[16] *Ibid.,* June 2, 1912; *City Club News* (Milwaukee), March 17, 1922; Leo Tiefenthaler, "The City Club of Milwaukee," *Chicago City Club Bulletin,* July 18, 1921; Paula Lynagh, *Groups in Milwaukee Which Participate in Civic Activities,* bulletin of Citizens' Research Bureau (Milwaukee, 1945), *passim.*

research staff came from the voluntary contributions of civic-minded individuals and firms interested in the promotion of effective local government through "fact finding, constructive suggestions based on facts, and vigorous reporting of the same to public officials and citizens." In spite of some curtailment of its activities during World War I, by the middle twenties the bureau had taken an active part in the achievement of a central purchasing board for the city, the development of budget procedures in both city and county, and the reorganization of the municipal health department and the business department of the public schools. Between 1924 and 1927, at the request of the school board, the Citizens' Bureau made a survey of the proposed city-wide playground system and served as the staff of the citizens' recreation council which promoted the necessary bond issues to carry out the playground program. During the thirties the activities of the bureau were pointed toward the simplification of local government, with the consequence that, although a constitutional amendment to permit city-county consolidation was blocked by the State legislature in 1935, the city and county park systems were merged early in 1937 and the park police integrated with the city force at the same time. When a deadlock arose over the method of transfer in 1936, the Citizens' Bureau served as mediator between the city and county governments with effective results. Throughout the generation, the Citizens' Bureau viewed its responsibility as one not so much of reducing the expenses of government as of making certain that the public received the largest possible return for the money spent. Its continued service to the citizenry and officialdom of the community, as well as the multiplication of similar fact-finding and planning agencies within the city government itself, attested an increasing recognition, during the period, of the utility of research in the administration of municipal affairs.[17]

[17] Bureau of Municipal Research of New York, *Preliminary Survey of Certain Departments of the City of Milwaukee* (New York, 1913); Norman N. Gill, *Municipal Research Bureaus* (Washington, D.C., 1944), 18, 22, 55-57, 60-63, 72, 82, 137; Norman N. Gill, *The 68.92% Question!* (dittoed reproduction of talk to Gyro Club, Milwaukee, Nov. 7, 1946); Bulletin of Citizens' Governmental Research Bureau of Milwaukee (mimeographed on Bureau's letterhead, Aug. 6, 1947); Milwaukee *Journal*, Oct. 9, 1924.

Milwaukee's record for municipal solvency was one of the civic achievements of the period which resulted from the combined efforts of the citizens organizations, the Socialist mayor, and career personnel who developed the techniques. The major planks in the platform of fiscal stability were adequate budgeting practices, a "pay-as-you-go" policy for the construction of public improvements, and the creation of a debt amortization fund which promised to make the city debt-free in less than fifty years. The foundation of scientific budgeting was laid in 1907 with the creation of the board of estimates; and further reforms were instituted during the Seidel administration when a centralized purchasing agency was created. The first Socialist administration abandoned the practice of issuing bonds for the city's share of street improvements, and in 1915 the comptroller went a step farther to sponsor a policy of paying contractors in cash even for the portion of improvements assessable against the benefited property, the owners of which could defer these charges for six years by paying 6 percent interest. One after another, the city departments were put on a cash basis until, after interruptions during the depression, all were so operating by 1939.[18]

The accumulation of interest on the deferred improvement payments prompted the idea of setting these earnings aside as a perpetual trust fund to eliminate the city's bonded debt, which then stood at $29,700,000. The council unanimously approved this plan, in essence providing the city with a "savings account"; and in 1923 the Public Debt Amortization Fund was created by the State legislature. Augmented by one-third of all other interest earned by the city and invested in interest-paying city bonds, delinquent tax certificates, and United States securities, the fund had grown to $8,640,544 by the end of 1939. Meanwhile, the council's refusal to issue general obligation bonds after 1932 further promoted what the city officials called Mil-

[18] *Milwaukee Civic News: 1938*, p. 4; Daniel W. Hoan, *Extricating a City from Financial Chaos*, pamphlet in Duke University Socialist Collection, n.d.; Daniel W. Hoan, *Mayor Hoan Answers Critics*, pamphlet—reprint of speech during public hearing before Common Council committee on scrip (Milwaukee, n.d.); William H. Wendt, *Milwaukee, a Debt Free City*, unpaged brochure (Milwaukee, 1941); Hoan, *City Government*, 133-35; *Annual Report . . . 1939*, p. 29-31.

waukee's progress out of "bondage." By December 1943 the amortization fund exceeded the existing debt of $10,654,000. Thus, after 1943, Milwaukee was "debt free" to the extent that no taxes were levied thereafter for the purpose of bond redemption and interest. The last bonds of the city were due to mature in 1951, but money was on hand in the fund to pay all outstanding debt charges.[19]

The fund proved to be a lifesaver for the municipality at the depth of the depression when its use for the purchase of $3,000,000 worth of delinquent tax certificates helped refill the city's fast emptying treasury. Early in the depression, the city was able to collect a large portion of the taxes on real estate and personal property from which more than 50 percent of its revenue was drawn. But as conditions darkened in 1932, tax delinquency mounted. Approximately 32 percent of the city's taxes remained uncollected at the end of the year; and a peak of $17,000,000, representing 75 percent of the total, went unpaid in 1933. City expenditures were drastically reduced, in spite of the mayor's much criticized opposition to indiscriminate budget slashing; and a popular referendum in 1932 supported tax and budget limitations. Fortunately for the city administration, public relief costs had been financed by the county since 1851. This made it possible to reduce city costs in spite of heavy expenditures for relief. The city tax rate per $1,000 of assessed value dropped from $26.05 in 1928 to $22.40 in 1932, and stood at $25.33 for 1940. At the same time, the county rate spiraled from $5.91 in 1928 to $10.57 in 1932 and $10.71 in 1940. It soon became apparent that the city must liquidize its depression-frozen tax assets; for high interest rates discouraged borrowing. As a result, the city gained legislative permission to issue tax redemption notes, referred to as "baby bonds"—four-year callable notes bearing interest at 5 percent on $100 and $10 denominations. Later, non-interest-bearing baby bonds (or scrip) were issued. Secured by city-owned delinquent tax certifi-

[19] *Ibid.*, p. 31; an article by Edwin E. Witte on Milwaukee's debt elimination plan, in unidentified paper, in Duke University Socialist Collection; Wendt, *Milwaukee, a Debt Free City*, passim. See also, Norman N. Gill and Paula Lynagh, "Debt Free Idea Loses Allure," *National Municipal Review*, 36:241 (May 1947).

cates, these baby bonds were used in part payment of wages and salaries to city employees. Between 1933 and 1938 a total of $14,600,000 in such bonds was issued. In the first rush of their use they dropped 10 percent in value, but by the close of 1934 they were being accepted at par. Through this device, the city weathered the financial crisis without resort to refunding operations or discontinuing payments on the principal and interest of its bonded debt.[20]

To carry out the "pay-as-you-go" policy a permanent improvement fund was established in 1936 and 1937. Endorsed by such organizations as the City Club and the Citizens' Bureau, the fund was to be accumulated from the levy of a tax "equal to the reduction in the amount annually required for sinking fund purposes." By 1940, critics of the community's outworn equipment and installations were contending that the administration had gone too far in its attempts to save and that the city's thriftiness might prove it to have been "penny wise" but "pound foolish" in the long run. In spite of these criticisms, however, many groups in the city were eager to take the credit for Milwaukee's nationally famous fiscal economies. In oft-repeated campaign argument, Mayor Hoan credited the Socialists with having restored to solvency a city whose every department was "in the red" upon their accession to office in 1910. While he admitted that one or two of the reform measures were initiated by the political opposition, he insisted that the effort would not have been sustained "without the leadership or driving force of a well-organized and well-disciplined party of workers." To be sure, the ideals of a worker party, "desirous of improving government so as to demonstrate that it is an admirable proprietor," undoubtedly gave real impetus to the achievement of the program—as did the graft-free tradition of the Hoan administrations over the years; but in assigning the credit for the city's solvency one certainly ought not to overlook the creative

[20] At the beginning of the depression the city had $15,000,000 in unused balances from the sale of bond issues. This cash was available for the payment of current expenses and was later replaced when delinquent taxes were paid. L. G. Meisenheimer, "Milwaukee's Finances from One War to Another," *Municipal Finance*, vol. 15, no. 4, pp. 4-6 (May 1943); *Municipal Activities . . . 1932*, pp. 17-18; *ibid. . . . 1933*, pp. 19-20, 25-26, 37-39; *ibid. . . . 1934*, p. 18; *ibid. . . . 1935*, pp. 42-43.

contribution of the city's administrative personnel, the support and encouragement of the citizens organizations, and the example of the conservative and thrifty citizenry itself.[21]

The concern for city beautification and planning, manifested during the first decade of the century, found increasing expression after 1910 in the efforts of the municipal administration, the citizens organizations, and the newspapers, especially the Milwaukee *Journal*. The example of both American and foreign cities was cited by the Metropolitan Park Commission, when in 1909 it recommended the grouping of public buildings in a civic center, to be bounded by Ninth, Fourth, Wells, and State streets, and the widening of Kilbourn Avenue, the thoroughfare which would connect the proposed new courthouse with lakeside Juneau Park. In 1910, the commission suggested the development of river parkways, inspired by the waterfronts of Düsseldorf and Vienna. The Socialist administration, under the influence of Charles B. Whitnall, the patriarch of the planning program, extended the commission's tenure, broadened its scope to provide for comprehensive over-all planning and regulated land use, and changed its name in 1911 to the City Planning Commission. Seidel's defeat in 1912 called a temporary halt to the work; but by 1915 the board of public land commissioners had been created, and in the following year, such citizens groups as the City Club, the Westminster League, and the South Side Civic Association were actively agitating for the adoption of a city plan.

By popular referendum, on April 6, 1920, the electorate endorsed the development of a civic center, to be built in the vicinity of the region proposed in 1909; and after considerable controversy, reminiscent of the sectional conflicts of the village period, contributory improvements were begun. The University of Wisconsin Extension Building and the Vocational

[21] Mayor Hoan pointed out in *City Government* that the depression forced more than 2,000 communities to default on existing debts or borrow money at higher rates of interest (p. 124). During the recession of 1938, tax receipts fell far below expectation and the year would have ended with a deficit but for the cooperation of all the departments in not spending all the funds that had been allotted. *Milwaukee, 1937*, pp. 15-16; *Milwaukee Civic News: 1938*, p. 4; *Milwaukee's Progress in 1940*, p. 55; Wendt, *Milwaukee, a Debt Free City;* Hoan, *Extricating a City from Financial Chaos*.

School were completed in 1928; the succeeding year saw not only the widening of Kilbourn Avenue from North Sixth Street to North Broadway but the construction of the Kilbourn Avenue bridge; and the completion of the City-County Safety Building (1930) and the courthouse (1931) followed. Nearly a decade of litigation over the condemnation and the assessment of benefits and damages procedures in public improvements was terminated in 1938 when the supreme court validated the Kline Benefit Assessment Law passed in 1931. The work of securing property had been carried on despite the litigation, and by 1941 a spacious and potentially impressive thoroughfare extended from Prospect Avenue to the courthouse. A comprehensive program of demolishing worthless and unsanitary buildings, begun in 1928, resulted in the destruction of nearly 6,000 such structures during the succeeding decade; but in spite of this, by 1936, the gradual decay of areas around the downtown business district was causing the planning department real concern. Meanwhile, Whitnall was exerting his creative influence; and by 1929, eighty-four miles of parkways, determined by the stream valleys of the county, were under way.[22]

Over-all city planning was facilitated by the zoning ordinance of November 15, 1920, which made Milwaukee the twelfth

[22] The personal element in city improvement is illustrated in Whitnall's account of the genesis of the planning program. "A small group of men and women many years ago attended lectures by a University of Wisconsin professor in South Side High School," he explained. "Before and after the lecture we discussed city and county problems. One night someone remarked that it was a pity cities levelled off hills and filled in valleys and later developed artificial parks on the same land. Some of us, including Colonel Charles Estabrook . . . and Emerson D. Hoyt, . . . decided to do something about it. We had a bill passed in the legislature authorizing the creation of a county park board. We then went to work." At various stages in city planning the city called upon such experts as Frederick Law Olmsted and John Nolen of New York for advice. Werner Hegemann, a well-known German planner, came to Milwaukee to stimulate planning in 1916. City Planning Commission, *Prelim. Repts.*, 4-6, 8, 12-24, 26-46; Charles B. Whitnall, "Milwaukee's Efforts in City and Regional Planning," *City Planning*, vol. 5, no. 4, pp. 205-6, 210, 213; Lloyd Gladfelter, "Park Pioneer Sees Greater Milwaukee as Garden City," Milwaukee *Journal*, Jan. 21, 1940; *ibid.*, March 28, 1924; Werner Hegemann, *City Planning for Milwaukee: Report* (Milwaukee, 1916); Elmer Krieger, *Brief History of the Widening of Kilbourn Avenue and the Location of Public Buildings along Its Axis since 1900* (dittoed report to Board of Public Land Commissioners, Milwaukee, June 11, 1947); *Municipal Activities . . . 1936*, p. 31; *Milwaukee Civic News: 1938*, pp. 1, 10, 15; *Milwaukee's Progress in 1940*, p. 6.

city of the nation to place comprehensive height, use, and area restrictions on buildings within the city limits. The City Planning Commission had been directed in 1911 to "provide residence areas apart from the commercial and factory zones"; but when the council set up piecemeal residential areas under the authority of an act passed by the State legislature in 1913, damage suits aggregating $76,000 were filed against the city on the ground that the owners had been deprived of property without due process of law, an opinion endorsed by Nonpartisan City Attorney Clifton Williams and Building Inspector Harper. Progress toward the achievement of zoning was nevertheless advanced by the example of New York City, where the first comprehensive zoning ordinance was passed in 1916; by the activities of the Public Land Commission, which turned to such national authorities on zoning as Edward M. Bassett and Arthur C. Comey to help prepare the ordinance and defend it before the leading citizens organizations of the city; and by the Milwaukee *Journal*, which insisted that the question of zoning was "bound up not only with property values, but with the health, the beautification, and the orderly development of the city." A resolution requesting the preparation of a comprehensive districting plan was presented to the council in December 1918; and subsequent pressure brought the passage of the ordinance two years later which, after some compromise, divided the city into use, height, and area districts according to the predominant types of buildings then existing or anticipated in the logical development of the community.[23]

Once zoning was achieved, Mayor Hoan and his supporters —on this issue the Milwaukee *Journal* as well as the citizens groups—were hard put to resist amendments that threatened to "tear the ordinance to shreds." Real estate speculators counted on Nonpartisan aldermen to change the measure to their

[23] "The Remarkable Spread of Zoning in American Cities," *American City*, 456-58 (December 1921); Milwaukee *Leader*, Aug. 25, 1915; Milwaukee *Sentinel*, Sept. 10, 1915; June 22, 1920; Board of Public Land Commissioners, *Zoning for Milwaukee, Tentative Report, June 21, 1920;* Milwaukee *Journal*, March 2, Dec. 2, 1918; Dec. 26, 29, 1919; March 7, April 11, July 18, 1920; for details of ordinance see "Zoning in Milwaukee," typescript, dated 1920, in Milwaukee Municipal Reference Library.

advantage; and Building Inspector Harper, whom the mayor was struggling to replace, enlisted the opposition of the labor unions to the height limitations in the measure by asserting that "millions would be expended on new buildings if these restrictions were lifted." In the later twenties, both the City Club and the Citizens' Bureau supported the mayor's veto of amendments to the zoning law; and a decade later, in spite of a generally prevailing popular endorsement of the principle of zoning, the conflict between mayor and council continued, with the *Journal* consistently seconding the mayor's determination to uphold the law. A decision of the Wisconsin Supreme Court, in a case concerning the Milwaukee ordinance, broadened the concept of police power in its relation to zoning in such a way as to advance this kind of regulation in the nation as well as in the Wisconsin metropolis. In the case of State ex rel. Carter v. Harper (1923), the court for the first time recognized planning as a means of promoting the public welfare and expanded the concept that aesthetic factors might be considered as incidents of regulation. "The rights of property should not be sacrificed to the pleasure of an ultra-aesthetic taste," the Justice wrote. "But whether they should be permitted to plague the average or predominant human sensibilities may well be pondered."[24]

Despite the fact that the expansion of heavy municipal improvements was affected by the violent economic fluctuations of the period, the generation of maturing cityhood saw overall advances in the provision of better streets, a purer water supply, and the more scientific disposal of the wastes produced in a populous urban society. Between the close of 1910 and the beginning of 1940, the number of miles of pavement within the city limits increased from 362 to 669, with asphalt and macadam predominating in contrast to the crushed stone and gravel com-

[24] Milwaukee *Journal*, Sept. 7, 1921; Nov. 23, 24, 1925; Feb. 12, March 1, 1928; July 15, 1931; May 30, 1935; Sept. 18, 1937; Milwaukee *Sentinel*, Dec. 31, 1925; May 11, 1926; Dec. 15, 1937; Jan. 19, 1938; *City Club News*, Dec. 10, 1926; Robert A. Walker, *The Planning Function in Urban Government* (New York, 1940), 70-71, 93. In 1925, Sol Ettenheim and Sons, real estate operators and builders, constructed a much-discussed black cottage at Park Place and Downer Avenue, as a protest against zoning regulations that prevented the building of an apartment house on the site. Milwaukee *Sentinel*, Aug. 29, 1925.

position of the earlier period. All records for construction were broken in the late twenties; and 1929, the peak year, saw the completion of 52.7 miles of streets and 23.4 miles of alleys, as well as 48.7 miles of water mains and 81.15 miles of storm and sanitary sewers. Special assessments on the tax rolls for 1929 totaled almost $3,650,000, the largest in the city's history. Street construction declined by 30 percent in 1930; and the dearth of projects thereafter reflected the economic difficulties of the ensuing years. Little more than a mile of streets was paved in 1933 and 1934 combined; and although federal projects for paving and repair ultimately brought a gradual increase in the totals, accomplishment remained slight by comparison with what had been achieved during the expansive twenties. As late as 1940, when 17.6 miles of pavement and 12.2 miles of sewers were constructed by persons employed with W.P.A. funds, construction paid for from city funds was limited to 9 miles of pavement, 2 of alleys, 5 of sidewalks, 12 of waterpipe, and 4 of sewers.[25]

The chief problem of the generation in connection with Milwaukee's municipally owned and operated waterworks sprang from the need of purifying the city water, a situation complicated by the fact that for topographical reasons the city was forced to dispose of its sewage, treated or untreated, in the same body of water from which it drew its water supply. Intermittent treatment of the water with chlorine was begun in June 1910; and after April 12, 1912, the use of this chemical, under laboratory control, continued without interruption. As a result, deaths from typhoid, which numbered 45 to 95 yearly before 1910, were greatly reduced. Continued concern for the purity of the water lent support to the movement for a water purification plant, which had been proposed as early as 1911. At last, in 1933, the council authorized its construction, to be financed by an issue of waterworks mortgage bonds totaling $3,675,000, a P.W.A. grant of $1,285,690, and a budget appro-

[25] Department of Public Works (Milwaukee), *Annual Report for the Year Ending December 31, 1910*, p. 126; Bureau of Engineers, City of Milwaukee, *Annual Report*, 1940, p. 21; *Municipal Government and Activities . . . 1928*, p. 4; *ibid. . . . 1929*, p. 28; *Municipal Activities . . . 1930*, p. 31; *ibid. . . . 1933*, p. 53; *ibid. . . . 1934*, p. 56; *Milwaukee's Progress in 1940*, p. 54.

priation of about $165,000. Construction of the $5,100,000 plant, to be of the mechanical, rapid-sand type with a capacity of 200,000,000 gallons a day, was begun in 1934; and after July 2, 1939, all water furnished the city was subjected to complete filtration treatment. The efficient management of the waterworks through the years resulted in the transfer of considerable revenue to the general city fund. Between 1892 and 1939 the amount so transferred, as a contribution to municipal expenses, reached a total of $12,787,965.[26]

Meanwhile, the desire for purer water had also led to the improvement of municipal sewage disposal facilities, as a result of which, after 1925, close to 95 percent of the polluted matter could be extracted from the sewage before discharging it into the lake. After study of the problem by a group of engineers in 1909, the legislature authorized the creation of a sewerage commission, in 1913; and with its organization, active work was begun on a complete system of intercepting sewers and on experiments which in 1920 resulted in a process for treating the sewage prior to disposing of it in the lake. By the time the Jones Island plant was ready for operation—on June 26, 1925—the legislature had created the Metropolitan Sewerage Commission (1921), authorized to construct intercepting sewers in the area contiguous to Milwaukee, thus permitting disposal at the Milwaukee plant. The treatment of the sewage—known as the "activated sludge" method—not only purified what was discharged into the lake but produced a by-product valuable as commercial fertilizer. By the close of 1927, the sewage disposal plant was treating 85,000,000 gallons of sewage—its capacity—every twenty-four hours; and returns of $500,000 were expected by the following year from the sale of Milorganite, its commercial by-product. The depression brought to a close the extensive sewer construction of the late twenties, but resort to the assistance of the federal works program in the mid-thirties permitted not only continued expansion of the sewerage system but the construction, under P.W.A., of an addition to the disposal plant. The former activity, carried on under W.P.A., had

[26] *Municipal Activities . . . 1930,* p. 40; *ibid. . . . 1932,* p. 72; *ibid. . . . 1933,* p. 63; *Milwaukee, 1937,* p. 44; *Annual Report . . . 1939,* pp. 68, 98-99.

cost the city $52,676 and the federal government $2,358,442 by December 31, 1936. The latter, which assumed operation in December 1935, permitted the treatment of more than 99 percent of the city's sewage during a normal day. In 1939, a sewer program estimated to cost $2,500,000 was carried out, largely through the application of federal funds under W.P.A. and P.W.A. By this date, the earnings from the sale of Milorganite were totaling about $700,000 yearly.[27]

The growth of the city and the development of the automobile led to revolutionary changes in the methods of municipal garbage collection by the early twenties. With the establishment of a separate bureau of garbage collection and disposal in 1923, the city's 131 small garbage wagons, each drawn by a single horse, gave way to a system of horse-drawn trailers, which, when filled, were hauled to the incinerator, four at a time, by tractor trucks. By 1939, safer, quieter, and more economical streamlined shuttle trucks were replacing the long four-trailer train units in service since 1923. Ashes from the incinerator, which was built in 1910, helped to fill in enough new land for the lake front drive and airport. The per capita cost of garbage disposal was reduced from about 75 cents in 1930 to 71 cents a decade later.[28]

In the realm of public utilities, and in spite of the city's reputation as socialistic, the efforts of the Electric Company and the Nonpartisan aldermen succeeded in staving off public ownership and operation except in the case of a municipal street lighting distribution system, which the city undertook to provide, after years of controversy, in 1916. According to a survey made in that year, "Milwaukee had with the possible exception of Jersey City, New Jersey, the poorest lighted streets of any city in America"; yet it was paying the Electric Company $65

[27] Charges of patent infringement, brought by Activated Sludge, Incorporated, led to a judgment of almost $5,000,000 against the city, which it settled for about 16 cents on the dollar. Gregory, *History*, 2:1143-45; *Municipal Government and Activities . . . 1923*, pp. 34-36; *ibid. . . . 1927*, pp. 26, 28; *Municipal Activities . . . 1933*, p. 67; *ibid. . . . 1934*, p. 62; *ibid. . . . 1935*, pp. 86-87; *ibid. . . . 1936*, p. 61; *Annual Report . . . 1939*, pp. 61-62; *Milwaukee's Progress in 1940*, p. 58.

[28] *Municipal Government and Activities . . . 1923*, p. 29-30; *ibid. . . . 1929*, pp. 33-34; *Annual Report . . . 1939*, pp. 64-65; *Milwaukee's Progress in 1940*, pp. 54-55.

a lamp for a demonstrably heterogeneous and antiquated system. In 1914 the company had offered to reduce the price to $55, if the city would enter into a ten-year contract; and two years later, as pressure for municipal lighting grew, it offered the city a "business proposition" of 10,631 lamps for $25.61 a lamp. The City Club and the Engineers' Society endorsed a $750,000 bond issue for municipal street lighting, arguing that a demonstration circuit installed by the city's consulting engineers promised not only better and more evenly distributed light at a reduction annually of from $65 to $37.50 per lamp, but also more artistically designed poles and lanterns as well as the elimination of overhead wires. Municipal control of street lighting was endorsed by the community in 1916, despite the Electric Company's assertions that the arguments of the City Club would "apply as well to the public ownership of grocery stores"; and in June of that year the installation of the city's distribution system was begun. By 1921, more than 3,600 new lighting units had been installed; and by the close of 1922, with the conversion of 1,500 gas units to electricity and the replacement of arc lamps with incandescent units, Milwaukee could boast of being "the first large city in the United States to have its streets entirely lighted by . . . incandescent tungsten lamps."[29]

The Electric Company succeeded, however, in holding on to the utility itself, in spite of the efforts, especially of the Socialists, to achieve public ownership and management of street railway and electric power facilities. Countering Mayor Hoan's desire to select a committee to investigate the acquisition of the utility, the council in 1919 authorized its president to make such an appointment; and in 1924 this group presented, in the form of an ordinance, a proposed "service-at-cost" contract between the Electric Company and the city, the result of a plan designed to assure good service at the lowest possible cost without immediate actual purchase of the property by the municipality. Such a solution was complicated by the difficulty of

[29] Emil Seidel, "Our City—Our Home," Milwaukee *Leader*, Dec. 13, 28, 1927; Milwaukee *Journal*, March 16, 28, 31, April 1, 11, 19, 1916; *Municipal Government and Activities* . . . *1921*, pp. 20-21; *ibid.* . . . *1922*, pp. 27-28.

arriving at a fair evaluation of the company's investment, which, in the opinion of the committee, appeared to involve about $4,000,000 in "watered" stock, and by the fact that the proposal failed to meet the Socialist demand for out-and-out ownership, if necessary, of a competing transit line. As a matter of fact, limitations on the bonded indebtedness of the city made immediate acquisition impossible, but Mayor Hoan pledged himself to follow a policy looking toward the realization of public ownership of the utility. Innovations introduced by the company as a means of reducing operating expenses were frequently interpreted by the mayor and his followers as an indication that under private management of the utility public safety was being sacrificed to private gain. Thus when one-man cars appeared on the city's most congested thoroughfares, the mayor condemned the practice as further evidence of the company's policy of "to hell with the public, hurrah for dividends." In 1936, a referendum on the question of public acquisition of the enterprise was again presented to the people; but a depression-weary electorate listened to arguments of the Taxpayers and Electricity Users Committee Incorporated; and, convinced that acquisition would increase already high debts and taxes and raise rather than lower rates, it defeated the proposal by a decisive majority.[30]

In spite of the mayor's contention that the Electric Company was more interested in dividends than in the public, innovations in equipment in the course of the generation brought improved service and greater convenience to users of the street-car lines. The most revolutionary development, after the appearance of the one-man "safety car," which was introduced in 1921, was the slow replacement of the rumbling, rail-bound street car with the streamlined motor bus and trackless trolley. Between April 1920 and May 1936, the mileage in bus lines in the city increased from less than 2 to more than 104 miles; and whereas by the end of 1921 there were only

[30] *Wisconsin News* (Milwaukee), Feb. 11, July 8, 1919; Milwaukee *Sentinel*, Aug. 29, 1919; Milwaukee *Leader*, Jan. 4, 1919; July 25, 1921; Dec. 24, 1925; Milwaukee *Journal*, May 7, 1923; April 8, 1936; *Municipal Government and Activities . . . 1924*, pp. 37-38.

2½ miles of bus lines to nearly 122 miles of street-car track, a gradual change by 1936 had reversed the trend until the mileage in both types of transit was approximately equal. The first trackless trolleys were installed on the North Avenue run in 1936; and by 1940 considerable progress had been made in extending this speedier service to other parts of the city. In 1930 the company inaugurated the $1.00 weekly pass system and put the so-called "liberal transfer" into service.[31]

Despite its achievements in connection with waste disposal, improved street lighting, and a purified water supply, it was in the promotion of health, public safety and order, and community recreation that the Wisconsin metropolis most clearly demonstrated its civic maturity in the generation from 1910 to 1940. In 1939, for the fourth time, the city won first place for public health within its population group, thus maintaining its reputation as the healthiest large city in the nation. For the ninth successive year, it ranked first for traffic safety. In addition to these distinctions, it led its population group in the field of fire prevention; its freedom from crime was widely recognized; and its public recreation program provided a model for the nation. What was attested in awards for such civic achievement was also revealed in the municipal budget. Between 1910 and 1940, per capita annual expenditures for police protection increased from $1.61 to $4.78; for fire protection, from $2.03 to $3.37; for the promotion of the public health, from 60 cents to $1.18; and for public library service, from 26 to 72 cents. And, as a matter of fact, save for police protection, the figures for 1940 were slightly under those of 1930 because of retrenchments prompted by the depressed conditions of the intervening decade.[32]

Its provision of speedy justice—for minor as well as major crimes—and its relatively non-political police force were important factors in building Milwaukee's reputation as the safest

[31] Milwaukee *Sentinel*, July 14, 1937; Austin, *The Milwaukee Story*, 197; *Municipal Activities . . . 1936*, pp. 18-19; *Milwaukee's Progress in 1940*, p. 7.
[32] For a comparative analysis of expenditures see chart, "Expenditures for Selected Urban Services in Milwaukee, 1861 to 1940," in appendix. See also *Annual Report . . . 1939*, p. 6, and Richard E. Krug, *The Keys to the Safest City*, unpaged pamphlet (Municipal Reference Library, Milwaukee, 1937).

city in the nation. Since 1885, the selection of fire and police chiefs had been vested in the mayor-appointed board of fire and police commissioners; but prior to 1911 the mayor was the official head of both the fire and police departments. In 1911, the law was amended so as to give the chiefs more direct responsibility over their respective departments. As a result, "Czar" Janssen, the veteran head of the police department, was in a position to flout the merit system in his appointments and to overlook, to some extent, the gambling, prostitution, and petty public thievery which decent elements in the community had been trying to correct since the close of the Rose régime. The death of Chief Janssen in 1921 provided Mayor Hoan with an opportunity to suggest to the commission the appointment of a successor on whom he could count to institute reform. Passing over Janssen's assistants, whom he associated with the prevailing corruption in the department, he recommended one of the detectives, his neighbor, Jacob G. Laubenheimer, regarded as a Nonpartisan in politics, on the understanding that "he would make all appointments and promotions subject to merit and the rules of the commission" and that he would not "use his department for or against any city administration that happened to be in power."

During the incumbency of the new chief, whose association with the department as early as 1893 made him by now a veteran in the service, the city was to advance from twenty-ninth among thirty-four major American cities in the adequacy of police protection to a position of unequaled eminence for crimelessness and public order. Chief Laubenheimer speedily augmented the force until by 1935 it numbered more than twice the personnel of 1910. He reorganized the detective bureau and introduced modern systems of records and crime accounting; and, adapting method to the mechanical innovations of the generation, he inaugurated a training school, a traffic bureau, a bureau of identification, and a medical bureau for instruction in first aid. In 1930 he instituted a police radio bureau to direct the work of radio squad cars; and by 1939 these were widely used for purposes of detection and arrest. Moreover, improved personnel relations, including the establishment of

TWENTIETH-CENTURY URBAN SERVICES WIN MILWAUKEE FAME FOR PUBLIC HEALTH AND SAFETY. *Top:* Modern methods of bridge construction and street repair and sanitation. *Center, left:* Local housewives look on as Health Department technician makes periodic check on moisture content of butter. *Center, right:* Young adults learn watch repairing at Milwaukee Vocational School. *Below:* Record-winning firemen and policemen on the job.

a pension system, gradual increases in salary, strict discipline, and promotions for demonstrated and recorded merit made it generally more profitable for policemen to be honest than otherwise. Despite the widespread unemployment of the thirties, Milwaukee maintained its record as a law-abiding community; and thanks to the vigilance and speedy justice to which transient vagrants were subjected, the downward trend of crime continued until 1937 when its increase in the nation at large was manifested in Milwaukee as well. Consideration for the public, exhibited by the city's ubiquitous policemen in these latter years, inspired an increasing respect for government on the part of a citizenry which itself assumed, to an unusual degree, a responsibility for the maintenance of public order; and the fundamental honesty of the municipal administration made no small contribution to the development of a force that continued to live up to its reputation as "the most efficient and cleanest police department in the country."[33]

The advent of Laubenheimer as chief of police coincided with the development of a program of traffic regulation necessitated by an almost ninefold increase in motor vehicles (from 3,608 to more than 30,000) in the city between 1913 and 1921. July 1921 saw official recognition of the Safety Commission, which had been created as a body advisory to the mayor, to study and give publicity to safety needs. The use of twenty-eight uniformed motorcycle policemen, attached to Chief Laubenheimer's newly created traffic bureau, deterred the recklessness of automobilists. During 1921 the police department began to experiment with mechanical "Stop" and "Go" signals; by 1922, the city owned two, and several others had been installed by the inventors; and in 1923, safety islands were being tried on Cedar Street and Biddle Street (now Kilbourn Avenue). Parking was further regulated in 1925; and during the ensuing fifteen years additional traffic-safety techniques, as well as

[33] Hoan, *City Government*, 197-223; *Municipal Government and Activities . . . 1921*, pp. 27-29; ibid. . . . *1922*, pp. 35-38; *Official Program, Milwaukee Mid-Summer Festival, 1936*, pp. 23-27; *Municipal Activities . . . 1936*, p. 47; *Milwaukee, 1937*, p. 31; *Annual Report . . . 1939*, p. 43. The death of Chief Laubenheimer in 1936 led to the appointment of Joseph T. Kluchesky, the first Socialist chief of police.

improved street lighting, cut the mounting traffic toll. By 1940 the city had 630 automatic traffic signals, 3,002 arterial stop signs, 256 safety islands, 162 street-car loading islands, 11 miles of one-way-traffic streets, and 148 miles of arterial highway. Engineering devices, enforcement of traffic violations, and a continuing and widespread educational campaign reflected the combined contribution of technical administration and community interest in holding traffic deaths in Milwaukee far below the average for cities of its size.[34]

Emphasis on the prevention as well as the extinction of fires and the introduction of new fire fighting techniques accounted for a reduction in per capita fire losses of from more than $5.00 to less than $1.00 in Milwaukee between 1921 and the middle thirties. Charges filed against Chief Thomas A. Clancy in 1910, alleging that proper inspection would have prevented many fires in the downtown area, led to the passage of ordinances enforcing the removal of fire hazards and to the creation in 1915 of a bureau of prevention. The advent of his successor, Peter J. Steinkellner, in 1925, brought the development of a widespread program of public education, including a Fire Prevention School and Fire Prevention Week, as well as continued inspections and both modernization and enforcement of the city's building codes. A new respect for the merit system improved the morale of the fire fighting force, which after 1923 was given systematic instruction in modern methods of fighting fire. Discussions during the convention of the International Association of Fire Engineers in 1911 led to the purchase in the following year of the city's first motor-driven apparatus for use in fighting fires; and by 1927 the equipment of the department was completely motorized.[35]

The findings and recommendations of the Socialists' Bureau of Economy and Efficiency, together with the services of their

[34] Hoan, *City Government*, 240-46; *Municipal Government and Activities . . . 1921*, pp. 28, 34; *ibid. . . . 1925*, p. 4; *ibid. . . . 1922*, p. 28; *ibid. . . . 1928*, p. 25; *Municipal Activities . . . 1936*, p. 70; *Milwaukee Civic News: 1938*, p. 1; *Milwaukee's Progress in 1940*, pp. 6, 116.

[35] Before becoming chief, Steinkellner had organized and served for five years as head of a fire fighters' union. Gill, *Career Personnel*, 9; Hoan, *City Government*, 224-39; *Mid-Summer Festival Program, 1936*, p. 31.

non-Socialist appointee, Dr. W. C. Rucker, gave an impulse to the development of a municipal health program which was carried forward with distinction during the incumbencies of Health Commissioners F. A. Kraft (October 1910 to 1914), G. C. Ruhland (to 1924), and John P. Koehler (to 1940). The activities of the health department helped to reduce the death rate in Milwaukee below that of most of the major cities of the nation; as a result of its work and of the improved health conditions in the country at large, the average life span in the city was lengthened from 27.6 years in 1900, to 38.7 in 1920, 52.6 in 1932, and 58.4 in 1940. In the last of these years, according to a municipal report, "Milwaukee experienced the best health conditions in its history." This achievement was the result of many activities. In connection with an extensive program of health supervision, representatives of the department visited the schools of the city—public, private, and parochial—conducting morning inspections, physical examinations, post-vacation checks for contagious diseases, and oral hygiene. Field nursing activities and child welfare clinics greatly reduced infant mortality as did augmented facilities for the isolation and treatment of contagious diseases and a broadened immunization program, such as that for the prevention of diphtheria, inaugurated early in the twenties. Health education was popularized through the use of contests, radio programs, and printed publicity; and intensified inspection of food, milk, factories, lodging places, beauty parlors, theaters, and dance halls, together with the achievement of a dependably pure water supply, helped to overcome the hazards to health associated with the congestion of urban living. Thanks to the continued vigilance of the health authorities, as well as to the curtailment of social activities and the intelligent distribution of food by relief agencies, the health of Milwaukeeans improved rather than declined during the depression-ridden thirties; and in 1934 the death rate of eight per 1,000 was the lowest in the city's history. By 1940, the health department was proposing the extension of its activities to include a broad program for detecting the existence of tuberculosis among industrial workers, in order to reduce the prevailing high death rate from this cause among men between twenty-five and forty-five; additional free dental treatment; specialized service for the discovery of postural and orthopedic defects in school children; facilities for inexpensive annual physical examinations; and, as a response to the increased incidence of the degenerative diseases of old age, "an inexpensive cooperative diagnostic and treatment service for cancer by the medical profession, hospital association, and health department."[36]

If the depression brought added responsibilities to the guardians of the city's health, it did so in even greater measure to those who guided its program of public recreation; for the municipal agencies that catered to the leisure-time needs of the citizenry were taxed to the limit of their resources in the era of the "unemployed thirties." By 1910 the number of books owned by the Public Library had increased from the 15,000 volumes of 1880 to some 218,870; and ten years later the collection totaled 386,175 volumes. The flush twenties brought a marked expansion not only in the facilities of the library but also in its use. The number of volumes increased from 386,175 in 1920 to 858,315 in 1930; and during that period the per capita circulation grew from 3.3 to 7.8. During the thirties, use of the library constituted a veritable barometer of the economic fluctuations of the decade. The 50 percent gain in circulation between 1929 and 1933 mirrored the downward trend of the business cycle. As employment picked up during the middle thirties, circulation fell; but an increase in lending beginning toward the end of 1937 reflected the recession which prevailed during 1938. By 1940, improved economic conditions had again reduced the library's use. At that date, per capita circulation had fallen from 8.4, the figure for 1932, to 6.7, approximately that of the middle twenties; and, since purchases had been curtailed during the depression, the total of 969,278

[36] Gregory, *History*, 2:1141; *Municipal Government and Activities . . . 1921*, pp. 34-39; ibid. . . . *1928*, p. 40; *Municipal Activities . . . 1931*, p. 93; ibid. . . . *1932*, pp. 94-115; ibid. . . . *1933*, p. 85; ibid. . . . *1934*, p. 90; *Annual Report . . . 1939*, pp. 60-61; *Milwaukee's Progress in 1940*, pp. 43, 47; Milwaukee *Journal*, Dec. 31, 1934. 1940 was the fourth consecutive year without a death from typhoid fever, a disease which in 1910 resulted in 171 deaths out of 1,605 cases. *Milwaukee's Progress in 1940*, p. 43.

volumes represented an increase of little more than 100,000 over the 1930 figure. Under the direction of Matthew S. Dudgeon, who served as librarian throughout the period of expansion and crisis, the policies of the library were shaped to meet the changing needs of the community. Departmentalized reference services and a readers' bureau broadened the utility of the library for research; while its role in the provision of leisure-time activities and community culture was expanded through the development of telephone and delivery service for shut-ins, a hospital and vacation book service, and the decentralization of its holdings into more than 2,500 separate collections, including those at eighteen branches, as well as at schools, drug stores, factories, and a variety of other locations. The depression years saw increased use of both the Public Museum, where W.P.A. funds were employed to advantage in improving the holdings, and the Milwaukee Art Institute. The latter, which had developed from the Milwaukee Art Society, founded in 1910, had had the benefit of city support since 1918. In 1922 the city agreed to increase its financial contribution to $20,000 annually with the understanding that it would ultimately acquire complete ownership of the institution.[37]

But it was the city's many playgrounds and social centers that won Milwaukee most renown for putting enforced idleness to worthwhile use. As early as 1908 to 1910, citizens groups like the North Side Civic League, the City Club, and the Woman's Club had initiated interest in the extension of playground facilities and the employment of the public schools for purposes of community recreation, in line with a program already being developed in Rochester, New York. Enabling legislation, passed in Madison in 1911, put the enterprise under the control of

[37] A study of community reading habits during the depression revealed that "while folks still read fiction to forget their troubles, they were turning more to non-fiction to learn about their jobs or acquire a philosophy after they lost theirs." During 1929 to 1933 the increase in fiction read was 51 percent; for science, 79 percent; for philosophy and religion, 88 percent; and for music and art, 123 percent. Milwaukee Public Library, *34th Annual Report, December 31st, 1911*, p. 25; *Municipal Government and Activities . . . 1929*, p. 76; *Municipal Activities . . . 1931*, pp. 148-49; *ibid. . . . 1932*, p. 135; *ibid. . . . 1933*, pp. 118, 121-22; *ibid. . . . 1935*, p. 114; *Milwaukee, 1937*, p. 54; *Milwaukee's Progress in 1940*, p. 105; *Municipal Government and Activities . . . 1922*, p. 69.

the public schools; and with the support of the incumbent Socialist city administration, the program was inaugurated under the pioneering leadership of Harold O. Berg, Dorothy Enderis, who succeeded him as director in 1920, L. H. Kottnauer, and Robert Witt. By 1912, four social centers had been established in underprivileged districts and the foundations laid for a program that expanded until by 1940 more than thirty such centers were offering leisure-time activities in fields ranging from cooking, chorus, and cabinetmaking to courses in home nursing, short-wave radio, and parliamentary law. Meanwhile, federal aid projects had speeded the development of a program for expanding recreation facilities, adopted in 1928, which contemplated the achievement of 112 play areas throughout the city. By 1940, civic support for Milwaukee's 52 supervised playgrounds, 20 athletic fields, and 32 social centers attested the city's confidence in municipal recreation as a preventative for urban crime.[38]

Unfortunately, the steady advance in the provision of urban services during the generation was not duplicated in the field of city charter reform, due to forces in part outside the city administration's control. Although home rule was achieved in 1924, all attempts at a renovation of the city's charter were blocked by the action of the State legislature; and as late as 1940, the city was still operating under the long obsolescent charter of 1874. Legislation in 1911 conferring powers of self-government on cities was negated by the supreme court as an undue delegation of legislative power; and a subsequent home-rule amendment, though approved in Milwaukee, lost in a State referendum in 1914. At last, in 1924, the State constitution was successfully amended so as to empower cities and villages "to determine their local affairs and government, subject

---

[38] It was estimated in the middle thirties that Milwaukee was "spending three times as much per capita as New York City in maintaining playgrounds, social centers, public parks, and other preventive measures; New York was spending eight times as much per capita for police and court maintenance." Milwaukee *Sentinel*, July 14, 1937; Milwaukee *Journal*, March 28, 1937; Nov. 16, 1924; "Social Center Movement in Milwaukee," MS, n.d., in Milwaukee Municipal Reference Library; Hoan, *City Government*, 286-90; *Municipal Government and Activities* . . . *1927*, p. 49; *Municipal Activities* . . . *1930*, p. 76; ibid. . . . *1932*, p. 65; *Milwaukee's Progress in 1940*, p. 59.

only to this constitution and to such enactments of the legislature of state-wide concern as shall with uniformity affect every city or every village." Thereafter, the legislature could interfere with Milwaukee's charter only by state-wide law, or by passing legislation of local concern which was optional with the city. Within the city, changes could be made by charter convention or by the enactment of charter ordinances which required a two-thirds vote in the council. Such ordinances could be initiated by 15 percent of the voters and were subject to popular referendum if 7 percent so desired.

Home rule, however, was an empty victory for the proponents of thorough-going charter reform. At the suggestion of the Citizens' Bureau, the City Charter League was organized in 1927 at a mass meeting called by the Civic Alliance, the League of Women Voters, and the Citizenship Division of the Federated Women's Clubs. A modernized charter, embodying the principles of a strong mayor, short ballot, proportional representation, and centralized administrative control, was formulated and presented to the electorate; but such comprehensive charter revision was effectively obstructed in the 1929 session of the legislature when a law was passed providing that ordinances accomplishing charter changes must specifically repeal all prior legislation affected by the change. Although this legislation was protested by the City Charter League, the City Club, and others on the ground that so complicated a requirement would make revision almost impossible, its support by twelve Nonpartisan aldermen won it the governor's approval. A bill amending the 1929 legislation so as to except complete revision from the law was supported in 1931 by the council, the mayor, the Socialist assemblymen, and numerous citizens groups; but it failed of passage in the legislature; and thus the 1929 legislation continued to stand in the way of such attempts as were made between the early thirties and 1940 to bring the city's charter up to date.[39]

[39] "History of the Milwaukee City Charter," MS, n.d., in Milwaukee Municipal Reference Library, 3-10; *Municipal Government and Activities . . . 1925*, p. 3. The legislation of 1929 imposed a definite barrier to the adoption of a new charter by requiring that a new charter must designate specifically the parts of the mass of law comprising the Milwaukee charter which were amended or

A similar pattern of citizen support and legislative opposition characterized the movement for city-county consolidation, which, though proposed as early as 1870, had not been realized by 1940. For reasons of efficiency, the relief of urban congestion, and city promotion, the municipal administration undertook a program of annexation in 1922 which by 1933 had increased the area of the city from about 26 to 44 square miles. But as late as 1940, eighteen communities, including Wauwatosa, Shorewood, West Allis, and Cudahy, though within the county, still lay outside the annexed area. The logic of consolidation was demonstrated not only in the overlapping of city and county functions but also in the fact that as more of the city's workers moved their residences to the suburbs, the outlying communities became an increasingly integral part of the greater city. As early as 1906 to 1908, such citizens organizations as the Greater Milwaukee Association, the Westminster Civic League, and the Merchants' and Manufacturers' Association endorsed the reform; by the middle twenties Mayor Hoan, the City Club, and the Citizens' Bureau were advocating the change; and prompted by the concern for economy during the depressed thirties, a renewed movement for consolidation was launched by both the Socialists and the Nonpartisans in the city hall, together with some fifty civic groups through whose efforts the Citizens' Joint Committee on Consolidation was organized in 1934. In that year, a committee including fifteen citizens appointed by the common council and fifteen chosen by the county board undertook to study the question of consolidation; and in an ensuing advisory referendum, which they recommended, the principle of consolidation was supported by large majorities in both the city and county vote.[40]

repealed. Such a requirement presented an almost impossible task and made any new instrument vulnerable to invalidation by the courts should any amendment or repeal be omitted. *Wisconsin Session Laws,* 1929, chap. 267.

[40] In arguing for annexation, Milwaukee's promoters held: "Metropolitan Milwaukee is really one city and should be given credit for the entire population rather than merely for that part which is included within its corporate city limits. . . . The larger the population, the easier it is to attract new industrial and commercial establishments, conventions, . . . headquarters of national organizations, etc." Theodore E. Whiting, The Theory of Public Works Control Applied to the City of Milwaukee, p. 20, MS, M.A. thesis, dated 1931, University of Wisconsin; *Free Press* (Milwaukee), Oct. 10, 1906; Milwaukee *Sentinel,* Nov. 9,

The legislature, however, lent a more willing ear to the opinions of the county and suburban officials whose positions would be affected and to the suburban opponents of consolidation, especially in Wauwatosa and West Allis, who likened Milwaukee to "the big snake that eats the little snakes" and accused the "big city" of trying to "make the man living in the small house move in with the man in the big house to help pay the rent." Even the Socialists, perhaps skeptical of the effect of consolidation on their current strength in city politics, cooled toward the change; and as a result, legislative measures to implement what the city had endorsed failed to pass in 1935 and again in 1937. During the later thirties, the issue became a subject of contest between Mayor Hoan and the Socialists, on the one hand, and citizens groups backed by the *Journal*, on the other. With an eye to tax reduction, the latter group favored the transfer of departments to the county board, whenever possible, as in proposals to relinquish control of the health department to the county and merge the city, suburban, and county parks. To such piecemeal mergers the Socialists remained resolutely opposed, arguing that partial consolidation would diminish the prestige of the city government and might obstruct the "final consummation of one unified government for Milwaukee under a modernized charter." As a result of these conflicts, the only mergers accomplished by 1940 were the consolidation of the city and county park systems and the merger of the park police with the city force on January 1, 1937.[41]

1906; Merchants' and Manufacturers' Association (Milwaukee), *Bulletin*, November 1908; Milwaukee *Leader*, Oct. 4, 1932; Jan. 27, 31, 1934; *Wisconsin News*, June 9, 1924; Milwaukee *Journal*, Aug. 10, 1925; July 17, 1932; Aug. 15, 1933; Feb. 14, Aug. 12, 1934; "City County Consolidation," MS in Milwaukee Municipal Reference Library; *Municipal Activities . . . 1934*, pp. 20-21; *Metropolitan Milwaukee . . . A Study of Economic Unity and Political Decentralization*, directed by Paula Lynagh and submitted by Joint Committee on Consolidation in Milwaukee County (Milwaukee, 1936); Werba and Grunwald, *Making Milwaukee Mightier*. See also *Proposed Constitutional Amendments to Permit Milwaukee City-County Consolidation*, prepared by Citizens' Governmental Research Bureau (dittoed, Milwaukee, 1947). For a graphic representation of the expansion of the city through annexation, see map in appendix entitled, "Composite Map, City of Milwaukee, Showing Growth, 1846-1940."

[41] "Record of the Wisconsin Legislature on Consolidation," typescript, dated 1934, prepared by Milwaukee Municipal Reference Library; Milwaukee *Sentinel*,

BY THE LATE 1930's both Milwaukee and Wisconsin were celebrating the century that had passed since the beginning of the territory and the lake shore village at the river's mouth; and the reluctance of the satellite communities to join the central city did not impair its people's pride in what had been accomplished in a meager hundred years.[42] From a nucleus of tiny, speculative townsites, centering upon the river's bend, had risen a metropolis whose central city occupied some 44 square miles and housed well over half a million souls. Eight hundred miles of streets extended highways arduously begun in village days; and 18,000 lighting units gave a kind of street illumination of which the early settlers scarcely dreamed. A police force numbering 1,200 men supplied a guarantee of public order which the town constables of the village period could ill insure; and professional firemen, 800 strong, replaced the volunteers who fought the frequent fires of early days. Traversing the experience of many another city in the nation, by 1940 Milwaukee had evolved from a simple village community whose yearly expenditures hardly approximated $5,000 to a metropolis whose annual budget totaled more than $30,000,000. Its administrative personnel, once frequently rotated among the commercial and professional leaders of the community, now comprised career-specialists in cost accounting, sanitary engineering, crime detection, city planning, and public health. And whereas the municipality formerly had furnished only the rudimentary guarantees of community welfare and public order, it now supplied the child welfare clinics, water purification, electrical traffic control, immunization against disease, and radio techniques for combating crime which suggest the scientific, highly technical, and professionally specialized public services of the mature metropolis.[43]

Dec. 29, 1934; March 13, 1935; Feb. 25, 1937; Milwaukee *Leader*, Jan. 14, March 14, 1935; Jan. 14, 1936; *Wisconsin News*, March 28, 1935; Milwaukee *Journal*, Jan. 16, April 6, July 19, 1935; Jan. 15, Dec. 9, 1936; Feb. 12, Nov. 18, 1937; Wauwatosa *News*, Aug. 18, 1932; West Allis *Star*, Jan. 28, Feb. 25, Aug. 12, 1937; *Municipal Activities . . . 1935*, pp. 18-19; *ibid*. . . . *1936*, pp. 15-16; *Milwaukee, 1937*, pp. 11-14.

[42] For centennial editions, see *Wisconsin News*, July 16, 1936; Milwaukee *Sentinel*, July 14, 1937. See also *Official Program, Milwaukee Mid-Summer Festival, 1936*.

[43] For comparative statistics on the expansion of the city in area, services, and administrative personnel, see *City of Milwaukee General Statistics as of*

The physical and commercial expansion of this fast-growing community, though not unaffected by the resources of its hinterland, was primarily the product of promotion. The efforts of the pioneer speculators to attract settlers and business to the original townsites encouraged city growth, as did the promotional achievements of the railroad builders in succeeding years. The quest of individual industries for national markets made the city known; and organizations like the board of trade, the Merchants' Association, the Association of Commerce, and the city's own harbor commission sought to realize conditions through which the business community could expand. In the later nineteenth century, organized activity, supported by the press, was largely responsible for encouraging the flow of capital into manufacturing pursuits. As a result, by 1910 industry had come to be regarded as more significant than commerce to the city's growth; and indeed by 1940 manufacturing, especially of heavy machines, was the predominant activity in the diversified commercial-industrial economy of the mature community.

In its social pattern, twentieth-century Milwaukee showed more variety than did the largely Protestant Yorker-Yankee village of a hundred years before. German names, remnants of German architecture, the sturdy physique of the inhabitants, and the Germanic idiom of their speech still recalled the once self-contained *Deutsch-Athen* which by the nineties had lent a uniquely Teutonic quality to the urban scene. But the intensely Polish, Italian, or Negro constituency of whole sections of the twentieth-century city, like the multiplication of Catholic church spires in its skies, suggested the nationality and religious heterogeneity of the modern metropolis. More elaborate, too, was the cultural pattern of city life. The general practice of the village period gave way to specialization in the fields of medicine, merchandising, education, and the arts; and radio and motion pictures limited the personal performance of music and the drama, entertainment which reached a peak of merit previous to World War I. The advent of the specialist and the

December 31 [1921-46], compiled from the Common Council, *Annual Reports,* by Mrs. Paula Lynagh, Citizens' Governmental Research Bureau (dittoed, Milwaukee, 1947). For the chronological expansion of urban services in the city, see Citizens' Governmental Research Bureau, *Growth of Milwaukee's City Governmental Activities, 1846 to 1947, Inclusive.*

machine made further inroads on the city dweller's self-sufficiency of life; but like the development of streamlined transportation, by both rail and air, it shaped the city's culture ever closer to the nation's mold.

As in the promotion of its economic and cultural advance, individual and organized effort within the city, as well as forces operating from without, propelled Milwaukee toward the maturity which characterized its civic behavior after 1910. To be sure, the city was never a free agent politically: from territorial days to the twentieth century it was always subject to the will of the State legislature and affected by the play of politics in the territory and the State. The termination of construction on the Milwaukee and Rock River Canal, resulting from Doty's appointment as territorial governor, gave evidence of this dependence in village days. It was equally apparent in 1929 when the legislature, despite the home rule law of 1924, obstructed the community's expressed desire for charter change. The broad powers granted the aldermen at the outset of cityhood reflected the legislature's preference for the lawmaking arm; and as late as 1940, the municipal government was still hampered by a dispersion of executive authority which was in general more acceptable to the legislators of the State than to the citizens of its major city. This is not, however, to deny the salutary influence exerted by the State's more progressive lawmakers in supporting measures for municipal reform and providing the necessary legislative sanction for many of the activities which the city desired to undertake.

But in the main, the forces which generated Milwaukee's social progress lay within the community itself. Despite the final authority of the legislature in matters of structure and finance and indeed the inspiration derived from other urban centers in America and abroad, it was primarily civic-minded individuals, the press, and the numerous citizens organizations within the metropolis itself that promoted the city's ever-widening concern for the safety, health, and comfort of its people.[44] At the outset of cityhood, the provision of water,

---

[44] In view of allegations with respect to the reactionary influence of the

waste disposal, and library facilities was supplied through individual effort or voluntary subscription; and the need for fire and police protection, the abatement of nuisances, and the construction of streets and bridges brought only such inadequate responses as of necessity had been made a century earlier in the older cities of the Atlantic Coast. The expansion of these primary services, after the mid-century, was motivated as much by the desire to attract population and industry as by a concern for human welfare; but the broad elaboration of municipal activity which began shortly after the turn of the twentieth century attested the work of the reformers and reflected the awakening of a civic conscience which coincided both with the flowering of progressivism in national thought and with the increased influence of the working-class in city life. The problems of the depressed 1930's imposed further responsibilities upon the municipality; but in this crisis the city turned for relief, as never before, to the State and federal governments. It applied to the national scene the principle of social interdependence, long since accepted as a justification for municipal regulation and control, and charged the nation at large with responsibility for the well-being of the industrial—and hence the urban—economy. In these later years the emphasis was placed increasingly upon administration—not only in the provision of additional services but in the improvement of techniques by which older ones could be supplied more effectively, more efficiently, and, if possible, at smaller cost. Thus, brighter and more evenly distributed street lights were installed, the water supply was purified, sewage was more adequately treated, the public debt was amortized, garbage collection was improved through introducing motorized equipment, and increasingly scientific methods were applied to crime detection and provisions for the public health.[45]

The expanding vigor of this municipal activity, together

press in many cities, it should be pointed out that as a general rule the Milwaukee newspapers played a significant role in promoting the city's growth and encouraging forward-looking solutions to the practical problems of urban life. On this point see Allen, *Our Fair City*, 12, 191.

[45] In 1941 it was estimated that the average house and lot in Milwaukee was assessed at $5,000. The city tax of $125.15, paid on this property, was distributed

with the continued endorsement of a Socialist mayor, gave rise to the popular impression that, to an extent not true of other large American cities, the government of twentieth-century Milwaukee was "socialistic." Actually, despite the twenty-four-year incumbency of Mayor Hoan, the Socialists had really dependable control of the city for only one two-year term. Moreover, as late as 1940, the Wisconsin metropolis had encroached far less directly upon individual enterprise in the fields of public utilities and public entertainment than had such cities as Detroit, Cleveland, San Francisco, and New York. Unhappily, this popular preoccupation with the city's "socialism" tended to obscure more fundamental aspects of the urban scene. For the real merit of Milwaukee's government lay less in the magnitude of its activity than in the integrity which characterized its administration; and the city's chief claim to distinction lay less in the political philosophy of its people than in their practical and honestly managed solutions to the problems of urban living and in their generally prosperous, progressive, and law-abiding way of life.

In accounting for these really significant attributes of the urban society, many factors must be recalled:[46] the abundant as follows:

Department	Amount	Department	Amount
Administration	$ 5.80	Harbor	$ .50
Police	11.20	Weights and Measures	.11
Fire	8.20	Public Health (General)	.10
Public Works (General)	2.33	Vital Statistics	.03
Street Construction	4.54	Child Welfare	.07
Street Sanitation	5.49	Field Nurses	.77
Lighting	2.66	School Hygiene	.36
Bridges, Buildings	3.07	Tuberculosis	.07
Sewers	2.40	Venereal Diseases	.03
Garbage	1.65	Health Centers	.03
Engineers	.65	Johnston Emergency	.30
Plumbing Inspection	.09	South View	.43
Equipment	.79	Laboratory	.11
Courts	.33	Food Inspection	.53
Forestry	.79	Education	43.93
Sewage Disposal	1.95	Library	1.71
City Planning	.26	Museum	1.24
Building Inspection	.55	Injuries and Pensions	4.40
Smoke and Boiler	.07	Debt Charges	17.61

These figures were drawn from *Milwaukee's Progress in 1940*, p. 73.

[46] "A city is like an individual. It is what it is because of its antecedents, its environment, its fixations." Allen, *Our Fair City*, 7.

resources of the hinterland and the early opportunities for growth coincident with the expansion of a nation on the march; the activities of the reformer-promoters whether as individuals or in church, civic, or commercial association; and the democratic temper of the political environment from the outset of villagehood, as well as the generally progressive atmosphere of the State of which the city is a part. To these must be added, with even greater emphasis than for many another American city, the contribution of the foreign-born. Their craftsmanship and industry stimulated the city's industrial advance, and their thrifty conservatism and loyalty as civil servants encouraged municipal honesty and effective administration. Moreover, the enthusiasm in some of their number for the ideal of a socially active government contributed to the receptiveness of the local community in this respect. And beyond the influence of the foreign-born was the play of twentieth-century politics. Not only did this bring about a mayoral tenure of sufficient length to assure a kind of executive leadership for which the charter failed to provide, but it presented the socially wholesome political situation in which two closely-matched partisan groupings were constantly compelled to vie for popular support.[47]

But implicit in all these factors is the force of the people themselves. They, in the last analysis, were responsible, both as individuals and in groups, for the economic progress and civic order of the city and the extensive services its government performed. There were, of course, the Byron Kilbourns and the Alexander Mitchells, whose dynamic ambitions for the commercial and financial development of young Milwaukee prompted their occasional defiance of legislative rule; the Increase Laphams and the Lydia Elys, whose enthusiasm for learning and the arts nurtured the refinements of life in a frequently unresponsive frontier scene; the Frederick Pabsts and the E. P. Allises, whose promotional drive sent the products of Milwau-

[47] According to Professor John M. Pfiffner, the administrative coordination provided by Mayor Hoan helps explain the fact that "during the last quarter century . . . Milwaukee has given the nation a splendid example of honest government based on competent administration, although that city has a very weak charter." See Pfiffner, *Municipal Administration*, 32-34. The conservative qualities of Milwaukee society, as well as other characteristics of the city, are discerningly described in Davis, "Milwaukee, Old Lady Thrift," in Allen, *Our Fair City*, 189-210.

kee industry around the globe; and the Francis Huebschmanns and the Daniel Hoans, through whose political leadership the municipal government was shaped to fit the realities of changing times. But such vigorous types were only in the van of the citizens themselves—the merchants, newspaper editors, professional men, civic agency representatives, clubwomen, volunteer firemen, policemen on the beat, career servants in the city hall, and members of the Young Men's Association, the labor unions, and the bundle brigade—whose political participation and personal promotion, to an extent not true in the national scene, made the twentieth-century city what it ultimately became. It is perhaps not without significance that the founding of the lake shore city coincided with the era of American democracy in which the common man first showed his power. Certainly the century of city building that followed bore witness to the contribution of the sovereign citizen in underwriting urban growth. And as the generation of the emerging metropolis gave way to one in which administration was the first concern, again it was the actions of the average man which lent a distinguishing integrity and geniality to the local scene and shaped the way of life which won Milwaukee fame.

Appendix: Tables and Maps

1. Total Population and Sex Distribution in Milwaukee and the State of Wisconsin, 1840 to 1940
2. Age Distribution in Milwaukee and the State of Wisconsin for Selected Decades, 1840 to 1940
3. Origins of the Native-born Population of Milwaukee Showing the States Most Numerously Represented, 1850 to 1940
4. Percentage of Foreign-born in Milwaukee, 1850 to 1940, Listed in the Order of Predominance of the Nationality Group
5. Establishments, Persons, and Capital Engaged in Industry in Milwaukee, 1860 to 1939
6. Occupational Distribution of the Population of Milwaukee, 1870 to 1940, Showing the Number of Persons per Thousand in the Population Engaged in Selected Occupations
7. Expenditures for Selected Urban Services in Milwaukee, 1861 to 1940
8. The Growth of Governmental Activities in Milwaukee, 1846 to 1940
9. Presidential Vote in Milwaukee County Compared with That in the Remainder of the State of Wisconsin, 1848 to 1940
10. The Growth of Milwaukee, 1846 to 1940: a Series of Maps Showing the Expansion of the City through Annexation, the Evolution of the Ward Structure, and the Milwaukee Metropolitan Area

TABLE 1.—TOTAL POPULATION AND SEX DISTRIBUT

TOTAL POPULATION AND

	1840		1850		1860		1870		1880	
	NUMBER	PER-CENT	NUMBER	PER-CENT	NUMBER	PER-CENT	NUMBER	PER-CENT	NUMBER	C
Male	974	56.9	10,490	52.3	22,398	49.5	35,275	49.4		
Female	738	43.1	9,571	47.7	22,848	50.5	36,165	50.6		
Total	1,712		20,061		45,246		71,440		115,587	
Percentage of increase over preceding decade			1,071.8		125.5		57.9		61.8	

TOTAL POPULATION AND S

	1840		1850		1860		1870		1880	
	NUMBER	PER-CENT	NUMBER	PER-CENT	NUMBER	PER-CENT	NUMBER	PER-CENT	NUMBER	CF
Male	18,862	61.0	164,716	53.9	407,449	52.5	544,886	51.7	680,069	5
Female	12,083	39.0	140,675	46.1	368,432	47.5	509,784	48.3	635,428	4
Total	30,945		305,391		775,881		1,054,670		1,315,497	
Percentage of increase over preceding decade			886.9		154.1		35.9		24.7	

[1] EXPLANATORY NOTES: [a] U. S. Census, Tenth, 1880, Population gives no breakdown by sex for citie [b] These figures deviate from original figures given in the census for 1890 because of the inclusion population (6,450) of Indian reservations specially enumerated.

SOURCES: U. S. Census, Thirteenth, 1910, Population, 3:1048; U. S. Census, Sixth, 1840, Compendium 92-94; U. S. Census, Seventh, 1850, p. 922; U. S. Census, Eighth, 1860, Population, 530-32, 539; U. S. Ce sus, Ninth, 1870, vol. 1, Population, 606, 638, 656; U. S. Census, Tenth, 1880, Population, 642-43; U.

APPENDIX

MILWAUKEE AND STATE OF WISCONSIN, 1840 TO 1940[1]

[DI]STRIBUTION IN MILWAUKEE

	1890		1900		1910		1920		1930		1940	
[NU]MBER	PER-CENT	NUMBER	PER-CENT	NUMBER	PER-CENT	NUMBER	PER-CENT	NUMBER	PER-CENT	NUMBER	PER-CENT
[1]00,773	49.3	140,536	49.3	189,488	50.7	228,614	50.0	290,648	50.3	289,118	49.2
[1]03,695	50.7	144,779	50.7	184,369	49.3	228,533	50.0	287,601	49.7	298,354	50.8
[2]04,468		285,315		373,857		457,147		578,249		587,472	
76.9		39.5		31.0		22.3		26.5		1.6	

[DI]STRIBUTION IN WISCONSIN

	1890[b]		1900		1910		1920		1930		1940	
[NU]MBER	PER-CENT	NUMBER	PER-CENT	NUMBER	PER-CENT	NUMBER	PER-CENT	NUMBER	PER-CENT	NUMBER	PER-CENT
[6]78,238	51.9	1,067,562	51.6	1,208,578	51.8	1,356,718	51.5	1,510,815	51.4	1,600,176	51.0
[6]15,092	48.1	1,001,480	48.4	1,125,282	48.2	1,275,349	48.5	1,428,191	48.6	1,537,411	49.0
[1,2]93,330		2,069,042		2,333,860		2,632,067		2,939,006		3,137,587	
28.7		22.2		12.8		12.8		11.7		6.8	

[Ce]nsus, Tenth, 1880, *Compendium*, pt. 1, pp. 327, 605; *U. S. Census, Eleventh*, 1890, *Compendium*, [pt]. 1, *Population*, 471, 579, 662-63; *U. S. Census, Twelfth*, 1900, vol. 1, *Population*, pt. 1, pp. xcii, [xci]4; *U. S. Census, Thirteenth*, 1910, *Population*, 3:1048, 1076, 1101; *U. S. Census, Fourteenth*, 1920, [P]*opulation*, 2:282, 360; *U. S. Census, Fifteenth*, 1930, *Abstract*, 195, 210; *U. S. Census, Fifteenth*, [19]30, *Population*, 1:1179-80; *U. S. Census, Sixteenth*, 1940, *Population*, 1:1162; *U. S. Census, [Si]xteenth*, 1940, *Population*, vol. 2, pt. 1, p. 134; *U. S. Census, Sixteenth*, 1940, *Population*, [vo]l. 4, pt. 4, p. 853.

TABLE 2.—AGE DISTRIBUTION IN MILWAUKEE AND STATE

AGE GROUP	1840 NUMBER	1840 PERCENT	1870 NUMBER	1870 PERCENT	1900 NUMBER	1900 PERCENT	1910 NUMBER	1910 PERCENT
Under 5	5,155	16.7			256,734	12.4	256,171	11.0
5–9	3,485	11.3			251,152	12.1	247,878	10.6
10–14	2,592	8.4	354,016[h]	33.6	232,112	11.2	246,154	10.5
15–19	2,544	8.2			208,938	10.1	242,671	10.4
20–24	9,041[a]	29.2			182,253	8.8	222,097	9.5
25–29			371,331[i]	35.2	159,833	7.7	355,897[n]	15.2
30–34	4,771[b]	15.4			144,803	7.0		
35–39					253,424[j]	12.2	281,632[j]	12.1
40–44	1,803[c]	5.8						
45–49					165,353[k]	8.0		
50–54	914[d]	3.0					360,363[p]	15.4
55–59					108,492[l]	5.2		
60–64	329[e]	1.1						
65–69					103,192[m]	5.0	118,637[m]	5.1
70–74	115[f]	.4						
75 and over								
Unknown	196[g]	.6	329,323	31.2	2,756	.1	2,360	.1
TOTALS	30,945	100.1	1,054,670	100.0	2,069,042	99.8	2,333,860	99.9

AGE DISTRIBUTION

AGE GROUP	1840 NUMBER	1840 PERCENT	1870 NUMBER	1870 PERCENT	1900 NUMBER	1900 PERCENT	1910 NUMBER	1910 PERCENT
Under 5	302	17.6			34,971	12.3	37,834	10.1
5–9	191	11.2			33,988	11.9	33,721	9.0
10–14	116	6.8	22,225[h]	31.1	30,455	10.7	35,320	9.4
15–19	149	8.7			28,642	10.0	38,520	10.3
20–24	512[a]	29.9			28,067	9.8	42,531	11.4
25–29					25,099	8.8	70,025[n]	18.7
30–34	267[b]	15.6	27,353[i]	38.3	22,568	7.9		
35–39					37,518[j]	13.1	48,808[j]	13.1
40–44	100[c]	5.8						
45–49					21,918[k]	7.7		
50–54	38[d]	2.2					53,718[p]	14.4
55–59					12,090[l]	4.2		
60–64	12[e]	.7						
65–69								
70–74	3[f]	.2			9,655[m]	3.4	12,756[m]	3.4
75 and over								
Unknown	22[g]	1.3	21,862	30.6	344	.1	624	.2
TOTALS	1,712	100.0	71,440	100.0	285,315	100.0	373,857	100.0

EXPLANATORY NOTES:
[a] Aged 20 and under 30
[b] Aged 30 and under 40
[c] Aged 40 and under 50
[d] Aged 50 and under 60
[e] Aged 60 and under 70
[f] Aged 70 and over
[g] Includes all colored residents for this census
[h] Aged 5 to 18
[i] Aged 18 to 45 (estimate)
[j] Aged 35 to 44
[k] Aged 45 to 54
[l] Aged 55 to 64
[m] Aged 65 and over
[n] Aged 25 to 34
[p] Aged 45 to 64

OF WISCONSIN FOR SELECTED DECADES, 1840 TO 1940

STATE OF WISCONSIN

1920		1930		1940		
NUMBER	PERCENT	NUMBER	PERCENT	NUMBER	PERCENT	AGE GROUP
285,042	10.8	271,360	9.2	253,780	8.1	Under 5
277,458	10.5	291,222	9.9	253,205	8.1	5–9
259,707	9.9	286,477	9.7	275,247	8.8	10–14
238,132	9.0	271,427	9.2	284,805	9.1	15–19
228,384	8.7	244,104	8.3	261,805	8.3	20–24
222,623	8.5	225,333	7.7	249,595	8.0	25–29
200,986	7.6	217,286	7.4	232,329	7.4	30–34
182,980	7.0	217,780	7.4	219,470	7.0	35–39
152,228	5.8	194,881	6.6	210,702	6.7	40–44
137,384	5.2	168,758	5.7	203,747	6.5	45–49
119,390	4.5	142,987	4.9	182,552	5.8	50–54
100,992	3.8	115,965	3.9	148,365	4.7	55–59
83,500	3.2	97,731	3.3	119,803	3.8	60–64
57,931	2.2	79,947	2.7	95,081	3.0	65–69
38,380	1.5	57,178	1.9	68,705	2.2	70–74
44,095	1.7	54,934	1.9	78,396	2.5	75 and over
2,855	.1	1,636	.1			Unknown
2,632,067	100.0	2,939,006	99.8	3,137,587	100.0	TOTALS

IN MILWAUKEE

45,889	10.0	47,347	8.2	39,494	6.7	Under 5
43,256	9.5	48,613	8.4	39,811	6.8	5–9
37,979	8.3	47,738	8.3	44,820	7.6	10–14
37,052	8.1	50,266	8.7	48,155	8.2	15–19
44,781	9.8	56,982	9.9	51,452	8.8	20–24
47,421	10.4	55,865	9.7	52,473	8.9	25–29
42,448	9.3	51,058	8.8	49,735	8.5	30–34
36,918	8.1	49,136	8.5	47,322	8.1	35–39
29,243	6.4	42,216	7.3	44,922	7.6	40–44
24,423	5.3	34,830	6.0	43,099	7.3	45–49
20,575	4.5	28,442	4.9	37,819	6.4	50–54
16,093	3.5	20,641	3.6	28,833	4.9	55–59
12,822	2.8	16,539	2.9	22,089	3.8	60–64
8,121	1.8	12,597	2.2	15,894	2.7	65–69
4,865	1.1	8,475	1.5	10,746	1.8	70–74
4,821	1.1	7,191	1.2	10,808	1.8	75 and over
440	.1	313	.1			Unknown
457,147	100.1	578,249	100.2	587,472	99.9	TOTALS

SOURCES: *U. S. Census, Sixth*, 1840, *Compendium of the Enumeration of the Inhabitants and Statistics of the United States*, 92-94; *U. S. Census, Ninth*, 1870, vol. 1, *Population*, 638, 656; *U. S. Census, Twelfth*, 1900, vol. 2, *Population*, pt. 2, pp. 106-7, 136; *U. S. Census, Thirteenth*, 1910, *Population*, 3:1076, 1078; *U. S. Census, Fourteenth*, 1920, *Population*, 2:282-83, 360; *U. S. Census, Fifteenth*, 1930, *Abstract*, 195, 210; *U. S. Census, Sixteenth*, 1940, *Population*, vol. 2, pt. 1, pp. 65, 134.

TABLE 3.—ORIGINS OF NATIVE-BORN POPULATION OF MILWAUKEE

CENSUS	PER-CENT								PERCENTAGE OF TOTAL				
1850	36	Wis.	13	N.Y.	11	Mass.	1.7	Ohio	1.7	Pa.	1.6	Conn.	1.5
1860	50	Figures not available.											
1870	53	Wis.	40	N.Y.	5.8	Mass.	1.1	Ohio	.88	Pa.	.82	Ill.	.6
1880	60	Wis.	50	N.Y.	3.9	Ill.	1.1	Ohio	.71	Pa.	.66	Mass.	.6
1890	61	Wis.	52	N.Y.	2.3	Ill.	1.1	Ohio	.64	Mich.	.59	Pa.	.5
1900	69	Wis.	59	N.Y.	1.8	Ill.	1.7	Mich.	1.2	Ohio	.70	Pa.	.5
1910	70	Wis.	61	Ill.	1.9	Mich.	1.4	N.Y.	1.4	Ohio	.73	Pa.	.6
1920	76	Wis.	64	Ill.	2.3	Mich.	1.8	N.Y.	1.1	Minn.	.69	Pa.	.6
1930	81	Wis.	69	Ill.	2.8	Mich.	2.4	Minn.	2	Iowa	1.1	N.Y.	.8
1940	88	Wis.	72	Ill.	2.8	Mich.	2.2	Minn.	1.7	Iowa	1.1	N.Y.	.6

SOURCES: DeBow, *Compendium of the Seventh Census*, 399; *U. S. Census, Ninth*, 1870, vol. Population, 380-85; *U. S. Census, Tenth*, 1880, Population, 536-37; *U. S. Census, Eleventh*, 1890 Population, pt. 1, pp. 670-73; *U. S. Census, Twelfth*, 1900, vol. 1, Population, pt. 1, pp. 710-13

TABLE 4.—PERCENTAGE OF FOREIGN-BORN IN MILWAUKEE, 1850 TO 1940

CENSUS	PER-CENT								PERCENTAGE OF TOTAL				
1850	64	Ger.	38ᵃ	Ire.	14	Eng.	7.2ᵇ	Fr.	.64				
1860	50	Ger.	35	Ire.	7	Brit.	4	Br.-A.	1.1	Fr.	.32	Other	3.3
1870	47	Ger.	32	Brit. / Ire.	8	Boh.	2	Br.-A.	1.1	Hol.	1	Aus.	.80
1880	40	Ger.	27	Ire.	3.2	Brit.	2	Pol.	1.5	Boh.	1.3	Nor.	.89
1890	39	Ger.	27	Pol.	4.5	Ire.	1.7	Brit.	1.7	Nor.	.89	Boh.	.71
1900	31	Ger.	19	Pol.	6	Brit.	1	Ire.	.93	Br.-A.	.66	Boh.	.60
1910	30	Ger.	17ᶜ	Rus.	3.2ᶜ	Aus.	3ᶜ	Hung.	1.4	It.	.90	Brit.	.72
1920	24	Ger.	8.7	Pol.	5	Rus.	1.6	Aus.	1.2	Hung.	1	Cze.	.98
1930	19	Ger.	7.2	Pol.	3.4	Rus.	1.2	Aus.	1	Jug.	.98	It.	.86
1940	14	Ger.	4.8	Pol.	2.5	Aus.	1.13	Rus.	1.12	It.	.74	Jug.	.62

[1] EXPLANATORY NOTES: ᵃ Includes Prussians and Austrians; ᵇ Includes Welsh and Scotch; ᶜ Includes Poles. Key to abbreviations:

Aus.	Austria	Cze.	Czecho-Slovakia	Hol.	Holland	Nor.	Norway
Boh.	Bohemia	Eng.	England	Hung.	Hungary	Pol.	Poland
Brit.	Britain	Fr.	France	Ire.	Ireland	Rus.	Russia
Br.-A.	British America	Ger.	Germany	It.	Italy	Swd.	Sweden
Can.	Canada	Grc.	Greece	Jug.	Jugo-Slavia	Sws.	Switzerland

APPENDIX   575

...OWING STATES MOST NUMEROUSLY REPRESENTED, 1850 TO 1940

OPULATION OF CITY															
. 1.1	Me.	.78	Mich.	.61	Ill.	.45	N.H.	.41	N.J.	.40					
. .58	Conn.	.53	Mich.	.53	Me.	.33	N.J.	.24	N.H.	.22					
ich. .57	Vt.	.35	Conn.	.27	Iowa	.22	Ind.	.19	Me.	.19					
inn. .50	Iowa	.38													
inn. .54	Iowa	.46	Ind.	.36	Mo.	.28									
hio .61	Iowa	.57	Ind.	.46	Mo.	.39									
a. .66	Ohio	.64	Ind.	.64	Mo.	.57	N.D.	.27	Neb.	.23	Ga.	.23	Ky.	.21	
a. .59	Ind.	.58	Ohio	.56	Mo.	.53	Ga.	.38	Tenn.	.32	N.D.	.31	Ark.	.29	

. S. Census, Thirteenth, 1910, Population, 1:773-79; U. S. Census, Fourteenth, 1920, Population, 671, 674, 677, 680; U. S. Census, Fifteenth, 1930, Population, vol. 3, pt. 2, p. 1338; U. S. Census, ixteenth, 1940, Population, State of Birth of the Native Population, 67-73.

...ISTED IN THE ORDER OF PREDOMINANCE OF THE NATIONALITY GROUP[1]

OPULATION OF CITY															
or. .73															
r.-A. .84	Aus.	.82	Hol.	.61	Sws.	.36									
r.-A. .61	Aus.	.45	Hol.	.34	Sws.	.29									
or. .60	Aus.	.57	Rus.	.40	It.	.25	Swd.	.23	Sws.	.23					
or. .57	Ire.	.52	Br.-A.	.50	Grc.	.29	Sws.	.22	Swd.	.21					
ug. .91	It.	.88	Brit.	.61	Br.-A.	.45	Nor.	.40	Grc.	.40	Ire.	.31			
ze. .76	Hung.	.65	Brit.	.47	Nor.	.33	Grc.	.25	Swd.	.21	Sws.	.19	Ire.	.18	
ung. .622	Cze.	.5	Brit.	.36	Can.	.3	Nor.	.25	Grc.	.23					

OURCES: DeBow, Compendium of the Seventh Census, 399; U. S. Census, Eighth, 1860, Population, xxii; U. S. Census, Ninth, 1870, vol. 1, Population, 386-91; U. S. Census, Tenth, 1880, Population, 38-39; U. S. Census, Eleventh, 1890, Population, pt. 1, pp. 580-83; U. S. Census, Twelfth, 1900, vol. 1, Population, pt. 1, pp. 800-803; U. S. Census, Thirteenth, 1910, Population, 1:824; U. S. Census, ourteenth, 1920, Population, 2:729-31; U. S. Census, Fifteenth, 1930, Population, 2:209-11; U. S. ensus, Sixteenth, 1940, Population, vol. 2, pt. 7, p. 683.

TABLE 5.—ESTABLISHMENTS, PERSONS, AND CAPITAL

	1860[a]	1870[a]	1880[b]	1890[b]	1900
Establishments	558	828	844	2,879	3,34
Average number wage earners	3,406[d]	8,433[e]	20,886[e]	38,850	48,32
Percent total population	7.5	11.8	18.1	19.	16.
Officials and clerks				4,573	4,35
Proprietors					
Salaried officials and clerks					
Wage earners:					
Males	3,110	7,197[b]	16,015[j]	30,593[b]	37,83
Females	296	660[b]	3,922[j]	7,478[b]	7,50
Youth		576	949	779	2,99
Wages:					
Officials and clerks				$ 3,909,456	$ 4,481,82
Officials					
Clerks					
Wage earners	$ 900,085	$ 3,409,172	$ 6,946,105	$ 16,737,261	$ 20,240,65
Capital employed	$ 2,990,170	$ 8,109,199	$ 18,766,914	$ 69,145,814	$ 110,363,85
Total value of product	$ 6,659,070	$ 18,798,122	$ 43,473,812	$ 97,503,951	$ 123,786,44

[1] EXPLANATORY NOTES:

[a] These figures are for Milwaukee County, but nearly all the manufacturing in the county was done in the city at these dates.

[b] From this date forward, the figures are for the city of Milwaukee only. These figures are somewhat misleading inasmuch as the census takers listed carpenters', milliners', and dress makers' shops as manufacturing establishments until 1904.

[c] From this census forward, figures from the above types of shops have been omitted.

[d] It is presumed that the designation "hands employed" means that officials and clerks have not been included in these figures. There is no reference to workers' age.

[e] According to the Census of 1870, "hands employed" does not include officials, clerks, etc.

[f] This figure does not include salaried officers.

[g] This figure does not include salaried officers or employees or non-manufacturing wage earners.

[h] Males above 16, females above 15.

[j] Males above 16, females above 16.

APPENDIX

NGAGED IN INDUSTRY IN MILWAUKEE, 1860 TO 1939[1]

1905c	1910	1919	1929	1939	
1,532	1,764	2,093	1,769	1,489	Establishments
43,540	64,212	84,222	94,873f	61,672g	Average number wage earners
	17.2	18.4	16.4	10.5	Percent total population
1,395	1,472	1,554			Officials and clerks Proprietors
5,106	7,959	15,691			Salaried officials and clerks
		84,222k	94,873	61,672	Wage earners:
33,202i	50,710i				Males
8,093i	10,927i				Females
2,245	2,575				Youth
					Wages:
5,869,500					Officials and clerks
	$ 4,028,382	$ 15,288,918			Officials
	$ 5,377,098	$ 15,521,087			Clerks
20,910,009	$ 31,436,626	$ 89,921,118	$ 136,775,336	$ 84,922,173	Wage earners
162,129,641	$ 219,391,145	$ 421,619,463	$ 361,052,449m	$ 220,238,347m	Capital employed
138,881,545	$ 208,323,630	$ 576,161,312	$ 700,760,456	$ 437,444,671	Total value of product

Taking a representative day, on which wage earners totaled 90,573, the distribution was 7,563 males over 16; 19,111 females over 16; and 3,899 youths.
Cost of materials, containers, fuel.

SOURCES: *U. S. Census, Seventh,* 1850, gives no information on manufacturing in the city. *U. S. Census, Eighth,* 1860, *Manufactures,* 649; *U. S. Census, Ninth,* 1870, vol. 3, *Statistics of Wealth and Industry,* 582; *U. S. Census, Eleventh,* 1890, *Manufacturing Industries in the United States,* pt. 2, pp. 334-37; *U. S. Census, Twelfth,* 1900, vol. 8, *Manufactures,* pt. 2, pp. 998-99; U. S. Census Office, *Special Reports,* 1905, *Manufactures,* pt. 2, pp. 1206-7; *U. S. Census, Thirteenth,* 1910, vol. 9, *Manufactures,* 1360-61; *U. S. Census, Fourteenth,* 1920, vol. 9, *Manufactures,* 1646-47; *U. S. Census, Fifteenth,* 1930, *Manufactures, 1929,* 3:562; *U. S. Census, Sixteenth,* 1940, *Manufactures, 1939,* 3:1083.

TABLE 6.—OCCUPATIONAL DISTRIBUTION OF POPULATION OF MILWAUKEE, 1870 TO 1940 SHOWING NUMBER PER THOUSAND IN POPULATION IN SELECTED OCCUPATIONS[1]

CENSUS	TOTAL	NO. PER 1,000	MALES	FEMALES	TOTAL	NO. PER 1,000	MALES	FEMALES	TOTAL	NO. PER 1,000	MALES	FEMALES
	ACTORS AND SHOWMEN				ARCHITECTS				ARTISTS, SCULPTORS, ART TEACHERS			
1870									47[a]	.7	30	17
1880												
1890												
1900	106	.4	106		350	1.2	350		97	.3	97	
1910												
1920	180	.4	180		179	.4	179		213	.5	213	
1930	279	.5	212	67	159	.2	159		516	.9	376	140
1940	205	.3	123	82	125	.2	125		450	.7	330	120
	MUSICIANS, MUSIC TEACHERS				LAWYERS[c]				CLERGYMEN			
1870	[b]				108	1.5	107	1	68	.95	68	
1880	175	1.5	118	57	154	1.3	154		80	.7	80	
1890	394	1.9	253	141	274	1.3	274					
1900	594	2.	336	258	450	1.6	450		237	.8	237	
1910	968	2.6	478	490	491	1.3	491					
1920	922	2.	443	479	587	1.3	587		327	.7	327	
1930	1,009	1.8	600	409	773	1.3	773		428	.7	428	
1940	742	1.3	430	312	903	1.5	885	18	461	.8	447	14
	PHYSICIANS, SURGEONS				DENTISTS				NURSES			
1870	84	1.2	84									
1880	141	1.2	137	4								
1890					37	.35	37					
1900	440	1.5	440		188	.7	188		188	.9		188
1910	551	1.5	551						564	2.		564
1920	614	1.3	614		385	.8	385		392	1.		392
1930	733	1.3	733		555	1.	555		873[d]	1.9		873
1940	782	1.3	739	43	445	.8	436	9	1,610[d]	2.8		1,610
									2,459[e]	4.2	38	2,421

[1] EXPLANATORY NOTES: The figures for the census years from 1870 through 1930 represent the total males and females ten years of age and over in selected groups of occupations; the listing for 1940 is of "employed persons (except on public emergency work)." The consistency and validity of the figures are somewhat minimized because of differences in definition used by the census takers from decade to decade. Gaps are explained by the absence of figures in the census compilation of selected industries.
[a] Includes teachers of painting, dancing, and music.
[b] Included in "artist" column.
[c] In certain years, this category was listed as including judges and justices.

578

CENSUS	TOTAL	NO. PER 1,000	MALES	FEMALES	TOTAL	NO. PER 1,000	MALES	FEMALES
		SCHOOL TEACHERS*f*				COLLEGE PROFESSORS		
1870	350	5.	97	253				
1880	523	4.5	147	376				
1890	1,002	4.9	237	765				
1900	1,595	5.6	340	1,255				
1910	1,771	4.8	*ff*	1,771				
1920	2,939	6.4	433	2,506	221	.3	142	79
1930	3,856	6.7	722	3,134	296	.5	198	98
1940	4,177	7.1	941	3,236				
		DEALERS (RETAIL)				DEALERS (WHOLESALE)		
1870								
1880	1,989*b*	8.5	1,905	84				
1890								
1900	3,417*i*	12.	3,417		367	1.3	367	
1910	5,809	15.5	5,264	545	396	1.1	396	
1920	6,570	14.4	5,896	674	543	1.2	543	
1930	9,027*j*	15.6	8,295	732	562	1.	562	
1940	5,658*k*	9.6	4,779	879	1,239	2.1	1,201	38
		CLERKS IN STORES				SALES PERSONS IN STORES		
1870	1,496*l*	20.9	1,430	66	1,075	5.3	737	338
1880	2,432	20.8	2,172	260	4,555	16.	2,846	1,709
1890					5,023	13.4	3,304	1,719
1900								
1910	3,575	9.6	1,896	1,679	7,071	15.5	4,407	2,664
1920	2,335	5.1	948	1,387	13,877	24.	9,686	4,191
1930								
1940	2,710	4.7	1,022	1,688	11,170	19.	4,999	6,171
		JOURNALISTS, WRITERS						
1870								
1880								
1890	23	.35	23					
1900	72	.6	70	2				
1910								
1920	212*g*	.75	212					
1930	297	.5	231	66				
1940	278	.5	206	72				
		BOOKKEEPERS, ACCOUNTANTS				STENOGRAPHERS		
1870								
1880								
1890								
1900	2,327	8.2	1,756	571	183	.9	271	183
1910	3,810	10.2	2,275	1,535	1,168	4.1	394	897
1920	5,477	12.2	2,837	2,640	2,930	7.8	307	2,536
1930					5,562	12.2	307	5,255
1940	4,900	8.5	1,653	3,247	7,475	12.9	178	7,297
					8,121	13.8	389	7,732

f Includes college faculties until census of 1920.
ff The census does not list the number of male teachers for this year.
g Includes literary and scientific writers.
b Includes dealers (wholesale).
i Does not include 249 female retail and wholesale dealers who are listed in this census.
j Includes managers and superintendents.
k Does not include eating and drinking places.
l Includes clerks, salesmen, and accountants.

TABLE 6.—OCCUPATIONAL DISTRIBUTION OF POPULATION OF MILWAUKEE, 1870 TO 1940 SHOWING NUMBER PER THOUSAND IN POPULATION IN SELECTED OCCUPATIONS *(continued)*

CENSUS	TOTAL	NO. PER 1,000	MALES	FEMALES	TOTAL	NO. PER 1,000	MALES	FEMALES	TOTAL	NO. PER 1,000	MALES	FEMALES
		TELEPHONE OPERATORS				FIREMEN				POLICEMEN		
1870												
1880												
1890												
1900	352m	1.2	224	128	458	1.2	458		474	1.3	474	
1910	524	1.4		524	517	1.1	517		579	1.3	579	
1920	1,347	2.9		1,347	768	1.3	768		1,054	1.8	1,054	
1930	1,986	3.4		1,986	750	1.3	750		1,247	2.1	1,247	15
1940	1,510	2.6	73	1,437					1,262			
		BLACKSMITHS				LAUNDERERS, LAUNDRESSES				LAUNDRY OPERATIVES		
1870	262	3.7	262		134	1.9		134				
1880	424	3.8	424		197	1.7	10	187				
1890	786	3.8	786		539	2.6		539				
1900	959	3.4	959		1,177	4.1		1,177	132	.46	132	
1910	1,159	3.1	1,159		1,108	3.		1,108	593	1.6		593
1920	1,134	2.8	1,134		917	2.		917	434	.9		434
1930	593	1.	593		372	.6		372	1,046	1.8		1,046
1940	431	.7	429	2	127	.2	12	115	1,148n	2.	216	932
		DRESSMAKERS, SEAMSTRESSES				TAILORS, TAILORESSES				MILLINERS, MILLINERY DEALERS		
1870	423o	5.9	1	422	822r	11.5	431	391	o			
1880	3,461p	29.9	885	2,576	p				p			
1890	3,422o	16.7		3,422	1,710	8.3	1,110	600	o			
1900	4,176	14.6		4,176	2,128	7.5	1,338	790	771	2.6		771
1910	3,641q	9.7		3,641	1,815	4.9	1,201	614	1,264	3.4		1,264
1920	1,446	3.2		1,446	1,470	3.2	1,047	423	707	1.5		707
1930	713	1.2		713	1,180	2.	972	208	441	.8		441
1940	905	1.5	9	896	699	1.2	603	96	119	.2	2	117

m Includes telegraph operators.
n Does not include proprietors.
o The "dressmaker" category includes milliners in 1870 and 1890.
p The "dressmaker" category includes tailors, dressmakers, and milliners in 1880.

CENSUS	TOTAL	NO. PER 1,000	MALES	FEMALES	TOTAL	NO. PER 1,000	MALES	FEMALES	TOTAL	NO. PER 1,000	MALES	FEMALES
		SERVANTS, WAITERS, WAITRESSES, AND HOUSEKEEPERS				BARBERS, HAIR-DRESSERS, AND MANICURISTS				BARTENDERS, SALOONKEEPERS		
1870	3,040*s*	42.1	546	2,494	67	.93	66	1				
1880	4,094*s*	35.1	517	3,577	216	1.9	196	20				
1890	6,207	30.	610	5,597	414	2.	414		572*t*	4.9	555	17
1900	7,621	26.7	834	6,787	727	2.6	658	69	260*u*	1.3	260	
1910	7,882	21.1	620	7,262	1,032	2.8	812	220	505*u*	1.8	505	
1920	7,014	15.3	994	6,020	1,032	2.3	853	179	2,125*t*	5.8	2,125	
1930	10,580	18.2	1,716	8,864	2,119	3.6	1,348	771	1,410*t*	3.	1,410	
1940	10,071	17.1	1,404	8,667	2,204	3.8	971	1,233	1,599	2.7	1,474	125

s Includes hotel and restaurant keepers and employees.
t Includes saloonkeepers.
u Does not include saloonkeepers.

SOURCES: U. S. Census, Ninth, 1870, vol. 1, Population, 789; U. S. Census, Tenth, 1880, Population, 789; U. S. Census, Eleventh, 1890, Population, 886; U. S. Census, Eleventh, 1890, Population, pt. 2, pp. 692-93; U. S. Census, Twelfth, 1900, Special Reports, Occupations, 608-13; U. S. Census, Thirteenth, 1910, vol. 4, Population, Occupation Statistics, 565-66; U. S. Census, Fourteenth, 1920, Population, Occupations, 4:1140-44; U. S. Census, Fifteenth, 1930, Population, 4:1771-73; U. S. Census, Sixteenth, 1940, Population, vol. 3, pt. 5, pp. 981-83.

TABLE 7.—EXPENDITURES FOR SELECTED URBAN SERVICES IN MILWAUKEE, 1861 TO 1940[1]

SERVICE	1861	PER CAPITA	1872	PER CAPITA	1881	PER CAPITA
Police	$ 13,123	$ .29	$ 37,791	$ .53	$ 77,780	$ .67
Fire	10,359	.23	76,672	1.07	101,037	.87
Health[a]			3,978	.06	7,837	.07
Sewers			69,820	.98	83,210	.72
Bridges and buildings[b]	9,860	.22	73,824	1.03	57,742	.50
School board—operation[c]	30,440	.67	143,414	2.01	249,418	2.16

SERVICE	1890	PER CAPITA	1899	PER CAPITA	1910	PER CAPITA
Police	$ 204,829	$ 1.00	$ 321,168	$ 1.13	$ 600,160	$ 1.61
Fire	296,888	1.45	380,310	1.33	757,875	2.03
Health[a]	56,950	.28	104,352	.37	226,159	.60
Sewers	301,383	1.47	202,527	.71	291,151	.78
Street sanitation					414,178	1.11
Garbage disposal[a]					146,342	.39
Street construction					901,637	2.41
Bridges and buildings[b]	81,441	.40	92,495	.32	421,446	1.13
Parks	84,208	.41	110,021	.39	190,037	.51
Public Museum					136,770	.37
School board—trades					105,520	.28
School board—repairs					125,350	.34
School board—operation[c]	696,266	3.41	791,957	2.78	1,482,789	3.97
Public Library					98,606	.26

SERVICE	1920	PER CAPITA	1930	PER CAPITA	1940	PER CAPITA
Police	$ 1,151,234	$ 2.52	$ 2,586,837	$ 4.47	$ 2,806,072	$ 4.78
Fire	1,291,162	2.82	1,965,601	3.40	1,982,474	3.37
Health	480,412	1.05	752,382	1.30	692,341	1.18
Sewers	80,877[d]	.18	263,272	.46	289,826	.49
Street sanitation	1,379,969	3.02	1,845,459	3.19	1,471,096	2.50
Garbage disposal			436,132	.75	419,591	.71
Street construction	649,137	1.42	411,559	.71	357,655	.61
Bridges and buildings[b]	618,540	1.35	1,238,410	2.14	702,567	1.20
Parks	554,325	1.21	832,151	1.44		
Public Museum	202,364	.44	318,532	.55	222,245	.38
School board—extension dept.	187,017	.41	538,404	.93	556,763	.95
School board—trades	219,889	.48	646,925	1.12	565,966	.96
School board—repairs	224,442	.49	1,007,935	1.74	769,679	1.31
School board—operation	3,335,893	7.30	7,104,932	12.29	7,459,374	12.70
Board of industrial education	422,508	.92	1,064,225	1.84	1,216,069	2.07
Public Library	209,838	.46	489,128	.85	424,294	.72

[1] EXPLANATORY NOTES:

[a] Garbage disposal costs are included under "Health," for 1890 and 1899.
[b] Expenditures for natatoria and maintenance of other public buildings are included under "Bridges and Buildings" after 1913.
[c] "School Board—Operation" includes all expenditures under heading "public schools" through 1900.
[d] The decreased cost under "Sewers" after 1910 is explained by the fact that expenditures for flushing stations apparently were not included after that date.

SOURCES: In assembling these data it has been difficult to obtain comparable figures because of variations over the years in methods of accounting. From 1861 through 1900 the figures were drawn from Larson, *Financial and Administrative History*, 163-66. Figures for street construction in 1910 were taken from Department of Public Works, *Annual Report* for year ending December 31, 1910, pp. 131-39. All remaining figures for 1910 were taken from Comptroller of the City of Milwaukee, *City Finances Report* for the fiscal year ending December 31, 1910. Figures for the period after 1913, at which time a new accounting system was installed by the city comptroller, were taken from the Annual Reports compiled by the Milwaukee Municipal Reference Library. Per capita figures have been calculated on the basis of city population at closest decennial census.

TABLE 8.—GROWTH OF GOVERNMENTAL ACTIVITIES IN MILWAUKEE, 1846 TO 1940[1]

ORDINANCES AUTHORIZING

1846

Legislation
Recording of proceedings
Publication of proceedings
Registration of chattel mortgages*
General administration by chief executive
Conduct of elections
Assessment of miscellaneous revenue
Assessment of property taxes
Special assessment for sidewalks
Special assessment for street opening and widening
Collection of miscellaneous revenue
Custody of funds
Disbursement of funds
Collection of property taxes
Legal advice
Attorney in litigation
Prosecution of ordinance violations
Platting
Establishment of street grades
Maintenance of general public structures
Operation of general public buildings
Adjudication of ordinance violations
Adjudication of felony violations
Organized foot patrol
Control of retail liquor dispensing
Enforcement of ordinances
Volunteer fire department
Fire prevention
Maintenance of fire station
Licensing trades and occupations
Maintenance of contagious disease hospitals
Board of health††

Sidewalk construction and maintenance
House numbering
Street opening and widening
Construction and maintenance of bridges
Outdoor relief*
Hospitalization of the sick poor*
Free medical service
Almshouse*
Elementary day school
School census
Operation of school buildings
Maintenance of school buildings
Examination of school teachers†
Regulation of commercial recreation
Harbor
Regulation of ferries

1847

Recording financial transactions
Approval of claims
Control of weights and measures
Provision of vaccination service
Public markets
Harbor lighthouse

1848

Special assessment for filling lots

1849

Codification of city ordinances
Special assessment for alleys
Special assessment for dock repairs
Maintenance of paved streets or highways
Care of dependent children*

[1] Citizens' Governmental Research Bureau, *The Growth of Milwaukee's City Governmental Activities, 1846 to 1947, Inclusive.* This compilation, prepared under the supervision of Mrs. Paula Lynagh, includes the services under the jurisdictions of the Milwaukee Common Council, Milwaukee Board of School Directors, and Milwaukee Board of Vocational and Adult Education. It does not include those services which are under the jurisdiction of the Milwaukee County Board of Supervisors. Symbols, as follows, have been used to indicate the disposition, by 1947, of activities originally assumed by the city: *, to county; †, to State; **, to private contract; ††, discontinued.

1850

1851

1852

Preservation of public documents
Special assessments for street paving
Description of property (metes and bounds)
Inspection of explosives
Hand street cleaning
Alley cleaning
Street lighting (gas)

1853

Street paving
Maintenance of paved streets or highways

1854

1855

Street name signs
Police station

1856

Dog pound**
Ward health officers

1857

Sanitary inspection
Maintenance of general hospital*
Prison for misdemeanants (jail)
High school

1858

Detectives

1859

1860

1861

Control of public debt

1862

1863

1864

Registration of voters

1865

1866

Meat inspection

1867

1868

Fire alarm system

1869

Special assessment for lateral sewers
Inspection of inflammables
Sewerage
Sewer maintenance
Sewer cleaning
Sewer design
Inspection of sewer construction
Sewage disposal

1870

1871

Full time fire department
Inspection of gas
Snow removal

1872

Quarantine of contagious diseases

1873

Ash collection

1874

Inspection of boilers
Repair of corporation cuts
Water supply
Water pumping
Water distribution
Water storage (reservoir)
Microscopy laboratory

1875

Licensing drain layers

1876

1877

Police ambulance service

1878

Pensions for firemen
Inspection of elevators

Garbage collection
Garbage disposal
Kindergarten
General library
Promotion of private recreation
Bathing beaches*

1879

Inspection of dairy farms

1880

Regulation of pawnbrokers
Elementary evening classes
Library reading rooms
Periodical library
Reference library

1881

1882

Pensions for policemen
Systematic control of recovered property
Call box
Police alarm system
Natural history museum
Industrial exhibits
Historical exhibits

1883

Research and publications (museum)
Water metering

1884

1885

Selection of police personnel by merit
Selection of fire personnel by merit
Classes for deaf and hard of hearing

1886

1887

Milk inspection
River flushing

1888

Regulation of employment agencies
Maintenance of emergency hospital
Inspection of applicants for liquor license

1889

Assessment of water mains
Fire boats
Sewer pumping
Public baths (natatoria)
Parks*

1890

High-school evening classes

1891

Library binding

1892

Elementary summer school
High-school summer classes

1893

Inspection of swimming pools
Recording of vital statistics
Maintenance of bacteriological laboratory
Maintenance of chemical laboratory
Water testing

1894

Boat wells

1895

Examination and certification of employees
Inspection of buildings and plans
Inspection of signs
Attendance and welfare officers

1896

Inspection of bakeries

1897

Bertillon identification
Inspection of plumbing
Fireboat signal system
Examination of plumbers
Free textbooks

1898

Children's library
Branch libraries
Civic library

APPENDIX 587

Technological library
Fine arts and music library
Band concerts
General food inspection

1899

Psychiatric examination of offenders
Conservatory*

1900

Animal exhibits
Free lectures (museum)
Field tours (museum)
Identification service (mushrooms, etc.)

1901

Literature and drama library

1902

Voting machines††
Medical services to police officers (police surgeon)
Traffic control
Free evening lectures (schools)
Street vendor records

1903

Inspection of maternity hospitals
Garbage incineration

1904

Smoke abatement
School lunches

1905

Library for blind
Skating rinks on vacant lots

1906

Inspection of electric wiring

1907

Preparation of legislative budget
Pensions for teachers
Special assessments for collection of ashes and rubbish††
Preparation of budget estimates

Fingerprint identification
Maintenance of tuberculosis hospitals*
Rubbish collection
Grade separation
Technical high school
Evening technical high school
Classes for the blind and defective of vision
Supervised playgrounds
Auditorium (municipal)

1908

Maintenance of municipal reference library
Ungraded classes

1909

Planning of public improvements
Medical inspection of school children
Mental inspection of school children
Provision of oral hygienist
School nurses (consolidated into general nursing staff, 1919)
Street oiling
Design of paving construction
Fresh air classes
Classes for anemic
Classes for defective of speech
Classes for teaching English
Community centers

1910

Centralized storehouse
Motorcycle patrol
Selective enforcement of traffic ordinance
Sunday library service
Symphony concerts*
Chlorination of water

1911

Election commission
Examining and licensing engineers
Fire and police alarm system
Workmen's compensation
Tuberculosis preventorium*
Maintenance of children's clinic
Provision of public health education

Street flushing
Comfort stations
Asphalt plant
School cost accounting

1912

Central registration of voters
Permanent registration
Testing of materials
Police recall lights
Provision of tuberculosis control
Provision for child welfare nurses
Pavement chemist
Employment bureau (joint)†
Gardening promotion
Continuation and adult education school (vocational)
Training library personnel
Library for foreign languages
Forestry
Water chemist (water department)

1913

Election booths
Continuous audit
Auto patrol
Inspection of fire escapes

1914

Medical service to firemen
Motorized fire engines
Motor street sweeping
Safety islands
Golf courses*

1915

Hearings in cases of discipline or removal of civil service employees
Traffic signs
Pulmotor
Fire prevention bureau
Sanding intersections
Classes for mental defectives
Classes for backward and retarded
Bedside instruction for crippled and sick
Library service to suburbs
Park nursery*

1916

Centralized maintenance of motor vehicles
Centralized dispatch of motor vehicles
Inspection of gasoline tanks for filling stations
Inspection of food handlers
Maintenance of tuberculosis diagnostic clinic
Pavement marking
Book deposits
Municipal street lighting distribution system

1917

Standardization of salaries
Special assessment for shade trees
Centralized purchasing
Motion picture censorship
Maintenance of serology laboratory

1918

Minimum wage
Exhibits of art

1919

River and harbor patrol
Maintenance of diagnostic clinic
Maintenance of venereal disease clinic
Provision of public health nurses
Promotion of athletics

1920

Regulation of zoning
Examination of electricians
Safety promotion
Provision of immunization against typhoid and diphtheria
Instructor at children's hospital

1921

Centralized sale of property
Centralized purchase of property
Police training school
Crime records (*modus operandi*)
Inspection of moral conditions (morals squad)
Inspection of oil burners
Inspection of oil tanks (fuel)
Maintenance of dental clinic
Provision of obstetrical nurses
Reading guidance

APPENDIX

1922

Consolidated annual report
Traffic lights
Women police
Operation of refuse dump
Educational research
School of art
Instruction in instrumental music
Hospital library service††
Tourist camp††
Outdoor dancing

1923

Promotion of annexation
Firemen's training school
Curb cuts
Refectories*

1924

Inspection of taxi meters
Junior high school
Pre-vocational schools
Garden homes

1925

Special assessment for tree borders††
Inspection and regulation of day nurseries
Examination of laborers

1926

Traffic police
Burglar alarm system
Vocational guidance
Radio in schools (sound amplification)
School stadium

1927

Auto pound
Super-lighting
Project classes for very young and backward children
Wild life refuge
Lake front air-strip (intermittent operation by city)

1928

Provision of social hygiene instructor
Home hygiene nurses
Nutrition classes
Classes for crippled children
Transportation for crippled children
Greenhouses
Regulation of air traffic

1929

Centralized hiring of motor trucks
Mounted police
Municipal open dock

1930

Publication of land value maps††
Investigation of delinquent taxes
Radio control of auto patrol
Inspection of refrigerators
Aviary*

1931

Radio control of motorcycles
Radio service to suburban police and sheriff
Eye, ear, nose, and throat clinic
Municipal carferry terminal

1932

Accident investigation car
High pressure water system
Provision of health centers
Open air swimming pool*

1933

Municipal mooring basin

1934

Immunization against scarlet fever
Open air opera
Unemployment compensation for city employees
Licensing and regulation of shooting galleries
Licensing and regulation of wholesale itinerant produce dealers

1935

Regulation of loading of volatile or inflammable liquids
Regulation of secondhand automobile and parts sales

Licensing and regulation of wholesale vendors of soda water
Regulation of dishwashing methods in public eating places

1936

City-county commission on crime
Regulation of auction sales of gold, silver, etc.
Regulation of exterminator business
Licensing and regulation of bicycles

1937

Low rental housing (U.S. owned)
Pensions for general employees
School board employees under civil service (other than teachers)
Junior College day classes (at Vocational School)

1938

Licensing of motorized sidewalk sweepers and plows
Collection of statistics on a census tract basis
Investigation of jurors by police department

1939

Adoption of minimum dwelling standards
Iron lung for infantile paralysis
Hearing tests for school children
Tax compromise board
Radio broadcasts by Library
Water filtration
Industrial hygiene (health department)

1940

Voluntary fingerprinting of school students

TABLE 9.—PRESIDENTIAL VOTE IN MILWAUKEE COUNTY COMPARED WITH THAT IN THE REMAINDER OF THE STATE OF WISCONSIN, 1848 TO 1940[1]

ELECTION	CANDIDATE	PARTY	MILWAUKEE COUNTY VOTE	PERCENT OF VOTE	WISCONSIN VOTE OUTSIDE MILWAUKEE COUNTY	PERCENT OF VOTE
1848	TAYLOR	Whig	1,190	29.99	12,557	35.68
	Cass	Democrat	2,151	54.21	12,850	36.51
	Van Buren	Free Soil	627	15.80	9,791	27.82
TOTAL			3,968		35,198	
1852	PIERCE	Democrat	3,640	58.85	30,018	51.32
	Scott	Whig	2,018	32.63	20,192	34.52
	Hale	Free Soil	527	8.52	8,287	14.17
TOTAL			6,185		58,497	
1856	Fremont	Republican	2,798	27.95	63,292	57.80
	BUCHANAN	Democrat	7,188	71.80	45,655	41.69
	Fillmore	American	25	.25	554	.51
TOTAL			10,011		109,501	
1860	LINCOLN	Republican	4,831	41.53	81,282	57.83
	Douglas	Democrat	6,726	57.82	58,295	41.48
	Breckinridge	Democrat	39	.34	849	.60
	Bell	Union	37	.32	124	.09
TOTAL			11,633		140,550	
1864	LINCOLN	Republican	3,175	31.59	60,283	50.53
	McClellan	Democrat	6,875	68.41	59,009	49.47
TOTAL			10,050		119,292	
1868	GRANT	Republican	6,101	40.20	102,756	57.60
	Seymour	Democrat	9,074	59.80	75,633	42.40
TOTAL			15,175		178,389	
1872	GRANT	Republican	5,834	40.67	99,160	55.98
	Greeley	Democrat and Liberal Rep.	8,512	59.33	77,965	44.02
TOTAL			14,346		177,125	
1876	HAYES	Republican	9,981	45.35	120,687	51.89
	Tilden	Democrat	12,026	54.65	111,901	48.11
TOTAL			22,007		232,588	

[1] Statistics for the elections of 1864 through 1936 were taken from the Wisconsin Blue Books. Data on the elections of 1848, 1852, 1856, 1860, and 1940 were supplied by the Division of Records and Elections of the State of Wisconsin. Minor candidates frequently have not been listed.

TABLE 9.—PRESIDENTIAL VOTE IN MILWAUKEE COUNTY COMPARED WITH THAT IN THE REMAINDER OF THE STATE OF WISCONSIN, 1848 TO 1940 *(continued)*

ELECTION	CANDIDATE	PARTY	MILWAUKEE COUNTY VOTE	PERCENT OF VOTE	WISCONSIN VOTE OUTSIDE MILWAUKEE COUNTY	PERCENT OF VOTE
1880	GARFIELD	Republican	14,088	55.99	130,310	53.88
	Hancock	Democrat	10,997	43.71	103,647	42.85
	Weaver	Greenback	76	.30	7,910	3.27
TOTAL			25,161		241,867	
1884	Blaine	Republican	16,841	49.17	144,316	50.52
	CLEVELAND	Democrat	16,290	47.56	130,187	45.58
	St. John	Prohibition	221	.65	7,435	2.60
	Butler	Greenback	901	2.63	3,697	1.29
TOTAL			34,253		285,635	
1888	HARRISON	Republican	21,394	49.15	155,159	49.88
	Cleveland	Democrat	17,302	39.75	137,930	44.34
	Fisk	Prohibition	339	.78	13,938	4.48
	Streeter	Union Labor	4,494	10.32	4,058	1.30
TOTAL			43,529		311,085	
1892	CLEVELAND	Democrat	24,607	48.23	152,718	47.64
	Harrison	Republican	24,602	48.23	146,499	45.70
	Weaver	People's	1,286	2.52	8,733	2.72
	Bidwell	Prohibition	513	1.01	12,623	3.94
TOTAL			51,008		320,573	
1896	Bryan	Democrat	26,536	41.24	138,987	36.28
	Levering	Prohibition	640	.99	6,867	1.79
	MCKINLEY	Republican	35,939	55.85	232,196	60.62
	Palmer	National Dem.	520	.81	4,064	1.06
	Bentley	National	30	.05	316	.08
	Matchett	Soc. Labor	679	1.06	635	.17
TOTAL			64,344		383,065	
1900	Bryan	Democrat	25,596	38.64	133,567	35.50
	Woolley	Prohibition	751	1.13	9,276	2.47
	MCKINLEY	Republican	34,790	52.52	230,970	61.39
	Debs	Soc. Dem.	4,874	7.36	2,174	.58
	Malloney	Soc. Labor	232	.35	271	.07
TOTAL			66,243		376,258	

APPENDIX 593

TABLE 9.—PRESIDENTIAL VOTE IN MILWAUKEE COUNTY COMPARED WITH THAT IN THE REMAINDER OF THE STATE OF WISCONSIN, 1848 TO 1940 *(continued)*

ELECTION	CANDIDATE	PARTY	MILWAUKEE COUNTY VOTE	PERCENT OF VOTE	WISCONSIN VOTE OUTSIDE MILWAUKEE COUNTY	PERCENT OF VOTE
1904	Parker	Democrat	18,560	26.32	105,547	28.33
	Swallow	Prohibition	934	1.32	8,836	2.37
	ROOSEVELT	Republican	32,587	46.22	247,577	66.46
	Debs	Socialist	18,340	26.01	9,880	2.65
	Watson	People's	30	.04	500	.13
	Corregan	Soc. Labor	61	.09	162	.04
TOTAL			70,512		372,502	
1908	Bryan	Democrat	26,000	35.40	140,632	36.72
	Chafin	Prohibition	1,278	1.74	10,286	2.69
	TAFT	Republican	28,625	38.97	221,122	57.74
	Debs	Socialist	17,496	23.82	10,668	2.79
	Gillhaus	Soc. Labor	57	.08	257	.07
TOTAL			73,456		382,965	
1912	WILSON	Democrat	27,628	38.75	136,602	41.56
	Chafin	Prohibition	536	.75	8,048	2.45
	Taft	Republican	17,877	25.07	112,719	34.30
	Debs	Socialist	19,243	26.99	14,233	4.33
	Roosevelt	Progressive	5,939	8.33	56,509	17.19
	Reimer	Independent (Soc. Labor)	79	.11	553	.17
TOTAL			71,302		328,664	
1916	WILSON	Democrat	34,812	43.51	156,551	42.64
	Hanly	Prohibition	425	.53	6,893	1.88
	Hughes	Republican	27,831	34.78	192,991	52.57
	Benson	Socialist	16,943	21.18	10,688	2.91
TOTAL			80,011		367,123	
1920	Cox	Democrat	25,464	17.89	87,958	15.74
	Watkins	Prohibition	523	.37	8,124	1.45
	HARDING	Republican	73,410	51.58	425,166	76.06
	Debs	Socialist	42,914	30.16	37,721	6.75
TOTAL			142,311		558,969	
1924	Davis	Democrat	14,510	9.80	53,586	7.81
	Faris	Prohibition	261	.18		
	COOLIDGE	Republican	50,730	34.27	260,884	38.00
	La Follette	Progressive	81,687	55.18	371,991	54.19
	Foster	Workers'	570	.39		
	Johns	Soc. Labor	206	.14		
TOTAL			147,964		686,461	

TABLE 9.—PRESIDENTIAL VOTE IN MILWAUKEE COUNTY COMPARED WITH THAT IN THE REMAINDER OF THE STATE OF WISCONSIN, 1848 TO 1940 *(continued)*

ELECTION	CANDIDATE	PARTY	MILWAUKEE COUNTY VOTE	PER-CENT OF VOTE	WISCONSIN VOTE OUTSIDE MILWAUKEE COUNTY	PER-CENT OF VOTE
1928	Smith	Democrat	110,668	53.66	339,591	47.39
	Varney	Prohibition	158	.08	2,087	.29
	HOOVER	Republican	82,025	39.77	368,234	51.38
	Thomas	Socialist	12,934	6.27	5,279	.74
	Foster	Workers'	327	.16	1,201	.17
	Reynolds	Labor	125	.06	258	.04
TOTAL			206,237		716,650	
1932	ROOSEVELT	Democrat	170,202	65.62	537,208	62.80
	Upshaw	Prohibition	157	.06	2,515	.29
	Hoover	Republican	54,693	21.09	293,048	34.26
	Thomas	Socialist	32,874	12.67	20,505	2.40
	Foster	Communist	1,242	.48	1,870	.22
	Reynolds	Soc. Labor	220	.08	274	.03
TOTAL			259,388		855,420	
1936	ROOSEVELT	Democrat	221,512	74.59	581,472	60.47
	Landon	Republican	54,811	18.46	326,017	33.90
	Browder	Communist	946	.32	1,251	.13
	Colvin	Prohibition	92	.03	976	.10
	Thomas	Socialist	6,311	2.13	4,315	.45
	Aiken	Soc. Labor	186	.06	371	.04
	Lemke	Union	13,100	4.41	47,197	4.91
TOTAL			296,958		961,599	
1940	ROOSEVELT	Democrat	209,861	59.76	494,960	46.94
	Willkie	Republican	131,120	37.33	548,086	52.00
	Thomas	Socialist	8,484	2.42	6,587	.62
	Browder	Communist	1,028	.29	1,366	.13
	Babson	Prohibition	225	.06	1,923	.18
	Aiken	Soc. Labor	479	.14	1,403	.13
TOTAL			351,197		1,054,343	

APPENDIX 595

10. THE GROWTH OF MILWAUKEE, 1846 TO 1940

A SERIES OF MAPS SHOWING THE EXPANSION OF THE CITY THROUGH ANNEXATION, THE
EVOLUTION OF THE WARD STRUCTURE, AND THE MILWAUKEE METROPOLITAN AREA

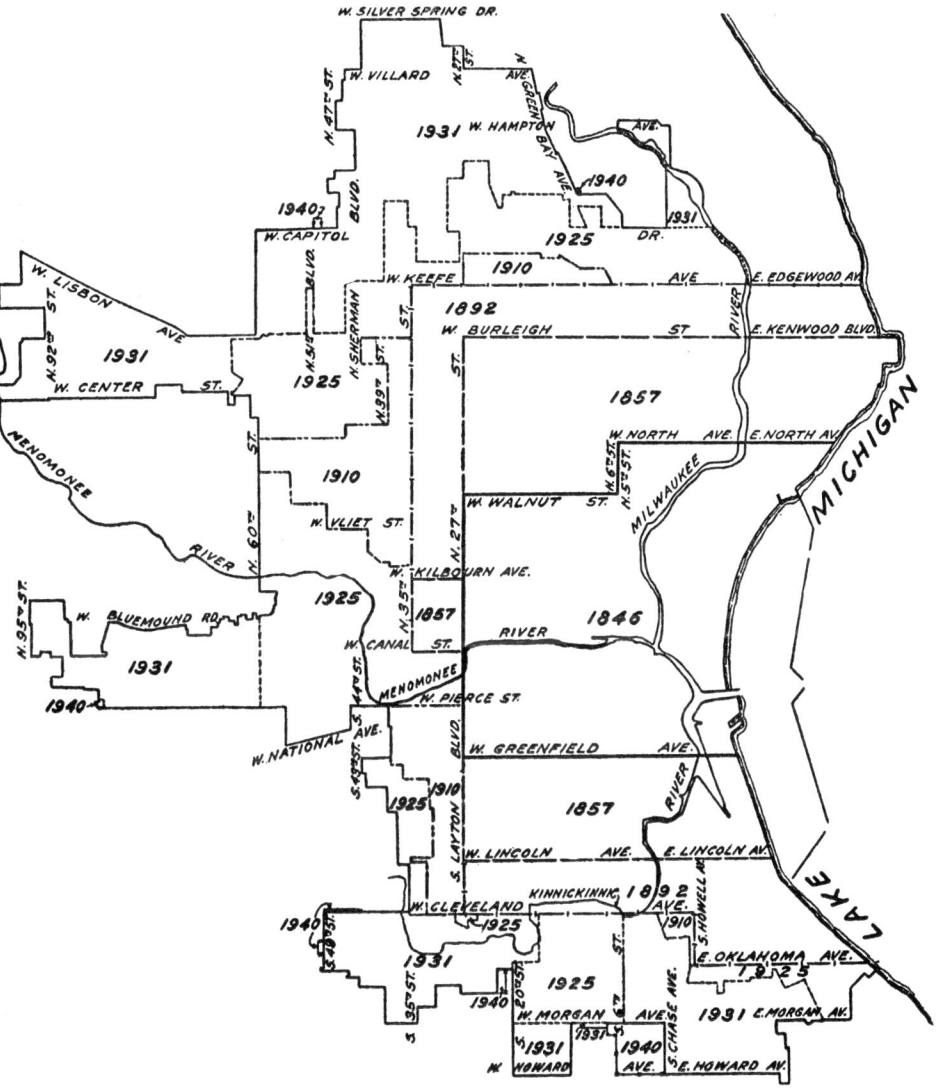

COMPOSITE MAP SHOWING PHYSICAL GROWTH OF MILWAUKEE, 1846 TO 1940

This map was drawn by John L. Wernette and was based on data supplied by the office of the city engineer, Milwaukee. It should be noted that the dates given on the map do not indicate the date of annexation but rather the dates at which given boundaries prevailed. Present-day street names have been used. Boundaries have been indicated as follows:——, boundary of city in 1846; ———, acquisitions by 1857; —·—·—, acquisitions by 1892; —··—, acquisitions by 1910; ----, acquisitions by 1925; ——, acquisitions by 1931;————, acqusitions by 1940.

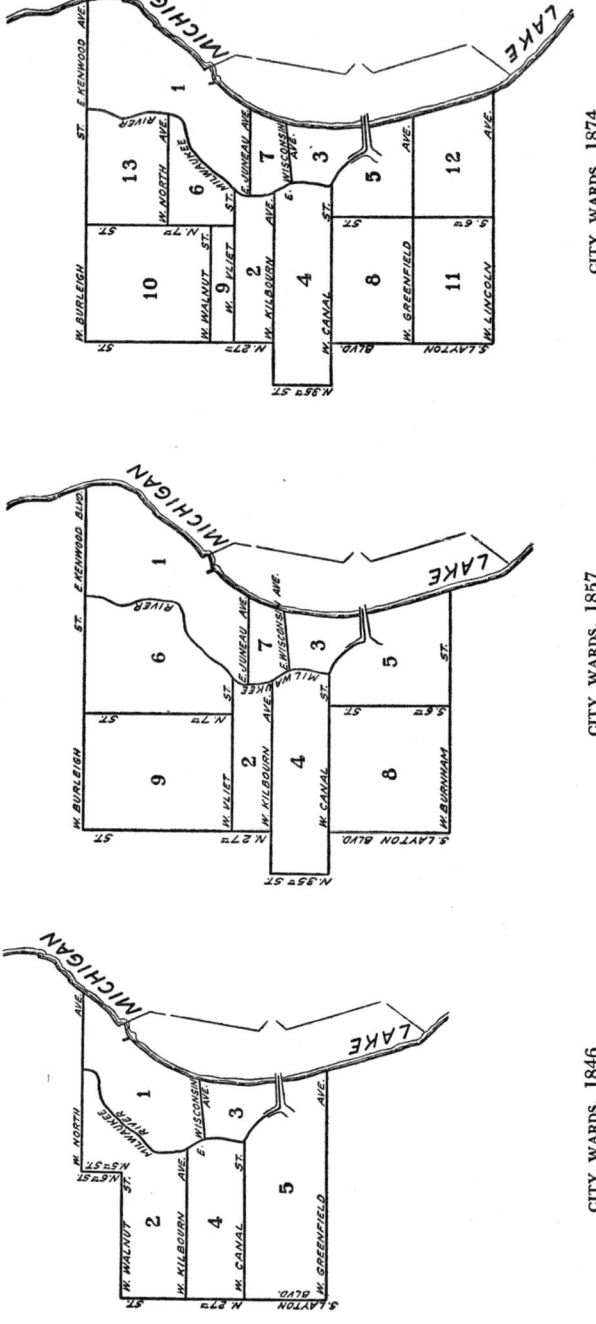

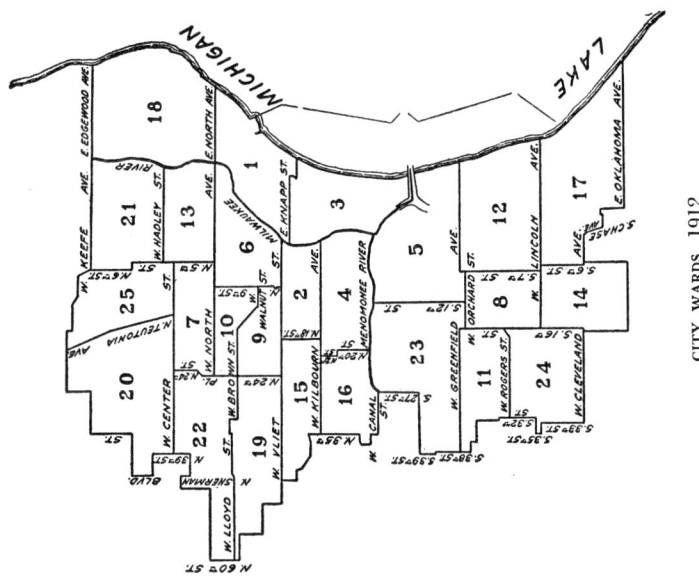

CITY WARDS, 1912

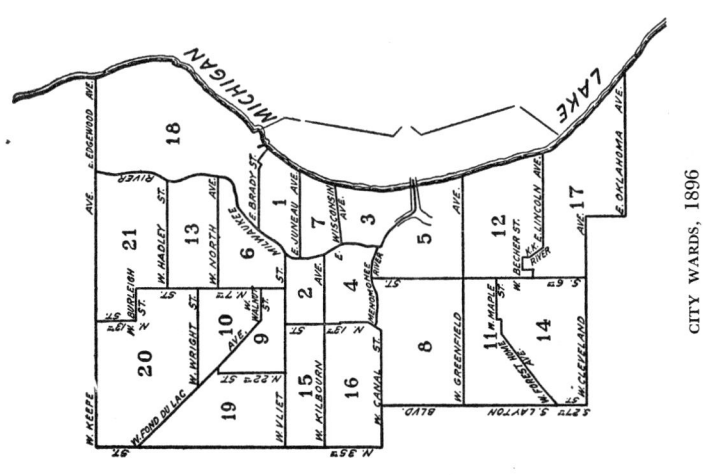

CITY WARDS, 1896

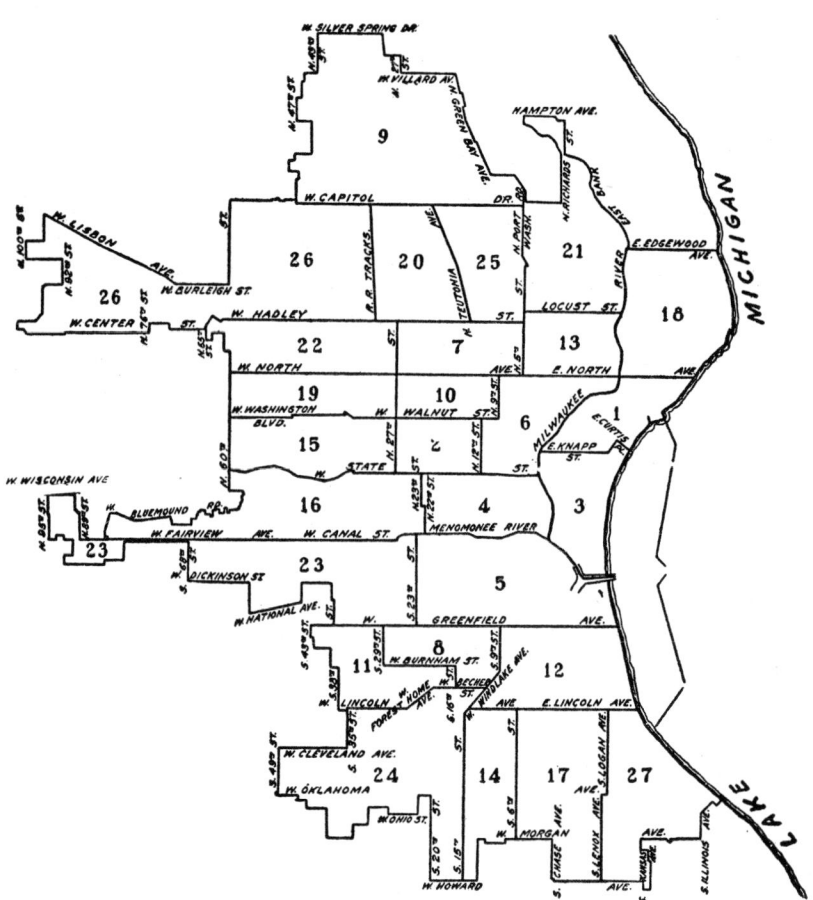

CITY WARDS, 1931

APPENDIX 599

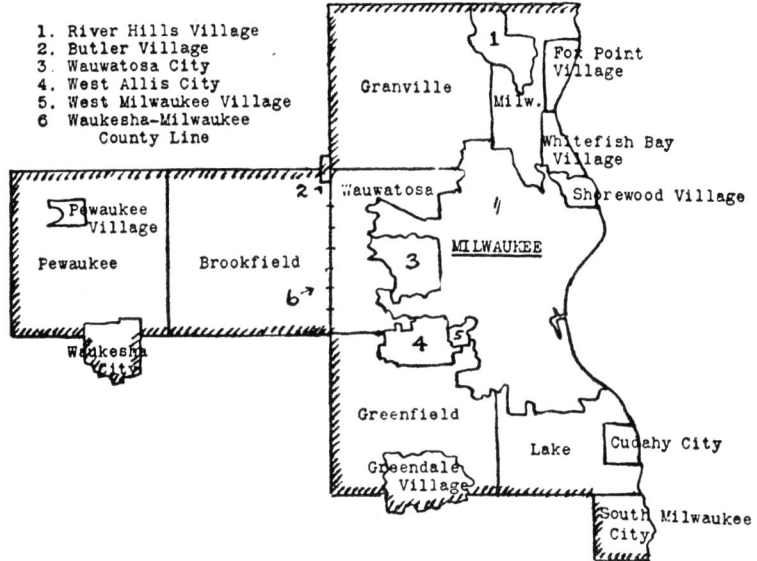

MILWAUKEE METROPOLITAN DISTRICT IN 1940

Wards	Date Approved	Date Effective
1, 2, 3, 4, 5	January 31, 1846	On passage
6, 7	February 21, 1856	On passage
8	October 11, 1856	March 31, 1857
9	February 20, 1857	March 31, 1857
10	March 23, 1872	March 31, 1872
11	February 27, 1873	March 31, 1873
12	February 27, 1873	March 4, 1873
13	March 10, 1874	Election, first Tuesday in April 1874
14	April 10, 1885	March 21, 1886
15	March 8, 1887	March 8, 1887
16	March 11, 1887	March 11, 1887
17	March 8, 1887	March 8, 1887
18	April 11, 1887	First Monday in March 1888
19, 20, 21	November 25, 1895	First Monday in March 1896
22, 23	March 11, 1901	March 11, 1901
24, 25	July 20, 1911	February 1, 1912
26, 27	December 29, 1930	May 1, 1931

The ward maps were drawn by John L. Wernette, and the information on the establishment of the wards was supplied by Mrs. Lucile M. Perry of the Milwaukee Municipal Reference Library. Wards 1 through 18 were created by legislative action; wards 19 through 27 were set up by council ordinance. Present-day street names have been used on the maps. The map of the metropolitan district follows *U. S. Census, Sixteenth, 1940, Population,* 1:1179.

Bibliographical Note

IN THE realm of primary sources, the newspaper presents the best over-all record of the rise and development of Milwaukee. The holdings of the Milwaukee Public Library in this field are highly representative and remarkably complete. They include, for the English press, the Milwaukee *Sentinel* (1837–date); *Daily Wisconsin* (1847–68), *Evening Wisconsin* (1868–1918), and *Wisconsin News* (1918–37), continued as Milwaukee *News* (1937–39); Milwaukee *Daily News,* variously titled (1855–1918); Milwaukee *Journal* (1882–date); *Free Press* (1901–18); and Milwaukee *Leader* (1911–39); for the German press, *Seebote* (1864–66, 1870, 1890–99); *Germania* (1873–1924); *Herold,* variously titled (1863–66, 1883–90, 1897–1932); and *Deutsche Zeitung* (1933–date); for the Polish press, *Nowiny Polskie* (1913–20) and *Kuryer Polski* (1885–date); and for the Slavic press, *Domacnost* (1916–18, 1920–23, 1925–30); *Jugoslovenski Obzor* (1929–38, complete; 1939–41, scattered); and *Cechoslovák* (1931–41). Many publications with a shorter existence, in both the English and the foreign-language field, are also represented. The newspaper division of the State Historical Society of Wisconsin contains, in addition to many publications for the later period, holdings which are especially valuable for the early years. Among other items, these include the Milwaukee *Advertiser* (July 1836–June 1837, 1838–40); *Wiskonsin-Banner,* first German paper (1844–55, scattered); *Wisconsin Banner und Volksfreund* (1855–85); Milwaukee *Courier* (1841–44, 1845–47); *Freidenker* (1872–1917); and *Wisconsin Vorwärts* (1894–98). Available at the Milwaukee County Historical Society are the Milwaukee *Leader,* the *Social-Democratic Herald* (1897–1913), and issues of *The Voice of the People.* A W.P.A. project to index the Milwaukee *Sentinel,* for the reason that it was the oldest Milwaukee newspaper with a continuous existence, resulted in the preparation of a card index, arranged by subject and personal name, for all local items appearing in the *Sentinel* between 1837 and 1879. This index is in the possession of the Reference Department of the Milwaukee Public Library. Highly useful files of clippings from the Milwaukee press on a wide variety of subjects pertaining to the city are maintained at the Milwaukee Municipal Reference Library (1911 to date) and in the Reference Department of the Public Library (1935 to date). In the latter there is a complete file of Milwaukee city directories from 1847 (the first issued) to date. The statistical outline of city growth, for which the newspaper articles supply the detail, must be gained from the *United States Census*, which, in spite of its exasperating deviations in method from decade to decade, remains the urban historian's most basic source.

The numerous editions of the charters and ordinances of Milwaukee, supplemented by the *Proceedings of the Common Council*, the *Wisconsin Territorial Laws*, and the *Laws of Wisconsin*, serve to document the constitutional development of the city and the activities of its government. Among these are the following: *Charter of the City of Milwaukee and Ordinances in Force, May 22, 1848* (2 vols. in one, Milwaukee, 1848); *Charter and Ordinances of the City of Milwaukee* (editions of 1852 and 1853); *Charter and Ordinances of the City of Milwaukee, with the constitution of the state and acts of the legislature, relating to the city* [as of] *December 5, 1856* (Milwaukee, 1857); *Charter of the City of Milwaukee, including a portion of the amendments thereto up to and including the year, A.D. 1861* [April 15], compiled by William A. Prentiss (Milwaukee, 1861); *Charter and Ordinances of the City of Milwaukee, with an appendix* [containing special laws and ordinances and amendments to the charter] (Milwaukee, 1875); *General Ordinances of the City of Milwaukee, with amendments thereto and an appendix* [containing special laws and ordinances] (Milwaukee, 1888); *Charter of the City of Milwaukee, being Chapter 184, Laws of 1874, as amended by subsequent acts of the legislature to and including the Acts of 1889*, compiled by Eugene S. Elliott (Milwaukee, 1889); *Charter of the City of Milwaukee, being Chapter 184, Laws of 1874, as amended by subsequent acts of the legislature to and including the Acts of 1891, and general laws operating as amendments thereto, up to and including those passed by the legislature of 1895*, compiled and annotated by Charles H. Hamilton (Milwaukee, 1895); *General Ordinances of the City of Milwaukee up to January 1, 1896, with amendments thereto and an appendix* [containing special laws and ordinances] (Milwaukee, 1896); *Ordinances of the City of Milwaukee granting franchises for quasi-public purposes up to and including those passed June 8, 1896*, compiled by Charles H. Hamilton

(Milwaukee, 1896); *Charter of the City of Milwaukee, being Chapter 184, Laws of 1874, as amended by subsequent acts of the legislature to and including the Laws of 1891, and general laws operating as amendments thereto, up to and including those passed by the legislature of 1903,* compiled and annotated by Charles E. Estabrook (Milwaukee, 1905); *General Ordinances of the City of Milwaukee to September 1, 1905, with amendments thereto and an appendix,* compiled and codified by Carl Runge (Milwaukee, 1906); *Laws enacted by the Legislature of the State of Wisconsin at the sessions of 1905 and 1907 relating to cities of the first class: Milwaukee city charter supplement, 1908* (Milwaukee, 1908); *Charter of the City of Milwaukee, being Chapter 184, Laws of 1874 as amended by subsequent acts of the legislature to and including the Laws of 1913,* compiled and annotated under the supervision of Daniel W. Hoan (Milwaukee, 1914); *Milwaukee Code of 1914: general ordinances of the City of Milwaukee in force May 25, 1914,* revised and codified by Leo Tiefenthaler (Milwaukee, 1914); *1921 Supplement to the Milwaukee Code of 1914, containing amendments to the code passed prior to January 1, 1922,* compiled by the Municipal Reference Library; *Charter of the City of Milwaukee, being Chapter 184, Laws of 1874 as amended by special acts of the legislature to and including Laws of 1891, and general laws not in printed statutes, up to and including those passed by the legislature of 1933,* compiled and annotated under the supervision of Max Raskin (Milwaukee, 1934); *Milwaukee Code of Ordinances, containing the general ordinances of the City of Milwaukee,* compiled and edited by Richard E. Krug and assistants (Milwaukee, 1941); *Charter Ordinances of the City of Milwaukee, containing all the charter ordinances passed by the common council . . . through November 25, 1946,* compiled by the Municipal Reference Library (Milwaukee, 1946). The *Proceedings of the Common Council* are available at the Public Library for the period May 3 to August 9, 1858, and August 16, 1858, to June 27, 1859, and at both the Public Library and the Municipal Reference Library for April 1869 to April 1872 (typed from newspaper clippings) and April 1873 to date (printed and bound). The *Manuals of the Common Council,* which were issued from 1878 to 1920, are useful for the biographical material on the members of the council, the departmental rosters, and other statistical data which they contain. All copies of the village ordinances appear to have been destroyed.

The reports of the municipal departments provide the best source on the development of urban services in the city. These were issued collectively as *City Documents,* beginning in 1861–62; and a complete set is available in the office of the city comptroller. Later such reports were separately issued. In 1922, the city began the practice of publishing an annual consolidated report of the common council designed to acquaint the public with the city's work. These, of which the first reported the activities of 1921, were originally entitled *Municipal Government and Activities of the City of Milwaukee;* but in recent years various titles have been used. They summarize the work of the various branches of the city government and draw upon the mimeographed or typewritten reports which the departments still issue for the use of a select clientele. The result is a consolidated account which serves as a highly useful summary of the year's accomplishments on the many fronts of municipal action. Such official publications as the *Annual Reports of the School Board* (1859–60 to date), the annually issued *Manual of the Milwaukee Public Schools,* and the reports of the board of harbor commissioners contribute to an understanding of social and economic as well as administrative developments in the city. Nongovernmental documents of interest for similar reasons are the collection of college bulletins held by the Public Library, including the Milwaukee College catalogues (1852–91), the annual reports prepared for the board of trade (1854, 1855, and 1856), and the annual reports of the Milwaukee Chamber of Commerce (1858 and following), the Milwaukee Grain and Stock Exchange (1931–32 to date), and the Milwaukee Association of Commerce and predecessors (scattered reports for early period). Many of these documents are available at the State Historical Society Library, the Milwaukee Public Library, and the Municipal Reference Library; and at the latter may be found the growing collection of studies of the urban economy prepared by specialists in such governmental agencies as the board of public land commissioners and in such citizens organizations as the Citizens' Governmental Research Bureau. A typical product of the former is the study by Robert Filtzer and William L. Slayton, *Manufacturing in Milwaukee and 22 Metropolitan Cities, 1919, 1929, 1939* (Board of Public Land Commissioners, Milwaukee, 1944) and of the latter that of the Citizens' Bureau of Milwaukee, *The Lake Front in Milwaukee County* (Milwaukee, 1940).

Personal papers describing the social, political, or industrial aspects of the developing city are understandably scarce. Once the initial novelty of townsite speculation had worn off, few city dwellers included any extensive comment on the city's growth in their letters or diaries; the informal personal intercourse of the urban community precluded the existence of much correspondence on local matters; and, unfortunately, neither the average business firm nor the average citizen had the foresight, the encouragement, or the desire to preserve their papers for historical purposes. The Grignon, Lawe, and Porlier Papers, being the business, personal, and official correspondence of three families engaged in the fur trade in the Great Lakes area, contribute to an understanding of fur trading operations in the vicinity of Milwaukee, as do the papers of the American Fur Company. For the period of townsite promotion, valuable material may be found in the correspondence between Solomon Juneau and Morgan L. Martin in the Morgan L. Martin Papers; in the letters from Byron Kilbourn to Micajah T. Williams, 1835–37; and in the Increase Lapham Papers, the Palmer Gardner correspondence, the reminiscences of Enoch Chase, and the Milwaukee County Claim Association Record Book, 1836–44. Detail on the developing city may be gained from the recollections of Amherst W. Kellogg; the family diary and record book of Edward D. Holton (1845–1907); the papers of John Jay Orton (1837–84), Milwaukee attorney and businessman; those of John H. Tweedy (1832–90), Milwaukee attorney and politician; the Mitchell Papers, which bear on the activities of Alexander Mitchell, financier and railroad promoter of the mid-century, and his son, John L. Mitchell, whose papers reveal local reactions to the panic of 1893; the Record Book of the Young Men's Association (1848–68), which reveals transactions which antedated the establishment of the Public Library; and the Henry C. Payne Papers (1885–1908), which touch upon the development of public utilities in the city. For further information on these materials, all of which are in the manuscript collection of the State Historical Society, with the exception of the American Fur Company Papers, see *Guide to the Manuscripts of the Wisconsin Historical Society,* edited by Alice E. Smith (Madison, 1944). The papers of the Wisconsin Marine and Fire Insurance Company of Milwaukee (1839–53) and those of the Plankinton Bank (1887–1907), both in the possession of the State Historical Society, are among the few collections of business papers available in public depositories, as are the Daniel Wells-Charles W. Norris correspondence (1818–1900) and the forty scrapbooks of the Pabst Brewery (publicity and advertising materials and clippings) held by the Milwaukee County Historical Society. Other important holdings of the latter are an extensive collection of materials pertaining to the Milwaukee Musical Society and the *Freie Gemeinde* and Christopher Bach music libraries. The County Historical Society also holds an especially rich collection of materials pertaining to the Milwaukee Socialist Party: the papers of the Milwaukee Socialist

Party, including annual convention proceedings, leaflets, and photographs; complete issues of the preambles and leaflets of the Social Democratic Party from 1897; the correspondence of Victor Berger as editor of the Milwaukee *Leader;* and correspondence and clippings of Daniel Hoan covering the period 1910 to 1940.[1] A published source of interest is the memoirs of William George Bruce, being the recollections of a local historian who was born in Milwaukee in 1856 and who for a full lifetime thereafter was actively associated with commercial and political developments in the city. These memoirs were published in the *Wisconsin Magazine of History,* 16:359–82; 17:3–71, 187–227, 307–40, 402–32; and 18:42–65. Somewhat amplified, they later appeared as William G. Bruce, *I Was Born in America* (Milwaukee, 1937). Daniel Hoan's *City Government* (New York, 1936) is a participant's account of the administrative development of the city from 1916 to 1936. Excerpts from many of the manuscripts in the possession of the State Historical Society have been reproduced in the publications of the Society, which include the *Collections,* the *Proceedings,* and the *Wisconsin Magazine of History.* For the location of many of these published items see Leroy Schlinkert, *Subject Bibliography of Wisconsin History* (Madison, 1947).

An informing source of contemporary comment on the developing city is provided in the writings of foreign travelers and American feature writers who found in the expanding West and, later, in the emerging city a subject with reader appeal. Some of the more penetrating descriptions of the city resulting from this interest in the Wisconsin metropolis are provided in Sarah Margaret Fuller Ossoli, *Summer on the Lakes, in 1843* (Boston, 1844); Fredrika Bremer, *Homes of the New World* (2 vols., New York, 1854); Anthony Trollope, *North America* (2 vols., London, 1862); Ernest Duvergier de Hauranne, *Huits Mois en Amérique, Lettres et Notes*

---

[1] The Milwaukee County Historical Society, which has enjoyed a vigorous existence since its founding in 1935, has made a conscientious effort to preserve photographs, costumes, furniture, and other relics illustrative of Milwaukee's past, in addition to the documents mentioned above. Through its auspices, and that of its members, several structures of historical importance have been preserved or reconstructed within the limits of the county. These include the Benjamin Church house, later known as the Kilbourntown House, and relocated in Estabrook Park; the Lowell Damon House (1844–45) in Wauwatosa; a replica of Solomon Juneau's log cabin, constructed through the generosity of Mrs. Anna Huebschmann Hottelet, and located in Juneau Park; and the Terrace Avenue mansion of Otto H. Falk, which serves as an auxiliary to the Milwaukee Historical Museum which is located in the courthouse. The Society publishes the *Historical Messenger,* a pamphlet containing brief historical articles. See Frederic Heath, "The Milwaukee County Historical Society," *Wisconsin Magazine of History,* 31:178–85 (December 1947).

BIBLIOGRAPHICAL NOTE   607

de Voyage, 1864-1865 (2 vols., Paris, 1866); Gail Hamilton [Mary Abigail Dodge], *Wool-Gathering* (Boston, 1867); Willard Glazier, *Peculiarities of American Cities* (Philadelphia, 1884); Charles Dudley Warner, *Studies in the South and West* (New York, 1889); Julian Street, *Abroad at Home* (New York, 1916); Ernest Ingersoll, "Milwaukee," in *Harper's New Monthly Magazine*, 62:702-18 (April 1881); Charles King, "The Cream City," in *Cosmopolitan*, 10:549-60 (March 1891); William W. Howard, "The City of Milwaukee," in *Harper's Weekly*, 35:538-39 (July 18, 1891); Edmund Goes, "Milwaukee: The German City of America," in *The Chautauquan*, 27:659-61 (September 1898); Ernest L. Meyer, "Twilight of a Golden Age," in *American Mercury*, 29:456-64 (August 1933); and Zona Gale, "Milwaukee," in *Good Housekeeping*, 50:317-25 (March 1910). For an expansion of this subject, see Bayrd Still, "The Growth of Milwaukee as Recorded by Contemporaries," in *Wisconsin Magazine of History*, 21:262-92 (March 1938). Useful material on the social history of the city is available in the clipping and pamphlet collection of the State Historical Society Library. On the history of religious organizations, in addition to pertinent clippings, there are anniversary books and booklets, manuals, year books, historical sketches, worship programs, and bulletins; and for many of the city's clubs and societies (secret, social, and professional) there are similar materials, including membership lists and annual reports.

With the exception of H. Russell Austin's *The Milwaukee Story: The Making of an American City* (Milwaukee, 1946), a popular account published by the Milwaukee *Journal* as a centennial feature, the general histories of the city usually combine biographies of the citizens with the narrative of the city's growth. The most usefully comprehensive of these is John G. Gregory, *History of Milwaukee, Wisconsin* (4 vols., Chicago, 1931). Others include William G. Bruce, *History of Milwaukee City and County* (3 vols., Milwaukee, 1922); *History of Milwaukee from Its First Settlement to the Year 1895*, ed. by Howard L. Conard (3 vols., Chicago, n.d.); and *Memoirs of Milwaukee County*, ed. by Jerome A. Watrous (2 vols., Madison, 1909). The Conard and Watrous works were compiled with the assistance of prominent citizens of the city; thus the authors of some of the chapters were participants in the activities described. Two other general works are [Frank A. Flower], *History of Milwaukee, from Prehistoric Times to the Present Date*, published by the Western Historical Company, A. T. Andreas, proprietor (Chicago, 1881), and James S. Buck, *Pioneer History of Milwaukee* (2 vols., Milwaukee, 1876 [rev. ed., 1890], 1881) and *Milwaukee Under the Charter* (2 vols., 1884, 1886). Because of

Buck's personal identification with the early city, his work has some of the quality of a primary source. This is also to some extent true of A. C. Wheeler, *The Chronicles of Milwaukee* (Milwaukee, 1861). The institutional growth of the city in the mid-nineteenth century is compared with that of other major cities of the Great Lakes area in Bayrd Still, "Patterns of Mid-Nineteenth Century Urbanization in the Middle West," in *Mississippi Valley Historical Review*, 28:187–206 (September 1941). For an analysis of the city's development in the post-Civil War period, see Bayrd Still, "Milwaukee, 1870–1900: The Emergence of a Metropolis," in *Wisconsin Magazine of History*, 23:138–62 (December 1939) and "The Development of Milwaukee in the Early Metropolitan Period," in *Wisconsin Magazine of History*, 25:297–307 (March 1942).

Several studies dealing with Milwaukee only as a part of a more extensive area nevertheless contribute significantly to an understanding of the city's history. For the early period there are Louise P. Kellogg, *The French Régime in Wisconsin and the Northwest* (Madison, 1925) and *The British Régime in Wisconsin and the Northwest* (Madison, 1935) and Joseph Schafer, *Four Wisconsin Counties: Prairie and Forest* (Madison, 1927). On the social and cultural side there are Porter Butts, *Art in Wisconsin* (Madison, 1936) and Lillian Krueger, "Social Life in Wisconsin: Pre-Territorial through the Mid-Sixties," in *Wisconsin Magazine of History*, 22:156–75 (December 1938); 312–28 (March 1939); 396–426 (June 1939). In the field of commercial and industrial development there are Ray H. Whitbeck, *The Geography and Economic Development of Southeastern Wisconsin* (Wisconsin Geological and Natural History Survey, Bulletin no. 58, Madison, 1921); Elmer A. Riley, *The Development of Chicago and Vicinity as a Manufacturing Center Prior to 1880* (Chicago, 1911); John G. Thompson, *The Rise and Decline of the Wheat Growing Industry in Wisconsin* (Economics and Political Science Series, vol. 5, no. 3, Madison, 1909); L. B. Krueger, *History of Commercial Banking in Wisconsin* (University of Wisconsin Studies in the Social Sciences and History, no. 18, Madison, 1933); Frederick Merk, *Economic History of Wisconsin during the Civil War Decade* (Madison, 1916); Herbert W. Rice, "The Early History of the Chicago, Milwaukee and St. Paul Railway Company" (Abstracts in History IV, University of Iowa Studies, Studies in the Social Sciences, vol. 11, no. 3, Iowa City, 1941); and Ralph G. Plumb, "Early Harbor History of Wisconsin" (Wisconsin Academy of Sciences, Arts, and Letters, *Transactions*, vol. 17, pt. 1, Madison, 1914). Norman N. Gill's *Municipal Research Bureaus*

(Washington, D.C., 1944) recounts Milwaukee's experience in this field.

Monographs of scholarly proportions dealing exclusively with special aspects of the city's history are conspicuously rare. Outstanding in this category are Laurence M. Larson, *A Financial and Administrative History of Milwaukee* (Madison, 1908); Marvin Wachman, *History of the Social Democratic Party of Milwaukee, 1897–1910* (Illinois Studies in the Social Sciences, vol. 28, no. 1, Urbana, 1945); Selig Perlman, *History of Socialism in Milwaukee* (manuscript B.A. Thesis, University of Wisconsin, Madison, 1910); Frederick I. Olson, *The Milwaukee Socialist Party, 1897–1941* (manuscript Ph.D. Thesis, Harvard University, in process of completion); and Thomas C. Cochran, *The Pabst Brewing Company: The History of an American Business* (in preparation). Other accounts on special subjects include Annabel Douglas MacArthur, *Religion in Early Milwaukee* (Milwaukee, 1946) and Louis F. Frank, *The Medical History of Milwaukee, 1834–1914* (Milwaukee, 1915).

Extended treatment of the city's German society may be found in Rud[olph] A. Koss, *Milwaukee* (Milwaukee, 1871); Wilhelm Hense-Jensen and Ernest Bruncken, *Wisconsin's Deutsch-Amerikaner bis zum Schluss des Neunzehnten Jahrhunderts* (2 vols., Milwaukee, 1900–1902); and in an excellent series of articles written by J. J. Schlicher for the *Wisconsin Magazine of History*, which contribute to an understanding of the cultural activities of the Milwaukee-German society in the mid-nineteenth century. These include "Hans Balatka and the Milwaukee Musical Society," 27:40–55 (September 1943); "The Milwaukee Musical Society in Time of Stress," 27:178–93 (December 1943); "Eduard Schroeter the Humanist," 28:169–83 (December 1944) and 307–24 (March 1945); and "Bernhard Domschcke," 29:319–32 (March 1946) and 435–56 (June 1946).

For the Poles there are Waclaw Kruszka, *Historya Polska w Ameryce* (13 vols., Milwaukee, 1906) and *We, the Milwaukee Poles*, compiled by Thaddeus Borun (Milwaukee, 1946); for the Irish, Humphrey J. Desmond, "Early Irish Settlers in Milwaukee," in *Wisconsin Magazine of History*, 13:365–74 (June 1930); for the Italians, G. La Piana, *The Italians in Milwaukee, Wisconsin* (Milwaukee, 1915); for the Slovaks, Henry Kusik, Jr., *The Early Slovak Settlers of Milwaukee,* pamphlet of the Ninth Annual Convention of Catholic Slovak Students' Fraternity of America (Milwaukee, 1930); for the Hungarians, Mrs. A. L. Banyai and Frank Beleznay, *The Hungarians of the City of Milwaukee* (Milwaukee, 1929); and for the Negro, "Milwaukee's Negro Community," prepared by Mrs. Paula Lynagh, Citizens' Governmental Research Bureau of Milwaukee (Milwaukee, 1946).

The studies of both the municipal and the citizens research agencies, which comprise a growing bibliography of significance, and the increasing output of souvenir publications commemorating anniversaries of the city's churches, industries, and organizations provide a useful source of information on special subjects; but it goes without saying that there is a real need for further scholarly analysis and interpretation of many special aspects of the city's growth. The history of its administrative activities, so admirably begun by Larson, should now be brought up to date, with special attention to the development of the highly professional and technical public services of the recent period. Most of the major industries, especially the heavy machines industry, the tanning industry, and the packing industry, await intensive study, both in general and from the approach of individual firms. The comparative reactions of the urban society in times of prosperity and depression merit investigation, as do the story of commercial promotion in the city through the years, the social and political adjustments and interrelations of the various nationality groups, the role of the church in the urban community, the evolution of professional activities, labor organization, and lodges, clubs, and societies, the force of the urban press, and the relations of the city not only with its parent state, but with its metropolitan satellites and with its urban neighbors of the Great Lakes area. The completion of such a series of studies would not only make possible a really incisive and comprehensive history of Milwaukee itself but, since the history of its cities reflects increasingly the history of the nation, it would illumine a development of significance in the history of the United States at large.

Index

Abbott, Samuel, 52
Academy of Fine Arts, proposed, 409
Academy of Music, 119, 401–2, 406
A Capella Chorus, 451
Adams, J. P., 207
Adler, David, 277
Aero Club, 405
Aigner, Dr. ——, 116–17, 122
Air-mail Service, 512
Albany Hall Reform Movement, 147–49, 164, 376
Albany (N.Y.), example cited, 102, 214, 357
Aldermen, terms, 105–6, 134, 533; powers and duties, 106–7, 233, 238, 376; bicameral organization, 135, 147, 165, 376 (abandoned); criticism of, 141, 147, 233, 376; checks on, 142, 147; activities concerning municipal improvements, 145–46, 166, 238–39; constituency (1880), 282; (1888), 284, 286; (1890), 297; (1896), 302; (1898), 306; (1900), 308; (1910), 316; (1932), 528, 532–33; salaries advocated, 285; indicted for graft, 310; number reduced, 315, 376; conflict with mayor, 530–31, 533–34
Alexander, O., 249
Allen, George W., 71–72, 157, 187, 347
Allen, William, 71, 187
Allis, Edward P., 71–72, 92, 114, 157, 191, 293, 337–39, 341, 347–48, 354–55, 567; pictured, 292
Allis-Chalmers Company. See Allis-Chalmers Manufacturing Company.
Allis-Chalmers Industrial Union, 501
Allis-Chalmers Manufacturing Company, 292, 338–39, 380, 486, 488, 490, 500–501; foundry pictured, 488. See Reliance Iron Works.
Allis-Chalmers Rumely, Ltd., 488

Allis (Edward P.) and Company; Edward P. Allis Company. See Allis-Chalmers Manufacturing Company.
Allis Mutual Aid Society, 341
Altpeter, Oscar, 286
American Federation of Labor, 294–95, 498–501
American Freeman, 68
American Fur Company, 5, 31–32, 52–53
American Hellenic Educational and Protective Association, 471
American House, hostelry, 66, 224
American Protective Association, 301
American Red Cross, Milwaukee Chapter, 459
American Revolution, 6
American Women's Educational Association of New York, 222
Anderson, John, 63
Anderson, Rasmus, 261
Anderson, Thomas G., 4
Anderson, William E., 414
Anderson, William J., 301
Andrews, Marion, 452
Animals (hogs and cattle) on Streets, 103, 245
Anneke, Fritz, 129
Annexation, 560
Anson, Charles H., 309–10
Anti-Catholicism, 139
Anti-spitting Ordinance, 386
Apartments, 250, 397
Appelhagen, E., 295
Architecture, village period, 66; mid-forties to 1900, 259, 396–97; twentieth-century developments, 475, 490
Architects and builders, 66, 438, 469
Arion Music Club, 407–8, 451
Armenians, 471
Arminia (Milwaukee), 285
Armour, Philip D., 183, 187

611

Arnold, J. E., 104–5
Arnold, Louis A., 534
Arnold, William A., 314–15
Art, village period, 86–87; mid-forties to 1910, 210–11, 409–12, 438; exhibits, 211; 1910 to 1940, 557. See Panoramas.
Assessors, 148
Assize of Bread, 244
Association for the Advancement of Milwaukee, 348–50, 353
Association of Commerce, 352, 508–9, 511, 563. See Merchants' and Manufacturers' Association.
Atlantic and Pacific Tea Company, Great, 399, 448–49
Atlas (Milwaukee), 125
Auditorium Building, 347
Auer, Louis, 286, 383–84
Auer, Mrs. Louis, 456
Austin, Robert N., 72
Austrians, 131, 454
Automobiles, 391, 405 (prices), 436–37, 449, 496, 553 (car ownership)
Aviation, 405, 440, 511–13

Bach, Christopher, band, 118, 259, 262, 267, 348, 452
Bacon, E. P., 71
Bade, Albert, 134
"Badger," lake vessel, 23
Badger Illuminating Company, 366
Bading, Gerhard, 386, 391, 520–23
Baker, Frank E., 447
Balatka, Hans, 115–17, 119–20, 125, 252, 274, 406
Bank of Milwaukee, 56–59
Banks. See Currency and Banks.
Banner und Volksfreund, 125
Baptists, 90, 351, 420, 422–23, 472
Baran, Felix, 465
Barber, Edward, 353
Barber, George, 47, 73; shipbuilding company, 287
Barber, Lucius I., 26, 36, 94
Barnard, Henry, 85
Barnard (E. W.) and Company, 62
Barr, James, 533
Barrett, Lawrence, 401
Barstow, William A., 171
Barter, 56
Bartlett, E. W., 413
Bartlett, J. K., 225
Baseball, 227, 404–6

Bashford, Coles, 155
Bassett, Edward M., 544
Bathrooms, introduction of, 398
Baumgaertner, Henry J., 262, 286
Bayer (William) Commercial College, 223
Baylies, Aaron, Jr., 224
Bay State Iron Works, 338
Bay View, 380
Beale, Charles H., 526
Beaubien, John B., 4
Bechtner, Paul, 297–98
Beck, William, 232, 252
Becker, Sherburn M., 312–15, 531
Becker, Washington, 355, 368–69
Beecher, Catherine, 222–23, 417
Beecher, Henry Ward, 215
Beer, Milwaukee, promotion of, 332–33
Beer Gardens, Saloons, and Taverns, 79, 242, 259, 403, 426; "stall" saloons, 313, 426
Beethoven Society, 87
Beffel, J. M., 317–18
Beggs, John I., 371, 374, 489; pictured, 292
Belleview (Milwaukee) House, 65
Bennett, Charles B., 535
Bennett Law, 260–62, 296, 298
Bentley, John, 383
Berg, Harold O., 558
Berger, Mrs. Meta, 317, 456
Berger, Victor, 301, 303 (sketch), 304–5, 308, 311, 314–15, 317–20, 377, 460, 516, 521, 524; pictured, 464
Beringer, Hedwig, 264
Berlin (Germany), example cited, 300, 383
Berner, E. J., 304
Bernhardt, Sarah, 401
Best, Charles, 189
Best, Jacob, Sr., 188
Best, Phillip, 188, 329, 341
Best Brewing Company, 188. See Pabst Brewing Company.
Bicycles, 245, 391
Biederman, A. J., 118
Bielfeld, A. Henry, 78, 135, 234
Bielfeld's Gardens, 242
Binner, Paul, 414
Birchard, Harvey, 72
Birth Rate, 434
Black, John, 282, 284, 347
Black Hawk War, 7
Blackwell, Lucy Stone, 213

INDEX 613

Blast Furnaces. See Metal Trades.
Blatz, Emil, donor of bandshell, 452
Blatz, Valentin, 188–89, 284, 341, 347
Blatz (Val) Brewing Company, 189, 330–31, 494
Bleyer, Henry, 72
Blix, Ovid B., 535
Blodgett, F. S., 248
"Bloomer Girl," lake vessel, 404
Blossom, Levi, 172, 225, 234, 392
B'ne Jeshurun, Jewish congregation, 424
Board of Estimates, 539
Board of Fire and Police Commissioners, 300, 357–58, 376, 534, 552
Board of Harbor Commissioners, 507–8, 563
Board of Health, 385
Board of Park Commissioners, 376, 383
Board of Public Land Commissioners, 542, 544
Board of Public Works, 165–67, 250, 302, 363, 517. See Commissioner of Public Works.
Board of Trade, 179, 183 (established), 563
Board of Water Commissioners, 248, 362
Boards and Commissions, 135, 164–67, 241–42, 250–51, 376, 517, 521, 533, 542, 547
Bodden, Michael, 156, 282
Bodden Packing Company, 334
Boebel, Hans, 129
Bohemians, 462; early migration and settlement, 131, 268, 273–74, 454, 469–70; religious activities, 131, 274–75; organizations, 274–76
Bohmann, Henry P., 534
Bojanowski, Jerzy, 467, 469
Boncel, Frank, 530
Boncel Act, 500, 529
Bonduel, Florimond J., 89
Bonzel, A., 285
Book Store, first, 86, 213
Boot and Shoe Industry, 189–90, 192–93 (statistics), 494–95
Booth, Edwin, 206, 401
Booth, Sherman, 150–51
Borchardt, Francis, 271
"Boss rule." See Graft and Machine Politics.
Boston (Mass.), example cited, 520
Boston Store, 400, 499 (strike)

Bowman, George, 57
Bowyer, John, 6
Boyd, G. B., 225
Bradford, John, 225
Bradley, Alice, 428
Bradley, Charles T., 72, 196, 347
Braman, Percy, 524–25
Brand, Charles, 533
Brand, Sebastian, 347
Brand Stove Company, 293
Brandt, Marianne, 408
Braun, John, 189
Breed, A. O. T., 53, 102
Bremer, Fredrika, 112
Brewers' Relief Society, 291
Brewing, 64–65, 188–90, 192–93, 326, 328–33, 341–42, 477–78, 484, 486–87, 490–94; workers, 293, 341
Brewster, William, 52
Brick Making, 64, 192–93
Bridges, 22, 39–41, 98–99, 360; "Bridge War," 39–41, 104
Briggs and Stratton Corporation, 500
Briggs, Lucia R., 448
Brisbane, Arthur, 492
Brisbane Hall, 519–20, 523
Brisbin, Giles S., 57
British, 112
British-Americans, 131
British Local Government Board, example cited, 300
Brockhausen, F., 304
Brodhead, Edward H., 71, 157, 159, 171, 347–48, 362, 399
Brookes, Samuel M., 86
Brooklyn (N.Y), example cited, 283
Brosius, George, 92, 124
Brown, James H., 36
Brown, James S., 155
Brown, John, reaction to execution of, 152
Brown, Samuel, 12–13, 18, 100, 102
Brown, Thomas H., 282, 284, 297, 309, 319, 381
Brown, W. W., 225
Brown, William, Jr., 58
Brown's Picture Gallery, 210
Bruce, William G., 273, 312, 351–52, 390, 507; pictured, 464
Brucker, Joseph, 289–90
Bruncken, Ernest, 266, 456
Buck, Amasa, 221
Buck, James S., 56
Bucyrus-Erie Company, 500

Buczynski, Bonaventure, 131, 269
Buffalo (N.Y.), lake commerce with, 45, 47–48, 179, 182; migration via, 74–75; example cited, 102, 361; rail connections with, 201; association with, 288; milling at, 496
Buffalo Leather Company, 187
Buffalo Synod, 92
Building Regulation, 233, 388, 517–18
Building Trades Council, 497
Bull, Ole, 212
Bund Freier Menschen (Federation of Free People), 125
Burdick, William, 12, 71
Bureau of Economy and Efficiency, 516, 537, 554
Burlesque Theaters and Troupes, 403
Burnham, George, 64, 362
Burnham, Jonathan L., 64
Burt, William A., 15
Business, municipal regulation of, 243–44, 246, 372
Butler, Ammi R. R., 144, 149, 281
Butler, John A., 299–301, 388
Button, Henry H., 72

Cable Cars. See Urban Transit.
Cameron, J. E., 225
Campbell, Colin, 285–86
Canals. See Milwaukee and Rock River Canal Company.
Capron, George, 205
Car-ferry Traffic, 343, 506, 510–11
Carley, Quartus G., 12, 71
Carney, J. P., 523, 528–29
Caroline, Mother, School, 221
Carpenter, E. W., 153
Carpenter, S. D., 173
Caruso, Enrico, 409
Cary, Anna Louise, 409
Casimir Pulaski Council, 466
Catholic Youth Organization, 512
Catholics. See Roman Catholics.
Catlin, John, 171–72
Cecilian Choir, 407
Celebrations and Parades, 75, 77, 88, 115, 128, 130, 161, 173, 224–25, 258, 261–62, 266, 293, 452
Central Labor Union, 292–94
Central Trust Company, 371–72
Centralized Purchasing, 523, 528, 535, 538–39
Český Spolek Podporující Spolky (C.S.P.S.), 274

Chain Stores, 399, 448–49, 462
Chalifon, Peter, 17–18, 20
Chamber of Commerce, 159, 162, 178–79, 183–86, 194, 236–37, 322–23, 327–29, 333, 342–43, 345–47, 352, 477, 501, 504, 508. See Milwaukee Grain and Stock Exchange.
Chamberlin, Miss S. E., 54
Chandler, D. H., 225
Chapin, Caroline E., 417
Chapin, Mary, 417
Chapman, T. A., 72, 348, 354
Chapman (T. A.) and Company, 399 (founded), 400
Charters (1846), 85, 104–5, 233; movement to revise in 1849, 140–41; (1852), 141–42; amended in 1853, 143; amended in 1858, 147–48; movement to revise in 1859, 148; proposed revision in 1867, 165; (1874), 376; amended to change number of aldermen, 315; attempt to revise, 558–60; charter convention of 1908, 377–78
Chase, Enoch, 34, 94
Chase, Horace, 12, 34, 57, 71, 156
Chesbrough, E. S., 248, 362
Chicago (Ill.), 24; rivalry with, 27, 114, 176, 196–97, 241, 343–44, 508, 510–11; example cited, 84, 106, 215, 238, 249, 310, 361, 367, 386, 426; commercial competition with, 180, 182, 184–86, 198–99, 252, 345, 507, 510, 514; association with, 199, 206, 214–15, 288, 407–8, 451–52, 514; center of Socialist movement, 290
Chicago *American,* 28
Chicago and North Western Railway, 177, 182, 186, 201, 260, 343, 513
Chicago *Democrat,* 67, 197
Chicago Grand Opera Company, visits of, 451–52
Chicago, Milwaukee and St. Paul Railroad, 169, 177–78, 327, 336, 343, 351, 513
Chicago, St. Paul, and Fond du Lac Railroad, 173, 177. See Chicago and North Western Railway.
Chicago Symphony Orchestra, 452
Chicago *Tribune,* 68
Childs, Ebenezer, 16, 20–21
Chippewa. See Indians.
Cholera Epidemic, 240–41
Christian Church, 424
Christian Scientists, 420

INDEX 615

Christy's Minstrels, 87, 208
Cincinnati (Ohio), example cited, 249
Circuses and Menageries, 208
Citizens, role in city advance, 300, 355, 378, 564, 567–68; role in municipal reform, 359, 365, 378, 394, 515, 535–39, 541–44, 549, 553, 557, 559–61, 567. See Manufacturing, promotion of, and City Promotion.
Citizens' Aid Committee, 277
Citizens' Bureau. See Citizens' Governmental Research Bureau.
Citizens' Business League, 345, 352 (organized), 353, 389
Citizens' Committee of Ten, 310
Citizens' Committee on Unemployment, 497, 518
Citizens' Governmental Research Bureau, 342, 537–38, 541–42, 544, 559–60
Citizens' Joint Committee on Consolidation, 560
Citizens Organizations. See City Club, Citizens' Governmental Research Bureau, Voters' League, Service Organizations.
Citizens' Ticket, 280–81, 285–86, 297. See Politics.
City Artillery, 226
City Beautification, 104, 242, 317, 387–89, 391, 542
City Charter League, 559
City Club, 341, 390, 520, 536–37, 541–42, 544–45, 549, 557, 559–60
City-County Consolidation, 165, 306, 378, 538, 560–61
City Finances and Municipal Debt, 143, 145, 147–49, 164, 175, 528–30, 533, 536, 539–42, 562. See Centralized Purchasing.
City Hotel, 65
City Planning, 388, 523, 528, 542–45. See Zoning.
City Planning Commission, 542, 544
City Promotion, municipal activities in interest of, 160, 209, 215, 218, 223, 229, 238, 240, 249, 312, 317–18, 322, 324, 352, 393, 402, 506–8, 511, 563; forwarded by citizens groups, 342, 344–49, 352–53, 394, 508–9, 511, 563; promotional literature, 345, 351, 353–54. See Newspapers, role in townsite and city promotion.
City Service Commission, 299–300, 307, 376

Civic Center, 536, 542
"Civic Conscience," noted, 320, 351–52, 356–57, 363, 384–85, 390, 392–93, 395, 433, 515, 536, 562, 565
Civil Service Reform, 283–84, 300–302, 306, 308–9, 320, 357, 521
Civil Service Reform Association, 282
Civil War, participation of Milwaukeeans, 157–61, 187–88; women's activities, 158; recruiting and draft, 158–60; Turners in, 124; reaction to northern victory, 161; stimulus to manufacturing, 188, 191, 196, 287. See Germans, attitude toward free soil issue and Civil War.
Claflin, Increase, 18, 20
Clancy, Thomas A., 534, 554
Clark, George Rogers, 6
Clark, John, 90
Clas, A. C., 388
Clauder, Joseph, 452
Clement, S., 194
Cleveland (Ohio), example cited, 238, 242, 249, 361, 369, 376
"Cleveland," lake vessel, 47
Clinton, E. D., 170
Clothing Industry, 189–90, 192–93 (statistics), 328, 484, 487
Clybourn, Archibald, 19, 30
Coal Trade, 504
Cobb, Joshua, 171
Cochems, Henry F., 311
Coe (Mrs.) Select School, 221
Colby, Charles, 428
Cold Spring City Railway Company, 249
Coleman, W. W., 281, 304
College Women's Club, 428, 536
Comey, Arthur C., 544
Commerce. See Trade and Commerce.
Commercial Associations, role of, 345. See Association for the Advancement of Milwaukee, Association of Commerce, Board of Trade, Chamber of Commerce, Citizens' Business League, Commercial Club, Corn Exchange, Jobbers' and Manufacturers' Association, Merchants' and Manufacturers' Association, Milwaukee Grain and Stock Exchange.
Commercial Club, 351
Commission Business. See Forwarding and Commission Business.
Commissioner of Public Works, 517, 533–34

Committee of One Hundred, 377
Committee on Industrial Organization (C.I.O.), 500–501
Committee on the Homeless, 481
Common Council. See Aldermen.
Commons, John R., 516
Comptroller, 142, 533, 539
Comstock, Cicero, 143–44, 146–47, 149, 154
Comstock, Leander, 214
Concordia College, 417, 447
Congregationalists, 80, 90–91, 420, 423, 472
Connecticut, settlers from. See Yankee-Yorkers.
Conner, Mr. and Mrs. E. S., 207
Constitutional Conventions of Wisconsin, 78, 136–37, 157; (1846), 78–79, 81, 85; (1847–48), 78–79, 81, 85, 137
Conventions, held in city, 350–52, 509
Cooley, Robert L., 440
Coon, S. P., 225
Cooperative Labor Party, 301, 303. See Politics.
Corbett, Jim, 405
Corcoran, Cornelius L., 533
Corn Exchange, 183, 345
Cornell, Herbert W., 535
Cornering Market. See Forestalling and Cornering Market.
Corsair (Milwaukee), 152
Cotillion Club, 428
Cottage Inn, 65, 88; pictured, 472
Cotton, L. H., 101–2
Cotzhausen, Frederick W. von, 129, 260 (sketch), 286, 301
Council of Jewish Women, 478, 536
Cox, Jesse, 304
Cramer, Eliphalet, 51, 55, 71–72, 171–72
Cramer, William E., 68, 71–72, 223, 225
"Cream City," 64
Cream City Club, baseball team, 227, 404
Cream City Railway Line, 368, 370–71
Creedon, Dan, 405
Cricket, 227
Crocker, Hans, 23, 49–51, 58, 81, 91, 114, 142 (sketch), 147, 171–72, 208, 249
Cromwell, William N., 371, 374
Cross, James B., 139, 144–49 (mayor), 238
Cudahy, Michael, 187, 334
Cudahy, Patrick, 334, 380

Cudahy, suburb, 380, 560
Cultural Life, 108; retrogression in frontier days, 82, 85, 95, 108, 215, 228. See Art, Book Store, Libraries, Lyceum, Music, Opera, Public Museum, Schools, Theater.
Currency and Banks, 28–29, 55–56, 323, 325, 328, 341, 490, 529; Bank of Milwaukee, 56–58; hostility to banks, 58, 136; Wisconsin Marine and Fire Insurance Company, 58–60; banks endorsed, 137; after panic of 1893, 324
Currie Park Airport, 511
Currier, R. J., 12
Curtis, Alvord, 284
Curtis, George W., 215
Curtis, Joseph, 68
Cushing, William, 92
Cutler-Hammer Company, 486
C.W.A. See New Deal Subsidies.
Czechoslovaks. See Bohemians and Slovaks.
Czechs. See Bohemians.
Czerwinski, Ignatz, 273, 299
Czerwinski, Roman, 296, 301, 468

Daily Free Democrat (Milwaukee), 248
Dancing Academies, 210
Darnall, Daniel, 20
Davenport, Miss J. M., 206
Davidson Theatre, 401–2, 449, 451
Davis, C. D., 249
Davis, G. D., 248
Davis, John, 64
Davis, S. B., 147, 225
Dean, Julia, 206–7
Death Rate, 385–86, 434, 555
DeBoeye, Chevalier J. G., 221
Debs, Eugene, 280, 304, 309, 311
Decker and Seville. See Reliance Iron Works.
De Haas, Carl, 113
Delaware, settlers from, 72
De Leon, Daniel, 303
Democratic Party, 38, 76, 78, 133–38, 141, 144, 146–56, 160–67, 280–84, 288, 296–99, 301–2, 305–9, 311–16, 318–19, 365, 468, 520–21; appeal for foreign-born, 76, 133, 150, 160, 280, 311, 468. See Politics.
Dentists, 200, 205, 413–14, 438, 469, 472
Department Stores, 399–400
Depressions, (1861), 195–96; (1883), 324; (early 1920's), 478, 497; (1930's), 439,

INDEX

441, 443, 445–47, 467, 472–73, 476, 478–84, 496–98, 501–2, 507–8, 514, 540–41, 546, 551, 553, 555–56, 565
Dermott, G. C., 413
Dernburg, Bernhard, 456
Destinn, Emmy, 409
Detroit (Mich.), example cited, 102–3, 242
Detroit and Milwaukee Line, 175–76
Deuster, P. V., 114, 129, 260
Deutsch-Athen, 70, 74, 115, 267–68, 451, 453
Deutsche Gesellschaft, 74, 260, 298
Dietz, Carl, 317, 516
Dime Museum, 208, 402
Dodge, Henry, 67
Dodge, Nehemiah, 413
Doerflinger, Carl H., 300
Domacnost (Milwaukee), 274
Domschcke, Bernhard, 113, 152, 213, 229, 281
Doty, James D., 9, 12, 14–15, 38, 43, 46, 67, 564
Dousman, George D., 35–36, 91, 102, 183
Dousman, George G., 155, 225
Dousman, Michael, 9, 22, 30, 73
Dousman, Talbot, 33
Downer, Jason, 72, 417
Downer College (Fox Lake). See Milwaukee-Downer College.
Drei-Cents Verein, 115
Drew, Mrs. John, 206
Drew, John I., city treasurer, 529
Druggists, 93
Druids, lodge, 266
Dudgeon, Matthew S., 557
Duluth (Minn.), competition with, 326, 503
Duluth-Superior Harbor, 510, 514
Dunbar, Sylvester W., 57
Dunck, Garrett, 299
Dunlap, Emily P., 425
Durocher, Amable, 20, 25
Durward, Bernard I., 86, 210
Dyer, George, 247
Dziennik Polski (Milwaukee), 270

Eagle Foundry, 194
Edgerton, Benjamin H., 19, 24, 36, 91, 100, 138
Edison Electric Illuminating Company, 366
Education. See Schools.

Eight-hour Day, 285, 287, 292–93, 305, 316
Eight-hour League, 287
Eldred, Anson, 170–71
Eldred, Elisha, 51
Elections. See Politics.
Electric Lighting, 285, 366; municipal ownership and operation of electric light plant, 302, 307, 313, 318, 365–68, 523, 527
Eliot, Ida, 428
Ellis, A. G., 16, 21
Ellsworth, Isaac, 249, 347, 368, 371
Ellsworth, Lemuel, 358
Elmergreen, Ralph, 526–27
Elsner, R., 304
Ely, Mrs. Lydia, 410, 567
Emancipator, The, 290
Emanu-El, Jewish congregation, 93
Emerson, Ralph Waldo, 215
Emmett Guards, 81
Enderis, Dorothy, 558
Enders, Frank, 411
Engelmann, Peter, 122, 125, 252, 382, 414
Engelmann Museum of Natural History, 382
English. See British-Americans.
English Lutheran Churches, 421
Episcopalians, 91–92, 420, 422, 472
Eppert, Carl, 452
Erie Canal, migration via, 74; trade via, 179, 182
Ernst, Otto von, 412
Eschweiler and Eschweiler, architects, 475
Espenhain's Department Store, 399
Estabrook, Charles, 543
Evangelical Association, 424
Evangelical Church, 80, 424
Evening Wisconsin (Milwaukee), 265, 323, 353, 369, 372, 380, 394, 397
Example of Other Cities, as motive for urban development, 232–33, 235–39, 241–44, 246, 249, 283, 300, 349, 356, 360–63, 365, 372, 378, 383–84, 386, 388, 393, 520, 542. See cities by names.
Excelsior Society, 224
Exposition Building, 347, 382

Falk, Otto, 428, 488; pictured, 464
Falk Corporation, 487
Farmer, John, 7

Farnham, Alden B., 413
Farrar, Charles S., 410, 417
Farwell, L. J., 92
Fasolt, G., 78
Faville, A. G., 407
Federal Steel Company, 336
Federated Trades Council (A.F. of L.), 294–95, 301, 304, 308, 311, 496–97, 499–500
Federated Women's Clubs, 478, 559
Federation of Civic Societies, 378
Federation of Milwaukee Slovak Societies, 470
Federation of Organized Trades and Labor Unions of the United States and Canada, 288
Federation of Poles in America, 465
Federation of Trades, 292
Fehr, Herman, 301
"Felicity," lake vessel, 4
F.E.R.A. See New Deal Subsidies.
Ferebee, James L., 535
Ferguson, David, 347, 362
Fessel, Christian, 116–17
Ficker, Christian, 74, 77
Filer, Delos L., 340
Filer and Stowell Company, 340
Fillmore, John S., 50, 68, 114, 225
Fily, Laurent, 4
Finch, Asahel, 71, 91, 150, 162
Finch, Benoni, 34
Finkler, W., 114
Fire Companies, 100, 225–26, 233; German, 79, 100
Fire Department. See Fire Protection.
Fire Inspection, 101, 233–34, 359
Fire Protection, village period, 96–97, 100–102, 105; fire department organized, 101; mid-forties to 1910, 106, 230, 232–35, 250, 356, 358–59; question of pay for firemen, 234–36; 1910 to 1940, 551–54, 562
Firer, Andrew, 275
First Baptist Church, 422–23
First Wisconsin National Bank, 341, 490
Fisher, Lucius G., 60
Fitch, Grant, 405, 428
Fitzgerald, G. M., 134, 137
Fitzsimmons, Bob, 405
Fjell Line (Norwegian), 511
Flanders, James G., 300
Flechsig, Alwin, 308
"Floating Rights," 12, 16–18

Flour Milling, 63–64, 189–90, 192–93 (statistics), 326, 328–29, 495
Flugblätter, 126
Fons and Company, 466, 469
Food Products, production of, 487
Ford, Jonathan, 219
Ford, Julia, 413
Ford Motor Company, 477
Foreign-born, contribution of, 567; influence on politics: see Germans, political activities and attitudes, Irish, political activities, Poles, political activities; migration and settlement, see nationalities by name; numbers, see Milwaukee, statistics on foreign-born population.
Forestalling and Cornering Market, 54, 243, 327
Fortier, Laurent, 20
Forty-eighters, 80, 115, 119–26, 153, 260–61; contribution assessed, 126–27
Forwarding and Commission Business, 47, 62–63, 94, 183–85, 187, 346, 503–4
Foundries. See Metal Trades.
Fowler, Albert, 12 (sketch), 18–19, 36, 71
Fox Point, 434
Foxes. See Indians.
Frackleton, Mrs. Susan, 410
Frankfurth, William, 347, 381
Fratny, Frederick, 68, 122, 126–27, 152, 225, 260
Free Legal Service, proposed, 305
Free Medical Service, proposed, 305, 317
Free Soil and Abolition Issue, 150–53
Freethinkers, 92, 123, 125–26
Freidenker (Milwaukee), 261, 300
Freie Gemeinde (Free Congregation). See Freethinkers.
Freie Gemeinde Chorus, 451
Freiligrath, Ferdinand, 115
French, 471
Frick, William K., 421
Friend, Elias, 347–48
Friends of New Germany, 463
Fritz, Theodore, 307
Froeboese, George, 463–64
Fugitive Slave Law, reaction to, 153
Fuller, W. A. J., 225
Fulton, John, 348
Fur Trade, 4–7, 52–53
Furlong, John, 71, 130, 136
Furniture. See Household Activities

INDEX 619

and Equipment.
Fusion in Municipal Elections, 284–85, 294, 315, 319, 516, 520–21, 523, 527, 530–31

Gadski, Johanna, 409
Gaenslen (Frederick J.) School, for crippled children, 442
Gale, Zona, 258, 357
Gallun (A. F.) and Sons Corporation, 495
Gammon, Simeon, 16, 20
G.A.R., 23d National Encampment, 350
Garbage Disposal, 239, 306, 308, 363–65, 548
"Garbage Ring," 306
Garden, Mary, 451
Garden Homes Project, 528
Gardiner, E. L'H., 146, 149, 154
Gardner, William N., 91
Gas Lighting, 203, 246, 366; gas works, 246–47
Gauer, Paul, 516, 529–30
Geisburg, Charles, 87, 118, 138–39
Genor, John B., 17, 20
George, D., 79, 105
German Aid Club, 79
German-American Alliance, 267
German-American *Volksbund*, 463
German Day (1890), 261–62, 298
German Democratic Association, 77–78
German-English Academy, 122, 221, 306, 330, 414, 461
German Language, teaching of in schools, 122, 260–61, 453, 460, 462
German Relief Society, 236
German Society. See *Deutsche Gesellschaft*.
Germania Association, 264
Germania Society, 298
Germans, 70–71, 227, 236, 251, 264, 329, 453–64; press, 68, 77, 120, 125–26, 264–65, 455; migration, 72–74, 113–15; population figures, 72, 259, 453–55; cultural contribution, 73, 75, 79–80, 88, 115, 127, 129, 204–5, 224, 259, 263, 397, 410–11; political activities and attitudes, 75–78, 81, 105, 126, 134–38, 141, 144, 147, 149, 151–52, 154, 160, 166, 260, 262, 265, 280–82, 286, 289, 297–99, 301, 305; attitude toward Fatherland, 77, 129, 259, 261, 297, 455–56; fire companies, 79; military companies, 79, 128, 226; churches and religious activities, 79–80, 89, 92–93, 126–27, 153, 420, 422–24; schools, 79, 121–22, 127, 220, 260–61; musical activities, 87, 115–20, 406–8, 451; society described, 112, 267, 464; industrial activities, 112, 188–89, 266; theater, 120–21, 208, 210, 264, 266, 461; internal friction, 125–26; relations with Americans, 128, 224–26, 263–64; attitude toward free soil issue and Civil War, 129, 151–53, 157; assimilation, 226, 259, 262–63, 265–67, 429, 444, 463–64; amusements, 259, 403–4; organizations, 260, 425; decline of Germanism, 263, 265–67, 403, 460, 463–64; socialistic attitudes and activities, 289, 291, 295, 303, 320; reaction to Hitlerism, 463–64. See Turner Movement.
Gesu, Church of the, 420
Gettleman, Adam, 331
Gettelman Brewing Company, 331
Geuder, William, 262, 306
Geuder and Paeschke Manufacturing Company, 340
Gilbert, Thomas J., 81
Gimbel Brothers Department Store, 400
Ginal, Heinrich, 92
Glidden, Carlos, 195
Glover, fugitive slave, 151
Goff, Guy D., 311–12
Goldmann, Ferdinand, 113
Goldsmith, B., 282
Golf, 405
Goll, Julius, 185
Good Government Clubs, 300
Good Government League, 535
Goodrich, John R., 347–48
Goodrich, Joseph, 171, 173
Goodrich, William O., 428
Goplana, singing society, 273
Government, county and township, 33–34; village, 33–37, 96, 107; suffrage qualifications, 33–34, 36–37, 76, 78, 104–5, 141; city government created, 104–6; opposition to municipal expenditures, 139–40, 145–49, 155, 164; controversy over creating board of public works, 165–67; urban services pictured, 552. See Aldermen, Boards and Commissions, Charters, City-County Consolidation, Fire Protection, Garbage Disposal, Health Pro-

tection, Home Rule, Libraries, Mayor, New Deal Subsidies for Municipal Activity, Playgrounds and Social Centers, Police Protection, Public Baths, Schools, Sewage Disposal, Sidewalk Construction, Streets, construction, cleaning, lighting, Traffic Regulation, Water Supply.
Grace Lutheran Church, 92
Graft and Machine Politics, 134–35, 144–49, 238, 283–85, 306, 311–12, 358, 361, 375, 516; alleged Democratic machine, 155, 162–63, 166; grand jury indictments (1903), 310–11
Graham License Law, 265
Grain Trade, 502–4; wheat trade, 48, 62, 176, 178, 180–84, 195, 198, 321–22, 325–27, 502–3; primacy in wheat trade (by 1862), 181; trade in coarse grains, 326–28, 503
Grand Avenue Congregational Church, 423, 526
Grand Avenue (Methodist) Church, 422
Grand Opera House, 401, 407
Grand Trunk Railway System, 343
Gray, W. D., 338
Great Lakes-St. Lawrence Seaway, 508–9
Great Lakes-Tidewater Association, 509
Greek-American Protective Association, 471
Greek Orthodox Catholic Church, 471
Greeks, 276, 454–55, 471
Greeley, Horace, 215
Green Bay, Milwaukee, and Chicago Railroad. See Lake Shore Railroad.
Greendale, 482
Greulich, August, 79 (sketch), 114, 126, 134, 141, 147, 151
Greulich and Haertel, 74
Grignon, Paul and Christiana, 16, 20
Grottkau, Paul, 285, 292–95, 303–4; pictured, 292
Guild, George, 66
Gulski, Father ——, 269, 313
Gurda, Leon, 534
Guzo, Michael, 275

Hadley, Jackson, 144–49, 145 (sketch), 151
Haertel, Herman, 76, 114–15, 129, 134, 136
Hagerman, J. J., 336
Hale, Philetus C., 86

Hall, S. C., 171
Hamilton Aero Manufacturing Company, 512
Harbor Development, 44–46, 141, 178–80, 322; twentieth century, 505–8, 514, 523, 527
Harbor Festival, 75
Harley-Davidson Motor Company, 486, 500
Harmonia Male Choir, 273
Harnischfeger, Henry, 340
Harnischfeger Corporation, 340, 500
Harper, W. D., 534, 544–45
Harris Brothers Fair Store, 400
Hart's Mill, 379
Harvest Festival of Many Lands, 471
Haskins, Charles H., 366, 398–99
Hasse, Carl E., 113
Hatch, Allen W., 58
Hathaway, Joshua, 49, 51, 71, 91, 169
Haverland, Anna, 264
Hawks, Nelson P., 99–100
Hawley, Cyrus, 57, 91
Health Commissioner, 376
Health Protection, village period, 103–4; mid-forties to 1910, 237, 239–42, 250, 356, 382, 384–87; health conditions, 240–41, 363, 387, 434, 534, 551, 555–56; 1910 to 1940, 517, 538, 551, 555–56, 561
Heath, Frederic, 303–4, 307–8 (sketch), 312, 317
Hebrew Relief Society, 237
Hegemann, Werner, 543
Heil Company, 500
Heine, F. W., 411
Heinzen, Karl, 115, 127
Heiser's, "Ma," 259, 403
Heiss, Michael, 261, 297, 420
Hellenic-American Republican Club, 471
Hempsted, Henry N., 212
Henman, Samuel, 35
Henni, John Martin, 80, 89, 126, 210, 221, 270, 416, 420
Henry, Prince, of Prussia, visit, 263
Herbold, Alexander, 289
Herman, Jan, 274
Herzfeld, Carl, 400
Herzfeld-Phillipson Company, 400
Hibbard, E. C., 156
Hibbard, William B., 156, 173
Higby, Lewis J., 71, 91, 94, 183–84
Higby (L. J.) and Company, 62

INDEX

Hill, Robert, 347
Hinkley, George M., 338
Hinman, Samuel, 102
Hinsey, John A., 284, 369
Hinterland, development of, 168, 174–75, 186, 322, 326, 335, 337, 486, 502, 514
Hintze, Theresa, 118
Hitlerism, reaction to, 463–64, 468–69
Hoan, Daniel, 317, 468, 516 (sketch), 535; activities in depression of 1930's, 481–82, 528; mayor, 500, 522–32, 540–41, 544–45, 549–50, 560–61, 567–68; city attorney, 516–17, 521; pictured, 522; appointments, 533–35, 552
Hodges, Lyman F., 183
Hoffmann, Bernard, 464
Hoistendahl, Chr., 114
Holbrook, Arthur, 413
Holeproof Hosiery Company, 496
Hollanders, 92, 131, 454
Hollister, D. S., 56
Holton, Edward D., 36–37, 50, 53, 62, 84, 104–5, 150–51, 170–72, 179, 183, 218, 234, 252, 418; pictured, 144
Holton, Mrs. E. D., 223
Holton and Goodall, 62
Home of the Friendless, 237
Home Rule, 258, 306, 316–18, 377–78, 521, 536, 558–59
Homer, Louise, 409
Hooker, David G., 281
Hooker, Samuel T., 183
Hooker, W. F., 313
Hoover, J. A., 171–72
Hopkins, B. B., 348
Hopkins, Mark, 215
Hopper (De Wolf) and Company, 402
Horse Cars. See Urban Transit.
Hospodar, 274
Hotels and Inns, 65, 183, 288, 345, 366
Houghton, George G., 153
Household Activities and Equipment, 202, 397–99, 435, 475
Housing and Slum Clearance, 305, 317, 340, 389–90, 455, 475, 482, 528, 536, 543
Howard, William W., 349
Hoxey, Art, 405
Hoyt, Emerson D., 543
Hoyt, Frank, 300
Hubbard, H. M., 36
Hubbard and Converse, 362
Hubbell, Levi, 36, 71, 208, 225

Huck, Clara, 406
Huebschmann, Franz, 75 (sketch), 77–78, 87, 94, 104, 126–28, 134, 136, 144, 147, 151, 157, 172, 252, 260, 265, 568; pictured, 144
Hull, Lemuel, 83, 91
Humanist (Milwaukee), 123, 126
Humboldt, 379
Hungarian Reform Church, 471
Hungarians, 276, 470–71
Hustis, John, 36

Ide, Mrs. George, 387
Illinois, settlers from, 71, 258, 453
Illinois Steel Company, 336–37, 506–7
Ilsley, C. F., 156, 159, 249, 368
Ilsley, George F., music store, 212
Ilsley, James K., 405, 428
Ilsley, Spencer, 428
Immanuel Presbyterian Church, 423
Immigration, encouragement of, 113–14, 197, 246; "new immigration," 267–78, 396, 419–20, 454, 464–71
Imprints, early, 26
Inbusch, John G., 149
Incomes, of Milwaukeeans, 196, 273
Indians, Chippewa, 6–7; Foxes, 3, 6–7; Mascouten, 3; Menominee, 5–8, 14; Miami, 6; Ottawa, 6–7; Potawatomi, 3, 6–7, 14; Sauk, 6–7; Winnebago, 4, 6–7
Industrial Expositions, 347, 410
Industrial Promotion, as factor in city growth, 332–33, 339
Ingersoll, Ernest, 397
Internal Improvements. See Harbor Development, Transportation, Byron Kilbourn.
Initiative, proposed, 306, 316–18
International Harvester Company, 486
International Institute, 471
International Workingmen's Association, influence of, 289–90
Iowa, settlers from, 453
Irish, 71, 80–81, 268, 454; migration, 80, 112; numbers, 130; political activities, 75–77, 81, 105, 130, 134–35, 147, 281, 298; military companies, 81, 128, 226
Iron Foundries. See Metal Trades.
Irving, Henrietta, 206
Italian Civic Association, 470
Italian Language, teaching of in schools, 462

Italians, 268, 276–77, 309, 454–55, 462, 470
Iversen, J. C., 347

Jacobi, W. H., 114
Jacobs, William H., 341, 347
Jacques, John, 284
James, Charles, 225
Janssen, John T., 358, 375, 534, 552
Jefferson, Thomas, 38
Jenkins, James G., 156
Jews, 81, 92, 237, 268, 277–78, 424, 454, 472–74
Jiranka, Thomas, 274
Jobbers' and Manufacturers' Association, 345, 350–51 (organized)
Johnson, James, 241, 363, 385
Johnson, John W., 5
Johnson, Willard B., 102
Johnson, W. S., 248, 358, 368
Johnston, John, 300, 347–48, 381
Johnston, Robert A., 416–17
Jones Island, 363, 506
Jones's (Miss) Ladies Seminary, 221
Jourdain, Joseph, 17–18, 20
Journalisten Verein, 298
Juneau, Peter, 9, 11, 16, 20
Juneau, Solomon, 5–6 (sketch), 87, 102, 252; fur trader, 3, 7, 17, 32, 52–53; townsite promoter, 8–17, 19–22, 24–27, 29–34, 57, 59, 64–65, 67, 73, 89, 97, 107; village official, 35–36, 39, 45, 49, 68; pictured, 36; mayor, 135; in local politics, 136
Juneautown, original boundaries, 34
Junkerman, Mrs. C. G., 526
Juvenile Delinquency, 390

Kainz, Joseph, 264
Kalina, singing society, 273
Kane, Charles L., 225
Kansas City (Mo.), example cited, 348
Kansas-Nebraska Bill, opposition to, 151
Keeler, David M., 68
Keenan, Matthew, 362, 381
Kellogg, Amherst W., 66
Kellogg, Clara Louise, 409
Kellogg, Leverett S., 90
Kellogg, Levi H., 183
Kellogg, William A., 90
Kemble, Mrs. Fanny, 207
Kemper, Herman, 113
Kemper, Jackson, 91

Kendall (Miss M. E.) Select School, 221
Kennedy, Daniel, 358
Kentucky, settlers from, 71
Kern, C. J., 76
Kershaw, Charles J., 183, 343
Kilbourn, Byron, 71, 87, 225, 234, 252, 257, 567; townsite promotion, 9, 12, 13 (sketch), 14–15, 17–19, 21–23, 25–26, 30, 32, 39, 65–67, 104, 107, 243, 251; village official, 35, 39; pictured, 36; in local politics, 38–39, 136, 140, 144–45, 151; promotion of internal improvements, 42, 44–46, 49–50, 98, 144–45, 169–73, 179; mayor, 115, 137, 144, 217
Kilbourn, Dr. Byron L., 413
Kilbourntown, original boundaries, 34
King, Rufus, 54, 68, 70–71, 84, 94, 108, 136–37, 139, 146–47, 151–52, 157, 173, 179, 208, 214, 216–19, 225–26, 228, 252; pictured, 144
Kingsley, Charles F., 417
Kinkel, Gottfried, 115
Kinzie, James, 11
Kirby, Abner, 72, 156
Kirkland, Caroline M., 24, 26
Kittredge, W. E., 381
Kleczka, John C., 468
Kline Benefit Assessment Law, 543
Kluchesky, Joseph T., 553
Kluegel, P., 79
Kneeland, James, 71, 140, 143, 170–71, 234
Kneeland, Moses, 36, 136
Knights of Labor, 288, 293–95
Knights of St. Crispin, 287
Knights of St. Mary Lodge, 275
Knit Goods and Hosiery, production of, 496
Know Nothings, 128
Koch, John C., 260, 298, 301, 319
Kochanek, Anthony, 269
Koehler, John P., 533–34, 555
Koehler, Robert, 411
Koeppel, Richard, 308
Koeppen, George, 260
Koerner, Christian, 261
Kohler, Aviation Corporation, 512
Kosciuszko Guard, 270–71, 273, 296
Kotecki, Louis M., 468, 533
Kottnauer, L. H., 558
Kraft, F. A., 555
Krause, Pastor, 79
Kremers Family, 75

Kresge (S. S.) Company Stores, 448
Kroeger, Herman, 284, 286, 294
Krug, August, 188, 330
Kruszka, Michael, 270-72, 465; pictured, 464
Kruszka, Waclaw, 465
Kryl, Bohumir, band, 403
Kryszak, Mrs. Mary O., 466
Krytyka ([The Critic] Milwaukee), 270
Kucera, Max, 286
Kuehn, Ferdinand, 155-56
Kundig, Martin, 90
Kuryer Polski (Milwaukee), 271-72, 465
Kurz, Joseph, 120-21
Kusik, Imrich, 275

Labor, organizations: village period, 65; mid-forties to 1910, 209, 258, 273, 284-96, 304, 340; 1910 to 1940, 496-501, 544; political activities, 282, 284-87, 289-91, 294-95, 303-4, 307-8, 311-12, 315-20, 497, 519-20, 523, 530, 541; union membership figures, 294-95; force of labor assessed, 295-96, 302, 324, 355; statistics on industrial workers, 325, 339, 412, 436-37, 476, 479, 485, 496; relations with employers, 341; wages, 496, 498; internal friction, 500. For coordination of labor organizations, see Trades Assembly, Trades Council, Federation of Trades, Federated Trades Council. See also Eight-hour Day, Social Democratic Party, Strikes.
Labor Party of Illinois, 289-90
Labor Reform Association, 287
La Croix, Joseph, 4
La Crosse and Horicon Railroad, 175
La Crosse and Milwaukee Railroad, 144-45, 171-77, 180, 182. See Chicago, Milwaukee and St. Paul Railroad.
La Crosse Plow Company, 488
Ladies' Art and Science Class, 388, 410
Ladies' Benevolent Society, 236-37
Ladies' Education Society of Milwaukee, 222
La Due, Joshua, 156
"Lady Elgin," disaster, 153
La Follette Progressives. See Republican Party.
La Framboise, Alexander, 4
La Framboise, François, 4
La Framboise, Joseph, 4

Lake Michigan Hydraulic Company, 248
Lake Shore Railroad, 171
Lake Transport and Trade, 47-48, 180-81, 327, 343, 504-5, 507, 509-11; season of navigation, 181
Land Grants, requested for internal improvements (1835), 42; for canal, 42-43; for railroads, 49
Land Speculation. See Townsite Promotion.
Lane, Moses, 362
Langson, William J., 327
Langworthy (A. J.) Foundry and Machine Shop, 194
Lansing, Andrew J., 12
Lapham, Increase A., 23, 26 (sketch), 28-29, 36, 39, 42, 71, 73, 84, 97, 113, 174, 214, 216-19, 221-22, 228, 234, 567
Larigo (Charles F.) Mercantile Academy, 223
La Salle, Robert Cavelier de, 4
Lassalle, Ferdinand, influence of, 289-90
Lau, F. C., 414
Laubenheimer, Jacob G., 534, 552-53
Laventure, Francis, 20
Lawe, George W., 22
Lawe, John, 21
Lawyers, 94, 200, 438, 469, 472
Layton, Frederick, 64, 187, 249, 342, 368, 408, 411
Layton Art Gallery, 411-12
Lead Trade, 62
Leahy, E., 139
Le Claire, Antoine, 4-5
Lee, George F., 246
Le Fevre, Clement F., 92
Lehmann, Lilli, 408
Le Roy Seminary, 222
Letourneau, Indian chief, 6
Lewis, Calvin E., 383
Liberal Club, 304
Liberty Loan Drives, 459, 461
Libraries, circulating, 213-14; public, 214-16, 381-82, 551, 556-57
Liebhaber, J. A., 78, 136, 225
Liebhaberverein. See Germans, theater.
Liederkranz (1878), 407, 451, 462
Light Horse Squadron, 293
Lighting Commission, 367
Lincke, F. Oscar, 289
Lincoln, Abraham, vote for (1860),

153; attitude toward, 157; vote for (1864), 160; reaction to assassination of, 161
Lincoln, Lowell, 224
Lincoln Guards, 293
Lindemann-Hoverson Manufacturing Company, 500
Lind, Jenny, 212
Lindsay, E. J., 301
Lipa, 131, 274
Litt, Jacob, 402
Lockwood, John, 246-48, 362
Lohr, August, 411
London (England), example cited, 383-84
Longstreet, William R., 35, 49, 102
London Aid Committee (for Jewish refugees), 277
Loose, H., 125
Lorenz, Richard, 411-12
Love, Mrs. W. de L., 223
Lowell, James Russell, 215
Lucca, Pauline, 408
Ludington, Harrison, 49-50, 71, 91, 169, 234, 279, 281 (sketch), 282, 319, 322, 352, 360, 362
Ludington, James, 234
Ludwig, John C., 286
Ludwig's Garden, 79
Luening, Eugen, 406
Luening, F. A., 76, 122, 127, 260
Lush, Charles K., novelist, 375, 428
Lutheran Welfare Society, 474
Lutherans, 79, 92, 261, 297-99, 419-21, 472-74. See various synods.
Lyceum, 85-86
Lynde, Charles, 71
Lynde, William P., 71, 136, 150, 154, 155 (sketch), 234, 247
Lynde, Mrs. William P., 223, 236
Lynn and Powell's Detroit and Chicago Company, 87
Lyser, Gustav, 289-90

MacAlister, James, 381, 414
McAuliffe, Jack, 405
McCabe, Julius P. B., 81
McCarty, John, 18-21
McClintock, Emory, 282
McCormick, Andrew, 134
McCullough, John, 402
McGarry, Ed, 134
McGeoch, Peter, 327, 368, 371
McGeoch (Peter) Company, 334

McGregor and Western Railway, 177
Machine Politics. See Graft and Machine Politics.
Machine Shops. See Metal Trades.
Machinery, production of. See Metal Trades.
Mack, Connie (Cornelius McGillicuddy), 404
Mack, H. S., 347
McKeith, David N., 534
McLaren, W. P., 301, 347
McVicker, J. H., 206, 208, 401
Madden, Billy, 405
Mader's German Restaurant, 464
Maennerchor, 451, 462
Maerklin, ——, 125
Mahler, Mrs. Jacob, 117-18
Mai Fest, 128
Maine, settlers from. See Yankee-Yorkers.
Maitland Field, 512
Maler and Wend, 74-75
Mallory, James A., 286
Malt Syrups, production of, 493
Manegold, Charles, Jr., 383
Mann, Charles L., 282
Mann, Horace, 215
Mansfield, Richard, 401
Manufacturers' Association, 191
Manufacturers' Club, 350
Manufacturing, promotion of, 181, 186, 190-91, 194, 322-23, 348-50, 354, 508; work of citizens groups in promotion, 342, 344-51, 353, 508, 563; development of, 190-91, 194, 322-25, 328-41, 354, 476-86, 501, 563; statistics on, 192-94, 321, 323-25, 328-29, 333-34, 336-37, 340, 476-78, 480, 484, 487, 492, 494; consolidation and concentration in, 325, 334-37, 354, 370-72, 487-89; social consequences of, 340. See Boot and Shoe Industry, Brewing, Brick Making, Clothing Industry, Flour Milling, Food Products, Industrial Expositions, Knit Goods and Hosiery, Malt Syrup, Match Production, Meat Packing, Metal Trades, Milling Equipment, Motor Vehicles and Automotive Equipment, Wood Working.
Mapes, D. P., 348
Maretzek's Italian Opera Company, 408
Mariner, E., 392
Mariner, John W., 428

INDEX 625

Mariner, William, 428
Marlowe, Julia, 402
Marquette, Father Jacques, 4
Marquette University, 221, 414, 416–17, 446–47
Marr, Carl, 411
Marshall, Samuel, 72, 249, 368
Martin, James B., 56, 72
Martin, Morgan L., 8, 9 (sketch), 10–12, 14–17, 19, 21, 25, 27, 30–31, 38, 46, 90, 97; pictured, 36
Martin, Robert, 385
Marx, Karl, influence of, 289
Maryland, settlers from, 72
Mascouten. See Indians.
Massachusetts, settlers from. See Yankee-Yorkers.
Match Production, 64
Matthews, E. P., 347
Maxon, Glenway, 302
Mayer, Louis, 411–12
Maynard Electric Steel Casting Company, 469
Mayor, powers, 106, 141, 249–50, 552, 559; veto, 135, 147–48; term, 281, 567
Meat Packing, 64, 187, 328, 333–34, 477, 484, 486
Mechanic's Protection Society, 65
Mechanicsville, 379
Medical Society of Milwaukee County, 205
Medicines, patent, 204. See Physicians.
Medico-Chirurgical Club, 205
Meister, Robert, 304
Melms, C. T., 114
Melms, Edmund T., 304, 311, 317
Membré, Zenobius, 4
Mendel, Henry M., 282, 347, 398, 408
Menominee. See Indians.
Merchandising, village period, 29, 52–53, 60; display signs, 55, 244, 315; retail, 185, 191, 200–202, 398–400, 412, 448; wholesale, 185, 327–28, 332, 346, 351, 354, 398–99, 480, 514; nationally advertised products, 398; appeal to national market, 490. See Barter, Prices.
Merchants' and Manufacturers' Association, 343, 350 (organized), 351, 353–54, 378, 415, 560. See Association of Commerce.
Merchants' Association, 159, 186, 345–48, 350, 563
Merrill, D., 179

Merrill, Mrs. S. S., 416
Metal Trades, 191, 192–93 (statistics), 194, 324, 328, 335–40, 437, 477–80, 484–86, 488
Metcalf, William H., 92
Methodists, 90, 420–22, 472–73
Metropolitan Opera Company of New York, visit of, 409
Metropolitan Park Commission, 388, 542
Metropolitan Police Bill, 233, 250
Metropolitan Sewerage Commission, 547
Metropolitanism, consciousness of, 111, 229, 242, 245, 250–51, 253, 257–58, 362–63, 369, 372, 392–93, 397, 429, 560
Metz, M., 114
Mexican War, 157
Mexicans, 455, 471
Meyer, William, 413
Miami. See Indians.
Michigan, settlers from, 453
Michigan Lake, 3
"Michigan Money," 55
Mickler, William, 406
Mid-Summer Festivals, 452, 474
Migration to Milwaukee, details, 74
Military Companies, 103, 157, 226, 228; German, 79, 157–58, 293
Military Hall, 79, 87, 206
Miller, Benjamin K., 374
Miller, Ernest, 331, 342
Miller, Frederick, 189, 331
Miller, Henry, 36
Miller, William P., 428
Miller Brewing Company, 189, 331, 487, 492–94
Millette, Percival C., 221
Milling Equipment, production of, 337–38, 340, 488
Mills, David L., 171
Milorganite, 547–48
Milwaukee, city hall pictured, *frontispiece;* Indian background, 1–8; townsite promotion, 8–32; public land sales, 14; original purchases, 15–21, 24; map of land purchases, 16; original plats, 19; speculative mania, 25; description (1836), 26; (1845), 52, 70; (1855), 195; (1860), 200–201; (1861), 228; (mid-sixties), 228; (1869), 251; (1880), 266; (1881), 397; (1890), 268; (1910), 258, 267; (1940), 514, 563–64;

map of 1836, 60; population growth, 70, 107, 111, 180, 257, 381, 433; statistics on foreign-born population, 72, 108, 132, 258, 267, 278, 296, 453, 465; map of 1853, 120; occupational distribution, 200-201, 412, 435-38; early street pictured, 266; physical expansion, 340, 368-70, 374-75, 379-81, 429, 433-34, 514, 562; policemen and firemen pictured, 360; age characteristics, 435; aerial view of, 436; sensitivity to economic change, 485. See Foreign-born, women.
"Milwaukee," lake vessel, 47
Milwaukee, "A Magazine for Her Business Leaders," 509
Milwaukee Academy, nineteenth century, 221
Milwaukee Academy, successor to German-English Academy, 461
Milwaukee *Advertiser*, 13, 23, 29, 34, 42, 45, 66-67
Milwaukee *Arbeiter Zeitung*, 261, 285, 292-93, 303
Milwaukee and Beloit Railroad, 164
Milwaukee and Fond du Lac Railroad, 143, 171
Milwaukee and Horicon Railroad, 171
Milwaukee and Lake Shore Railroad Company, 260
Milwaukee and Minnesota Railroad, 175
Milwaukee and Mississippi Railroad, 143-44, 169 (chartered), 171-72, 175-77, 182
Milwaukee and Prairie du Chien Railroad, 175, 177, 180, 182
Milwaukee and Rock River Canal Company, 42-43, 49, 63, 564
Milwaukee and St. Paul Railroad. See Chicago, Milwaukee, and St. Paul Railroad.
Milwaukee and Superior Railroad, 164, 175
Milwaukee and Watertown Plank Road Company, 51, 58
Milwaukee and Watertown Railroad, 171-73
Milwaukee and Waukesha Railroad. See Milwaukee and Mississippi Railroad.
Milwaukee Art Association, 410, 412
Milwaukee Art Institute, 412, 557
Milwaukee Art Society, 557

Milwaukee Baptist Church Union, 423
Milwaukee City Council of Parent-Teacher Associations, 445
Milwaukee City Guards, 128
Milwaukee City Medical Association, 205
Milwaukee City Mission and Church Extension Society of the Methodist Episcopal Church, 421
Milwaukee City Railway Company, 249, 368, 371
Milwaukee City Rifles, 128
Milwaukee Civic Alliance, 537, 539
Milwaukee Civic Orchestra, 452
Milwaukee College. See Milwaukee-Downer College.
Milwaukee College Endowment Association, 388, 417
Milwaukee Collegiate Institute, 221
Milwaukee *Commerce*, 509
Milwaukee *Commercial Advertiser*, 135
Milwaukee Commercial College, 223
Milwaukee Country Club, 405
Milwaukee County, set up, 33
Milwaukee County Agricultural Society, 35
Milwaukee County Council of Defense (World War I), 458, 524
Milwaukee County Industrial Union Council, 501
Milwaukee County League of Women Voters, 536, 559
Milwaukee *Courier*, 29, 50, 67-68, 77, 81, 87, 105, 133, 135-36
Milwaukee *Daily Gazette*, 68
Milwaukee *Daily News*, 133, 135; political attitudes, 154-58, 160-61, 165-66
Milwaukee *Democrat*, 68
Milwaukee-Downer College, 35, 221-23, 409, 416-18, 446, 448
Milwaukee Dragoons, 226
Milwaukee Electric Railway Company, 370, 384
Milwaukee Electric Railway and Light Company, 342, 371-75, 489, 521-23, 529, 548-50; contest over franchise, 307-8, 367, 373-76; strikes, 498-99. See Wisconsin Electric Power Company.
Milwaukee Extension Division of the University of Wisconsin, 448, 467, 512
Milwaukee Federation of Churches, 474
Milwaukee Female College; Milwaukee

INDEX 627

Female Seminary. See Milwaukee-Downer College.
Milwaukee *Free Press,* 456
Milwaukee *Freie Presse,* 284
Milwaukee Garden, 293, 404
Milwaukee Gas Light Company, 239, 246–47, 366
Milwaukee *Germania,* 265; political attitudes, 260, 264, 299, 455, 457
Milwaukee *Germania Abend Post,* 265
Milwaukee *Germania Herold,* 455
Milwaukee Grain and Stock Exchange, 503
Milwaukee Grammar School, 221
Milwaukee *Herold,* 264, 281, 298
Milwaukee Hospital, 205, 237
Milwaukee House, 31, 65
Milwaukee Hydraulic Company, 248
Milwaukee Industrial Exposition Association, 347
Milwaukee Iron Company, 194, 335
Milwaukee *Journal,* 265, 318, 394, 444, 450, 453, 455, 463, 511, 520–22, 524–25, 527, 529, 542, 544–45, 561; activities during World War I, 456–57, 460–62, 524–25
Milwaukee Labor Reform Assembly, 287
Milwaukee *Leader,* 460, 520–21
Milwaukee Light and Power Company, 367
Milwaukee Light Guard, 226
Milwaukee Light, Heat, and Traction Company, 489
Milwaukee Medical and Surgical Club, 205
Milwaukee Medical College, 413, 417
Milwaukee Medical Society, 205
Milwaukee Museum of Fine Arts, 410
Milwaukee Musical Society, 116–20, 128, 209, 212, 225, 264, 406–8, 462
Milwaukee Normal. See Milwaukee State Teachers College.
Milwaukee Normal Institute and High School. See Milwaukee-Downer College.
Milwaukee Orphan Asylum, 237
Milwaukee Philharmonic Orchestra, 452
Milwaukee Pioneer Club, 251
Milwaukee Relief Society, 236
Milwaukee School Board, 442–44
Milwaukee School of Engineering, 448, 512

Milwaukee *Seebote,* 125–26, 261, 264, 297
Milwaukee *Sentinel,* organization, 67–68, 81; first daily, 68; miscellaneous comment, 28–29, 43, 49–50, 52, 59, 61, 65, 85–87, 99, 101, 103, 118, 181, 194, 198, 231, 233, 243, 246, 248, 265, 273, 294, 346, 351, 382, 389, 391, 393–94, 396, 479–80; political attitudes, 76–77, 105, 128, 135, 142, 146, 148, 150, 156, 161–63, 165, 281–82, 285–86, 309–10, 312, 314–15, 319, 378; circulation, 265
Milwaukee *Sentinel and Farmer,* 46
Milwaukee State Teachers College, 418–19, 446–48, 478
Milwaukee Steamboat Company, 22, 27
Milwaukee Street Railway Company, 371, 379, 489
Milwaukee *Turnverein,* 124
Milwaukee Vocational School, 440–41, 445
Milwaukee *Wiskonsin-Banner,* 68, 77, 120, 264
Milwaukee Woman's Club, 388, 536, 557
Milwaukie *Journal,* 45, 49, 62, 67–68, 101
Minerva Furnace, 336
Minneapolis (Minn.), competition with, 326, 328–29, 351, 514
Minnesota, settlers from, 453
Mirandeau, ——, blacksmith, 4
Mission Sunday Schools, 421
Missouri Synod, 92
Mitchell, Alexander, 36, 58–60, 155–56, 159, 170–73, 177–78, 182, 194, 196, 225, 234, 247–49, 251, 327, 336, 355, 362, 392, 567; pictured, 144
Mitchell, Mrs. Alexander, 223
Mitchell, Andrew, 147
Mitchell, William, 513
Mitchell Field, 513
Miter, J. J., 80, 91
Mitterwurzer, Frederick, 264
Mix, E. Townshend, 72
Modjeska, Helena, 401
Moeller, G. H., 452
Monitor, baseball club, 227
Montgomery Guards, 226
Morgan (James) Department Store, 399
Mortimer, Mary, 222–23, 417
Mossop, Mrs. See Mrs. John Drew.
Motion Pictures, 403, 449–51

628 INDEX

Motor Vehicles and Automotive Equipment, production of, 477–78, 480, 484–85, 487, 496
Mount Mary College, 447
Mudroch, John W., 528–29
Mueller, Alexander, 411
Muhlhaeuser, John, 92
Municipal Administration, character of, 252, 300, 531–35, 538, 541, 547–58, 551–53, 559, 562, 565–67
Municipal Car-ferry Terminal, 506, 510
"Municipal Conscience." See "Civic Conscience."
Municipal Debt. See City Finances and Municipal Debt.
Municipal Garbage Plant, 306
Municipal Ice Plant, proposed, 316–17
Municipal League, 279, 299–302, 307, 373, 388
Municipal Ownership, 247, 285, 302, 305–7, 309, 312, 314, 316, 320, 518–19, 521–22, 527–29, 549–50
Municipal Reform, 258, 296, 299–302, 310–12, 318–20, 377, 392, 394, 416, 515, 520, 535–38
Municipal Stone Quarry, 527
Murdoch, J. E., 207
Murphey, N. S., 297
Murphy, Richard, 76, 134
Music, village period, 87–88; mid-forties to 1910, 115–20, 209, 211–12, 384, 406–9, 438; symphony concerts proposed by Social Democrats, 305, 383, 408, 518; outdoor concerts, 384, 452; 1910 to 1940, 451–52, 466
Musikverein. See Milwaukee Musical Society.

Naprzod, 316
Naprstek, Vojta, 122, 126, 274
Natatoria. See Public Baths.
National Bell Telephone Company, 398–99
National Educational Association, convention, 351
National German-American Alliance, 455
National Municipal League, 299
National North American *Saengerbund,* meeting of, 407–8
National Park, 404
Nationality Background, 95. See various nationalities.

Nativism, 76, 80, 128–30, 138
Nazro, John, 157, 196, 392
Nazro, Mrs. John, 223
Nazro (Henry) and Company, 185
Neacy, Thomas J., 367–68
Negro Chamber of Commerce and Business Men's League, 472
Negroes, 162, 423 (churches), 454, 471–72
"Neptune," fire engine, 101
Neukirch, Franz, 113
Neukirch, Friedrich, 78, 114
Neustadtl, Isaac, 92, 274, 277
New Deal Subsidies for Municipal Activity, 482–84, 506–7, 512, 546–48, 557–58
New England, settlers from. See Yankee-Yorkers.
"New" Immigration. See Immigration.
New Jersey, settlers from, 72
New York (state), settlers from. See Yankee-Yorkers.
New York City, example cited, 102, 242, 283, 475, 544, 558; railroad connections with, 201; association with, 288, 537; production of engines for New York subway, 339
Newhall, Daniel, 146, 157, 182–83
Newhall House, 183, 288, 345, 359 (fire), 366
Newhouse, Henry, 92
Newspapers, role in townsite and city promotion, 23, 41–43, 66–67, 69, 196, 252, 349, 353, 382, 389, 394, 511, 563; agitation for internal improvements, 45–46, 49–51, 99, 173, 175–176, 238, 247–48; promotion of economic advance, 59, 62, 68–69, 108, 185, 190, 194, 198, 349, 352, 563; promotion of cultural facilities, 84–86, 118, 218; promotion of public order, 100–101, 103–4, 231–33, 356, 391, 393, 564; literary publications, 213; circulation, 264–65; as channel of expression for foreign-language groups, see various nationalities, press.
Neyman, Edgar A., 413
Nichols, Henry A., 183
Nicholson, Joseph W., 535
Niedecken, Henry, 87
Niedermann, H., 78
Niel Norris Farm, 426
Night Watch, suggested, 103, 231–32
Nilsson, Christine, 409

INDEX

Noise, prohibition of, 239, 244, 317, 391
Nolen, John, 543
Nonpartisans, 515, 522, 532–34, 537, 541, 544, 548, 559–60, 567. See Fusion in Municipal Elections.
Noonan, Josiah A., 23, 67–68, 71, 191, 234
Norris, C. W., 301
North American Company, 371
North Chicago Rolling Mill Company, 293, 336
North Greenfield, 380
North Side Civic League, 390, 557
North West Fur Company, 3, 5
Northwest Airlines, 512
Northwest Airways, Inc., 512
Northwestern *Saengerbund*, 118
Northwestern *Saengerfest*, 119
Norwegians, 81, 114, 131
Novak, Mrs. Capek, 470
Nowiny Polskie, 272, 469
Nunnemacher, Herman, 401
Nunnemacher, Jacob, 401

Oak Creek, 379
Oakman, Walter G., 371
O'Brien, Timothy, 130, 144, 245
Occupations. See Milwaukee, occupational distribution.
Ocean-going Watercraft, 511
Odenbrett, George L., 405
Odontological Society, 413
O'Farrall, Francis K., 57–58
Ohio, settlers from, 111, 258
O'Kelley, Patrick, 90
Old School Presbyterians, 423
Old Settlers' Club, 251
Olin, Nelson, 60, 97–98
Olin, Thomas, 98
Oliver, Joe, 33
Olmsted, Frederick L., 384, 543
Onaugesa ("Old Flour"), 7
O'Neill, Edward, 130, 134, 147, 156, 162–63, 233, 241–42, 281–82, 357, 362, 392
"Open Town." See Personal Liberty.
Opera, 117 (first performed in Northwest), 118, 209, 212, 406–9, 451–52, 466 (Polish)
Oranje Line (Dutch), 511
O'Rourke, John, 67
Orton, J. J., 162
Ottawa. See Indians.
"Our Lady of Lourdes," lodge, 275

Outdoor Art Association, 389
Owens, Richard, 64

Pabst, Frederick, 329–32, 341, 347, 355, 362, 567; pictured, 292
Pabst, Gustave, 384, 428, 492
Pabst, Mrs. Gustave, 456
Pabst Brewing Company, 188, 329–31, 333, 341, 489–90, 494
Pabst Building, 464
Pabst Theatre, 402, 451
Page, Herman L., 149, 358
Paine, H. J., 153
Pan-Germanism, 263
Panics, (1837), 27–29, 49, 58, 90; (1857), 119, 195, 215, 219–20, 223, 233, 236, 238; (1873), 288–89, 323; (1893), 301, 324, 335, 370, 380; (1907–8), 277, 325, 335, 497. For panic of 1929, see Depression of 1930's.
Panoramas, 86, 211, 410–11
Park Board Band, 452
Parklawn, 482
Parks, Rufus, 57, 242
Parks, Commercial, and Pleasure Resorts, 404. See Public Parks.
Parochial Schools. See Schools, private schools.
Parsons, William L., 222
Parsons, Mrs. William L., 222
Passavant, W. A., 237
Patti, Adelina, 212
Paul Binner School, 414, 441
Paving, 360–61, 394, 482, 517, 521, 527, 545–46
Pawinski, Peter, 299, 309
Pawlett, William, 64
Pawling, Alonzo, 340
Payne, Henry C., 281, 298, 371–75, 399
Payne, William, 91
Pearse, Carroll G., 447
Peck, George W., 260, 296–97 (sketch)
Peckham, G. W., 282, 416
Penney (J. C.) Company Stores, 449, 469
Pennsylvania, settlers from, 111, 224
Pennsylvania Airlines, 512
People's Council, Milwaukee branch, 460
People's Institute, 416
People's Party, 290, 294, 301, 303
People's Pulpit, 426
People's Ticket, 133–34, 139, 142–44, 146, 149, 153, 163. See Politics.

People's Reform Party, 281
Pere Marquette Railway, 343, 510
Pereles, Nathan, 93, 147, 154, 274, 277
Personal Liberty, 285, 313, 315, 358, 426, 526
Petit, L. J., 428
Petroleum Products, trade in, 505
Pewaukee, 434
Pfeiffer, Alexander, 121
Pfister and Vogel, 188, 196
Pfister and Vogel Tanning Company, 334, 495
Pfister, Charles, 375, 399, 403
Pfister, Guido, 188, 238, 362, 392
Philadelphia (Pa.), example cited, 239, 247, 347, 386
Philharmonic Society, 119, 209; of 1870, 407
Phillips, Joseph, 155, 163 (sketch), 362
Phillips, Wendell, 215
Phoenix, 125
Phoenix Hosiery Company, 496
Phonological Institute, 414
Physicians, 93–94, 200, 204–5, 413, 438, 469, 472
Piasecki, Peter, 465
Pierce, Charles L., 347
Pierce, R. W., match factory, 64
Piers, Commercial, 47, 246
Pilgrim's Festival, 224
Plank Road Brewery, 189
Plankinton, Elizabeth, 426
Plankinton, John, 64, 72, 154–55, 163, 187, 196, 249, 327, 334, 342, 347, 355, 362, 368, 381, 407; pictured, 144
Plankinton, William, 348
Plankinton and Armour, 333
Plankinton Bank, 324
Plankinton (John) and Company, 334
Plankinton Packing Company, 334
Plats, original, 19
Playgrounds and Social Centers, 312–13, 382, 390, 483, 518, 538, 557–58
Pleasure Resorts, 404
Plymouth (First) Congregational Church, 58, 423–24
Poles, migration and settlement, 131, 268–69, 453–55, 464–69; religious activities, 131, 268–71, 273, 275, 446, 465, 468; described, 268, 273, 278; organizations, 269–70, 272, 465–66; press, 269–72, 465, 567; political activities, 271–72, 283, 286, 296–99, 301, 304, 308–9, 311–13, 315–16, 467–68,

525–26, 531, 534; industrial and commercial activities, 273, 293, 466–67; cultural contribution, 273, 466–67, 469; assimilation, 468–69
Police Protection, village period, 96–97, 102–3; mid-forties to 1910, 230–33, 246, 250, 356–58; 1910–40, 538, 551–54, 561–62
Polish Fine Arts Club, 467
Polish Language, teaching of in schools, 272, 453, 462, 465, 467
Polish Merchants' and Business Men's Association, 273
Polish National Alliance, 272, 465–66
Polish National Church, 465
Polish Relief Committee, 469
Polish Roman Catholic Union, 272
Polish Women's Alliance of America, 272, 466
Polish Women's Voice, The, 466
Politics, first township election, 33; first election in town as organized in 1839, 36; territorial contests, 38; newspapers and politics, 67–68; municipal elections (1846), 135; (1847), 136–37; (1848), 137–38; (1849), 138; (1850), 139; (1851), 141; (1852), 142; (1853), 143–44; (1854), 144; (1855, 1856, 1857), 144, 146; (1858), 149; (1859), 149–50; (1860), 153–55; (1861), 155; (1862–64), 156; (1865–67), 162; (1868–70), 163; (1871–76), 281; (1878), 281–82; (1880), 282, 301; (1882), 282, 286, 291; (1884), 260, 283; (1886), 283; (1888), 284–86, 294; (1890), 260, 296; (1892), 297–98, 301; (1893), 260, 298–99; (1894), 260, 301, 303; (1896), 260, 301–3; (1898), 303–6; (1900), 262, 307–8; (1902), 262, 309–10; (1904), 311–12; (1906), 312–15; (1908), 315–16; (1910), 316–20; (1912), 520–21; (1914), 521–22; (1916), 522–23; (1918, 1920), 524–25; (1924), 526–27; (1928), 528; (1932), 528–29; (1936), 530; (1940), 530–31; presidential elections, 78, 151–53, 160–61, 280, 289, 457, 530. See Foreign-born, Free Soil and Abolition Issue, Fusion in Municipal Elections, Graft and Machine Politics, Nativism, Nonpartisans, several political parties.
Polonia Assembly, 285
Pomeroy, Fenimore C., 220
"Popocrats," 305–6

INDEX 631

Populist Party, 288, 295, 302-3, 305-7
Port Huron Convention (1853), 179
Porth, George W., 284
Potawatomi. See Indians.
Potter, Milton C., 443
Powell and Dunn Dramatic Troupe, repertoire, 207
Pre-emption, 11, 17-18
Premier Malt Products Company, 489
Prentiss, William A., 35-36, 49-50, 72, 102, 146, 149 (mayor), 154, 156, 164, 169, 179, 234, 292
Presbyterian and Congregational Convention of Wisconsin, 91
Presbyterians, 90-91, 423-24, 472-73
Prices, (1835-42), 54; (1845), 48; (1875), 399-400; (of automobiles), 405
Prieger, Ernst, 127
Pringle, Thomas J., 315
Pritzlaff, John, 163
Private Schools. See Schools.
Prize-fighting Exhibitions, 405
Progressives, La Follette. See Republican Party: La Follette Progressives.
Prohibition, 470, 478, 491-94; repeal of, 493-94
Promotional Literature. See City Promotion, promotional literature.
Prostitution, 309, 317, 426-27
Proudfit, William P., 71
Provident Association, 236
Pryor, Arthur, band, 403
Public Baths, 285, 305, 356, 382
Public Comfort Stations, proposed, 308, 391
Public Crematory, proposed, 308
Public Debt Amortization Fund, 539-40
Public Debt Commission, 164, 249-50
Public Market, 243
Public Museum, 382, 483, 557
Public Parks, 283, 317, 356, 382-84, 387, 538, 543, 561; Washington Park bandshell, 452. See Parks, Commercial and Pleasure Resorts.
Public Pawn Shops, advocated, 302
Public Sale of Coal, Wood, Ice, and Milk, proposed, 285, 308, 317, 383, 529
Public School Art League, 388
Pulaski High School, 443
P.W.A. See New Deal Subsidies.

Quarles, Joseph V., 300
Quarles, William C., 367

Quentin, Charles, 147
Quinn, Jeremiah, 163

Raab, George, 411
Raabe, William, 289
Radio, 450-51
Railroad Commissioner, 143
Railroads, 44, 51, 169, 176, 180-81, 195, 501, 513; promotion and organization, 48-50, 169-78, 323, 346, 352; municipal loans to, 140, 144, 164, 170-71, 174, 322; and municipal politics, 143, 147, 155, 172; federal aid for, 173; effect on city growth, 199, 343, 345-46; connections with New York, 201, 506, 513; lines, (1870), 327, 342; (1908), 343; (1940), 512; streamliners, 512
Randall, Francis, 84, 91, 171
Raskin, Max, 528, 530
Rauschenberger, William J., 260, 302, 319, 377
Ray, Adam E., 171
Read, John T., 16, 20
Rebecca Lodge, 209
Recall of Municipal Officials, 285, 316-18
Recreation, village period, 88; mid-forties to 1910, 209-10, 215, 224-27, 384, 390, 404-5; 1910 to 1940, 452-53, 518, 551, 556-58
Reed, George, 25, 30, 91
Reed, Harrison, 67-69
Referendum, proposed, 306, 316-18
Reform (Jewish) Temple, 424
Reformed Church of Milwaukee, First, 92
Reformer, 284
Reicher, Emanuel, 264
Reinertsen, Mrs. R. C., 386
Reliance Iron Works, 194, 293, 337-38. See Allis-Chalmers Manufacturing Company.
Relief, village period, 104; mid-forties to 1910, 235-37; 1910 to 1940, 479-84, 540, 555
Religion, village period, 89-93; list of churches (1845), 93; mid-forties to 1910, 419-24, 438; "institutional" church, 424; 1910 to 1940, 472-74. See denominations by name.
Republican Party, growth and activities of, 147, 149-56, 161-64, 280-84; 296-99, 301-2, 306-9, 311-17, 319,

632 INDEX

365, 378, 391, 457, 520–21; claims credit for civil service reform, 283; appeal to German voters, 283, 297–99, 301–2, 306–7, 309; La Follette Progressives, 309, 311–13, 316. See Politics.
Rescue Mission, 481
Reutelshöfer, ——, pioneer brewer, 64
Reynolds, Edwin, 338
Rhodes, Jesse, 57
Rice, John B., 206–8
Rich, A. W., 347, 350
Rich (A. W.) and Company, 399
Richards, Daniel H., 23, 35–36, 66–67, 102
Ricker, John S., 347
Ries, Florian J., 358
Ringer, Carl F., 517
Ritchie, John, 153
River and Harbor Convention (1847), 178
River and Lake Shore City Railway Company, 248–49, 368
Roads. See Trails and Roads.
Robber's Revenge, The, 120
Roberts, Mrs. Allan J., 526
Robertson, Samuel, 4
Robinson, C. D., 213
Rochester (N.Y.), example cited, 102, 390, 557
Rogers, C. C., 349
Rogers, D. G., 153
Rogers, James H., 35 (sketch), 36, 39, 42, 49–50, 58, 65, 71, 91, 99–100, 102, 104, 107, 154, 169, 179, 195, 225, 234, 247–48, 251–52; pictured, 36
Roithmayr, Anna, 264
Rolling Mills. See Metal Trades.
Roman Catholics, 80, 89, 139, 261, 268–71, 273–75, 277, 286, 297–98, 301, 308, 311, 419–20, 465, 470, 472–74
Roosevelt, Franklin D., 508
Rose, David G., 305, 306 (sketch), 307–9, 311–16, 357, 367, 374–75, 378, 388–89, 403, 526–27; pictured, 292
Rosebeck, J., 114, 134
Ross, Laura J., 205
Roundy, J. A., 347
Rouse, Lewis, 17, 20
Rousseau, Achilles J., 67
Rublee, Horace, 72
Rucker, W. C., 555
Rudzinski, August, 269–71
Rudzinski, Theodore, 271, 284

Ruhland, George C., 533, 555
Russell, George H., 428
Russell, Sol Smith, 402
Russell Sage Foundation, 389
Russians, 454, 474
Ryan, Tommy, 405

Sabin, Ellen C., 417–18, 448
Sack Company, 234
Safety Commission, 553
Sag Nicht, organization, 128
St. Cosme, Jean F. B. de, 4
St. John's Cathedral, 89–90
St. John's Infirmary, 205
St. Josaphat's (Catholic) Basilica, 465, 469
St. Louis (Mo.), example cited, 234, 249; competition with, 328
St. Mary's Hospital, 205, 237
St. Paul's (Episcopal) Church, 91, 422, 526
St. Paul's (Lutheran) Church, 92, 421
St. Peter's (Catholic) Church, 88–89
St. Pierre, Joseph, 4
St. Rose's Orphanage, 237
St. Stanislaus (Catholic) Church, 131, 269, 469
St. Vincent, Amand, 126
Salomon, Edward, 283
Salvation Army, 426
Sanderson, James, 57
Sanger, Caspar, 281
Sauk. See Indians.
Savage (Henry W.) Opera Company, 409
Sawyer, Amos, 225
Scandinavians, 454
Schade, Robert, 411
Schallitz, Charles, 528
Schandein, Emil, 286, 330, 341, 397
Schilling, Robert, 284, 292–93, 295, 302, 305
Schindler, Alwine, 121
Schlitz, Joseph, 114, 188, 330, 341
Schlitz (Joseph) Brewing Company, 188, 330–33, 404, 490–91, 493–94; buildings and product pictured, 188
Schlitz Palm Garden, 259, 403, 464
Schlitz Park, 404, 409
Schloemilch, Frederick, 87
Schmelz, Reinhard, 406
Schoeffler, Moritz, 77–78, 125–27, 129, 134, 136–37, 173, 225, 260
Schoenecker, Vincenz J., 318

INDEX

Schools, village period, 81–85; public schools (1846), 85; teachers salaries, 82–83, 217, 219, 414, 445, 536; private schools, 82–83, 216, 220–21, 260–61, 269–70, 272, 296–97, 446; buildings, 82–83, 85, 217–19, 415–16, 440, 442–43, 482; colleges and universities, 84, 219, 221–24, 409, 413–14, 416–19, 446–48; mid-forties to 1910, 216–24, 285, 359–60, 414–19; high schools, 218–20, 415, 439, 442; kindergarten, 359, 414; schools for handicapped, 360, 414, 439, 441–42; vocational and adult education, 360, 414–15, 439–41, 445, 471; teacher training, 414, 418–19, 446–48; 1910 to 1940, 438–39; costs, 445. See Germans, Poles, Rufus King, Increase Lapham, Textbooks.
Schroeder Hotel, pictured, 472
Schroeter, Eduard, 123, 126
Schubert, Martin, 299
Schulte, Victor, 66
Schultz, Eduard, 124
Schulverein. See Germans, schools.
Schulz, F. M., 386
Schumann-Heink, Ernestine, 409
Schurz, Carl, 118, 120, 127
Schuster's Department Stores, 400, 462
Schütz, George, 289
Schwarz, C. W., 78
Scotch, 60, 81, 224, 454
Scottish-Illinois Land Investment Company, 61
Seaman Body Corporation, 486, 500 (strike)
Sears, Roebuck, and Company, 449, 469
Seaver, Lucas, 225
Sectionalism, Ward, origins in original incorporation, 34; village period, 37–41; city period, 106–8, 140, 142, 165, 171, 231, 241–42, 250, 252–53, 258, 363, 415
Seidel, Emil, 279, 312, 315–19, 368, 497, 539; administration, 515–20; sketch, 516; pictured, 522
Seidensticker, Oswald, 115
Semi-centennial Anniversary, 262
Senn, Nicholas, 413
Service Organizations, listed, 537
Seventh Day Adventists, 424
Severance, Mrs. D., 284
Seville, James, 181
Sewage Disposal, 99, 241–42, 356, 363–64, 482, 521, 523, 528, 545, 547–48

Sewerage Commission, 242, 250, 364 (1903), 364 (1913), 547
Sexton, Lester, 196, 234
Sexton and Wing, 238
Shannon, Mr. and Mrs. E. L., private school, 221
Sheldon, George R., 371, 374
Sheridan Guards, 293
Sherman, Asa, 16, 20
Sherman, S. S., 417
Sherry, Mrs. Laura, 451
Shinners, Joseph J., 530
Sholes, Charles, 68
Sholes, Christopher L., 195
Shorewood, 380, 405, 434, 560
Short, Charles W., 84
Shoyer, Emanuel, 277
Sicilians. See Italians.
Sidewalk Construction, 97–98, 143, 237, 239, 546
Simons (Julius) Department Store, 400
Skupniewicz, Michael, 131
Slaughter Houses, 241
Slavery. See Free Soil and Abolition Issue.
Slovaks, 275–76, 470
Slovenians, 454
Slum Clearance. See Housing and Slum Clearance.
Smallpox Epidemics, 240–41, 384
Smith, Mr. and Mrs. A. D., 136, 236
Smith, Angus, 183–84
Smith, George, 58–60
Smith, Henry, 282, 284, 301–2, 305
Smith, John, 20
Smith, John B., 135, 138–39
Smith, Uriel B., 53
Smith (A. O.) Corporation, 486, 491, 500
Smoke Abatement, 317, 391, 536
Sobolewski, ———, 119
Social Affairs, village period, 88–89, 102; mid-forties to 1910, 224–28, 428, 456
Social Centers. See Playgrounds and Social Centers.
Social Democratic Party, 279–80, 303–7, 309, 311–20, 365, 378, 387, 392–94, 460, 515–32, 541–42, 558, 560–61, 567; organized, 304; appeal to Poles, 309, 317; bundle brigade, 311, 317, 521, 568; change in political tactics and appeal, 312, 314–17, 319–20; control of common council, 516, 528–29. See Politics.

Social Democratic Party of North America, 289–90
Social Economics, club, 388
Social Political Workingmen's Society of Cincinnati, 290
Social Registers, 427
Social *Turnverein*, 124
Socialism, 279–80, 285–86, 289–91, 293–96, 303–4, 308–9, 314, 317–18, 320, 460, 468, 520, 522, 530, 565–66
Socialist Labor Party, 285–86, 290, 303–4, 308, 311
Socialist Party of America, organized, 304
Society of German Physicians, 205
Society of Milwaukee Artists, 412
Soldiers' Home, 380; fair, 410
Solomon, E., 114
"Solomon Juneau," fire engine, 235
"Solomon Juneau," lake vessel, 47
Somers, P. J., 282, 297–99
Sons of Hermann, 126–27, 266
Sons of New England, 224
Sons of Pennsylvania, 224
Sons of the South, 224
Sorma, Agnes, 264, 402
Sothern, E. H., 401–2, 451
Soule, Samuel, 195
South Milwaukee, 379–80
South Side Civic Association, 542
Southern Wisconsin Railroad Company, 172
Stowell, John M., 71, 277, 282, 286, 288, 291, 340–41, 378
Sozialist, Der, 289–90
Specialization, lack of in village period, 93–94, 108, 252; later evidences of, 200–201, 205, 227, 229–31, 250–52, 322, 359–60, 399–400, 412–14, 429, 435–38, 532, 562–63
Spencerian College, 223
Spiritualists, 424
Spring Street Female Seminary, 221
Spring Street Ferry, 39
Stadt Theatre, 121, 264, 266–67, 290
Stambaugh, S. C., 8
Staples, C. A., 236
Stark, Charles G., 347, 399
Stark, Joshua, 72, 300, 381
Starr, Elisha, 36, 68, 71
State Legislature, relations with, 241–42, 376–77, 518, 520, 558–59, 561, 564–65, 567
Stedman, Seymour, 304, 309, 311

Steel Works. See Metal Trades.
Steichen, Edward J., 412
Stein, Matthias, 36, 73, 78
Steinkellner, Peter J., 534, 554
Stern, Henry, 185
Stern, Leo, 456, 462
Stevens, Horatio G., 47
Stippick, John, 301
Stirn, August, 347
Stock, Frederick, 409
Stoelting, Roland E., 534
Stolze, F., 92
Stone, Nat, 400
Stone Brothers, 400
Stowe, Harriet Beecher, 222
"Straight Cut." See Harbor Development.
Strakosch, Maurice, 212
Stratification, Social, 266, 273, 428–29, 469
Street Commissioners, 147, 164, 166, 237–38, 241, 250
Street Railways. See Urban Transit.
Street, construction, 24, 27, 30–31, 96–97, 103, 141–43, 230, 237–39, 311, 360–61, 482, 517, 528, 539, 545–46; citizens labor on, 96, 98, 230; cleaning, 103–4, 239, 285, 386–88; lighting, 239, 365–68, 523, 527, 548–49, 562. See Electric Lighting.
Strehlow, A., 304
Strikes, 287–88, 291–92, 341, 371–72, 497–500, 529; of 1886, 291–95
Strothmann, Wilhelm, 72
Subscription and Voluntary Service, to meet urban needs, 96, 107, 114, 230, 251, 392, 481, 564–65; bridges, 39, 99, 392; harbor, 46, 99, 179; piers, 47, 99; roads, 50; newspapers, 77; maintenance of order, 79, 102–3, 226, 230–31; fire protection, 79, 100, 230, 233–35, 358; relief, 79, 104, 235–37; churches, 91; streets, 96, 98, 230, 237, 239; encouraging immigration, 114; entertainment, 118–19, 206–8, 215, 452; educational facilities, 122, 215–16, 219, 222; in Civil War, 158–59; railroads, 170; library, 213–14; later civic activities of commercial and industrial leaders, 342; inducing manufactures, 349, 353
Suburbs, Development of, 340, 370, 378–81, 433–34, 560–61
Suffrage. See Government.

INDEX 635

Sullivan, John L., 405
Sullivan, William H., 81
Swedes, 81
Sweet, Alanson, 43, 45, 71, 91, 140, 183, 225, 234
Swietlik, Francis X., 466
Swift, L. K., 225
Swiss, 81
Syrians, 471

Talking Pictures, 450
Tallmadge, J. J., 156, 162 (sketch)
Tallmadge, N. P., 77
Tanning, 187–89, 192–93 (statistics), 328, 334–35, 477–78, 484–86, 494–95
Tarrant, Warren D., 310
Tax League, 377
Tax Rate, city, 352, 540, 565–66
Taxpayers' Groups, 529, 537 (listed), 550, 561
Taylor, Bayard, 209, 215
Teachers Cooperative Council, 445
Teatr Polski (Polish Theater), 273, 466
Telephone, 398–99, 449
Temperance Issue, 128, 138–39, 265, 283–84
Tenements. See Housing and Slum Clearance.
Territorial Liberty Association, 150
Terry, E. S., 503
Tesch, John H., 153–56
Textbooks, 82, 218, 220, 415; free textbooks advocated, 302, 305–6, 316; provided, 357, 360
Theater, village period, 87; German theater, 120–21, 208, 210, 264, 266, 403, 451, 461; mid-forties to 1910, 206–9, 399–403; 449–50 (motion pictures); 1910 to 1940, 451; little theater movement, 451
Thomas, Elizabeth, 317
Thomas (Theodore) Orchestra, of Chicago, 407–9
Thompson, Carl D., 317
Thompson, Linus, 20
Thompson, Sheldon, 15
Thomssen, J., 78
Thumb, Tom, 208
Titsworth, Judson, 423
Tomlins, William L., 407–8
Toronto (Can.), example cited, 300
Toser, Herman, *Wein Stube*, 259, 403
Townsite promotion. See Milwaukee.
Trade and Commerce, village period, 52–63, 199; exports (1846), 61; decline of Mississippi River route, 176, 180, 196; mid-forties to 1910, 181–87, 196, 321, 324–28, 344; promotion of, 186, 348, 351, 354; 1910 to 1940, 501–5, 509–11, 513–14; products (1939), 504–5. See Car-ferry Traffic, Coal Trade, Commercial Associations, Grain Trade, Hinterland, Lead Trade, Lake Transport, Petroleum Products.
Trade Excursions, 348, 351
Trade Unions. See Labor.
Trades Assembly, 287 (first), 288
Trades Assembly Ticket (1882), 282, 284, 291
Trades Association, 65
Trades Council, 288
Trading Pit, inaugurated, 184, 327
Traffic Regulation and Safety Techniques, 244–46, 391, 517, 553–54
Trails and Roads, 41–42, 50; plank roads, 51
Train, George Francis, 209
Transportation. See Lake Transport and Trade, Milwaukee and Rock River Canal Company, Piers, Railroads, Trails and Roads.
Trayser, Louis, 73
Treat, Curt M., 349
Trinity (Lutheran) Church, 92, 421
Trollope, Anthony, 228
Trostel (A. O.) and Sons Company, 495
Trostel and Gallun, 188
Trowbridge, William S., 19
Troy (N.Y.), example cited, 215
Troy Stove Works, 349
Trumpff, Gustave C., 162, 381
Turner Movement (*Turnverein*), 123–25, 129, 131, 266–67, 298, 303, 310, 462; North American *Turnerbund*, 262
Turnverein Sokol, 131, 274, 470
Turton and Sercomb, 194
Tuttle, Howard, 309
Tweedy, J. H., 405 (younger generation)
Tweedy, John H., 23, 35, 92, 135–36, 147, 170–71, 179
Tweedy, Robert B., 428
Typewriter, invention of, 194–95
Typographical Union, 287

Uihlein, Alfred, 330
Uihlein, August, 330, 341, 347, 355

INDEX

Uihlein, Henry, 330
Uihlein, Joseph, 319, 492
Uihlein, Paula, 456
Uihlein, William J., 331
Ulrich, John, 301
Unemployment. See Relief.
Union Bethel Mission Societies, 237
Union College, 72
Union Labor Party, 284-85, 294-95
Union Ticket. See Politics.
Unitarians, 92, 424
United States Hotel, 65, 100
United States Leather Company, 335, 354
United States Steel Corporation, 337, 354
Universalists, 92, 424
Universities and Colleges. See Schools and the several universities and colleges by name.
University of Milwaukee, 223
Upham, D. A. J., 36, 72, 104-5, 136, 138 (sketch), 144, 225, 236
Upton, Louise R., 418
Urban League, 472
Urban Services. See Government.
Urban Transit, 47, 368-75, 393; horse railroads, 248-49 (first trip), 368-69; electric street railways, 302, 314, 369 (first trip), 369-75, 379, 517, 522, 550-51; cable cars, 369-70; motor buses, 550-51. See Milwaukee Electric Railway and Light Company.
Utica (N.Y.), example cited, 215

Vaccination, opposition to, 240
Van den Broek, Theodore J., 89
Van Dyke, John H., 336
Van Kirk, Nelson, 327
Van Vechten, Peter, 163
Vaudeville, Orpheum Circuit, 403
Velocipede, 227, 245
Verein Freier Maenner (Society of Free Men), 123-25
Vermont, settlers from. See Yankee-Yorkers.
Vianden, Henry, 210, 252, 411
Vieau, Andrew, 25
Vieau, Jacques, 3-5, 9
Vieux, James, 20
Vigilance Committee, 102
Villard, Henry, 116, 127, 371, 374
Virginia, settlers from, 71
Vliet, Garret, 19, 72

Vogel, Fred, 188
Voice of the People, The (Milwaukee), 317
Volksblatt (Milwaukee), 292
Volksfreund (Milwaukee), 68, 120, 126, 141, 152, 264
Volkshalle (Milwaukee), 141
Volunteer Effort. See Fire Companies, Military Companies, Subscription and Voluntary Service.
Volunteers of America, 426
Voters' Council, 535
Voters' League, 279, 310 (organized), 524-25, 535

WAAK, radio station, 450
Wabiszewski Family, 469
Wachsner, Leon, 264
Wahl, Agnes, 428
Wahl, Christian, 383-84
Wahl, Hedwig, 428
Waldo, Otis H., 154, 345
Walgreen Company Stores, 448, 469
Walker, George H., 34, 36, 39, 50, 71, 107, 136-37, 140, 142, 144, 171-72, 208, 225, 234, 248, 252; sketch, 12; pictured, 36; mayor, 141, 143
"Walker's Point," 12, 22, 99, 217; added to village of Milwaukee, 36
Wallber, Emil, 129, 260, 283, 293, 382-83
Wall, Caleb, 89, 114, 245
Waller, Frank, 452
Ward, E. B., 194, 336
Ward, Joseph, 53
Ward, Lindsey, 36, 53, 104, 156
Wardner, Frederick, 53
Washington (D.C.), example cited, 361
Washington Guard, 79, 157, 226
Washington Park Zoo, 384
Wasielewski, Thaddeus, 468
Wasson, Robert, 358
Water Supply, 99-100, 103, 230, 247-48, 250, 338, 356, 362-63, 523, 545-46, 555
Watkins, Charles K., 147
Waukesha, 50, 434
Wauwatosa, 379-80, 434, 560-61
Way, Sylvester B., 489, 499
Weber and Stuber Restaurant, 403, 426
Weber, Frank J., 301, 304, 315, 497; pictured, 464
Wedemeyer, W., 92
Weekly Wisconsin (Milwaukee), 68

INDEX

Weeks, Lemuel W., 36, 72, 104, 114, 157, 170–71, 179, 183, 248
Weights and Measures, Supervision of, 243
Weil, B. M., 349
Weil, Bernard S., 277
Weisner, Edward, 75
Weiss, G. E., 381
Wells, D. L., 399
Wells, Daniel, Jr., 24, 35–36, 58, 65, 72
Wells, Horatio N., 36, 136–37
Welsh, 81
Wendt, William H., 533
West, Edward, school teacher, 83
West, Edward K., president of Chamber of Commerce, 301, 323
West Allis, 379–80, 560–61
West Milwaukee, 434
West Side Passenger Railway Company, 249
West Side Street Railway Company, 368–71
West Water Street Railway Company, 249
Western Union Railroad, 178
Westminster Civic League, 520, 542, 560
Wetmore, Charles W., 374
Wettstein, Theodore, 65, 113, 122, 127
WHAD, radio station, 450
Whig Party, 38, 76, 78, 133–37, 151. See People's Ticket.
Whitcomb, H. F., 399
Whitcomb, Mrs. Henry, 426
White, John, 75, 77, 130, 134, 234
White and Evans, 18
Whitefish Bay, 380, 434
Whitefish Bay Resort, 404
Whitmore, Holmes, 526
Whitnall, Charles B., 317, 516–17, 542–43
Wight, O. W., 385
"Wild-cat" Money, 28, 55
Wilder, Amos P., 300
Wiley, Charles, 223
Williams, C. H., 179
Williams, Clifton, 524–25, 544
Williams, Kitty, 427
Williams, Micajah T., 11–14, 18–19, 30
Willich, August, 124
Willis, Nathaniel, 200
Willmanns, Fred, 162
Wilson, William D., 68
Wingate, U. O. B., 365, 386
Winkler, Frederick C., 347
Winnebago. See Indians.
Wisconsin (outside Milwaukee), settlers from, 111, 258, 453
Wisconsin Aid Society, 158
Wisconsin Brewers' Association, 491
Wisconsin Central Railway, 343
Wisconsin Club, 461
Wisconsin College of Physicians and Surgeons, 413–14
Wisconsin Conservatory of Music, 417
Wisconsin Electric Power Company, 489
Wisconsin Enterprise Blade (Milwaukee), 472
Wisconsin Federation of Women's Clubs, 418
Wisconsin German-American Alliance, 456–57, 462
Wisconsin Iron Company, 335–36
Wisconsin Loyalty Legion, 460
Wisconsin Marine and Fire Insurance Company, 58–60
Wisconsin News (Milwaukee), 500, 511
Wisconsin Players, 451
Wisconsin Russian Aid Society, 277
Wisconsin Synod, 92
Wisconsin Theatre, 450
Wisconsin Vorwärts (Milwaukee), 303
Witt, Robert, 558
Wolcott, Erastus B., 63, 71, 170–71, 249
Woman's School Alliance, 388, 416
Women, 158, 387–88, 426–27, 434–38, 459, 462, 526, 536; fashions, 54–55, 200; in industry, 412, 425, 436–38, 497; organizations, 293, 410, 536
Women's Labor Organizations, 293
Wood Working, 64, 192–93 (statistics)
Woolworth (F. W.) Company Stores, 448, 469
Workingmen's Party of the United States, 290
World War I, attitude toward, 455–58, 463, 524; participation of Milwaukeeans in, 457, 463; effect on city's Germanism, 461, 463–64; reaction to Armistice, 462–63; consequences, 463, 465, 492, 497, 501; stimulus to industry, 477, 484, 494; Socialist stand, 524
W.P.A. See New Deal Subsidies.
Wright, E. P., 422
Wright, R. E., 478
WTMJ, radio station, 450–51

Yankee-Yorkers, early migration, 70–72, 86; later migrants, 111, 258, 453; contribution, 108, 132, 217, 224–25, 228, 397; attitudes, 207, 429
Yates, Peter, 50
Young, Alexander M., 327
Young, William, 327
Young Men's Association, 199, 209, 214 (organized), 215–16, 381, 568
Young Men's Christian Association, 419, 425, 513; German branch, 425
Young Men's Republican Club, 281
Young Men's Sherburn M. Becker Club, 313
Young Women's Christian Association, 419, 425–26

Zabel, Winfred C., 427
Zeidler, Carl, 468, 531–32 (sketch)
Zeidler, Frank P., 532
Ziegler, Alexander, 113
Zoning, 388, 528, 536, 543–45
Zum Deutschen Haus, hostelry, 65
Zur Deutschen Little Tavern, 73

DEC 11 1989
AUG 23 1993
DEC 2 1999

DEC 1 9 2003

MAR 3 0 2009
MAY APR 2 1 2010
15 2012
SEP 18 2012

DEC 07 2010

DEC 27 2013
FEB 2 5 2014

APR 2 4 1990